D1147654

Collins World Atlas

MINI EDITION

Collins

COLLINS WORLD ATLAS
MINI EDITION

Collins
An imprint of HarperCollins Publishers
Westerhill Road, Bishopbriggs,
Glasgow
G64 2QT

First Published as Collins Mini Atlas of the World 1999
Second edition 2004
Third Edition 2007
Fourth Edition 2009

Fifth Edition 2013
Reprinted 2013
Reprinted with changes 2014

Copyright © HarperCollins Publishers 2014
Maps © Collins Bartholomew Ltd 2014

Printed in Hong Kong

British Library Cataloguing in Publication Data.
A catalogue record for this book is available from the British Library.

ISBN 978-0-00-794177-3

All mapping in this atlas is generated from Collins Bartholomew™
digital databases. Collins Bartholomew™, the UK's leading
independent geographical information supplier, can provide a digital,
custom, and premium mapping service to a variety of markets.
For further information:
Tel: +44 (0) 208 307 4515
e-mail: collinsbartholomew@harpercollins.co.uk
or visit our website at: www.collinsbartholomew.com

Follow us on Twitter @collinsmaps

Pages	Title	Scale

GEOGRAPHICAL INFORMATION

Pages	Title	Scale
6–19	**COUNTRIES of the WORLD**	
20–21	**OCEANIA** Physical Features	
22–23	**ASIA** Physical Features	
24–25	**EUROPE** Physical Features	
26–27	**AFRICA** Physical Features	
28–29	**NORTH AMERICA** Physical Features	
30–31	**SOUTH AMERICA** Physical Features	
32–33	**OCEANS and POLES** Physical Features	
34–35	**CLIMATE**	
36–37	**LAND COVER**	
38–39	**POPULATION**	
40–41	**URBANIZATION**	
42–43	**SYMBOLS and ABBREVIATIONS**	

WORLD

Pages	Title	Scale
44–45	**WORLD** Physical Features	1:170 000 000
46–47	**WORLD** Countries	1:170 000 000

OCEANIA — 1:70 000 000

Pages	Title	Scale
50–51	**AUSTRALIA**	1:25 000 000
52–53	**AUSTRALIA** Southeast	1:10 000 000
54	**NEW ZEALAND**	1:10 000 000

ANTARCTICA — 1:60 000 000 (55)

ASIA — 1:70 000 000 (56–57)

Pages	Title	Scale
58–59	**SOUTHEAST ASIA**	1:30 000 000
60–61	**MALAYSIA and INDONESIA** West	1:15 000 000
62–63	**CONTINENTAL SOUTHEAST ASIA**	1:15 000 000
64	**PHILIPPINES**	1:15 000 000

CONTENTS

Pages	Title	Scale
65	**NORTH KOREA and SOUTH KOREA**	1:9 000 000
66–67	**JAPAN**	1:10 000 000
68–69	**CHINA and MONGOLIA**	1:30 000 000
70–71	**CHINA** Central	1:15 000 000
72–73	**SOUTH ASIA**	1:20 000 000
74–75	**PAKISTAN, INDIA and BANGLADESH**	1:15 000 000
76–77	**CENTRAL ASIA**	1:20 000 000
78–79	**ARABIAN PENINSULA**	1:15 000 000
80–81	**EAST MEDITERRANEAN**	1:15 000 000
82–83	**RUSSIA**	1:42 000 000
84–85	EUROPE	1:40 000 000
86–87	**EUROPEAN RUSSIA**	1:20 000 000
88–89	**NORTHEAST EUROPE**	1:8 000 000
90–91	**UKRAINE and MOLDOVA**	1:8 000 000
92–93	**SCANDINAVIA and ICELAND**	1:10 000 000
94–95	**BRITISH ISLES**	1:8 000 000
96	**SCOTLAND**	1:4 000 000
97	**IRELAND**	1:4 000 000
98–99	**ENGLAND and WALES**	1:4 000 000
100–101	**NORTHWEST EUROPE**	1:4 000 000
102–103	**CENTRAL EUROPE**	1:8 000 000
104–105	**FRANCE and SWITZERLAND**	1:8 000 000
106–107	**SPAIN and PORTUGAL**	1:8 000 000
108–109	**ITALY and THE BALKANS**	1:8 000 000
110–111	**GREECE, ROMANIA and BULGARIA**	1:8 000 000
112–113	AFRICA	1:60 000 000
114–115	**NORTHWEST AFRICA**	1:26 000 000

Pages	Title	Scale
116–117	**NORTHEAST AFRICA**	1:26 000 000
118–119	**CENTRAL AFRICA**	1:20 000 000
120–121	**SOUTHERN AFRICA**	1:20 000 000
122–123	**SOUTH AFRICA**	1:10 000 000
124–125	NORTH AMERICA	1:70 000 000
126–127	**CANADA**	1:30 000 000
128–129	**CANADA** West	1:15 000 000
130–131	**CANADA** East	1:15 000 000
132–133	**UNITED STATES OF AMERICA**	1:25 000 000
134–135	**USA** West	1:11 000 000
136–137	**USA** North Central	1:11 000 000
138–139	**USA** South Central	1:11 000 000
140–141	**USA** Northeast	1:11 000 000
142–143	**USA** Southeast	1:11 000 000
144–145	**MEXICO**	1:15 000 000
146–147	**CARIBBEAN**	1:20 000 000
148–149	SOUTH AMERICA	1:70 000 000
150–151	**SOUTH AMERICA** North	1:25 000 000
152–153	**SOUTH AMERICA** South	1:25 000 000
154–155	**BRAZIL** Southeast	1:10 000 000
	OCEANS	
156–157	**PACIFIC OCEAN**	1:120 000 000
158	**ATLANTIC OCEAN**	1:120 000 000
159	**INDIAN OCEAN**	1:120 000 000
160	**ARCTIC OCEAN**	1:60 000 000
161–256	INDEX	

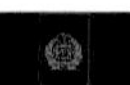

AFGHANISTAN
Islamic State of Afghanistan
Capital Kābul

Area sq km	652 225	**Currency**	Afghani
Area sq miles	251 825	**Languages**	Dari, Pashto
Population	32 358 000		(Pashtu), Uzbek,
			Turkmen

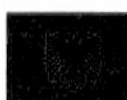

ALBANIA
Republic of Albania
Capital Tirana (Tiranë)

Area sq km	28 748	**Currency**	Lek
Area sq miles	11 100	**Languages**	Albanian, Greek
Population	3 216 000		

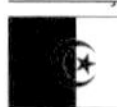

ALGERIA
People's Democratic Republic of Algeria
Capital Algiers (Alger)

Area sq km	2 381 741	**Currency**	Algerian dinar
Area sq miles	919 595	**Languages**	Arabic, French,
Population	35 980 000		Berber

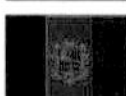

ANDORRA
Principality of Andorra
Capital Andorra la Vella

Area sq km	465	**Currency**	Euro
Area sq miles	180	**Languages**	Catalan, Spanish,
Population	86 000		French

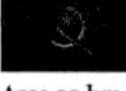

ANGOLA
Republic of Angola
Capital Luanda

Area sq km	1 246 700	**Currency**	Kwanza
Area sq miles	481 354	**Languages**	Portuguese,
Population	19 618 000		Bantu, local lang.

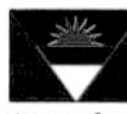

ANTIGUA AND BARBUDA
Capital St John's

Area sq km	442	**Currency**	East Caribbean
Area sq miles	171		dollar
Population	90 000	**Languages**	English, creole

ARGENTINA
Argentine Republic
Capital Buenos Aires

Area sq km	2 766 889	**Currency**	Argentinian peso
Area sq miles	1 068 302	**Languages**	Spanish, Italian,
Population	40 765 000		Amerindian lang.

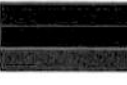

ARMENIA
Republic of Armenia
Capital Yerevan (Erevan)

Area sq km	29 800	**Currency**	Dram
Area sq miles	11 506	**Languages**	Armenian, Yezidi
Population	3 100 000		

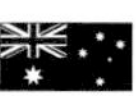

AUSTRALIA
Commonwealth of Australia
Capital Canberra

Area sq km	7 692 024	**Currency**	Australian dolla
Area sq miles	2 969 907	**Languages**	English, Italian,
Population	22 606 000		Greek

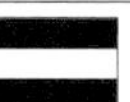

AUSTRIA
Republic of Austria
Capital Vienna (Wien)

Area sq km	83 855	**Currency**	Euro
Area sq miles	32 377	**Languages**	German,
Population	8 413 000		Croatian, Turkis

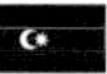

AZERBAIJAN
Republic of Azerbaijan
Capital Baku (Bakı)

Area sq km	86 600	**Currency**	Azerbaijani mar
Area sq miles	33 436	**Languages**	Azeri, Armeniar
Population	9 306 000		Russian, Lezgia

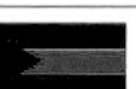

THE BAHAMAS
Commonwealth of The Bahamas
Capital Nassau

Area sq km	13 939	**Currency**	Bahamian dolla
Area sq miles	5 382	**Languages**	English, creole
Population	347 000		

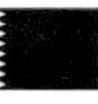

BAHRAIN
Kingdom of Bahrain
Capital Manama (Al Manāmah)

Area sq km	691	**Currency**	Bahraini dinar
Area sq miles	267	**Languages**	Arabic, English
Population	1 324 000		

BANGLADESH
People's Republic of Bangladesh
Capital Dhaka (Dacca)

Area sq km	143 998	**Currency**	Taka
Area sq miles	55 598	**Languages**	Bengali, English
Population	150 494 000		

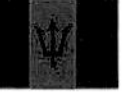

BARBADOS
Capital Bridgetown

Area sq km	430	**Currency**	Barbados dollar
Area sq miles	166	**Languages**	English, creole
Population	274 000		

BELARUS
Republic of Belarus
Capital Minsk

Area sq km	207 600	**Currency**	Belarus rouble
Area sq miles	80 155	**Languages**	Belorussian,
Population	9 559 000		Russian

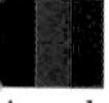

BELGIUM
Kingdom of Belgium
Capital Brussels (Bruxelles)

Area sq km	30 520	**Currency**	Euro
Area sq miles	11 784	**Languages**	Dutch (Flemish),
Population	10 754 000		French (Walloon),
			German

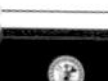

BELIZE
Capital Belmopan

Area sq km	22 965	**Currency**	Belize dollar
Area sq miles	8 867	**Languages**	English, Spanish,
Population	318 000		Mayan, creole

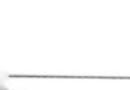

BENIN
Republic of Benin
Capital Porto-Novo

Area sq km	112 620	**Currency**	CFA franc*
Area sq miles	43 483	**Languages**	French, Fon,
Population	9 100 000		Yoruba, Adja,
			local lang.

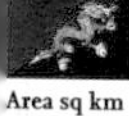

BHUTAN
Kingdom of Bhutan
Capital Thimphu

Area sq km	46 620	**Currency**	Ngultrum,
Area sq miles	18 000		Indian rupee
Population	738 000	**Languages**	Dzongkha,
			Nepali, Assamese

BOLIVIA
Plurinational State of Bolivia
Capital La Paz/Sucre

Area sq km	1 098 581	**Currency**	Boliviano
Area sq miles	424 164	**Languages**	
Population	10 088 000		Spanish, Quechua,
			Aymara

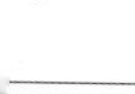

BOSNIA-HERZEGOVINA
Republic of Bosnia and Herzegovina
Capital Sarajevo

Area sq km	51 130	**Currency**	Marka
Area sq miles	19 741	**Languages**	Bosnian, Serbian,
Population	3 752 000		Croatian

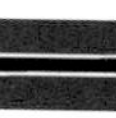

BOTSWANA
Republic of Botswana
Capital Gaborone

Area sq km	581 370	**Currency**	Pula
Area sq miles	224 468	**Languages**	English, Setswana,
Population	2 031 000		Shona, local lang.

BRAZIL
Federative Republic of Brazil
Capital Brasília

Area sq km	8 514 879	**Currency**	Real
Area sq miles	3 287 613	**Languages**	Portuguese
Population	196 655 000		

BRUNEI
State of Brunei Darussalam
Capital Bandar Seri Begawan

Area sq km	5 765	**Currency**	Brunei dollar
Area sq miles	2 226	**Languages**	Malay, English,
Population	406 000		Chinese

BULGARIA
Republic of Bulgaria
Capital Sofia (Sofiya)

Area sq km	110 994	**Currency**	Lev
Area sq miles	42 855	**Languages**	Bulgarian,
Population	7 446 000		Turkish, Romany,
			Macedonian

BURKINA FASO
Democratic Republic of Burkina Faso
Capital Ouagadougou

Area sq km	274 200	**Currency**	CFA franc*
Area sq miles	105 869	**Languages**	French, Moore
Population	16 968 000		(Mossi), Fulani,
			local lang.

BURUNDI
Republic of Burundi
Capital Bujumbura

Area sq km	27 835	**Currency**	Burundian franc
Area sq miles	10 747	**Languages**	Kirundi (Hutu,
Population	8 575 000		Tutsi), French

CAMBODIA
Kingdom of Cambodia
Capital Phnom Penh

Area sq km	181 035	**Currency**	Riel
Area sq miles	69 884	**Languages**	Khmer,
Population	14 305 000		Vietnamese

* CFA Communauté Financière Africaine

COUNTRIES OF THE WORLD

CAMEROON
Republic of Cameroon
Capital Yaoundé

Area sq km	475 442	**Currency**	CFA franc*
Area sq miles	183 569	**Languages**	French, English,
Population	22 254 000		Fang, Bamileke,
			other local lang.

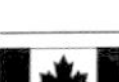

CANADA
Capital Ottawa

Area sq km	9 984 670	**Currency**	Canadian dollar
Area sq miles	3 855 103	**Languages**	English, French,
Population	35 182 000		other local lang.

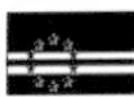

CAPE VERDE (CABO VERDE)
Republic of Cabo Verde
Capital Praia

Area sq km	4 033	**Currency**	Cape Verde
Area sq miles	1 557		escudo
Population	499 000	**Languages**	Portuguese, creole

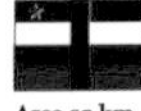

CENTRAL AFRICAN REPUBLIC
Capital Bangui

Area sq km	622 436	**Currency**	CFA franc*
Area sq miles	240 324	**Languages**	French, Sango,
Population	4 616 000		Banda, Baya,
			other local lang.

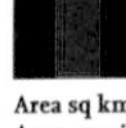

CHAD
Republic of Chad
Capital Ndjamena

Area sq km	1 284 000	**Currency**	CFA franc*
Area sq miles	495 755	**Languages**	Arabic, French,
Population	12 825 000		Sara, other local
			lang.

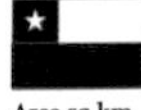

CHILE
Republic of Chile
Capital Santiago

Area sq km	756 945	**Currency**	Chilean peso
Area sq miles	292 258	**Languages**	Spanish,
Population	17 620 000		Amerindian lang.

CHINA
People's Republic of China
Capital Beijing (Peking)

Area sq km	9 606 802		Yuan, HK dollar,
Area sq miles	3 709 186		Macao pataca
Population	1 369 993 000	**Languages**	Mandarin
			(Putonghua), Wu,
			Cantonese, Hsiang,
			regional lang.

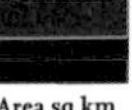

COLOMBIA
Republic of Colombia
Capital Bogotá

Area sq km	1 141 748	**Currency**	Colombian peso
Area sq miles	440 831	**Languages**	Spanish,
Population	48 321 000		Amerindian lan.

COMOROS
Union of the Comoros
Capital Moroni

Area sq km	1 862	**Currency**	Comoros franc
Area sq miles	719	**Languages**	Shikomor
Population	735 000		(Comorian),
			French, Arabic

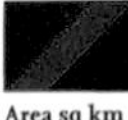

CONGO
Republic of the Congo
Capital Brazzaville

Area sq km	342 000	**Currency**	CFA franc*
Area sq miles	132 047	**Languages**	French, Kongo,
Population	4 448 000		Monokutuba,
			other local lang.

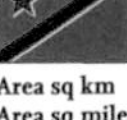

CONGO, DEMOCRATIC REPUBLIC OF THE
Capital Kinshasa

Area sq km	2 345 410	**Currency**	Congolese franc
Area sq miles	905 568	**Languages**	French, Lingala,
Population	67 514 000		Swahili, Kongo,
			other local lang.

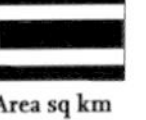

COSTA RICA
Republic of Costa Rica
Capital San José

Area sq km	51 100	**Currency**	Costa Rican colón
Area sq miles	19 730	**Languages**	Spanish
Population	4 872 000		

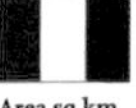

CÔTE D'IVOIRE (IVORY COAST)
Republic of Côte d'Ivoire
Capital Yamoussoukro

Area sq km	322 463	**Currency**	CFA franc*
Area sq miles	124 504	**Languages**	French, creole,
Population	20 316 000		Akan, other local
			lang.

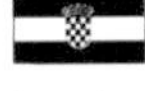

CROATIA
Republic of Croatia
Capital Zagreb

Area sq km	56 538	**Currency**	Kuna
Area sq miles	21 829	**Languages**	Croatian, Serbian
Population	4 290 000		

CUBA
Republic of Cuba
Capital Havana (La Habana)

Area sq km	110 860	**Currency**	Cuban peso
Area sq miles	42 803	**Languages**	Spanish
Population	11 266 000		

CYPRUS
Republic of Cyprus
Capital Nicosia (Lefkosia)

Area sq km	9 251	**Currency**	Euro
Area sq miles	3 572	**Languages**	Greek, Turkish,
Population	1 141 000		English

CZECH REPUBLIC
Capital Prague (Praha)

Area sq km	78 864	**Currency**	Czech koruna
Area sq miles	30 450	**Languages**	Czech, Moravian,
Population	10 702 000		Slovakian

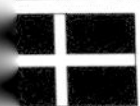

DENMARK
Kingdom of Denmark
Capital Copenhagen (København)

Area sq km	43 075	**Currency**	Danish krone
Area sq miles	16 631	**Languages**	Danish
Population	5 619 000		

DJIBOUTI
Republic of Djibouti
Capital Djibouti

Area sq km	23 200	**Currency**	Djibouti franc
Area sq miles	8 958	**Languages**	Somali, Afar,
Population	873 000		French, Arabic

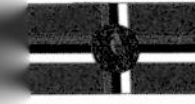

DOMINICA
Commonwealth of Dominica
Capital Roseau

Area sq km	750	**Currency**	East Caribbean
Area sq miles	290		dollar
Population	72 000	**Languages**	English, creole

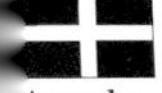

DOMINICAN REPUBLIC
Capital Santo Domingo

Area sq km	48 442	**Currency**	Dominican peso
Area sq miles	18 704	**Languages**	Spanish, creole
Population	10 404 000		

EAST TIMOR (TIMOR-LESTE)
Democratic Republic of Timor-Leste
Capital Dili

Area sq km	14 874	**Currency**	US dollar
Area sq miles	5 743	**Languages**	Portuguese, Tetun,
Population	1 133 000		English

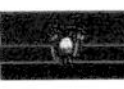

ECUADOR
Republic of Ecuador
Capital Quito

Area sq km	272 045	**Currency**	US dollar
Area sq miles	105 037	**Languages**	Spanish, Quechua,
Population	15 738 000		Amerindian lang.

EGYPT
Arab Republic of Egypt
Capital Cairo (Al Qāhirah)

Area sq km	1 000 250	**Currency**	Egyptian pound
Area sq miles	386 199	**Languages**	Arabic
Population	82 056 000		

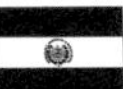

EL SALVADOR
Republic of El Salvador
Capital San Salvador

Area sq km	21 041	**Currency**	El Salvador colón,
Area sq miles	8 124		US dollar
Population	6 340 000	**Languages**	Spanish

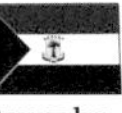

EQUATORIAL GUINEA
Republic of Equatorial Guinea
Capital Malabo

Area sq km	28 051	**Currency**	CFA franc*
Area sq miles	10 831	**Languages**	Spanish, French,
Population	757 000		Fang

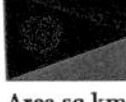

ERITREA
State of Eritrea
Capital Asmara

Area sq km	117 400	**Currency**	Nakfa
Area sq miles	45 328	**Languages**	Tigrinya, Tigre
Population	6 333 000		

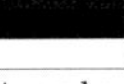

ESTONIA
Republic of Estonia
Capital Tallinn

Area sq km	45 200	**Currency**	Euro
Area sq miles	17 452	**Languages**	Estonian, Russian
Population	1 287 000		

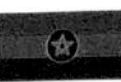

ETHIOPIA
Federal Democratic Republic of Ethiopia
Capital Addis Ababa (Ādīs Ābeba)

Area sq km	1 133 880	**Currency**	Birr
Area sq miles	437 794	**Languages**	Oromo, Amharic,
Population	84 734 000		Tigrinya,
			local lang.

FIJI
Republic of Fiji
Capital Suva

Area sq km	18 330	**Currency**	Fiji dollar
Area sq miles	7 077	**Languages**	English, Fijian,
Population	868 000		Hindi

FINLAND
Republic of Finland
Capital Helsinki (Helsingfors)

Area sq km	338 145	**Currency**	Euro
Area sq miles	130 559	**Languages**	Finnish, Swedish
Population	5 385 000		

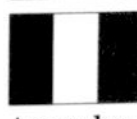

FRANCE
French Republic
Capital Paris

Area sq km	543 965	**Currency**	Euro
Area sq miles	210 026	**Languages**	French, Arabic
Population	63 126 000		

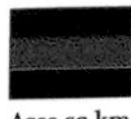

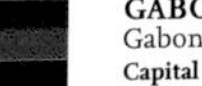

GABON
Gabonese Republic
Capital Libreville

Area sq km	267 667	**Currency**	CFA franc*
Area sq miles	103 347	**Languages**	French, Fang,
Population	1 534 000		local lang.

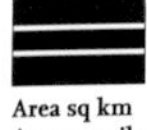

THE GAMBIA
Republic of The Gambia
Capital Banjul

Area sq km	11 295	**Currency**	Dalasi
Area sq miles	4 361	**Languages**	English, Malinke,
Population	1 776 000		Fulani, Wolof

Gaza
Semi-autonomous region
Capital Gaza

Area sq km	363	**Currency**	Israeli shekel
Area sq miles	140	**Languages**	Arabic
Population	1 535 120		

GEORGIA
Republic of Georgia
Capital Tbilisi

Area sq km	69 700	**Currency**	Lari
Area sq miles	26 911	**Languages**	Georgian, Russia
Population	4 329 000		Armenian, Azeri,
			Ossetian, Abkhaz

GERMANY
Federal Republic of Germany
Capital Berlin

Area sq km	357 022	**Currency**	Euro
Area sq miles	137 849	**Languages**	German, Turkish
Population	82 163 000		

GHANA
Republic of Ghana
Capital Accra

Area sq km	238 537	**Currency**	Cedi
Area sq miles	92 100	**Languages**	English, Hausa,
Population	24 966 000		Akan, local lang.

GREECE
Hellenic Republic
Capital Athens (Athina)

Area sq km	131 957	**Currency**	Euro
Area sq miles	50 949	**Languages**	Greek
Population	11 390 000		

GRENADA
Capital St George's

Area sq km	378	**Currency**	East Caribbean
Area sq miles	146		dollar
Population	105 000	**Languages**	English, creole

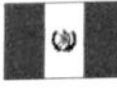

GUATEMALA
Republic of Guatemala
Capital Guatemala City

Area sq km	108 890	**Currency**	Quetzal, US dolla
Area sq miles	42 043	**Languages**	Spanish,
Population	14 757 000		Mayan lang.

GUINEA
Republic of Guinea
Capital Conakry

Area sq km	245 857	**Currency**	Guinea franc
Area sq miles	94 926	**Languages**	French, Fulani,
Population	10 222 000		Malinke,
			local lang.

GUINEA-BISSAU
Republic of Guinea-Bissau
Capital Bissau

Area sq km	36 125	**Currency**	CFA franc*
Area sq miles	13 948	**Languages**	Portuguese,
Population	1 547 000		crioulo, local lang.

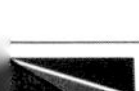

GUYANA
Co-operative Republic of Guyana
Capital Georgetown

Area sq km	214 969	**Currency**	Guyana dollar
Area sq miles	83 000	**Languages**	English, creole,
Population	756 000		Amerindian lang.

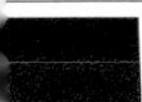

HAITI
Republic of Haiti
Capital Port-au-Prince

Area sq km	27 750	**Currency**	Gourde
Area sq miles	10 714	**Languages**	French, creole
Population	10 124 000		

HONDURAS
Republic of Honduras
Capital Tegucigalpa

Area sq km	112 088	**Currency**	Lempira
Area sq miles	43 277	**Languages**	Spanish,
Population	7 755 000		Amerindian lang.

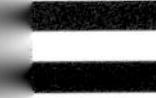

HUNGARY
Capital Budapest

Area sq km	93 030	**Currency**	Forint
Area sq miles	35 919	**Languages**	Hungarian
Population	9 966 000		

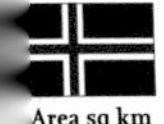

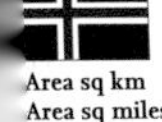

ICELAND
Republic of Iceland
Capital Reykjavík

Area sq km	102 820	**Currency**	Icelandic króna
Area sq miles	39 699	**Languages**	Icelandic
Population	324 000		

INDIA
Republic of India
Capital New Delhi

Area sq km	3 064 898	**Currency**	Indian rupee
Area sq miles	1 183 364	**Languages**	Hindi, English,
Population	1 241 492 000		many regional lang.

INDONESIA
Republic of Indonesia
Capital Jakarta

Area sq km	1 919 445	**Currency**	Rupiah
Area sq miles	741 102	**Languages**	Indonesian,
Population	242 326 000		local lang.

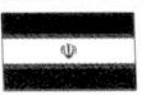

IRAN
Islamic Republic of Iran
Capital Tehrän

Area sq km	1 648 000	**Currency**	Iranian rial
Area sq miles	636 296	**Languages**	Farsi, Azeri,
Population	74 799 000		Kurdish,
			regional lang.

IRAQ
Republic of Iraq
Capital Baghdäd

Area sq km	438 317	**Currency**	Iraqi dinar
Area sq miles	169 235	**Languages**	Arabic, Kurdish,
Population	32 665 000		Turkmen

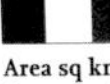

IRELAND
Capital Dublin (Baile Átha Cliath)

Area sq km	70 282	**Currency**	Euro
Area sq miles	27 136	**Languages**	English, Irish
Population	4 526 000		

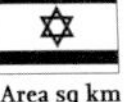

ISRAEL
State of Israel
Capital Jerusalem* (Yerushalayim) (El Quds)

Area sq km	20 770	**Currency**	Shekel
Area sq miles	8 019	**Languages**	Hebrew, Arabic
Population	7 562 000		

* De facto capital. Disputed.

ITALY
Italian Republic
Capital Rome (Roma)

Area sq km	301 245	**Currency**	Euro
Area sq miles	116 311	**Languages**	Italian
Population	60 789 000		

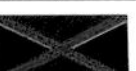

JAMAICA
Capital Kingston

Area sq km	10 991	**Currency**	Jamaican dollar
Area sq miles	4 244	**Languages**	English, creole
Population	2 751 000		

JAPAN
Capital Tōkyō

Area sq km	377 727	Currency	Yen
Area sq miles	145 841	Languages	Japanese
Population	127 144 000		

JORDAN
Hashemite Kingdom of Jordan
Capital 'Ammān

Area sq km	89 206	Currency	Jordanian dinar
Area sq miles	34 443	Languages	Arabic
Population	7 274 000		

KAZAKHSTAN
Republic of Kazakhstan
Capital Astana (Akmola)

Area sq km	2 717 300	Currency	Tenge
Area sq miles	1 049 155	Languages	Kazakh, Russian,
Population	16 441 000		Ukrainian, German,
			Uzbek, Tatar

KENYA
Republic of Kenya
Capital Nairobi

Area sq km	582 646	Currency	Kenyan shilling
Area sq miles	224 961	Languages	Swahili, English,
Population	44 354 000		other local lang.

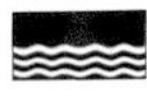

KIRIBATI
Republic of Kiribati
Capital Bairiki

Area sq km	717	Currency	Australian dollar
Area sq miles	277	Languages	Gilbertese,
Population	102 000		English

KOSOVO
Republic of Kosovo
Capital Prishtinë (Priština)

Area sq km	10 908	Currency	Euro
Area sq miles	4 212	Languages	Albanian, Serbian
Population	1 815 606		

KUWAIT
State of Kuwait
Capital Kuwait (Al Kuwayt)

Area sq km	17 818	Currency	Kuwaiti dinar
Area sq miles	6 880	Languages	Arabic
Population	3 369 000		

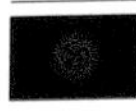

KYRGYZSTAN
Kyrgyz Republic
Capital Bishkek (Frunze)

Area sq km	198 500	Currency	Kyrgyz som
Area sq miles	76 641	Languages	Kyrgyz, Russian,
Population	5 548 000		Uzbek

LAOS
Lao People's Democratic Republic
Capital Vientiane (Viangchan)

Area sq km	236 800	Currency	Kip
Area sq miles	91 429	Languages	Lao, other local
Population	6 770 000		lang.

LATVIA
Republic of Latvia
Capital Rīga

Area sq km	64 589	Currency	Euro
Area sq miles	24 938	Languages	Latvian, Russian
Population	2 050 000		

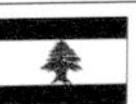

LEBANON
Lebanese Republic
Capital Beirut (Beyrouth)

Area sq km	10 452	Currency	Lebanese pound
Area sq miles	4 036	Languages	Arabic, Armenian,
Population	4 822 000		French

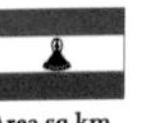

LESOTHO
Kingdom of Lesotho
Capital Maseru

Area sq km	30 355	Currency	Loti,
Area sq miles	11 720		S. African rand
Population	2 074 000	Languages	Sesotho, English,
			Zulu

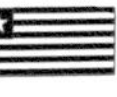

LIBERIA
Republic of Liberia
Capital Monrovia

Area sq km	111 369	Currency	Liberian dollar
Area sq miles	43 000	Languages	English, creole,
Population	4 294 000		other local lang.

LIBYA
State of Libya
Capital Tripoli (Ṭarābulus)

Area sq km	1 759 540	Currency	Libyan dinar
Area sq miles	679 362	Languages	Arabic, Berber
Population	6 202 000		

LIECHTENSTEIN
Principality of Liechtenstein
Capital Vaduz

Area sq km	160	Currency	Swiss franc
Area sq miles	62	Languages	German
Population	37 000		

LITHUANIA
Republic of Lithuania
Capital Vilnius

Area sq km	65 200	**Currency**	Euro
Area sq miles	25 174	**Languages**	Lithuanian,
Population	3 017 000		Russian, Polish

LUXEMBOURG
Grand Duchy of Luxembourg
Capital Luxembourg

Area sq km	2 586	**Currency**	Euro
Area sq miles	998	**Languages**	Letzeburgish,
Population	530 000		German, French

MACEDONIA (F.Y.R.O.M.)
Republic of Macedonia
Capital Skopje

Area sq km	25 713	**Currency**	Macedonian denar
Area sq miles	9 928	**Languages**	Macedonian,
Population	2 107 000		Albanian, Turkish

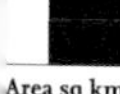

MADAGASCAR
Republic of Madagascar
Capital Antananarivo

Area sq km	587 041	**Currency**	Malagasy franc
Area sq miles	226 658		Malagasy ariary
Population	22 925 000	**Languages**	Malagasy, French

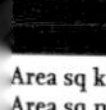

MALAWI
Republic of Malawi
Capital Lilongwe

Area sq km	118 484	**Currency**	Malawian kwacha
Area sq miles	45 747	**Languages**	Chichewa,
Population	16 363 000		English, other
			local lang.

MALAYSIA
Capital Kuala Lumpur/Putrajaya

Area sq km	332 965	**Currency**	Ringgit
Area sq miles	128 559	**Languages**	Malay, English,
Population	29 717 000		Chinese, Tamil,
			other local lang.

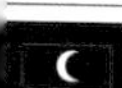

MALDIVES
Republic of the Maldives
Capital Male

Area sq km	298	**Currency**	Rufiyaa
Area sq miles	115	**Languages**	Divehi
Population	345 000		(Maldivian)

MALI
Republic of Mali
Capital Bamako

Area sq km	1 240 140	**Currency**	CFA franc*
Area sq miles	478 821	**Languages**	French, Bambara,
Population	15 302 000		other local lang.

MALTA
Republic of Malta
Capital Valletta

Area sq km	316	**Currency**	Euro
Area sq miles	122	**Languages**	Maltese, English
Population	429 000		

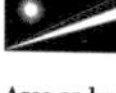

MARSHALL ISLANDS
Republic of the Marshall Islands
Capital Delap-Uliga-Djarrit

Area sq km	181	**Currency**	US dollar
Area sq miles	70	**Languages**	English,
Population	53 000		Marshallese

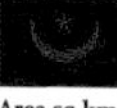

MAURITANIA
Islamic Republic of Mauritania
Capital Nouakchott

Area sq km	1 030 700	**Currency**	Ouguiya
Area sq miles	397 955	**Languages**	Arabic, French,
Population	3 890 000		other local lang.

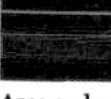

MAURITIUS
Republic of Mauritius
Capital Port Louis

Area sq km	2 040	**Currency**	Mauritius rupee
Area sq miles	788	**Languages**	English, creole,
Population	1 244 000		Hindi, Bhojpuri,
			French

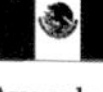

MEXICO
United Mexican States
Capital Mexico City

Area sq km	1 972 545	**Currency**	Mexican peso
Area sq miles	761 604	**Languages**	Spanish,
Population	122 332 000		Amerindian lang.

MICRONESIA, FEDERATED STATES OF
Capital Palikir

Area sq km	701	**Currency**	US dollar
Area sq miles	271	**Languages**	English, Chuukese,
Population	104 000		Pohnpeian, other
			local lang.

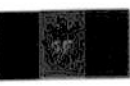

MOLDOVA
Republic of Moldova
Capital Chişinău (Kishinev)

Area sq km	33 700	**Currency**	Moldovan leu
Area sq miles	13 012	**Languages**	Romanian,
Population	3 545 000		Ukrainian,
			Gagauz, Russian

MONACO
Principality of Monaco
Capital Monaco-Ville

Area sq km	2	**Currency**	Euro
Area sq miles	1	**Languages**	French,
Population	35 000		Monégasque,
			Italian

MONGOLIA
Capital Ulan Bator (Ulaanbaatar)

Area sq km	1 565 000	**Currency**	Tugrik (tögrög)
Area sq miles	604 250	**Languages**	Khalka
Population	2 800 000		(Mongolian),
			Kazakh,
			local lang.

MONTENEGRO
Republic of Montenegro
Capital Podgorica

Area sq km	13 812	**Currency**	Euro
Area sq miles	5 333	**Languages**	Serbian
Population	632 000		(Montenegrin),
			Albanian

MOROCCO
Kingdom of Morocco
Capital Rabat

Area sq km	446 550	**Currency**	Moroccan dirham
Area sq miles	172 414	**Languages**	Arabic, Berber,
Population	32 273 000		French

MOZAMBIQUE
Republic of Mozambique
Capital Maputo

Area sq km	799 380	**Currency**	Metical
Area sq miles	308 642	**Languages**	Portuguese,
Population	23 930 000		Makua, Tsonga,
			local lang.

MYANMAR (Burma)
Republic of the Union of Myanmar
Capital Nay Pyi Taw

Area sq km	676 577	**Currency**	Kyat
Area sq miles	261 228	**Languages**	Burmese, Shan,
Population	48 337 000		Karen, local lang.

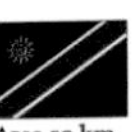

NAMIBIA
Republic of Namibia
Capital Windhoek

Area sq km	824 292	**Currency**	Namibian dollar
Area sq miles	318 261	**Languages**	English, Afrikaans
Population	2 324 000		German, Ovambo
			local lang.

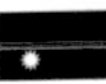

NAURU
Republic of Nauru
Capital Yaren

Area sq km	21	**Currency**	Australian dollar
Area sq miles	8	**Languages**	Nauruan, English
Population	10 000		

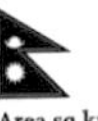

NEPAL
Federal Democratic Republic of Nepal
Capital Kathmandu

Area sq km	147 181	**Currency**	Nepalese rupee
Area sq miles	56 827	**Languages**	Nepali, Maithili,
Population	30 486 000		Bhojpuri, English
			local lang.

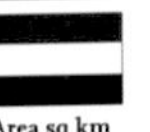

NETHERLANDS
Kingdom of the Netherlands
Capital Amsterdam/The Hague ('s-Gravenha...

Area sq km	41 526	**Currency**	Euro
Area sq miles	16 033	**Languages**	Dutch, Frisian
Population	16 665 000		

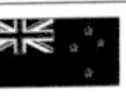

NEW ZEALAND
Capital Wellington

Area sq km	270 534	**Currency**	New Zealand
Area sq miles	104 454		dollar
Population	4 415 000	**Languages**	English, Maori

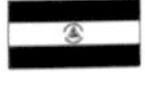

NICARAGUA
Republic of Nicaragua
Capital Managua

Area sq km	130 000	**Currency**	Córdoba
Area sq miles	50 193	**Languages**	Spanish,
Population	5 870 000		Amerindian lang

NIGER
Republic of Niger
Capital Niamey

Area sq km	1 267 000	**Currency**	CFA franc*
Area sq miles	489 191	**Languages**	French, Hausa,
Population	16 069 000		Fulani, local lang

NIGERIA
Federal Republic of Nigeria
Capital Abuja

Area sq km	923 768	**Currency**	Naira
Area sq miles	356 669	**Languages**	English, Hausa,
Population	162 471 000		Yoruba, Ibo,
			Fulani, local lang.

NORTH KOREA
Democratic People's Republic of Korea
Capital P'yŏngyang

Area sq km	120 538	**Currency**	North Korean won
Area sq miles	46 540	**Languages**	Korean
Population	24 451 000		

NORWAY
Kingdom of Norway
Capital Oslo

Area sq km	323 878	**Currency**	Norwegian krone
Area sq miles	125 050	**Languages**	Norwegian
Population	4 925 000		

OMAN
Sultanate of Oman
Capital Muscat (Masqaṭ)

Area sq km	309 500	**Currency**	Omani riyal
Area sq miles	119 499	**Languages**	Arabic, Baluchi,
Population	2 846 000		Indian lang.

PAKISTAN
Islamic Republic of Pakistan
Capital Islamabad

Area sq km	803 940	**Currency**	Pakistani rupee
Area sq miles	310 403	**Languages**	Urdu, Punjabi,
Population	176 745 000		Sindhi, Pashto
			(Pashtu), English,
			Balochi

PALAU
Republic of Palau
Capital Melekeok (Ngerulmud)

Area sq km	497	**Currency**	US dollar
Area sq miles	192	**Languages**	Palauan, English
Population	21 000		

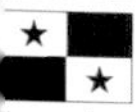

PANAMA
Republic of Panama
Capital Panama City

Area sq km	77 082	**Currency**	Balboa
Area sq miles	29 762	**Languages**	Spanish, English,
Population	3 571 000		Amerindian lang.

PAPUA NEW GUINEA
Independent State of Papua New Guinea
Capital Port Moresby

Area sq km	462 840	**Currency**	Kina
Area sq miles	178 704	**Languages**	English,
Population	7 014 000		Tok Pisin (creole),
			local lang.

PARAGUAY
Republic of Paraguay
Capital Asunción

Area sq km	406 752	**Currency**	Guaraní
Area sq miles	157 048	**Languages**	Spanish, Guaraní
Population	6 568 000		

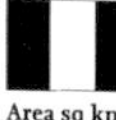

PERU
Republic of Peru
Capital Lima

Area sq km	1 285 216	**Currency**	Nuevo sol
Area sq miles	496 225	**Languages**	Spanish, Quechua,
Population	29 400 000		Aymara

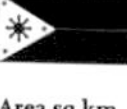

PHILIPPINES
Republic of the Philippines
Capital Manila

Area sq km	300 000	**Currency**	Philippine peso
Area sq miles	115 831	**Languages**	English, Filipino,
Population	94 852 000		Tagalog, Cebuano,
			local lang.

POLAND
Polish Republic
Capital Warsaw (Warszawa)

Area sq km	312 683	**Currency**	Złoty
Area sq miles	120 728	**Languages**	Polish, German
Population	38 299 000		

PORTUGAL
Portuguese Republic
Capital Lisbon (Lisboa)

Area sq km	88 940	**Currency**	Euro
Area sq miles	34 340	**Languages**	Portuguese
Population	10 690 000		

QATAR
State of Qatar
Capital Doha (Ad Dawḥah)

Area sq km	11 437	**Currency**	Qatari riyal
Area sq miles	4 416	**Languages**	Arabic
Population	1 870 000		

ROMANIA
Capital Bucharest (Bucureşti)

Area sq km	237 500	**Currency** Romanian leu
Area sq miles	91 699	**Languages** Romanian,
Population	21 699 000	Hungarian

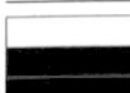

RUSSIA
Capital Moscow (Moskva)

Area sq km	17 075 400	**Currency** Russian rouble
Area sq miles	6 592 849	**Languages** Russian, Tatar,
Population	142 834 000	Ukrainian, other local lang.

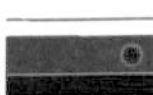

RWANDA
Republic of Rwanda
Capital Kigali

Area sq km	26 338	**Currency** Rwandan franc
Area sq miles	10 169	**Languages** Kinyarwanda,
Population	11 777 000	French, English

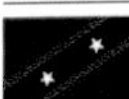

ST KITTS AND NEVIS
Federation of St Kitts and Nevis
Capital Basseterre

Area sq km	261	**Currency** East Caribbean
Area sq miles	101	dollar
Population	54 000	**Languages** English, creole

ST LUCIA
Capital Castries

Area sq km	616	**Currency** East Caribbean
Area sq miles	238	dollar
Population	182 000	**Languages** English, creole

ST VINCENT AND THE GRENADINES
Capital Kingstown

Area sq km	389	**Currency** East Caribbean
Area sq miles	150	dollar
Population	109 000	**Languages** English, creole

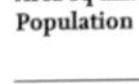

SAMOA
Independent State of Samoa
Capital Apia

Area sq km	2 831	**Currency** Tala
Area sq miles	1 093	**Languages** Samoan, English
Population	190 000	

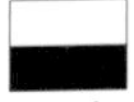

SAN MARINO
Republic of San Marino
Capital San Marino

Area sq km	61	**Currency** Euro
Area sq miles	24	**Languages** Italian
Population	31 000	

SÃO TOMÉ AND PRÍNCIPE
Democratic Rep. of São Tomé and Prínci
Capital São Tomé

Area sq km	964	**Currency** Dobra
Area sq miles	372	**Languages** Portuguese, creo
Population	193 000	

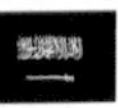

SAUDI ARABIA
Kingdom of Saudi Arabia
Capital Riyadh (Ar Riyāḍ)

Area sq km	2 200 000	**Currency** Saudi Arabian
Area sq miles	849 425	riyal
Population	28 829 000	**Languages** Arabic

SENEGAL
Republic of Senegal
Capital Dakar

Area sq km	196 720	**Currency** CFA franc*
Area sq miles	75 954	**Languages** French, Wolof,
Population	14 133 000	Fulani, other loc lang.

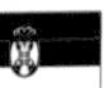

SERBIA
Republic of Serbia
Capital Belgrade (Beograd)

Area sq km	77 453	**Currency** Serbian dinar,
Area sq miles	29 904	**Languages** Serbian,
Population	7 181 505	Hungarian

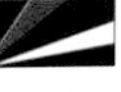

SEYCHELLES
Republic of Seychelles
Capital Victoria

Area sq km	455	**Currency** Seychelles rupee
Area sq miles	176	**Languages** English, French,
Population	93 000	creole

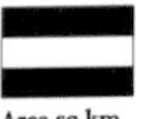

SIERRA LEONE
Republic of Sierra Leone
Capital Freetown

Area sq km	71 740	**Currency** Leone
Area sq miles	27 699	**Languages** English, creole,
Population	6 092 000	Mende, Temne, other local lang.

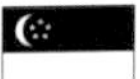

SINGAPORE
Republic of Singapore
Capital Singapore

Area sq km	639	**Currency** Singapore dollar
Area sq miles	247	**Languages** Chinese, English
Population	5 412 000	Malay, Tamil

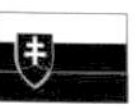

SLOVAKIA
Slovak Republic
Capital Bratislava

Area sq km	49 035	**Currency**	Euro
Area sq miles	18 933	**Languages**	Slovak,
Population	5 450 000		Hungarian, Czech

SLOVENIA
Republic of Slovenia
Capital Ljubljana

Area sq km	20 251	**Currency**	Euro
Area sq miles	7 819	**Languages**	Slovene, Croatian,
Population	2 072 000		Serbian

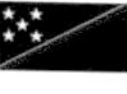

SOLOMON ISLANDS
Capital Honiara

Area sq km	28 370	**Currency**	Solomon Islands
Area sq miles	10 954		dollar
Population	561 000	**Languages**	English, creole,
			other local lang.

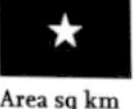

SOMALIA
Federal Republic of Somalia
Capital Mogadishu (Muqdisho)

Area sq km	637 657	**Currency**	Somali shilling
Area sq miles	246 201	**Languages**	Somali, Arabic
Population	10 496 000		

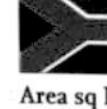

SOUTH AFRICA
Capital Pretoria (Tshwane)/ Cape Town/Bloemfontein

Area sq km	1 219 090	**Currency**	Rand
Area sq miles	470 693	**Languages**	Afrikaans,
Population	52 776 000		English, nine
			official local lang.

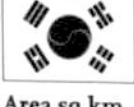

SOUTH KOREA
Republic of Korea
Capital Seoul (Sŏul)

Area sq km	99 274	**Currency**	South Korean
Area sq miles	38 330		won
Population	49 263 000	**Languages**	Korean

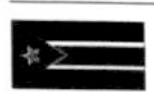

SOUTH SUDAN
Republic of South Sudan
Capital Juba

Area sq km	644 329	**Currency**	South Sudan
Area sq miles	248 775		pound
Population	11 296 000	**Languages**	English, Arabic,
			Dinka, Nuer, other
			local lang.

SPAIN
Kingdom of Spain
Capital Madrid

Area sq km	504 782	**Currency**	Euro
Area sq miles	194 897	**Languages**	Spanish (Castilian),
Population	46 927 000		Catalan, Galician,
			Basque

SRI LANKA
Democratic Socialist Republic of Sri Lanka
Capital Sri Jayewardenepura Kotte

Area sq km	65 610	**Currency**	Sri Lankan rupee
Area sq miles	25 332	**Languages**	Sinhalese,
Population	21 273 000		Tamil, English

SUDAN
Republic of the Sudan
Capital Khartoum

Area sq km	1 861 484	**Currency**	Sudanese pound
Area sq miles	718 725		(Sudani)
Population	37 964 000	**Languages**	Arabic, English,
			Nubian, Beja, Fur,
			other local lang.

SURINAME
Republic of Suriname
Capital Paramaribo

Area sq km	163 820	**Currency**	Suriname guilder
Area sq miles	63 251	**Languages**	Dutch,
Population	539 000		Surinamese,
			English, Hindi

SWAZILAND
Kingdom of Swaziland
Capital Mbabane

Area sq km	17 364	**Currency**	Emalangeni,
Area sq miles	6 704		South African
Population	1 250 000		rand
		Languages	Swazi, English

SWEDEN
Kingdom of Sweden
Capital Stockholm

Area sq km	449 964	**Currency**	Swedish krona
Area sq miles	173 732	**Languages**	Swedish, Sami
Population	9 571 000		

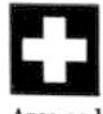

SWITZERLAND
Swiss Confederation
Capital Bern (Berne)

Area sq km	41 293	**Currency**	Swiss franc
Area sq miles	15 943	**Languages**	German, French,
Population	8 078 000		Italian, Romansch

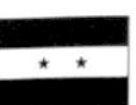

SYRIA
Syrian Arab Republic
Capital Damascus (Dimashq)

Area sq km	185 180	**Currency**	Syrian pound
Area sq miles	71 498	**Languages**	Arabic, Kurdish,
Population	20 766 000		Armenian

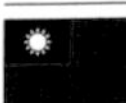

TAIWAN
Republic of China
Capital Taibei

Area sq km	36 179	**Currency**	Taiwan dollar
Area sq miles	13 969	**Languages**	Mandarin
Population	23 164 000		(Putonghua), Min,
			Hakka, local lang.

The People's Republic of China claims Taiwan as its 23rd province.

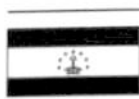

TAJIKISTAN
Republic of Tajikistan
Capital Dushanbe

Area sq km	143 100	**Currency**	Somoni
Area sq miles	55 251	**Languages**	Tajik, Uzbek,
Population	6 977 000		Russian

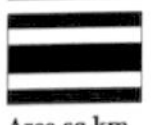

TANZANIA
United Republic of Tanzania
Capital Dodoma

Area sq km	945 087	**Currency**	Tanzanian shilling
Area sq miles	364 900	**Languages**	Swahili, English,
Population	46 218 000		Nyamwezi,
			local lang.

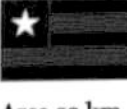

THAILAND
Kingdom of Thailand
Capital Bangkok (Krung Thep)

Area sq km	513 115	**Currency**	Baht
Area sq miles	198 115	**Languages**	Thai, Lao,
Population	69 519 000		Chinese, Malay,
			Mon-Khmer lang.

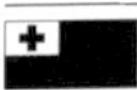

TOGO
Republic of Togo
Capital Lomé

Area sq km	56 785	**Currency**	CFA franc*
Area sq miles	21 925	**Languages**	French, Ewe,
Population	6 155 000		Kabre, local lang.

TONGA
Kingdom of Tonga
Capital Nuku'alofa

Area sq km	748	**Currency**	Pa'anga
Area sq miles	289	**Languages**	Tongan, English
Population	105 000		

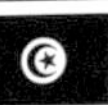

TRINIDAD AND TOBAGO
Republic of Trinidad and Tobago
Capital Port of Spain

Area sq km	5 130	**Currency**	Trinidad and
Area sq miles	1 981		Tobago dollar
Population	1 346 000	**Languages**	English, creole,
			Hindi

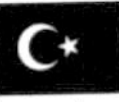

TUNISIA
Republic of Tunisia
Capital Tunis

Area sq km	164 150	**Currency**	Tunisian dinar
Area sq miles	63 379	**Languages**	Arabic, French
Population	10 594 000		

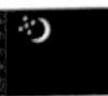

TURKEY
Republic of Turkey
Capital Ankara

Area sq km	779 452	**Currency**	Lira
Area sq miles	300 948	**Languages**	Turkish, Kurdish
Population	73 640 000		

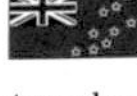

TURKMENISTAN
Republic of Turkmenistan
Capital Aşgabat (Ashkhabad)

Area sq km	488 100	**Currency**	Turkmen manat
Area sq miles	188 456	**Languages**	Turkmen, Uzbek,
Population	5 105 000		Russian

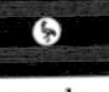

TUVALU
Capital Vaiaku

Area sq km	25	**Currency**	Australian dollar
Area sq miles	10	**Languages**	Tuvaluan, English
Population	10 000		

UGANDA
Republic of Uganda
Capital Kampala

Area sq km	241 038	**Currency**	Ugandan shilling
Area sq miles	93 065	**Languages**	English, Swahili,
Population	34 509 000		Luganda,
			local lang.

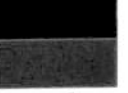

UKRAINE
Capital Kiev (Kyiv)

Area sq km	603 700	**Currency**	Hryvnia
Area sq miles	233 090	**Languages**	Ukrainian,
Population	45 190 000		Russian

UNITED ARAB EMIRATES
Federation of Emirates
Capital Abu Dhabi (Abū Ẓaby)

Area sq km	77 700	**Currency**	UAE dirham
Area sq miles	30 000	**Languages**	Arabic, English
Population	7 891 000		

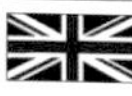

UNITED KINGDOM
United Kingdom of Great Britain and
Northern Ireland
Capital London

Area sq km	243 609	**Currency**	Pound sterling
Area sq miles	94 058	**Languages**	English, Welsh,
Population	62 417 000		Gaelic

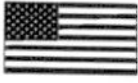

UNITED STATES OF AMERICA
Capital Washington D.C.

Area sq km	9 826 635	**Currency**	US dollar
Area sq miles	3 794 085	**Languages**	English, Spanish
Population	313 085 000		

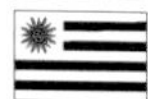

URUGUAY
Oriental Republic of Uruguay
Capital Montevideo

Area sq km	176 215	**Currency**	Uruguayan peso
Area sq miles	68 037	**Languages**	Spanish
Population	3 380 000		

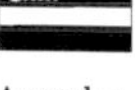

UZBEKISTAN
Republic of Uzbekistan
Capital Tashkent

Area sq km	447 400	**Currency**	Uzbek som
Area sq miles	172 742	**Languages**	Uzbek, Russian,
Population	27 760 000		Tajik, Kazakh

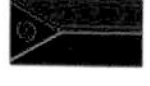

VANUATU
Republic of Vanuatu
Capital Port Vila

Area sq km	12 190	**Currency**	Vatu
Area sq miles	4 707	**Languages**	English,
Population	246 000		Bislama (creole),
			French

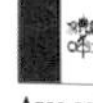

VATICAN CITY
Vatican City State or Holy See
Capital Vatican City

Area sq km	0.5	**Currency**	Euro
Area sq miles	0.2	**Languages**	Italian
Population	800		

VENEZUELA
Bolivarian Republic of Venezuela
Capital Caracas

Area sq km	912 050	**Currency**	Bolívar fuerte
Area sq miles	352 144	**Languages**	Spanish,
Population	29 437 000		Amerindian lang.

VIETNAM
Socialist Republic of Vietnam
Capital Ha Nôi (Hanoi)

Area sq km	329 565	**Currency**	Dong
Area sq miles	127 246	**Languages**	Vietnamese, Thai,
Population	88 792 000		Khmer, Chinese,
			local lang.

West Bank
Disputed territory

Area sq km	5 860	**Currency**	Jordanian dinar,
Area sq miles	2 263		Israeli shekel
Population	2 513 283	**Languages**	Arabic, Hebrew

Western Sahara
Disputed territory (Morocco)
Capital Laâyoune

Area sq km	266 000	**Currency**	Moroccan dirham
Area sq miles	102 703	**Languages**	Arabic
Population	548 000		

YEMEN
Republic of Yemen
Capital Şan'ā'

Area sq km	527 968	**Currency**	Yemeni riyal
Area sq miles	203 850	**Languages**	Arabic
Population	24 800 000		

ZAMBIA
Republic of Zambia
Capital Lusaka

Area sq km	752 614	**Currency**	Zambian kwacha
Area sq miles	290 586	**Languages**	English, Bemba,
Population	13 475 000		Nyanja, Tonga,
			local lang.

ZIMBABWE
Republic of Zimbabwe
Capital Harare

Area sq km	390 759	**Currency**	Zimbabwean
Area sq miles	150 873		dollar (suspended)
Population	12 754 000	**Languages**	English, Shona,
			Ndebele

Total Land Area 8 844 516 sq km / 3 414 868 sq miles
(includes New Guinea and Pacific Island nations)

HIGHEST MOUNTAIN
Puncak Jaya
4 884 m / 16 023 feet

Oceania cross section

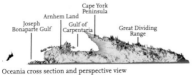

Joseph
Bonaparte Gulf

Arnhem Land

Cape York
Peninsula

Gulf of
Carpentaria

Great Dividing
Range

Oceania cross section and perspective view

Cook Strait

North Island

North Cape

Tasman Sea

HIGHEST MOUNTAINS	metres	feet	Map page
Puncak Jaya, Indonesia	4 884	16 023	59 D3
Puncak Trikora, Indonesia	4 730	15 518	59 D3
Puncak Mandala, Indonesia	4 700	15 420	59 D3
Puncak Yamin, Indonesia	4 595	15 075	—
Mt Wilhelm, Papua New Guinea	4 509	14 793	59 D3
Mt Kubor, Papua New Guinea	4 359	14 301	—

LARGEST ISLAND
New Guinea
808 510 sq km /
312 166 sq miles

LARGEST ISLANDS	sq km	sq miles	Map page
New Guinea	808 510	312 166	59 D3
South Island (Te Waipounamu)	151 215	58 384	54 B2
North Island (Te Ika-a-Māui)	115 777	44 701	54 B1
Tasmania	67 800	26 178	51 D4

LONGEST RIVERS	km	miles	Map page
Murray-Darling	3 672	2 282	52 B2
Darling	2 844	1 767	52 B2
Murray	2 375	1 476	52 B3
Murrumbidgee	1 485	923	52 B2
Lachlan	1 339	832	53 C2
Cooper Creek	1 113	692	52 B1

LARGEST LAKES	sq km	sq miles	Map page
Kati Thanda-Lake Eyre	0–8 900	0–3 436	52 A1
Lake Torrens	0–5 780	0–2 232	52 A1

LARGEST LAKE AND LOWEST POINT
Kati Thanda-Lake Eyre
0-8 900 sq km / 0-3 436 sq miles
16 m / 52 feet below sea level

LONGEST RIVER AND
LARGEST DRAINAGE BASIN
Murray-Darling
3 672 km / 2 282 miles
1 058 000 sq km / 409 000 sq miles

Total Land Area 45 036 492 sq km / 17 388 589 sq miles

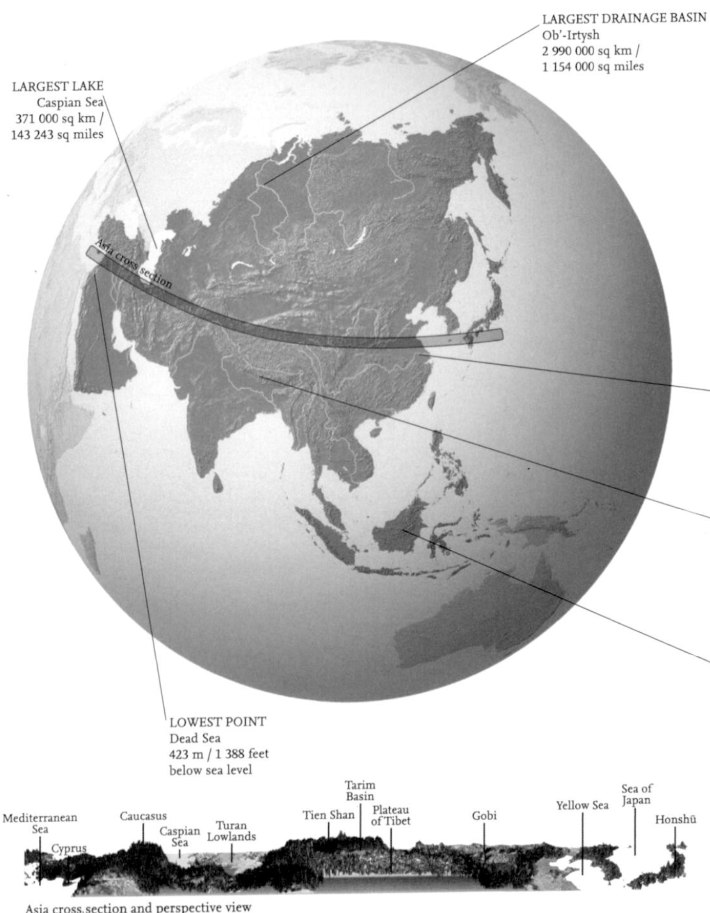

LARGEST DRAINAGE BASIN
Ob'-Irtysh
2 990 000 sq km /
1 154 000 sq miles

LARGEST LAKE
Caspian Sea
371 000 sq km /
143 243 sq miles

Asia cross section

LOWEST POINT
Dead Sea
423 m / 1 388 feet
below sea level

Mediterranean
Sea
Cyprus
Caucasus
Caspian
Sea
Turan
Lowlands
Tien Shan
Tarim
Basin
Plateau
of Tibet
Gobi
Yellow Sea
Sea of
Japan
Honshū

Asia cross section and perspective view

HIGHEST MOUNTAINS	metres	feet	Map page
Mt Everest (Sagarmatha/ Qomolangma Feng), China/Nepal	8 848	29 028	75 C2
K2 (Qogir Feng), China/Pakistan	8 611	28 251	74 B1
Kangchenjunga, India/Nepal	8 586	28 169	75 C2
Lhotse, China/Nepal	8 516	27 939	—
Makalu, China/Nepal	8 463	27 765	—
Cho Oyu, China/Nepal	8 201	26 906	—

LARGEST ISLANDS	sq km	sq miles	Map page
Borneo	745 561	287 861	61 C1
Sumatra (Sumatera)	473 606	182 859	60 A1
Honshū	227 414	87 805	67 B3
Celebes (Sulawesi)	189 216	73 056	58 C3
Java (Jawa)	132 188	51 038	61 B2
Luzon	104 690	40 421	64 B1

LONGEST RIVERS	km	miles	Map page
Yangtze (Chang Jiang)	6 380	3 965	70 C2
Ob'-Irtysh	5 568	3 460	86 F2
Yenisey-Angara-Selenga	5 550	3 449	83 H3
Yellow (Huang He)	5 464	3 395	70 B2
Irtysh	4 440	2 759	86 F2
Mekong	4 425	2 750	63 B2

LARGEST LAKES	sq km	sq miles	Map page
Caspian Sea	371 000	143 243	81 C1
Lake Baikal (Ozero Baykal)	30 500	11 776	69 D1
Lake Balkhash (Ozero Balkash)	17 400	6 718	77 D2
Aral Sea (Aral'skoye More)	17 158	6 625	76 B2
Ysyk-Köl	6 200	2 394	77 D2

LONGEST RIVER
Yangtze (Chang Jiang)
6 380 km /
3 965 miles

HIGHEST MOUNTAIN
Mt Everest
8 848 m / 29 028 feet

LARGEST ISLAND
Borneo
745 561 sq km /
287 861 sq miles

Total Land Area 9 908 599 sq km / 3 825 710 sq miles

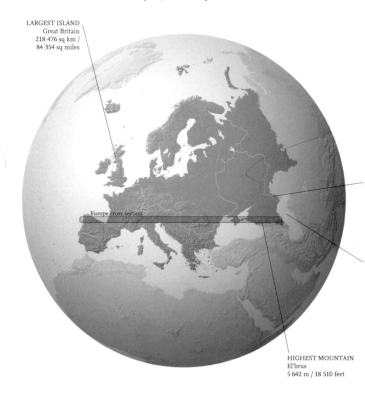

LARGEST ISLAND
Great Britain
218 476 sq km /
84 354 sq miles

Europe cross section

HIGHEST MOUNTAIN
El'brus
5 642 m / 18 510 feet

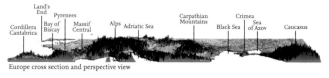

Cordillera
Cantabrica

Land's
End

Bay of
Biscay

Pyrenees

Massif
Central

Alps

Adriatic Sea

Carpathian
Mountains

Black Sea

Crimea

Sea
of Azov

Caucasus

Europe cross section and perspective view

HIGHEST MOUNTAINS	metres	feet	Map pages
El'brus, Russian Federation	5 642	18 510	87 D4
Gora Dykh-Tau, Russian Federation	5 204	17 073	—
Shkhara, Georgia/Russian Federation	5 201	17 063	—
Kazbek, Georgia/Russian Federation	5 047	16 558	76 A2
Mont Blanc, France/Italy	4 810	15 781	105 D2
Dufourspitze, Italy/Switzerland	4 634	15 203	—

LARGEST ISLANDS	sq km	sq miles	Map pages
Great Britain	218 476	84 354	95 C3
Iceland	102 820	39 699	92 A3
Ireland	83 045	32 064	97 C2
Ostrov Severnyy (part of Novaya Zemlya)	47 079	18 177	86 E1
Spitsbergen	37 814	14 600	82 C1

LONGEST RIVER AND
LARGEST DRAINAGE BASIN
Volga
3 688 km / 2 292 miles
1 380 000 sq km / 533 000 sq miles

LONGEST RIVERS	km	miles	Map pages
Volga	3 688	2 292	89 F2
Danube	2 850	1 771	110 A1
Dnieper	2 285	1 420	91 C2
Kama	2 028	1 260	86 E3
Don	1 931	1 200	89 E3
Pechora	1 802	1 120	86 E2

LARGEST LAKE AND LOWEST POINT
Caspian Sea
371 000 sq km / 143 243 sq miles
28m / 92 feet below sea level

LARGEST LAKES	sq km	sq miles	Map pages
Caspian Sea	371 000	143 243	81 C1
Lake Ladoga (Ladozhskoye Ozero)	18 390	7 100	86 C2
Lake Onega (Onezhskoye Ozero)	9 600	3 707	86 C2
Vänern	5 585	2 156	93 F4
Rybinskoye Vodokhranilishche	5 180	2 000	89 E2

Total Land Area 30 343 578 sq km / 11 715 655 sq miles

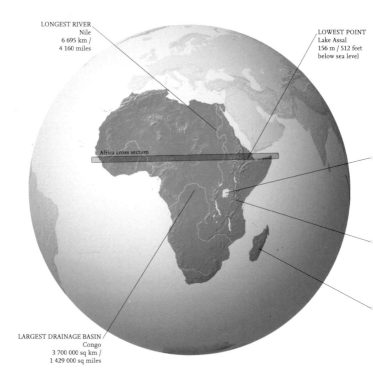

LONGEST RIVER
Nile
6 695 km /
4 160 miles

LOWEST POINT
Lake Assal
156 m / 512 feet
below sea level

Africa cross section

LARGEST DRAINAGE BASIN
Congo
3 700 000 sq km /
1 429 000 sq miles

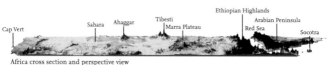

Africa cross section and perspective view

Cap Vert — Sahara — Ahaggar — Tibesti — Marra Plateau — Ethiopian Highlands — Red Sea — Arabian Peninsula — Socotra

HIGHEST MOUNTAINS	metres	feet	Map page
Kilimanjaro, Tanzania	5 892	19 330	119 D3
Mt Kenya (Kirinyaga), Kenya	5 199	17 057	119 D3
Margherita Peak, Democratic Republic of the Congo/Uganda	5 110	16 765	119 C2
Meru, Tanzania	4 565	14 977	119 D3
Ras Dejen, Ethiopia	4 533	14 872	117 B3
Mt Karisimbi, Rwanda	4 510	14 796	—

LARGEST ISLANDS	sq km	sq miles	Map page
Madagascar	587 040	226 656	121 D3

LONGEST RIVERS	km	miles	Map page
Nile	6 695	4 160	116 B1
Congo	4 667	2 900	118 B3
Niger	4 184	2 600	115 C4
Zambezi	2 736	1 700	120 C2
Webi Shabeelle	2 490	1 547	117 C4
Ubangi	2 250	1 398	118 B3

LARGEST LAKES	sq km	sq miles	Map page
Lake Victoria	68 870	26 591	52 B2
Lake Tanganyika	32 600	12 587	119 C3
Lake Nyasa (Lake Malawi)	29 500	11 390	121 C1
Lake Volta	8 482	3 275	114 C4
Lake Turkana	6 500	2 510	119 D2
Lake Albert	5 600	2 162	119 D2

LARGEST LAKE
Lake Victoria
68 870 sq km /
26 591 sq miles

HIGHEST MOUNTAIN
Kilimanjaro
5 892 m / 19 330 feet

LARGEST ISLAND
Madagascar
587 040 sq km /
226 656 sq miles

Total Land Area 24 680 331 sq km / 9 529 076 sq miles
(including Hawaiian Islands)

HIGHEST MOUNTAIN
Mt McKinley
6 194 m / 20 321 feet

LARGEST ISLAND
Greenland
2 175 600 sq km /
839 999 sq miles

North America cross section

LOWEST POINT
Death Valley
86 m / 282 feet
below sea level

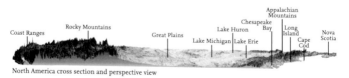

Coast Ranges Rocky Mountains Great Plains Lake Michigan Lake Huron Lake Erie Chesapeake Bay Appalachian Mountains Long Island Cape Cod Nova Scotia

North America cross section and perspective view

HIGHEST MOUNTAINS	metres	feet	Map page
Mt McKinley, USA	6 194	20 321	124 F2
Mt Logan, Canada	5 959	19 550	126 B2
Pico de Orizaba, Mexico	5 610	18 405	145 C3
Mt St Elias, USA	5 489	18 008	126 B2
Volcán Popocatépetl, Mexico	5 452	17 887	145 C3
Mt Foraker, USA	5 303	17 398	—

LARGEST LAKE
Lake Superior
82 100 sq km /
31 699 sq miles

LARGEST ISLANDS	sq km	sq miles	Map page
Greenland	2 175 600	839 999	127 I2
Baffin Island	507 451	195 927	127 G2
Victoria Island	217 291	83 896	126 D2
Ellesmere Island	196 236	75 767	127 F1
Cuba	110 860	42 803	146 B2
Newfoundland	108 860	42 031	131 E2
Hispaniola	76 192	29 418	147 C2

LONGEST RIVERS	km	miles	Map page
Mississippi-Missouri	5 969	3 709	133 D3
Mackenzie-Peace-Finlay	4 241	2 635	126 C2
Missouri	4 086	2 539	137 E3
Mississippi	3 765	2 340	142 C3
Yukon	3 185	1 979	126 A2
St Lawrence	3 058	1 900	131 D2

LONGEST RIVER AND
LARGEST DRAINAGE BASIN
Mississippi-Missouri
5 969 km / 3 709 miles
3 250 000 sq km / 1 255 000
sq miles

LARGEST LAKES	sq km	sq miles	Map page
Lake Superior	82 100	31 699	140 B1
Lake Huron	59 600	23 012	140 C2
Lake Michigan	57 800	22 317	140 B2
Great Bear Lake	31 328	12 096	126 C2
Great Slave Lake	28 568	11 030	128 C1
Lake Erie	25 700	9 923	140 C2
Lake Winnipeg	24 387	9 416	129 E2
Lake Ontario	18 960	7 320	141 D2

Total Land Area 17 815 420 sq km / 6 878 534 sq miles

LARGEST LAKE
Lago Titicaca
8 340 sq km /
3 220 sq miles

South America cross section

LARGEST ISLAND
Isla Grande de Tierra del Fuego
47 000 sq km / 18 147 sq miles

Andes

Selvas

Planalto do
Mato Grosso

Bahia de
São Marcos

Cabo de
São Roque

South America cross section and perspective view

HIGHEST MOUNTAINS	metres	feet	Map page
Cerro Aconcagua, Argentina	6 959	22 831	153 B4
Nevado Ojos del Salado, Argentina/Chile	6 908	22 664	152 B3
Cerro Bonete, Argentina	6 872	22 546	—
Cerro Pissis, Argentina	6 858	22 500	—
Cerro Tupungato, Argentina/Chile	6 800	22 309	—
Cerro Mercedario, Argentina	6 770	22 211	—

LARGEST ISLANDS	sq km	sq miles	Map page
Isla Grande de Tierra del Fuego	47 000	18 147	153 B6
Isla de Chiloé	8 394	3 241	153 A5
East Falkland	6 760	2 610	153 C6
West Falkland	5 413	2 090	153 B6

LONGEST RIVER AND
LARGEST DRAINAGE BASIN
Amazon
8 516 km / 4 049 miles
7 050 000 sq km / 2 722 000 sq miles

LONGEST RIVERS	km	miles	Map page
Amazon (Amazonas)	6 516	4 049	150 C1
Río de la Plata-Paraná	4 500	2 796	153 C4
Purus	3 218	2 000	150 B2
Madeira	3 200	1 988	150 C2
São Francisco	2 900	1 802	151 E3
Tocantins	2 750	1 709	151 D2

HIGHEST MOUNTAIN
Cerro Aconcagua
6 959 m / 22 831 feet

LARGEST LAKES	sq km	sq miles	Map page
Lake Titicaca	8 340	3 220	152 B2

LOWEST POINT
Laguna del Carbón
105 m / 345 feet below sea level

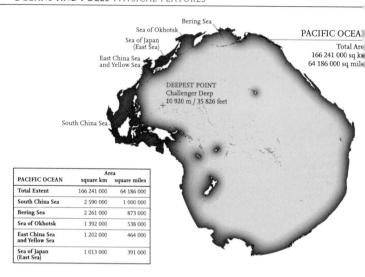

PACIFIC OCEAN

Total Area
166 241 000 sq km
64 186 000 sq miles

Bering Sea
Sea of Okhotsk
Sea of Japan
(East Sea)
East China Sea
and Yellow Sea
South China Sea

DEEPEST POINT
Challenger Deep
10 920 m / 35 826 feet

PACIFIC OCEAN	Area square km	square miles
Total Extent	166 241 000	64 186 000
South China Sea	2 590 000	1 000 000
Bering Sea	2 261 000	873 000
Sea of Okhotsk	1 392 000	538 000
East China Sea and Yellow Sea	1 202 000	464 000
Sea of Japan (East Sea)	1 013 000	391 000

ANTARCTICA

Total Land Area 12 093 000 sq km /
4 669 107 sq miles (excluding ice shelves)

HIGHEST MOUNTAINS	Height metres	feet
Mount Vinson	4 897	16 066
Mt Tyree	4 852	15 918
Mt Kirkpatrick	4 528	14 855
Mt Markham	4 351	14 275
Mt Sidley	4 285	14 058
Mt Minto	4 165	13 665

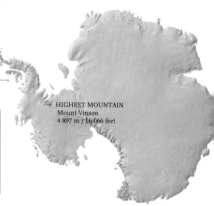

HIGHEST MOUNTAIN
Mount Vinson
4 897 m / 16 066 feet

ATLANTIC OCEAN

Arctic Ocean

Total Area
86 557 000 sq km
33 420 000 sq miles

Hudson Bay

Baltic Sea

North Sea   Black Sea

Gulf of Mexico

DEEPEST POINT
Milwaukee Deep
8 605 m / 28 231 feet

Mediterranean Sea

Caribbean Sea

ATLANTIC OCEAN	Area square km	square miles
Total Extent	86 557 000	33 420 000
Arctic Ocean	9 485 000	3 662 000
Caribbean Sea	2 512 000	970 000
Mediterranean Sea	2 510 000	969 000
Gulf of Mexico	1 544 000	596 000
Hudson Bay	1 233 000	476 000
North Sea	575 000	222 000
Black Sea	508 000	196 000
Baltic Sea	382 000	148 000

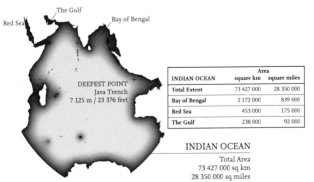

The Gulf

Red Sea

Bay of Bengal

DEEPEST POINT
Java Trench
7 125 m / 23 376 feet

INDIAN OCEAN	Area square km	square miles
Total Extent	73 427 000	28 350 000
Bay of Bengal	2 172 000	839 000
Red Sea	453 000	175 000
The Gulf	238 000	92 000

INDIAN OCEAN

Total Area
73 427 000 sq km
28 350 000 sq miles

MAJOR CLIMATIC REGIONS AND SUB-TYPES
Köppen classification system
Winkel Tripel Projection
scale 1:200 000 000

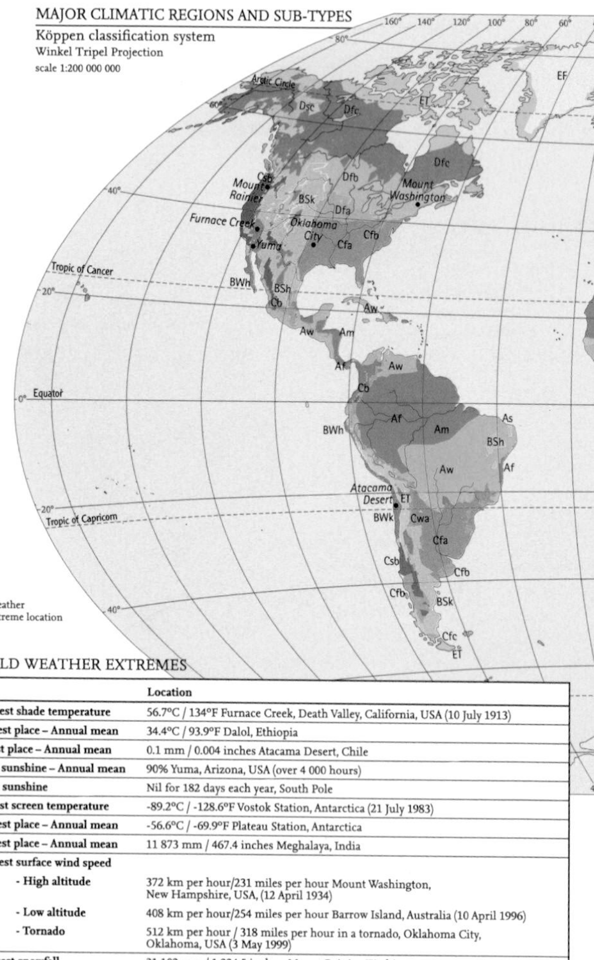

- Weather
  extreme location

WORLD WEATHER EXTREMES

	Location
Highest shade temperature	56.7°C / 134°F Furnace Creek, Death Valley, California, USA (10 July 1913)
Hottest place – Annual mean	34.4°C / 93.9°F Dalol, Ethiopia
Driest place – Annual mean	0.1 mm / 0.004 inches Atacama Desert, Chile
Most sunshine – Annual mean	90% Yuma, Arizona, USA (over 4 000 hours)
Least sunshine	Nil for 182 days each year, South Pole
Lowest screen temperature	-89.2°C / -128.6°F Vostok Station, Antarctica (21 July 1983)
Coldest place – Annual mean	-56.6°C / -69.9°F Plateau Station, Antarctica
Wettest place – Annual mean	11 873 mm / 467.4 inches Meghalaya, India
Highest surface wind speed	
- High altitude	372 km per hour/231 miles per hour Mount Washington, New Hampshire, USA, (12 April 1934)
- Low altitude	408 km per hour/254 miles per hour Barrow Island, Australia (10 April 1996)
- Tornado	512 km per hour / 318 miles per hour in a tornado, Oklahoma City, Oklahoma, USA (3 May 1999)
Greatest snowfall	31 102 mm / 1 224.5 inches Mount Rainier, Washington, USA (19 February 1971 – 18 February 1972)

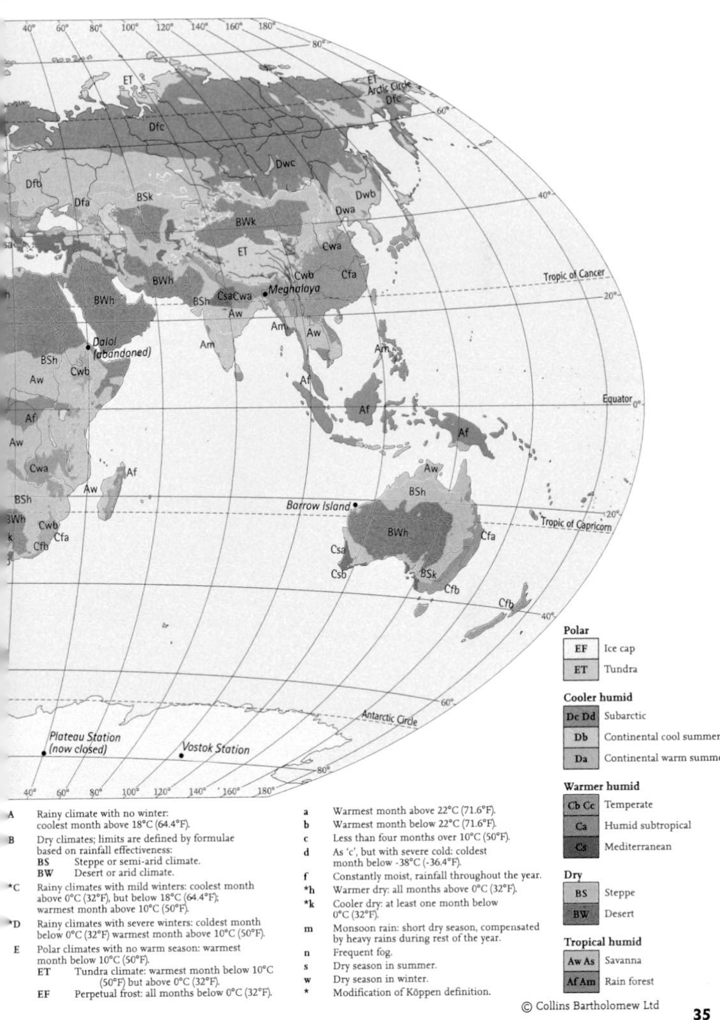

Polar

| EF | Ice cap |
| ET | Tundra |

Cooler humid

Dc Dd	Subarctic
Db	Continental cool summer
Da	Continental warm summer

Warmer humid

Cb Cc	Temperate
Ca	Humid subtropical
Cs	Mediterranean

Dry

| BS | Steppe |
| BW | Desert |

Tropical humid

| Aw As | Savanna |
| Af Am | Rain forest |

A Rainy climate with no winter: coolest month above 18°C (64.4°F).

B Dry climates; limits are defined by formulae based on rainfall effectiveness:
BS Steppe or semi-arid climate.
BW Desert or arid climate.

*C Rainy climate with mild winters: coolest month above 0°C (32°F), but below 18°C (64.4°F); warmest month above 10°C (50°F).

*D Rainy climates with severe winters: coldest month below 0°C (32°F) warmest month above 10°C (50°F).

E Polar climates with no warm season: warmest month below 10°C (50°F).
ET Tundra climate: warmest month below 10°C (50°F) but above 0°C (32°F).
EF Perpetual frost: all months below 0°C (32°F).

a Warmest month above 22°C (71.6°F).
b Warmest month below 22°C (71.6°F).
c Less than four months over 10°C (50°F).
d As 'c', but with severe cold: coldest month below -38°C (-36.4°F).
f Constantly moist, rainfall throughout the year.
*h Warmer dry: all months above 0°C (32°F).
*k Cooler dry: at least one month below 0°C (32°F).
m Monsoon rain: short dry season, compensated by heavy rains during rest of the year.
n Frequent fog.
s Dry season in summer.
w Dry season in winter.
* Modification of Köppen definition.

© Collins Bartholomew Ltd

35

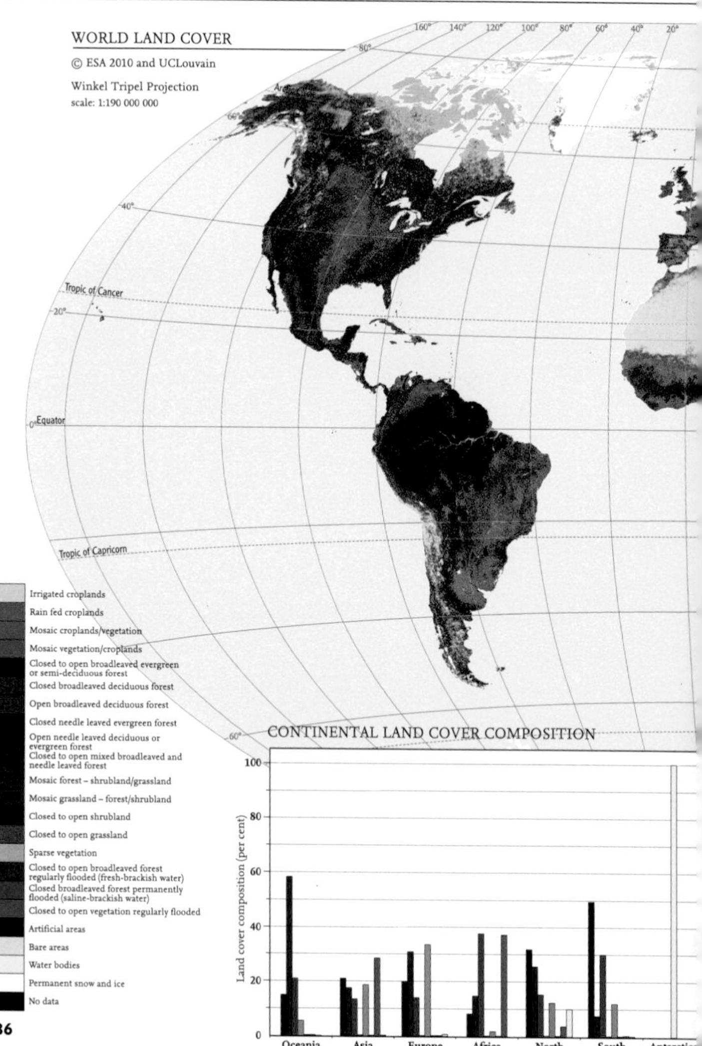

WORLD LAND COVER

© ESA 2010 and UCLouvain

Winkel Tripel Projection
scale: 1:190 000 000

Tropic of Cancer

Equator

Tropic of Capricorn

Irrigated croplands
Rain fed croplands
Mosaic croplands/vegetation
Mosaic vegetation/croplands
Closed to open broadleaved evergreen or semi-deciduous forest
Closed broadleaved deciduous forest
Open broadleaved deciduous forest
Closed needle leaved evergreen forest
Open needle leaved deciduous or evergreen forest
Closed to open mixed broadleaved and needle leaved forest
Mosaic forest – shrubland/grassland
Mosaic grassland – forest/shrubland
Closed to open shrubland
Closed to open grassland
Sparse vegetation
Closed to open broadleaved forest regularly flooded (fresh-brackish water)
Closed broadleaved forest permanently flooded (saline-brackish water)
Closed to open vegetation regularly flooded
Artificial areas
Bare areas
Water bodies
Permanent snow and ice
No data

CONTINENTAL LAND COVER COMPOSITION

Land cover composition (per cent)

Oceania   Asia   Europe   Africa   North America   South America   Antarctica

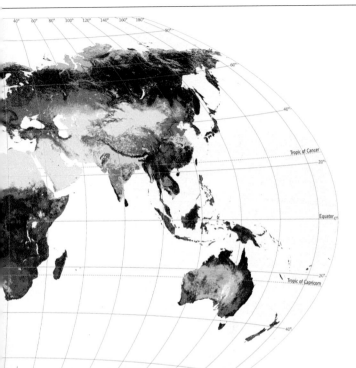

LAND COVER GRAPHS - CLASSIFICATION

Class description	Map classes
Forest/Woodland	Evergreen needleleaf forest
	Evergreen broadleaf forest
	Deciduous needleleaf forest
	Deciduous broadleaf forest
	Mixed forest
Shrubland	Closed shrublands
	Open shrublands
Grass/Savanna	Woody savannas
	Savannas
	Grasslands
Wetland	Permanent wetlands
Crops/Mosaic	Croplands
	Cropland/Natural vegetation mosaic
Urban	Urban and built-up
Snow/Ice	Snow and Ice
Barren	Barren or sparsely vegetated

GLOBAL LAND COVER COMPOSITION

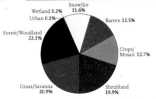

Wetland 0.2%
Snow/Ice 11.6%
Urban 0.1%
Barren 12.5%
Forest/Woodland 22.1%
Crops/Mosaic 12.7%
Grass/Savanna 20.9%
Shrubland 19.9%

© Collins Bartholomew Ltd

WORLD POPULATION DISTRIBUTION

Population Density
Winkel Tripel Projection
scale 1:190 000 000

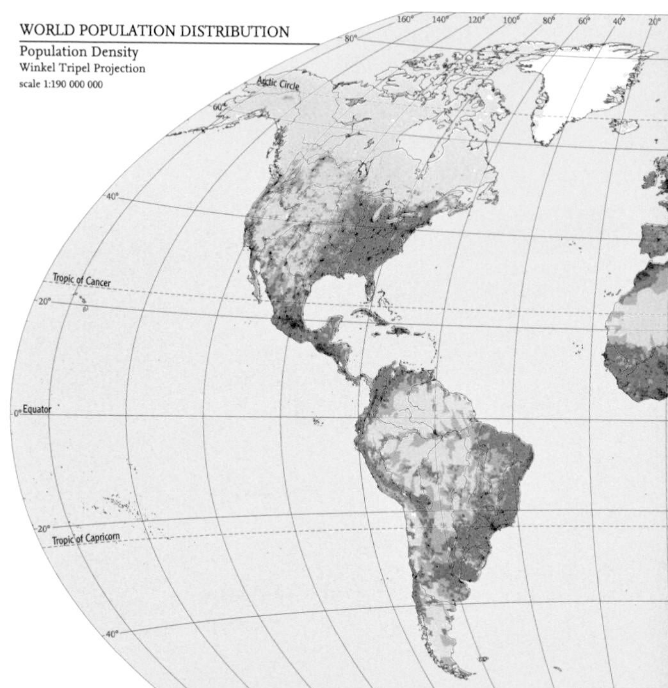

KEY POPULATION STATISTICS FOR MAJOR REGIONS

	Population 2013 (millions)	Growth (per cent)	Infant mortality rate	Total fertility rate	Life expectancy (years)
World	7 162	1.1	37	2.5	70
More developed regions[1]	1 253	0.3	6	1.7	78
Less developed regions[2]	5 909	1.3	40	2.6	67
Africa	1 111	2.5	64	4.7	58
Asia	4 299	1.0	31	2.2	71
Europe[3]	742	0.1	6	1.6	76
Latin America and the Caribbean[4]	617	1.1	18	2.2	75
North America	355	0.9	6	1.9	79
Oceania	38	1.4	20	2.4	78

1. Europe, North America, Australia, New Zealand and Japan.

2. Africa, Asia (excluding Japan), Latin America and the Caribbean and Oceania (excluding Australia and New Zealand).

3. Includes Russia.

4. South America, Central America (including Mexico) and all Caribbean Islands.

Except for population (2013) the data are annual averages projected for the period 2010–2015.

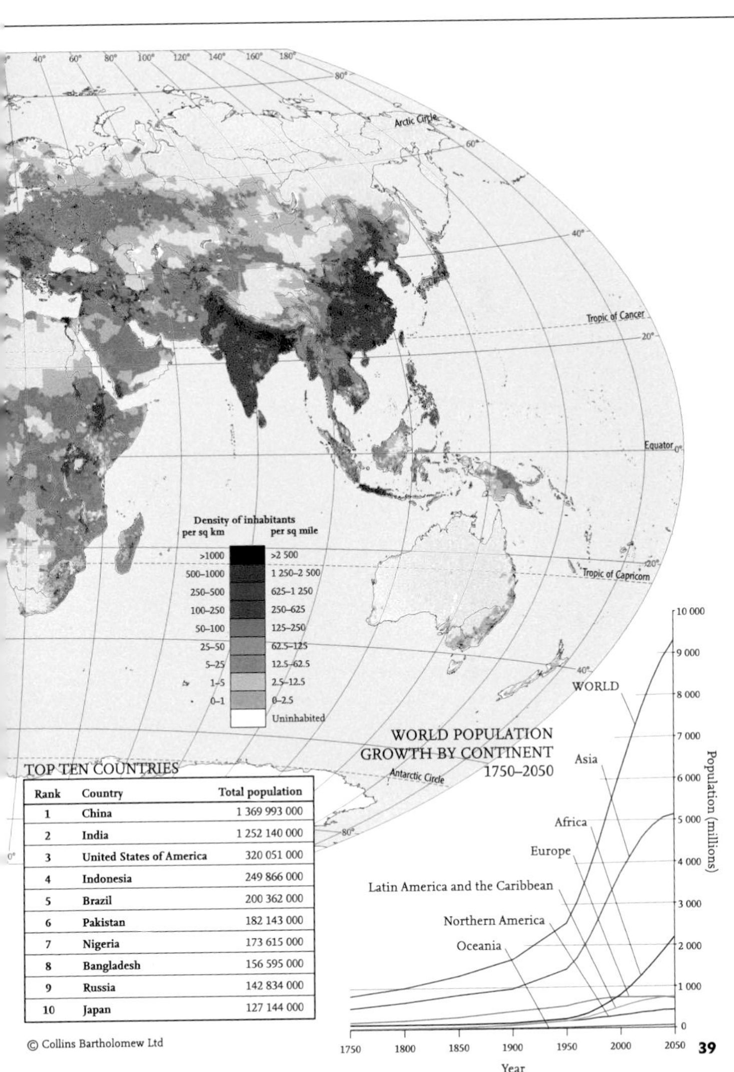

Density of inhabitants

per sq km	per sq mile
>1000	>2 500
500–1000	1 250–2 500
250–500	625–1 250
100–250	250–625
50–100	125–250
25–50	62.5–125
5–25	12.5–62.5
1–5	2.5–12.5
0–1	0–2.5
Uninhabited	

TOP TEN COUNTRIES

Rank	Country	Total population
1	China	1 369 993 000
2	India	1 252 140 000
3	United States of America	320 051 000
4	Indonesia	249 866 000
5	Brazil	200 362 000
6	Pakistan	182 143 000
7	Nigeria	173 615 000
8	Bangladesh	156 595 000
9	Russia	142 834 000
10	Japan	127 144 000

WORLD POPULATION GROWTH BY CONTINENT 1750–2050

WORLD

Asia

Africa

Europe

Latin America and the Caribbean

Northern America

Oceania

Population (millions)

Year

THE WORLD'S MAJOR CITIES

Urban agglomerations with over
1 million inhabitants.
Winkel Tripel Projection
scale 1:190 000 000

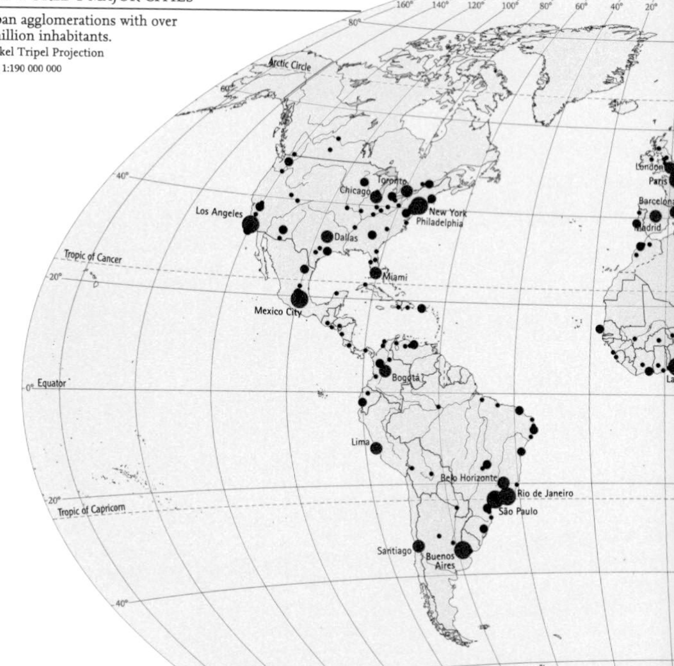

LEVEL OF URBANIZATION BY MAJOR REGION 1970–2030

Urban population as a percentage of total population

	1970	2010	2030
World	36.1	50.5	59.0
More developed regions[1]	64.7	75.2	80.9
Less developed regions[2]	25.3	45.1	55.0
Africa	23.6	40.0	49.9
Asia	22.7	42.2	52.8
Europe[3]	62.8	72.8	78.4
Latin America and the Caribbean[4]	57.1	79.6	84.9
Northern America	73.8	82.1	86.7
Oceania	70.8	70.2	71.4

1. Europe, North America, Australia,
New Zealand and Japan.

2. Africa, Asia (excluding Japan), Latin
America and the Caribbean, and
Oceania (excluding Australia and
New Zealand).

3. Includes Russian Federation.

4. South America, Central America
(including Mexico) and all Caribbean
Islands.

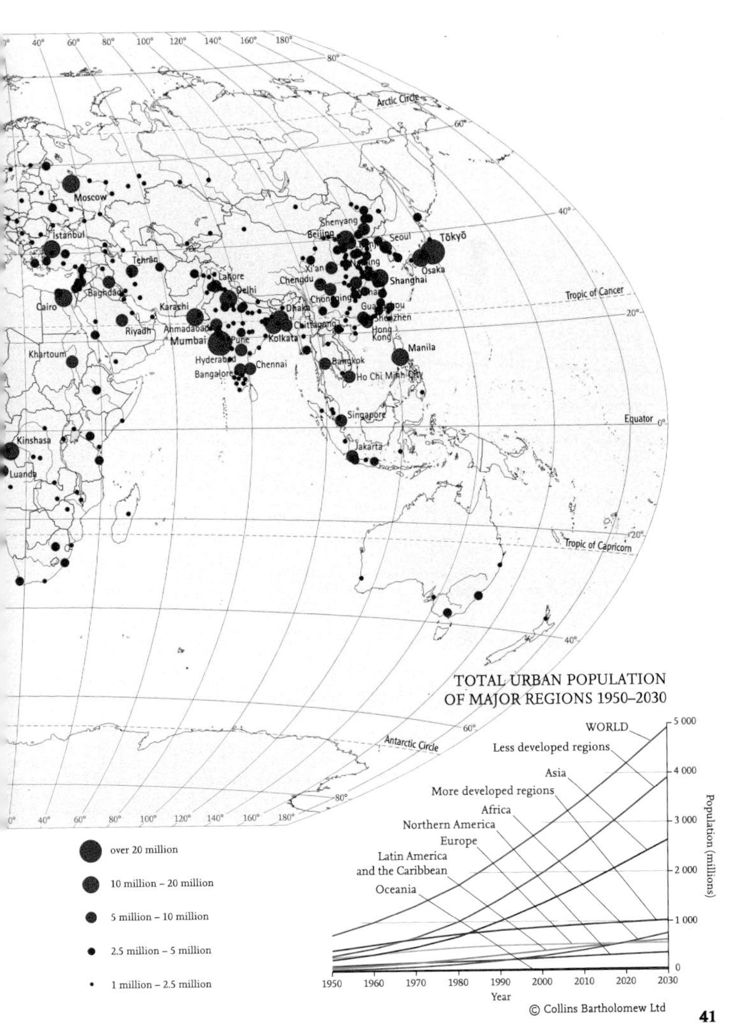

Moscow
Istanbul
Tehrān
Cairo
Baghdad
Riyadh
Khartoum
Karāchi
Lahore
Delhi
Dhaka
Ahmadābād
Mumbai
Hyderabād
Bangalore
Chennai
Kolkata
Chongqing
Chengdu
Shenyang
Beijing
Seoul
Tōkyō
Ōsaka
Shanghai
Guangzhou
Shenzhen
Hong Kong
Bangkok
Ho Chi Minh City
Manila
Singapore
Jakarta
Kinshasa
Luanda

Arctic Circle
Tropic of Cancer
Equator
Tropic of Capricorn
Antarctic Circle

TOTAL URBAN POPULATION
OF MAJOR REGIONS 1950–2030

WORLD
Less developed regions
Asia
More developed regions
Africa
Northern America
Europe
Latin America
and the Caribbean
Oceania

Population (millions)

5 000
4 000
3 000
2 000
1 000
0

1950 1960 1970 1980 1990 2000 2010 2020 2030
Year

over 20 million

10 million – 20 million

5 million – 10 million

2.5 million – 5 million

1 million – 2.5 million

© Collins Bartholomew Ltd

SYMBOLS

Map symbols used on the map pages are explained here. The status of nations and their boundaries are shown in this atlas as they are in reality at time of going to press, as far as can be ascertained. Where international boundaries are subject of disputes the aim is to take a strictly neutral viewpoint, based on advice from expert consultants. Settlements are classified in terms of both population and administrative significance. The abbreviations listed are those used in place names on the map pages and within the index.

BOUNDARIES

- International boundary
- Disputed international boundary or alignment unconfirmed
- Undefined international boundary in the sea. All land within this boundary is part of state or territory named.
- Disputed territory boundary
- Administrative boundary Shown for selected countries only.
- Ceasefire line or other boundary described on the map

TRANSPORT

- Motorway
- Main road
- Track
- Main railway
- Canal
- ⊕ Main airport

LAND AND WATER FEATURES

- Lake
- Impermanent lake
- Salt lake or lagoon
- Impermanent salt lake
- Dry salt lake or salt pan
- River
- Impermanent river
- Ice cap / Glacier
- 123 Pass height in metres
- 123 Summit △ height in metres
- 1234 Volcano ▲ Height in metres
- ∴ Site of special interest
- ∿∿∿ Wall

CITIES AND TOWNS

Built-up area
SCALE 1:4 000 000 only

Population	National Capital	Administrative Capital Shown for selected countries only	Other City or Town
over 10 million	**BEIJING** ■	São Paulo ◉	New York ◉
5 to 10 million	**MADRID** ■	Toronto ◉	Philadelphia ◉
1 to 5 million	**KUWAIT** ■	Sydney ◉	Seattle ○
500 000 to 1 million	**BANGUI** ■	Winnipeg ◉	Warangal ○
100 000 to 500 000	WELLINGTON ■	Edinburgh ◉	Apucarana ○
50 000 to 100 000	PORT OF SPAIN ■	Bismarck ◉	Invercargill ○
under 50 000	MALABO ■	Charlottetown ◉	Ceres ○

STYLES OF LETTERING

Cities and towns are explained separately

		Physical features	
Country	**FRANCE**	Island	*Gran Canaria*
Overseas Territory/Dependency	**Guadeloupe**	Lake	*Lake Erie*
Disputed Territory	WESTERN SAHARA	Mountain	*Mt Blanc*
Administrative name Shown for selected countries only.	**SCOTLAND**	River	*Thames*
Area name	PATAGONIA	Region	*LAPPLAND*

CONTINENTAL MAPS

BOUNDARIES

———— International boundary

------- Disputed international boundary

•••••••• Ceasefire line

CITIES AND TOWNS

National capital

Kuwait ■

Other city or town

Seattle ○

ABBREVIATIONS

Arch.	Archipelago			
B.	Bay			
	Bahia, Baía	Portuguese	bay	
	Bahía	Spanish	bay	
	Baie	French	bay	
C.	Cape			
	Cabo	Portuguese, Spanish	cape, headland	
	Cap	French	cape, headland	
Co	Cerro	Spanish	hill, peak, summit	
E.	East, Eastern			
Est.	Estrecho	Spanish	strait	
Gt	Great			
I.	Island, Isle			
	Ilha	Portuguese	island	
	Islas	Spanish	island	
Is	Islands, Isles			
	Islas	Spanish	islands	
Khr.	Khrebet	Russian	mountain range	
L.	Lake			
	Loch	(Scotland)	lake	
	Lough	(Ireland)	lake	
	Lac	French	lake	
	Lago	Portuguese, Spanish	lake	
M.	Mys	Russian	cape, point	
Mt	Mount			
	Mont	French	hill, mountain	
Mt.	Mountain			

Mts	Mountains			
	Monts	French	hills, mountains	
N.	North, Northern			
O.	Ostrov	Russian	island	
Pt	Point			
Pta	Punta	Italian, Spanish	cape, point	
R.	River			
	Rio	Portuguese	river	
	Río	Spanish	river	
	Rivière	French	river	
Ra.	Range			
S.	South, Southern			
	Salar, Salina, Salinas	Spanish	saltpan, saltpans	
Sa	Serra	Portuguese	mountain range	
	Sierra	Spanish	mountain range	
Sd	Sound			
S.E.	Southeast, Southeastern			
St	Saint			
	Sankt	German	saint	
	Sint	Dutch	saint	
Sta	Santa	Italian, Portuguese, Spanish	saint	
Ste	Sainte	French	saint	
Str.	Strait			
W.	West, Western			
	Wadi, Wādī	Arabic	watercourse	

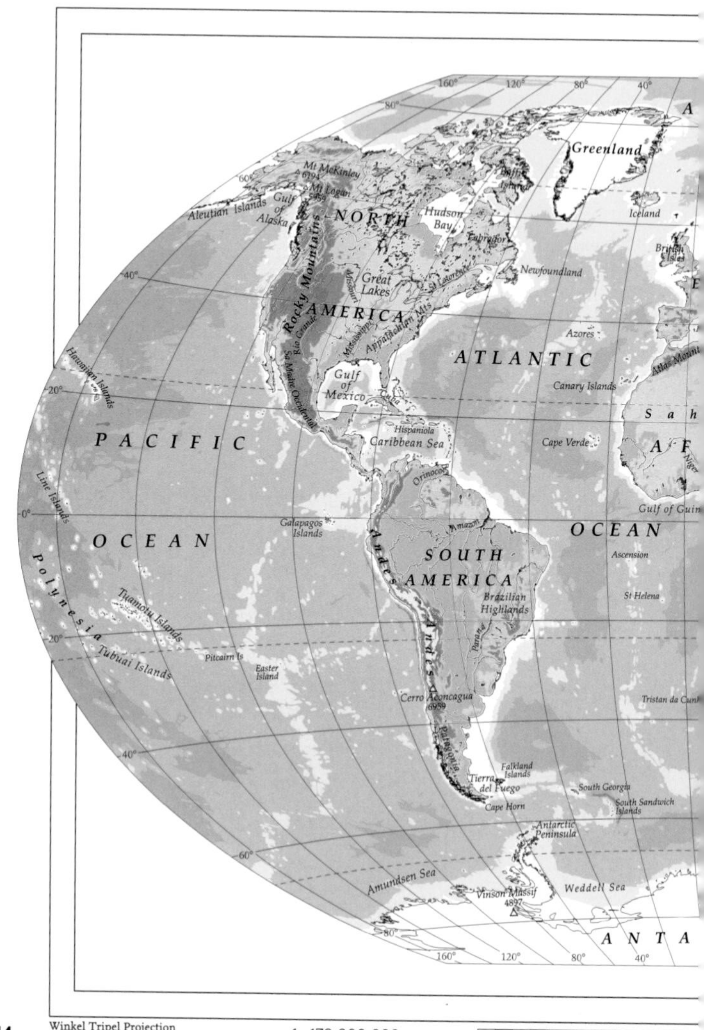

80° **160°** **120°** **80°** **40°** **A**

Greenland

60°

Mt McKinley
Mt Logan
Aleutian Islands   Gulf of   NORTH   Hudson
Alaska   AMERICA   Bay   Iceland

40°   Rocky Mountains   Great   British
Lakes   Labrador   Isles   E
AMERICA   Appalachian Mts   Newfoundland

Mississippi   Azores

20°   Hawaiian Islands   Gulf   ATLANTIC   Canary Islands
of
Mexico   S a h
PACIFIC   Hispaniola
Caribbean Sea   Cape Verde   A F

Orinoco   Gulf of Guin
Galapagos   Niger
0°   Islands   OCEAN

Line Islands   Amazon

OCEAN   SOUTH   Ascension
AMERICA   St Helena
Brazilian
Highlands

Polynesia   Tuamotu Islands

20°   Tubuai Islands   Pitcairn Is   Paraná
Easter
Island   Cerro Aconcagua   Tristan da Cunh
6959

40°   Falkland
Islands   South Georgia
Tierra   South Sandwich
del Fuego   Islands
Cape Horn   Antarctic
Peninsula
60°   Amundsen Sea   Weddell Sea
Vinson Massif
4897   A N T A

80°
160° **120°** **80°** **40°**

Winkel Tripel Projection   1 : 170 000 000   MILES 0   1000   2000   3000

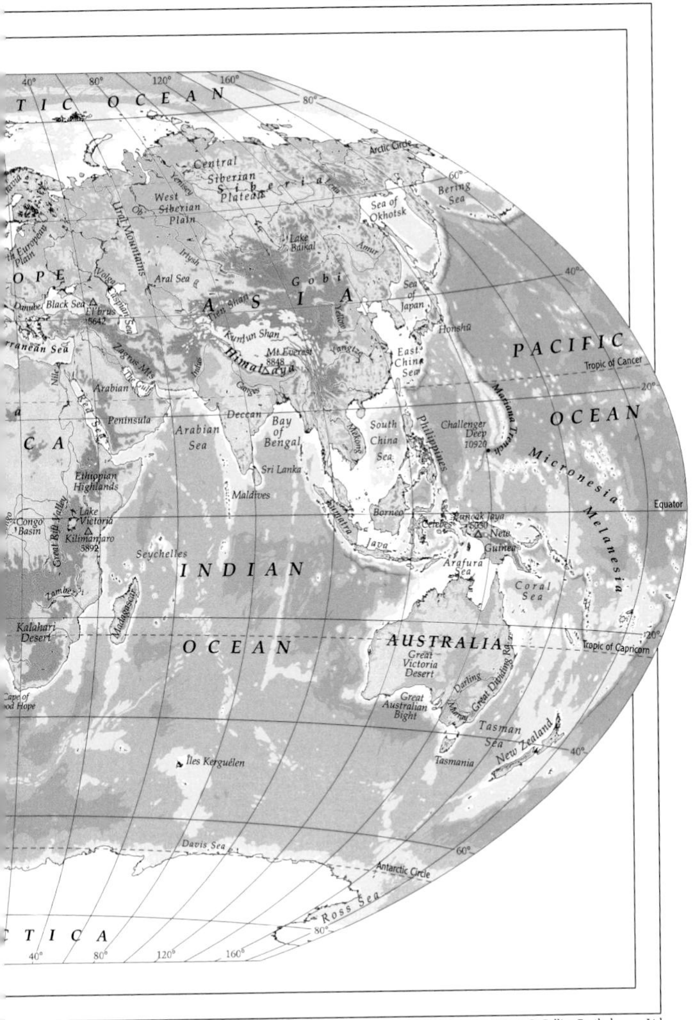

TIC OCEAN
Arctic Circle
Central Siberian Plateau
Siberia
Lena
Yenisey
West Siberian Plain
Ob
Ural Mountains
Sea of Okhotsk
Bering Sea
Lake Baikal
Amur
Irtysh
Aral Sea
Volga
Caspian Sea
Gobi
ASIA
Tien Shan
Black Sea
El'brus 5642
Danube
Sea of Japan
Honshu
Kunlun Shan
Mt Everest 8848
Himalaya
Yangtze
East China Sea
Zagros Mts
The Gulf
Indus
Arabian Peninsula
Red Sea
Nile
Ganges
PACIFIC OCEAN
Tropic of Cancer
Mariana Trench
Deccan
Bay of Bengal
Arabian Sea
Mekong
South China Sea
Philippines
Challenger Deep 10920
Micronesia
Ethiopian Highlands
Sri Lanka
Maldives
Borneo
Equator
Congo Basin
Great Rift Valley
Lake Victoria
Kilimanjaro 5892
Sumatra
Celebes
Puncak Jaya 5030
New Guinea
Melanesia
Java
Seychelles
INDIAN OCEAN
Arafura Sea
Coral Sea
Zambezi
Madagascar
Kalahari Desert
AUSTRALIA
Great Victoria Desert
Great Dividing Ra.
Tropic of Capricorn
Darling
Murray
Great Australian Bight
Cape of Good Hope
Tasman Sea
New Zealand
Tasmania
Îles Kerguélen
Davis Sea
Antarctic Circle
Ross Sea
TICA
40° 80° 120° 160°
0 1000 2000 3000 4000 5000 KILOMETRES

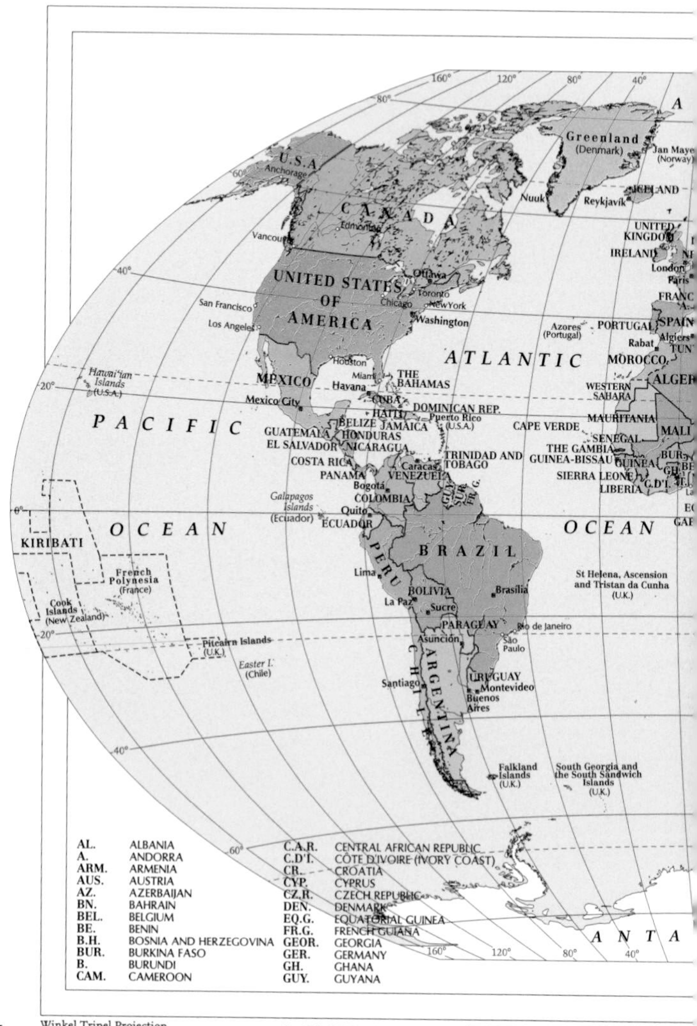

KIRIBATI

French
Polynesia
(France)

Cook
Islands
(New Zealand)

Pitcairn Islands
(U.K.)

Easter I.
(Chile)

PACIFIC OCEAN

Hawaiian
Islands
(U.S.A.)

U.S.A.

Anchorage

CANADA

Edmonton

Vancouver

San Francisco

Los Angeles

UNITED STATES
OF
AMERICA

Ottawa
Toronto
Chicago
New York
Washington

Houston

MEXICO

Mexico City

Havana

Miami

THE
BAHAMAS

CUBA

HAITI

DOMINICAN REP.
Puerto Rico
(U.S.A.)

JAMAICA

GUATEMALA
EL SALVADOR
COSTA RICA

BELIZE
HONDURAS
NICARAGUA

PANAMA

Caracas

TRINIDAD AND
TOBAGO

VENEZUELA

Bogotá

COLOMBIA

Galapagos
Islands
(Ecuador)

Quito

ECUADOR

Lima

PERU

La Paz

BOLIVIA

Sucre

Brasília

BRAZIL

São
Paulo

Rio de Janeiro

PARAGUAY

Asunción

ARGENTINA

Santiago

URUGUAY

Montevideo
Buenos
Aires

Falkland
Islands
(U.K.)

South Georgia and
the South Sandwich
Islands
(U.K.)

Greenland
(Denmark)

Jan Mayen
(Norway)

ICELAND

Nuuk

Reykjavík

UNITED
KINGDOM

IRELAND

London

Paris

FRANC

SPAIN

PORTUGAL

Azores
(Portugal)

Rabat

MOROCCO

Algiers

TUN

ALGE

WESTERN
SAHARA

MAURITANIA

CAPE VERDE

SENEGAL

THE GAMBIA
GUINEA-BISSAU

MALI

GUINEA

SIERRA LEONE

LIBERIA

C.D'I.

BURS
B

G

EQ

GAB

St Helena, Ascension
and Tristan da Cunha
(U.K.)

ATLANTIC OCEAN

OCEAN

A

ANTA

AL.   ALBANIA
A.   ANDORRA
ARM.   ARMENIA
AUS.   AUSTRIA
AZ.   AZERBAIJAN
BN.   BAHRAIN
BEL.   BELGIUM
BE.   BENIN
B.H.   BOSNIA AND HERZEGOVINA
BUR.   BURKINA FASO
B.   BURUNDI
CAM.   CAMEROON

C.A.R.   CENTRAL AFRICAN REPUBLIC
C.D'I.   CÔTE D'IVOIRE (IVORY COAST)
CR.   CROATIA
CYP.   CYPRUS
CZ.R.   CZECH REPUBLIC
DEN.   DENMARK
EQ.G.   EQUATORIAL GUINEA
FR.G.   FRENCH GUIANA
GEOR.   GEORGIA
GER.   GERMANY
GH.   GHANA
GUY.   GUYANA

46 Winkel Tripel Projection

1 : 170 000 000

MILES 0   1000   2000   3000

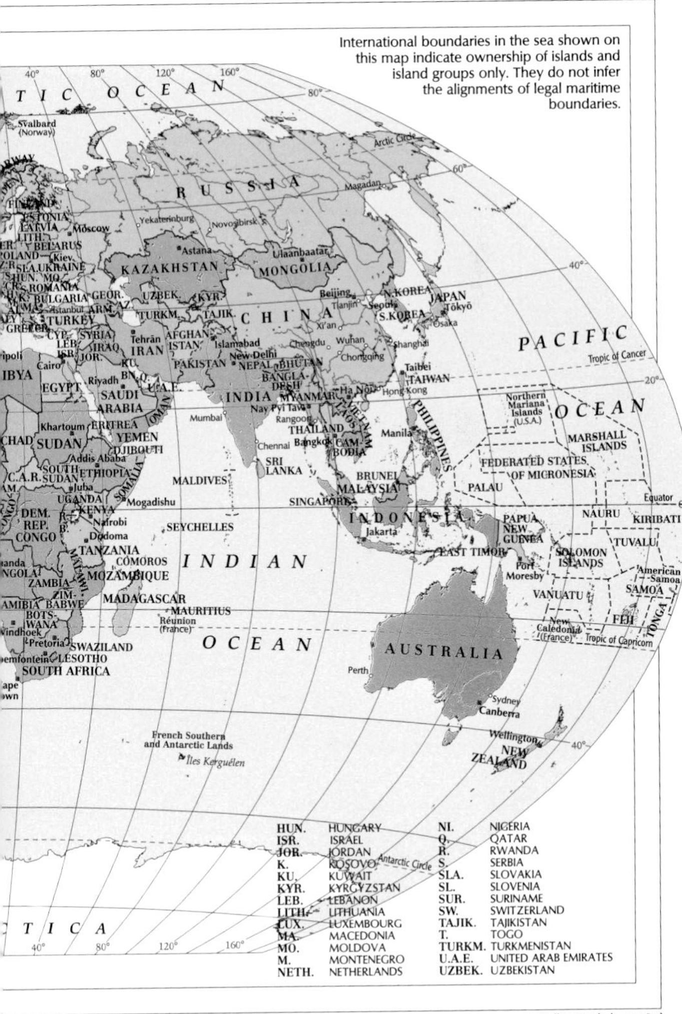

International boundaries in the sea shown on this map indicate ownership of islands and island groups only. They do not infer the alignments of legal maritime boundaries.

HUN.	HUNGARY	NI.	NIGERIA
ISR.	ISRAEL	Q.	QATAR
JOR.	JORDAN	R.	RWANDA
K.	KOSOVO	S.	SERBIA
KU.	KUWAIT	SLA.	SLOVAKIA
KYR.	KYRGYZSTAN	SL.	SLOVENIA
LEB.	LEBANON	SUR.	SURINAME
LITH.	LITHUANIA	SW.	SWITZERLAND
LUX.	LUXEMBOURG	TAJIK.	TAJIKISTAN
MA.	MACEDONIA	T.	TOGO
M.	MONTENEGRO	TURKM.	TURKMENISTAN
MO.	MOLDOVA	U.A.E.	UNITED ARAB EMIRATES
NETH.	NETHERLANDS	UZBEK.	UZBEKISTAN

0 1000 2000 3000 4000 5000 KILOMETRES

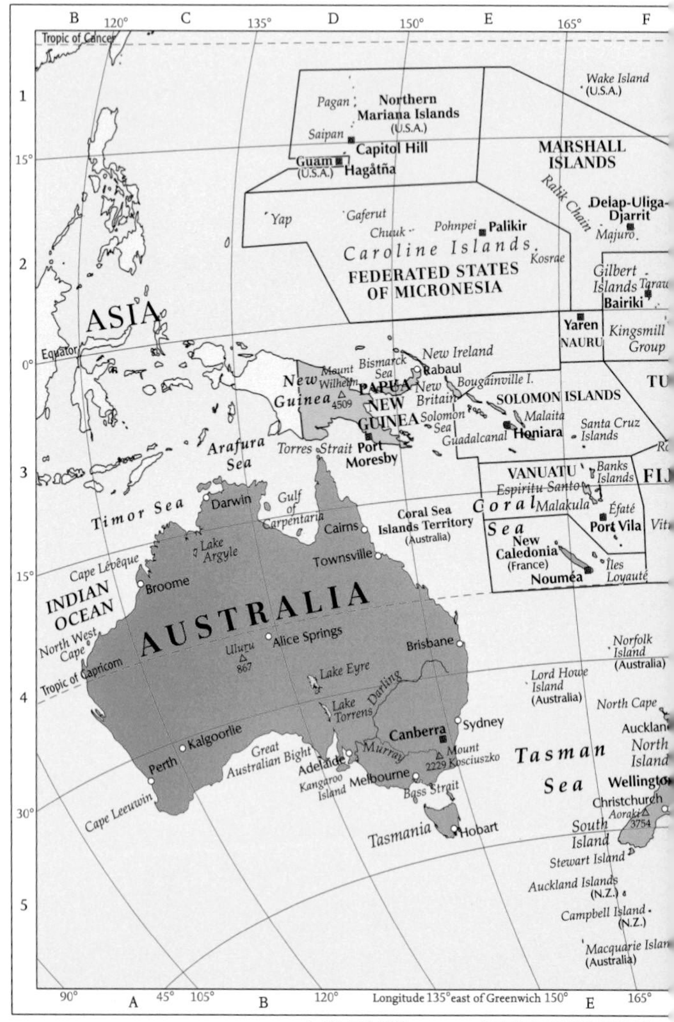

B
120°
C
135°
D
150°
E
165°
F
Tropic of Cancer
1
2
3
4
5
15°
0°
30°
Pagan
Northern
Mariana Islands
(U.S.A.)
Saipan
Capitol Hill
Guam
(U.S.A.)
Hagåtña
Wake Island
(U.S.A.)
MARSHALL
ISLANDS
Ralik Chain
Delap-Uliga-
Djarrit
Majuro
Yap
Gaferut
Chuuk
Pohnpei
Palikir
Caroline Islands
Kosrae
FEDERATED STATES
OF MICRONESIA
Gilbert
Islands
Tarau
Bairiki
ASIA
Yaren
NAURU
Kingsmill
Group
Equator
New Ireland
Bismarck
Sea
Rabaul
Mount
Wilhelm
4509
New
Guinea
PAPUA
NEW
GUINEA
New
Britain
Bougainville I.
SOLOMON ISLANDS
Solomon
Sea
Malaita
Honiara
Guadalcanal
Santa Cruz
Islands
Arafura
Sea
Torres Strait
Port
Moresby
VANUATU
Banks
Islands
Espiritu Santo
Malakula
Éfaté
Port Vila
Timor Sea
Darwin
Gulf
of
Carpentaria
Cairns
Coral Sea
Islands Territory
(Australia)
Coral
Sea
New
Caledonia
(France)
Nouméa
Îles
Loyauté
Lake
Argyle
Townsville
Cape Lévêque
Broome
INDIAN
OCEAN
AUSTRALIA
North West
Cape
Uluru
867
Alice Springs
Brisbane
Norfolk
Island
(Australia)
Tropic of Capricorn
Lake Eyre
Darling
Lord Howe
Island
(Australia)
Lake
Torrens
North Cape
Sydney
Auckland
Kalgoorlie
Great
Australian Bight
Canberra
Murray
Mount
2229 Kosciuszko
Tasman
Sea
North
Island
Wellington
Perth
Adelaide
Kangaroo
Island
Melbourne
Bass Strait
Christchurch
Aoraki
3754
Cape Leeuwin
Tasmania
Hobart
South
Island
Stewart Island
Auckland Islands
(N.Z.)
Campbell Island
(N.Z.)
Macquarie Island
(Australia)
90°
A
45°
105°
B
120°
Longitude 135° east of Greenwich 150°
E
165°
1 : 72 000 000
MILES 0
500
1000

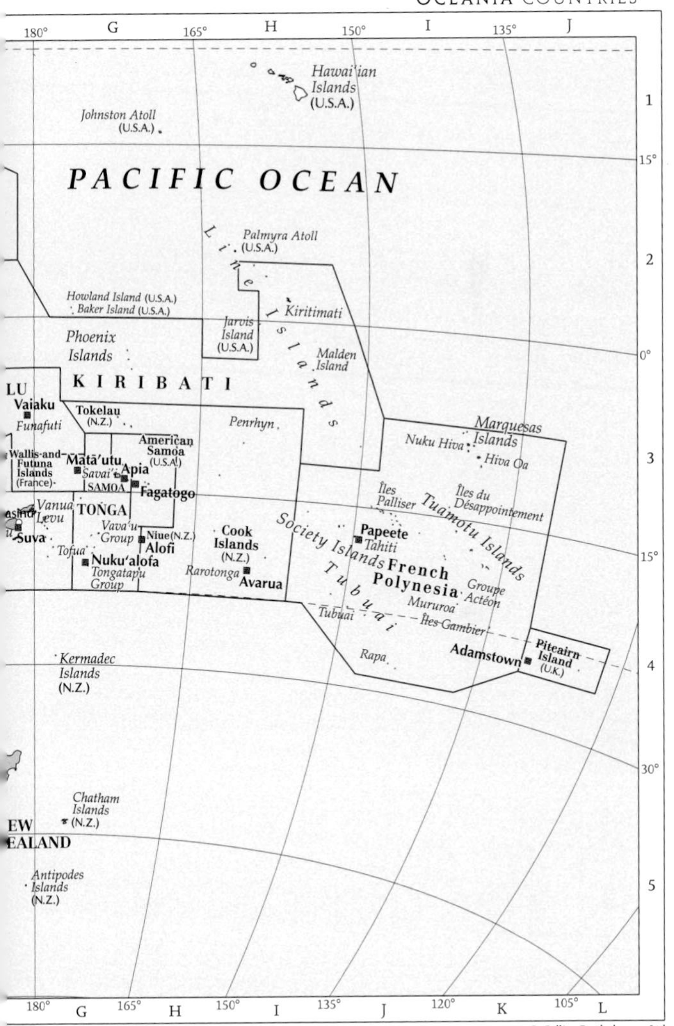

180°   G   165°   H   150°   I   135°   J

Hawai'ian Islands (U.S.A.)

Johnston Atoll (U.S.A.)

1

15°

PACIFIC OCEAN

Palmyra Atoll (U.S.A.)

2

Howland Island (U.S.A.)
Baker Island (U.S.A.)

Kiritimati

Jarvis Island (U.S.A.)

Phoenix Islands

Malden Island

0°

K I R I B A T I

Line Islands

Marquesas Islands

LU
Vaiaku
■ *Funafuti*

Tokelau (N.Z.)

Penrhyn

Nuku Hiva • *Hiva Oa*

3

Wallis-and-Futuna Islands (France)

American Samoa (U.S.A.)

Matā'utu ■
Savai'i ■ **Apia**
SAMOA

Fagatogo

Îles Palliser

Îles du Désappointement

Tuamotu Islands

asho
Vanua Levu
■
Suva

TONGA

Vava'u Group

■**Alofi**
Niue (N.Z.)

Cook Islands (N.Z.)

Society Islands

Papeete ■
Tahiti

French Polynesia

15°

Tofua ■
Nuku'alofa
Tongatapu Group

Rarotonga ■

Avarua

T u b u a i

Groupe Actéon

Mururoa • *Îles Gambier*

Tubuai ·

Pitcairn Island (U.K.)

Kermadec Islands (N.Z.)

Rapa ·

Adamstown ■

4

30°

EW
EALAND

Chatham Islands (N.Z.)

Antipodes Islands (N.Z.)

5

180°   G   165°   H   150°   I   135°   J   120°   K   105°   L

0   500   1000   1500 KILOMETRES

© Collins Bartholomew Ltd

49

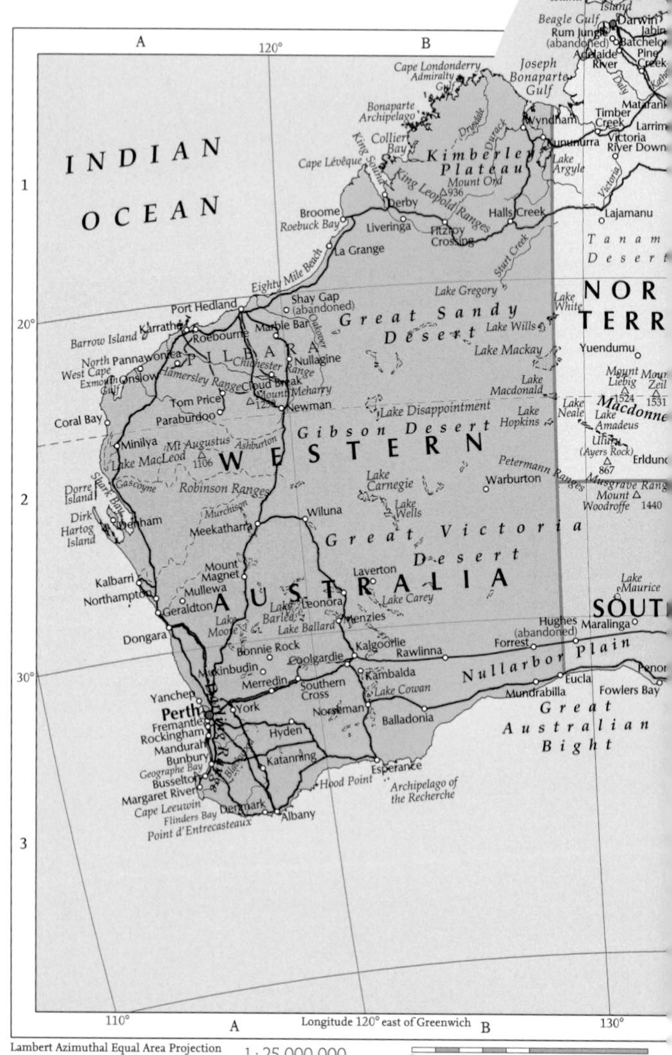

INDIAN

OCEAN

A · 120° · B

Bathurst Island · Melville Isl... Island
Beagle Gulf · Darwin · Jabin...
Rum Jungle · Batchelo...
Adelaide · Pine...
River · Creek
Mataran...
Timber · Larrim...
Creek · Victoria
Wyndham · Kununurra · River Down...

Cape Londonderry
Admiralty
Bonaparte
Archipelago · Joseph
Collier · Bonaparte
Bay · Gulf
Cape Lévêque · Kimberley
Plateau
King Leopold Ranges · Mount Ord
936
Broome · Derby · Halls Creek · Lajamanu
Roebuck Bay · Fitzroy
Liveringa · Crossing · Sturt Creek · Tanam...
La Grange · Deser...

NOR...
TERR...

Eighty Mile Beach
Port Hedland · Shay Gap · (abandoned)
Barrow Island · Karratha · Marble Bar · Great Sandy · Lake
West Cape · Roebourne · Desert · Lake Wills · White
North Pannawonica · PILBARA · Nullagine
Exmouth Onslow · Hamersley Range · Chichester · Lake Mackay · Yuendumu
Gulf · Tom Price · Range · Mount Meharry · Newman · Mount
Coral Bay · Paraburdoo · 1249 · Liebig · Zeil
Minilya · Mt Augustus · Ashburton · Gibson Desert · Lake Disappointment · Lake · Macdonne...
Lake MacLeod · 1106 · WESTERN · Hopkins · Uluru · Erldund...
Dorre · Robinson Ranges · Lake · (Ayers Rock)
Island · Gascoyne · Carnegie · Petermann Ranges · 867 · Musgrave Range...
Dirk · Murchison · Lake · Warburton · Mount
Hartog · Denham · Meekatharra · Wells · Woodroffe · 1440
Island
Great Victoria
Kalbarri · Mount · Wiluna · Desert
Northampton · Magnet · Lake · SOUT...
Mullewa · AUSTRALIA · Laverton · Lake Carey
Geraldton · Lake · Leonora · Hughes
Barlee · Menzies · (abandoned) · Maralinga
Dongara · Lake · Rawlinna · Forrest · Fowlers Bay
Moore · Kalgoorlie · Nullarbor Plain · Peno...
Mukinbudin · Bonnie Rock · Coolgardie · Kambalda · Eucla
Merredin · Southern · Lake Cowan · Mundrabilla · Great
Yanchep · Cross · Norseman · Australian
Perth · York · Bight
Fremantle · Hyden
Rockingham · Balladonia
Mandurah · Katanning · Esperance
Bunbury · Hood Point
Geographe Bay · Busselton · Archipelago of
Margaret River · the Recherche
Cape Leeuwin · Denmark · Albany
Flinders Bay
Point d'Entrecasteaux

110° · A · Longitude 120° east of Greenwich · B · 130°

Lambert Azimuthal Equal Area Projection · 1 : 25 000 000 · MILES 0 · 250 · 500

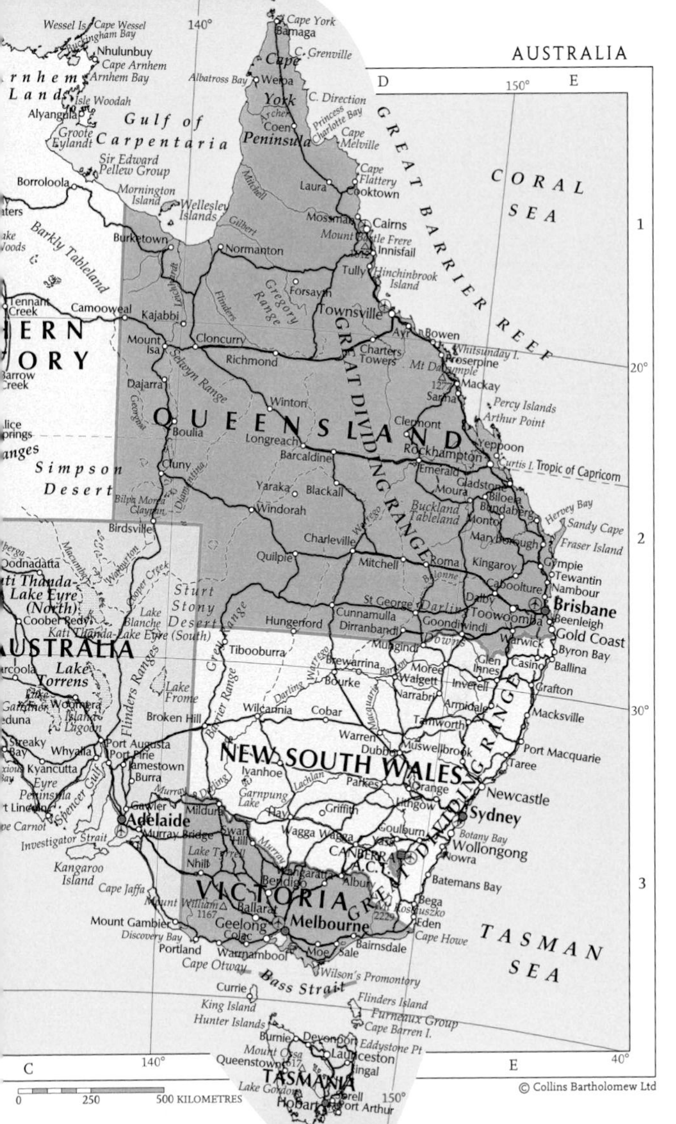

Wessel Is. Cape Wessel
ingham Bay
Nhulunbuy
Cape Arnhem
Alyangula Isle Woodah
Groote
Eylandt
Sir Edward
Pellew Group
Borroloola Mornington
Island
Wellesley
Islands
aters
Burketown
Normanton

Arnhem
Land
Gulf of
Carpentaria

Albatross Bay Weipa
Cape
York
Peninsula
Coen
Princess
Charlotte Bay
Laura

Cape York
Bamaga
C. Grenville
C. Direction

C. Melville
Cape
Flattery
Cooktown
Mossman
Cairns
Mount Bartle Frere
Innisfail
Tully
Hinchinbrook
Island

CORAL
SEA

Great Barrier Reef

1

ake
oods

NORTHERN
TERRITORY

arrow
reek

lice
prings
anges
exa

Barkly Tableland

Tennant
Creek
Camooweal
Burketown
Kajabbi
Mount
Isa
Cloncurry
Dajarra
Richmond

Simpson
Desert

Birdsville

AUSTRALIA

Odnadatta
Coober Pedy
Kati Thanda-
Lake Eyre
(North)
arcoola
Lake
Torrens
eduna

ious
Kyancutta
ay
Eyre
Peninsula
e Carnot
Streaky
Bay
Whyalla
Cleve
Port Augusta
Port Pirie
Jamestown
Burra

Investigator Strait
Adelaide
Murray Bridge
Kangaroo
Island
Cape Jaffa

Mount Gambier
Discovery Bay
Portland
Cape Otway

Forsayth
QUEENSLAND
Winton
Boulia
Longreach
Cluny
Barcaldine
Yaraka Blackall
Windorah

Townsville
Charters
Towers
Mt Dare
Clermont

Ayr
Bowen
Whitsunday I.
Proserpine
Mackay

Percy Islands
Arthur Point
Yeppoon
Rockhampton
Curtis I. Tropic of Capricorn
Gladstone
Emerald
Moura
Buckland
Tableland
Monto
Bundaberg
Hervey Bay
Sandy Cape
Fraser Island

20°

Charleville
Quilpie
Mitchell

Maryborough
Gympie
Tewantin
Nambour
Kingaroy
Roma
St George
Cunnamulla
Dirranbandi
Goondiwindi
Warwick

Brisbane
Beenleigh
Gold Coast
Byron Bay
Ballina
Casino

2

Tibooburra
Hungerford

Bilpa Morea
Claypan

Sturt Stony
Desert

Great Barrier Reef

Coober Pedy
Kati Thanda-Lake Eyre (South)
Lake
Blanche
Lake
Frome

Broken Hill
Wilcannia

Mungindi Moree
Brewarrina
Bourke
Cobar
Warren Dubbo

Narrabri
Walgett
Inverell
Tamworth
Armidale
Grafton
Glen
Innes
Macksville
Port Macquarie

30°

Flinders Ranges

NEW SOUTH WALES

Iyanhoe
Griffith
Lachlan
Parkes
Orange

Taree

Newcastle
Sydney
Botany Bay
Wollongong

Gawler
Swan Reach
Wagga Wagga
Goulburn
Mildura
Murray Bridge

CANBERRA
A.C.T.

Nowra
Batemans Bay

Kyneton
Horsham
Mount
William 1167
Ballarat
VICTORIA
Geelong
Colac
Warrnambool

Albury
Wodonga
Mt Kosciuszko
Bombala
Cape Howe

Bega

3

TASMAN
SEA

Bendigo
Melbourne
Sale
Bairnsdale

Wilson's Promontory

Bass Strait
Flinders Island
Furneaux Group

Currie
King Island
Hunter Islands

Mount Ossa
Queenstown
TASMANIA
Lake Gordon
Hobart

Devonport
Launceston
Fingal

Eddystone Pt
Cape Barren I.

Port Arthur

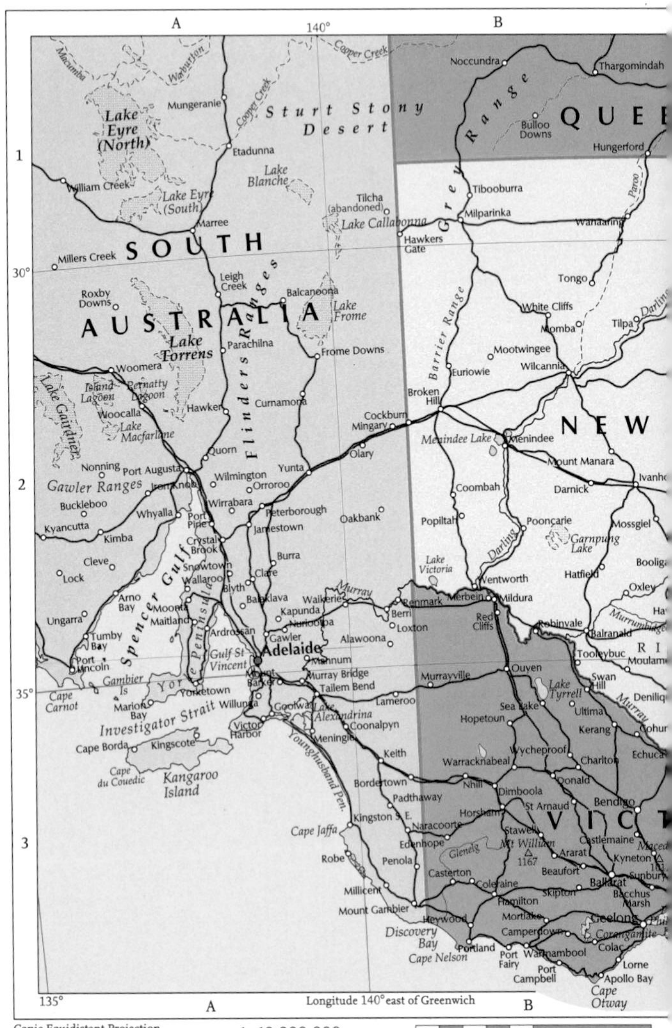

A   140°   B

Macumba

Warburton

Noccundra   Thargomindah

Lake
Eyre
(North)

Mungeranie

Cooper Creek

Sturt Stony
Desert

Grey Range

Bulloo
Downs

QUEE

Hungerford

William Creek

Etadunna

Lake
Blanche

1

Tilcha
(abandoned)

Lake Callabonna

Tibooburra

Barcoo

Marree

Lake Eyre
(South)

Hawkers
Gate

Milparinka

Wanaaring

30°

Millers Creek

SOUTH

Leigh
Creek

Balcanoona

Tongo

Roxby
Downs

Lake
Frome

White Cliffs

Momba

Tilpa

Darling

AUSTRALIA

Lake
Torrens

Flinders Ranges

Parachilna

Frome Downs

Mootwingee

Euriowie

Wilcannia

Woomera

Pernatty
Lagoon

Lake Gairdner

Island
Lagoon

Hawker

Curnamona

Cockburn
Mingary

Broken
Hill

NEW

Woocalla

Lake
Macfarlane

Nonning

Port Augusta

Quorn

Yunta

Olary

Menindee Lake   Menindee

Mount Manara

Ivanho

Gawler Ranges

Iron Knob

Wilmington

Ororroo

Coombah

Darnick

Buckleboo

Whyalla

Port
Pirie

Wirrabara

Peterborough

Oakbank

Popiltah

Pooncarie

Garnpung
Lake

Mossgiel

Kyancutta

Kimba

Crystal
Brook

Jamestown

Darling

Booliga

Cleve

Lock

Snowtown

Burra

Lake
Victoria

Wentworth

Hatfield

Oxley

Ungarra

Tumby
Bay

Arno
Bay

Maitland

Wallaroo

Blyth

Clare

Balaklava

Walkerie

Kapunda

Nuriootpa

Berri

Renmark   Merbein

Mildura

Robinvale

Murrumb

Ha

Balranald

Port
Lincoln

Ardrossan

Gawler

Loxton

Red
Cliffs

Tooleybuc

Moulame

Cape
Carnot

Marion
Bay

Yorketown

Gulf St
Vincent

Adelaide

Nangawooka

Murray Bridge

Tailem Bend

Alawoona

Murrayville

Ouyen

Lake
Tyrrell

Swan
Hill

Deniliqu

35°

Yorke Peninsula

Willunga

Goolwa

Meningie

Lameroo

Sea
Lake

Ultima

Kerang

Cohur

Murray

Investigator Strait

Victor
Harbor

Alexandrina

Coonalpyn

Hopetoun

Wycheproof

Charlton

Echuca

Cape Borda

Kingscote

Youngshusband Pen.

Keith

Warracknabeal

Donald

Bendig

Cape
du Couedic

Kangaroo
Island

Bordertown

Padthaway

Nhill

Dimboola

St Arnaud

Castlemaine

Kyneton

Mace

Sunbur

Horsham

Naracoorte

Stawell

Mt William
1167

Ararat

Beaufort

VICT

Bacchus
Marsh

3

Cape Jaffa

Edenhope

Penola

Glenelg

Mortlake

Casterton

Coleraine

Skipton

Ballarat

Geelong

Corangamite

Robe

Millicent

Heywood

Hamilton

Camperdown

Colac

Lorne

Mount Gambier

Discovery
Bay

Cape Nelson

Portland

Port
Fairy

Warrnambool

Apollo Bay

Cape
Otway

135°

A   Longitude 140° east of Greenwich   B

Conic Equidistant Projection   1 : 10 000 000   MILES 0   100   200

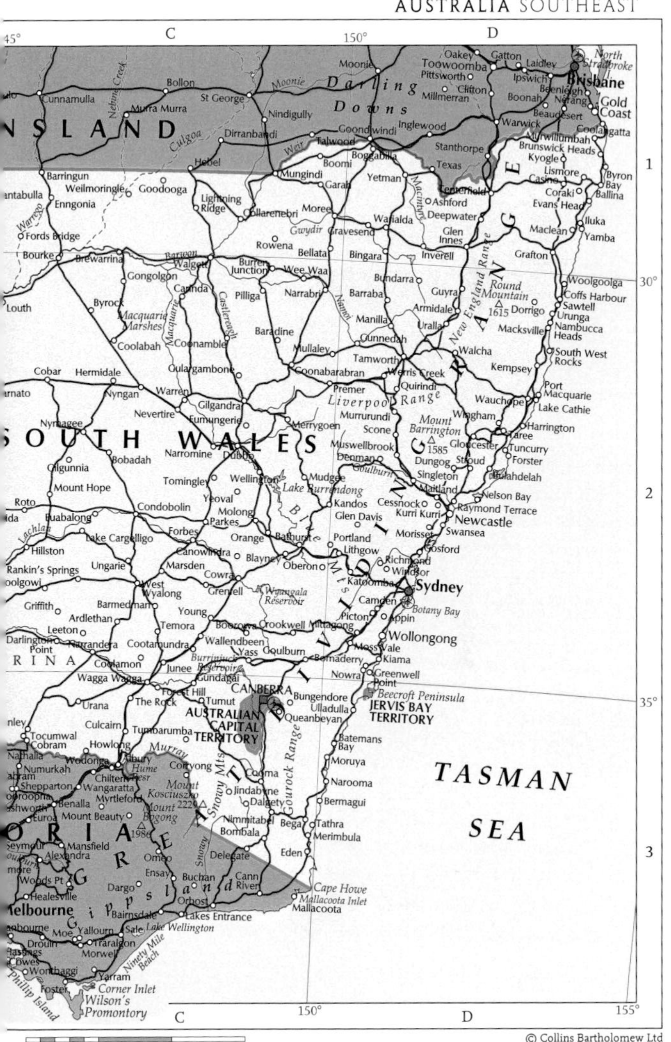

Oakey Gatton
Moonie Toowoomba Laidley North
Bollon Pittsworth Stradbroke
Cunnamulla Murra Murra St George Millmerran Clifton Ipswich Brisbane
Nindigully Boonah Nerang Gold
Barringun Dirranbandi Warwick Coast
Weilmoringle Goodooga Talwood Stanthorpe Willumbah Coolangatta
Enngonia Boomi Texas Brunswick Heads
Yetman Kyogle
Hebel Boggabilla Tenterfield Casino Byron
Fords Bridge Mungindi Garah Ashford Deepwater Coraki Bay
Bourke Brewarrina Rowena Moree Wahalda Glen Evans Head
Gongolgon Collarenebri Bellata Bingara Inverell Innes Maclean
Byrock Lightning Narrabri Barraba Guyra Round Iluka
Louth Walgett Ridge Pilliga Bundarra Mountain Yamba
Burren Manilla Armidale 1615 Dorrigo Woolgoolga
Nyngan Junction Wee Waa Uralla Macksville Coffs Harbour
Cobar Coonamble Baradine Gunnedah Walcha Urunga
Hermidale Mullaley Tamworth Kempsey Nambucca
Nevertire Gilgandra Premer Werris Creek Heads
Warren Coonabarabran Quirindi Wauchope South West
Gulargambone Murrurundi Mount Port Rocks
Dubbo Scone Barrington Gloucester Macquarie
Narromine Merrygoen Muswellbrook 1585 Stroud Lake Cathie
Tomingley Wellington Mudgee Singleton Dungog Taree
Condobolin Yeoval Kandos Maitland Tuncurry
Mount Hope Molong Parkes Glen Davis Cessnock Nelson Bay Forster
Roto Lake Cargelligo Forbes Portland Kurri Kurri Raymond Terrace
Ungarie Marsden Blayney Lithgow Morisset Newcastle
Hillston Canowindra Oberon Richmond Swansea
West Grenfell Cowra Katoomba Windsor Gosford
Rankin's Springs Wyalong Young Boorowa Crookwell Sydney
Griffith Barmedman Cootamundra Wallendbeen Yass Botany Bay
Ardlethan Temora Murringo Goulburn Appin Wollongong
Leeton Junee Wagga Wagga Gundagai Bungendore Kiama
Coolamon Canberra Greenwell
The Rock Tumut AUSTRALIAN Queanbeyan Point Nowra
Tocumwal Culcairn Turnbarumba CAPITAL Bungendore JERVIS BAY Ulladulla
Cobram Howlong TERRITORY Cooma TERRITORY Batemans
Nathalia Wodonga Albury Jindabyne Bay
Numurkah Chiltern Mount Dalgety Moruya
Shepparton Wangaratta Kosciuszko Bombala Narooma
Benalla Myrtleford 2228 Nimmitabel Bermagui
Alexandra Mansfield Mount Bonbala Bega TASMAN
Woods Pt Bogong Delegate Merimbula
Dargo Omeo Cann Eden SEA
Healesville Bairnsdale Ensay Buchan River
Melbourne Sale Orbost Cape Howe
Drouin Traralgon Lakes Entrance Mallacoota Inlet
Warragul Morwell Lake Wellington Mallacoota
Wonthaggi Yarram Ninety Mile
Foster Beach
Corner Inlet
Wilson's
Promontory

NSLAND
Darling Downs
RANGE
SOUTH WALES
Liverpool Range
New England Range
GREAT DIVIDING RANGE
RINA
Snowy Mts
Bogong Range
G i p p s l a n d

0   100   200   300 KILOMETRES

© Collins Bartholomew Ltd   **53**

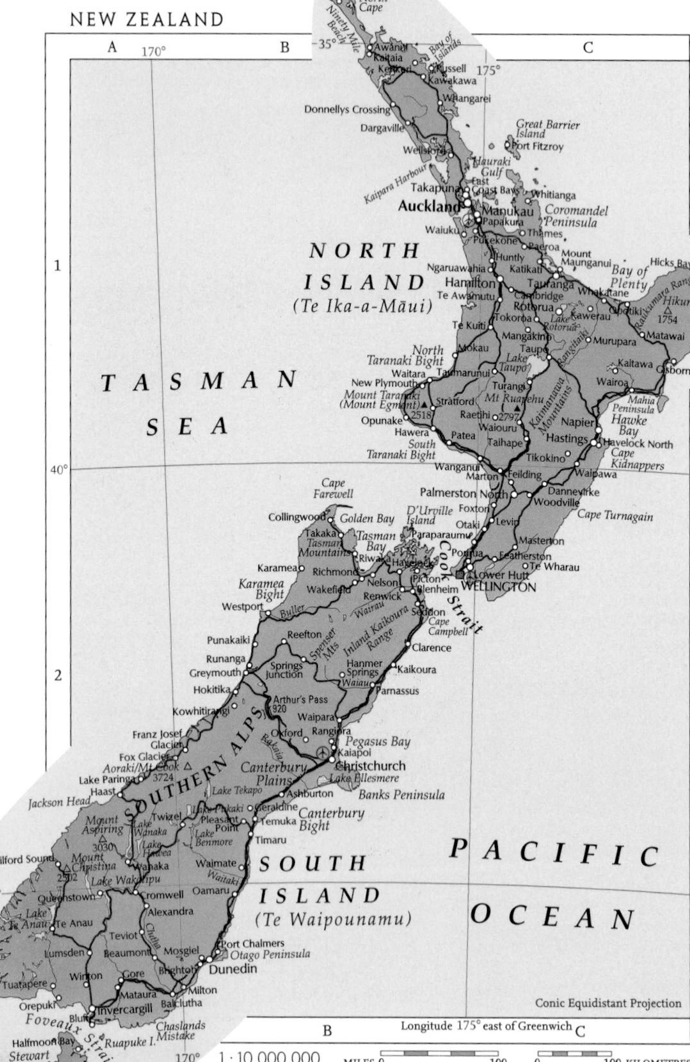
NEW ZEALAND
A
B
C
170°
175°
-35°
40°
-45°
1
2
Te Paki
North Cape
Ninety Mile Beach
Awanui
Kaitaia
Kerikeri
Bay of Islands
Russell
Kawakawa
Whangarei
Donnellys Crossing
Dargaville
Great Barrier Island
Port Fitzroy
Wellsford
Hauraki Gulf
Kaipara Harbour
Takapuna
East Coast Bays
Whitianga
Auckland
Manukau
Coromandel Peninsula
Papakura
Waiuku
Thames
Pukekohe
Paeroa
NORTH ISLAND
(Te Ika-a-Māui)
Huntly
Mount Maunganui
Hicks Bay
Ngaruawahia
Katikati
Bay of Plenty
Hamilton
Tauranga
Whakatane
Raukumara Range
Te Awamutu
Cambridge
Hikurangi
Rotorua
Opotiki
1754
Lake Rotorua
Kawerau
Te Kuiti
Tokoroa
Matawai
Mangakino
Murupara
Mokau
Taupo
North Taranaki Bight
Lake Taupo
Kaitawa
Waitara
Taumarunui
Gisborne
New Plymouth
Turangi
Wairoa
Mount Taranaki (Mount Egmont)
Mt Ruapehu
Kaimanawa Mountains
Mahia Peninsula
Stratford
2518
Raetihi
2797
Opunake
Waiouru
Napier
Hawke Bay
Hawera
Patea
Taihape
Hastings
Havelock North
South Taranaki Bight
Tikokino
Cape Kidnappers
TASMAN SEA
Wanganui
Marton
Feilding
Waipawa
Cape Farewell
Palmerston North
Dannevirke
Woodville
D'Urville Island
Foxton
Cape Turnagain
Collingwood
Golden Bay
Otaki
Levin
Takaka
Tasman Bay
Paraparaumu
Tasman Mountains
Masterton
Porirua
Featherston
Riwaka
Havelock
Te Wharau
Karamea
Richmond
Cook Strait
Picton
Lower Hutt
Nelson
WELLINGTON
Karamea Bight
Wakefield
Blenheim
Renwick
Westport
Buller
Wairau
Seddon
Cape Campbell
Inland Kaikoura Range
Reefton
Spenser Mts
Punakaiki
Clarence
Runanga
Springs Junction
Hanmer Springs
Kaikoura
Greymouth
Waiau
Parnassus
Hokitika
Arthur's Pass
920
Kowhitirangi
Waipara
SOUTHERN ALPS
Franz Josef Glacier
Oxford
Rangiora
Pegasus Bay
Rakaia
Kaiapoi
Fox Glacier
Aoraki/Mt Cook
3724
Christchurch
Canterbury Plains
Lake Paringa
Lake Ellesmere
Haast
Lake Tekapo
Banks Peninsula
Jackson Head
Ashburton
Lake Pukaki
Geraldine
Mount Aspiring
Twizel
Canterbury Bight
Pleasant Point
Temuka
Lake Wanaka
Lake Benmore
3030
Lake Hawea
Timaru
PACIFIC OCEAN
Milford Sound
Mount Christina
Wanaka
Waimate
2502
SOUTH ISLAND
Lake Wakatipu
Waitaki
Queenstown
Cromwell
Oamaru
(Te Waipounamu)
Lake Te Anau
Te Anau
Alexandra
Teviot
Clutha
Port Chalmers
Lumsden
Beaumont
Mosgiel
Otago Peninsula
Brighton
Dunedin
Winton
Gore
Tuatapere
Milton
Mataura
Balclutha
Orepuki
Invercargill
Conic Equidistant Projection
Bluff
Chaslands Mistake
Longitude 175° east of Greenwich
Foveaux Strait
Ruapuke I.
Halfmoon Bay
Stewart Island
1 : 10 000 000
MILES 0
100
0
100 KILOMETRES

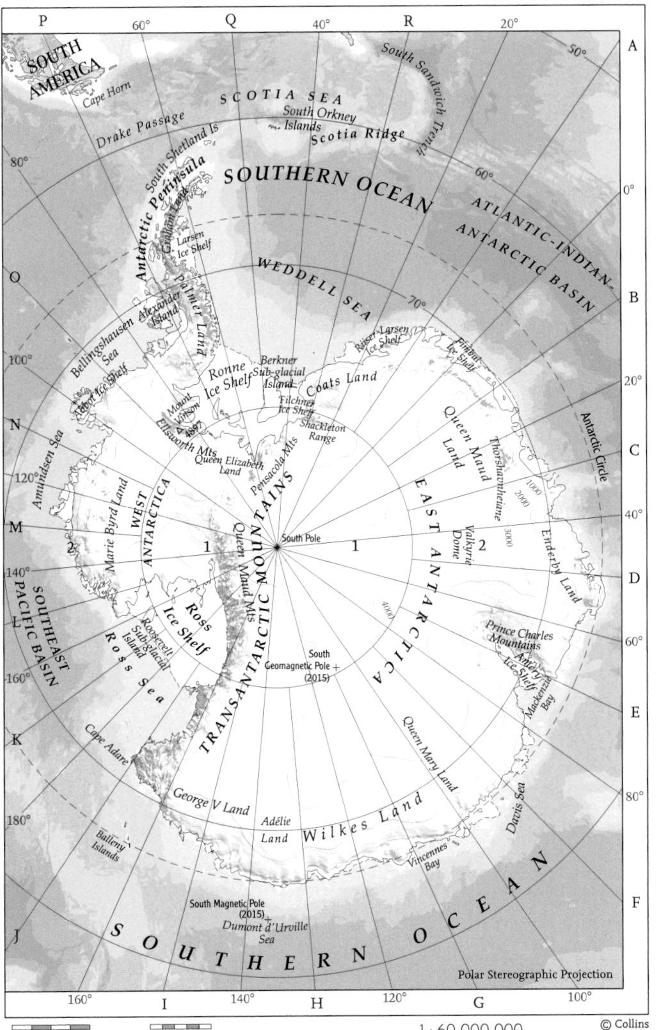

South America
Cape Horn
SCOTIA SEA
South Orkney Islands
Scotia Ridge
Drake Passage
South Sandwich Trench
South Shetland Is
Antarctic Peninsula
Graham Land
SOUTHERN OCEAN
ATLANTIC-INDIAN-ANTARCTIC BASIN
Larsen Ice Shelf
WEDDELL SEA
Bellingshausen Sea
Alexander Island
Palmer Land
Robert Larsen Ice Shelf
Brunt Ice Shelf
Riiser-Larsen Ice Shelf
George VI Ice Shelf
Ronne Ice Shelf
Berkner Sub-glacial Island
Coats Land
Mount Vinson
Filchner Ice Shelf
Shackleton Range
Ellsworth Mts
Queen Elizabeth Land
Pensacola Mts
Queen Maud Land
Thorshavnheane
Antarctic Circle
Enderby Land
Amundsen Sea
Marie Byrd Land
WEST ANTARCTICA
South Pole
EAST ANTARCTICA
Valkyrie Dome
TRANSANTARCTIC MOUNTAINS
SOUTHEAST PACIFIC BASIN
Ross Ice Shelf
Roosevelt Island
Ross Sea
South Geomagnetic Pole (2015)
Prince Charles Mountains
Amery Ice Shelf
Mac. Robertson Land
Prydz Bay
Cape Adare
Queen Mary Land
Davis Sea
Balleny Islands
George V Land
Adélie Land
Wilkes Land
Vincennes Bay
South Magnetic Pole (2015)
Dumont d'Urville Sea
SOUTHERN OCEAN

Polar Stereographic Projection

0   400 MILES   0   500 KILOMETRES

1 : 60 000 000

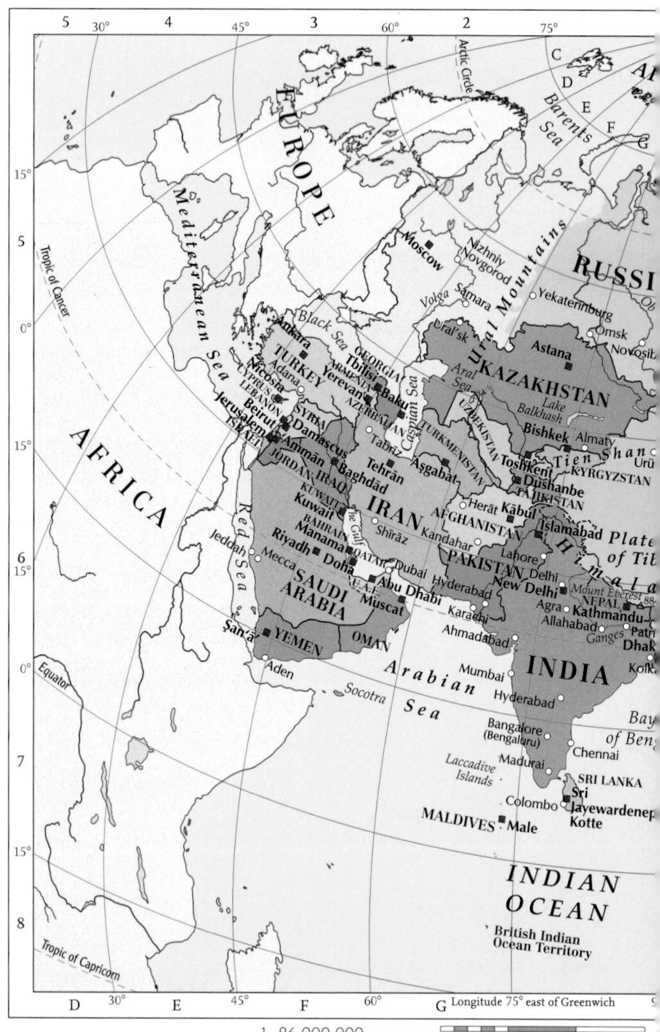

5 30° 4 45° 3 60° 2 75°

EUROPE

Arctic Circle

Barents
Sea

C
D
E
F
G

AR

RUSSI

Tropic of Cancer

Mediterranean Sea

Moscow

Nizhniy
Novgorod

Volga

Samara

Yekaterinburg

Omsk

Novosi

Ob

Black Sea GEORGIA
TURKEY Tbilisi
Ankara ARMENIA Baku
Adana Yerevan AZERBAIJAN
SYRIA
Nicosia
CYPRUS
Beirut Damascus
LEBANON
Jerusalem ISRAEL
JORDAN

Ural'sk

Aral
Sea

Astana

KAZAKHSTAN

Lake
Balkhash

Caspian Sea

Bishkek Almaty

UZBEKISTAN Toshkent

TURKMENISTAN

Tabrīz Tehrān

Tien Shan

Urü

KYRGYZSTAN

Dushanbe

IRAQ Baghdād
Amman

Aşgabat

Herāt Kābul

Plate
of Til

Kuwait The Gulf
KUWAIT
Manama Shīrāz
BAHRAIN
Riyadh Doha
QATAR Dubai
U.A.E.
Mecca Abu Dhabi Muscat
SAUDI
ARABIA OMAN

AFGHANISTAN

Kandahar

Islamabad

Lahore

PAKISTAN

Hyderabad

New Delhi

Himalaya

Mount Everest
Kathmandu
NEPAL Patn

AFRICA

Red Sea

Jeddah

Jerusalem

6
15°

Karāchi

Agra
Allahabad

Dhak

Ganges

Kol

15°

0°
Equator

San'a YEMEN

Aden

Socotra

Arabian Sea

Ahmadabad

Mumbai

INDIA

Hyderabad

Bay
of Ben

Bangalore
(Bengaluru)

Chennai

Laccadive
Islands

Madurai

SRI LANKA
Sri
Jayewardenep
Kotte

MALDIVES Male

Colombo

15°

8

INDIAN
OCEAN

British Indian
Ocean Territory

Tropic of Capricorn

D 30° E 45° F 60° G Longitude 75° east of Greenwich 9

56

1 : 86 000 000

MILES 0   500   1000   1500

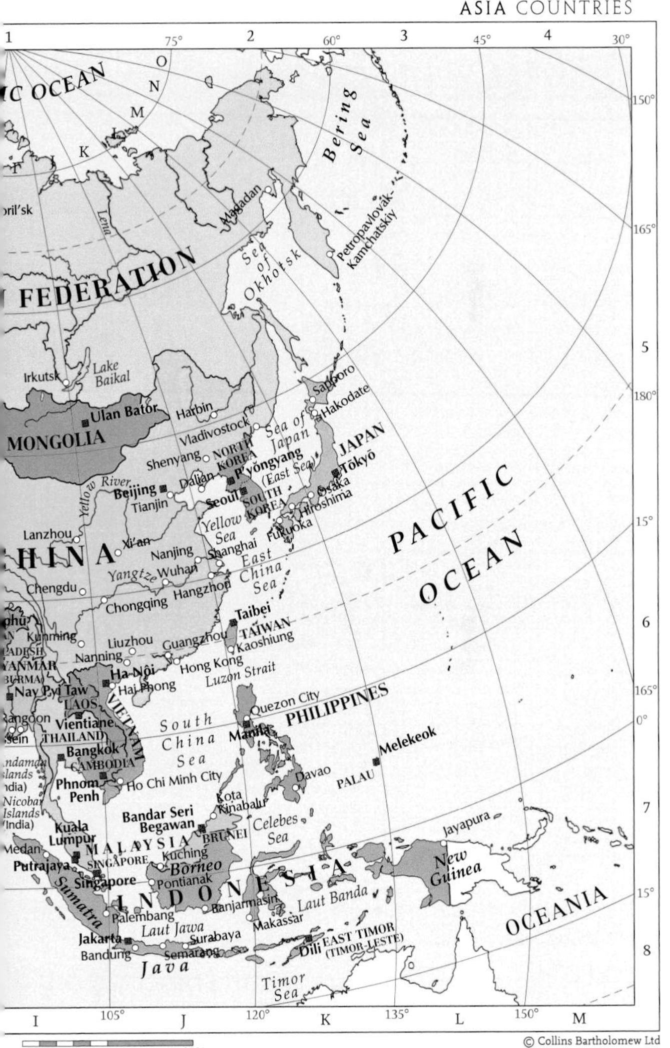

ASIA COUNTRIES

C OCEAN

Koril'sk

N
O
M
K
L

FEDERATION

Irkutsk
Lake
Baikal

Lena

Bering
Sea

Magadan

Sea of
Okhotsk

Petropavlovsk-
Kamchatskiy

MONGOLIA

Ulan Bator

Harbin

Vladivostock

Sapporo

Shenyang

Sea of
Japan
(East Sea)

Hakodate

JAPAN

Beijing

Yellow River

Dalian

NORTH
KOREA

P'yŏngyang

Tōkyō

Tianjin

Seoul

SOUTH
KOREA

Ōsaka

Hiroshima

CHINA

Lanzhou

Xi'an

Yellow
Sea

Fukuoka

Nanjing

Shanghai

PACIFIC

Chengdu

Yangtze

Wuhan

East
China
Sea

Chongqing

Hangzhou

OCEAN

Kunming

Liuzhou

Guangzhou

Taibei

TAIWAN

Kaoshiung

PRADESH

MYANMAR
BURMA

Nanning

Hong Kong

Nay Pyi Taw

Ha-Nôi

Hai Phong

Luzon Strait

LAOS

Rangoon
tein

Vientiane

THAILAND

South
China
Sea

Quezon City

PHILIPPINES

Bangkok

Manila

Andaman
Islands
(India)

Phnom
Penh

CAMBODIA

Ho Chi Minh City

Davao

Melekeok

PALAU

Nicobar
Islands
(India)

Bandar Seri
Begawan

Kota
Kinabalu

Celebes
Sea

Jayapura

Medan

Kuala
Lumpur

MALAYSIA

BRUNEI

Kuching

Borneo

Putrajaya

SINGAPORE

Singapore

INDONESIA

New
Guinea

Sumatra

Palembang

Banjarmasin

Laut Banda

OCEANIA

Jakarta

Laut Jawa

Makassar

Bandung

Semarang

Surabaya

Java

Dili

EAST TIMOR
(TIMOR-LESTE)

Timor
Sea

I   105°   J   120°   K   135°   L   M

0   1000   2000 KILOMETRES

© Collins Bartholomew Ltd

57

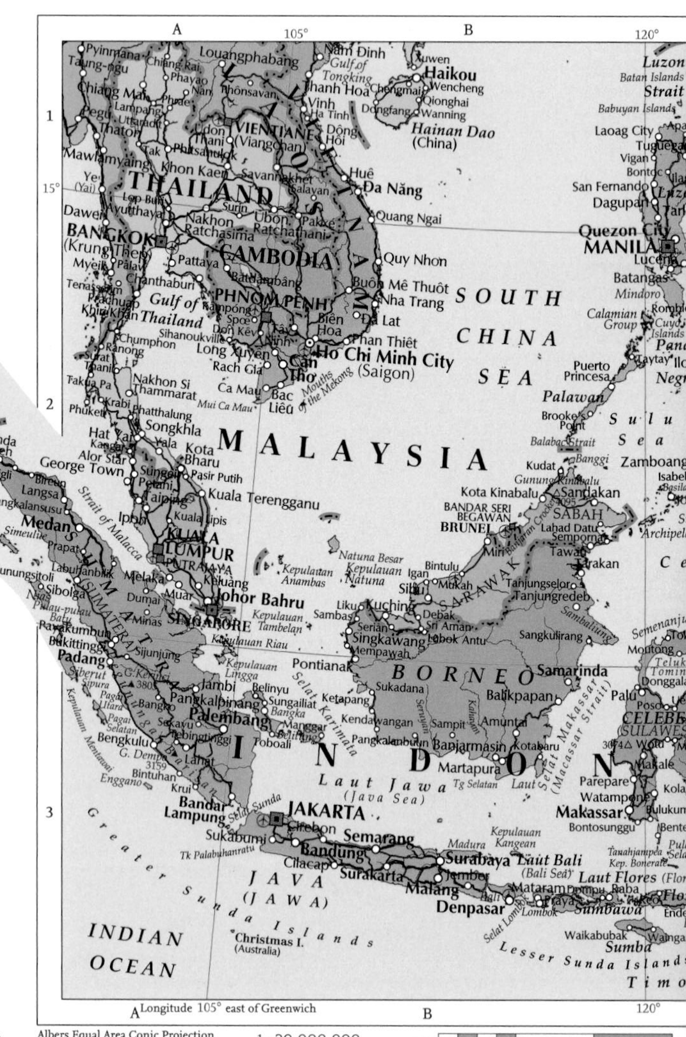

A · 105° · B · 120°

Pyinmana · Louangphabang · Nam Dinh · Suwen · Luzon
Taung-ngu · Chiang Rai · Phayao · Wencheng · Batan Islands
Chiang Mai · Nan · Thônsavan · Thanh Hoa · Haikou · Qionghai · Babuyan Islands
Lampang · Phrae · Ha Tinh · Dongfang · Wanning · Laoag City
Lamphun · Uttaradit · Phitsanulok · Dong Hoi · Hainan Dao · Tuguera
Mawlamyaing · Tak · Khon Kaen · Savannakhet · Huê · (China) · Vigan · Bontoc
Ye · (Yai) · Yutthaya · Udon Thani · Kalasin · Balayan · Đa Nẵng · San Fernando
Dawei · THAILAND · Lop Buri · Surin · Ubon · Pakxe · Quang Ngai · Dagupan
BANGKOK · Nakhon · Ratchasima · Si Sa Ket · Quy Nhơn · Quezon City
(Krung Thep) · Pattaya · CAMBODIA · Buôn Mê Thuột · MANILA
Myeik · Palaw · Chanthaburi · Battambang · Nha Trang · Batangas
Tenasserim · PHNOM PENH · Biên · Đà Lạt · Mindoro · Romblo
Pathiu · Khlong Khlan · Sihanoukville · Spoc · Hòa · Biên · Calamian · Cuyo
Chumphon · Long Xuyen · Cần · Ho Chi Minh City · Group · Islands · Pana
Ranong · Sóc · Kep · Thơ · (Saigon) · Phan Thiết · Puerto · Palawan · Negr
Takua Pa · Nakhon Si · Rach Gia · Bạc · Princesa · Sulu
Phuket · Thammarat · Cà Mau · Liêu · Mui Cà Mau · Mouths of · the Mekong · SOUTH · Sea
Krabi · Phatthalung · Balabac Strait · Brooke's · Point · Banggi · Zamboang
Hat Yai · Songkhla · Kota · CHINA · Kudat · Gunung Kinabalu · Isabel
Alor Star · Bharu · Pasir Putih · SEA · Kota Kinabalu · SABAH · Santakan · Basila
Sungai · Petani · Taiping · Kuala Terengganu · BANDAR SERI · BEGAWAN · Lahad Datu · Tawau · Sempo
George Town · Ipoh · Kuala Lipis · BRUNEI · Miri · Tarakan
Medan · Kuala Kangsar · Natuna Besar · Kepulauan · Igan · Tanjungselor · Ce
Gunungsitoli · Labuanbatu · KUALA · Kluang · Natuna · Mukah · Tanjungredeb
Sibolga · LUMPUR · PUTRAJAYA · Anambas · Bintulu · SARAWAK
Payakumbuh · Minas · Melaka · Kuching · Debak · Sangkulirang
Bukittinggi · Dumai · Muar · Johor Bahru · Liku · Sri Aman · Sibu · Serian · Boy Antu
Padang · SINGAPORE · Kepulauan · Tambelan · Singkawang · Semenonya · Moutong
Sijunjung · Kepulauan Riau · Sambas · Pempawang · Samarinda · Teluk · Tomini · Donggala
Kepulauan · Lingga · Pontianak · BORNEO · Balikpapan · Palu
Jambi · Belinyu · Ketapang · Sukadana · Amuntai · Poso · CELEBES
Pangkalpinang · Sungailiat · Sampit · Kotabaru · Parepare · (SULAWES)
Palembang · Bangka · Pangkalanbun · Banjarmasin · Martapura · Watampone · Wowon
Bengkulu · Mangar · Toboali · Martapura · Tg Selatan · Makassar · Kola
Bintuhan · Lahat · Laut Jawa · (Java Sea) · Bontosunggu · Bente
Bandar · Lampung · JAKARTA · Cirebon · Semarang · Surabaya · Laut Bali · Tawahiampea · Kep. Bonerate · Pula
Sukabumi · Bandung · Surakarta · Malang · Jember · Mataram · Flores
JAVA · Cilacap · Denpasar · Sumbawa · Ende
(JAWA) · Christmas I. · (Australia) · Waikabubak · Wangar
INDIAN · Greater · Sunda · Islands · Lesser Sunda Islands · Sumba · Timo
OCEAN · Tk Pelabuhanratu · Kepulauan · Kangean · Madura · Selat Lombok · Lombok

15°

SOUTH
CHINA
SEA

MALAYSIA

INDONESIA

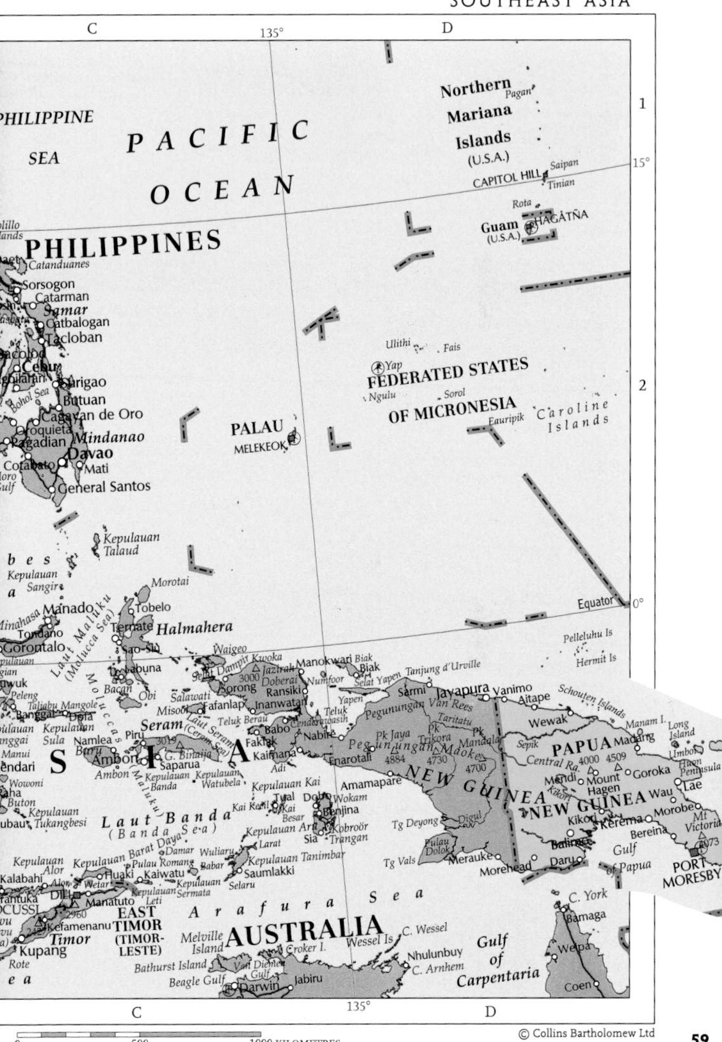

PHILIPPINE
SEA

PACIFIC
OCEAN

PHILIPPINES

Northern
Mariana
Islands
(U.S.A.)

Pagan

CAPITOL HILL ● Saipan
Tinian

Guam
(U.S.A.) ● HAGÅTÑA
Rota

Jolillo
Islands
Catanduanes
Sorsogon
Catarman
Samar
Catbalogan
Tacloban

Cebu
Surigao
Butuan
Cagayan de Oro
Mindanao
Davao
Cotabato
Mati
General Santos
Moro
Gulf

Ulithi
Fais
Yap
Ngulu
FEDERATED STATES
OF MICRONESIA
Sorol
Eauripik
Caroline
Islands

PALAU
MELEKEOK

b e s
Kepulauan
Talaud
a
Kepulauan
Sangir
inahasa Manado
Tondano
Gorontalo
Tobelo
Ternate Halmahera
Sao-bolu
tabuna
Waigeo
Selat Dampit Kwoka
Sorong
Ransiki
Manokwari Biak
Numfoor
Selat Yapen Tanjung d'Urville
Sarmi
Jayapura
Vanimo
Aitape
Wewak
Schouten Islands
Hermit Is
Pelleluhu Is
Manam I
Long
Island

Bacan
Obi
Salawati
Misool
Doberai
Teluk Berau
Babo
Nabire
Fakfak
Kaimana

Yapen
Teluk
Cenderawasih

Taritatu
Pegunungan Van Rees
Mamberamo
Mandala
4700
PAPUA
Sepik
Madang
Central Ra.
Mount
4509
Hagen
Mendi
Goroka
Lae

S I A
endari
Wowoni
Buton
Kepulauan
aha
Kalabahi
Tukangbesi

Ambon
Seram
Saparua
Ambon
Namlea
Banda
Watubela

Pk Jaya
Pk
Trikora
4884
NEW GUINEA
4000
NEW GUINEA
Kikori
Kerema
Morobe
Bereina
Wau
Huon
Peninsula
Umboi
Victoria
4073

Laut Banda
(Banda Sea)
Kepulauan Kai
Kai Kecil
Kai Besar
Dobo
Wokam
Tual
Kepulauan Aru
Kobroor
Trangan
Pulau
Dolak
Tg Deyong
Digul
Merauke
Morehead
Daru
PORT
MORESBY
Gulf
of
Papua

Kepulauan Barat Daya
Damar
Wuliaru
Babar
Kepulauan Tanimbar
Saumlakki
Sermata
Selaru
Tg Vals

Kepulauan
Leti
Wetar
Kisar
Kepulauan
Kepulauan
Alor
Romang

Arafura Sea

C. York
Bamaga
Wepa

EAST
TIMOR
(TIMOR-
LESTE)
DILI
Kefamenanu
Timor
Kupang
Rote

Manatuto
Melville
Island
Bathurst Island
Van Diemen
Gulf
Beagle Gulf
Darwin
Jabiru

AUSTRALIA
Croker I.
C. Wessel
Wessel Is
Nhulunbuy
C. Arnhem

Gulf
of
Carpentaria

Coen

Equator

0 500 1000 KILOMETRES

© Collins Bartholomew Ltd

59

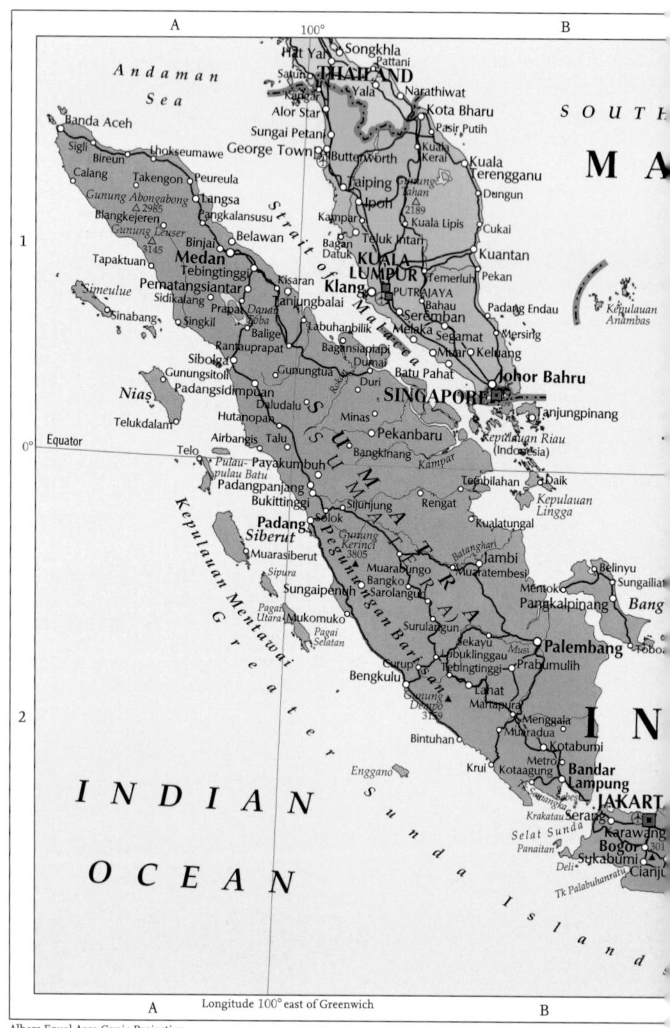

A

100°

B

Andaman
Sea

Hat Yai Songkhla
Pattani
Satun THAILAND
Alor Star Yala Narathiwat
Sungai Petani Kota Bharu
Banda Aceh Pasir Putih
Sigli Kuala
Bireun Lhokseumawe George Town Butterworth Kerai Kuala
Calang Takengon Peureula Terengganu
Blangkejeren Tangsa Taiping Sungai Dungun
Gunung Abongabong Pangkalansusu Ipoh Kuala Lipis
△2985 Belawan Kampar Cukai
Gunung Leuser Binjai Bagan Teluk Intan Kuantan
△3145 Medan Datuk KUALA
Tapaktuan Tebingtinggi LUMPUR
Pematangsiantar Kisaran Klang PUTRAJAYA Pekan
Simeulue Sidikalang Tanjungbalai Temerluh Padang Endau
Sinabang Prapat Bahau Seremban
Singkil Balige Labuhanbatu Melaka Mersing
Rantauprapat Bagansiapiapi Segamat Kluang
Sibolga Gunungtua Dumai Batu Pahat OMuar
Nias Gunungsitoli Duri Johor Bahru
Padangsidimpuan SINGAPORE
Hutanopan Daludalu Tanjungpinang
Telukdalam Airbangis Talu Minas Pekanbaru *Kepulauan Riau*
Equator 0° Telo Bangkinang (Indonesia)
Pulau Payakumbuh *Kampar* Tembilahan Daik
pulau Batu Padangpanjang Rengat *Kepulauan*
Bukittinggi Sijunjung Kualatungal *Lingga*
Padang Solok
Siberut *Gunung Kerinci* Batanghari
Muarasiberut 3805 Muarabungo Jambi
Sipura Bangko Muaratembesi Belinyu
Sungaipenuh Sarolangu Sungaliat
Pagan Mukomuko Surulangun Memtok Pangkalpinang *Bang*
Utara Sekayu *Musi*
Pagai Lubuklinggau Palembang Toba
Selatan Bengkulu Tebingtinggi Prabumulih
Curup Lahat
Gunung Martapura
Dempo Menggala
△ Muaradua
Bintuhan Kotabumi
Metro
Enggano Krui Kotaagung Bandar
Lampung
JAKARTA
Serang
Krakatau Karawang
Selat Sunda Bogor
Panaitan Sukabumi
Deli Cianju
Tk Palabuhanratu

Kepulauan
Anambas

SOUTH

M A

Kepulauan
Lingga

I N

Gunung Leuser

SUMATRA

Pegunungan Barisan

Kepulauan Mentawai

Greater Sunda Islands

I N D I A N

O C E A N

Equator 0°

1

2

Longitude 100° east of Greenwich

A   B

60 Albers Equal Area Conic Projection   1 : 15 000 000   MILES 0   100   200   300

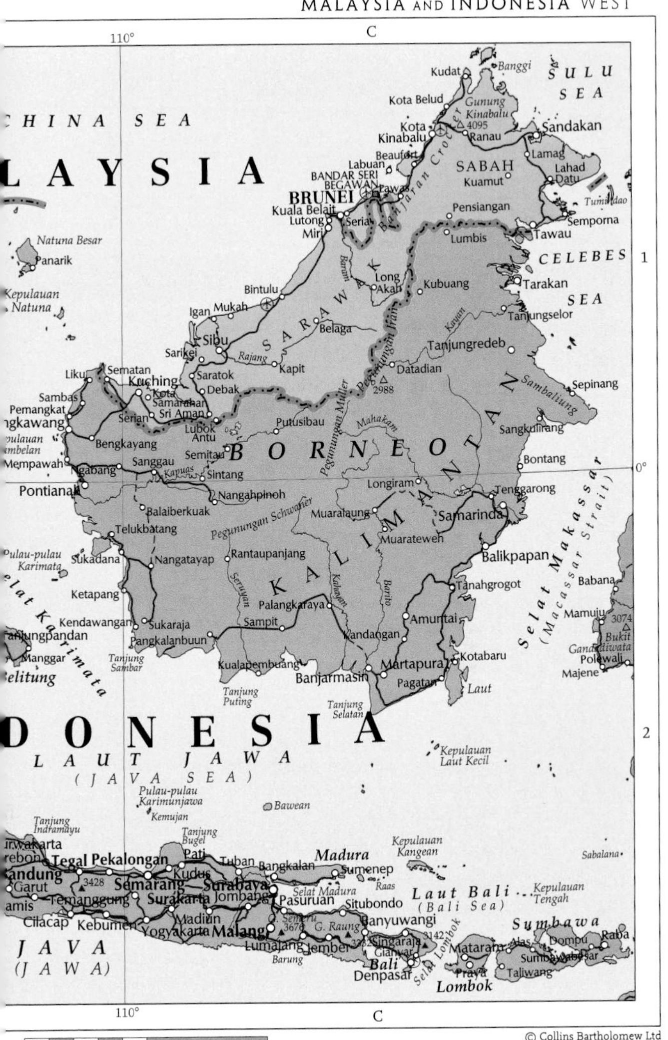

C

110°

SULU SEA

CHINA SEA

LAYSIA

Kudat
Banggi
Kota Belud
Kota Kinabalu
Gunung Kinabalu 4095
Ranau
Sandakan
Beaufort
Labuan
Lamag
Lahad Datu
Kuala Belait
BANDAR SERI BEGAWAN
BRUNEI
Kuamut
Pensiangan
Semporna
Lutong
Seria
Lumbis
Tawau
Miri
Tunku
Tarakan
CELEBES
SEA
Long Akah
Kubuang
Natuna Besar
Panarik
Kepulauan Natuna
Bintulu
Igan
Mukah
Belaga
Tanjungredeb
Tanjungselor
Sibu
Sarikei
Rajang
Kapit
SARAWAK
Datadian
2988
Sepinang
Liku
Sematan
Kuching
Saratok
Debak
Kota
Putusibau
Sambas
Pemangkat
gkawang
Sri Aman
Antu
Lubok
Semitau
Sintang
BORNEO
Sangkulirang
Bengkayang
Sanggau
Kapuas
Bontang
Mempawah
Pontianak
Nangahpinoh
Longiram
Samarinda
Balaiberkuak
Muaralaung
Tenggarong
Telukbatang
Pegunungan Schwaner
Muarateweh
Balikpapan
Babana
Pulau-pulau Karimata
Sukadana
Nangatayap
Rantaupanjang
KALIMANTAN
Barito
Tanahgrogot
Mamuju
Ketapang
Palangkaraya
Amuntai
Bukit
Kendawangan
Sukaraja
Sampit
Kandangan
Polewali
njungpandan
Pangkalanbuun
Kualapembuang
Martapura
Kotabaru
Majene
elitung
Tanjung Sambar
Banjarmasin
Pagatan
Laut
Tanjung Puting
Tanjung Selatan

DONESIA

LAUT JAWA
(JAVA SEA)

Kepulauan Laut Kecil

Pulau-pulau Karimunjawa
Bawean
Kepulauan Kangean
Sabalana

Tanjung Indramayu
rebon
Tegal
Pekalongan
Pati
Tuban
Bangkalan
Madura
Sumenep
Raas
Laut Bali
(Bali Sea)
andung
Garut
3428
Temanggung
Semarang
Kudus
Jombang
Surabaya
Pasuruan
Sumbawa
amis
Kebumen
Surakarta
Madiun
Malang
Raba
Cilacap
Yogyakarta
Situbondo
Banyuwangi
Dompu
JAVA
(JAWA)
Lumajang
Jember
Singaraja
Gianyar
Mataram
Sumbawabesar
Taliwang
Bali
Denpasar
Praya
Lombok

2

110°

C

0   250   500 KILOMETRES

© Collins Bartholomew Ltd

61

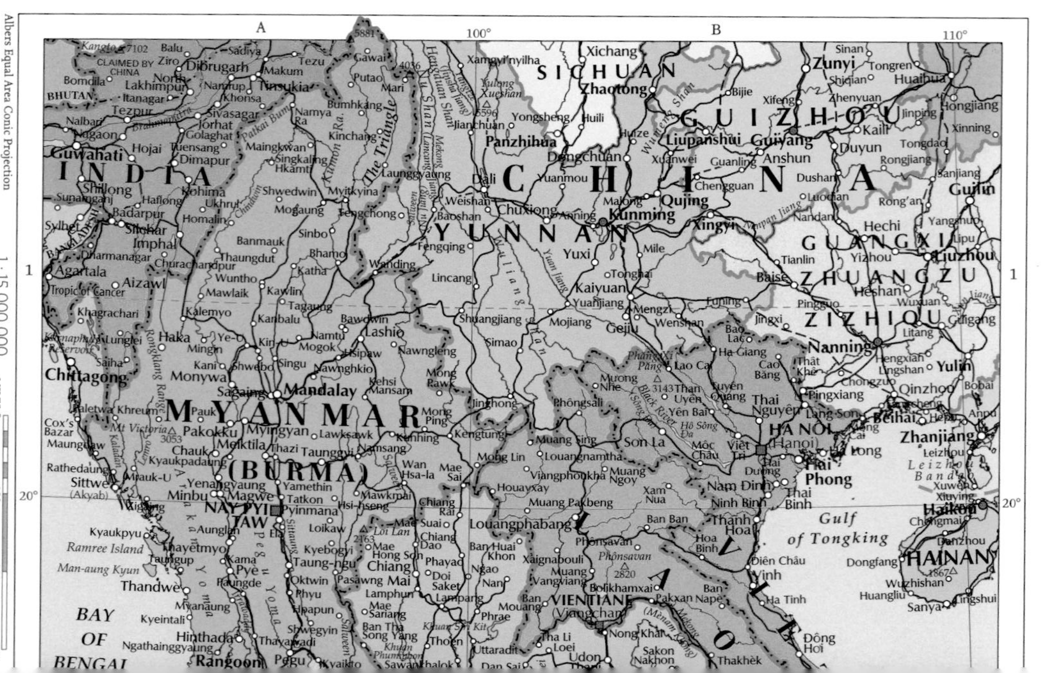

Albers Equal Area Conic Projection   1 : 15 000 000   MILES 0   100   200   300

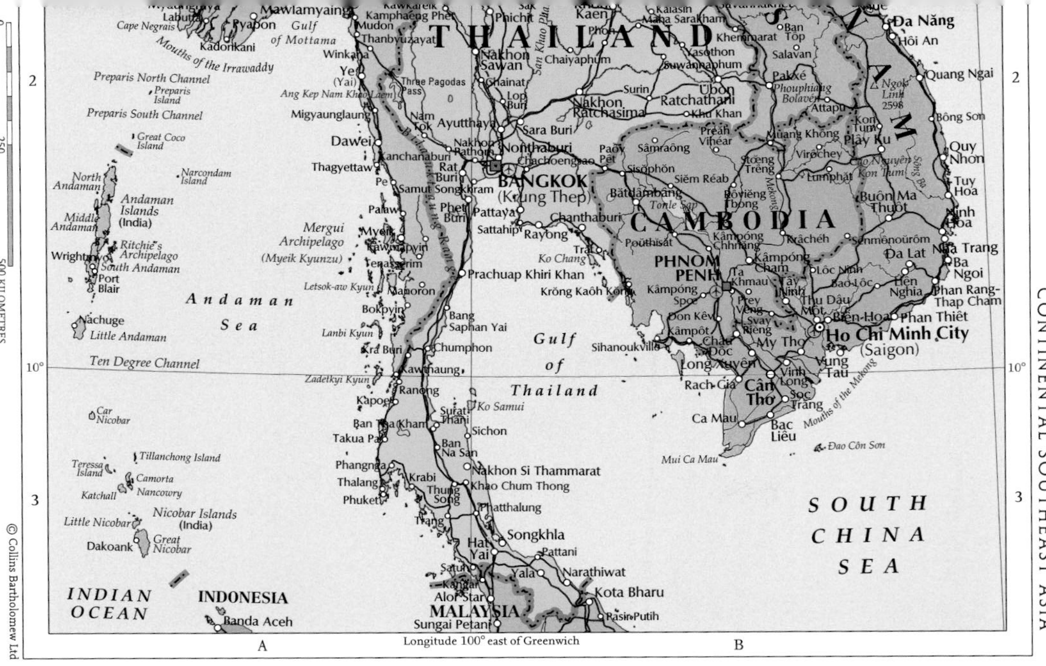

© Collins Bartholomew Ltd

0   250   500 KILOMETRES

THAILAND
CAMBODIA
MALAYSIA
INDONESIA
INDIAN OCEAN
SOUTH CHINA SEA
Andaman Sea
Gulf of Thailand
Gulf of Mottama
Mouths of the Irrawaddy
Mouths of the Mekong
Mergui Archipelago (Myeik Kyunzu)
Andaman Islands (India)
Nicobar Islands (India)
Ten Degree Channel
Preparis North Channel
Preparis South Channel
Preparis Island
Great Coco Island
Narcondam Island
North Andaman
Middle Andaman
South Andaman
Ritchie's Archipelago
Port Blair
Little Andaman
Car Nicobar
Tillanchong Island
Teressa Island
Camorta
Nancowry
Katchall
Little Nicobar
Great Nicobar
Dakoank
Banda Aceh
BANGKOK (Krung Thep)
PHNOM PENH
Ho Chi Minh City (Saigon)
Da Năng
Hôi An
Quang Ngai
Bông Son
Quy Nhon
Tuy Hoa
Nha Trang
Ba Ngoi
Phan Rang-Thap Cham
Phan Thiêt
Da Lat
Buôn Ma Thuôt
Play Ku
Kon Tum
Ngok Linh 2598
Mekong
Tonle Sap
Siĕm Réab
Bătdâmbâng
Sisŏphŏn
Pouthĭsăt
Kâmpóng Chhnăng
Kâmpóng Cham
Krâchéh
Sênmonoŭrôm
Lôc Ninh
Bao Lôc
Liên Nghia
Biên Hoa
Thu Dâu Môt
Tây Ninh
Svay Riĕng
Prey Vêng
Ta Khmau
Kâmpóng Spoe
Don Kêv
Kâmpôt
Chau Dôc
Long Xuyên
My Tho
Vung Tau
Vinh Long
Cân Tho
Soc Trang
Bac Liêu
Ca Mau
Mui Ca Mau
Rach Gia
Dao Côn Son
Sihanoukville
Krŏng Kaôh Kŏng
Trat
Ko Chang
Chanthaburi
Rayong
Sattahip
Pattaya
Chachoengsao
Nonthaburi
Nakhon Pathom
Ratchaburi
Phetchaburi
Samut Songkhram
Ayutthaya
Sara Buri
Lop Buri
Chainat
Nakhon Sawan
Phichit
Chaiyaphum
Nakhon Ratchasima
Surin
Ubon Ratchathani
Khu Khan
Yasothon
Suwannaphum
Khemmarat
Maha Sarakham
Kalasin
Salavan
Ban Tôp
Pakxé
Phouphiang Bolavén
Attapu
Muang Không
Virôchey
Lumphăt
Stœng Trĕng
Preăh Vihéar
Sâmraông
Paôy Pêt
Bôvĭeng Tbong
Kanchanaburi
Three Pagodas Pass
Nam Tok
Bilauktaung Range
San Khao Phang
Prachuap Khiri Khan
Bang Saphan Yai
Chumphon
Kra Buri
Kawthaung
Ranong
Kapoe
Ban Taba Kham
Takua Pa
Surat Thani
Ko Samui
Sichon
Ban Na San
Nakhon Si Thammarat
Khao Chum Thong
Phatthalung
Phangnga
Thalang
Phuket
Krabi
Thung Song
Trang
Songkhla
Hat Yai
Pattani
Yala
Narathiwat
Satun
Kangar
Alor Star
Sungai Petani
Kota Bharu
Pasir Putih
Mawlamyaing
Mudon
Thanbyuzayat
Kamphaeng Phet
Kawkareik
Labutta
Pyapon
Kadonkani
Cape Negrais
Winkana
Ye (Yai)
Ang Kep Nam Khao Laem
Migyaunglaung
Dawei
Thagyettaw
Pe
Palaw
Myeik
Kawmapyin
Tenasserim
Mamoron
Letsok-aw Kyun
Bokpyin
Lanbi Kyun
Zadetkyi Kyun
Nachuge
Wrightmyo
Longitude 100° east of Greenwich
3
10°

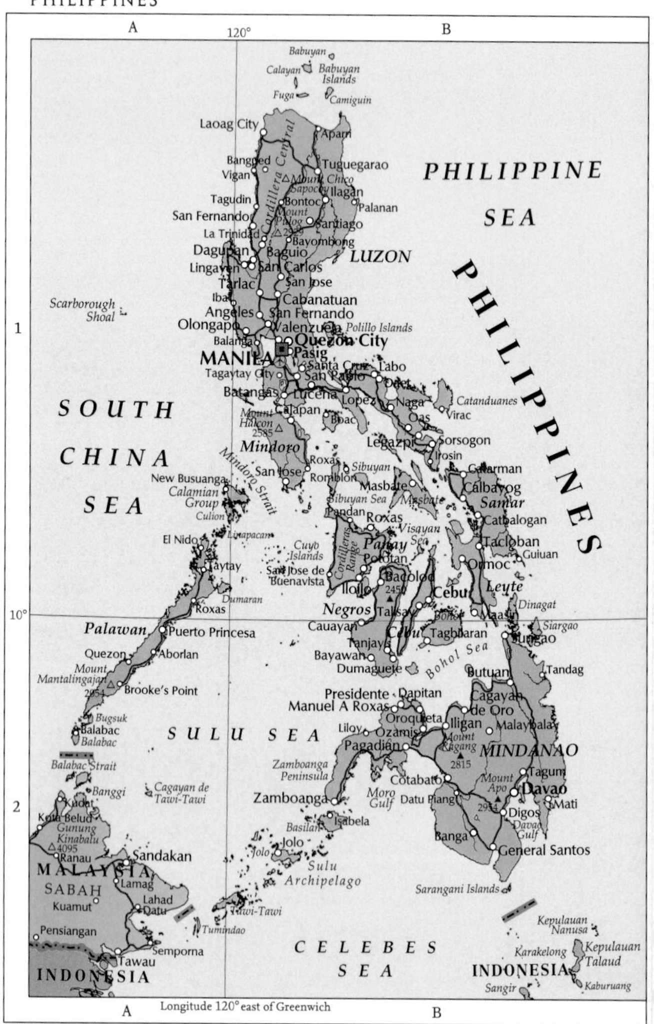

A   120°   B

Babuyan
Calayan *Babuyan*
Islands
Fuga *Camiguin*

Laoag City · *Aparri*

PHILIPPINE
SEA

Bangued ·Tuguegarao
Vigan · *Bapocol* ·Ilagan
Tagudin ·Bontoc *Mount* ·Palanan
San Fernando· *Chico* ·Santiago
La Trinidad· *Mount* ·Bayombong
Baguio · *Nga*
Dagupan· San Carlos
Lingayen· San Jose
Tarlac· ·Cabanatuan
Angeles ·San Fernando
Olongapo· ·Valenzuela *Polillo Islands*
Balanga· **Quezon City**
MANILA ·Pasig
Tagaytay City· Santa Cruz ·Labo
Batangas· San Pablo ·Daet
Mount ·Lucena *Lopez* ·Naga ·Virac
Halcon ·Calapan *Oas* *Catanduanes*
Mindoro ·Legaspi ·Sorsogon
San Jose· Roxas *Sibuyan* ·Irosin ·Calarman
New Busuanga· *Calamian* Romblon *Masbate* **Calbayog**
Group *Sibuyan Sea* **Samar**
Culion ·Roxas *Masbate* ·Catbalogan
El Nido· *Cuyo* *Pandan* *Visayan* ·Tacloban
Islands ·Kalibo *Sea* ·Guiuan
Taytay· *Linapacan* San Jose de ·Roxas **Leyte**
Dumaran Buenavista· *Iloilo* Bacolod· **Cebu** ·Ormoc *Dinagat*
Negros Talisa· *Siargao*
Roxas· *Cebu* Tagbilaran· ·Surigao
Palawan Cauayan· ·Tanjay
Puerto Princesa· Bayawan· *Bohol Sea* ·Tandag
Quezon· Dumaguete· ·Butuan
Mount Aborlan· Presidente Dapitan· Cagayan
Mantalingajan Manuel A Roxas· de Oro ·Malaybalay
2085 Brooke's Point· Liloy· Oroquieta· ·Iligan
Bugsuk Ozamis· *Mount*
Balabac *Zamboanga* Pagadian· *Kitanglad* **MINDANAO**
Balabac SULU SEA *Peninsula* *2815*
Balabac Strait *Cagayan de* Zamboanga· Cotabato· ·Tagum
Tawi-Tawi *Moro* Datu Piang· *Mount* **Davao**
Banggi *Gulf* *Apo* *2954*
Kudat *Isabela* ·Digos
Kota Belud *Basilan* Banga· *Davao*
Gunung *Jolo* *Gulf*
Kinabalu *Sulu* ·General Santos
4095 ·Ranau Sandakan· *Archipelago* *Sarangani Islands*
MALAYSIA Lamag·
SABAH Lahad· *Kepulauan*
Kuamut· Datu *Tawi-Tawi* *Nanusa*
Pensiangan· *Tinindao* *Karakelong* *Kepulauan*
CELEBES *Talaud*
Semporna· SEA
Tawau· *INDONESIA* *Sangir* *Kaburuang*
INDONESIA

1

SOUTH

CHINA

SEA

Scarborough
Shoal

Mindoro Strait

LUZON

Cordillera Central
Mount Chico

Luzon Strait

Sibuyan

Cordillera

Palay
Iloilo

10°

2

A   Longitude 120° east of Greenwich   B

Albers Equal Area Conic
Projection

1 : 15 000 000   MILES 0   100   0   250 KILOMETRES

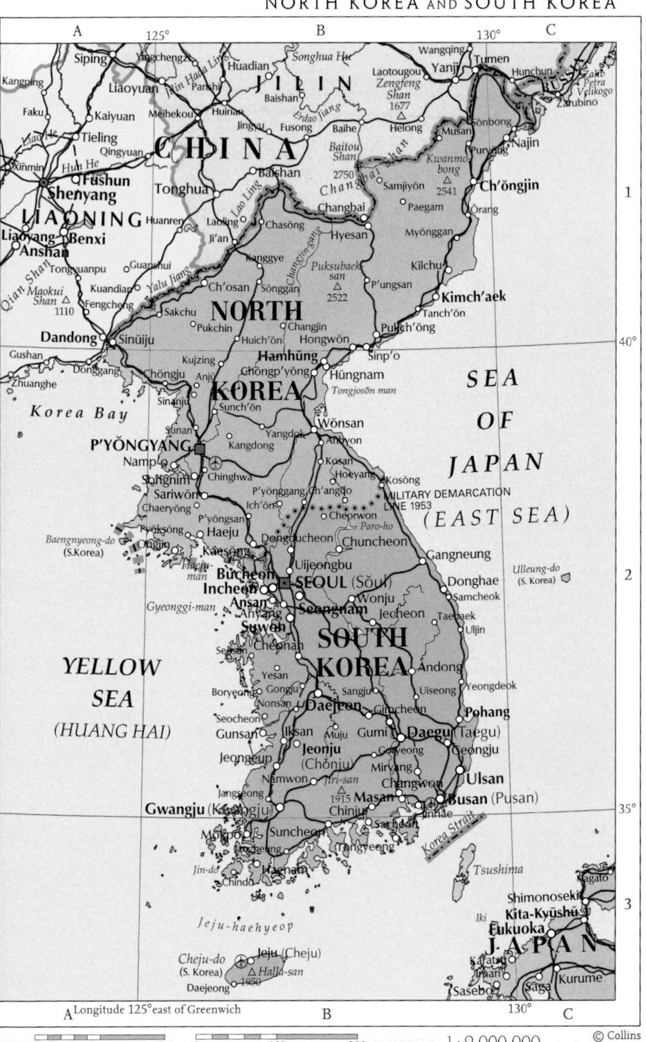

A 125° B 130° C

Siping Shuangchengzi Songhua He Wangqing
Kangping Liaoyuan Huadian Laotougou Yanji Tumen Hunchun
Faku Kaiyuan Meihekou Baishan Jingyu Fusong Zengfeng Sonbong Petra
JILIN Shan Velikogo
Tieling Huinan Baihe Helong Musan 1677 Puryŏng Najin Zarubino
Fushun Tonghua Baitou Samjiyŏn Musan Ch'ŏngjin
CHINA Shan Ch'ŏngjin
Shenyang Huanren Laoling Ji'an Chasŏng 2750 Changbai Paegam Kwanmo Ŏrang 1
LIAONING Qingyuan Kanggye Changbai Hyesan Myŏnggan bong 2541
Benxi Tonghua Yalu River Changjin Kilchu
Anshan Guanshui Songgan Puksubaek Tanch'ŏn Kimch'aek
Qian Shan Tongyuanpu Ch'osan san
Maokui Shan Kuandian P'ungsan 2522 P'ungsan 40°
1110 Fengcheng Sakchu Pukch'in Changlin Hongwŏn
Dandong Sinŭiju Pukch'ŏng NORTH Huich'ŏn Hongwŏn Pukch'ŏng
Gushan Dongganog Kujang Hamhŭng Sinp'o
Zhuanghe Sinanju Chŏngp'yŏng Hŭngnam
Korea Bay Anju Sunch'ŏn KOREA Tongjosŏn man SEA
P'YŎNGYANG Sŭngho Yangdŏk Wŏnsan OF
Namp'o Chinghwa Kangdong Anbyŏn JAPAN
Songnim P'yŏngsan Kosŏng
Sariwŏn P'yŏnggang-Ch'angdo MILITARY DEMARCATION (EAST SEA)
Chaeryŏng Ich'ŏn Ch'ŏrwŏn LINE 1953
Pyoksong Haeju Paro-ho
Baengnyeong-do Onjin Kaesŏng Dongducheon Chuncheon Gangneung Ulleung-do 2
(S.Korea) Haeju Uijeongbu (S. Korea)
Huju man Incheon SEOUL (Sŏul) Donghae
Gyeonggi-man Bucheon Wonju Samcheok
Ansan Anyang Seongnam Jecheon Taebaek Uljin
Suwon Cheonan Andong Yeongdeok
YELLOW Seosan SOUTH
SEA Yesan Sangju Uiseong Pohang
(HUANG HAI) Boryeong Gongju KOREA Gimcheon
Gunsan Seocheon Daejeon Gumi Daegu (Taegu) Gyeongju
Jeonju Iksan Muju Gimcheon Geumseong Ulsan
(Chŏnju) Jirisan Miryang Geonhae
Jeongeup Namwon 1915 Changwon Busan (Pusan) 35°
Jangseong Chinju Masan
Gwangju (Kaŏngju) Mokp'o Suncheon Sacheon Korea Strait
Molpo Gangjin Tongyeong Tsushima
Jin-do Haenam Kita-Kyūshū
Jeju-haehyeop Fukuoka
Shimonoseki JAPAN
Iki Saga 3
Cheju-do Jeju (Cheju) Kurume
(S.Korea) Halla-san
Daejeong Sasebo

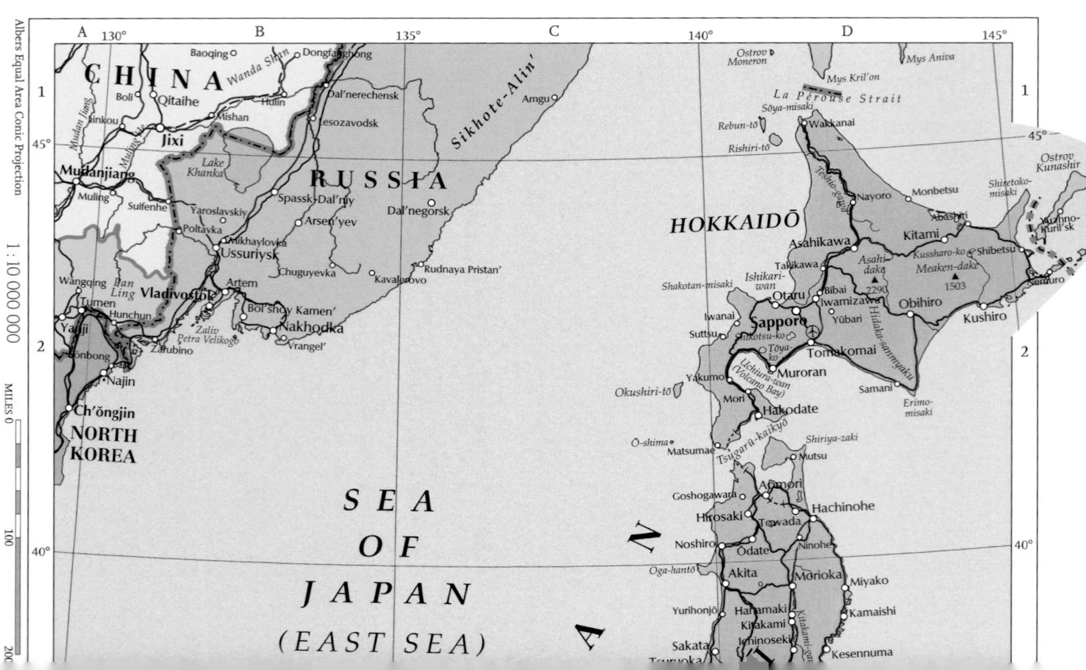

Albers Equal Area Conic Projection   1 : 10 000 000   MILES 0   100   200

CHINA

RUSSIA

NORTH KOREA

HOKKAIDŌ

SEA OF JAPAN (EAST SEA)

Sikhote-Alin'

La Pérouse Strait

Ostrov Kunashir
Ostrov Moneron
Rishiri-tō
Rebun-tō
Okushiri-tō
O-shima

Baoqing
Qitaihe
Boli
Jixi
Jidong
Wanda Shan
Hulin
Mishan
Jiamusi
Muling
Suifenhe
Dongning
Hunchun
Wangqing
Tumen
Yanji
Tuman
Zahvino
Najin
Chŏngjin
Mudanjiang
Dunhua
Dal'nerechensk
Lesozavodsk
Spassk-Dal'niy
Arsen'yev
Chuguyevka
Kavalerovo
Rudnaya Pristan'
Dal'negorsk
Ariadnoye
Tayezhnoye
Kamen'-Rybolov
Lake Khanka
Yaroslavskiy
Oktyabr'skiy
Pogranichnyy
Ussuriysk
Artem
Bol'shoy Kamen'
Nakhodka
Vrangel'
Vladivostok
Zaliv Petra Velikogo

Mys Kril'on
Mys Aniva
Shiretoko-misaki
Sōya-misaki
Shakotan-misaki
Suttsu
Iwanai
Wakkanai
Monbetsu
Kitami
Abashiri
Kushiro-ko
Shabetsu
Moshiri-dake
1503
Obihiro
Nayoro
Asahikawa
Asahi-dake
2290
Takikawa
Ashibetsu
Yūbari
Iwamizawa
Bibai
Hidaka-sammyaku
Samani
Ermo-misaki
Tomakomai
Mutsu
Shiriya-zaki
Otaru
Sapporo
Chitose
Ishikari-wan
Shokotsu-misaki
Yoichi
Shizunai
Urakawa
Uchiura-wan
Oshima-hantō
Yakumo
Mori
Hakodate
Muroran
Matsumae
Tsugaru-kaikyō
Ōma
Goshogawara
Noshiro
Hirosaki
Ōdate
Towada
Aomori
Oga-hantō
Akita
Hachinohe
Misawa
Towada-ko
Kitakami-gawa
Iwate-san
Morioka
Miyako
Kamaishi
Miyako
Hanamaki
Yokote
Kitakami
Ōfunato
Yuzawa
Ichinoseki
Kesennuma
Yurihonjō
Sakata
Tsuruoka

N

A

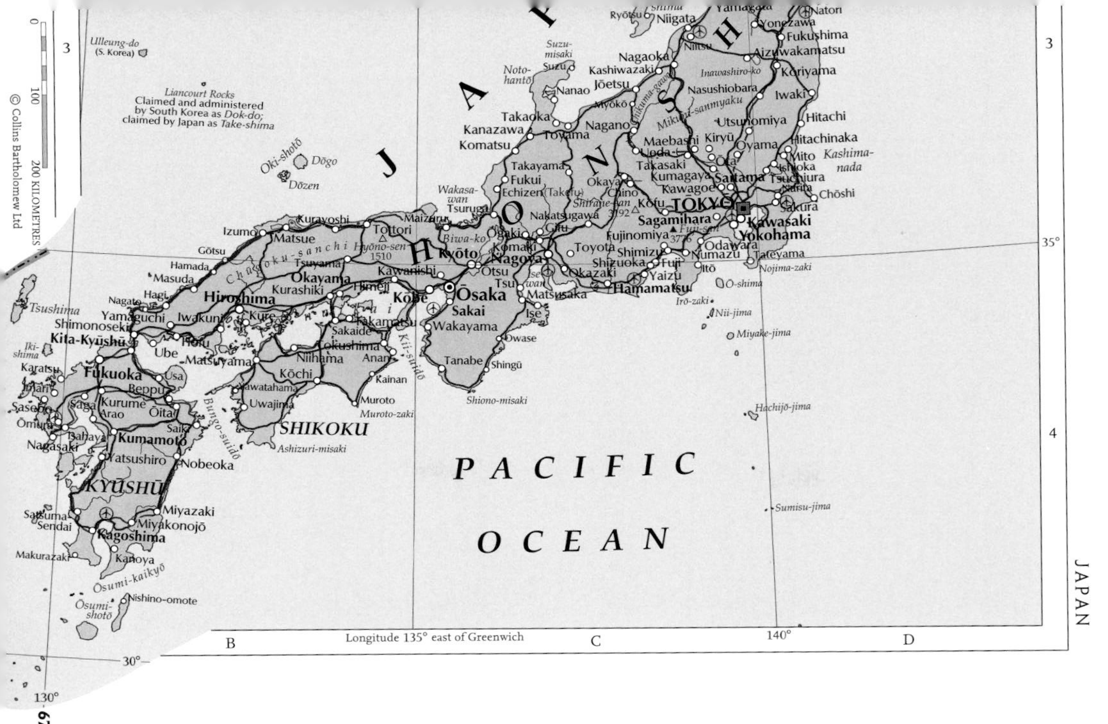

JAPAN

3

35°

4

D

3

C

B

Longitude 135° east of Greenwich

Ullŭng-do
(S. Korea)

Claimant Rocks
Claimed and administered
by South Korea as Dok-do;
claimed by Japan as Take-shima

Oki-shotō
Dōgo
Dōzen

Kyoga-misaki

Suzu-misaki
Noto-hantō

Sado

Niigata

Fukushima

Aizuwakamatsu

Kōriyama

Hitachi

Hitachinaka

Kashima-nada

Chōshi

Nojima-zaki

Ō-shima

Katsuura

Tateyama

Hamamatsu

Iō-jima

Hachijō-jima

Miyake-jima

Nii-jima

Sumisu-jima

Nagaoka

Kashiwazaki

Jōetsu

Nagano

Komatsu

Kanazawa

Toyama

Takaoka

Fukui

Echizen

Maizuru

Tottori

Matsue

Izumo

Gōtsu

Hamada

Masuda

Iwakuni

Yamaguchi

Ube

Shimonoseki

Kita-Kyūshū

Fukuoka

Kurume

Saga

Ōmuta

Nagasaki

Sasebo

Unzen

Kumamoto

Yatsushiro

Minamata

Kagoshima

Miyakonojō

Miyazaki

Nobeoka

Ōita

Beppu

Saiki

Matsuyama

Imabari

Niihama

Kōchi

Sukumo

Tosashimizu

Uwajima

Ashizuri-misaki

Muroto-misaki

Muroto

Anan

Tokushima

Naruto

Kōbe

Ōsaka

Sakai

Wakayama

Kainan

Tanabe

Shingū

Owase

Shiono-misaki

Kyōto

Ōtsu

Nara

Nabari

Tsu

Ise

Toba

Nagoya

Toyota

Okazaki

Hekinan

Toyohashi

Gifu

Ōgaki

Shizuoka

Fuji

Shimizu

Yaizu

Numazu

Odawara

Atami

Itō

Yokohama

Sagamihara

Hiratsuka

Kawagoe

TŌKYŌ

Chiba

Utsunomiya

Kiryū

Maebashi

Takasaki

Matsumoto

Nakatsugawa

Kōfu

Saitama

Hiroshima

Kure

Fukuyama

Onomichi

Okayama

Kurashiki

Takamatsu

Tokushima

SHIKOKU

KYŪSHŪ

Tsushima

Iki

Ikoma

Kōya

Satsuma-sendai

Makurazaki

Sata-misaki

Ōsumi-shotō

Tane-shima

Yaku-shima

Kuchinoerabu-jima

Nakano-shima

Tsurugi-san
1955

PACIFIC

OCEAN

Hatchōri

Morioka

Kamaishi

Ichinoseki

Ōfunato

Sendai

Fukushima

Kōriyama

0   100   200 KILOMETRES

© Collins Bartholomew Ltd

67

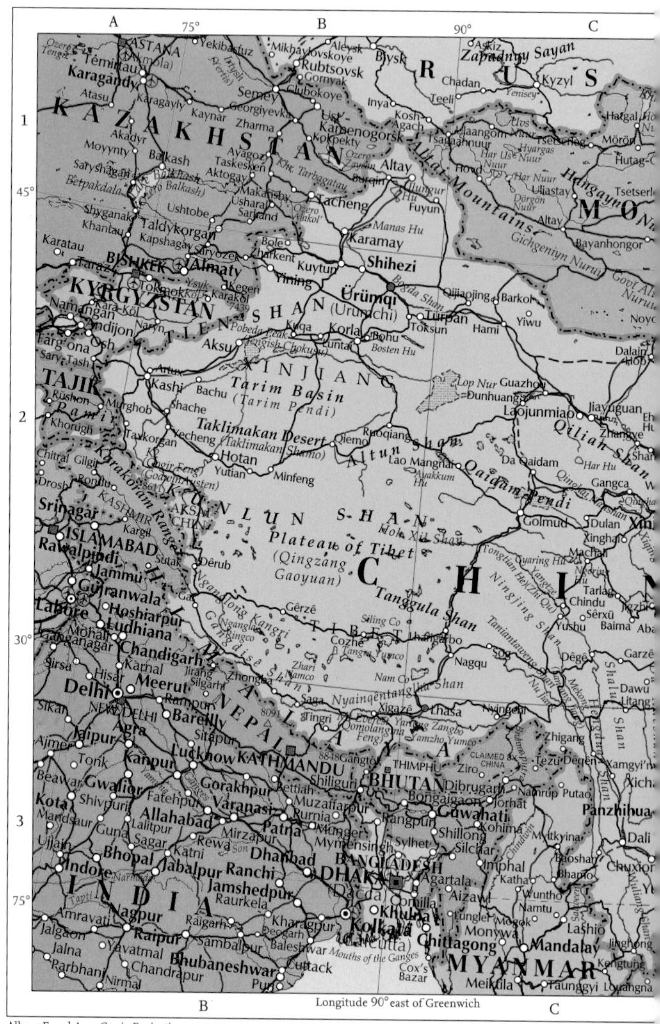

Albers Equal Area Conic Projection   1 : 30 000 000   MILES 0   200   400   600

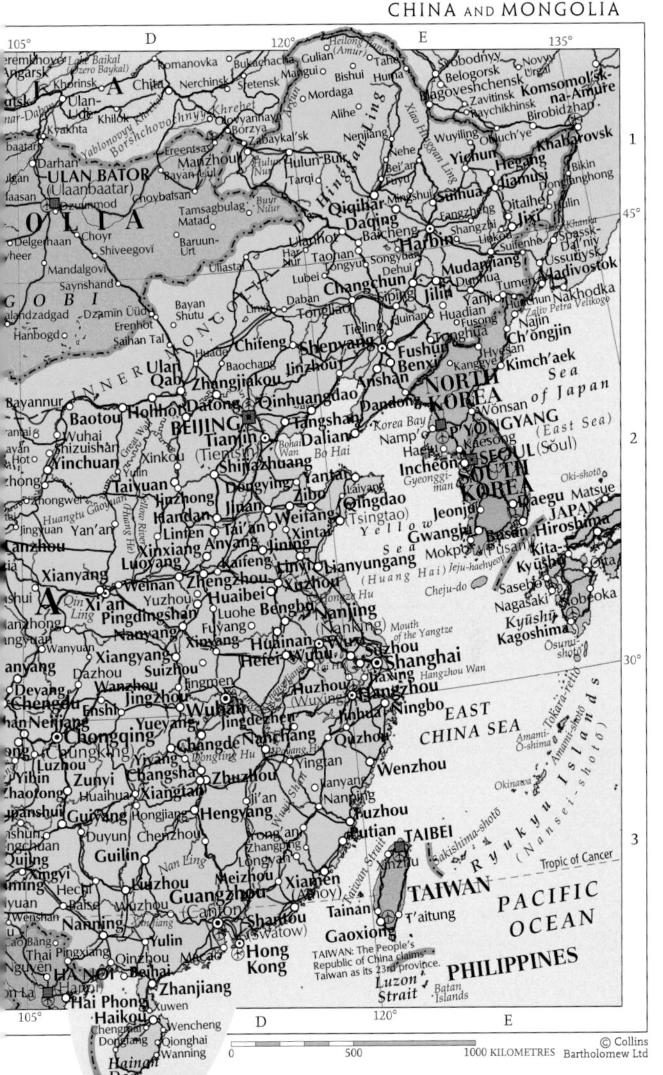
ULAN BATOR
(Ulaanbaatar)
BEIJING
Tianjin
(Tientsin)
Shanghai
Chongqing
(Chungking)
Guangzhou
(Canton)
Hong Kong
Macao
HANOI
P'YONGYANG
SEOUL (Sŏul)
TAIBEI
NORTH KOREA
SOUTH KOREA
JAPAN
TAIWAN
PHILIPPINES
INNER MONGOLIA
GOBI
Yellow Sea
(Huang Hai)
Sea of Japan
(East Sea)
EAST CHINA SEA
PACIFIC OCEAN
Ryukyu Islands
(Nansei-shotō)
Tropic of Cancer
Bo Hai
Korea Bay
Luzon Strait
Taiwan Strait
Hainan Dao
Lake Baikal
(Ozero Baykal)
Heilong Jiang
(Amur)
Da Hinggan Ling
Xiao Hinggan Ling
Harbin
Shenyang
Dalian
Qingdao
(Tsingtao)
Nanjing
(Nanking)
Wuhan
Xi'an
Chengdu
Kunming
Nanning
Fuzhou
Xiamen
(Amoy)
Hangzhou
Vladivostok
Khabarovsk
Qiqihar
Changchun
Jilin
Hohhot
Baotou
Lanzhou
Yinchuan
Taiyuan
Shijiazhuang
Jinan
Zhengzhou
Hefei
Nanchang
Changsha
Guiyang
Haikou
Kaohsiung
Gaoxiong
Hiroshima
Kagoshima
Busan
(Pusan)
Daegu
Incheon
TAIWAN: The People's Republic of China claims Taiwan as its 23rd province.
0
500
1000 KILOMETRES
105°
120°
135°
45°
30°
D
E
1
2
3
© Collins Bartholomew Ltd

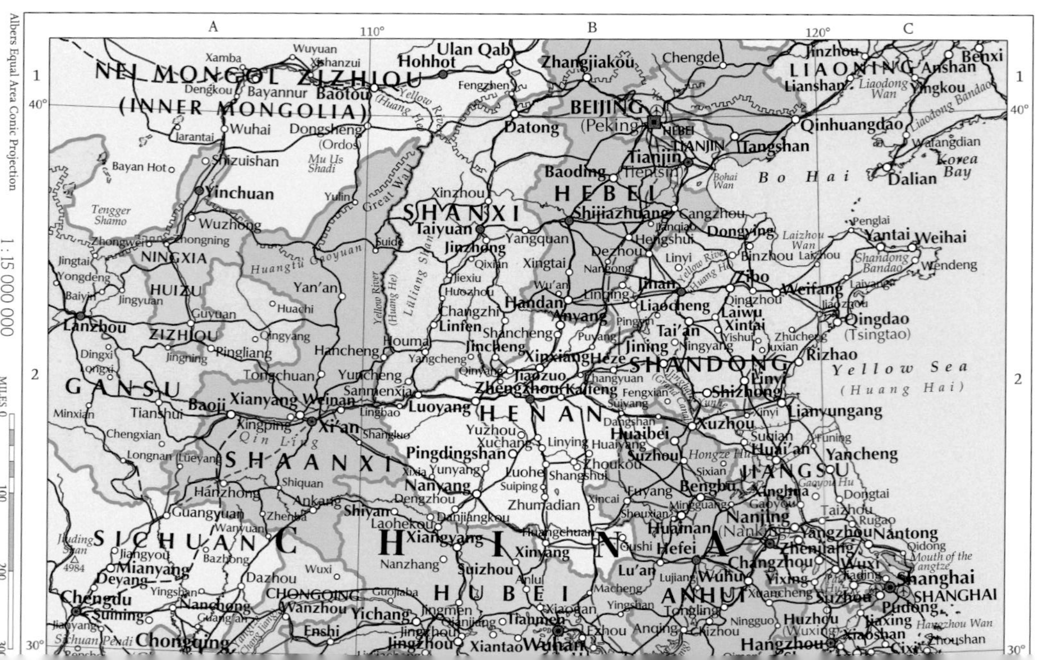

Albers Equal Area Conic Projection

1 : 15 000 000

MILES 0   100   200   300

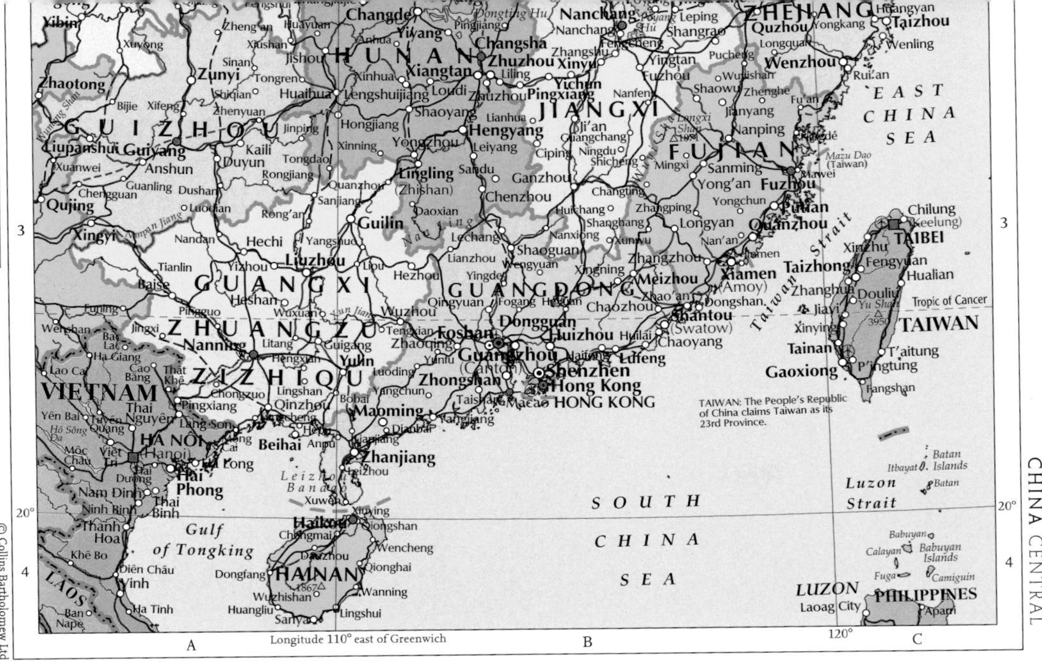

© Collins Bartholomew Ltd

0   250   500 KILOMETRES

ZHEJIANG
HUNAN
JIANGXI
FUJIAN
GUIZHOU
GUANGDONG
GUANGXI ZHUANGZU ZIZHIQU
HAINAN
TAIWAN
VIETNAM
LAOS
PHILIPPINES
LUZON
HONG KONG
EAST CHINA SEA
SOUTH CHINA SEA
Taiwan Strait
Luzon Strait
Gulf of Tongking
Tropic of Cancer
TAIWAN: The People's Republic of China claims Taiwan as its 23rd Province.
Longitude 110° east of Greenwich
Changsha
Nanchang
Fuzhou
Guangzhou (Canton)
Guiyang
Nanning
Haikou
Xiamen (Amoy)
Shantou (Swatow)
Shenzhen
Hong Kong
Macao
TAIBEI
Gaoxiong
HA NÔI (Hanoi)
Hai Phong
Zhanjiang
Guilin
Wenzhou
Taizhou
Chilung (Keelung)
Tainan
20°
120°
3
4

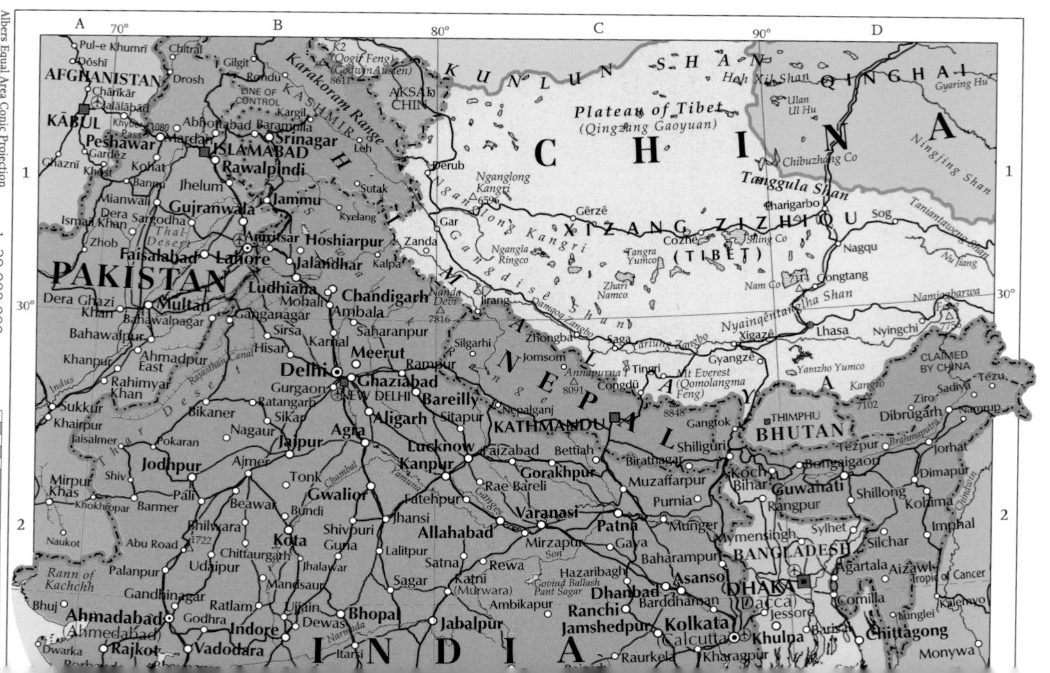

Albers Equal Area Conic Projection

1 : 20 000 000

MILES 0   100   200   300   400

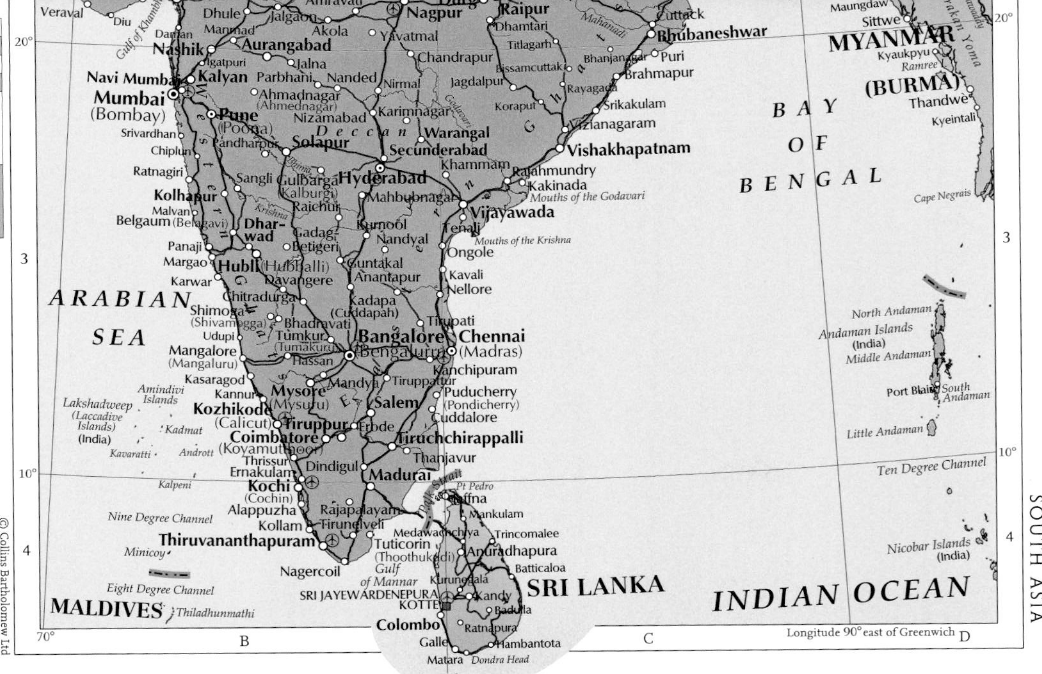

MYANMAR (BURMA)

rakan Yoma

Maungdaw
Sittwe
Kyaukpyu
Ramree
Thandwe
Kyeintali

Cape Negrais

B A Y   O F   B E N G A L

North Andaman
Andaman Islands (India)
Middle Andaman
Port Blair South Andaman
Little Andaman

Ten Degree Channel

Nicobar Islands (India)

INDIAN OCEAN

Cuttack
Bhubaneshwar
Puri
Brahmapur
Bhanjanagar
Rayagada Srikakulam
Titlagarh
Jeypore Vizianagaram
Koraput Vishakhapatnam
Kakinada
Rajahmundry
Mouths of the Godavari
Khammam
Warangal
Vijayawada
Mouths of the Krishna
Ongole

Raipur
Nagpur
Amravati
Akola
Yavatmal
Chandrapur
Adilabad
Nizamabad Karimnagar
Nirmal
Secunderabad
Hyderabad
Nalgonda
Mahbubnagar
Kurnool
Nandyal
Kadapa (Cuddapah)
Anantapur
Tirupati
Nellore
Kavali

Dhule
Jalgaon
Nashik
Kalyan
Navi Mumbai
Mumbai (Bombay)
Pune (Poona)
Sangli
Kolhapur
Ratnagiri
Chiplun
Malvan
Panaji
Margao
Karwar

Aurangabad
Jalna
Parbhani Nanded
Ahmadnagar
Gulbarga (Kalburgi)
Solapur
Bijapur
Bagalkot
Gadag
Davangere
Chitradurga
Shimoga (Shivamogga)
Bhadravati
Tumkur (Tumakuru)
Hassan

Dhantari
Titlagarh
Jagdalpur

Chikmagalur
Kozhikode (Calicut)
Udupi
Mangalore (Mangaluru)
Kasaragod
Kannur
Koyilandy

Dharwad
Hubli (Hubballi)
Belgaum (Belagavi)

Shahada

Bangalore (Bengaluru)
Mysore (Mysuru)
Salem
Chennai (Madras)
Kanchipuram
Vellore
Puducherry (Pondicherry)
Cuddalore

Coimbatore
Tiruppur
Erode
Tiruchirappalli
Thanjavur

Thrissur
Ernakulam
Kochi (Cochin)
Alappuzha
Kollam

Dindigul
Madurai
Virudhunagar
Rajapalayam

A R A B I A N   S E A

Veraval
Diu
Daman
Gulf of Khambhat

Lakshadweep (Laccadive Islands) (India)
Amindivi Islands
Kadmat
Androth
Kavaratti
Kalpeni

Nine Degree Channel
Kalpeni
Minicoy

Eight Degree Channel
Thiladhunmathi

MALDIVES

Nagercoil
Thiruvananthapuram

Kanniyakumari
Nagercoil
Tuticorin (Thoothukudi)
Tirunelveli

Gulf of Mannar

SRI LANKA

Jaffna
Mullaittivu
Mankulam
Trincomalee
Medawachchiya
Anuradhapura
Batticaloa
Kurunegala
Kandy
SRI JAYEWARDENEPURA KOTTE
Colombo
Galle
Matara Dondra Head
Ratnapura
Hambantota

Palk Strait
Gulf of Mannar

0   200   400   600 KILOMETRES

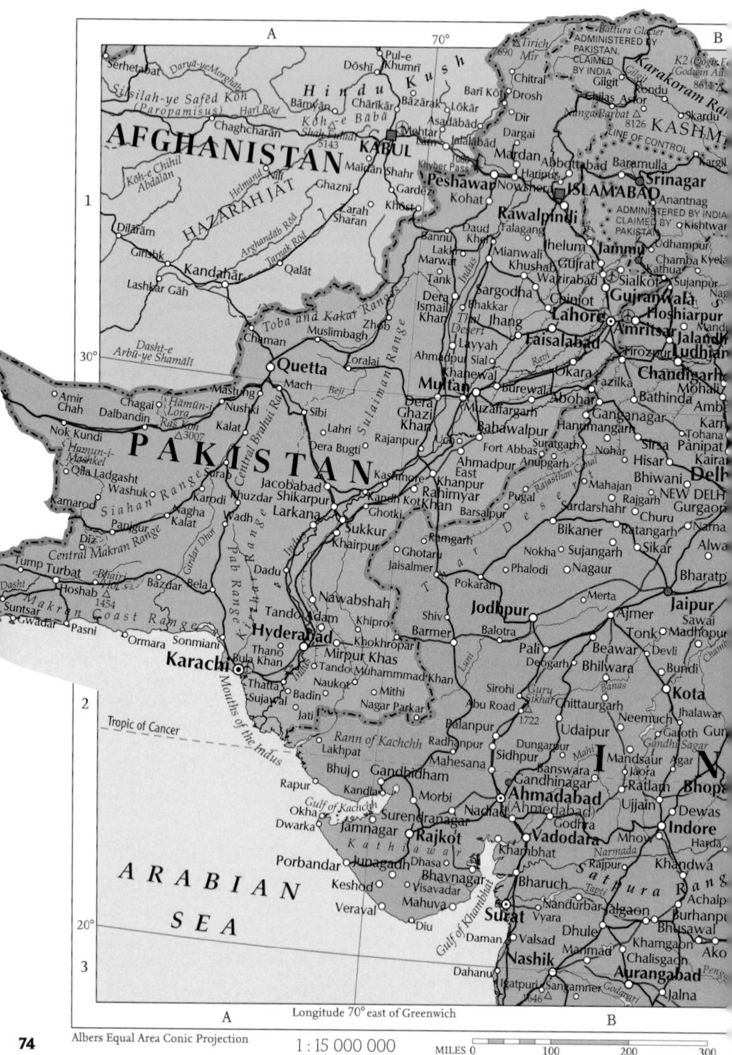

A
70°
B
1
2
3
30°
20°
AFGHANISTAN
PAKISTAN
KASHMIR
ARABIAN SEA
KABUL
ISLAMABAD
Hindu Kush
Karakoram Range
ADMINISTERED BY PAKISTAN, CLAIMED BY INDIA
ADMINISTERED BY INDIA CLAIMED BY PAKISTAN
LINE OF CONTROL
Tirich Mir
K2 (Qogir Feng) (Godwin Austen)
8611
Nanga Parbat
8126
Koh-e Baba
Shah Fuladi
5143
Silsilah-ye Safed Koh
(Paropamisus)
Hari Rod
Darya-ye Morghab
Koh-e Chihil Abdalan
HAZARAH JAT
Helmand
Arghandab Rod
Tarnak Rod
Dasht-e Arbu-ye Shamali
Toba and Kakar Range
Sulaiman Range
Central Brahui Range
Kirthar Range
Pab Range
Siahan Range
Central Makran Range
Makran Coast Range
Hamun-i-Lora
Hamun-i-Mashkel
Ras Koh
3007
Thal Desert
Thar Desert
Indus
Ravi
Rajasthan Canal
Luni
Girdar Dhor
Bhairi Hol
1454
Mouths of the Indus
Tropic of Cancer
Rann of Kachchh
Gulf of Kachchh
Gulf of Khambhat
Kathiawar
Satpura Range
Narmada
Tapti
Mahi
Banas
Chambal
Godavari
Guru Sikhar
1722
1646
Serhetabat
Pul-e Khumri
Doshi
Chitral
Drosh
Bari Kot
Dir
Dargai
Gilgit
Chilas
Skardu
Kargil
Srinagar
Anantnag
Kishtwar
Baramulla
Abbottabad
Haripur
Mardan
Bamyan
Charikar
Bazarak
Lokar
Asadabad
Jalalabad
Mehtar Lam
Khyber Pass
Chaghcharan
Maidan Shahr
Ghazni
Gardez
Khost
Nili
Zarah Sharan
Peshawar
Nowshera
Kohat
Rawalpindi
Talagang
Daud Khel
Bannu
Lakki Marwat
Tank
Mianwali
Khushab
Jhelum
Gujrat
Jammu
Udhampur
Chamba
Kathua
Wazirabad
Sialkot
Sujanpur
Gujranwala
Sargodha
Bhakkar
Dera Ismail Khan
Chiniot
Lahore
Amritsar
Hoshiarpur
Jhang
Faisalabad
Jalandhar
Ludhiana
Layyah
Firozpur
Sial
Ahmadpur Sial
Khanewal
Okara
Fazilka
Chandigarh
Mohali
Multan
Burewala
Abohar
Bathinda
Dilaram
Girishk
Kandahar
Qalat
Lashkar Gah
Chaman
Muslimbagh
Zhob
Loralai
Quetta
Mach
Mastung
Nushki
Sibi
Beji
Chagai
Amir Chah
Dalbandin
Nok Kundi
Kalat
Lahri
Dera Bugti
Rajanpur
Dera Ghazi Khan
Muzaffargarh
Bahawalpur
Uch
Ganganagar
Hanumangarh
Suratgarh
Nohar
Sirsa
Tohana
Panipat
Hisar
Fort Abbas
Anupgarh
Ahmadpur East
Bhiwani
Delhi
NEW DELHI
Gurgaon
Qila Ladgasht
Washuk
Surab
Kamarod
Karodi
Nagha Kalat
Khuzdar
Jacobabad
Shikarpur
Kashmore
Khanpur
Rahimyar Khan
Kandh Kot
Ghotki
Larkana
Wadh
Sukkur
Khairpur
Mahajan
Rajgarh
Pugal
Sardarshahr
Churu
Barsalpur
Bikaner
Ratangarh
Panjgur
Diz
Tump
Turbat
Dasht
Hoshab
Bazdar
Bela
Dadu
Ramgarh
Ghotaru
Jaisalmer
Nokha
Sujangarh
Sikar
Phalodi
Nagaur
Pokaran
Suntsar
Gwadar
Pasni
Ormara
Sonmiani
Karachi
Bula Khan
Thano Bula Khan
Nawabshah
Tando Adam
Hyderabad
Khipro
Shiv
Barmer
Jodhpur
Merta
Ajmer
Jaipur
Sawai Madhopur
Tonk
Balotra
Khokhropar
Mirpur Khas
Tando Muhammmad Khan
Pali
Beawar
Devli
Bundi
Deogarh
Bhilwara
Kota
Thatta
Sujawal
Naukot
Badin
Mithi
Jati
Nagar Parkar
Sirohi
Abu Road
Chittaurgarh
Jhalawar
Neemuch
Palanpur
Udaipur
Garoth
Gandhi Sagar
Lakhpat
Radhanpur
Dungarpur
Sidhpur
Mahesana
Mandsaur
Agar
Bhuj
Gandhidham
Banswara
Jaora
Gandhinagar
Ratlam
Bhopal
Rapur
Kandla
Morbi
Ahmadabad
(Ahmedabad)
Okha
Dwarka
Surendranagar
Nadiad
Ujjain
Dewas
Jamnagar
Rajkot
Godhra
Vadodara
Mhow
Indore
Harda
Khambhat
Porbandar
Junagadh
Dhasa
Rajpur
Khandwa
Bhavnagar
Bharuch
Keshod
Visavadar
Mahuva
Achalpur
Veraval
Nandurbar
Jalgaon
Burhanpur
Surat
Vyara
Diu
Dhule
Bhusawal
Daman
Valsad
Manmad
Khamgaon
Akola
Nashik
Chalisgaon
Dahanu
Aurangabad
Igatpuri
Sangamner
Jalna
Narnaul
Alwar
Bharatpur
Kaithal
Karnal
Ambala
Longitude 70° east of Greenwich
Albers Equal Area Conic Projection
1 : 15 000 000
MILES 0
100
200
300

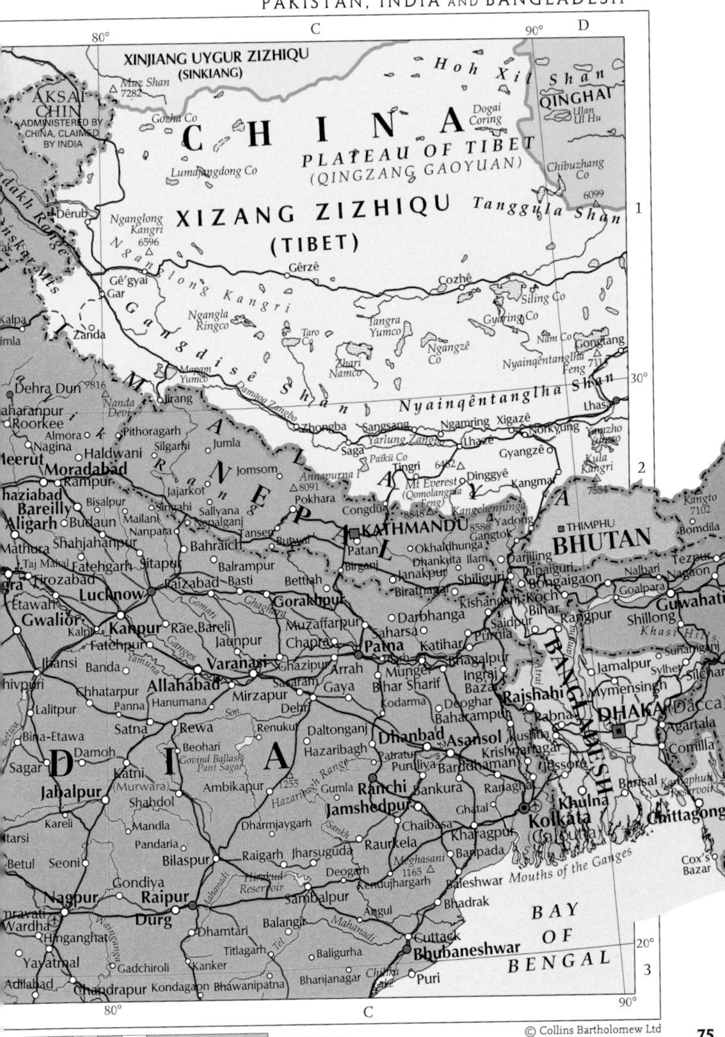
C
D
80°
90°
XINJIANG UYGUR ZIZHIQU
(SINKIANG)
Hoh Xil Shan
QINGHAI
AKSAI CHIN
ADMINISTERED BY CHINA, CLAIMED BY INDIA
Dogai Coring
Ulan Ul Hu
CHINA
PLATEAU OF TIBET
(QINGZANG GAOYUAN)
Gozha Co
Lumajangdong Co
Chibuzhang Co
6099
XIZANG ZIZHIQU
(TIBET)
Tanggula Shan
1
Dêrub
Nganglong Kangri
6596
Nganglong Kangri
Gêrzê
Gê'gyai
Gar
Gangdisê Shan
Cozhê
Siling Co
Ngangla Ringco
Tangra Yumco
Gyaring Co
Zanda
Taro Co
Nam Co
Gongtang
Ngangzê Co
Zhari Namco
Nyainqêntanglha Feng
7111
30°
Déhra Dun
7816
Nanda Devi
Nyainqêntanglha Shan
Lhasa
Roorkee
Pithoragarh
Zhongba
Sangsang
Ngamring
Xigazê
Almora
Silgarhi
Jumla
Yarlung Zangbo
Lhazê
Nagina
Haldwani
Saga
Gyangzê
Meerut
Moradabad
Jomsom
Paikü Co
Tingri
6482
Kula Kangri
2
Rampur
Annapurna I
8091
Mt Everest (Qomolangma Feng)
8848
Dinggyê
Kangmar
Ghaziabad
Jajarkot
Pokhara
7554
Bareilly
Bisalpur
Singahi
Sallyana
Congdü
Kangchenjunga
8586
Yadong
Kangto
7102
Aligarh
Budaun
Mailani
Nepalganj
NEPAL
KATHMANDU
THIMPHU
Bomdila
Mathura
Shahjahanpur
Nanpara
Tansen
Butwal
Patan
Okhaldhunga
Gangtok
BHUTAN
Taj Mahal
Fatehgarh
Sitapur
Bahraich
Birganj
Dhankuta
Ilam
Darjiling
Tezpur
Firozabad
Balrampur
Janakpur
Jalpaiguri
Nalbari
Nagaon
Faizabad
Basti
Bettiah
Shiliguri
Bongaigaon
Etawah
Lucknow
Gorakhpur
Biratnagar
Goalpara
Guwahati
Gomati
Ghaghara
Kishanganj
Koch Bihar
Gwalior
Kanpur
Rae Bareli
Muzaffarpur
Darbhanga
Rangpur
Shillong
Kalpi
Saharsa
Saidpur
Khasi Hills
Fatehpur
Jaunpur
Chapra
Patna
Katihar
Purnia
Jhansi
Banda
Yamuna
Ganges
Varanasi
Ghazipur
Arrah
Bhagalpur
BANGLADESH
Sunamganj
Allahabad
Sasaram
Munger
Jamalpur
Sylhet
Silchar
Chhatarpur
Mirzapur
Gaya
Bihar Sharif
Rajshahi
Mymensingh
Lalitpur
Panna
Hanumana
Son
Dehri
Kodarma
Deoghar
Baharampur
DHAKA (Dacca)
Satna
Rewa
Renukut
Daltonganj
Pabna
Agartala
Bina-Etawa
Beohari
Hazaribagh
Dhanbad
Asansol
Kushtia
Damoh
Govind Ballash Pant Sagar
Patratu
Purulia
Krishnanagar
Comilla
Sagar
INDIA
Barddhaman
Jessore
Katni (Murwara)
Ambikapur
1255
Gumla
Ranchi
Bankura
Ranaghat
Barisal
Jabalpur
Hazaribagh Range
Karnaphuli Reservoir
Shahdol
Jamshedpur
Ghatal
Khulna
Kareli
Mandla
Dharmjaygarh
Chaibasa
Kharagpur
Kolkata (Calcutta)
Chittagong
Itarsi
Pandaria
Raurkela
Baripada
Betul
Seoni
Bilaspur
Raigarh
Jharsuguda
Meghasani
1165
Cox's Bazar
Hirakud Reservoir
Deogarh
Keonjhargarh
Baleshwar
Mouths of the Ganges
Gondiya
Mahanadi
Nagpur
Raipur
Sambalpur
Bhadrak
Durg
Angul
BAY OF BENGAL
Wardha
Hinganghat
Dhamtari
Balangir
Cuttack
20°
Titlagarh
Tel
Baligurha
Bhubaneshwar
Yavatmal
Gadchiroli
Kanker
3
Adilabad
Chandrapur
Kondagaon
Bhawanipatna
Bhanjanagar
Chilika Lake
Puri
80°
C
90°
0
250
500 KILOMETRES

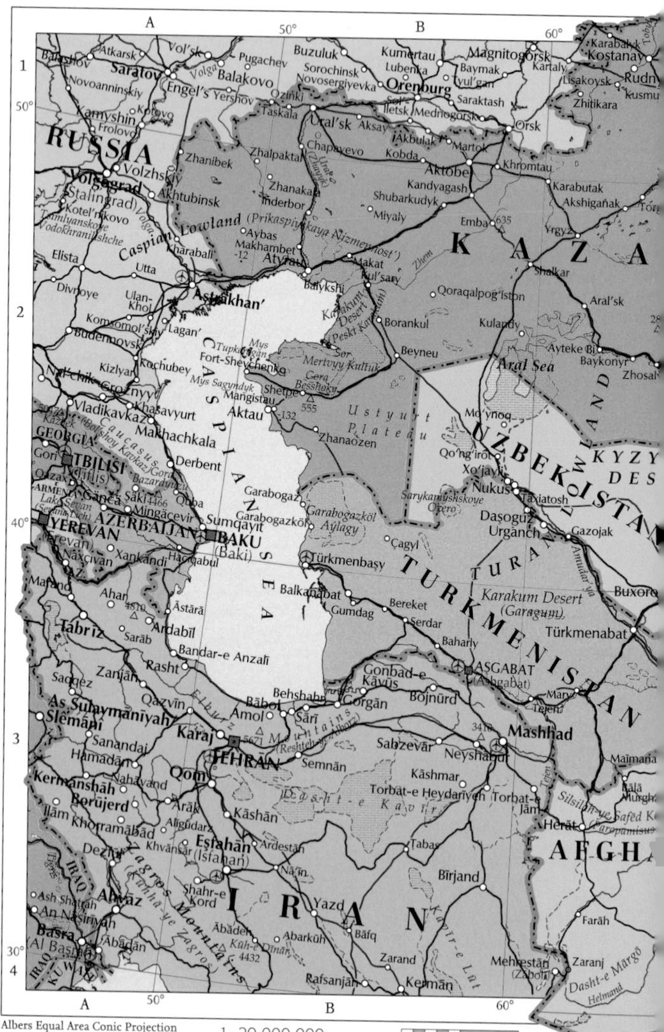
RUSSIA
KAZA
UZBEKISTAN
TURKMENISTAN
AZERBAIJAN
GEORGIA
ARMENIA
IRAN
IRAQ
KUWAIT
AFGHA
CASPIAN SEA
Aral Sea
Caspian Lowland (Prikaspiyskaya Nizmennost')
Ustyurt Plateau
Turan Lowland
Karakum Desert (Garagum)
Dasht-e Kavir
Elburz Mountains (Reshteh-ye Alborz)
Zagros Mountains (Kuhha-ye Zagros)
Caucasus (Bol'shoy Kavkaz)
TBILISI
YEREVAN
BAKU (Baki)
AŞGABAT (Ashgabat)
TEHRĀN
Volgograd (Stalingrad)
Saratov
Astrakhan'
Orenburg
Aktobe
Atyrau
Ural'sk
Aktau
Mashhad
Eşfahān (Isfahan)
Tabrīz
Basra (Al Başrah)
Albers Equal Area Conic Projection
1 : 20 000 000
MILES 0 100 200

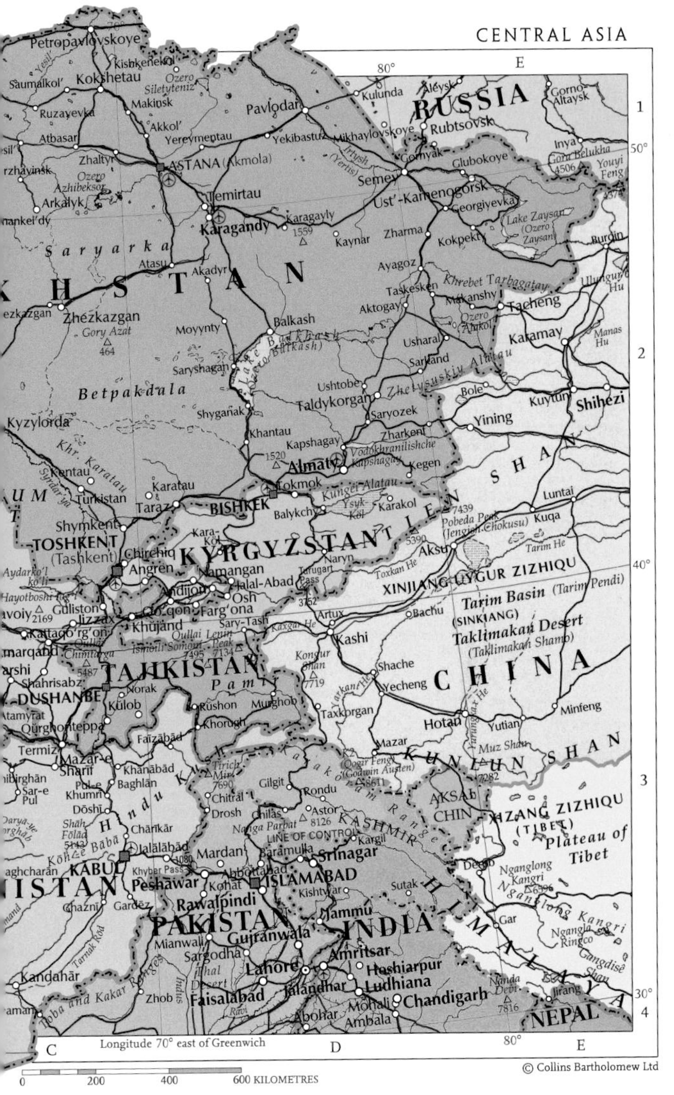

RUSSIA
KAZAKHSTAN
KYRGYZSTAN
TAJIKISTAN
CHINA
PAKISTAN
INDIA
NEPAL
XINJIANG UYGUR ZIZHIQU
(SINKIANG)
XIZANG ZIZHIQU
(TIBET)
ASTANA (Akmola)
BISHKEK
TOSHKENT
(Tashkent)
DUSHANBE
KABUL
ISLAMABAD
Petropavlovskoye
Kishkenekol'
Kokshetau
Saumalkol'
Ozero Siletyteniz
Makinsk
Ruzayevka
Akkol'
Atbasar
Yereymentau
Zhaltyr
Ozero Azhibeksor
Arkalyk
Pavlodar
Yekibastuz
Kulunda
Aleysk
Gorno-Altaysk
Rubtsovsk
Mikhaylovskoye
Irtysh (Yertis)
Gornyak
Inya
Gora Belukha 4506
Youyi Feng
Glubokoye
Semey
Ust'-Kamenogorsk
Georgiyevka
Lake Zaysan (Ozero Zaysan)
Temirtau
Karagandy
Karagayly
1559
Kaynar
Zharma
Kokpekty
Burqin
Saryarka
Atasu
Akadyr
Ayagoz
Khrebet Tarbagatay
Ulungur Hu
Taskesken
Makanshy
Tacheng
Ozero Alakol'
Karamay
Manas Hu
Zhezkazgan
Gory Azat
464
Moyynty
Balkash
Aktogay
Lake Balkhash (Ozero Balkash)
Usharal
Sarkand
Zhetysuskiy Alatau
Saryshagan
Betpakdala
Ushtobe
Taldykorgan
Bole
Kuytun
Shihezi
Shyganak
Saryozek
Yining
Kyzylorda
Khantau
Zharkent
Kapshagay
Vodokhranilishche Kapshagay
Khr. Karatau
1520
Almaty
Kegen
Kentau
Syrdar'ya
Karatau
Tokmok
Kungei Alatau
Turkistan
Taraz
Balykchy
Ysyk-Köl
Karakol
Luntai
Shymkent
7439
Pobeda Peak (Jengish Chokusu)
Kuqa
Kara-Köl
5390
Aksu
Tarim He
Chirchiq
Angren
Naryn
Toxkan He
Namangan
Jalal-Abad
Turugart Pass
3752
Andijon
Osh
Qo'qon
Farg'ona
Guliston
Bachu
Tarim Basin (Tarim Pendi)
Taklimakan Desert (Taklimakan Shamo)
Jizzax
Khujand
Sary-Tash
Artux
Kaxgar He
Kashi
Qullai Lenin
Ismoili Somoni Peak
7495
7134
Kongur Shan
7719
Shache
Yecheng
Yarkant He
5487
Shahrisabz
Norak
Pamir
Kulob
Rushon
Murghob
Taxkorgan
Hotan
Yurungkax He
Minfeng
Yutian
Khorugh
Faizabad
Mazar
Muz Shan
Termiz
Mazar-e Sharif
K2 (Qogir Feng) (Godwin Austen) 8611
KUNLUN SHAN
Khanabad
Baghlan
Tirich Mir 7690
Gilgit
Rondu
Karakoram Range
7282
AKSAI CHIN
Pul-e Khumri
Doshi
Chitral
Drosh
Chilas
Astor
8126
Nanga Parbat
KASHMIR
Charikar
LINE OF CONTROL
Kargil
Plateau of Tibet
Jalalabad
Baramulla
Srinagar
Mardan
Khyber Pass
Abbottabad
Nganglong Kangri
6596
Peshawar
Kohat
Kishtwar
Sutak
Ghazni
Gardez
Rawalpindi
HIMALAYA
Jammu
Gar
Nganglong Kangri
Ngangla Ringco
Mianwali
Gujranwala
Gangdisê Shan
Sargodha
Amritsar
Hoshiarpur
Kandahar
Thal Desert
Lahore
Ludhiana
Jalandhar
Chandigarh
Nanda Devi 7816
Jirang
Toba and Kakar Ranges
Zhob
Indus
Faisalabad
Ravi
Mohali
Abohar
Ambala
80°
50°
40°
30°
E
C
D
1
2
3
4
Longitude 70° east of Greenwich
0
200
400
600 KILOMETRES

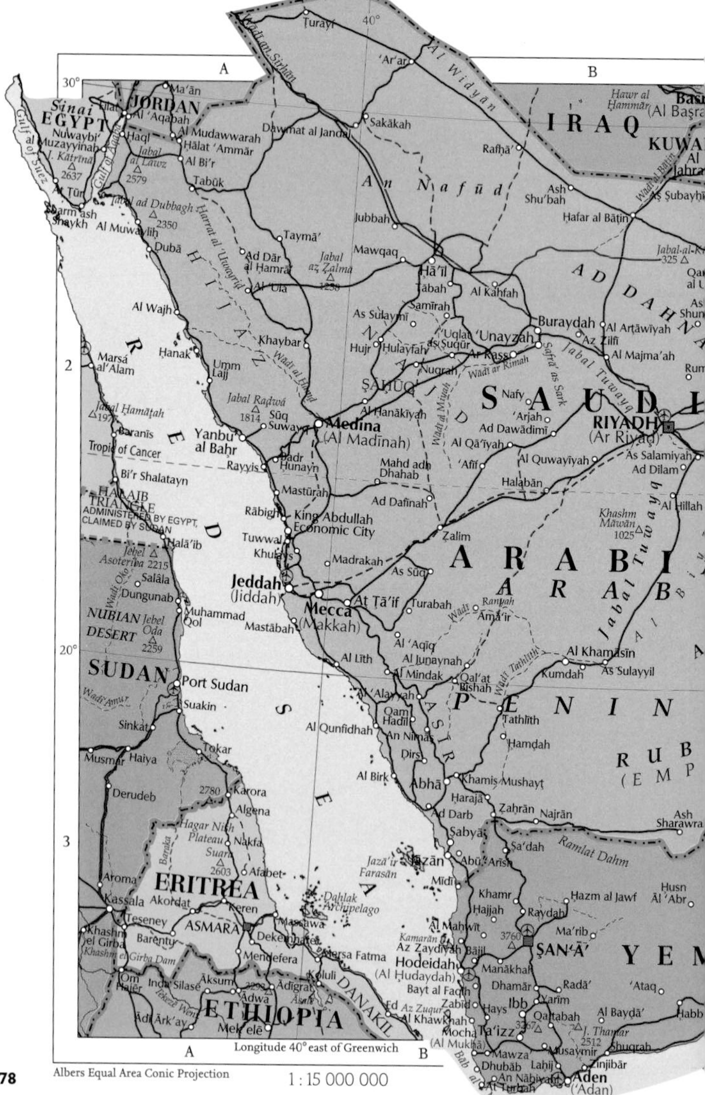

Turayf 40°
'Ar'ar
Hawr al Hammār
Başra

JORDAN
Ma'ān
'Aqaba
Al Mudawwarah
Ḥālat 'Ammār
Al Bi'r
Al Muwayliḥ
Dubā

Nuwaybi'
Muzayyinah
Jabal
al Lawz
2579
Tabūk
Ḥaql
IRAQ
KUWAIT
Jahra
Al Başra

EGYPT
Sinai
Gulf of Suez
Sharm ash Shaykh
Jabal
Kātrīna
2637
Ṭūr
Jabal ad Dubbagh
△ 2350
Ḥarrat al 'Uwayrid

Dawmat al Jandal
Sakākah
Rafḥā
Ash Shu'bah
Ḥafar al Bāṭin
Wādī al Bāṭin
Jabal-al-K
325 △
Qa'r

An Nafūd

Taymā'
Mawqaq
Ḥā'il
Jabah
Al Kahfah
AD DAHNA

Jubbah
Jabal az Zalma

Ad Dār al Ḥamra
Jabal
az Zalma

Al Wajh
Ḥanak
Umm Lajj
As Sulaymi
Samirah

Khaybar
Hujr
Ḥulayfah
'Uqlat aṣ Ṣuqūr
Nuqrah
Ra's al Khaimah
'Unayzah
Burayḍah
Al Arṭāwiyah
Az Zilfī
Al Majma'ah

Jabal Raḍwá
1814
Sūq
Yanbu'
al Baḥr
Suwayq
Al Ḥanākiyah
Nafy
'Arjah
Sūq al Juma'ah
Jabal Ṭuwayq

HIJAZ
NAJD
SAUDI
RIYADH
(Ar Riyāḍ)

Rayyis
Ḥunayn
Badr
Ḥunayn
Mahd adh Dhahab
'Afīf
Ad Dawādimi
Al Qā'īyah
As Salamiyah
Ad Dilam
Hillah

Marsá
al 'Alam
Jabal Ḥamāṭah
△191
Baranis
Tropic of Cancer
Bi'r Shalatayn

RED
SEA
Maṣṭūrah
Ad Dafīnah
Halabān
Al Quwayh
Khashm Mawān
1025 △
Jabal Ṭuwayq

HALAIB
TRIANGLE
ADMINISTERED BY EGYPT
CLAIMED BY SUDAN

Rābigh
King Abdullah
Economic City
Tuwwāl
Khulaïs
Madrakah
As Suq
Zalim
ARABIA

Jeddah
(Jiddah)
Mecca
(Makkah)
Aṣ Ṣalālā
Dungunab
Muhammad Qol
Mastābāh
At Ṭā'if
Turabah
Ranyah
Amā'ir
Wādī Tathlith
Al Khamāsīn
As Sulayyil
Kumdah

NUBIAN
DESERT
Jebel Oda
2259
Asoteriba 2215

SUDAN
Port Sudan
Suakin
Wādī 'Amur

Al Līth
Al 'Aqiq
Al Junaynah
Al Mindak
Qal'at Bishah
'Alayah
Qam Ḥadil
An Nimāṣ
ASER
PENIN
RUB'
(EMP

Sinkat
Musmar
Haiya
Tokar
Al Qunfidhah
Dirs
Tathlīth
Ḥamdah

Derudeb
2780
Karora
Algena
Al Birk
Abhā
Khamīs Mushayṭ
Harajah
Najrān
Hazm al Jawf
Āl 'Abr

Aroma
Hagar Nish Plateau
Suara
2603
Nakfa
Ad Darb
Zahrān
Sabyā
Ṣa'dah
Ramlat Daḥm
Ash Sharawra

Kassala
Akordat
Teseney
Barentu
Dekemhare
Jaza'ir Farasan
Jazan
Abū 'Arīsh
Midi
Khamr
Ḥajjah
Raydah
Ma'rib
Husn
Āl 'Abr

ERITREA
ASMARA
Keren
Massawa
Dahlak Archipelago
Kamarān
Az Zaydīyah
Ḥajjī
Maḥwit
Mawza
3760
SAN'A'
YEMEN

Mendefera
Adi Keyh
Marsa Fatma
DANAKIL
Koluli
Hodeidah
(Al Hudaydah)
Manākhah
Dhamār
Radā'
'Ataq
Habb

Om Hager
Adwa
Adigrat
Ed Zuqur
Bayt al Faqih
Zabīd
Hays
Ibb
Yarīm
Qaflabah
Al Bayḍā'

Inda Silase
Aksum
Al Khawkhah
Ta'izz
Mocha
Āl Thamar
2512
Shuqrah

ETHIOPIA
Mek'ele
Longitude 40° east of Greenwich
Dhubāb
Laḥij
Mawza
An Nabīyah
'Addan Tehbo
Aden
(Adan)
Zinjibār

A
B

78 Albers Equal Area Conic Projection   1 : 15 000 000

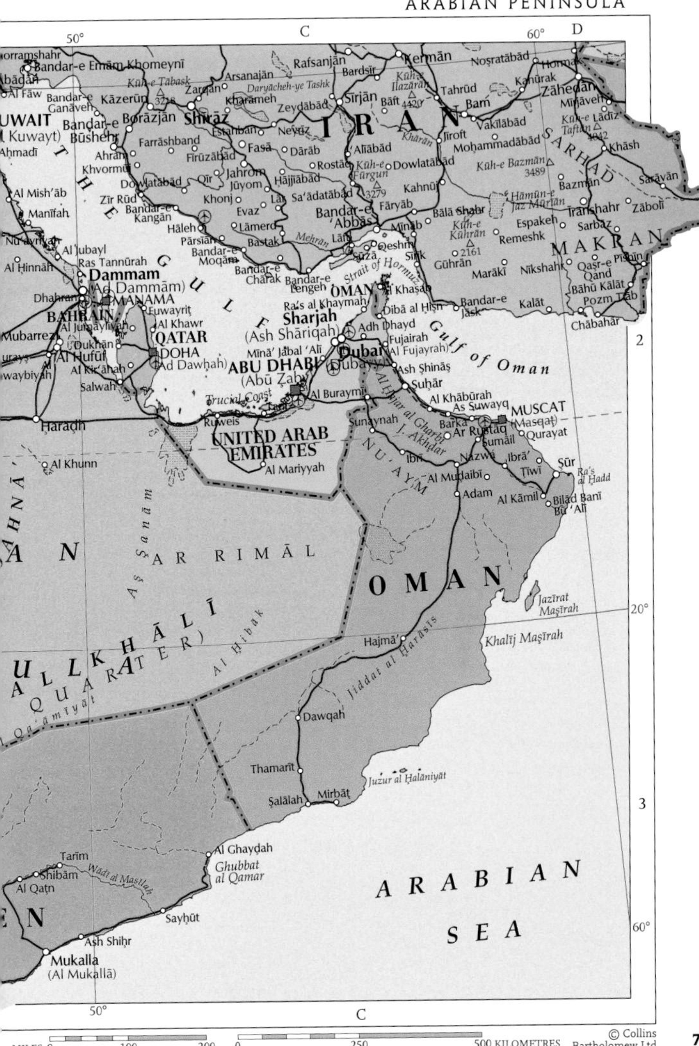

ARABIAN

SEA

© Collins
Bartholomew Ltd

MILES 0   100   200   0   250   500 KILOMETRES

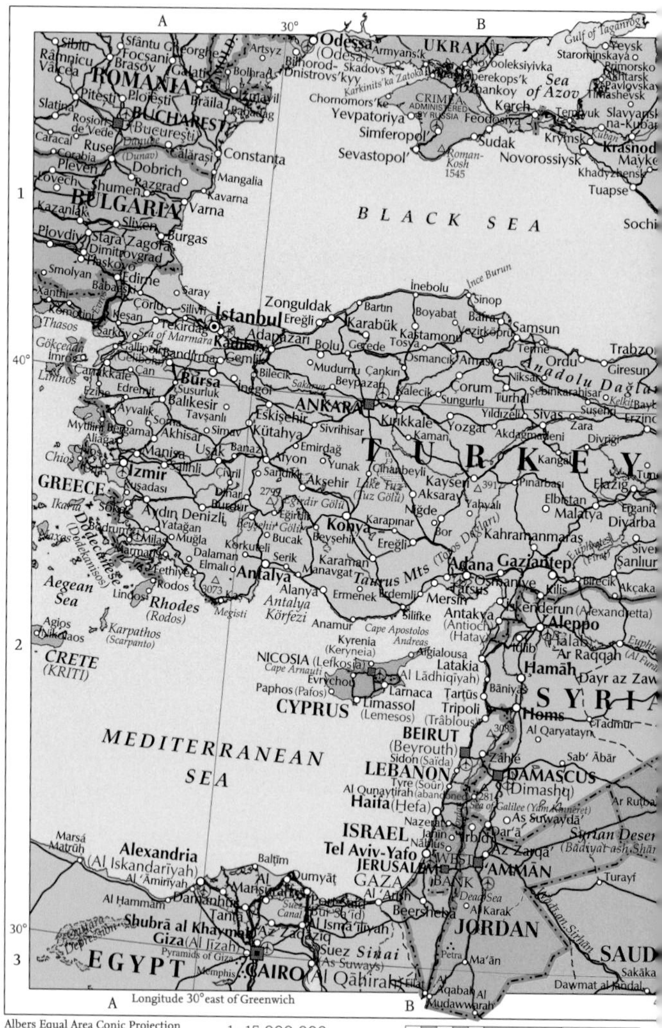

80

Albers Equal Area Conic Projection

1 : 15 000 000

MILES 0 · · · 100 · · · 200 · · · 300

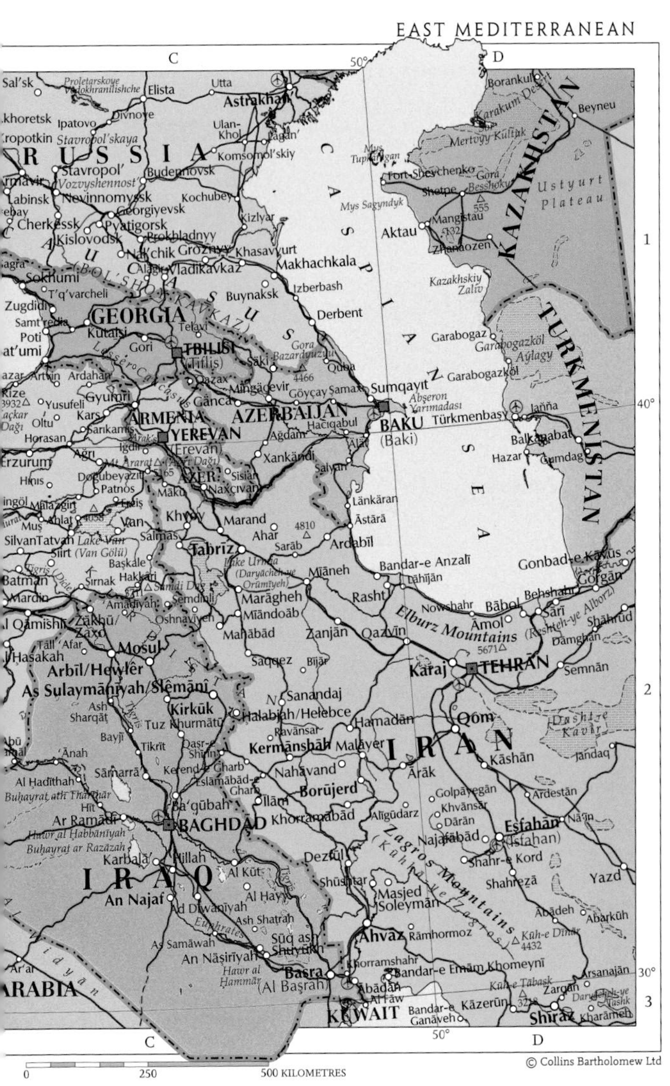

0   250   500 KILOMETRES

© Collins Bartholomew Ltd

1
3
40°
30°
RUSSIA
GEORGIA
ARMENIA
AZERBAIJAN
KAZAKHSTAN
TURKMENISTAN
IRAN
IRAQ
KUWAIT
CASPIAN SEA
TBILISI
YEREVAN
BAKU
TEHRAN
BAGHDAD
Elburz Mountains
Zagros Mountains

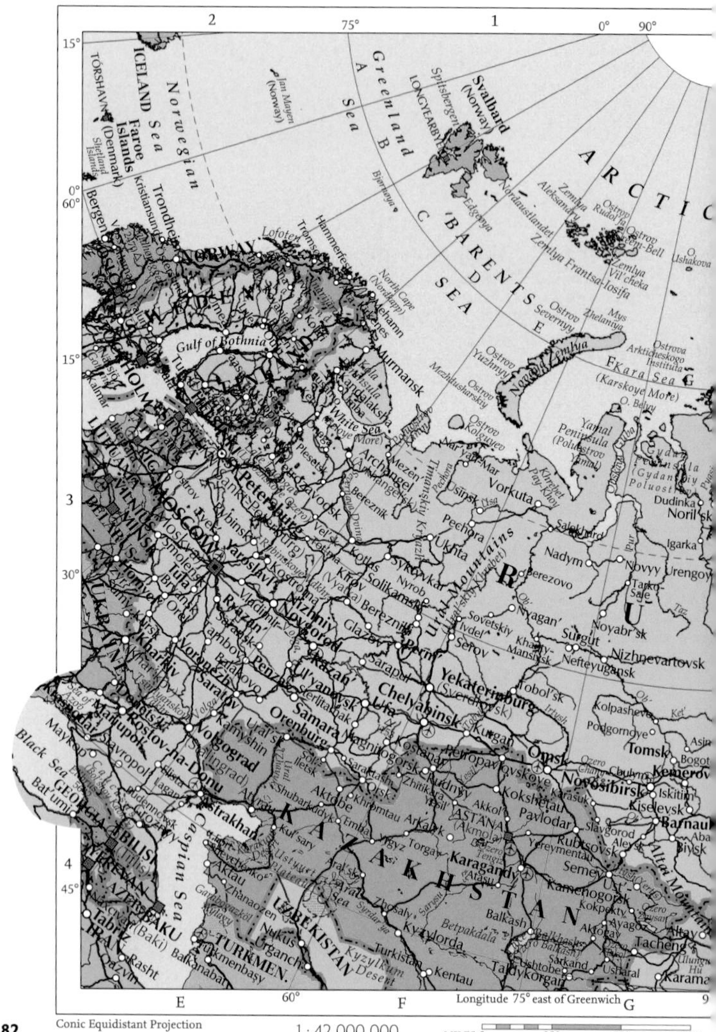

15°

ICELAND
TÓRSHAVN Norwegian
Faroe
Islands
(Denmark)
Bergen

Jan Mayen
(Norway)

Greenland Sea

Svalbard
(Norway)

Spitsbergen

Bjørnøya

A R C T I C

Zemlya
Aleksandry
Ostrov
Rudol'fa
Ostrov
Greem Bell
Ushakova

0°
60°

NORWAY

Lofoten

North Cape
(Norway)
Hammerfest

B A R E N T S

Nordaustlandet

Zemlya
Frantsa Iosifa

Mys
Zhelaniya

Ostrova
Arkticheskogo
Instituta

15°

Gulf of Bothnia

Murmansk

S E A

Ostrov
Yuzhnyy

Novaya
Zemlya

E

Kara Sea
(Karskoye More)

G

White Sea

Ostrov
Kolguyev

Yamal
Peninsula
(Poluostrov
Yamal)

O. Belyy

Gydan
(Gydanskiy
Poluostrov)

3

St. Petersburg

Arkhangel'sk

Pechora

Timanskiy

Vorkuta

Salekhard

Dudinka
Noril'sk

Igarka

R

U

30°

MOSCOW
Yaroslavl'
Tula
Ryazan'

Nizhniy
Novgorod

Solikamsk
Berezniki
Glazov
Perm'

Syktyvkar

Ukhta

U
r
a
l

M
o
u
n
t
a
i
n
s

Nadym

Berezovo

Novyy Urengoy

Tazovskiy
Salekhard

Noyabr'sk

Surgut
Khanty-
Mansiysk

Nizhnevartovsk

Ul'yanovsk
Penza
Saratov

Samara

Ufa
Magnitogorsk

Yekaterinburg
(Sverdlovsk)

Chelyabinsk

Tobol'sk

Kolpashevo

Podgornoye

Asino

Rostov-na-Donu
Volgograd
(Stalingrad)

Orenburg

Kurgan

Omsk

Tomsk

Kemerovo

Bogot

Astrakhan'

Ural'sk

Caspian Sea

K A Z A K H S T A N

Aktobe
(Aktyubinsk)

Kostanay

Petropavlovsk

ASTANA
(Akmola)

Pavlodar

Novosibirsk

Barnaul

Iskitim
Kiselevsk

Bab

Bor

Black Sea
Bat'umi
TBILISI
Rasht

BAKU
(Baki)
Tabriz

TURKMEN.
Turkmenbashy

Nukus

UZBEKISTAN
Nukus

Aral Sea

Kyzylorda

Karagandy

Balkash

Ozero
Balkhash

Semey
Ayagoz

Altay
Tacheng

45°

4

E   60°   F   Longitude 75° east of Greenwich G   9

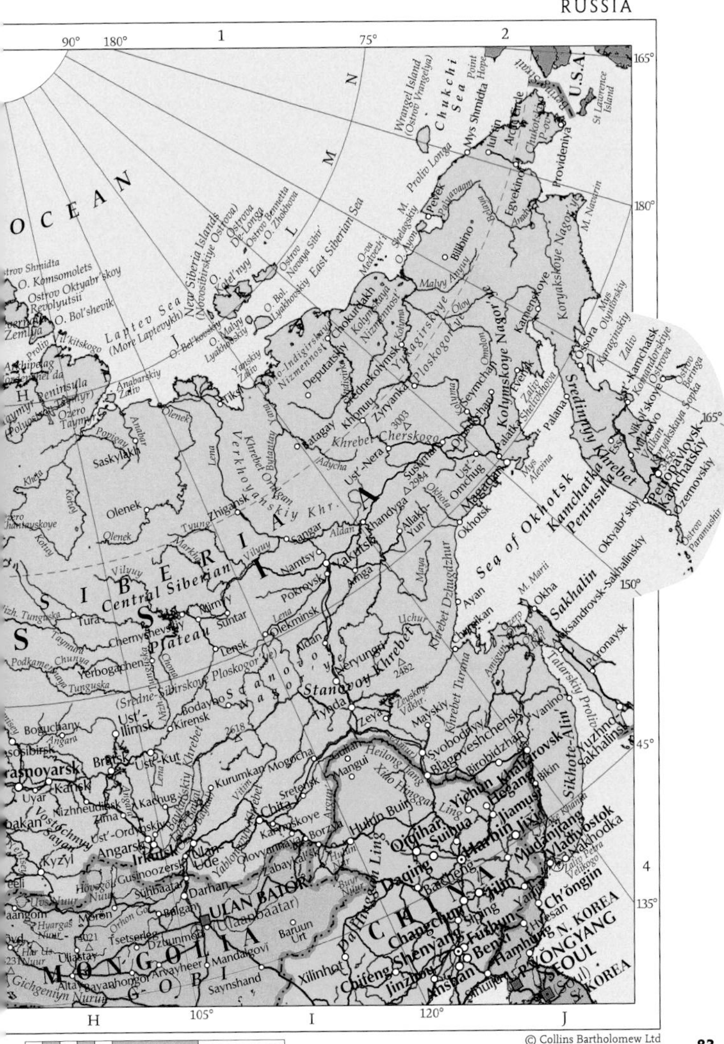

0   500   1000   1500 KILOMETRES

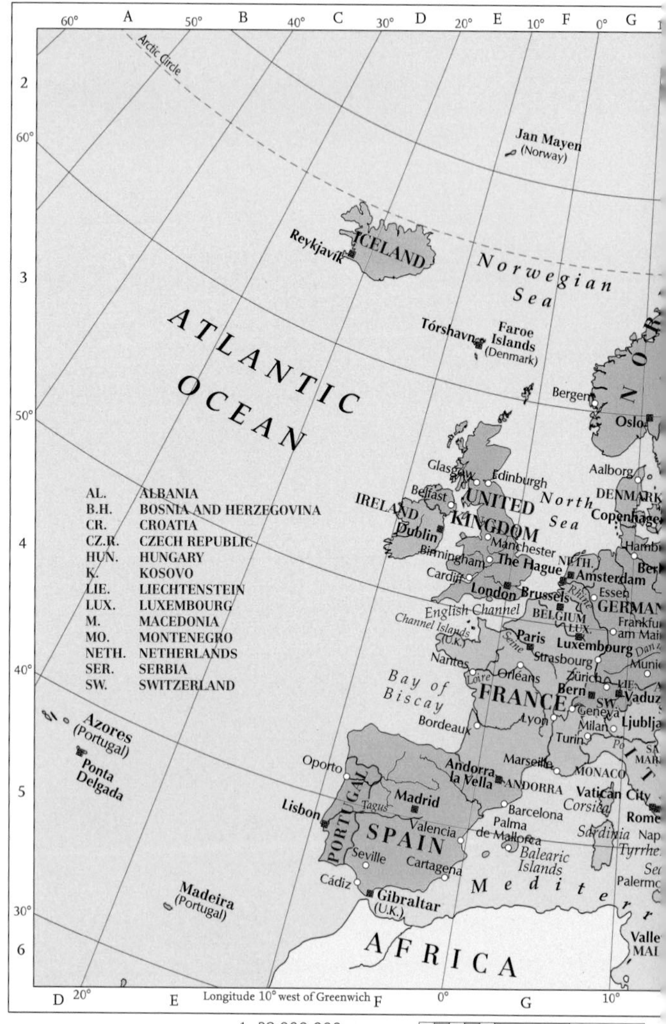

84

Arctic Circle

Jan Mayen
(Norway)

Reykjavik ICELAND

*Norwegian
Sea*

Tórshavn • Faroe
Islands
(Denmark)

A T L A N T I C

Bergen

O C E A N

N...
Oslo

Glasgow • Edinburgh
Belfast *North*
IRELAND UNITED *Sea*
Dublin KINGDOM
Birmingham • Manchester NETH.
Cardiff • The Hague
London • Brussels
English Channel BELGIUM
Channel Islands Paris
Nantes Strasbourg Luxembourg

Aalborg
DENMARK
Copenhagen

Hamb...
Ber...
Amsterdam
Essen GERMA...
Frankfurt
am Main
Munic...

AL.	ALBANIA
B.H.	BOSNIA AND HERZEGOVINA
CR.	CROATIA
CZ.R.	CZECH REPUBLIC
HUN.	HUNGARY
K.	KOSOVO
LIE.	LIECHTENSTEIN
LUX.	LUXEMBOURG
M.	MACEDONIA
MO.	MONTENEGRO
NETH.	NETHERLANDS
SER.	SERBIA
SW.	SWITZERLAND

*Bay of
Biscay*
Bordeaux
Orleans Zürich LIE.
Bern Vaduz
FRANCE Geneva
Lyon Milan Ljublja
Turin

Azores
(Portugal)

Ponta
Delgado

Oporto

Marseille MONACO
Andorra
la Vella Corsica Rome
ANDORRA Vatican City
Madrid Barcelona Sardinia Nap...
Lisbon Valencia Palma Tyrrhe...
PORTUGAL de Mallorca Sea
SPAIN Palerme
Seville *Balearic
Islands*
Cádiz Cartagena *M e d i t e r*

Madeira
(Portugal)

Gibraltar
(U.K.)

A F R I C A

Valle
MAI

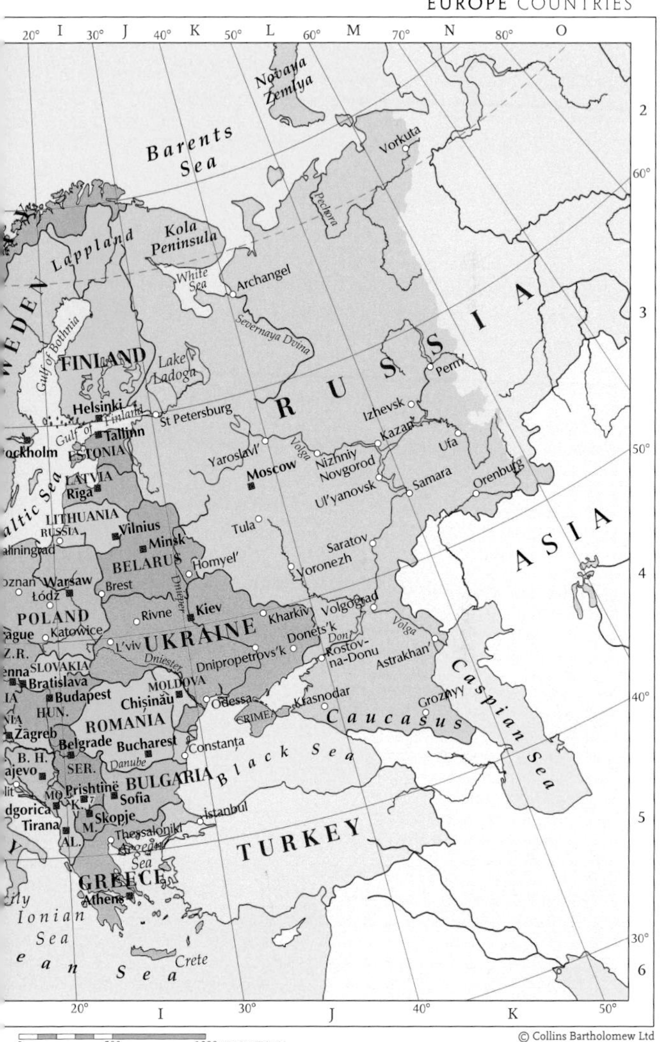

© Collins Bartholomew Ltd

0   500   1000 KILOMETRES

Novaya Zemlya
Barents Sea
Vorkuta
Pechora
Kola Peninsula
Lappland
White Sea
Archangel
Severnaya Dvina
Gulf of Bothnia
FINLAND
Lake Ladoga
Helsinki
Gulf of Finland
Tallinn
ESTONIA
St Petersburg
R U S S I A
Perm'
Izhevsk
Kazan'
Ufa
Yaroslavl'
Volga
Moscow
Nizhniy Novgorod
Ul'yanovsk
Samara
Orenburg
LATVIA
Rīga
LITHUANIA
Vilnius
RUSSIA
Minsk
BELARUS
Homyel'
Tula
Saratov
Voronezh
A S I A
Warsaw
Łódź
Brest
POLAND
Katowice
Rivne
Kiev
Dnieper
Kharkiv
Volgograd
UKRAINE
L'viv
Donets'k
Don
Rostov-na-Donu
Astrakhan'
Dnipropetrovs'k
Dniester
SLOVAKIA
Bratislava
Budapest
HUN.
MOLDOVA
Chișinău
Odessa
CRIMEA
Krasnodar
Groznyy
Caucasus
Caspian Sea
ROMANIA
Zagreb
Belgrade
Bucharest
Constanța
Danube
Black Sea
B. H.
SER.
BULGARIA
Prishtinë
Sofia
Skopje
Tirana
AL.
Istanbul
Thessaloniki
Aegean Sea
TURKEY
GREECE
Athens
Ionian Sea
Crete
Stockholm
Baltic Sea
Kaliningrad
Poznań
Prague
Vienna
Podgorica
Sarajevo
SWEDEN
I J K L M N O
20° 30° 40° 50° 60° 70° 80°
2 3 4 5 6
60° 50° 40° 30°

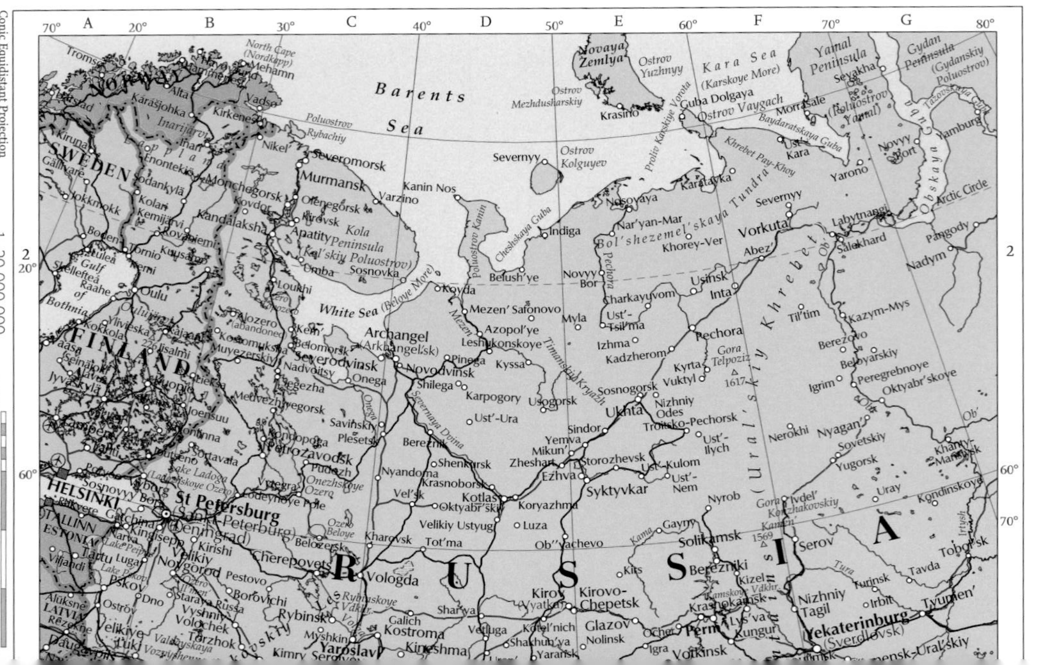

Conic Equidistant Projection

1 : 20 000 000

MILES 0   100   200   300   400

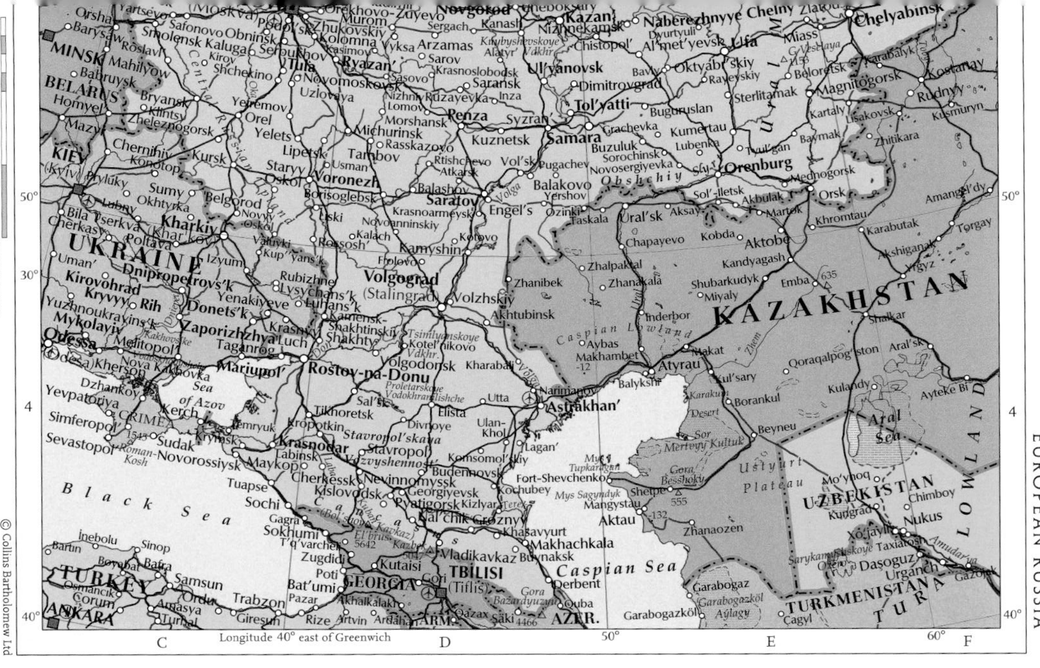

Longitude 40° east of Greenwich

0   200   400   600 KILOMETRES

© Collins Bartholomew Ltd

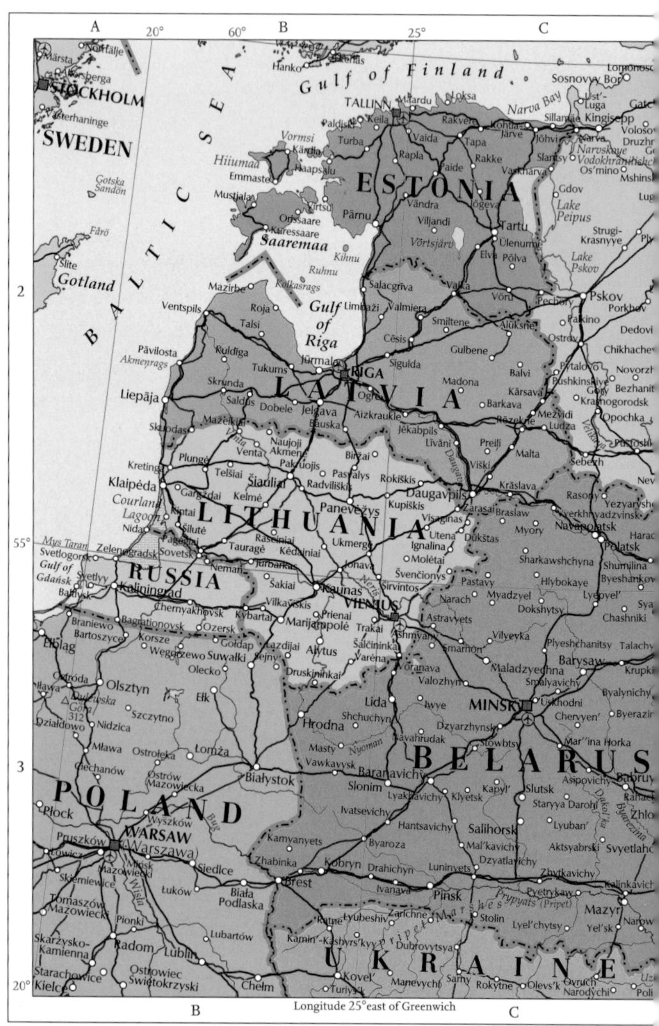

Conic Equidistant Projection   1 : 8 000 000   MILES 0   50   100   150

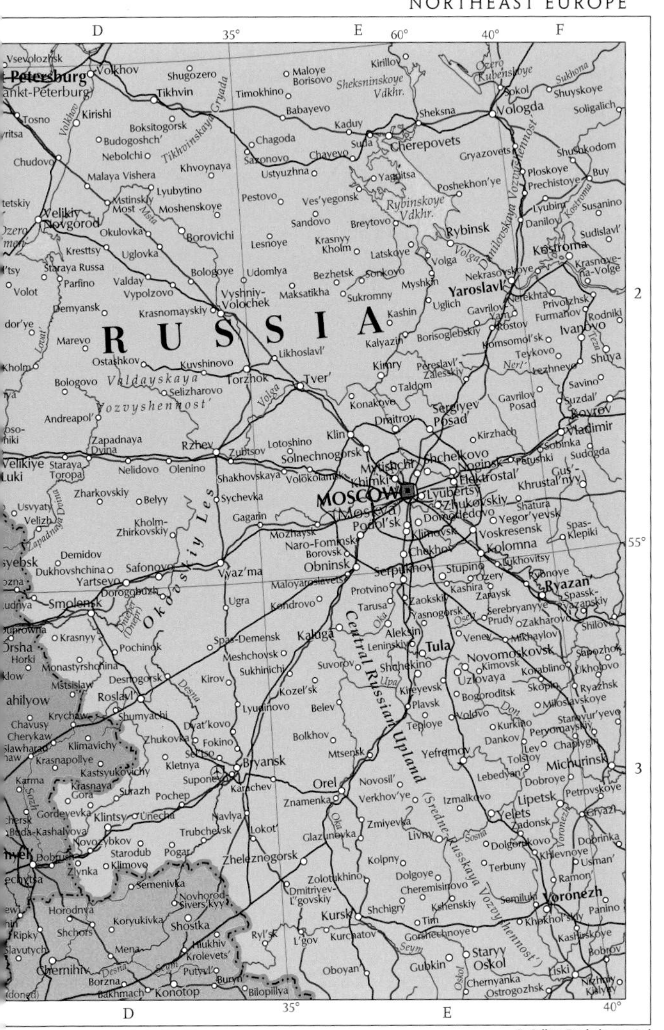

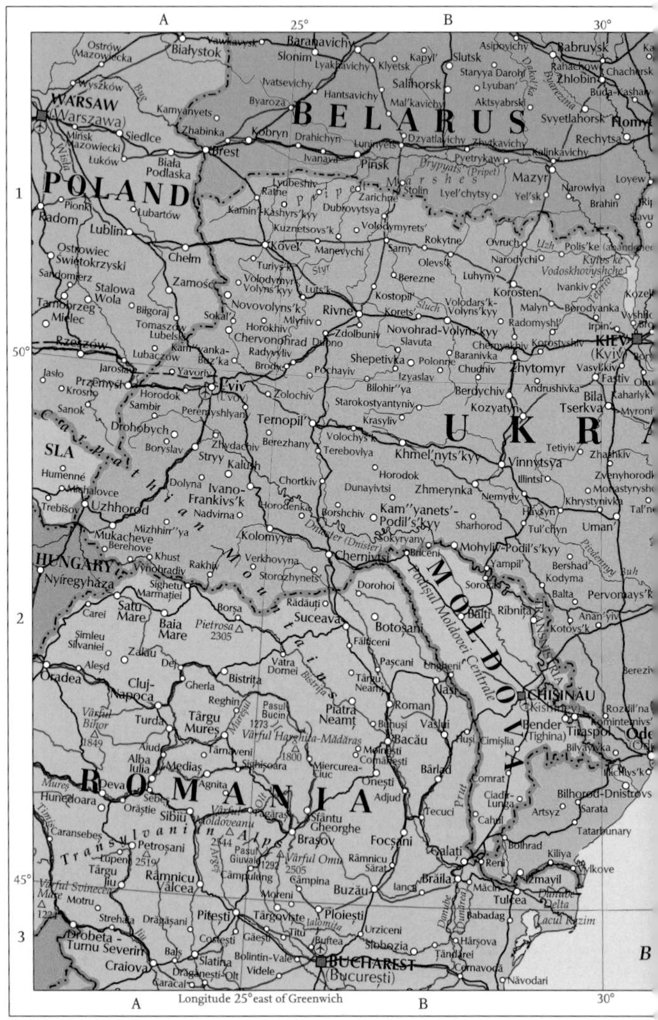

A — 25° — B — 30°

BELARUS

Ostrów
Mazowiecka
WARSAW
(Warszawa)
Wyszków
Białystok
Vawkavysk
Baranavichy
Slonim
Lyakhavichy
Klyetsk
Kapyl'
Asipovichy
Slutsk
Starya Darohi
Lyuban'
Babruysk
Rahachow
Zhlobin
Chacheisk
Buda-Kashalyova
Homy

Kamyanyets
Zhabinka
Siedlce
Biała
Podlaska
Brest
Kobryn
Drahichyn
Ivanava
Pinsk
Luninyets
Hantsavichy
Salihorsk
Starobin
Byaroza
Mal'kavichy
Aktsyabrski
Svyetlahorsk
Rechytsa

POLAND
Mińsk
Mazowiecki
Łuków
Lubartów
Ratne
Kamin'-Kashyrs'ky
Dubrovytsya
Zarichne
Stolin
Lyel'chytsy
Yel'sk
Narowla
Brahin
Loyew

Radom
Lublin
Kovel'
Manevychi
Sarny
Rokytne
Ovruch
Narodychi
Polis'ke (abandoned)
Ivankiv
Loyw

Ostrowiec
Świętokrzyski
Chełm
Zamość
Turiys'k
Volodymyr-
Volyns'kyy
Styr
Berezne
Luhyny
Korosten'
Malyn
Borodyanka
KIEV
(Kyyiv)
Irpin'
Kozel

Sandomierz
Stalowa
Wola
Mielec
Biłgoraj
Tomaszów
Lubelski
Sokal
Novovolyns'k
Horokhiv
Mlyniv
Rivne
Korets'
Novohrad-Volyns'kyy
Polonne
Slavuta
Radomyshl'
Fastiv
Vasyl'kiv

Tarnobrzeg
Rzeszów
Jarosław
Przemyśl
Lubaczów
Chervonohrad
Brody
Dubno
Zdolbuniv
Shepetivka
Baranivka
Chudniv
Berdychiv
Andrushivka
Zhytomyr
Bila
Tserkva
Kaharlyk
Myroniv

UKR

Jasło
Krosno
Horodok
Sambir
Peremyshlyany
Lviv
Zolochiv
Pochayiv
Izyaslav
Starokostyantyniv
Krasyliv
Kozyatyn
Tetiyiv
Tarashcha
Zhashkiv

SLA
Humenné
Drohobych
Boryslav
Stryy
Zhydachiv
Berezhany
Ternopil'
Volochys'k
Khmel'nyts'kyy
Vinnytsya
Illintsi
Zvenyhorodka
Monastyryshche
Khrystynivka
Talne

Michalovce
Uzhhorod
Dolyna
Kalush
Ivano-
Frankivs'k
Chortkiv
Terebovlya
Horodok
Zhmerynka
Nemyriv
Haysyn
Tul'chyn
Uman'

Trebišov
Mukacheve
Berehove
Khust
Nadvirna
Horodenka
Borshchiv
Kam"yanets'-
Podil's'kyy
Sharhorod
Mohyliv-Podil's'kyy
Bershad'
Kodyma
Balta
Pervomays'k

HUNGARY
Nyíregyháza
Vynohradiv
Sighetu
Marmației
Rakhiv
Verkhovyna
Sokyryany
Chernivtsi
Bucecea
Yampil'
Soroca
Ribnita
Ananyiv
Kotovs'k

Satu
Mare
Carei
Borşa
Pietrosu
2305
Storozhynets'
Dorohoi
Rădăuți
Dorokhoi
MOLDO
Bălți
Pervomays'k

Baia
Mare
Zalău
Dej
Vatra
Dornei
Suceava
Fălticeni
Botoşani
Bălți
Rozdil'na
Ode

Simleu
Silvaniei
Bistriţa
Pascani
Iaşi
Ungheni
CHIŞINĂU
Bender
(Tighina)
Tiraspol
Hrihoriopil'
Bilyayivka

Oradea
Gherla
Reghin
Pasul
Bucin
1273
Piatra
Neamţ
Roman
Vaslui
Comrat
Cimişlia
Căuşani
Bilhorod-Dnistrovs'kyy

Cluj-
Napoca
Turda
Vârful
Bihor
1849
Târgu
Mureş
Vârful Harghita-Mădăraş
1800
Băcau
Bârlad
Cahul
Ciadâr-
Lunca
Artsyz
Sarata
Tatarbunary

Alba
Iulia
Aiud
Târnăveni
Mediaş
Agnita
Miercurea-
Ciuc
Oneşti
Adjud
Tecuci
Comrat
Bolhrad
Kiliya

Deva
Hunedoara
Orăştie
Sebeş
Sibiu
Sighişoara
Moldoveanu
2544
Sfântu
Gheorghe
Braşov
Focşani
Galaţi
Reni
Izmayil
Vylkove

ROMANIA
Caransebeş
Petroşani
Lupeni
2519
Târgu
Jiu
Pasul
Giuvala
1292
Câmpulung
Vârful Omu
2505
Râmnicu
Sărat
Buzău
Ianca
Brăila
Măcin
Tulcea
Lacul Razim

Vârful Surianu
2061
Motru
Strehaia
Drăgăşani
Piteşti
Târgovişte
Ploieşti
Mizil
Slobozia
Ţăndărei
Hârşova
Babadag
Năvodari

Drobeta-
Turnu Severin
Balş
Slatina
Bolintin-Vale
Videle
Buftea
Urziceni
BUCHAREST
(Bucureşti)
Olteniţa
Călăraşi
Feteşti
Cernavodă

Craiova
Caracal
Drăgăneşti-Olt
Găeşti
Costeşti

Longitude 25° east of Greenwich

A — B — 30°

Trans ylvanian Alps
Carpathian Mountains
Moldavian Carpathians
Pripet Marshes
Prypyats' (Pripet)
Dnister (Dniester)
Prut
Danube
Danube Delta

Conic Equidistant Projection
1 : 8 000 000
MILES 0   50   100   150

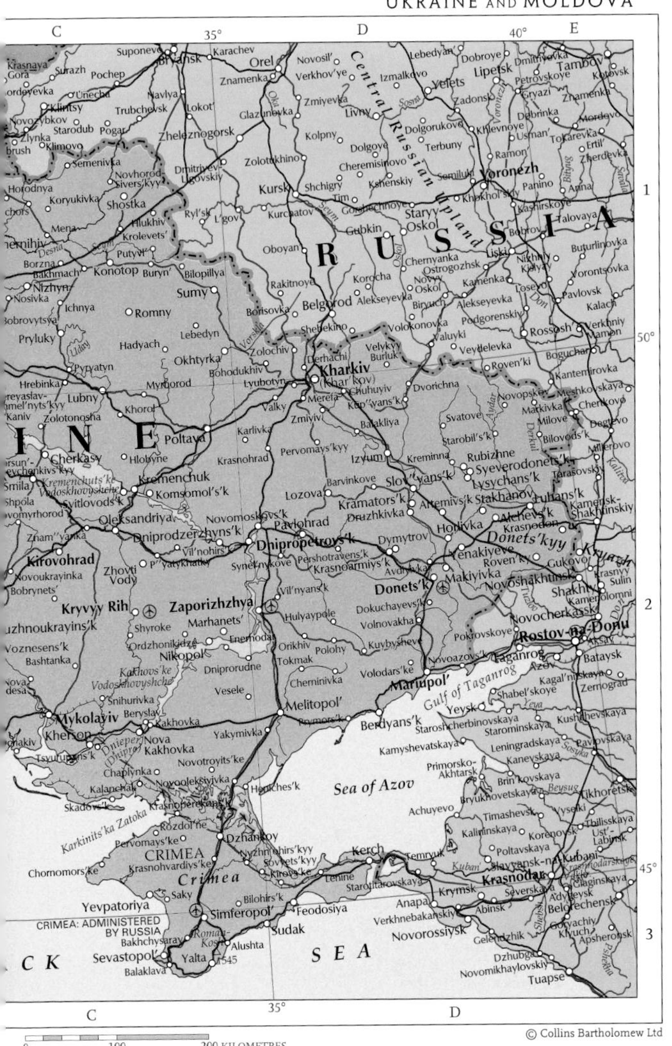

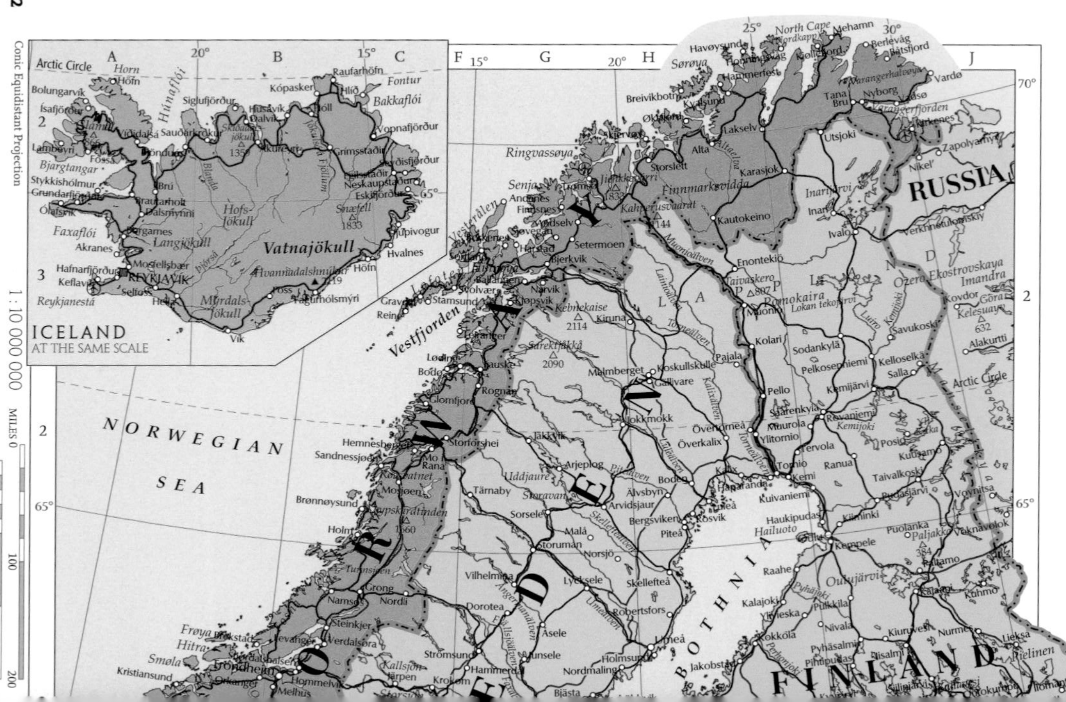

Conic Equidistant Projection

ICELAND
AT THE SAME SCALE

1 : 10 000 000

MILES 0   100   200

KILOMETRES 0   100   200   300

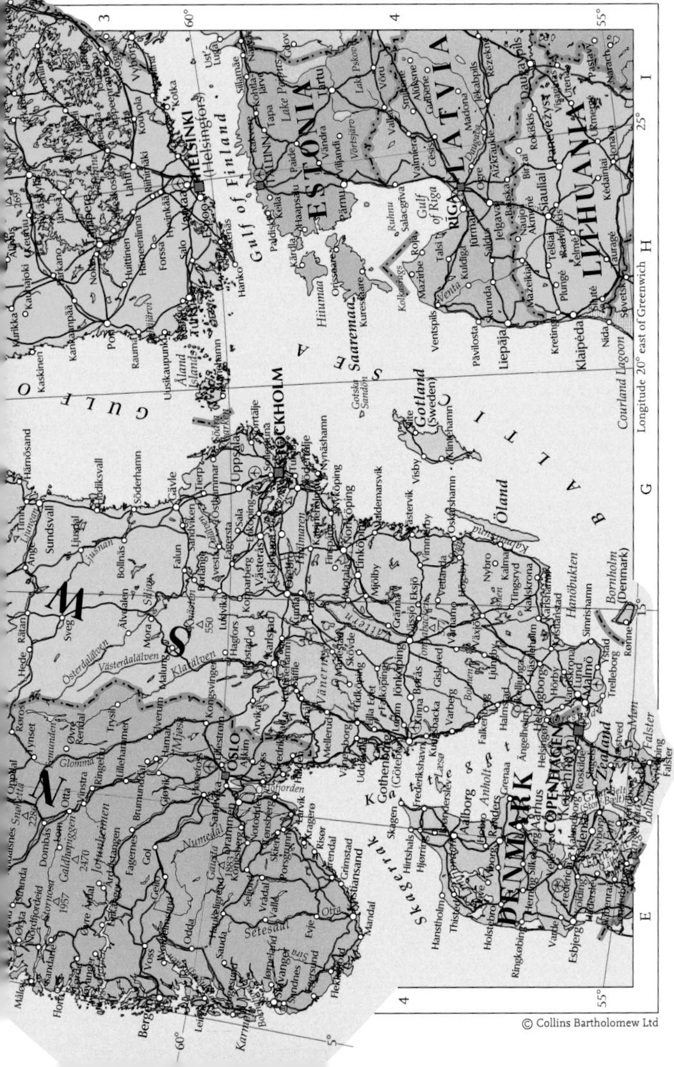

HELSINKI (Helsingfors)

ESTONIA

LATVIA

LITHUANIA

RIGA

Gulf of Finland

Gulf of Riga

Saaremaa

Hiiumaa

Åland Islands (Ahvenanmaa)

GULF

BALTIC

SEA

Gotland (Sweden)

Öland

STOCKHOLM

Uppsala

SWEDEN

OSLO

DENMARK

COPENHAGEN

Bornholm (Denmark)

Skagerrak

Gothenburg (Göteborg)

Aalborg

Århus

Odense

Esbjerg

Kattegat

Vänern

Vättern

Kristiansand

Bergen

Longitude 20° east of Greenwich

© Collins Bartholomew Ltd

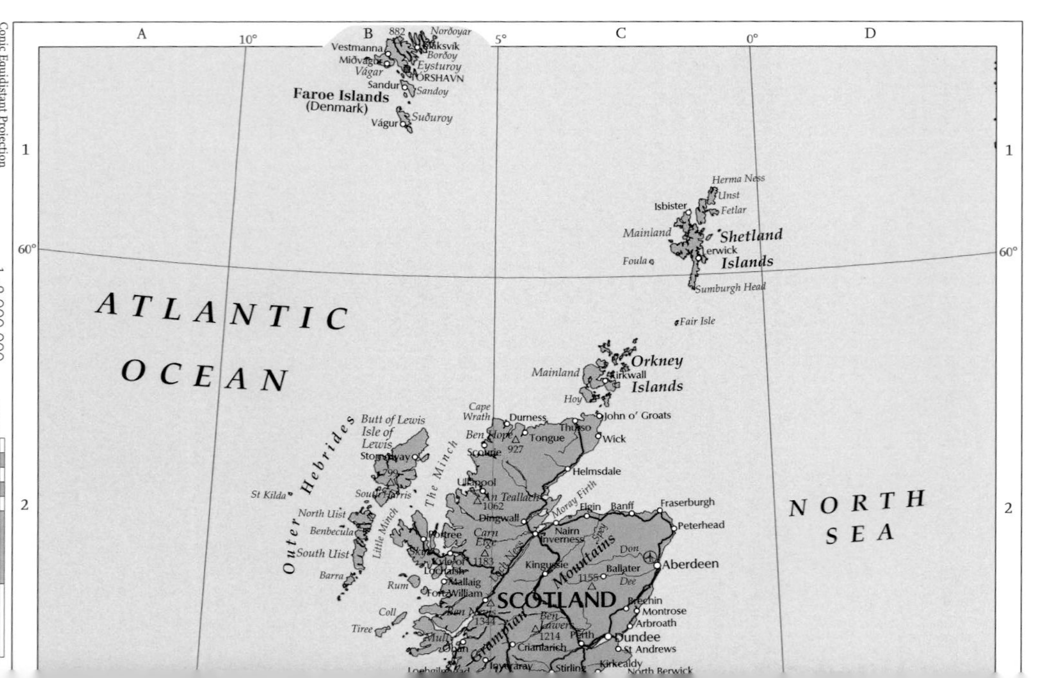

D

0°

C

5°

A

10°

B

ATLANTIC

OCEAN

NORTH

SEA

SCOTLAND

Outer Hebrides

The Minch

Little Minch

Shetland Islands

Herma Ness
Unst
Fetlar
Isbister
Mainland
Foula
Berwick
Sumburgh Head

Fair Isle

Orkney Islands
Mainland
Kirkwall
Hoy
John o' Groats
Wick

Cape
Wrath
Durness
Tongue
Thurso
Helmsdale

Ben More

Kyle of Lochalsh

Ben Nevis
Fort William

Butt of
Lewis
Isle of
Lewis
Stornoway

North Uist
Benbecula
South Uist
Barra

St Kilda

Rum
Eigg

Coll
Tiree

Mull

Inverness
Nairn
Kingussie

Carn
Dalwhinnie

Banff
Fraserburgh
Peterhead

Aberdeen

Dee

Ballater

Brechin
Montrose
Arbroath

Dundee

St Andrews

Perth
Stirling

North Berwick

927

1214

Faroe Islands
(Denmark)

Nordtoqur
Eysturoy
THORSHAVN
Vestmanna
Bordoy
Sandur
Vagur
Suduroy
882

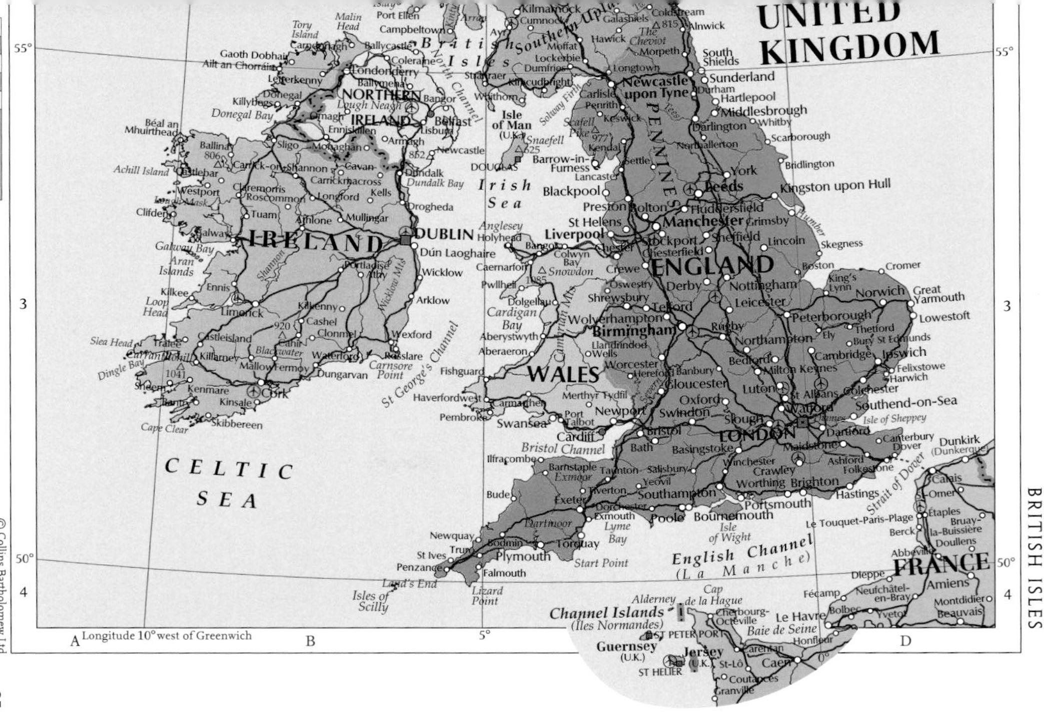

© Collins Bartholomew Ltd

0   100   200 KILOMETRES

UNITED KINGDOM
IRELAND
NORTHERN IRELAND
ENGLAND
WALES
FRANCE
PENNINES
CELTIC SEA
Irish Sea
English Channel
(La Manche)
Bristol Channel
St George's Channel
North Channel
Strait of Dover
Cardigan Bay
Galway Bay
Donegal Bay
Dundalk Bay
Solway Firth
British Isles
Channel Islands
(Îles Normandes)
Isle of Man
(U.K.)
Isle of Wight
Anglesey
Aran Islands
Isles of Scilly
Lough Neagh
Cambrian Mts
Wicklow Mts
Southern Uplands
The Cheviot
LONDON
DUBLIN
Birmingham
Manchester
Liverpool
Leeds
Newcastle upon Tyne
Sheffield
Bristol
Cardiff
Swansea
Belfast
Londonderry
Cork
Limerick
Galway
Waterford
Plymouth
Southampton
Portsmouth
Norwich
Cambridge
Oxford
Kingston upon Hull
York
Nottingham
Leicester
Brighton
Dover
Calais
Amiens
Le Havre
Caen
Cherbourg-Octeville
Guernsey
(U.K.)
Jersey
(U.K.)
ST PETER PORT
ST HELIER
Land's End
Lizard Point
Start Point
Cape Clear
Malin Head
Longitude 10° west of Greenwich
55°
50°
5°
3
4

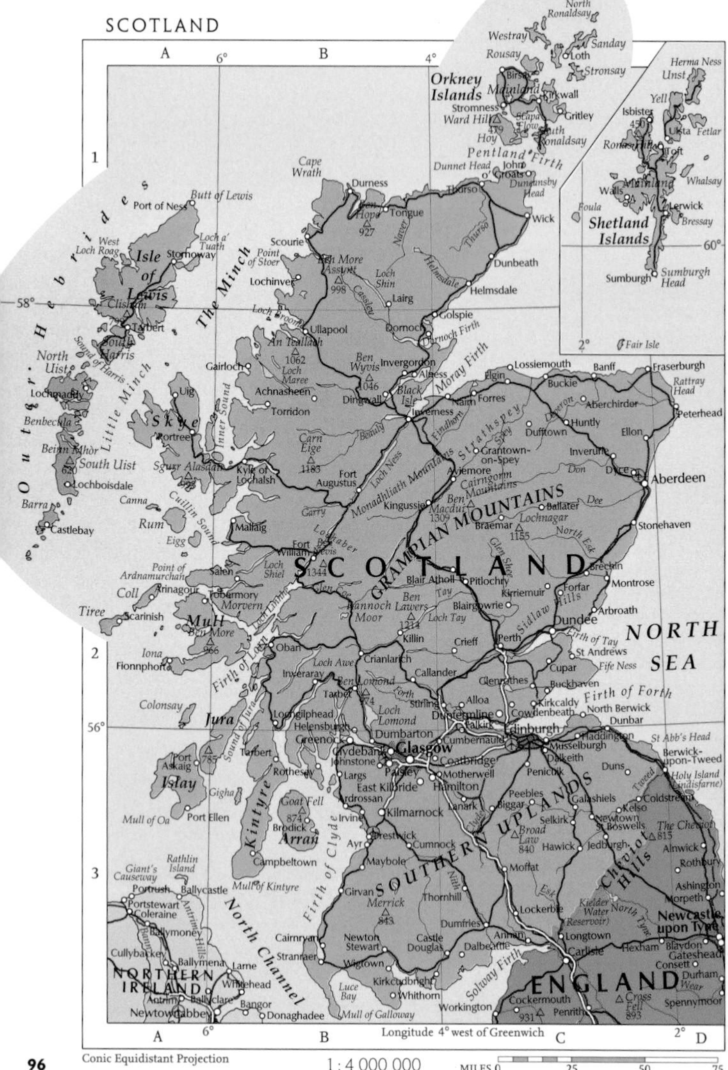
SCOTLAND
Orkney Islands
Shetland Islands
Outer Hebrides
SCOTLAND
GRAMPIAN MOUNTAINS
SOUTHERN UPLANDS
NORTH SEA
ENGLAND
NORTHERN IRELAND
North Channel
The Minch
Little Minch
Firth of Forth
Firth of Clyde
Moray Firth
Pentland Firth
Solway Firth
Isle of Lewis
Skye
Mull
Jura
Islay
Arran
Kintyre
Glasgow
Edinburgh
Aberdeen
Dundee
Inverness
Perth
Stirling
Fort William
Oban
Ullapool
Thurso
Wick
Kirkwall
Lerwick
Stornoway
Dumfries
Carlisle
Newcastle upon Tyne
Longitude 4° west of Greenwich
Conic Equidistant Projection
1 : 4 000 000
MILES 0 25 50 75

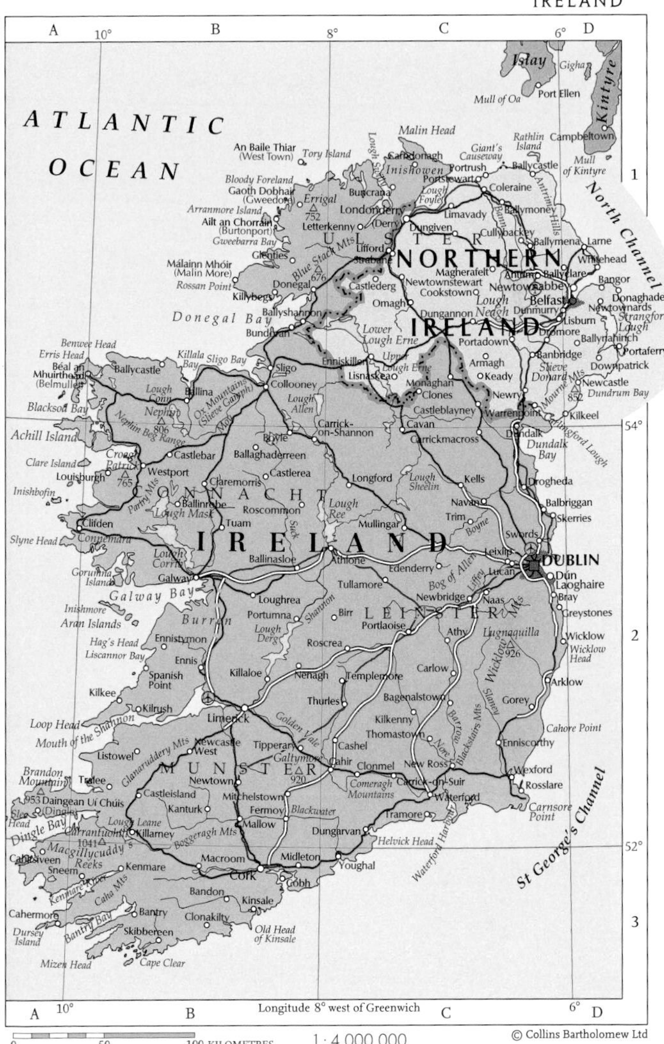

Longitude 8° west of Greenwich

0   50   100 KILOMETRES   1 : 4 000 000

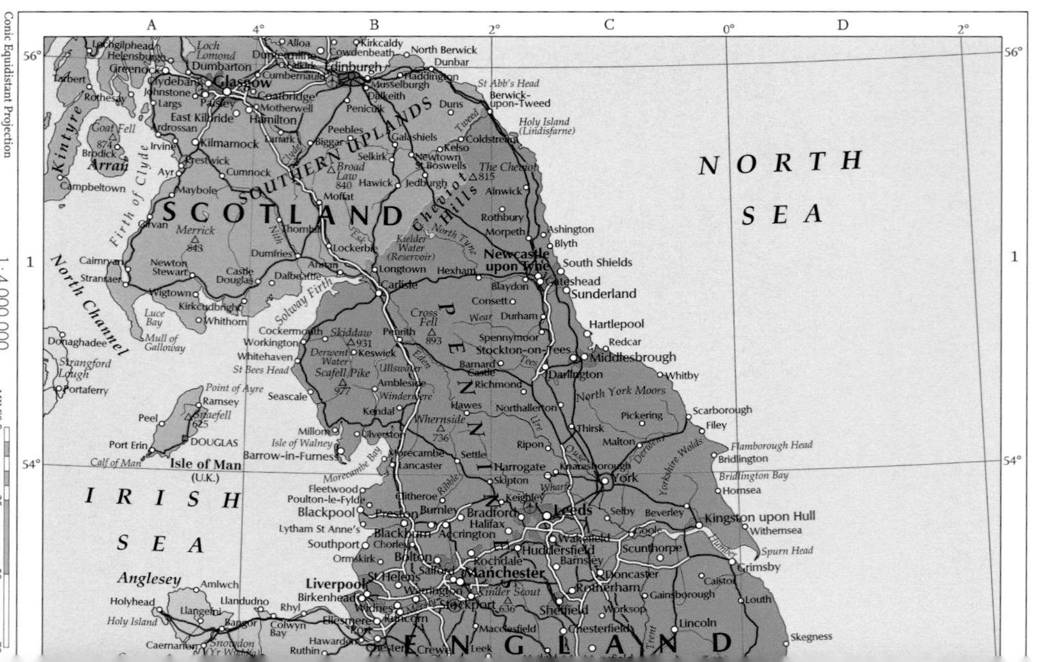

Conic Equidistant Projection

1 : 4 000 000

MILES 0   25   50   75

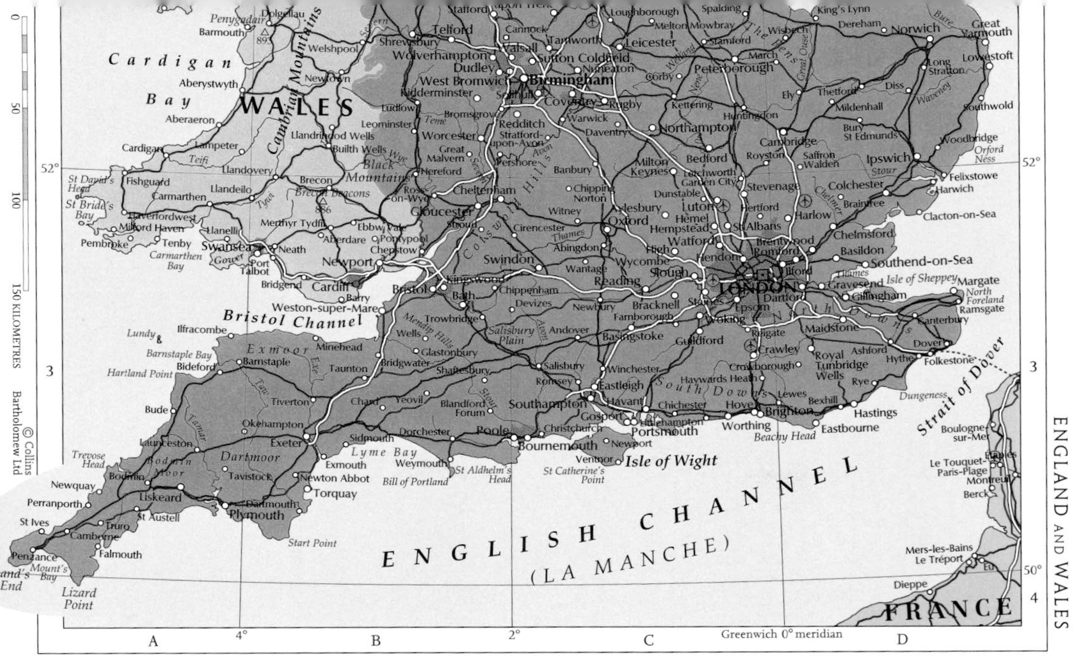

0   50   100   150 KILOMETRES   © Collins Bartholomew Ltd

ENGLISH CHANNEL
(LA MANCHE)
Bristol Channel
Cardigan Bay
Strait of Dover
WALES
FRANCE
LONDON
Isle of Wight
Isle of Sheppey
Cambrian Mountains
Black Mountains
Brecon Beacons
Exmoor
Dartmoor
Bodmin Moor
Mendip Hills
Salisbury Plain
South Downs
North Downs
The Fens
Cotswold Hills
Lyme Bay
Barnstaple Bay
Carmarthen Bay
St Bride's Bay
Mount's Bay
Land's End
Lizard Point
Start Point
Hartland Point
Lundy
Bill of Portland
St Aldhelm's Head
St Catherine's Point
Beachy Head
Dungeness
North Foreland
Orford Ness
Trevose Head
St David's Head
Great Yarmouth
Lowestoft
Norwich
Southwold
Ipswich
Felixstowe
Harwich
Clacton-on-Sea
Colchester
Chelmsford
Southend-on-Sea
Margate
Ramsgate
Canterbury
Dover
Folkestone
Hythe
Ashford
Maidstone
Gillingham
Gravesend
Basildon
Hastings
Eastbourne
Brighton
Hove
Worthing
Crawley
Royal Tunbridge Wells
Lewes
Bexhill
Rye
Chichester
Portsmouth
Southampton
Bournemouth
Poole
Weymouth
Dorchester
Salisbury
Winchester
Basingstoke
Guildford
Reading
Slough
Oxford
Swindon
Bath
Bristol
Gloucester
Cheltenham
Worcester
Hereford
Birmingham
Coventry
Wolverhampton
Leicester
Northampton
Peterborough
Cambridge
Bedford
Luton
Watford
Stevenage
Milton Keynes
Newport
Cardiff
Swansea
Neath
Port Talbot
Barry
Bridgend
Merthyr Tydfil
Brecon
Carmarthen
Aberystwyth
Cardigan
Fishguard
Pembroke
Milford Haven
Haverfordwest
Tenby
Llanelli
Ilfracombe
Barnstaple
Bideford
Bude
Minehead
Taunton
Exeter
Exmouth
Torquay
Plymouth
Tiverton
Okehampton
Tavistock
Launceston
Liskeard
Bodmin
St Austell
Truro
Falmouth
Camborne
Newquay
Perranporth
St Ives
Penzance
Boulogne-sur-Mer
Le Touquet-Paris-Plage
Montreuil
Berck
Mers-les-Bains
Le Tréport
Dieppe
Greenwich 0° meridian
52°

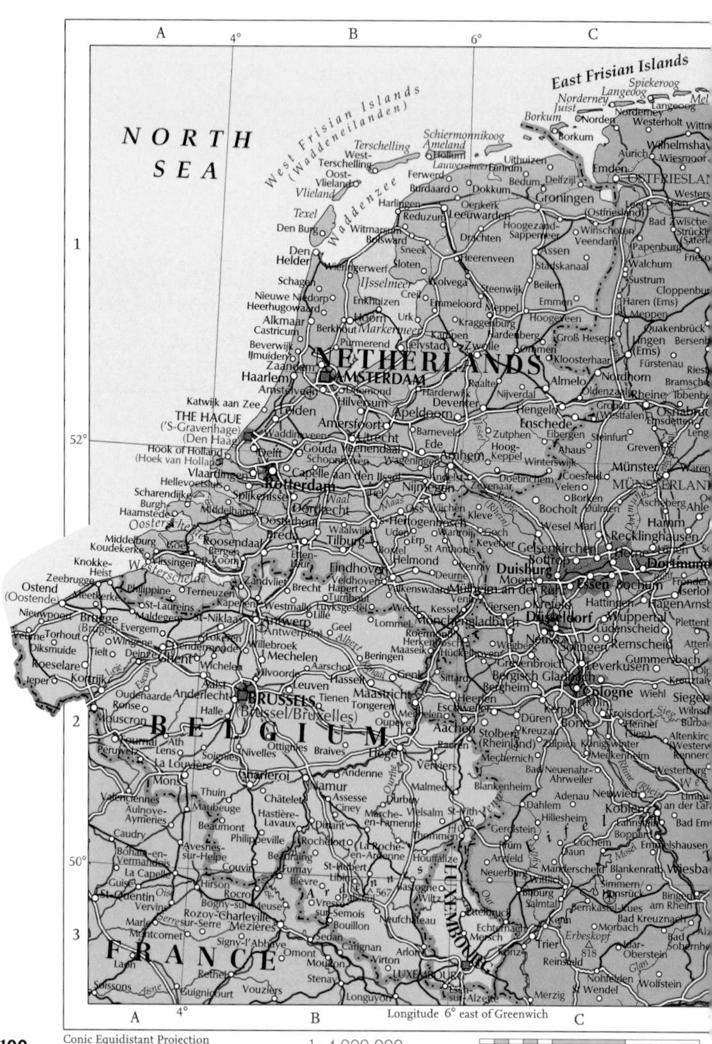

A 4° B 6° C

NORTH SEA

East Frisian Islands
Spiekeroog
Norderney Langeoog
Juist Langeoog Mel
Baltrum
Borkum Norden Westerholt Witt
Borkum Nordermeer Wilhelmshaven
Aurich Wiesmoor
OSTFRIESLAN
Emden Westers

West Frisian Islands
(Waddeneilanden)
Terschelling
West- Schiermonnikoog
Terschelling Ameland
Oost- Lauwersmeer
Vlieland Ferwerd Uithuizen Delfzijl
Vlieland Burdaard Dokkum Bedum Groningen Ostfriesland
Texel Oenkerk Leeuwarden Winschoten Bad Zwische
Harlingen Reduzum Hoogezand- Strücke
Den Burg Bolsward Drachten Sappemeer Papenburg Frieso
Den Bolsward Sneek Assen Veendam Walchum
Helder Workum Kolvega Steenwijk Stadskanaal Sustrum
Schagen Lemmer Beilen Cloppenburg
Nieuwe Niedorp Emmeloord Hoogeveen Emmen Haren (Ems) Quakenbrück
Heerhugoward Koppel Hardenberg Meppen Bersenb
Alkmaar Markermeer Kampen Hoogeveen ingen (Ems)
Castricum Berkhout Zwolle Kraggenburg Nordhorn Fürstenau Bramsch
Beverwijk Purmerend Ommen Kloosterhaar Nordhorn Osnab
IJmuiden Zaan AMSTERDAM Lelystad Raalte Almelo Oldenzaal Ibbenb
Zaandam NETHERLANDS Harderwijk Nijverdal Hengelo Rheine
Haarlem Amstelveen Hilversum Apeldoorn Deventer Enschede Steinfurt
Katwijk aan Zee Amersfoort Ede Hoog- Eibergen Ahaus Greven
THE HAGUE Leiden Utrecht Barneveld Zutphen Winterswijk Münster
('S-Gravenhage) Woerden Wageningen Arnhem Keppel Bocholt Coesfeld MÜNSTER
(Den Haag) Gouda Nieuwegein Veenendaal Ede Doetinchem Borken Dülmen
Hook of Holland Vlaardingen Capelle aan den IJssel Rhenen Nijmegen Kleve Wesel Marl Haltern
(Hoek van Holland) Rotterdam Waal 's-Hertogenbosch Kevelaer Bottrop Recklinghausen
Schiedam Dordrecht Gorinchem Grave Goch Geldern Gelsenkirchen Dortmund
Scharendijke Zwijndrecht Waalwijk Oss Uden Straelen Moers Essen Bochum Iserlohn
Burgh Oosterhout Tilburg Helmond St Anthonis Krefeld Duisburg Hattingen Hagen
Haamstede Middelburg Breda Eindhoven Venray Viersen Mönchengladbach Düsseldorf Wuppertal
Oosters... Roosendaal Eindhoven Deurne Venlo Willich Neuss Solingen
Koudekerke Bergen op Zoom Brecht Geel Weert Roermond Mönchengladbach Leverkusen Remscheid
Knokke- Westmalle Bree Maaseik Erkelenz Grevenbroich Bergisch Gladbach Gummersbach
Heist Terneuzen Kapellen Nuenen Kessel Geilenkirchen Jülich Cologne Wiehl
Ostend Philippine Turnhout Westerlo Beringen Maaseik Heinsberg Bedburg Bergheim Siegb
(Oostende) Brugge Sint-Niklaas Antwerpen Herentals Genk Hasselt Maastricht Eschweiler Düren Bonn Troisdorf
Nieuwpoort Bruges Lokeren Aarschot Diest Tongeren Aachen Stolberg Euskirchen Bad
Diksmuide Torhout Mechelen Leuven Beek Geilenkirchen (Rheinland) Zülpich Mecken
Ieper Gent Wetteren BELGIUM Hasselt Hoeilaart Tienen Sint-Truiden Visé Herve Verviers Mechernich Adenau Neuwied Koblenz
Roeselare Deinze BRUSSELS Leuven Eupen Malmedy Blankenheim Bad Neuenahr- an der
Kortrijk Michelen (Brussel/Bruxelles) Overijse Hannut Huy Dahlem Ahrweiler Mayen Lahn
Oudenaarde Anderlecht Namur Andenne Braives Verviers St Vith Hillesheim Adenau Neuwied Boppard Bad Em
Ronse Aalst Nivelles Ottignies Braives Andenne Malmedy Gerolstein Daun Mayen Emmelshausen Wiesba
Muscron Ath Mons Braine Gembloux Huy Prüm Manderscheid Kelberg Koblenz Simmern Bingerb
Péruwelz Lessines Charleroi Namur Marche- Neuerburg Wittlich Morbach Bad Kreuznach
Valenciennes La Louvière Thuin Châtelet Andenne en-Famenne Houffalize Bitburg Trier Hunsrück Oberstein Simmern
Aulnoye- Maubeuge Nivelles Ciney Marche- Bastogne Echternach Morsch Idar- Oberstein Sobern
Aymeries Beaumont Philippeville Rochefort Han- Houffalize Diekirch Erbeskopf Bad Kreuznach
Caudry Avesnes- Philippeville Dinant sur-Lesse La Roche-en- Ettelbruck Reinsfeld Oder-
Le Cateau Philippeville Couvin Beauraing St-Hubert Ardenne LUXEMBOURG Merzig Nohfelden Wendel
Bohain-en- Chimay Givet Wellin Libin Nufchâteau Arlon Saarburg Merzig Wollstein
Vermandois Hirson Rocroi Bogny-sur- Fumay Bouillon Florenville Virton LUXEMBOURG Wellin
La Capelle Vervins Rozoy- Charleville- Meuse Vresse-sur-Semois Bouillon Arlon Saarburg Merzig
St-Quentin Vervins sur-Serre Mézières Sedan Carignan Virton
Marle Rethel Omont Mouzon Montmédy
Guise Signy-l'Abbaye Mouzon
Montcornet Signy-l'Abbaye Stenay
Laon Rethel FRANCE Vouziers Longuyon
Soissons Béthel Buzancy-court

A 4° B Longitude 6° east of Greenwich C

52°

50°

1

2

3

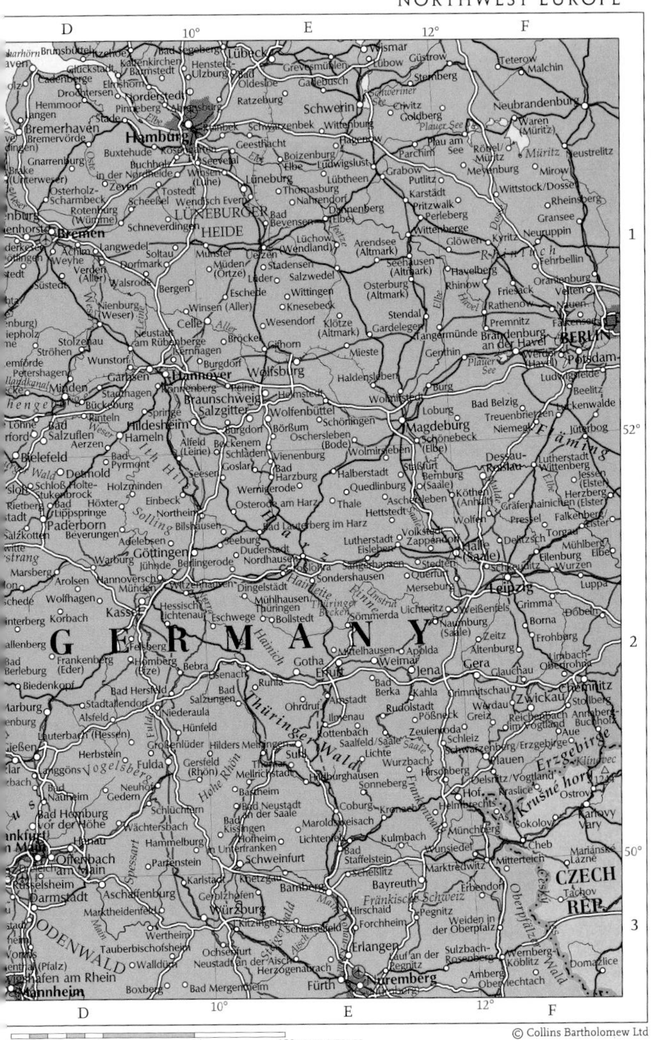

0   50   100   150 KILOMETRES

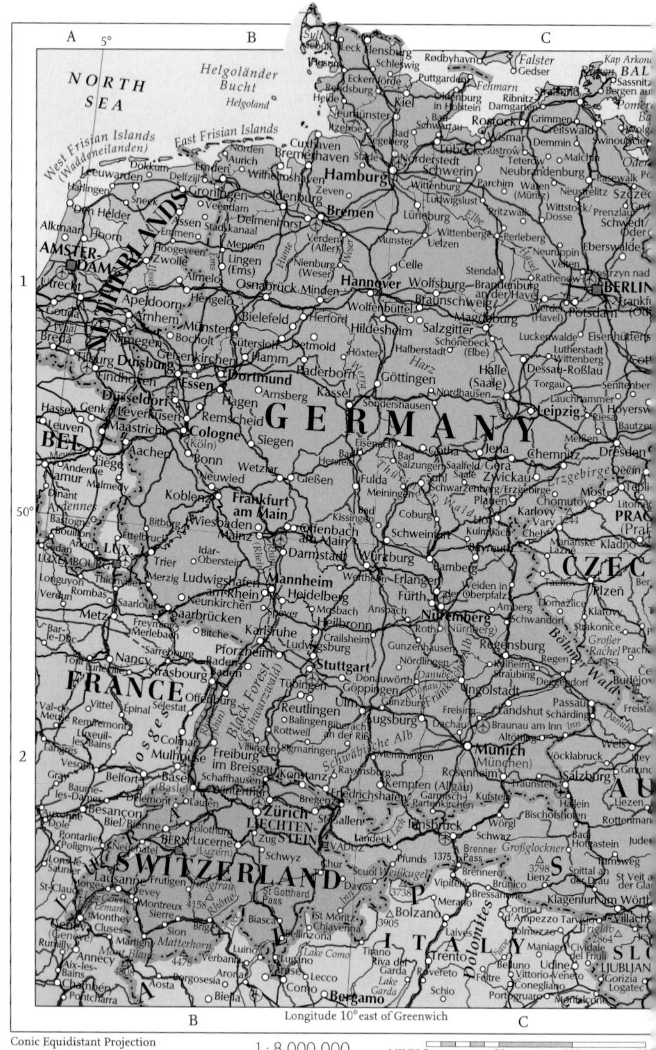

Longitude 10° east of Greenwich

1 : 8 000 000   MILES 0   50   100   15

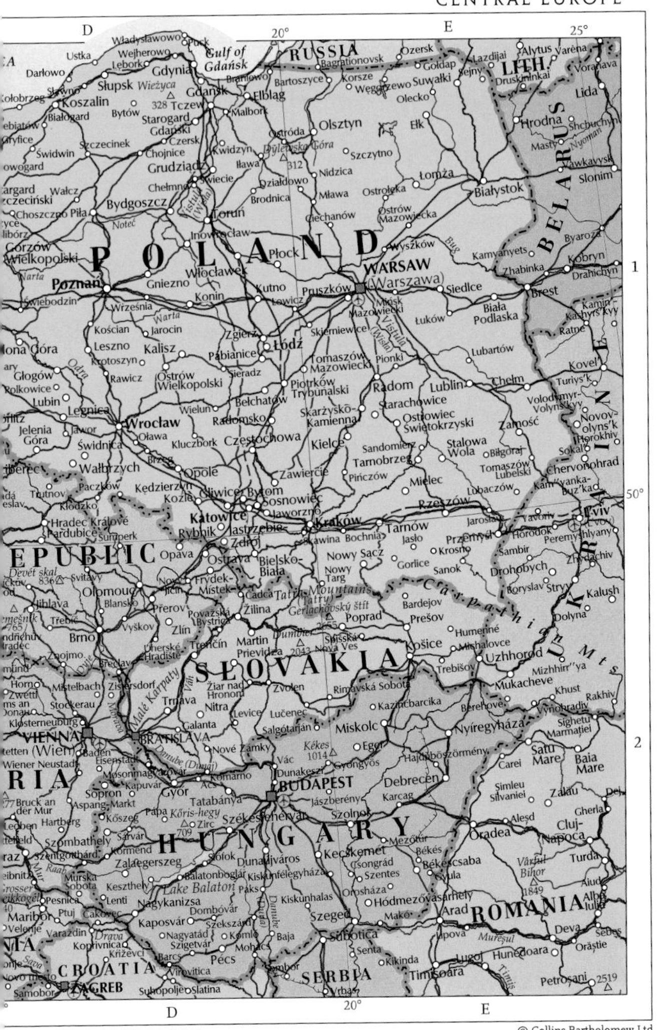

Władysławowo
Ustka Wejherowo Gulf of
Darłowo Łeba Gdańsk RUSSIA Ozersk Lazdijai Alytus Varena
Kołobrzeg Słupsk Wierżyca Gdynia Braniewo Bagrationovsk Goldap Suwałki LITH Voranava
Skawina Koszalin Lębork Gdańsk Pasłęczyce Korsze Olecko Sejny Druskininkai Lida
ebianow Świdwin Bytów 328 Tczew Elbląg Ełk Hrodna Nioman Ivawksi
owogard Białogard Starogard Malbork Ostróda Olsztyn Szczytno Łomża Białystok Słonim
argard Wałcz Czarnków Gdański Kwidzyn Dylewska Góra 312 Nidzica Mława Ostrołęka Kamyanyets Byaro
czecinski Piła Chojnice Czersk Grudziądz Chełmno Działdowo Ciechanów Ostrów Mazowiecka Zhabinka Korbyn Drahichyn
Łobżenica Bydgoszcz Brodnica Płock Wyszków Bug Siedlce Brest Ratne
Gorzów Noteć Toruń Inowrocław POLAND WARSAW (Warszawa) Biała Podlaska Kovel
Wielkopolski Gniezno Konin Kutno Pruszków Łuków Lubartów Volodymyr Volyns'k
Poznań Września Koło Łowicz Skierniewice Mazowiecki Radzyń Chełm Turiys'k Novov Olyns'k
Zielona Góra Leszno Kalisz Jarocin Zgierz Łódź Tomaszów Mazowiecki Pionki Radom Lublin Krasnystaw chervonohrad
Głogów Rawicz Ostrów Wielkopolski Sieradz Piotrków Trybunalski Skarżysko Kamienna Starachowice Kraśnik Tomaszów Lubelski Zhovkva
Polkowice Wieluń Bełchatów Ostrowiec Świętokrzyski Sandomierz Stalowa Wola Łukaczów buz'ka L'viv
Lubin Legnica Oława Wrocław Kluczbork Częstochowa Kielce Tarnobrzeg Stalowa Mielec Rzeszów Yavoriv
Jelenia Góra Świdnica Opole Zawiercie Pińczów Jarosław Horodok Peremyshlyany CARPATHIAN
Wałbrzych Paczków Kędzierzyn Kłodzko Koźle Gliwice Bytom Sosnowiec Kraków Tarnów Jasło Przemyśl Sambir Drohobych Kalush
Kłodzko Prudnik Katowice Jaworzno Chrzanów Bochnia Krosno Sanok Boryslav Stryy Dolyna
EPUBLIC Opava Rybnik Jastrzębie Nowy Sącz Gorlice Uzhhorod Zhydachiv
Ostrava Frydek Bielsko Biała Tatra Mountains Gerlachovský štít Poprad Bardejov Prešov Humenné Mukacheve Khust Rakhiv
Olomouc Mistek Žilina Martin Považská Bystrica Prievidza Košice Trebišov Uzhhorod Mts
Brno Vyškov Zlín Dubnica SLOVAKIA Rimavská Sobota Miskolc Sátoraljaújhely Berehove Vynohradiv Sighetu Marmaţiei
Mistelbach Hronov Trenčín Zvolen Lučenec Kazincbarcika Nyíregyháza Satu Mare Baia Mare
VIENNA (Wien) BRATISLAVA Nové Zámky Komárno Vác Gyöngyös Eger Hajdúböszörmény Carei Cluj
Bruck an der Mur Eisenstadt Kapuvár Győr Tatabánya BUDAPEST Jászberény Debrecen Karcag Şimleu Silvaniei Zalău Gherla
Szombathely Körmend Pápa Zirc Székesfehérvár Kecskemét Békés Oradea Aleşd Cluj Napoca Turda
HUNGARY Dunaújváros Mezőtúr Csongrád Szentes Békéscsaba Gyula Vărşand Bihor Aiud
Keszthely Lake Balaton Siófok Paks Kalocsa Hódmezővásárhely Makó Arad ROMANIA
Nagykanizsa Dombóvár Szekszárd Baja Szeged Subotica Lipova Mureşul Lugoj Hunedoara Deva Orăştie
Varaždin Drava Szigetvár Pécs Sombor SERBIA Kikinda Timişoara Petroşani 2519
ZAGREB Slavonska Slatina CROATIA Sulipolje Našice SERBIA

D   20°   E   25°

1

50°

LTH

2

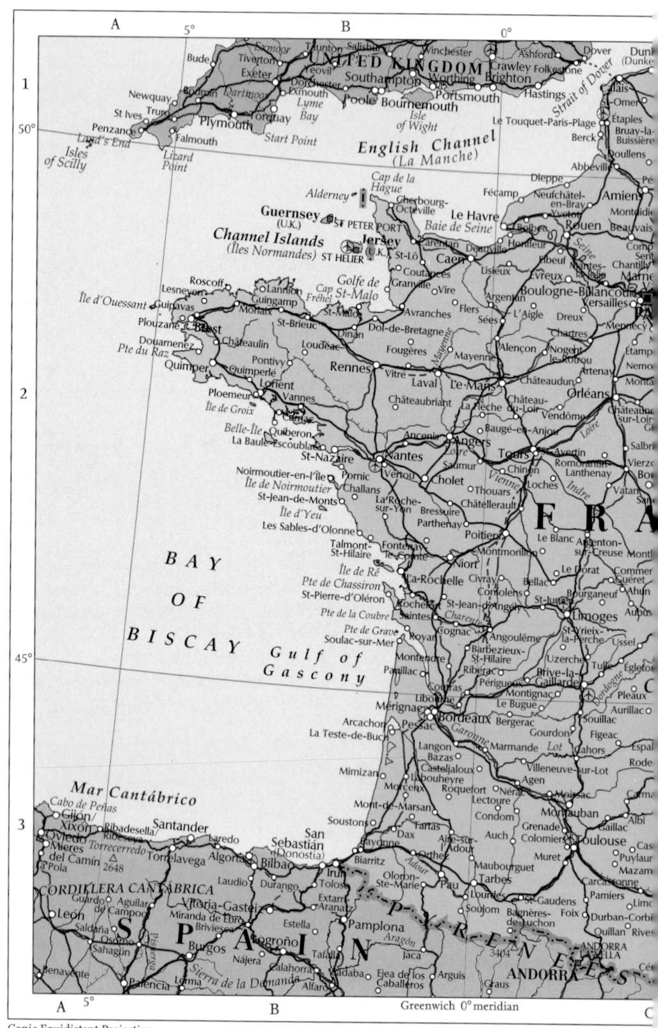

104 Conic Equidistant Projection   1 : 8 000 000   MILES 0   50   100   150

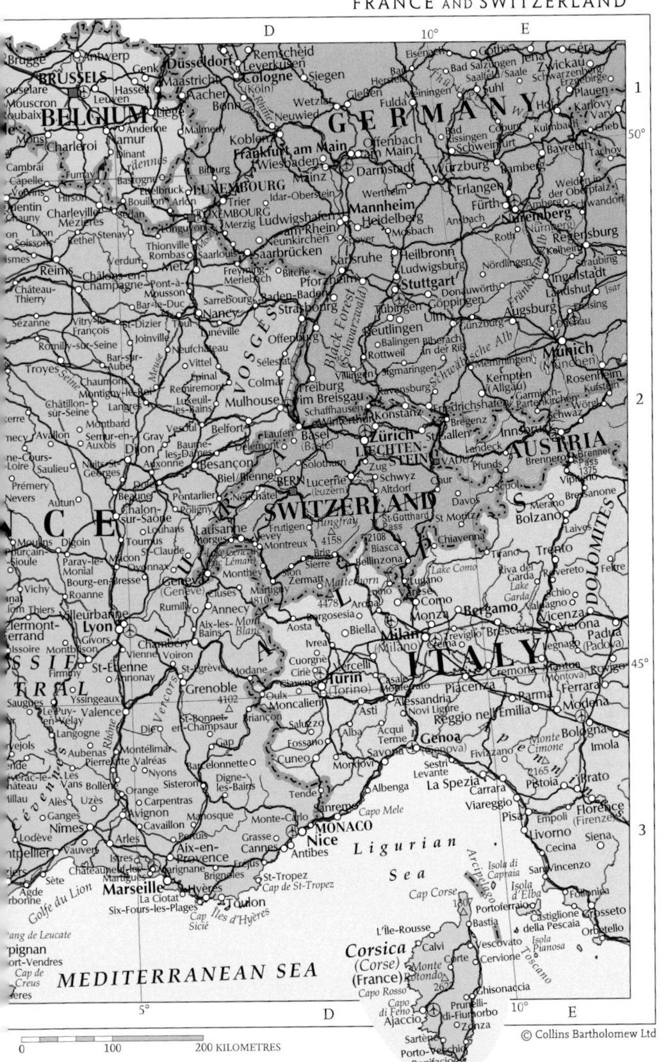

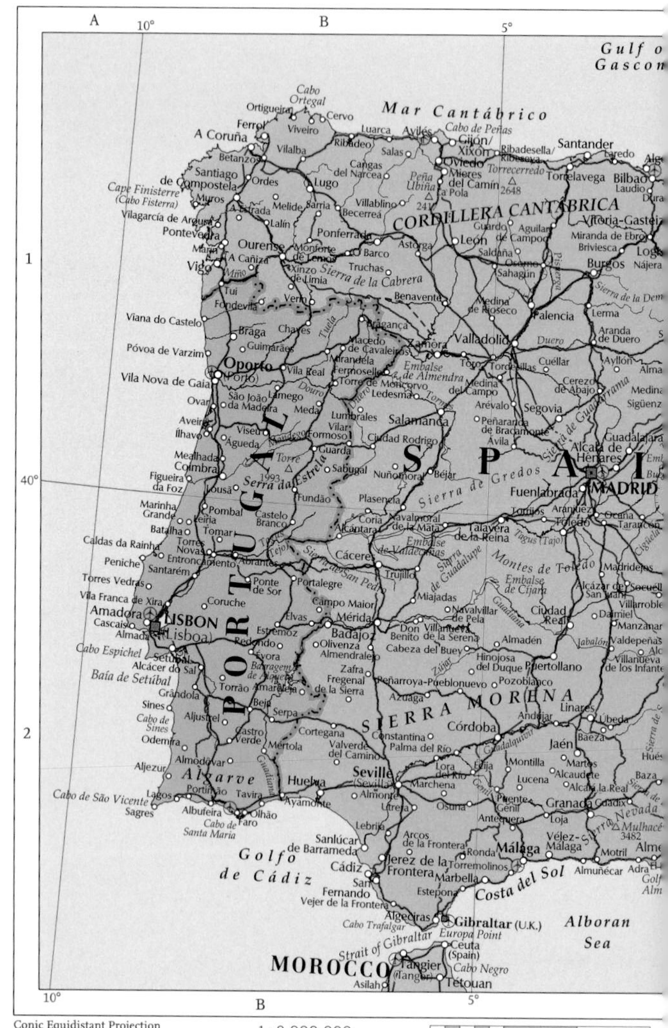

A   10°   B   5°   Gulf o
Gascon

Mar Cantábrico

Cabo
Ortegal
Ortigueira   Cervo
Ferrol   Vivaro   Luarca   Avilés   Cabo de Peñas
A Coruña   Ribadeo   Gijón/   Ribadesella   Santander
Betanzos   Salas   Xixón   Laredo   Alga
Cangas   Oviedo   Torrecerredo   Torrelavega   Bilbao
Santiago   Ordes   Lugo   del Narcea   Mieres   2648   Vitoria-Gasteiz   Laudio   Dura
de Compostela   Melide   Sarria   Peña   del Camin   La Pola
Cape Finisterre   Estrada   Villablino   Ubiña   Miranda de Ebro
(Cabo Fisterra)   Muros   Monforte   2417   CORDILLERA CANTÁBRICA   Guardo   Briviesca   Logr
Vilagarcía de Arousa   de Lemos   Ponferrada   Aguilar   de Campoo   Nájera
Pontevedra   Ourense   Barco   Astorga   León   Sierra de la Dem   S
Vigo   A Cañiza   Sierra de la Cabrera   Saldaña   Sahagún   Burgos
Tui   Verín   Trubes   Benavente   Medina   Palencia   Lerma
Viana do Castelo   Fonsagrada   Barco   Valladolid   de Rioseco   Aranda   Ayllón   Alma
Braga   Chaves   Macedo   Zamora   Duero   de Duero   Almazán
Póvoa de Varzim   Guimarães   de Cavaleiros   Embalse   Toro   Tordesillas   Cuéllar   Cerezo   Medina
Vila Nova de Gaia   Vila Real   Miranda   de Almendra   Medina   de Abajo   Sigüenza
Oporto   Ferreedo   Torre de Moncorvo   del Campo   Arévalo   Segovia   Guadalajara
Ovar   São João   Lamego   Ledesma   Peñaranda   Ávila   Alcalá de   Emb
Aveiro   da Madeira   Viseu   Lumbrales   Salamanca   de Bracamonte   Henares   MADRID
Ílhavo   Águeda   Meda   Vilar   Ciudad Rodrigo   Sierra de Gredos   Fuenlabrada
Mealhada   Tondela   Guarda   Torre   Nuñomoral   Ávila   Torres   Aranju   Ocaña
Coimbra   1993   Sabugal   Plasencia   Alcorcón   Toledo   Tarancón
Figueira   da Estrela   Fundão   Arenas   Talavera   Madridejos
da Foz   Lousã   Serra da Estrela   Coria   Navalmoral   de la Mata   de la Reina   Tajo   Alcázar de San Juan
Marinha   Pombal   Castelo   de la Mata   Embalse   Montes de Toledo   Villarrob
Grande   Batalha   Branco   Abrantes   Cáceres   de Valdecañas   Ciudad Real   Daimiel   Manzanar
Caldas da Rainha   Torres   Portalegre   Campo Maior   Trujillo   Embalse   Almadén   Valdepeñas
Peniche   Novas   Tomar   Ponte   Miajadas   de Cíjara   Jabalón   Alco
Torres Vedras   Santarém   de Sor   Elvas   Mérida   Navalvillar   Villanueva
Vila Franca de Xira   Coruche   Estremoz   Badajoz   de Pela   Ciudad Real   de los Infante
Amadora   LISBON   Évora   Olivenza   Don Villaromán   Puertollano
Cascais   (Lisboa)   Torrão   Barragem   Almendralejo   Benito de la Serena   Hinojosa   Pozoblanco
Cabo Espichel   Setúbal   de Vigia   Zafra   Cabeza del Buey   del Duque
Alcácer do Sal   Beja   Fregenal   Peñarroya-Pueblonuevo
Baía de Setúbal   Grândola   de la Sierra   Azuaga   SIERRA MORENA
Sines   Serpa   Andújar   Linares
Cabo de   Aljustrel   Cortegana   Constantina   Córdoba   Úbeda
Sines   Castro   Palma del Río   Jaén   Baeza
Odemira   Verde   Mértola   Valverde   Montilla   Martos   Hués
Aljezur   Almodôvar   del Camino   Sevilla   Lora   Lucena   Alcaudete   Baza
Algarve   Huelva   del Río   Marchena   Osuna   Granada   vada
Cabo de São Vicente   Lagos   Portimão   Tavira   Ayamonte   Almonte   Utrera   Antequera   Genil   Mulhacé
Sagres   Albufeira   Olhão   Lebrija   Arcos   Ronda   3482   Alme
Cabo de   Faro   Sanlúcar   de la Frontera   Torremolinos   Málaga   Motril   Almuñécar   Adra
Santa Maria   de Barrameda   Cádiz   Jerez de la   Marbella   Costa del Sol
Golfo   San   Frontera   Estepona   Almería
de Cádiz   Fernando   Vejer de la Frontera   Algeciras   Gibraltar   Alborán
Cabo Trafalgar   Europa Point   (U.K.)   Sea
Strait of Gibraltar   Ceuta   Alm
MOROCCO   Tangier   (Spain)   Cabo Negro
Asilah   Tetouan

10°   B   5°

Conic Equidistant Projection   1 : 8 000 000   MILES 0   50   100   150

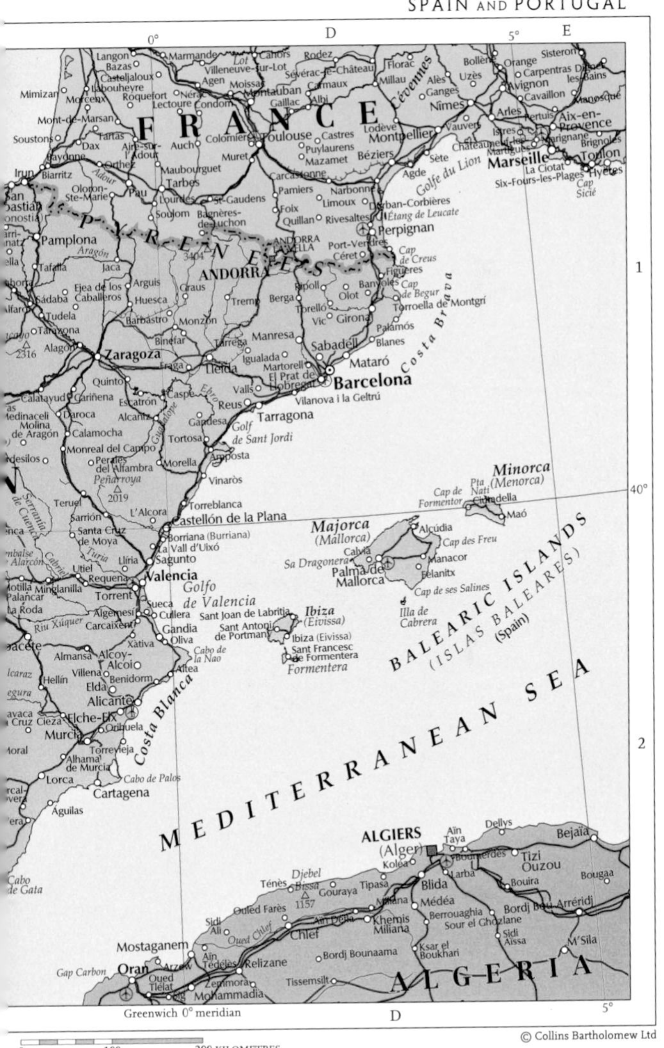

© Collins Bartholomew Ltd

Greenwich 0° meridian

0   100   200 KILOMETRES

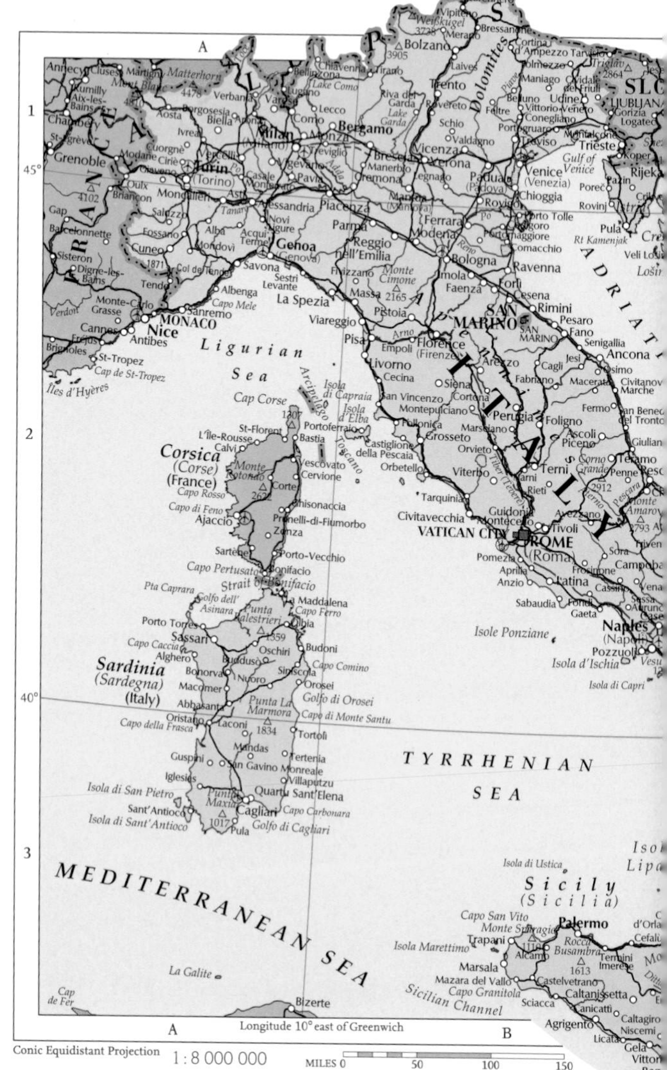

108 Conic Equidistant Projection   1 : 8 000 000   MILES 0   50   100   150

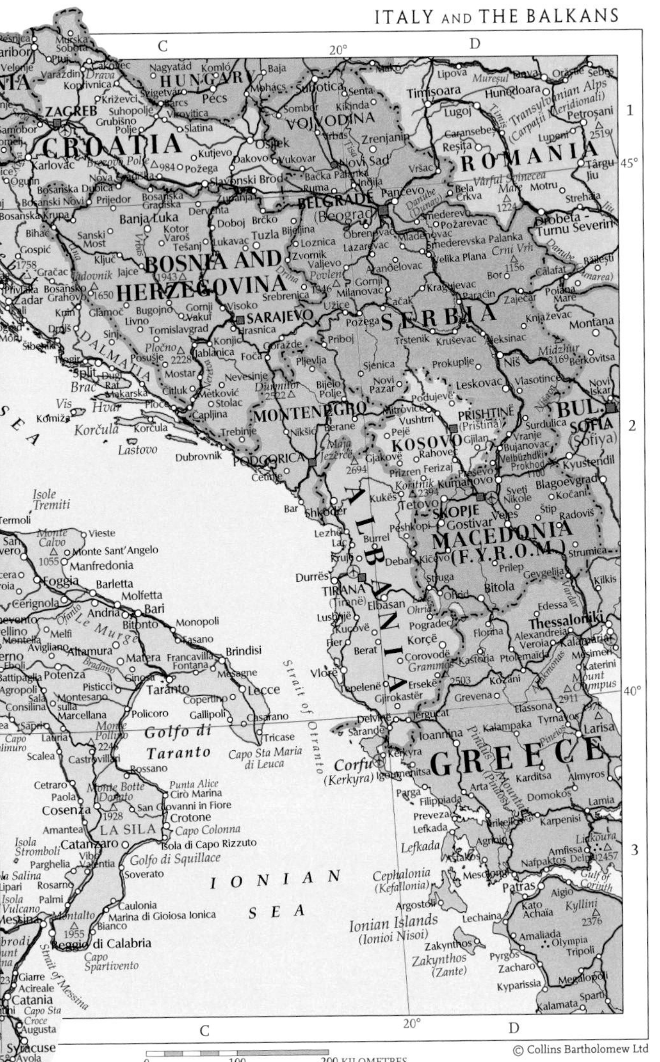

CROATIA
HUNGARY
VOJVODINA
ROMANIA
BOSNIA AND HERZEGOVINA
SERBIA
MONTENEGRO
KOSOVO
ALBANIA
MACEDONIA (F.Y.R.O.M.)
BUL.
GREECE
ZAGREB
BELGRADE (Beograd)
SARAJEVO
PODGORICA
PRISHTINË (Priština)
SKOPJE
TIRANA (Tiranë)
SOFIA (Sofiya)
IONIAN SEA
Strait of Otranto
Golfo di Taranto
Strait of Messina
Ionian Islands (Ionioi Nisoi)
DALMATIA
Transylvanian Alps (Carpaţii Meridionali)
Pindus Mountains (Pindos)

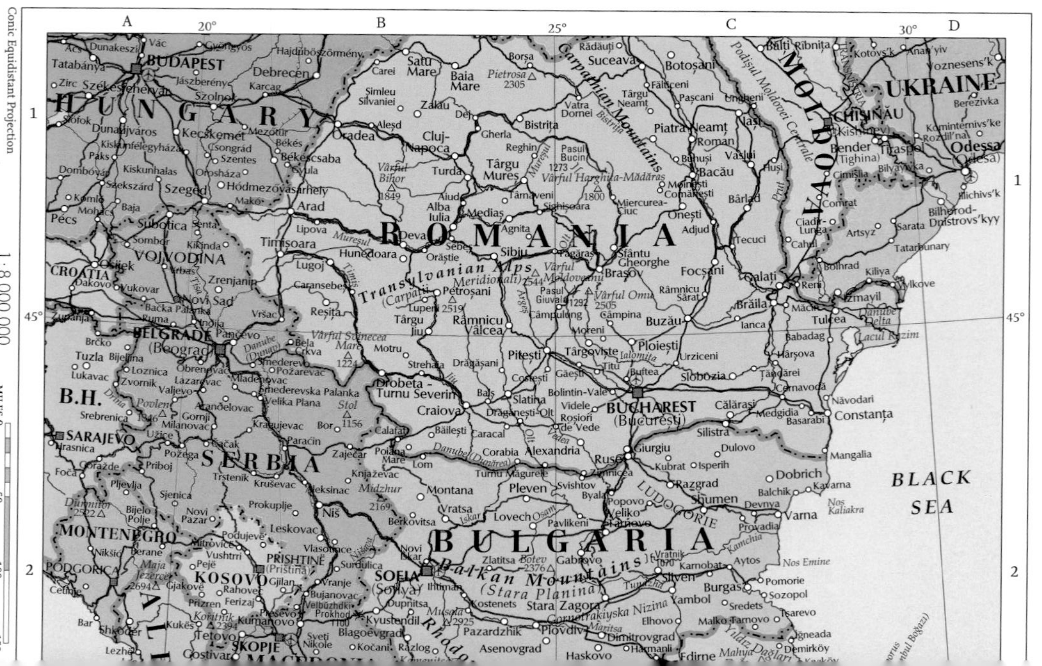

110   Conic Equidistant Projection   1 : 8 000 000   MILES 0   50   100   150

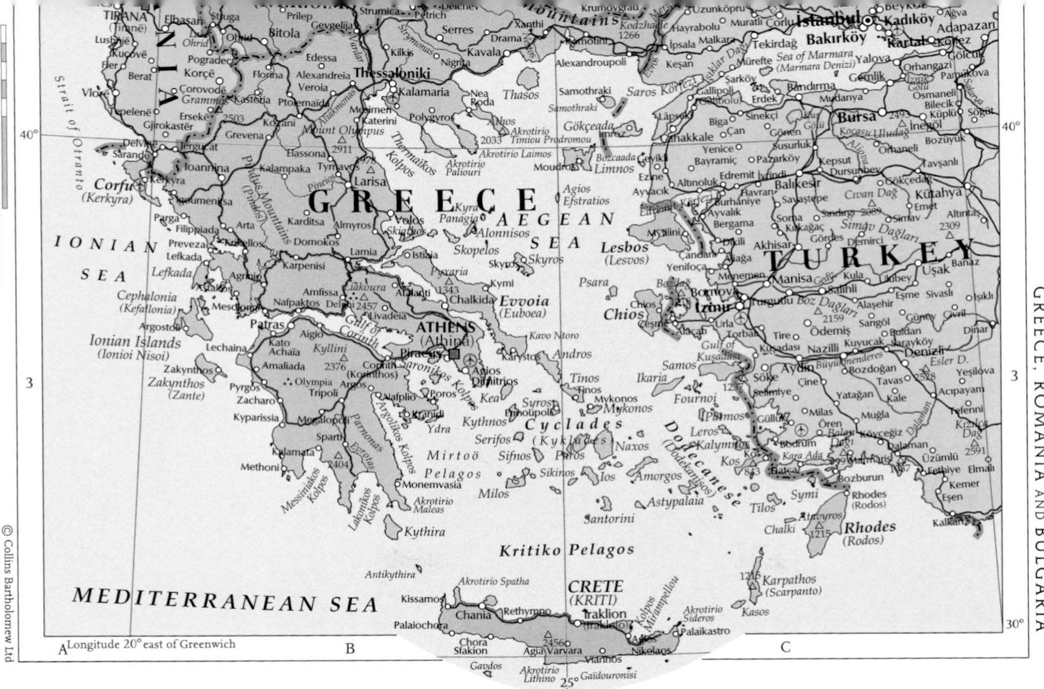
GREECE
TURKEY
AEGEAN SEA
IONIAN SEA
MEDITERRANEAN SEA
CRETE
(KRITI)
Kritiko Pelagos
Mirtoö Pelagos
Cyclades
(Kyklades)
Dodecanese
(Dodekanisos)
ATHENS
(Athina)
Thessaloniki
Istanbul
İzmir
Bursa
Lesbos
(Lesvos)
Chios
Rhodes
(Rodos)
Evvoia
(Euboea)
Ionian Islands
(Ionioi Nisoi)
Corfu
(Kerkyra)
Cephalonia
(Kefallonia)
Zakynthos
(Zante)
Pindus Mountains
(Pindos)
Strait of Otranto
Sea of Marmara
(Marmara Denizi)
Longitude 20° east of Greenwich
A
B
C
3
40°
30°
25°
0
100
200 KILOMETRES

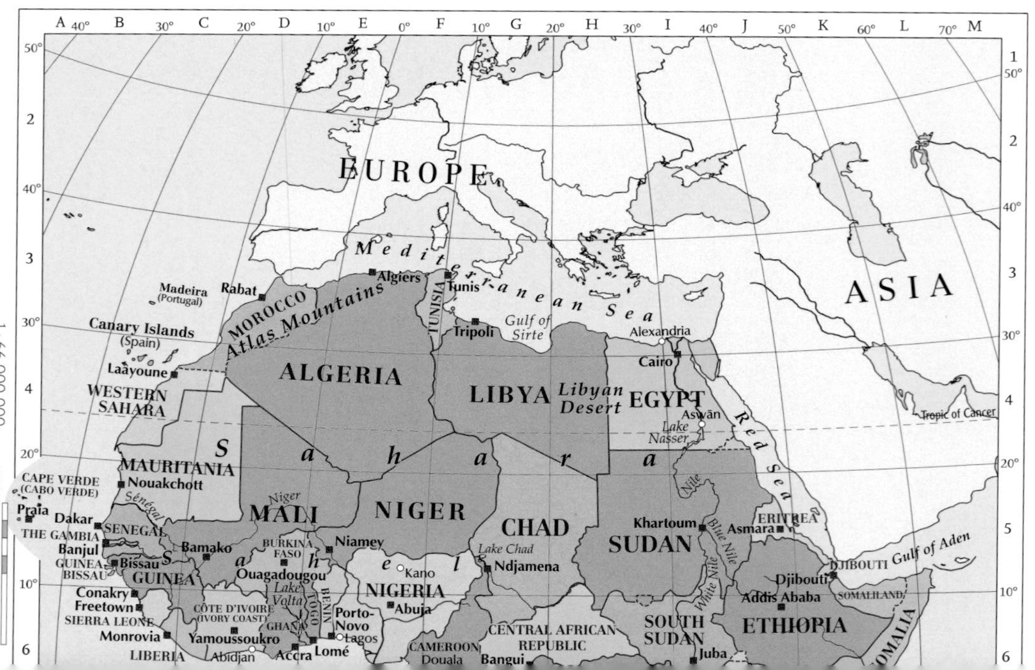

A B C D E F G H I J K L M
40° 30° 20° 10° 0° 10° 20° 30° 40° 50° 60° 70°
1 2 3 4 5 6
50° 40° 30° 20° 10°
EUROPE
ASIA
Mediterranean Sea
Madeira (Portugal)
Rabat
Algiers
Tunis
MOROCCO
Atlas Mountains
TUNISIA
Canary Islands (Spain)
Tripoli
Gulf of Sirte
Alexandria
Cairo
Laâyoune
ALGERIA
LIBYA
Libyan Desert
EGYPT
WESTERN SAHARA
Aswān
Lake Nasser
Red Sea
Tropic of Cancer
Sahara
MAURITANIA
Nouakchott
CAPE VERDE (CABO VERDE)
Praia
Sénégal
Niger
MALI
NIGER
CHAD
SUDAN
Nile
Khartoum
Blue Nile
ERITREA
Asmara
Dakar
SENEGAL
THE GAMBIA
Banjul
GUINEA-BISSAU
Bissau
Bamako
BURKINA FASO
Niamey
Lake Chad
Ndjamena
GUINEA
Ouagadougou
Kano
DJIBOUTI
Gulf of Aden
Djibouti
Conakry
Freetown
SIERRA LEONE
Lake Volta
TOGO
BENIN
NIGERIA
White Nile
Addis Ababa
SOMALILAND
CÔTE D'IVOIRE (IVORY COAST)
GHANA
Porto-Novo
Abuja
Monrovia
Yamoussoukro
Lagos
CENTRAL AFRICAN REPUBLIC
SOUTH SUDAN
ETHIOPIA
SOMALIA
LIBERIA
Abidjan
Accra
Lomé
CAMEROON
Douala
Bangui
Juba
1:66 000 000
MILES 0 400 800

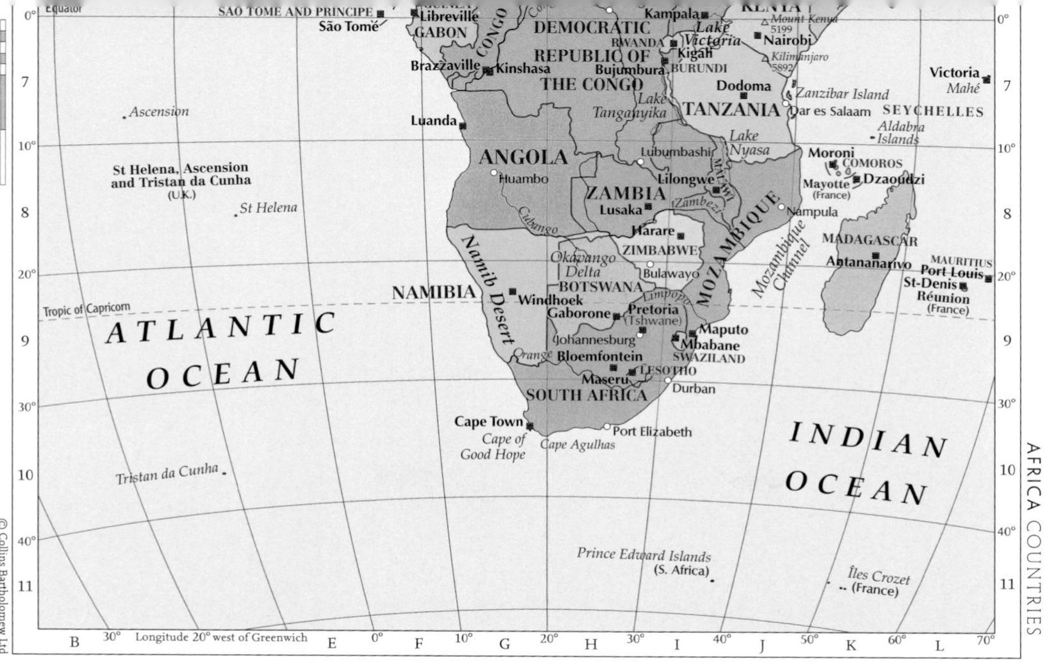

SÃO TOMÉ AND PRÍNCIPE ■ São Tomé ■

Victoria ■ Mahé

SEYCHELLES

Aldabra Islands

COMOROS
Moroni ●
Mayotte ● Dzaoudzi
(France)

MAURITIUS
Port Louis ■
St-Denis ● Réunion
(France)

Libreville ■
GABON
Brazzaville ■
Kinshasa ■

CONGO

REPUBLIC OF
THE CONGO

DEMOCRATIC

Kampala ●
Kigali ●
RWANDA
BURUNDI
Bujumbura ●

Lake
Victoria
△ Mount Kenya
5199
Nairobi ●
Kilimanjaro
5892

KENYA

Dodoma ■
TANZANIA
Dar es Salaam
Zanzibar Island

ANTANANARIVO

MADAGASCAR
Antananarivo ■

INDIAN

OCEAN

Îles Crozet
(France)

Luanda ■

ANGOLA

Huambo ■

Namib Desert

NAMIBIA

Windhoek ■

Okavango
Delta

Cubango

BOTSWANA

Gaborone ■

Lubumbashi ●
Lilongwe ■
MALAWI
Lake
Nyasa

ZAMBIA
Lusaka ■
Lake
Tanganyika

Harare ■
ZIMBABWE
Bulawayo ●

Limpopo

Pretoria ■
Johannesburg ●

Lake
Nasa

Zambezi

Nampula ●

MOZAMBIQUE

Mozambique
Channel

Maputo ■
Mbabane ■
SWAZILAND

LESOTHO
Maseru ■

Lake

Orange (Gariep)

SOUTH AFRICA

Bloemfontein ●

Durban ●

Port Elizabeth ●

Cape Town ■
Cape of
Good Hope
Cape Agulhas

Prince Edward Islands
(S. Africa)

Ascension

St Helena

St Helena, Ascension
and Tristan da Cunha
(U.K.)

ATLANTIC

OCEAN

Tropic of Capricorn

Tristan da Cunha

Longitude 20° west of Greenwich

© Collins Bartholomew Ltd

0   500   1000   1500   KILOMETRES

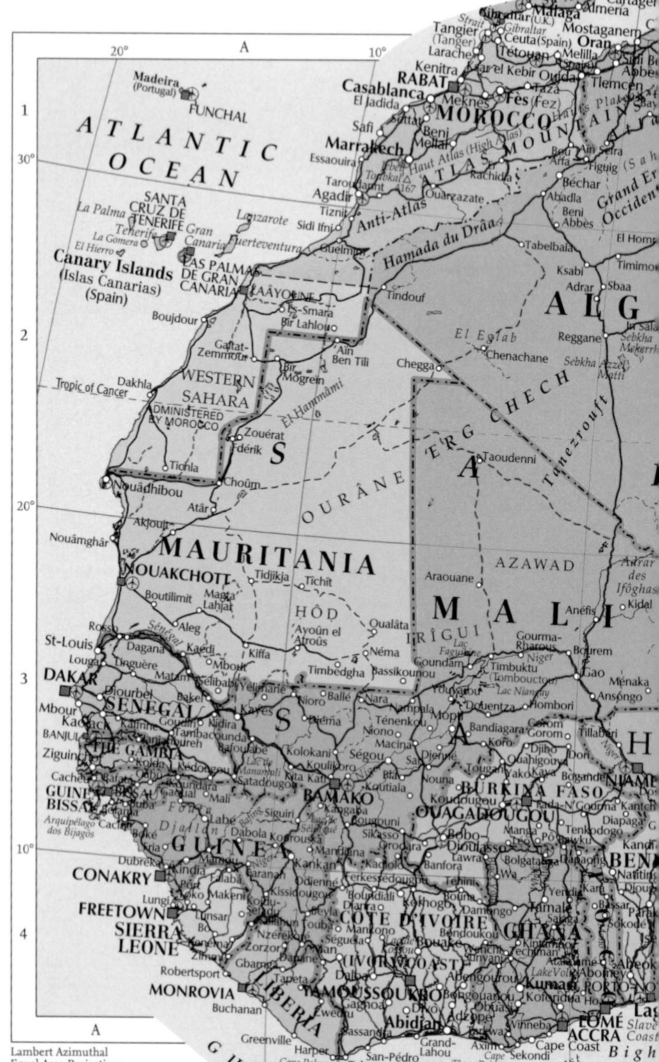

114

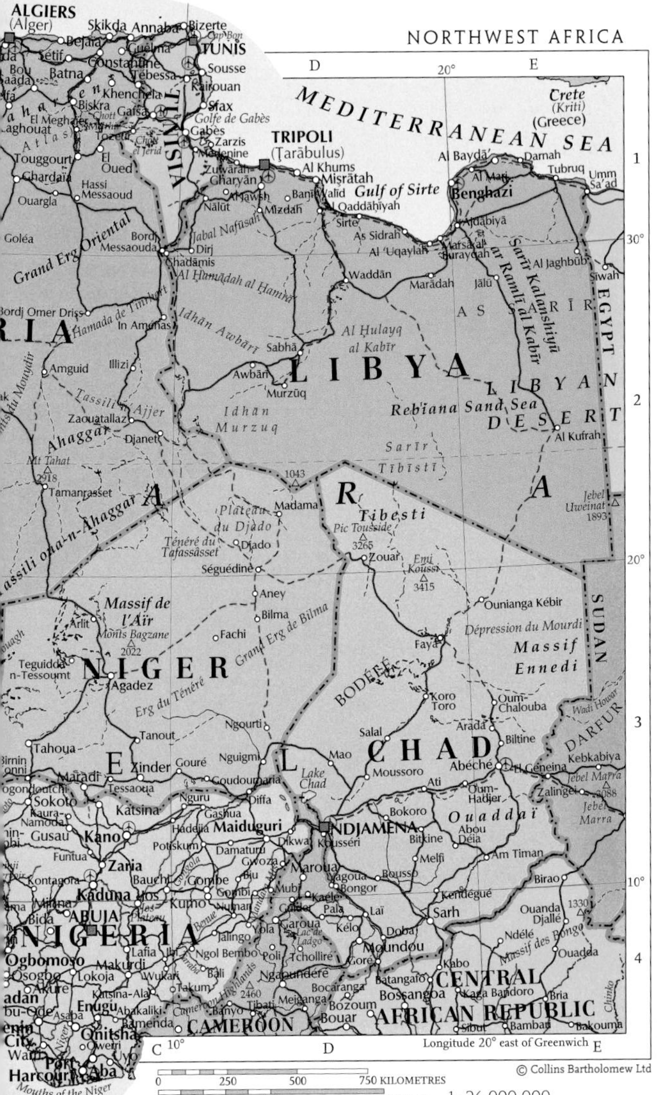

ALGIERS
(Alger)
Skikda Annaba Bizerte
Sétif Constantine Kroumire TUNIS
Bou Batna Guelma Tébessa Sousse
Khenchela Kairouan
El Meghri Biskra Gafsa Sfax
Touggourt Golfe de Gabès
Hassi Gabès
Ghardaïa Messaoud Zarzis
Ouargla Chott Djerid MEDITERRANEAN SEA
El Oued
Bordj Messaouda Nalūt TRIPOLI Al Khums Al Bayḍā' Darnah
Goléa Hassi Ḍirj (Ṭarābulus) Misrātah Crete
Grand Erg Oriental Ghadāmis Jabal Nafūsah Gharyān Banī Walīd Tubruq (Kriti)
Ghadāmis Mizdah Sirte Qaddāḥīyah As Sidrah Umm (Greece)
Hamadah de Tinrhert Gulf of Sirte Benghazi Sa'ad
Hamada al Hamra As Sidrah Al Marj
In Amenas Waddān Al 'Uqaylah Marsá al Al Jaghbūb
Al Ḥamādah al Ḥamrā' Ajdābiyā Burayqah
Amguid Marādah Jālū Siwah
Tassili-n'Ajjer Al Ḥulayq Sarīr Kalanshiyū
Illizi al Kabīr Sarīr Rimāl al Kabīr
Zaouatallaz Sabhā LIBYA Rebiana Sand Sea DESERT
Ahaggar Djanet Awbārī LIBYAN
Mt Tahat Murzūq Sarīr Al Kufrah
Tamanrasset Idhān Tibistī
Tassili oua-n-Ahaggar Murzuq 1043 Jebel
Madama Uweinat
Plateau du Djado Tibesti 1893
Séguédine Pic Toussidé SUDAN
Massif de Zouar 3265
l'Aïr Djado Emi
Monts Bagzane Aney Koussi Ounianga Kébir
Arlit 2022 Bilma 3415 Dépression du Mourdi
Teguidda Fachi Massif
n-Tessoumt Grand Erg de Bilma Faya Ennedi
Agadez BODÉLÉ Koro Oum-
Erg du Ténéré Toro Chalouba
Tanout Ngourti Arada Biltine Kebkabiya
Tahoua Zinder Gouré Salal Mao CHAD Abéché El Geneina Jebel Marra
NIGER Ngigmi Moussoro Oum- Zalingei 3088
Maradi Tessaoua Coudoumaria Ati Hadjer Jebel Marra
Nguru Diffa Lake Bokoro Ouaddaï Abou Am Timan
Gusau Katsina Gashua Chad Deïa
Kano Hadejia Maiduguri NDJAMENA Dikwa Melfi Birao 1330
Zaria Potiskum Damaturu Kousséri Bitkine Ounda
Bauchi Gombe Biu Maroua Massakory Bousso Kendégué Djalle
Kaduna Jos Kumo Gwoza Bongor Am Dam Massif des Bongo
ABUJA Gombi Mubi Kélo Lai Ouadda
NIGERIA Lafia Ngol Bembo Mora Doba Sarh Ndélé
Ogbomosho Makurdi Garoua Pala Moundou CENTRAL
Osogbo Lokoja Wukari Jalingo Tcholliré Batangafo
Akure Takum Béli Ngaoundéré Bocaranga Bossangoa AFRICAN REPUBLIC
Bali Meiganga Bozoum Bouar
CAMEROON Bouar Bozoum Bambari
Onitsha Bamenda Tibati Bambari Sibut Bambam
Owerri CAMEROON Tibati
Port Mouths of the Niger

1043
Tibesti
Pic Toussidé 3265
Emi Koussi 3415

Madama
Plateau du Djado
Ténéré du Tafassasset

1: 26 000 000

© Collins Bartholomew Ltd

Longitude 20° east of Greenwich

0 250 500 750 KILOMETRES
0 250 500 MILES

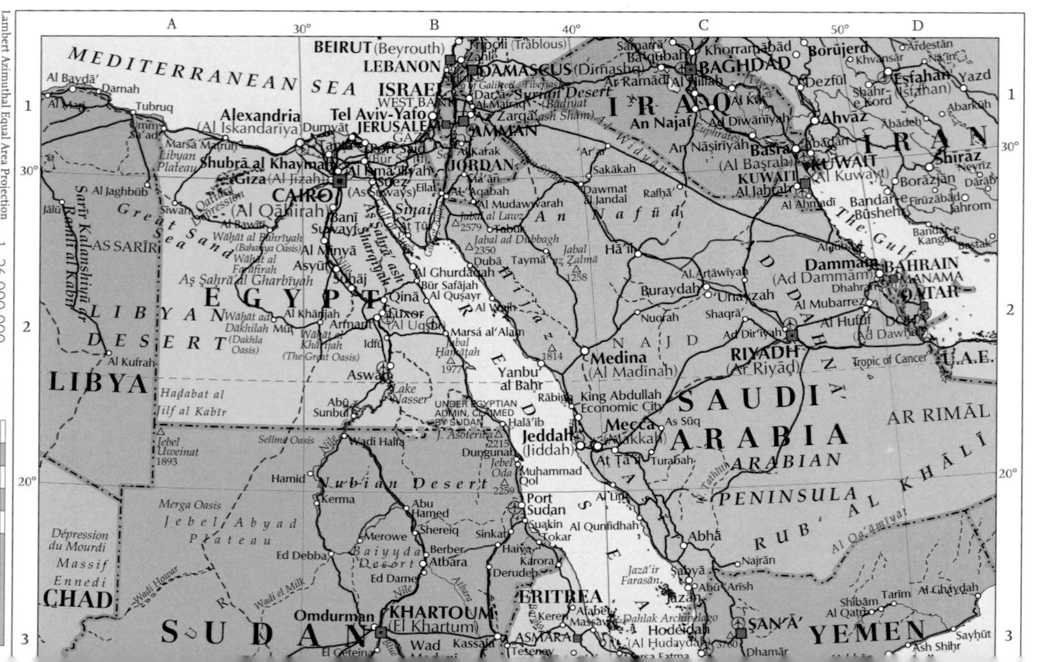

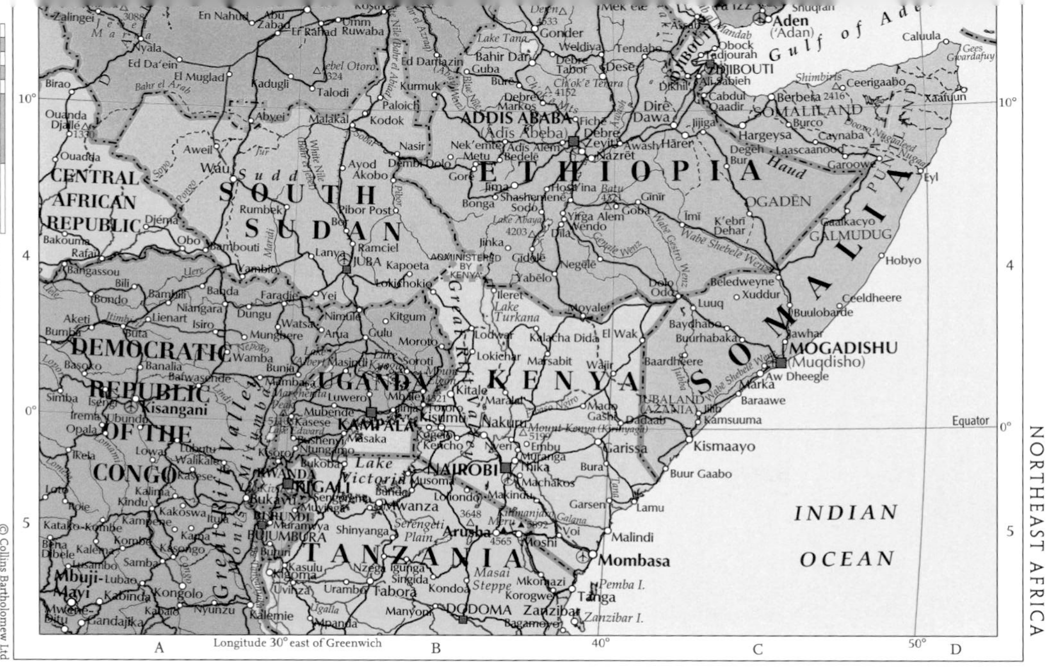

© Collins Bartholomew Ltd

0   250   500   750 KILOMETRES

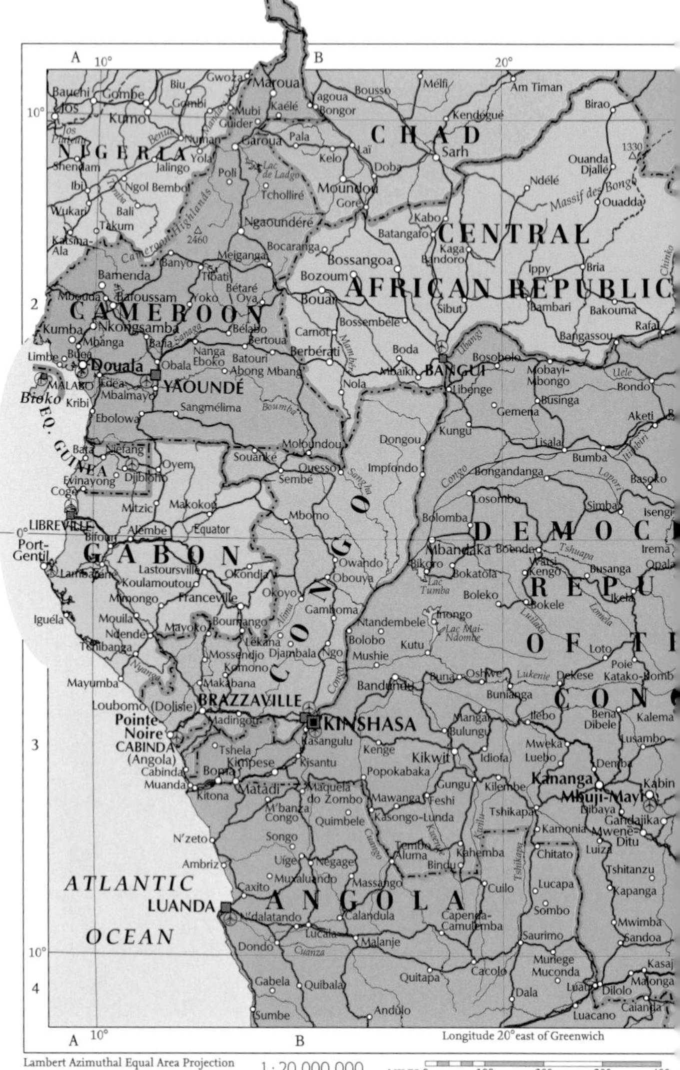

A 10° B 20°

Los Jos Gombe Biu Gwoza Maroua Bousso Mélfi Am Timan
Bauchi Gombe Mubi Kaélé Bongor Kendegue Birao
Kumo Guider Pala Sarh Ouanda 1330
NIGERIA Yola Garoua Kelo Djallé
Shendam Poli Doba Ndélé Bongo Ouadda
Ngol Bembol Tcholliré Gore Kabo Massif des CENTRAL
Wukari Takum Bali Ngaoundéré Bocaranga Batangafo Kaga Ippy Bria
Bamenda Banyo Yoko Meiganga Bandoro AFRICAN REPUBLIC
Mbouda Bafoussam Bétaré Bozoum Bambari Bakouma
Bafia Oya Bouar Sibut Rafaï
CAMEROON Belabo Bertoua Carnot Bossembele Bangassou
Kumba Nkongsamba Nanga Eboko Berbérati Boda Bosobolo Uele
Limbe Buea Mbanga Obala Batouri Bangui Mobayi- Bondo
MALABO Douala Abong Mbang Nola Mbongo Businga Aketi
Bata Mbalmayo YAOUNDÉ Ngbenge Gemena Lisala
EQ. GUINEA Ebolowa Sangmélima Dongou Kungu Bumba
Bioko Kribi Moloundou Impfondo Bongandanga Basoko Simba
Nkan Oyem Souanké Owesso Losombo DEMOC
Mitzic Djibloho Sembé CONGO Bolomba REPU
Cogo Makokou Mbomo Mbandaka Boende OF T
LIBREVILLE Alembe Equator Bokatola Irema
Port- GABON Lastoursville Okondja Owando Bikoro Ikela
Gentil Koulamoutou Obouaya Boleko Bokele Loto CON
Mouila Franceville Okoyo Lac Ntandembele Mushie Poie
Lambaréné Mayoko Boumango Bolobo Kutu Dekese Katako-Bomb
Iguéla Ndendé Zanaga Tekana Djambala Bandundu Lukenie Lusambo
Tshibanga Komono Mossendjo Makaba BRAZZAVILLE KINSHASA Ilebo Benal Kalema
Mayumba Loubomo (Dolisie) Madingou Kikwit Dibele
Pointe- Tshela Kimpese Yasangulu Idiofa Mweka Lueba Demba
Noire Risantu Popokabaka Kenge Kilembe Kananga Kabin
CABINDA Muanda Matadi Mbanza- Gungu Feshi Tshikapa Kamonia Gandajika
(Angola) Kitona Congo Mawanga-Lunda Kasongo-Lunda Mbuji-Mayi
N'zeto Songo Uige Negage Tembo Kahemba Chitato Ditu
Ambriz Mucaba Aluma Bindu Cuilo Luiza Kapanga
ATLANTIC Caxito Massango Tshitanzu
LUANDA Muxaluando Calandula Sombo Mwimba
OCEAN N'dalatando Lucapa Saurimo Sandoa
Dondo Malanje Kasaj
Gabela Quibala Cacolo Dala Dilolo Matonga
Quitapa Munege Calanha
Sumbe Andulo Muconda Luacano

Longitude 20° east of Greenwich

A 10° B

118 Lambert Azimuthal Equal Area Projection 1 : 20 000 000 MILES 0 100 200 300 400

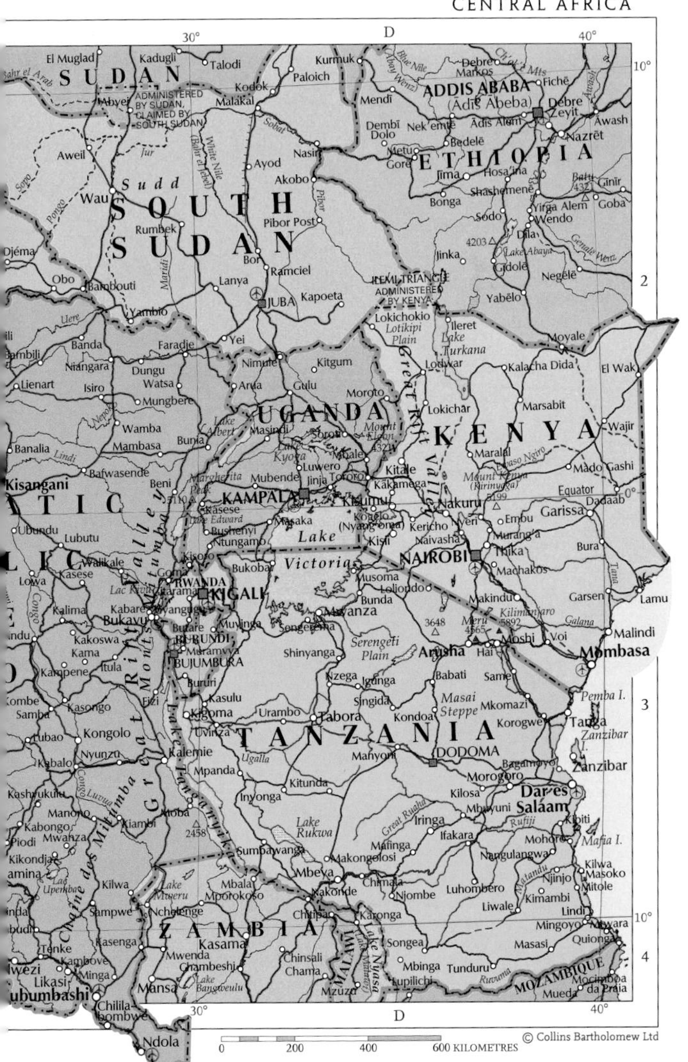

0   200   400   600 KILOMETRES

© Collins Bartholomew Ltd

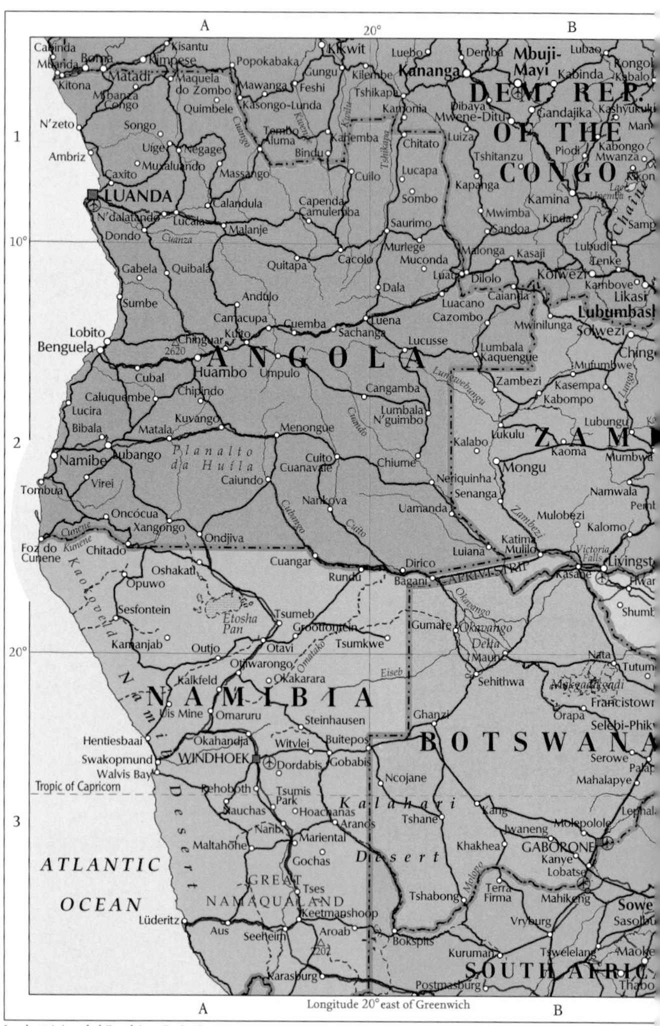

Lambert Azimuthal Equal Area Projection   1 : 20 000 000   MILES 0   100   200   300   400

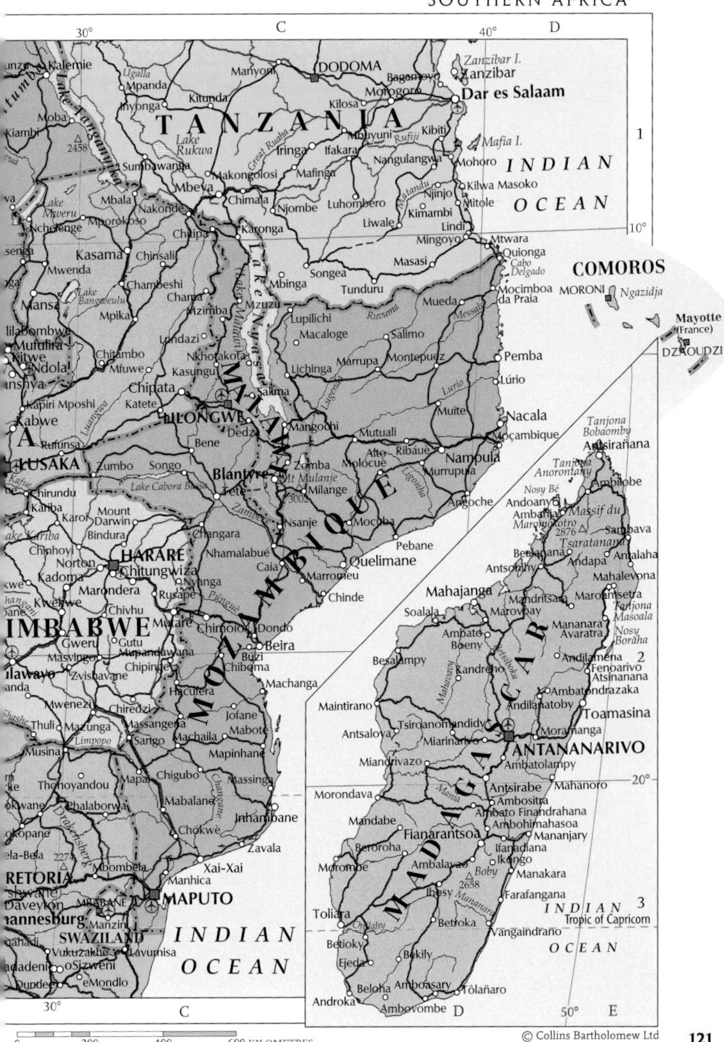

© Collins Bartholomew Ltd

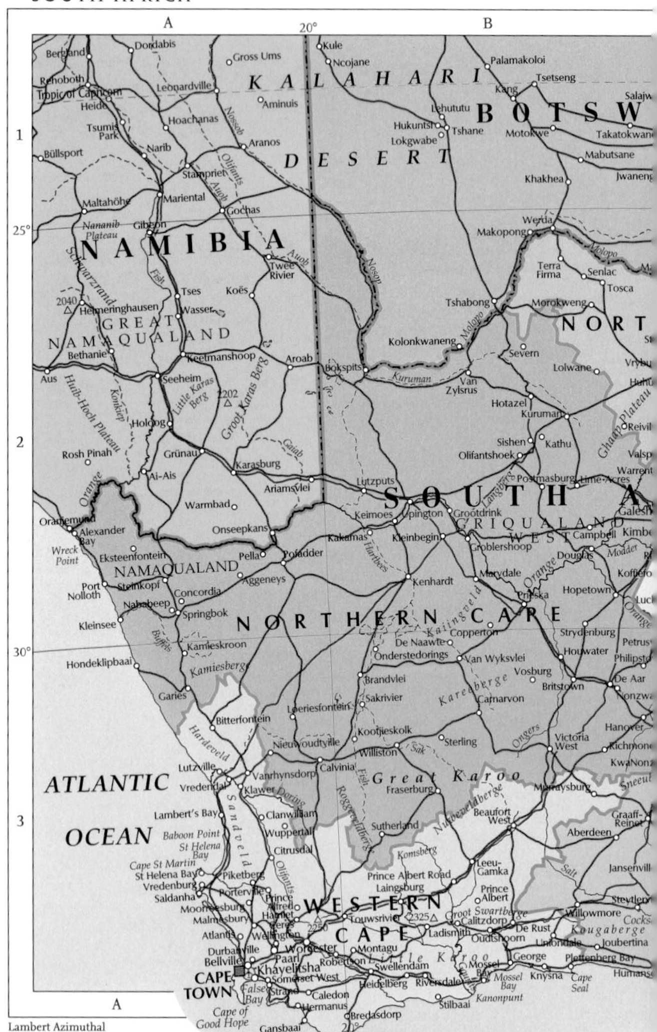

Lambert Azimuthal
Equal Area Projection

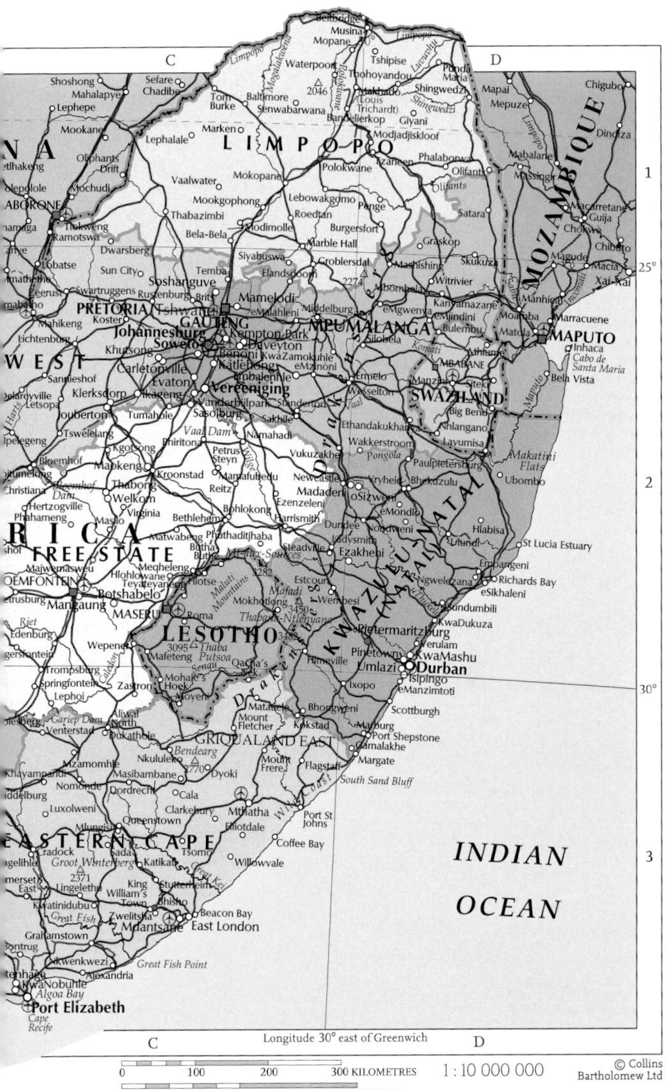

INDIAN

OCEAN

Longitude 30° east of Greenwich

0   100   200   300 KILOMETRES   1 : 10 000 000

0   100   200 MILES

© Collins
Bartholomew Ltd

123

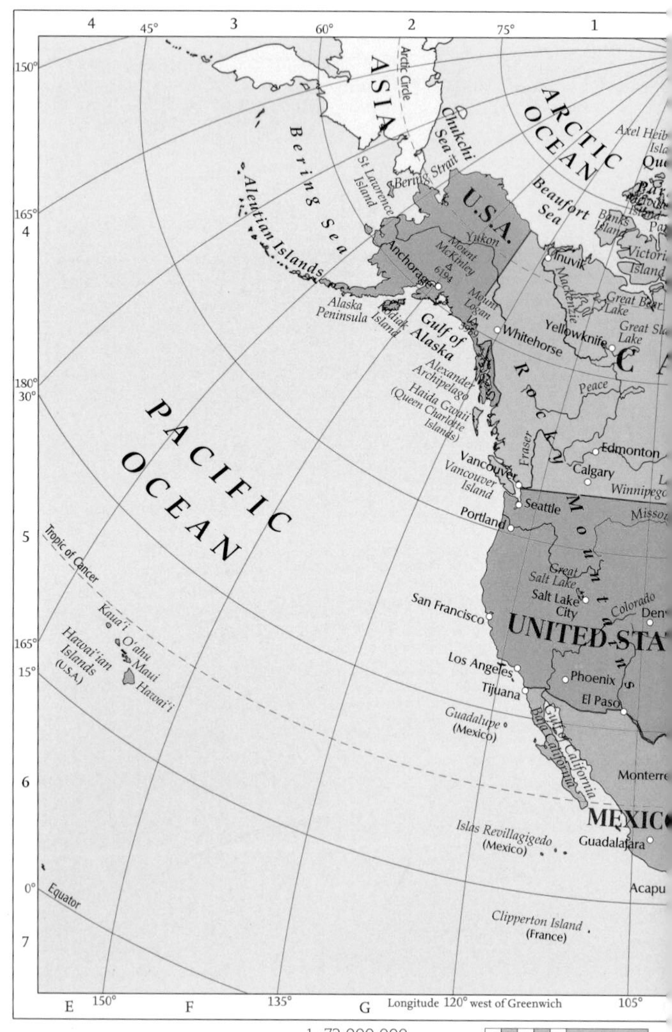

1 : 72 000 000   MILES 0   500   1000

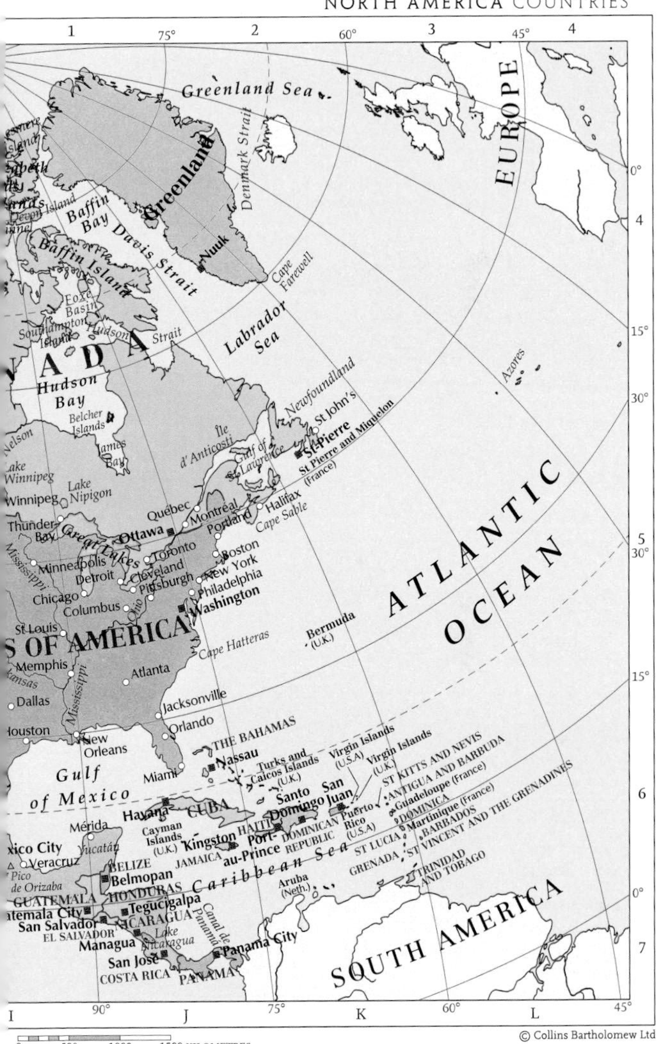

Greenland Sea

EUROPE

Greenland

Denmark Strait

Baffin
Bay

Baffin Island

Davis Strait

Nuuk

Cape Farewell

0°

Foxe
Basin

Southampton Island

Hudson Strait

Labrador
Sea

CANADA

Hudson
Bay

Belcher Islands

James Bay

Newfoundland

Azores

St John's

Ile d'Anticosti

Gulf of St Lawrence

St-Pierre and Miquelon (France)

ATLANTIC

Lake Winnipeg

Winnipeg

Lake Nipigon

Québec

Montréal

Thunder Bay

Great Lakes

Ottawa

Toronto

Halifax

Portland

Cape Sable

Minneapolis

Detroit

Cleveland

Boston

Chicago

Pittsburgh

New York

Columbus

Philadelphia

Washington

OCEAN

St Louis

UNITED STATES OF AMERICA

Cape Hatteras

Bermuda (U.K.)

Memphis

Atlanta

Kansas

Dallas

Jacksonville

Houston

Orlando

New Orleans

THE BAHAMAS

Nassau

Virgin Islands

Virgin Islands (U.S.A.)

Gulf
of Mexico

Miami

Turks and Caicos Islands (U.K.)

ST KITTS AND NEVIS

ANTIGUA AND BARBUDA

CUBA

Havana

Santo Domingo

San Juan

Guadeloupe (France)

Mérida

Cayman Islands (U.K.)

Kingston

HAITI

Puerto Rico (U.S.A.)

DOMINICA

México City

Veracruz

Yucatán

JAMAICA

DOMINICAN REPUBLIC

Port-au-Prince

Martinique (France)

ST LUCIA

BARBADOS

Pico de Orizaba

BELIZE

Belmopan

Caribbean Sea

Aruba (Neth.)

GRENADA

ST VINCENT AND THE GRENADINES

GUATEMALA

HONDURAS

Tegucigalpa

TRINIDAD AND TOBAGO

Guatemala City

NICARAGUA

Lake Nicaragua

Canal de Panamá

EL SALVADOR

Managua

San José

Panama City

COSTA RICA

PANAMA

SOUTH AMERICA

0   500   1000   1500 KILOMETRES

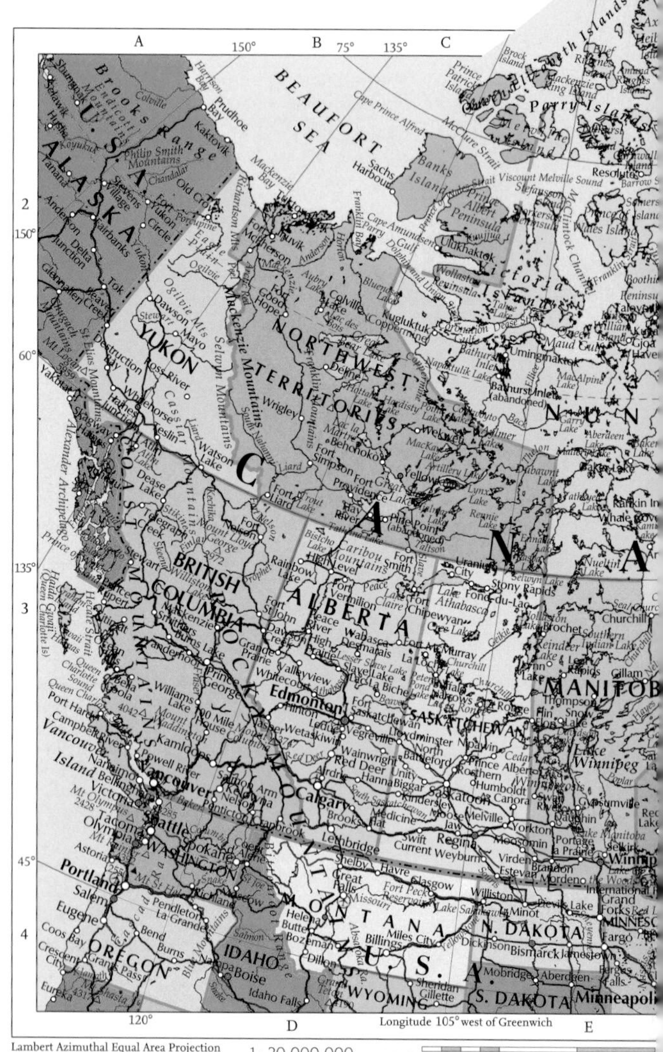

Lambert Azimuthal Equal Area Projection   1 : 30 000 000   MILES 0   200   400   60

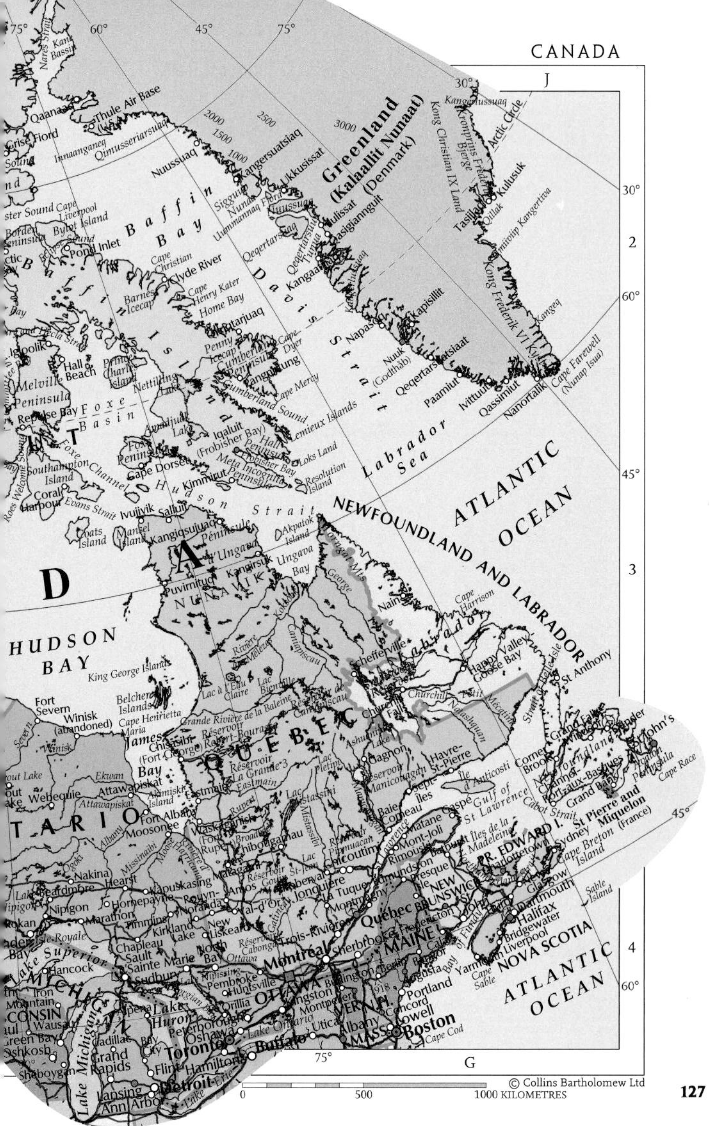

CANADA

Narwhal Kane
Qaanaaq Basin
Thule Air Base
Tuanangneq
Qimussertarsuaq

Cristol Fiord
Nuussuaq

Greenland
(Kalaallit Nunaat)
(Denmark)

Kangerlussuaq
Arctic Circle

Baffin
Bay

Sigguk
Qeqertarsuaq
Nuussuatsiaq
Ikusissat

Kong Christian IX Land

Tasiilaq
Kulusuk

Ittoqqortoormiit Kangertittivaq

Kangaatsiaq
Sisimiut

Aasiaat

Kong Frederik VI Kyst

Cape Christian
Clyde River
Home Bay

Penny Ice
Cap

Napasoq

Qasigiannguit

Kangerlussuaq

Kangeq

Barnes
Icecap
Cape Henry Kater

Nuuk
(Godthåb)

Maniitsoq

Paamiut

Ivittuut

Qaqortoq
Qassimiut

Nanortalik

Cape Farewell
(Nunap Isua)

Pangnirtung

Qeqertarsuatsiaq

Davis
Strait

Cumberland
Sound

Labrador
Sea

ATLANTIC
OCEAN

Cape
Dorset

Iqaluit
(Frobisher Bay)

Meta Incognita
Peninsula

Lemieux Islands

Cape
Mercy

Resolution
Island

Lake Harbour
Kimmirut

Big Island

NEWFOUNDLAND AND LABRADOR

Hudson Strait

Foxe
Channel

Coral
Harbour

Southampton
Island

Coats
Island

Evans Strait

Mansel
Island

Ivujivik

Akpatok
Island

Ungava
Bay

Cape
Harrison

D

HUDSON
BAY

King George Islands

Belcher
Islands

Puvirnituq

Kangiqsujuaq

Kangiqsualujjuaq

Schefferville

Happy Valley-
Goose Bay

St Anthony

Fort
Severn

Cape Henrietta
Maria

Inukjuak

Grande Rivière de la Baleine

Réservoir de
Caniapiscau

Churchill

Winisk
(abandoned)

JAMES
BAY

Lac à l'Eau
Claire

QUÉBEC

Lac
Bienville

Manicouagan

Gulf of
St Lawrence

Grand Bank

Cape Race

St. John's

Trout Lake

Webequie

Fort
George

Eastmain

Grande 2

Réservoir
de La Grande 3

Réservoir
Gouin

Baie-
Comeau

Anticosti
Island

Cabot Strait

Sable
Island

ONTARIO

Fort Albany

Moosonee

Attawapiskat

Kapiskau

Rupert

Matagami

Chisasibi

Mistassini

Lac
Mistassini

Lac St-Jean

Chicoutimi

Havre-
St-Pierre

Îles de la
Madeleine

CAPE BRETON I.

Sydney

Lake Superior

Nakina

Hearst

Kapuskasing

Cochrane

Kirkland
Lake

La Tuque

Trois-Rivières

Québec

P. EDWARD I.

Miquelon
(France)

NOVA SCOTIA

ATLANTIC
OCEAN

Nipigon

Marathon

Sault
Sainte Marie

North
Bay

Sudbury

Ottawa

Montréal

Sherbrooke

NEW
BRUNSWICK

MAINE

Fredericton

Saint John

Halifax

Bridgewater

Yarmouth

Liverpool

WISCONSIN

Wausau

Iron
Mountain

Oshkosh

Sheboygan

Grand
Rapids

Lansing

Ann Arbor

Lake Michigan

Green
Bay

Lake Huron

Orillia

Barrie

Peterborough

Kingston

Utica

VERMONT

N.H.

Portland

MASS.

Boston

Cape Cod

Toronto

Buffalo

Flint

Detroit

Hamilton

Lake Erie

Lake Ontario

Oswego

Syracuse

Lowell

© Collins Bartholomew Ltd

127

0   500   1000 KILOMETRES

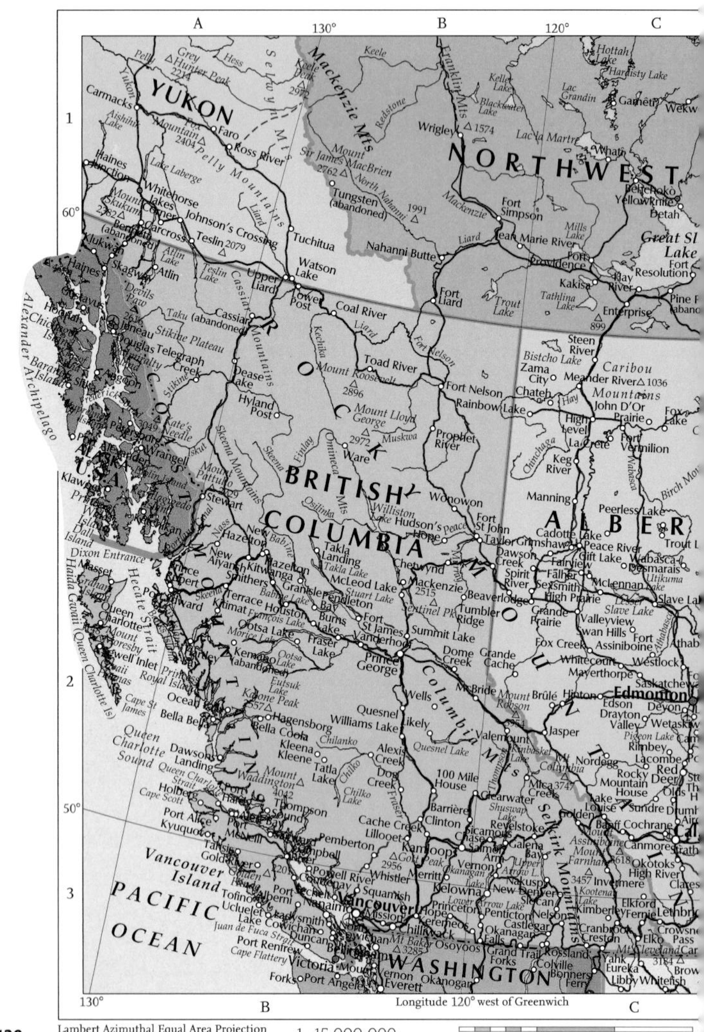

1 : 15 000 000

MILES 0   100   200   300

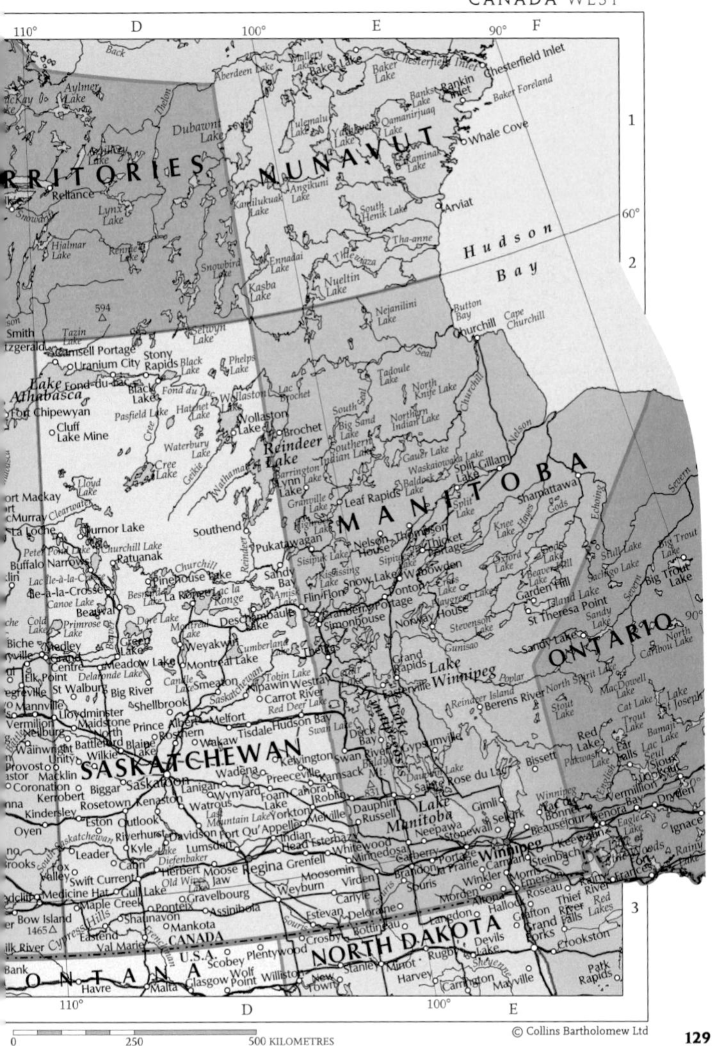

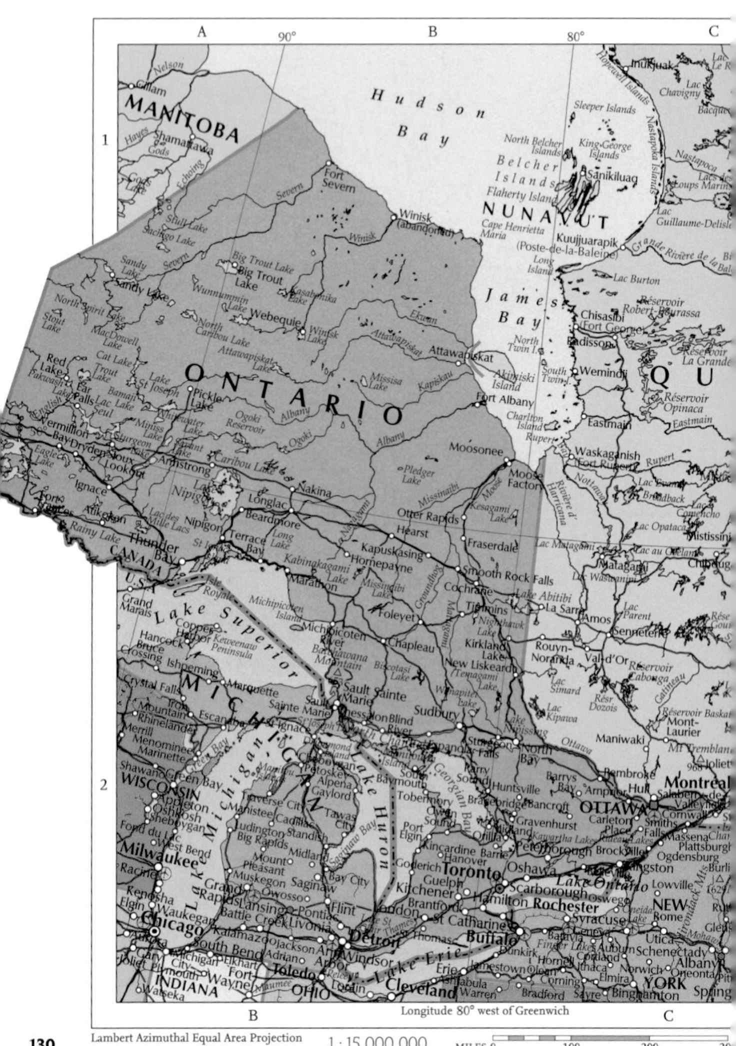

Lambert Azimuthal Equal Area Projection
1 : 15 000 000
MILES 0   100   200   30

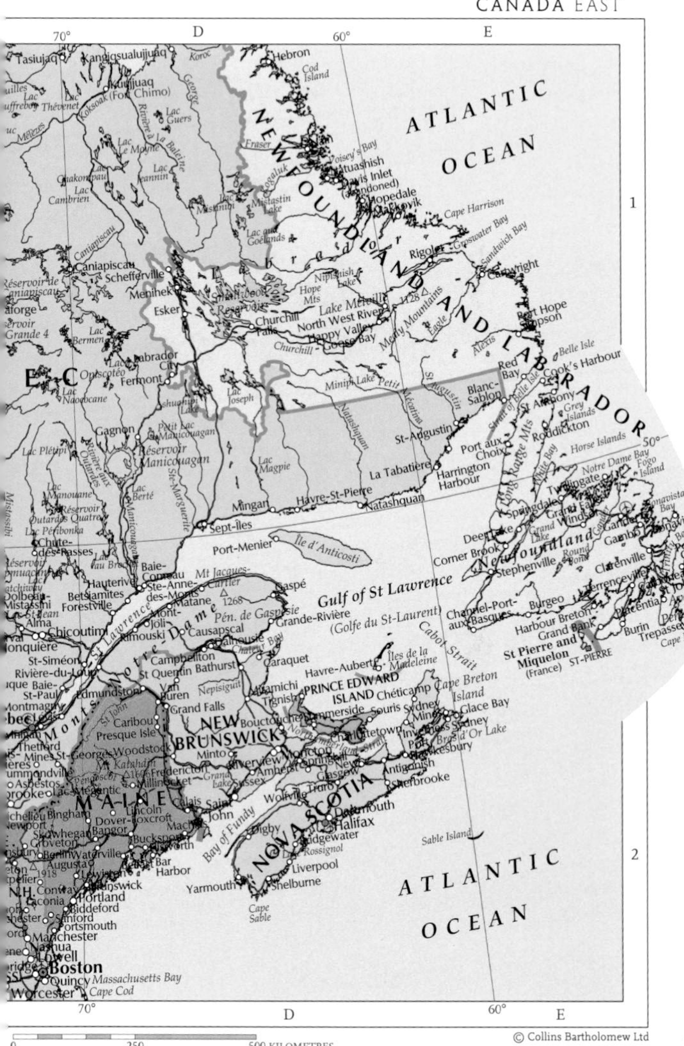

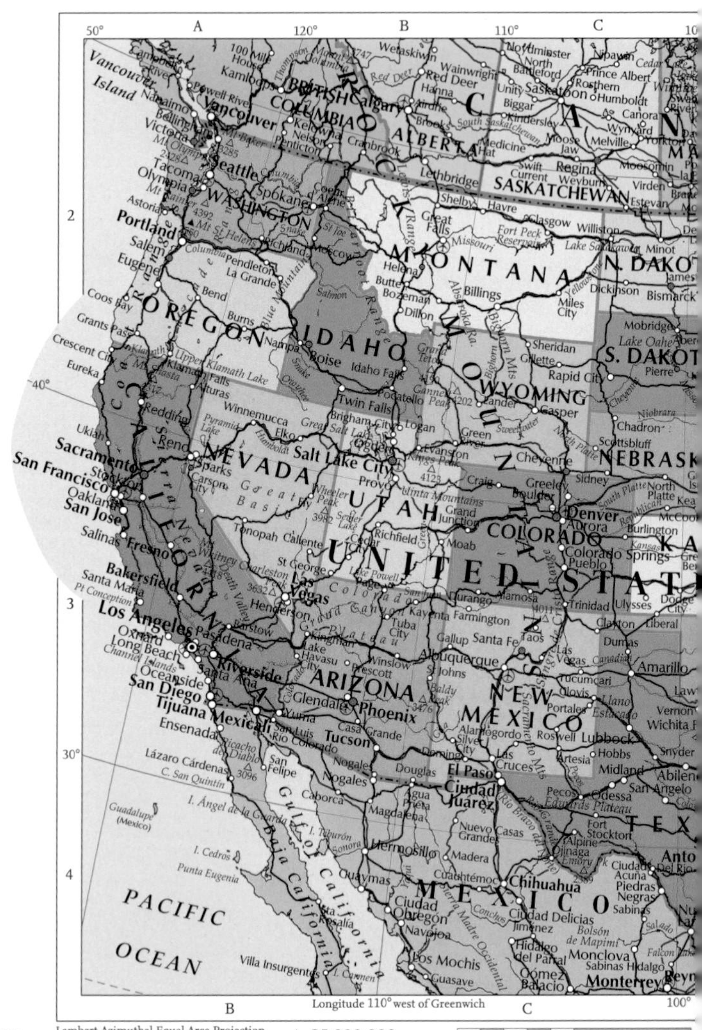

Lambert Azimuthal Equal Area Projection   1 : 25 000 000   MILES 0   250   500

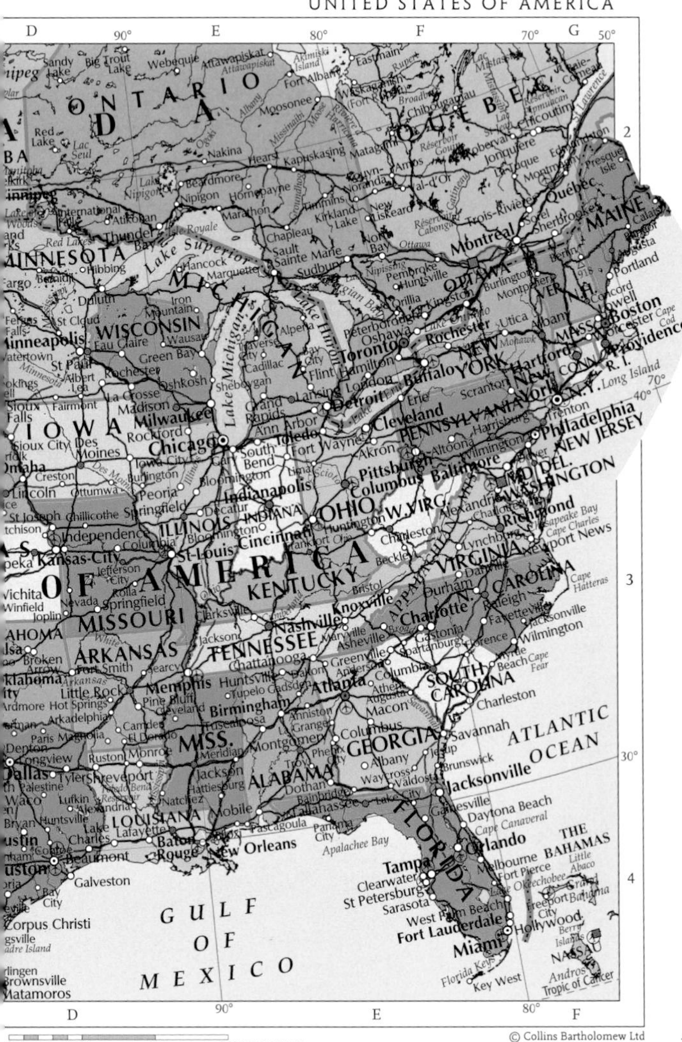

© Collins Bartholomew Ltd

0   250   500   750 KILOMETRES

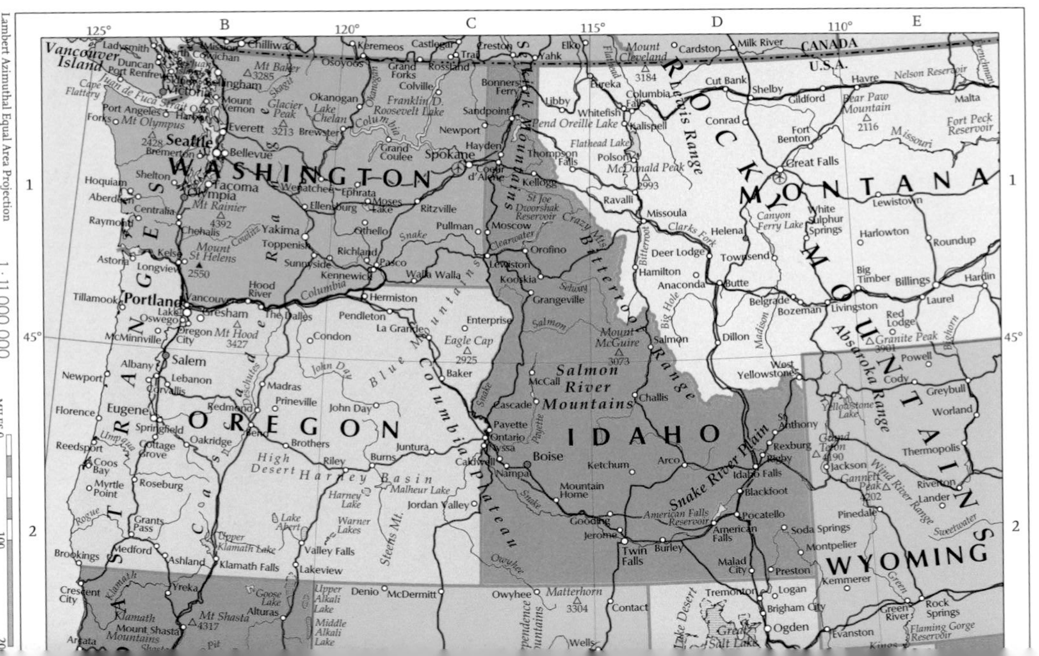

Lambert Azimuthal Equal Area Projection   1 : 11 000 000   MILES 0   100   200

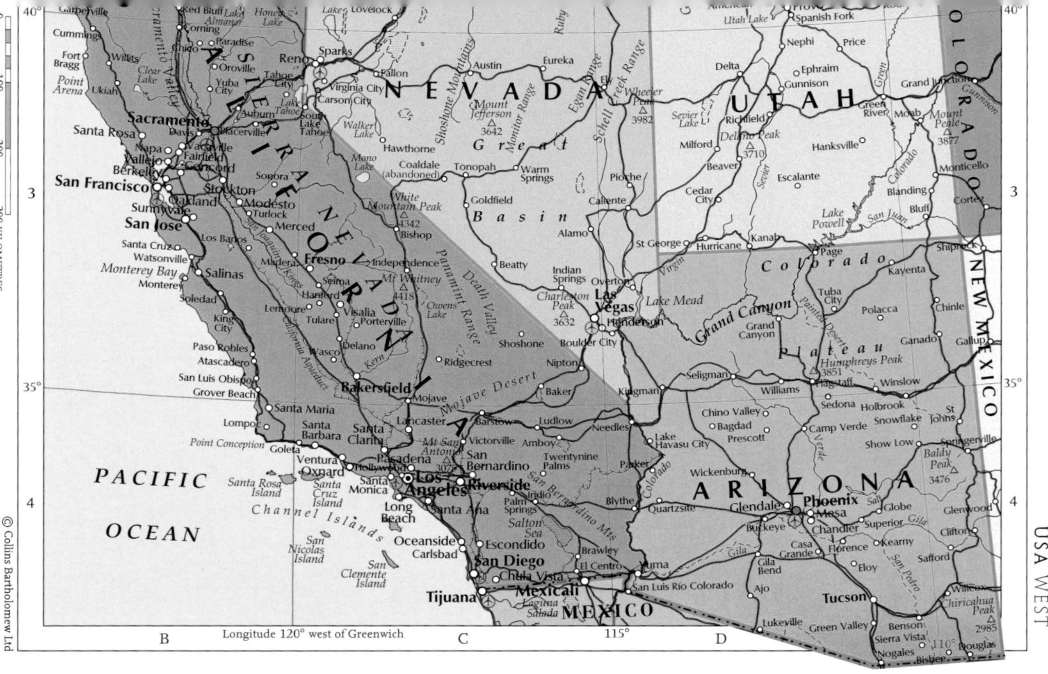

0   100   200   300 KILOMETRES

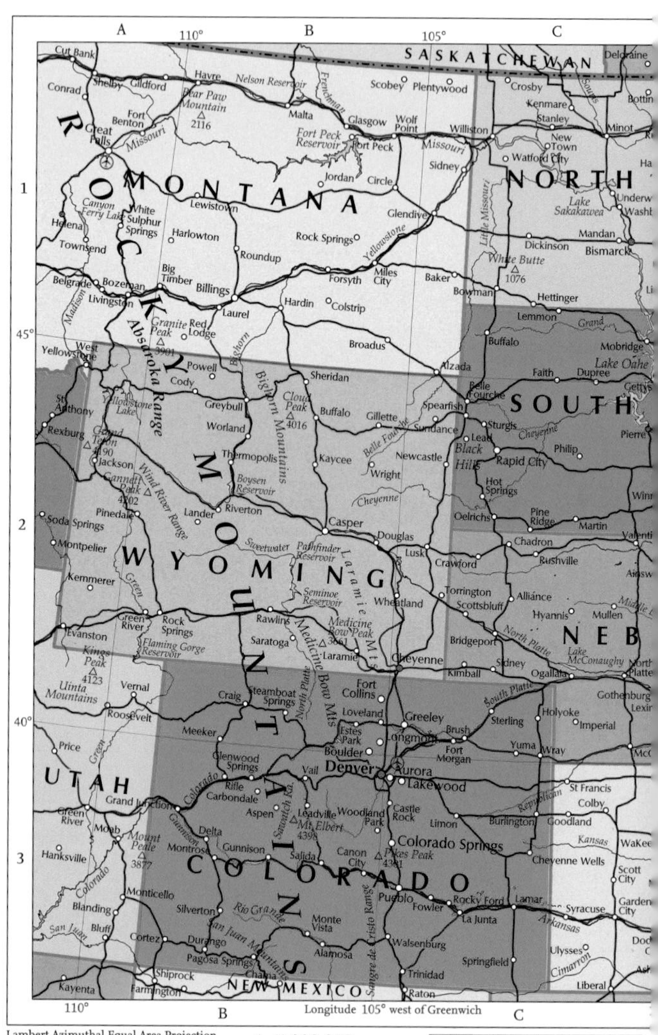

A   110°   B   105°   C

SASKATCHEWAN

Deloraine
Cut Bank
Conrad Shelby Gildford Havre Nelson Reservoir Scobey Plentywood Crosby Kenmare Bottin
Fort Bear Paw Malta Glasgow Wolf Williston Stanley New Minot
Great Benton Mountain Fort Peck Point Watford Town Underwi
Falls 2116 Reservoir Fort Peck Sidney City Lake Washt
Missouri Jordan Circle Missouri Sakakawea

R O C K Y   M O N T A N A   N O R T H

1

Canyon White Lewistown Glendive Dickinson Mandan
Ferry Lake Sulphur Harlowton Rock Springs Yellowstone Baker White Butte Bismarck
Helena Springs Roundup Forsyth Miles 1076 Hettinger
Townsend Big Billings Hardin City Bowman Lemmon
Belgrade Timber Laurel Colstrip Alzada Buffalo Grand Mobridge
Livingston Red Broadus Belle Faith Dupree Gettys
45° Lodge Sheridan Fourche Lake Oahe
Yellowst West Cody Clouds Buffalo Spearfish Sturgis S O U T H
Anthony Yellowstone Greybull Peak Gillette Sundance Leat Black Rapid City Philip Pierre
Rexburg Lake Worland 4016 Kaycee Newcastle Hills Hot
Jackson Thermopolis Wright Cheyenne Springs Pine Winn
Boysen Ridge Martin
Pinedale Lander Riverton Casper Douglas Lusk Oelrichs Chadron Rushville Valenti
Soda Springs Sweetwater Crawford Ainsw
2 Montpelier W Y O M I N G Pathfinder Torrington Alliance NEB
Kemmerer Reservoir Seminoe Wheatland Scottsbluff Hyannis Mullen
Green Reservoir Bridgeport North Platte Lake
Evanston Rock Rawlins Medicine Cheyenne Sidney Ogallala McConaughy Platte
Springs Saratoga Bow Peak Laramie Kimball South Platte Gothenburg Lexir
Flaming Gorge Fort Sterling Holyoke Imperial McCo
Uinta Reservoir Collins Greeley Brush Yuma Wray
Mountains Vernal Craig Steamboat Loveland Longmont Fort St Francis
Price Roosevelt Springs Estes Morgan Burlington Goodland Colby WaKee
Meeker Park Boulder Denver Limon Kansas
40° Glenwood Rifle Aurora Castle McC
Green Springs Lakewood Rock Scott
River Moab Grand Junction Carbondale Leadville Woodland Colorado Springs Cheyenne Wells City
U T A H Aspen Mt Elbert Park Pikes Peak Garde
Delta 4399 4341 Rocky Ford Syracuse City
Hanksville Montrose Gunnison Salida Canon Pueblo Lamar
3 C O L O R A D O City Fowler La Junta Dod
Monticello Silverton Rio Grande Ulysses C
Blanding San Juan Mountains Monte Walsenburg
Bluff Durango Vista Alamosa Springfield Liberal
Cortez Pagosa Springs Trinidad Raton
Kayenta Shiprock Farmington N E W   M E X I C O

110° B Longitude 105° west of Greenwich C

136   Lambert Azimuthal Equal Area Projection   1 : 11 000 000   MILES 0   100   200

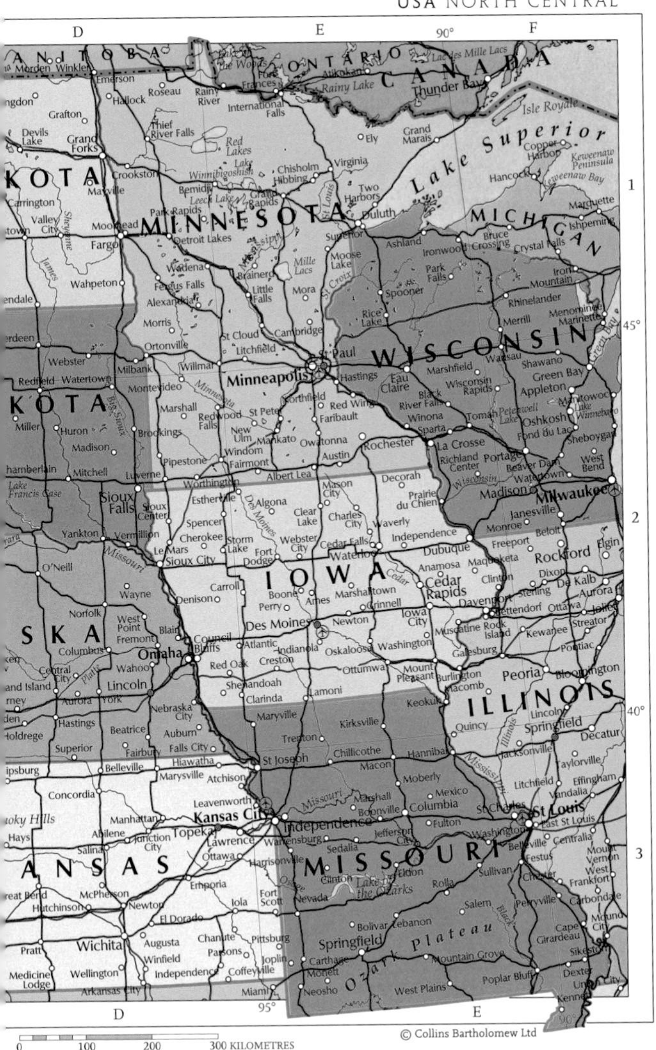

0   100   200   300 KILOMETRES

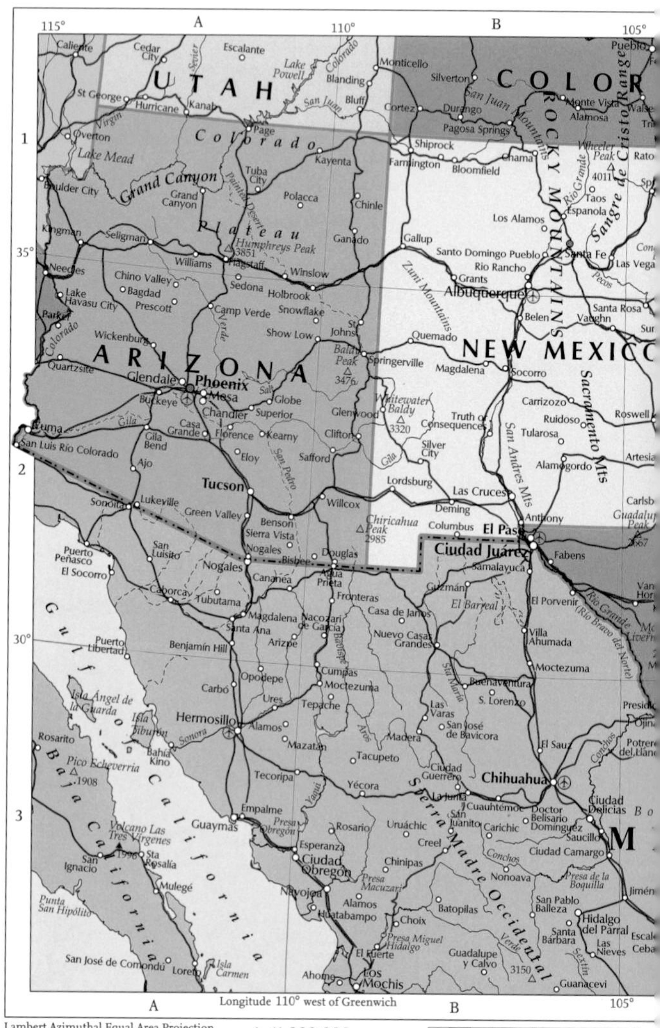

Lambert Azimuthal Equal Area Projection   1 : 11 000 000   MILES 0   100   200

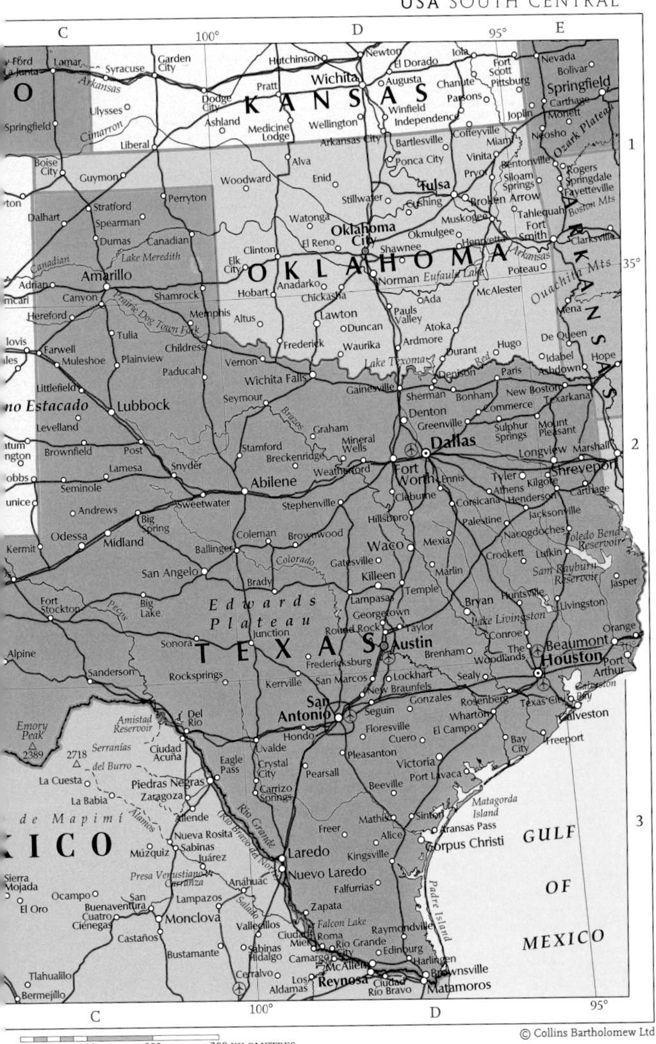

0   100   200   300 KILOMETRES

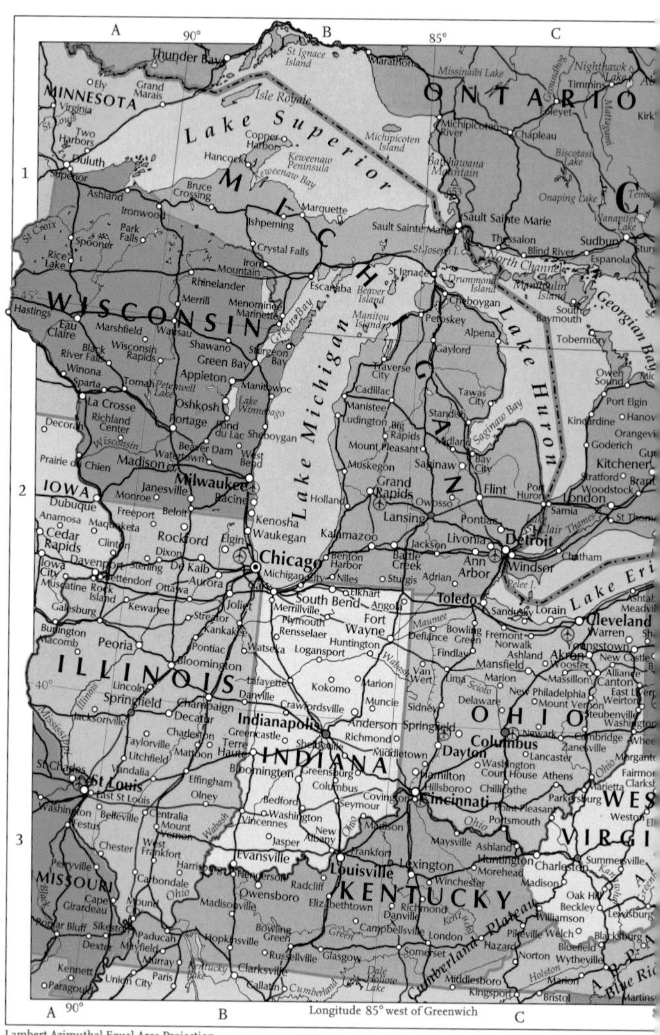

Lambert Azimuthal Equal Area Projection   1 : 11 000 000   MILES 0   100   200

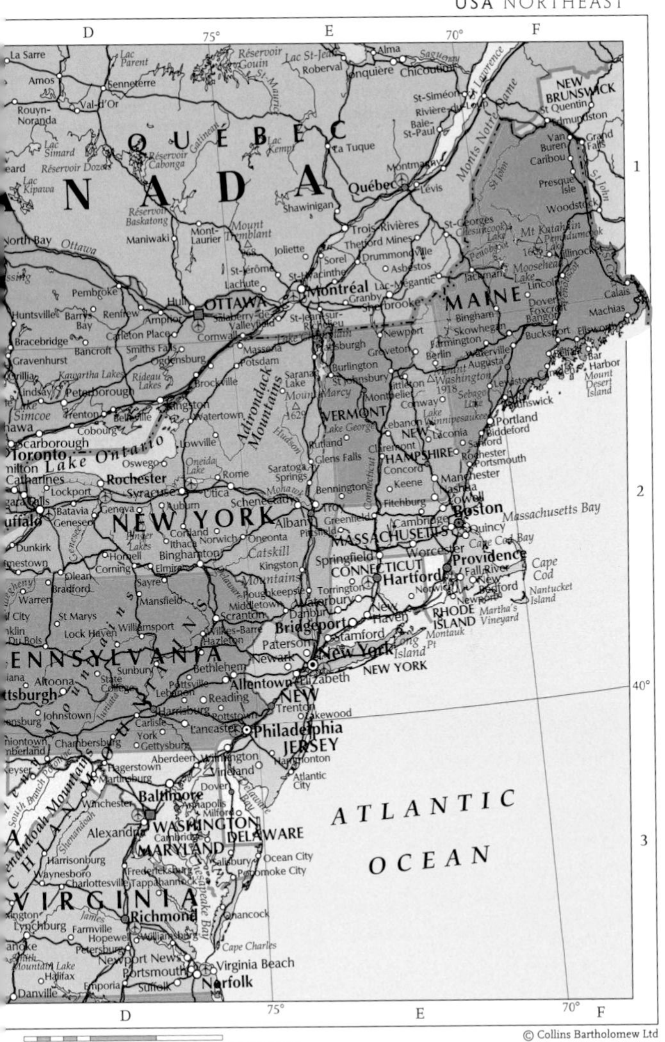

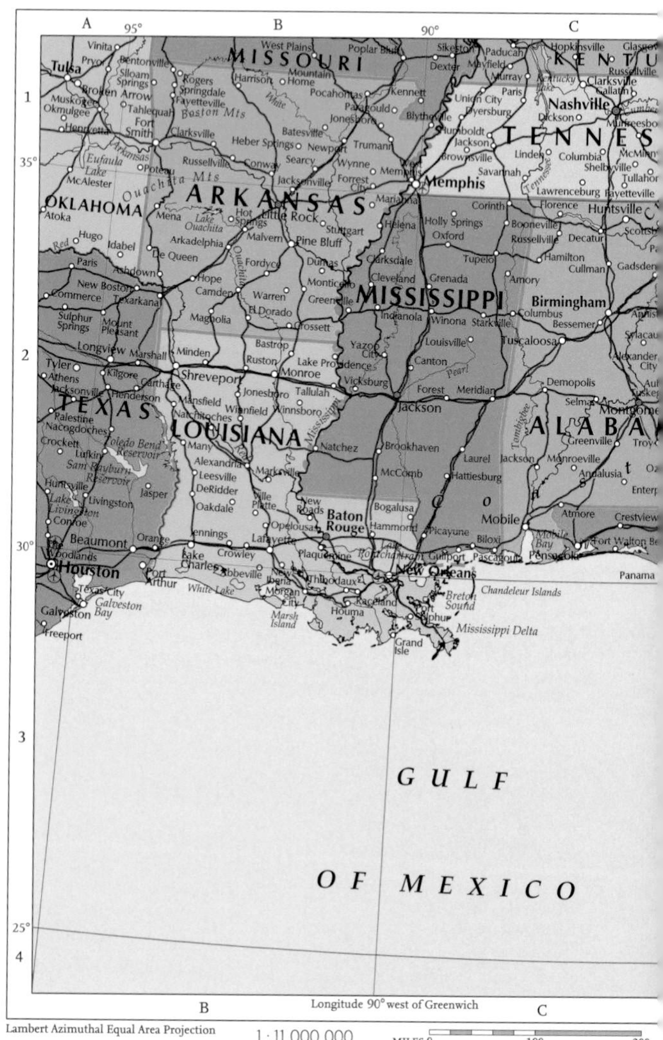

Lambert Azimuthal Equal Area Projection   1 : 11 000 000   MILES 0   100   200

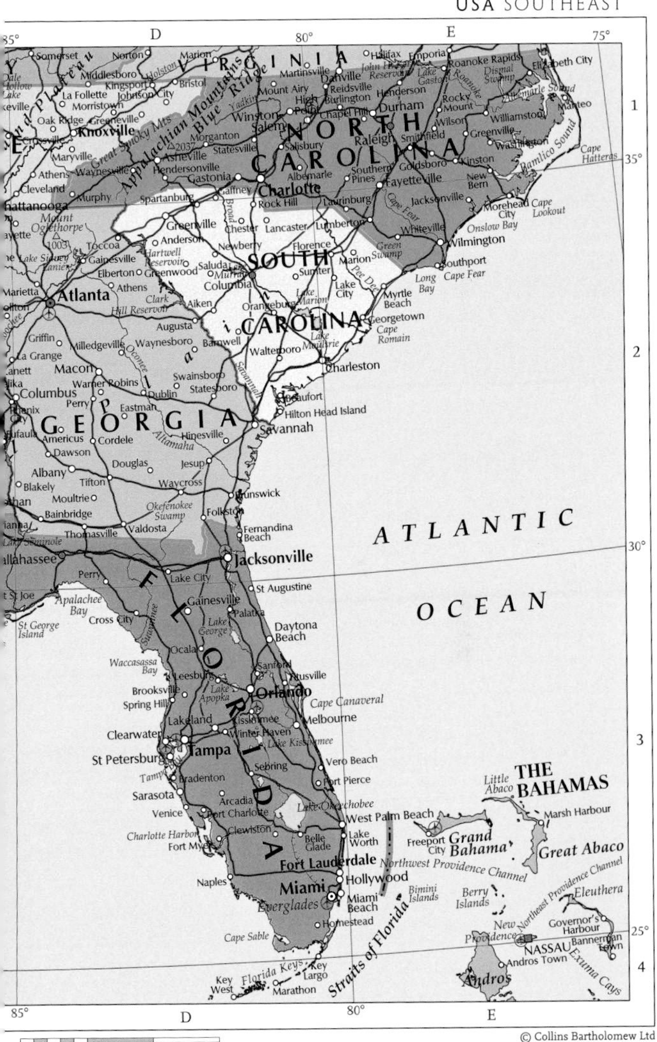

ATLANTIC OCEAN

THE BAHAMAS

© Collins Bartholomew Ltd

0   100   200   300 KILOMETRES

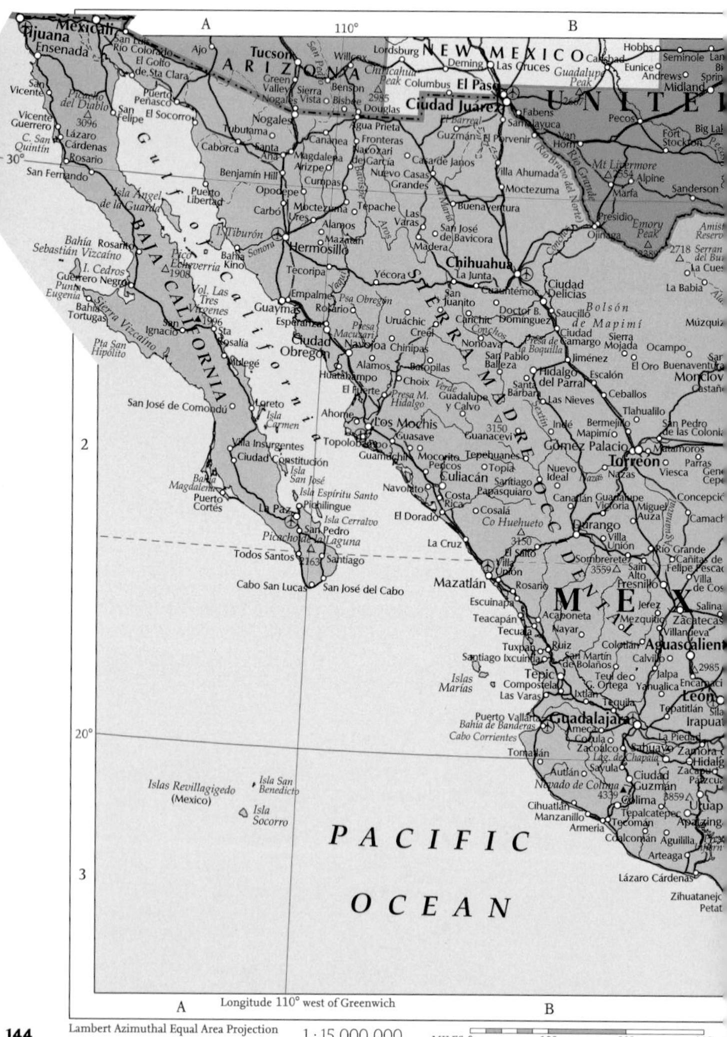

144

Lambert Azimuthal Equal Area Projection

1 : 15 000 000

MILES 0   100   200   300

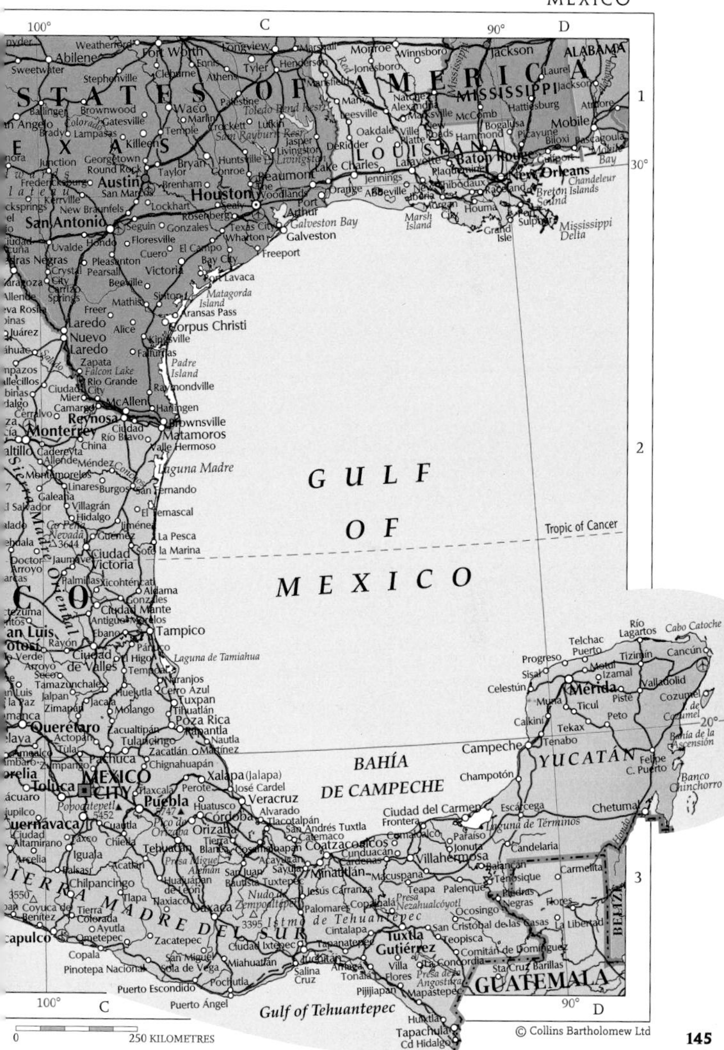

© Collins Bartholomew Ltd

GULF
OF
MEXICO
BAHÍA
DE CAMPECHE
Gulf of Tehuantepec
Tropic of Cancer
STATES OF AMERICA
TEXAS
LOUISIANA
MISSISSIPPI
ALABAMA
YUCATÁN
GUATEMALA
BELIZE
SIERRA MADRE DEL SUR
Istmo de Tehuantepec
Houston
San Antonio
Austin
Fort Worth
Abilene
Waco
Beaumont
Lake Charles
Baton Rouge
New Orleans
Jackson
Mobile
Galveston
Galveston Bay
Corpus Christi
Laredo
Nuevo Laredo
Brownsville
Matamoros
Reynosa
Monterrey
McAllen
Laguna Madre
Ciudad Victoria
Tampico
Laguna de Tamiahua
Tuxpan
Poza Rica
MEXICO CITY
Puebla
Veracruz
Xalapa (Jalapa)
Orizaba
Cuernavaca
Toluca
Querétaro
Oaxaca
Coatzacoalcos
Minatitlán
Villahermosa
Ciudad del Carmen
Laguna de Términos
Campeche
Mérida
Progreso
Cancún
Cozumel
Chetumal
Tuxtla Gutiérrez
Tapachula
Acapulco
Puerto Escondido
Puerto Ángel
Mississippi Delta
Chandeleur Islands
Matagorda Island
Padre Island
Marsh Island
Cabo Catoche
Banco Chinchorro
Bahía de la Ascensión
100°
90°
30°
20°
1
2
3
0
250 KILOMETRES

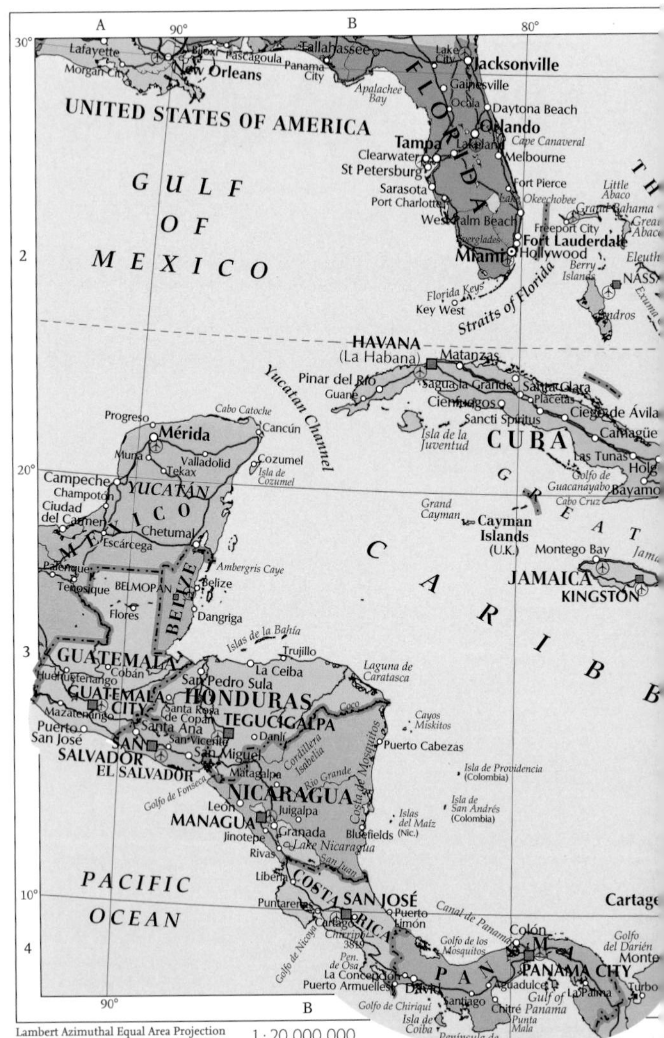

A 90° **B** 80°

30°

Lafayette
Morgan City
New Orleans · Biloxi · Pascagoula · Panama · Tallahassee · Lake · **Jacksonville**
City · City · Gainesville
Apalachee · Ocala · Daytona Beach

UNITED STATES OF AMERICA

G U L F
O F
M E X I C O

Apalachee Bay · Ocala · **Orlando**
Tampa Lakeland · Cape Canaveral
Clearwater · **Melbourne**
St Petersburg · Fort Pierce
Sarasota · Lake · Little
Port Charlotte · Okeechobee · Grand Bahama
West Palm Beach · Great
Everglades · Freeport City · Abaco
Miami · Hollywood · Berry · Eleuthe
Fort Lauderdale · Islands · NASS
Florida Keys · Ndros
Key West · **HAVANA** · Straits of Florida
(La Habana) · Matanzas
Pinar del Río · Sagua la Grande · Santa Clara
Guane · Cienfuegos · Placetas · Ciego de Ávila
Cabo Catoche · Sancti Spíritus · Camagüe
Progreso · Cancún · **CUBA** · Holg
Mérida · Cozumel · Las Tunas
Valladolid · Isla de · Guacanayabo · Bayamo
Motul · Tekax · Cozumel · Cabo Cruz
Campeche · **YUCATÁN**
Champotón · Grand · **Cayman** · Montego Bay · Jamo
Ciudad · **C O** · Cayman · **Islands**
del Carmen · Chetumal · (U.K.) · **JAMAICA**
Escárcega · **KINGSTON**
Palenque · Ambergris Caye · **C**
Tenosique · BELMOPAN · Belize · **A**
Flores · Dangriga · **R**
Islas de la Bahía · Trujillo · **I**
GUATEMALA · La Ceiba · Laguna de · **B**
Cobán · San Pedro Sula · Caratasca
Huehuetenango · **HONDURAS** · **B**
GUATEMALA · Santa Rosa · **TEGUCIGALPA**
CITY · de Copán · Santa Ana · Cayos
Mazatenango · San Vicente · Danlí · Miskitos
Puerto · San Miguel · Cordillera · Puerto Cabezas
San José · **SAN** · Matagalpa · Isabelia
SALVADOR · Río Grande · Isla de Providencia
EL SALVADOR · **NICARAGUA** · (Colombia)
Golfo de Fonseca · Costa de Mosquitos
León · Isla de
MANAGUA · Juigalpa · San Andrés
Jinotepe · Granada · Bluefields · (Colombia)
Rivas · Lake Nicaragua · Islas
del Maíz (Nic.)
Liberia · **COST** · **PACIFIC**
Puntarenas · **SAN JOSÉ** · **Canal de Panamá** · Cartage
OCEAN · Chirripó · Puerto · **Colón**
3891 · Limón · **M** · Golfo
La Concepción · Golfo de los · del Darién
Pen. · Mosquitos · **PANAMÁ CITY** · Monte
de Osa · Gulf of Panama · Turbo
Puerto Armuelles · David · **P A**
Santiago · Aguadulce · La Palma
Chitré · Panamá · Punta
Golfo de Chiriquí · Isla de · Mala
Coiba · Peninsula de · 80°
Azuero

20°

2

3

10°

4

90° **B** 80°

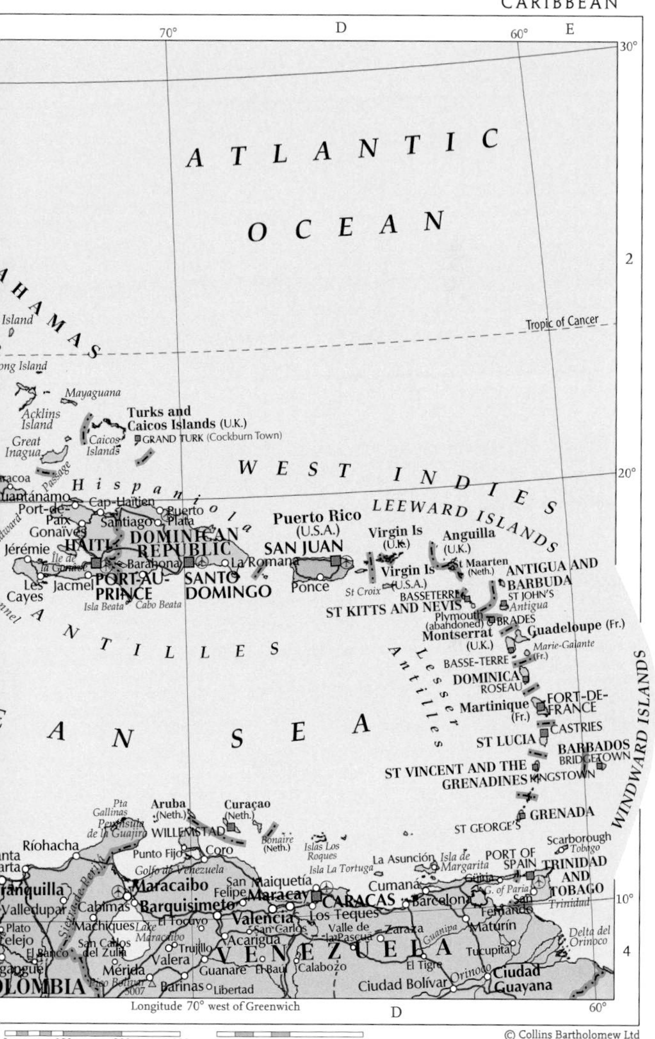

© Collins Bartholomew Ltd

ATLANTIC
OCEAN
WEST INDIES
LEEWARD ISLANDS
WINDWARD ISLANDS
Hispaniola
ANTILLES
Lesser Antilles
Tropic of Cancer
Mayaguana
Acklins Island
Great Inagua
Turks and Caicos Islands (U.K.)
GRAND TURK (Cockburn Town)
Caicos Islands
Cap-Haïtien
Port-de-Paix
Gonaïves
Jérémie
HAITI
Île de la Gonâve
Les Cayes
Jacmel
PORT-AU-PRINCE
Isla Beata
Cabo Beata
Santiago
Puerto Plata
DOMINICAN REPUBLIC
Barahona
SANTO DOMINGO
La Romana
Puerto Rico (U.S.A.)
SAN JUAN
Ponce
Virgin Is (U.K.)
Virgin Is (U.S.A.)
St Croix
Anguilla (U.K.)
St Maarten (Neth.)
ANTIGUA AND BARBUDA
ST JOHN'S
Antigua
BASSETERRE
ST KITTS AND NEVIS
Plymouth (abandoned)
BRADES
Montserrat (U.K.)
Guadeloupe (Fr.)
Marie-Galante (Fr.)
BASSE-TERRE
DOMINICA
ROSEAU
Martinique (Fr.)
FORT-DE-FRANCE
CASTRIES
ST LUCIA
BARBADOS
BRIDGETOWN
ST VINCENT AND THE GRENADINES
KINGSTOWN
GRENADA
ST GEORGE'S
Scarborough
Tobago
PORT OF SPAIN
TRINIDAD AND TOBAGO
Trinidad
San Fernando
Delta del Orinoco
Pta Gallinas
Península de la Guajira
Aruba (Neth.)
Curaçao (Neth.)
WILLEMSTAD
Bonaire (Neth.)
Islas Los Roques
Isla La Tortuga
La Asunción
Isla de Margarita
Ríohacha
Punto Fijo
Coro
Golfo de Venezuela
Maracaibo
Lake Maracaibo
Cabimas
Machiques
San Carlos del Zulia
El Banco
Valledupar
Sierra de Perijá
Barquisimeto
El Tocuyo
Trujillo
Valera
Mérida
Pico Bolívar 5007
Barinas
Libertad
Guanare
El Baul
Acarigua
San Carlos
San Felipe
Maiquetía
Maracay
CARACAS
Valencia
Los Teques
Valle de la Pascua
Calabozo
Zaraza
Cumaná
Barcelona
Güiria
G. of Paria
Maturín
Tucupita
El Tigre
Guanipa
Orinoco
Ciudad Bolívar
Ciudad Guayana
VENEZUELA
COLOMBIA
70°
60°
30°
20°
10°
2
4
Longitude 70° west of Greenwich
0 100 200 300
0 200 400 KILOMETRES

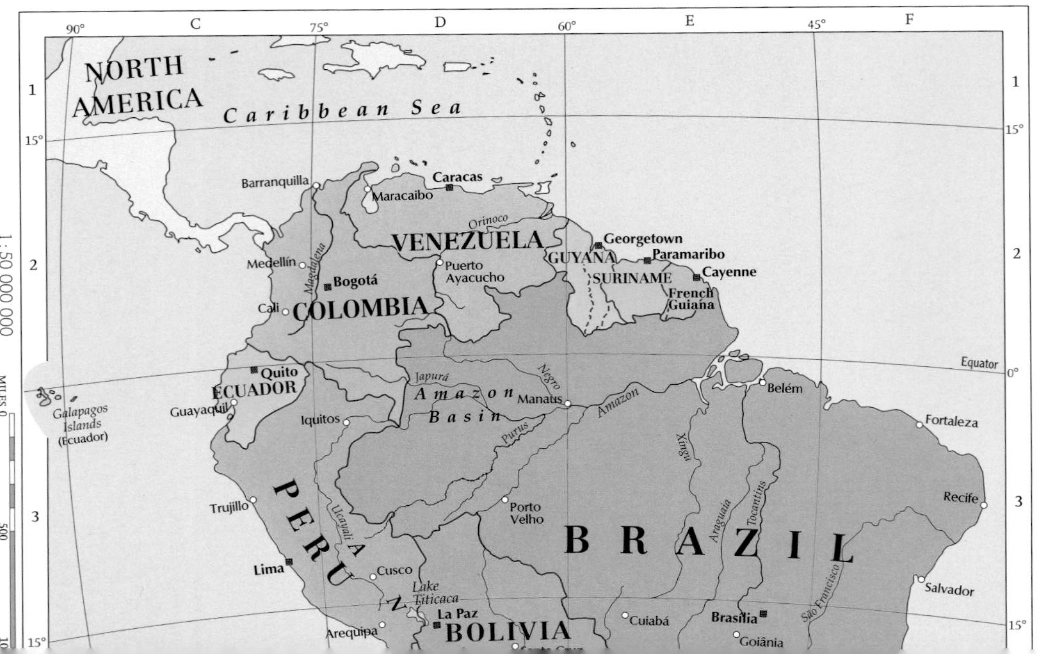

NORTH AMERICA

Caribbean Sea

Barranquilla
Maracaibo
Caracas
VENEZUELA
Puerto Ayacucho
Orinoco

Medellín
Bogotá
COLOMBIA
Cali
Magdalena

Quito
ECUADOR
Guayaquil

Galapagos Islands (Ecuador)

Georgetown
GUYANA
Paramaribo
SURINAME
Cayenne
French Guiana

Negro
Manaus
A m a z o n B a s i n
Japurá
Iquitos
Ucayali
Purus
Madeira
Porto Velho
Amazon

PERU
Trujillo
Lima
Cusco
Lake Titicaca
La Paz
BOLIVIA

Equator
Fortaleza
Recife
Salvador

Belém
Tocantins
Araguaia
Brasília
Goiânia
Cuiabá

B R A Z I L

Xingu
São Francisco

15°   45°   60°   75°   90°   15°

1   2   3

0°   15°

F   E   D   C

1 : 50 000 000

MILES 0   500   10

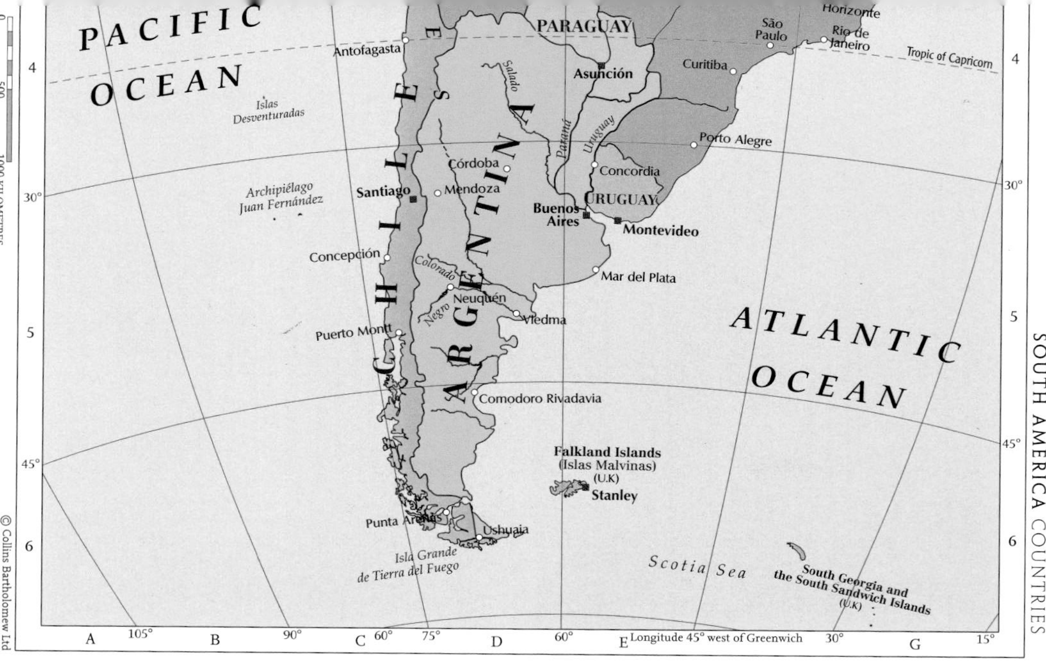

PACIFIC OCEAN

ATLANTIC OCEAN

Scotia Sea

Tropic of Capricorn

Horizonte

Rio de Janeiro

São Paulo

Curitiba

Porto Alegre

PARAGUAY

Asunción

Pilcomayo

Paraguay

Paraná

CONCORDIA

URUGUAY

Montevideo

Buenos Aires

Mar del Plata

Salado

Córdoba

Mendoza

Santiago

Concepción

Puerto Montt

Neuquén

Viedma

Colorado

Negro

Comodoro Rivadavia

Falkland Islands
(Islas Malvinas)
(U.K)

Stanley

ARGENTINA

CHILE

Punta Arenas

Ushuaia

Isla Grande
de Tierra del Fuego

Antofagasta

Islas
Desventuradas

Archipiélago
Juan Fernández

South Georgia and
the South Sandwich Islands
(U.K)

E Longitude 45° west of Greenwich

15°
30°
45°
60°
75°
90°
105°

15°
30°
45°

0   500   1000 KILOMETRES

© Collins Bartholomew Ltd

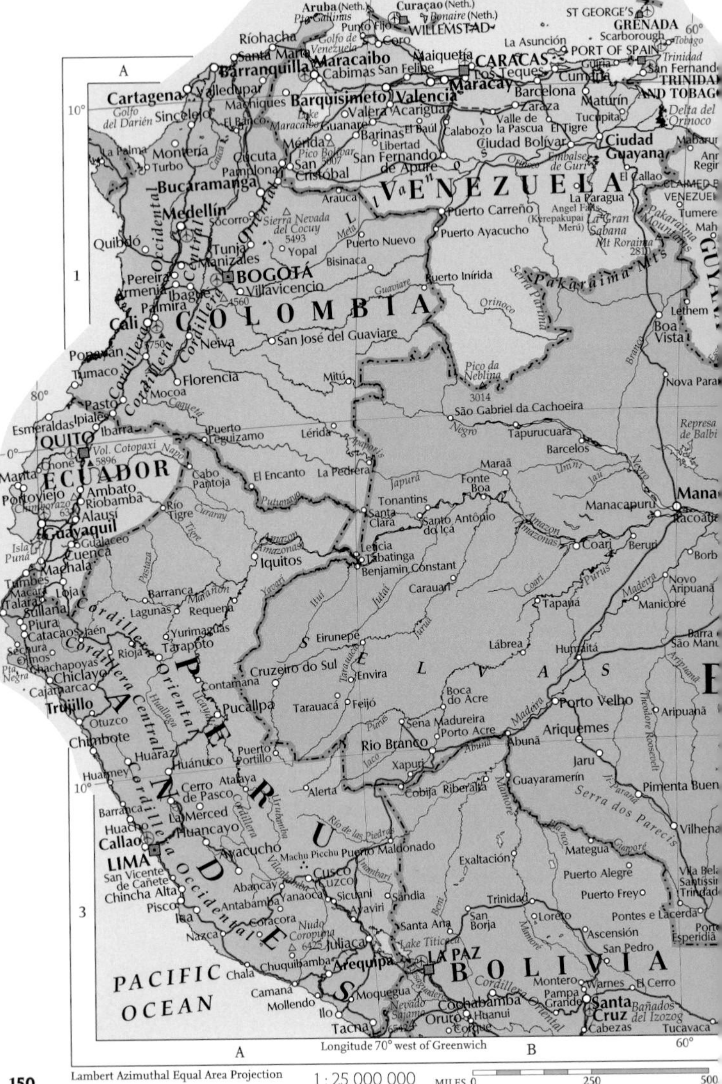

Lambert Azimuthal Equal Area Projection   1 : 25 000 000   MILES 0   250   500

Longitude 70° west of Greenwich

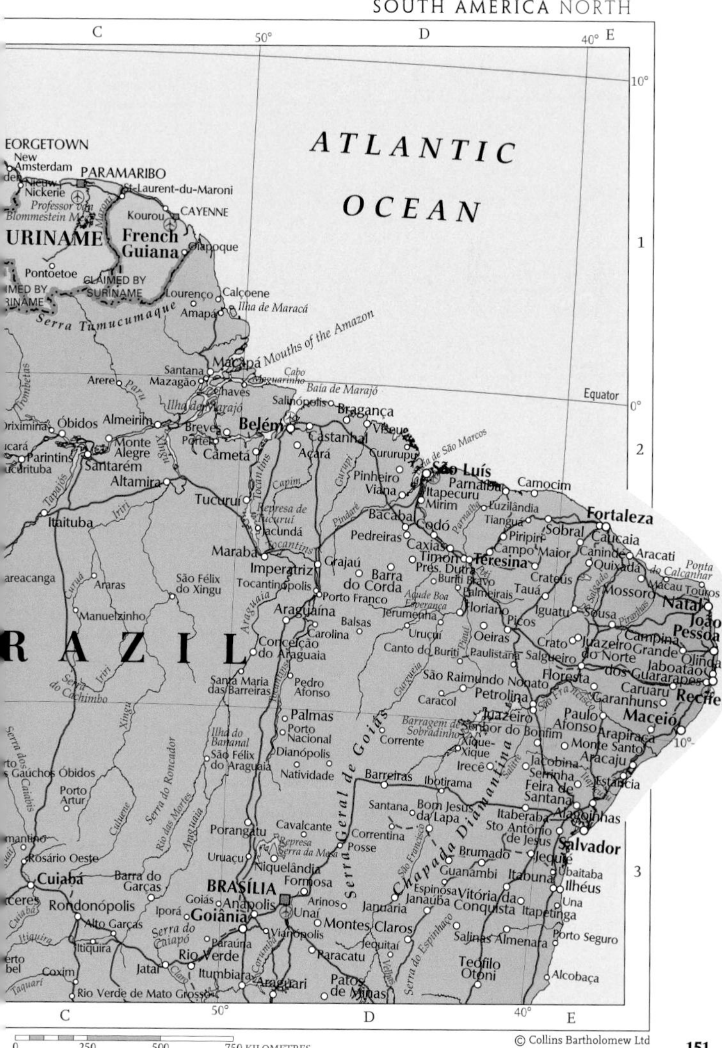

ATLANTIC

OCEAN

EORGETOWN
New
Amsterdam
Nickerie
PARAMARIBO
St-Laurent-du-Maroni
Professor Dr
Blommestein Me
Kourou
CAYENNE
URINAME **French
Guiana**
Pontoetoe
CLAIMED BY
SURINAME
RINAME
Lourenço
Oiapoque
Calçoene
Serra Tumucumaque
Amapá
Ilha de Maracá
Santana
Arere
Mazagão
Macapá
Mouths of the Amazon
Cabo
Orgurinho
Norte
oriximiná
Óbidos
Almeirim
Jari
Chaves
Baía de Marajó
icará
Breves
Porto
Santana
Equator
Monte
Alegre
Ilha de Marajó
Belém
Salinópolis
Bragança
Parintins
untuba
Santarém
Cametá
Acará
Vigia
Castanhal
Iriri
Altamira
Tucuruí
Pinheiro
Vizeu
Bacabal
São Luís
Camocim
Itaituba
Tapajós
Represa de
Tucuruí
Itapecuru
Parnaíba
Acajatuba
Marabá
Grajaú
Pedreiras
Codó
Tianguá
Fortaleza
areacanga
Araras
São Félix
do Xingu
Imperatriz
Barra
do Corda
Timon
Prés. Dutra
Teresina
Maior
Caninde
Caucaia
Aracati
Quixadá
Ponta
de Calcanhar
Manuelzinho
Tocantinópolis
Porto Franco
Jerumenha
Crateús
Tauá
Iguatu
Sousa
Mossoró
Natal
B R A Z I L
Araguaína
Carolina
Balsas
Floriano
Oeiras
Picos
Crato
Juazeiro
do Norte
Campina
Grande
João
Pessôa
Conceição
do Araguaia
Santa Maria
das Barreiras
Pedro
Afonso
Uruçuí
Canto do Buriti
São Raimundo
Paulistana
Salgueiro
Floresta
Jaboatão
dos Guararapes
Olinda
Recife
Serra
do Cachimbo
s Gaúchos
Óbidos
Porto
Artur
Palmas
Porto
Nacional
Dianópolis
Natividade
Corrente
Petrolina
Juazeiro
Paulo
Afonso
Monte Santo
Garanhuns
Caruaru
Maceió
antiqo
Rosário Oeste
Manuelzinho
Ilha do
Bananal
Parque
Nacional
Barragem de
Sobradinho
Xique-
Xique
Irecê
Jacobina
Serrinha
Estância
mantino
Barra do
Garças
Porangatu
Uruaçu
Cavalcante
Posse
Correntina
Santana
Bom Jesus
da Lapa
Ibotirama
Feira de
Santana
Sto Antônio
de Jesus
Alagoinhas
Maragogipe
Salvador
ceres
Cuiabá
Rondonópolis
Alto Garças
Barra do
Garças
Goiás
Iporá
Niquelândia
BRASÍLIA
Formosa
Unaí
Januária
Brumado
Guanambi
Espinosa
Itaberaba
Jequié
Conquista
Itabuna
Ilhéus
Una
Ibitiara
Porto Seguro
Jataí
Itiquira
Alto Garças
Rio
Verde
Paraúna
Vianópolis
Montes
Claros
Salinas
Almenara
Teófilo
Otoni
Alcobaça
Coxim
Rio Verde de Mato Grosso
Itumbiara
Araguari
Patos
de Minas
Paracatu
Jequitaí

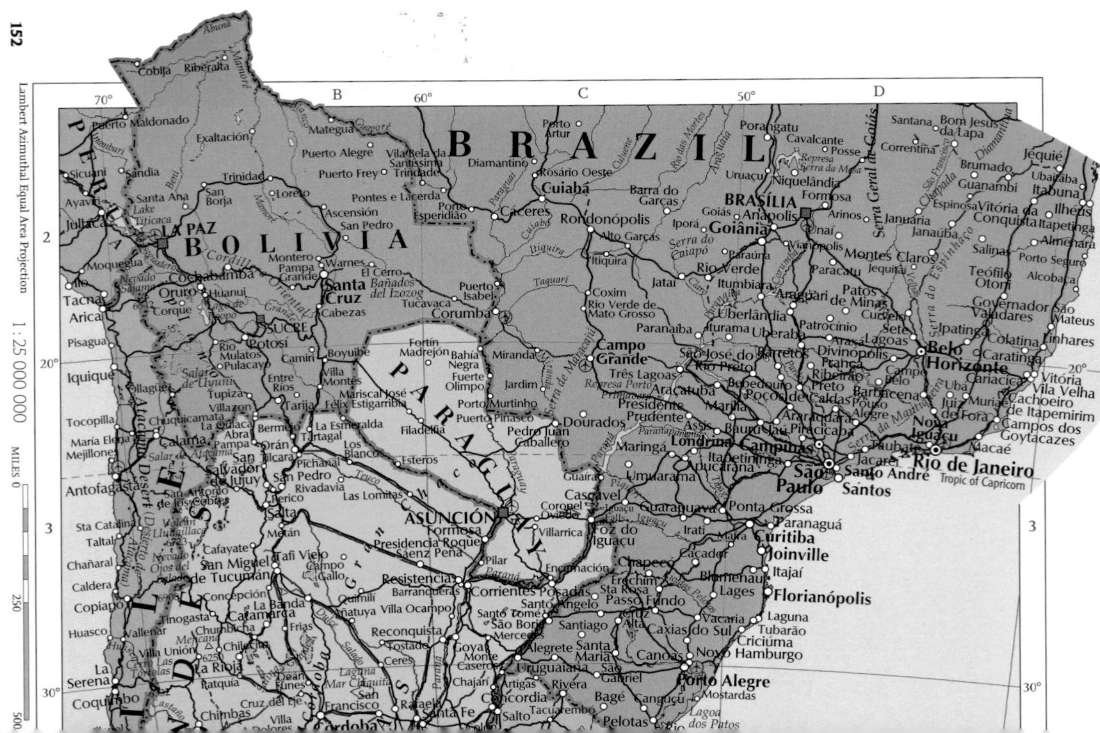

Lambert Azimuthal Equal Area Projection   1 : 25 000 000   MILES 0   250   500

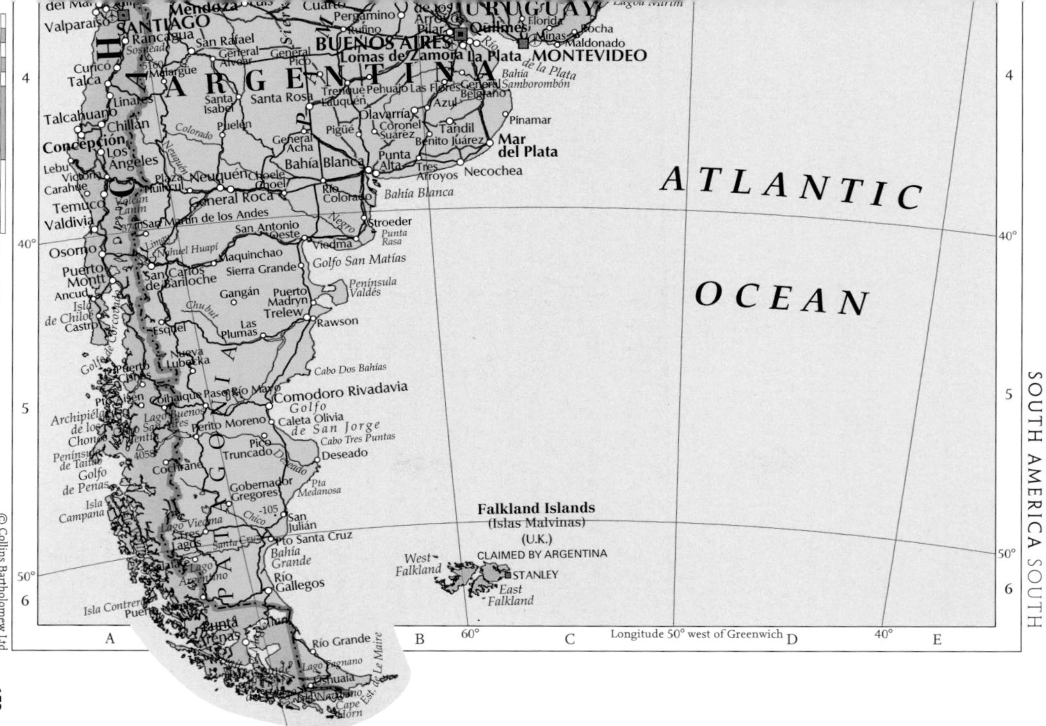

ATLANTIC

OCEAN

URUGUAY
MONTEVIDEO
Maldonado

Punta del Este
Rocha

Florida
Minas
San Carlos
Sombrónbón

Mar del Plata

Ostamar

Necochea

Azul

Tandil
Benito Juárez
Arroyos

Coronel Suárez

Bahía Blanca

Tres Arroyos

Las Flores

BUENOS AIRES
Lomas de Zamora la Plata

Pergamino

ARGENTINA

Falkland Islands
(Islas Malvinas)
(UK)
CLAIMED BY ARGENTINA

STANLEY

West
Falkland

East
Falkland

Peninsula
Valdés

Golfo San Matías

Puerto
Madryn

Trelew
Rawson

Cabo Dos Bahías

Comodoro Rivadavia

Golfo
San Jorge

Caleta Olivia

Cabo Tres Puntas

Deseado

Puerto
Moreno

Pta
Medanosa

Bahía
Grande

San
Julián

Gobernador
Gregores

Puerto
Santa Cruz

Río
Gallegos

Río Grande

Est. de Le Maire

SANTIAGO

Valparaíso

Mendoza

San Rafael

Curicó
Talca
Talcahuano
Chillán
Concepción
Los Ángeles
Lebu
Temuco
Valdivia
Osorno

Puerto
Montt

Ancud

Castro

Archipiélago
de los
Chonos

Península
de Taitao

Golfo
de Penas

Isla
Campana

Isla Contreras

Río Negro

Río Colorado

General Roca

Neuquén
San Antonio

Choele Choel

Viedma

Carmen de Patagones

San Carlos
de Bariloche

Esquel

Gobernador
Costa

Sarmiento

Perito
Moreno

0   250   500   750 KILOMETRES

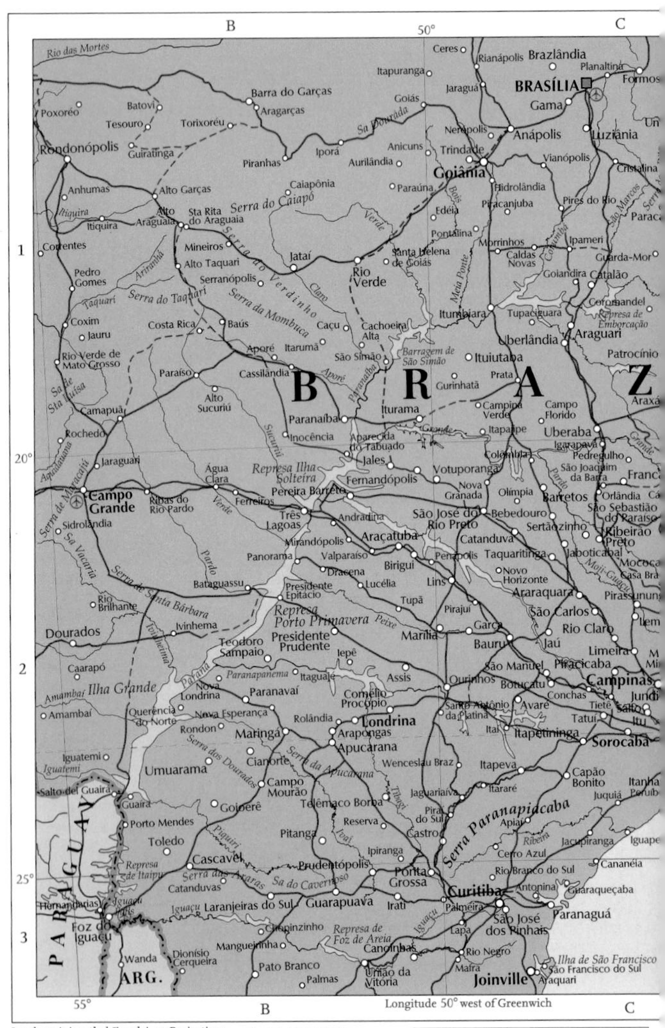

B 50° C

Rio das Mortes

Ceres · Rianápolis Brazlândia

Itapuranga · Planaltina

Poxoréo · Jaraguá BRASÍLIA Formos

Batovi · Goiás Gama

Barra do Garças Aragarças Nemópolis Un

Tesouro · Torixoréu Iporá Anicuns Anápolis Luziânia

Rondonópolis · Guiratinga Piranhas Aurilândia Trindade Vianópolis

Anhumas Caiapônia Paraúna Goiânia Hidrolândia Cristalina

Alto Garças Sta Rita do Araguaia Edéia Piracanjuba Pires do Rio Parac

Itiquira Alto Araguaia Jataí Santa Helena de Goiás Pontalina Morrinhos Ipameri

Correntes Mineiros Rio Verde Caldas Novas Goiandira Guarda-Mor Catalão

Pedro Gomes Alto Taquari Serra do Caiapó Itumbiara Tupaciguara Corumbaíba

Coxim Serranópolis Cachoeira Alta Uberlândia Represa de Emborcação Araguari

Jauru Costa Rica Baús Aporé Itarumã São Simão Gurinhatã Prata Patrocínio

Rio Verde de Mato Grosso Serra do Taquari Serra da Mombuca Cassilândia Barragem de São Simão Ituiutaba B R A Z Araxá

Paraíso Alto Sucuriú Paranaíba Iturama Campina Verde Campo Florido Uberaba

Camapuã Inocência Aparecida do Taboado Itapagipe Igarapava

Rochedo Jaraguari Votuporanga Colômbia Pedregulho

Água Clara Represa Ilha Solteira Jales Nova Granada Olímpia São Joaquim da Barra Franc

Campo Grande Ribas do Rio Pardo Ferreira Pereira Barreto Fernandópolis São José do Rio Preto Bebedouro Barretos Orlândia Ca

Sidrolândia Três Lagoas Andradina Catanduva Sertãozinho Ribeirão Preto São Sebastião do Paraíso

Rio Brilhante Sta Bárbara Mirandópolis Araçatuba Penápolis Taquaritinga Jaboticabal Mococa Casa Bra

Panorama Valparaíso Birigui Novo Horizonte Araraquara Pirassununga

Dourados Batayguassu Dracena Lucélia Tupã Lins Garça São Carlos Rio Claro Iten

Caarapó Ilha Grande Presidente Epitácio Represa Porto Primavera Peixe Jaú Limeira Mi

Amambaí Teodoro Sampaio Presidente Prudente Marília São Manuel Bauru Piracicaba Campinas

Querência do Norte Ivinhema Paranapanema Iepé Comélio Procópio Avaré Botucatu Conchas Jundi

Iguatemi Londrina Nova Esperança Itaguajé Assis Santo Antônio da Platina Itaí Tietê Salto Itu

Amambaí Rondon Paranavaí Rolândia Wenceslau Braz Itapetininga Sorocaba

Salto del Guairá Guaíra Maringá Arapongas Apucarana Jaguariaíva Itapeva Itararé Capão Bonito Itanha

Umuarama Cianorte Serra da Apucarana Piraí do Sul Apiaí Juquiá Perib

Porto Mendes Campo Mourão Telêmaco Borba Reserva Castro Serra Paranapiacaba Jacupiranga Iguape

Toledo Goioerê Pitanga Ipiranga Cerro Azul Cananéia

Cascavel Prudentópolis Ponta Grossa Rio Branco do Sul Guaraqueçaba

Catanduvas Serra da Esperança Sa do Cavernoso Irati Palmeira Antonina Ilha de São Francisco

Hernandárias Iguaçu Laranjeiras do Sul Guarapuava Curitiba Paranaguá

Foz do Iguaçu Dionísio Cerqueira Chapinzinho Represa de Foz de Areia Lapa São José dos Pinhais São Francisco do Sul

Wanda Mangueirinha Canoinhas Rio Negro Araquari

ARG. Pato Branco União da Vitória Mafra Joinville

55° B Longitude 50° west of Greenwich C

154 Lambert Azimuthal Equal Area Projection 1 : 10 000 000 MILES 0 100 200

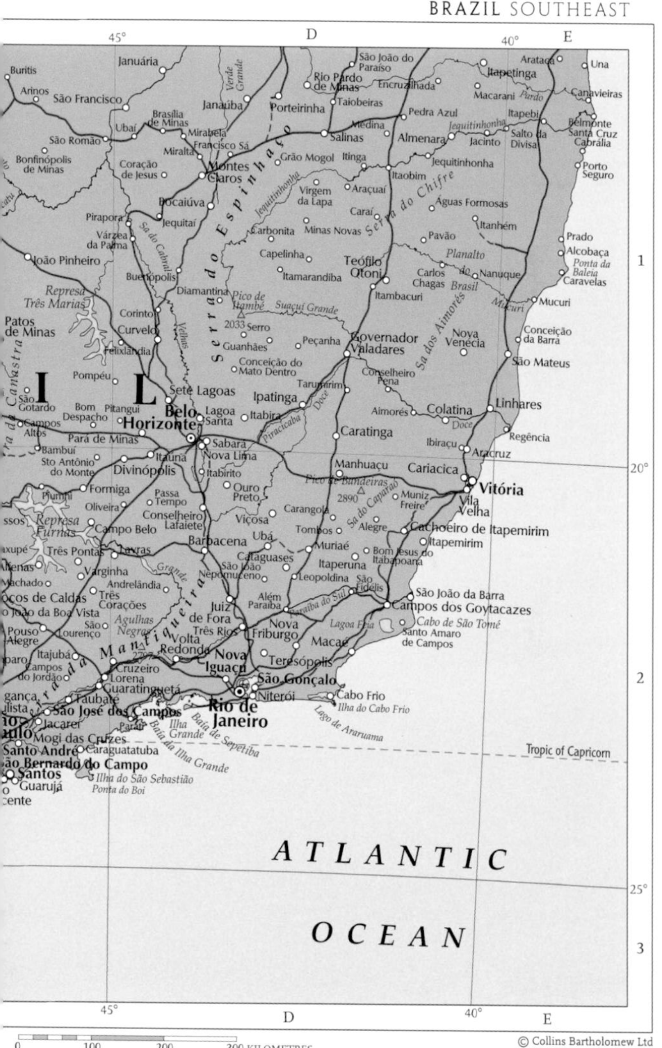
45°
D
40°
E
1
2
3
20°
25°
Januária
Buritis
Arinos
São Francisco
Janaúba
Porteirinha
Rio Pardo de Minas
São João do Paraíso
Encruzilhada
Taiobeiras
Salinas
Medina
Pedra Azul
Almenara
Macarani
Itapetinga
Arataca
Una
Canavieiras
Itapebi
Belmonte
Santa Cruz Cabrália
Porto Seguro
Salto da Divisa
Jacinto
Jequitinhonha
Brasília de Minas
Ubaí
São Romão
Mirabela
Francisco Sá
Miralta
Montes Claros
Coração de Jesus
Bonfinópolis de Minas
Grão Mogol
Itinga
Araçuaí
Itaobim
Virgem da Lapa
Serra do Espinhaço
Serra do Chifre
Águas Formosas
Caraí
Bocaiúva
Pirapora
Jequitaí
Várzea da Palma
Carbonita
Minas Novas
Itanhém
Pavão
Prado
Alcobaça
Ponta da Baleia
Caravelas
João Pinheiro
Capelinha
Teófilo Otoni
Itamarandiba
Carlos Chagas
Planalto do Brasil
Nanuque
Buenópolis
Diamantina
Pico de Itambé
Itambacuri
Mucuri
Represa Três Marias
Suaçuí Grande
Corinto
Curvelo
Patos de Minas
Serro
2033
Guanhães
Peçanha
Governador Valadares
Sa dos Aimorés
Nova Venécia
Conceição da Barra
São Mateus
Felixlândia
Conceição do Mato Dentro
Conselheiro Pena
Pompéu
Sete Lagoas
Tarumirim
Ipatinga
São Gotardo
Bom Despacho
Pitangui
Belo Horizonte
Lagoa Santa
Itabira
Aimorés
Colatina
Linhares
Campos Altos
Caratinga
Doce
Piracicaba
Regência
Pará de Minas
Sabará
Ibiraçu
Aracruz
Bambuí
Itaúna
Nova Lima
Sto Antônio do Monte
Divinópolis
Itabirito
Manhuaçu
Cariacica
Vitória
Vila Velha
Formiga
Ouro Preto
Pico da Bandeira
2890
Muniz Freire
Piumhi
Passa Tempo
Oliveira
Conselheiro Lafaiete
Carangola
Sa do Caparaó
Represa Furnas
Campo Belo
Viçosa
Tombos
Alegre
Cachoeiro de Itapemirim
Itapemirim
Barbacena
Ubá
Muriaé
Bom Jesus do Itabapoana
Três Pontas
Lavras
Cataguases
Itaperuna
Varginha
São João Nepomuceno
Leopoldina
Grande
Andrelândia
São Fidélis
Poços de Caldas
Três Corações
Além Paraíba
Paraíba do Sul
São João da Barra
Campos dos Goytacazes
São João da Boa Vista
Juiz de Fora
Agulhas Negras
São Lourenço
Três Rios
Nova Friburgo
Lagoa Feia
Cabo de São Tomé
Santo Amaro de Campos
Pouso Alegre
Volta Redonda
Macaé
Serra da Mantiqueira
Itajubá
Campos do Jordão
2797
Nova Iguaçu
Teresópolis
Cruzeiro
Lorena
Guaratinguetá
São Gonçalo
Taubaté
Niterói
Cabo Frio
Ilha do Cabo Frio
São José dos Campos
Rio de Janeiro
Jacareí
Paraty
Ilha Grande
Baía de Sepetiba
Lago de Araruama
Mogi das Cruzes
Caraguatatuba
Baía da Ilha Grande
Santo André
São Bernardo do Campo
Santos
Guarujá
Ilha do São Sebastião
Ponta do Boi
Tropic of Capricorn
ATLANTIC
OCEAN
0
100
200
300 KILOMETRES

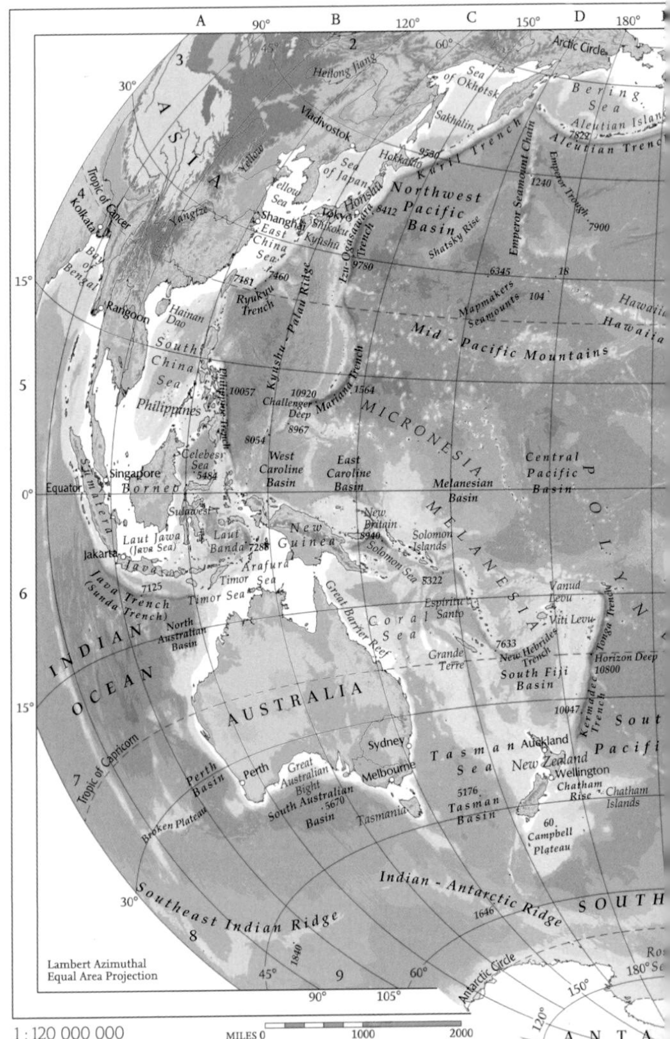

ASIA

Heilong Jiang

Sea of Okhotsk

Arctic Circle

Bering Sea

Aleutian Islands

Aleutian Trench

Vladivostok

Sakhalin

Kuril Trench

9540

Sea of Japan

Hokkaidō

Northwest Pacific Basin

Emperor Seamount Chain

7822

Izu Trench 7240

Empiror Trough 7900

Yellow Sea

Honshu

Tokyo

Yangtze

Tropic of Cancer

Shikoku

6412

Kyushu

Shatsky Rise

6345

18

Kōlkata

Shanghai

East China Sea

Izu Ogasawara Trench 9780

Hawaii

Hawaii

15°

Bay of Bengal

Rangoon

Hainan Dao

Ryukyu Trench

7381

7460

Kyushu - Palau Ridge

Mid - Pacific Mountains

Manmakers Seamounts 104

South China Sea

10057

Challenger Deep 8967

Mariana Trench 10920

1564

Philippines

8054

MICRONESIA

Singapore

Celebes Sea 5454

West Caroline Basin

East Caroline Basin

Melanesian Basin

Central Pacific Basin

P O L Y

Equator

Borneo

Sulawesi

Jakarta

Laut Jawa (Java Sea)

Laut Banda 7288

New Britain 8940

Solomon Islands

New Guinea

MELANESIA

Espiritu Santo

Vanua Levu

Sumatra

Java Trench (Sunda Trench)

7125

Timor Sea

Arafura Sea

Great Barrier Reef

Solomon Sea 9322

Viti Levu

6°

Timor Sea

North Australian Basin

Coral Sea

Grande Terre

New Hebrides Trench

7633

South Fiji Basin

Horizon Deep 10800

INDIAN

AUSTRALIA

15°

OCEAN

Tropic of Capricorn

Sydney

10047

Tasman Sea

Auckland

New Zealand

South Pacific

Perth

Perth Basin

Great Australian Bight

Melbourne

Wellington

Chatham Rise

Chatham Islands

Broken Plateau

South Australian Basin

5670

5176

Tasman Basin

Tasmania

60

Campbell Plateau

Southeast Indian Ridge

1560

45°

Indian - Antarctic Ridge

1646

SOUTH

ANTARCTIC

Antarctic Circle

180° Se

Ro

Lambert Azimuthal
Equal Area Projection

90°

105°

60°

150°

120°

ANTA

156 1 : 120 000 000

MILES 0   1000   2000

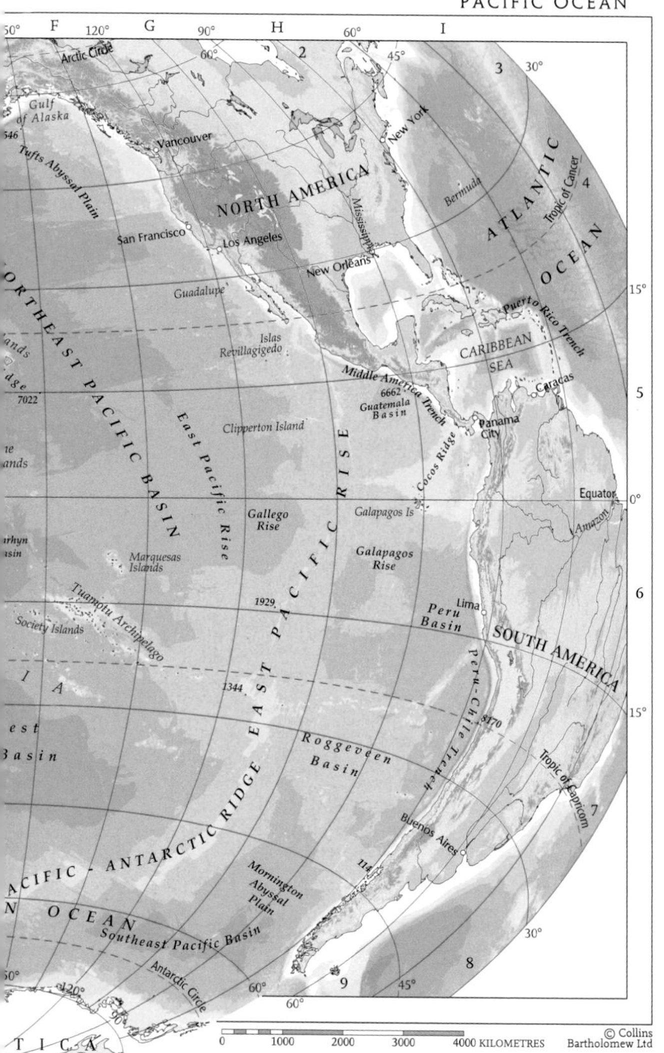

Arctic Circle

Gulf of Alaska

546

Tufts Abyssal Plain

Vancouver

NORTH AMERICA

San Francisco

Los Angeles

New York

Bermuda

Tropic of Cancer

ATLANTIC

OCEAN

Mississippi

Guadalupe

New Orleans

ORTHEAST PACIFIC BASIN

Islas Revillagigedo

Middle America Trench

Guatemala Basin

6662

CARIBBEAN SEA

Caracas

Puerto Rico Trench

Cocos Ridge

Panama City

7022

dge

te ands

Clipperton Island

East Pacific Rise

Galapagos Is

Equator

Amazon

arhyn asin

Gallego Rise

Galapagos Rise

Marquesas Islands

Lima

Peru Basin

SOUTH AMERICA

Tuamotu Archipelago

1929

Society Islands

Peru-Chile Trench

5870

I   A

1344

est Basin

EAST   PACIFIC   RISE

Roggeveen Basin

Tropic of Capricorn

Buenos Aires

PACIFIC - ANTARCTIC RIDGE

Mornington Abyssal Plain

114

N   OCEAN

Southeast Pacific Basin

Antarctic Circle

TICA

0   1000   2000   3000   4000 KILOMETRES

© Collins
Bartholomew Ltd

157

120° A 90° B 60° C 30° D 0° E 30° F 60°

Arctic Circle

Greenland

Iceland

Denmark Strait

Norwegian Basin

Norwegian Sea

Baltic

Hudson Bay

Reykjanes Ridge

Iceland Basin

Rockall Bank

North Sea

NORTH AMERICA

Labrador Sea

Celtic Shelf 38

British Isles

London

EUROPE

45°

Newfoundland

St John's

Grand Banks of Newfoundland

MID-ATLANTIC RIDGE

4938

Lisbon

Mediterranean Sea

5121

New York

5943

Azores

Algiers

2

30°

New Orleans

4556

Bermuda

Monaco Basin

Canary Is.

Nares Deep

Sargasso Sea

5508

Milwaukee Deep 8605

Puerto Rico Trench

6690

5491

Tropic of Cancer

Greater Antilles

AFRICA

Cayman Trench 7535

3

Caribbean Sea

5523

Cape Verde

Cape Verde Basin

Dakar

Niger

Lesser Antilles

Panama City

Caracas

Guiana Basin

Amazon Cone

Sierra Leone Basin

Gulf of Guinea

Guinea Basin

Lagos

5212

4

0°

Equator

Amazon

Ascension

5391

Luanda

Lima

SOUTH AMERICA

Brazil Basin

St Helena

Angola Basin

5

MID-ATLANTIC RIDGE

Congo

Rio de Janeiro

5460

Walvis Ridge

24

Orange Cone

Orange

6

30°

Tropic of Capricorn

Paraná

Rio Grande Rise

Tristan da Cunha

Cape Basin

5520

Cape of Good Hope

Cape Town

Buenos Aires

Agulhas Basin

6195

7

Argentine Basin

6681

Falkland Islands

Scotia Ridge

South Georgia

5066

Atlantic-Indian Ridge

1530

Cape Horn

Drake Passage

Scotia Sea

8325

Antarctic Peninsula

PACIFIC OCEAN

5750

8

60°

Antarctic Circle

Atlantic-Indian Antarctic Basin

90° 60° 30° 0° 30°

Lambert Azimuthal Equal Area Projection   1 : 120 000 000   MILES 0   1000   2000

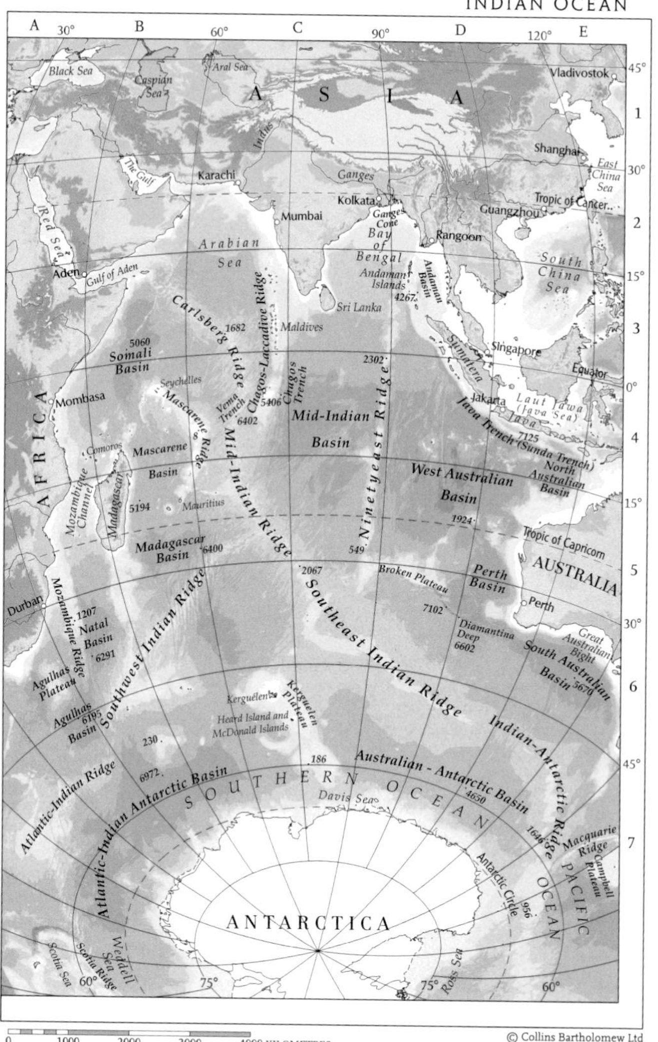

	30° A	60° B	C	90°	D	120° E

Black Sea
Caspian Sea
Aral Sea
Vladivostok

A S I A

The Gulf
Karachi
Ganges
Kolkata
Shanghai
East China Sea

Red Sea
Mumbai
Ganges
Bay of Bengal
Rangoon
Guangzhou
Tropic of Cancer

Aden
Gulf of Aden
Arabian Sea
Andaman Islands
4267
South China Sea

Carlsberg Ridge
1682
Chagos-Laccadive Ridge
Maldives
Sri Lanka
Andaman Basin

5060
Somali Basin
Seychelles
5406
Chagos Trench
Sumatra
Singapore
Equator

Mombasa
Vema Trench
6402
2302
Jakarta
Laut Jawa (Java Sea)
Mascarene Ridge
Mid-Indian Basin
Java Trench (Sunda Trench)
2125
North Australian Basin

A F R I C A
Comoros
Mascarene Basin

Mozambique Channel
5194
Mauritius
West Australian Basin

Madagascar
Madagascar Basin
6400
1924
Tropic of Capricorn

Ninetyeast Ridge
549
Broken Plateau
Perth Basin
AUSTRALIA
Perth

Durban
1207
Natal Basin
2067
7102
Diamantina Deep 6602
South Australian Basin
5670
Great Australian Bight

Mozambique Ridge
6291
Southwest Indian Ridge
Agu`lhas Plateau
Agu`lhas Basin
6195

Kerguélen
Kerguelen Plateau
Heard Island and McDonald Islands
Southeast Indian Ridge
Indian-Antarctic Ridge

Atlantic-Indian Ridge
230
186
Australian - Antarctic Basin
4650
Macquarie Ridge
Campbell Plateau

Atlantic-Indian Antarctic Basin
6972
S O U T H E R N   O C E A N
Davis Sea
PACIFIC

Antarctic Circle
Ross Sea

A N T A R C T I C A

Scotia Sea
South Sandwich Trench

0	1000	2000	3000	4000 KILOMETRES

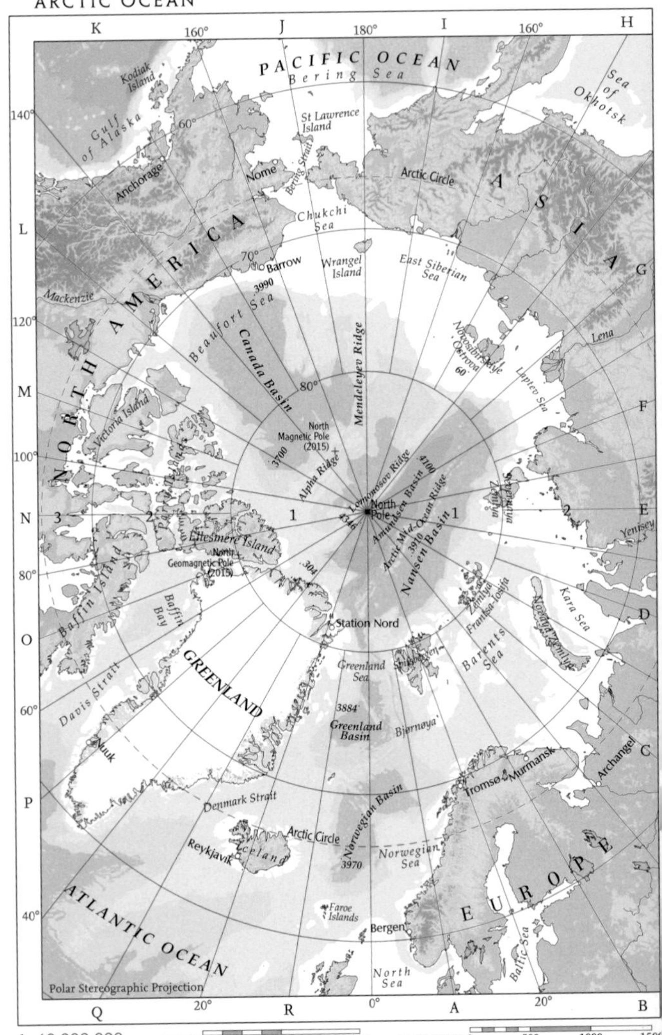

MILES 0   400   800

KILOMETRES 0   500   1000   1500

Polar Stereographic Projection

INTRODUCTION TO THE INDEX

The index includes all names shown on the maps in the Atlas of the World. Names are referenced by page number and by a grid reference. The grid reference correlates to the alphanumeric values which appear within each map frame. Each entry also includes the country or geographical area in which the feature is located. Entries relating to names appearing on insets are indicated by a small box symbol: □, followed by a grid reference if the inset has its own alphanumeric values.

Name forms are as they appear on the maps, with additional alternative names or name forms included as cross-references which refer the user to the entry for the map form of the name. Names beginning with Mc or Mac are alphabetized exactly as they appear. The terms Saint, Sainte, etc., are abbreviated to St, Ste, etc., but alphabetized as if in the full form.

Names of physical features beginning with generic, geographical terms are permuted – the descriptive term is placed after the main part of the name. For example, Lake Superior is indexed as Superior, Lake; Mount Everest as Everest, Mount. This policy is applied to all languages.

Entries, other than those for towns and cities, include a descriptor indicating the type of geographical feature. Descriptors are not included where the type of feature is implicit in the name itself.

Administrative divisions are included to differentiate entries of the same name and feature type within the one country. In such cases, duplicate names are alphabetized in order of administrative division. Additional qualifiers are also included for names within selected geographical areas.

INDEX ABBREVIATIONS

admin. div.	administrative division	**Fin.**	Finland	**Phil.**	Philippines
Afgh.	Afghanistan	**for.**	forest	**plat.**	plateau
Alg.	Algeria	**Fr.**	French	**P.N.G.**	Papua New Guinea
Arg.	Argentina	**g.**	gulf		
Austr.	Australia	**Ger.**	Germany	**Pol.**	Poland
aut. reg.	autonomous region	**Guat.**	Guatemala	**Port.**	Portugal
Azer.	Azerbaijan	**h.**	hill	**prov.**	province
b.	bay	**hd**	head	**r.**	river
Bangl.	Bangladesh	**Hond.**	Honduras	**reg.**	region
Bol.	Bolivia	**imp. l.**	impermanent lake	**resr.**	reservoir
Bos. & Herz.	Bosnia and Herzegovina	**Indon.**	Indonesia	**S.**	South
		i.	island	**str.**	strait
Bulg.	Bulgaria	**is**	Islands	**Switz.**	Switzerland
c.	cape	**isth.**	isthmus	**Tajik.**	Tajikistan
Can.	Canada	**Kazakh.**	Kazakhstan	**Tanz.**	Tanzania
C.A.R.	Central African Republic	**Kyrg.**	Kyrgyzstan	**terr.**	territory
		lag.	lagoon	**Thai.**	Thailand
chan.	channel	**Lith.**	Lithuania	**Trin. and Tob.**	Trinidad and Tobago
Col.	Colombia	**Lux.**	Luxembourg		
Czech Rep.	Czech Republic	**Madag.**	Madagascar	**Turkm.**	Turkmenistan
Dem. Rep. Congo	Democratic Republic of the Congo	**Maur.**	Mauritania	**U.A.E.**	United Arab Emirates
		Mex.	Mexico	**U.K.**	United Kingdom
depr.	depression	**Moz.**	Mozambique	**Ukr.**	Ukraine
des.	desert	**mt.**	mountain	**Uru.**	Uruguay
disp. terr.	disputed territory	**mun.**	municipality	**U.S.A.**	United States of America
Dom. Rep.	Dominican Republic	**N.**	North		
		Neth.	Netherlands	**Uzbek.**	Uzbekistan
esc.	escarpment	**Nic.**	Nicaragua	**val.**	valley
est.	estuary	**N.Z.**	New Zealand	**Venez.**	Venezuela
Eth.	Ethiopia	**Pak.**	Pakistan	**vol.**	volcano
		Para.	Paraguay		
		pen.	peninsula		

1

Page	Grid	Name
128	B2	**100 Mile House** Can.

A

Page	Grid	Name
93	E4	**Aabenraa** Denmark
100	C2	**Aachen** Ger.
93	E4	**Aalborg** Denmark
100	B2	**Aalst** Belgium
93	F4	**Aarhus** Denmark
100	B2	**Aarschot** Belgium
68	C2	**Aba** China
115	C4	**Aba** Nigeria
81	C2	**Ābādān** Iran
81	D2	**Ābādeh** Iran
114	B1	**Abadla** Alg.
115	C4	**Abakaliki** Nigeria
83	H3	**Abakan** Russia
150	A3	**Abancay** Peru
81	D2	**Abarkūh** Iran
66	D2	**Abashiri** Japan
117	B4	**Abaya, Lake** Eth.
		Ābay Wenz *r.* Eth./Sudan *see* **Blue Nile**
82	G3	**Abaza** Russia
108	A2	**Abbasanta** *Sardinia* Italy
104	C1	**Abbeville** France
142	B3	**Abbeville** U.S.A.
55	O2	**Abbot Ice Shelf** Antarctica
74	B1	**Abbottabad** Pak.
115	E3	**Abéché** Chad
114	B4	**Abengourou** Côte d'Ivoire
114	C4	**Abeokuta** Nigeria
99	A2	**Aberaeron** U.K.
96	C2	**Aberchirder** U.K.
99	B3	**Aberdare** U.K.
99	A2	**Aberdaron** U.K.
122	B3	**Aberdeen** S. Africa
96	C2	**Aberdeen** U.K.
141	D3	**Aberdeen** *MD* U.S.A.
137	D1	**Aberdeen** *SD* U.S.A.
134	B1	**Aberdeen** *WA* U.S.A.
129	E1	**Aberdeen Lake** Can.
134	B2	**Abert, Lake** U.S.A.
99	A2	**Aberystwyth** U.K.
86	F2	**Abez'** Russia
78	B3	**Abhā** Saudi Arabia
		Abiad, Bahr el *r.* Sudan/Uganda *see* **White Nile**
114	B4	**Abidjan** Côte d'Ivoire
137	D3	**Abilene** *KS* U.S.A.
139	D2	**Abilene** *TX* U.S.A.
99	C3	**Abingdon** U.K.
91	D3	**Abinsk** Russia
130	B2	**Abitibi, Lake** Can.
81	C1	**Abkhazia** *disp. terr.* Georgia
		Åbo Fin. *see* **Turku**
74	B1	**Abohar** India
114	C4	**Abomey** Benin
60	A1	**Abongabong, Gunung** *mt.* Indon.
118	B2	**Abong Mbang** Cameroon
64	A2	**Aborlan** Phil.
115	D3	**Abou Déia** Chad
106	B2	**Abrantes** Port.
152	B3	**Abra Pampa** Arg.
136	A2	**Absaroka Range** *mts* U.S.A.
81	C1	**Abşeron Yarımadası** *pen.* Azer.
78	B3	**Abū 'Arīsh** Saudi Arabia
79	C2	**Abu Dhabi** U.A.E.
116	B3	**Abu Hamed** Sudan
115	C4	**Abuja** Nigeria
81	C2	**Abū Kamāl** Syria
152	B1	**Abunã** *r.* Bol./Brazil
150	B2	**Abunã** Brazil
74	B2	**Abu Road** India
116	B2	**Abū Sunbul** Egypt
117	A3	**Abu Zabad** Sudan
		Abū Zabī U.A.E. *see* **Abu Dhabi**
117	A4	**Abyei** Sudan
145	B2	**Acambaro** Mex.
106	B1	**A Cañiza** Spain
144	B2	**Acaponeta** Mex.
145	C3	**Acapulco** Mex.
151	D2	**Acará** Brazil
150	B1	**Acarigua** Venez.
145	C3	**Acatlán** Mex.
145	C3	**Acayucán** Mex.
114	B4	**Accra** Ghana
98	B2	**Accrington** U.K.
74	B2	**Achalpur** India
97	A2	**Achill Island** Ireland
101	D1	**Achim** Ger.
96	B2	**Achnasheen** U.K.
91	D2	**Achuyevo** Russia
111	C3	**Acıpayam** Turkey
109	C3	**Acireale** *Sicily* Italy
147	C2	**Acklins Island** Bahamas
153	B4	**Aconcagua, Cerro** *mt.* Arg.
106	B1	**A Coruña** Spain
108	A2	**Acqui Terme** Italy
103	D2	**Ács** Hungary
145	C2	**Actopán** Mex.
139	D2	**Ada** U.S.A.
79	C2	**Adam** Oman
49	J4	**Adamstown** Pitcairn Is
		'Adan Yemen *see* **Aden**
80	B2	**Adana** Turkey
111	D2	**Adapazarı** Turkey
		Adapazari Turkey *see* **Adapazarı**
108	A1	**Adda** *r.* Italy
78	B2	**Ad Dafīnah** Saudi Arabia
78	B2	**Ad Dahnā'** *des.* Saudi Arabia
78	B2	**Ad Dahnā'** *des.* Saudi Arabia
		Ad Dammām Saudi Arabia *see* **Dammam**
78	A2	**Ad Dār al Ḥamrā'** Saudi Arabia
78	B3	**Ad Darb** Saudi Arabia
78	B2	**Ad Dawādimī** Saudi Arabia
		Ad Dawḥah Qatar *see* **Doha**
78	B2	**Ad Dilam** Saudi Arabia
116	C2	**Ad Dir'īyah** Saudi Arabia
117	B4	**Addis Ababa** Eth.
81	C2	**Ad Dīwānīyah** Iraq
52	A2	**Adelaide** Austr.
50	C1	**Adelaide River** Austr.
101	D2	**Adelebsen** Ger.
55	J2	**Adélie Land** Antarctica
78	B3	**Aden** Yemen
117	C3	**Aden, Gulf of** Somalia/Yemen
100	C2	**Adenau** Ger.
79	C2	**Adh Dhayd** U.A.E.
59	C3	**Adi** *i.* Indon.
78	A3	**Ādī Ārk'ay** Eth.
116	B3	**Ādīgrat** Eth.
75	B3	**Adilabad** India
141	E2	**Adirondack Mountains** U.S.A.
		Ādīs Ābeba Eth. *see* **Addis Ababa**
117	B4	**Ādīs Alem** Eth.
110	C1	**Adjud** Romania
50	B1	**Admiralty Gulf** Austr.
128	A2	**Admiralty Island** U.S.A.
104	B3	**Adour** *r.* France
106	C2	**Adra** Spain
114	B2	**Adrar** Alg.
140	C2	**Adrian** *MI* U.S.A.
139	C1	**Adrian** *TX* U.S.A.
108	B2	**Adriatic Sea** Europe
116	B3	**Ādwa** Eth.
83	K2	**Adycha** *r.* Russia
91	D3	**Adygeysk** Russia
114	B4	**Adzopé** Côte d'Ivoire
111	B3	**Aegean Sea** Greece/Turkey
101	D1	**Aerzen** Ger.
106	B1	**A Estrada** Spain
116	B3	**Afabet** Eritrea
76	C3	**Afghanistan** *country* Asia
78	B2	**'Afīf** Saudi Arabia
80	B2	**Afyon** Turkey
115	C3	**Agadez** Niger
114	B1	**Agadir** Morocco
74	B2	**Agar** India
75	D2	**Agartala** India
81	C1	**Ağdam** Azer.
81	C2	**Ağdam (abandoned)** Azer.
105	C3	**Agde** France
104	C3	**Agen** France
122	A2	**Aggeneys** S. Africa
111	C3	**Agia Varvara** Greece
111	B3	**Agios Dimitrios** Greece
111	C3	**Agios Efstratios** *i.* Greece
111	C3	**Agios Nikolaos** Greece
110	B1	**Agnita** Romania
75	B2	**Agra** India
81	C2	**Ağrı** Turkey
		Ağrı Dağı *mt.* Turkey *see* **Ararat, Mount**
108	B3	**Agrigento** *Sicily* Italy
111	B3	**Agrinio** Greece
109	B2	**Agropoli** Italy
154	B2	**Água Clara** Brazil
146	B4	**Aguadulce** Panama
144	B2	**Aguanaval** *r.* Mex.
144	B1	**Agua Prieta** Mex.
144	B2	**Aguascalientes** Mex.
155	D1	**Águas Formosas** Brazil
106	B1	**Águeda** Port.
106	C1	**Aguilar de Campoo** Spain
107	C2	**Águilas** Spain
144	B3	**Aguililla** Mex.
122	B3	**Agulhas, Cape** S. Africa
155	D2	**Agulhas Negras** *mt.* Brazil
111	C2	**Ağva** Turkey
115	C2	**Ahaggar** *plat.* Alg.
115	C2	**Ahaggar, Tassili oua-n-** *plat.* Alg.
81	C2	**Ahar** Iran
100	C1	**Ahaus** Ger.
81	C2	**Ahlat** Turkey
100	C2	**Ahlen** Ger.
74	B2	**Ahmadabad** India
73	B3	**Ahmadnagar** India
74	B2	**Ahmadpur East** Pak.
74	B1	**Ahmadpur Sial** Pak.
		Ahmedabad India *see* **Ahmadabad**
		Ahmednagar India *see* **Ahmadnagar**
144	B2	**Ahome** Mex.
79	C2	**Ahram** Iran
101	E1	**Ahrensburg** Ger.
104	C2	**Ahun** France
81	C2	**Ahvāz** Iran
122	A2	**Ai-Ais** Namibia
80	B2	**Aigialousa** Cyprus
111	B3	**Aigio** Greece
143	D2	**Aiken** U.S.A.
97	B1	**Ailt an Chorráin** Ireland
155	D1	**Aimorés** Brazil
155	D1	**Aimorés, Serra dos** *hills* Brazil
114	B2	**'Aïn Ben Tili** Maur.
107	D2	**Aïn Defla** Alg.
114	B1	**Aïn Sefra** Alg.
136	D2	**Ainsworth** U.S.A.
		Aintab Turkey *see* **Gaziantep**
107	D2	**Aïn Taya** Alg.
107	D2	**Aïn Tédélès** Alg.

115 C3 Aïr, Massif de l' mts Niger
60 A1 Airbangis Indon.
128 C2 Airdrie Can.
104 B3 Aire-sur-l'Adour France
101 E3 Aisch r. Ger.
128 A1 Aishihik Lake Can.
100 A3 Aisne r. France
59 D3 Aitape P.N.G.
110 B1 Aiud Romania
105 D3 Aix-en-Provence France
105 D2 Aix-les-Bains France
62 A1 Aizawl India
88 C2 Aizkraukle Latvia
67 C3 Aizuwakamatsu Japan
105 D3 Ajaccio Corsica France
115 E1 Ajdābiyā Libya
115 C2 Ajjer, Tassili n' plat. Alg.
74 B2 Ajmer India
138 A2 Ajo U.S.A.
77 D2 Akadyr Kazakh.
87 E3 Akbulak Russia
80 B2 Akçakale Turkey
80 B2 Akdağmadeni Turkey
88 A2 Åkersberga Sweden
118 C2 Aketi Dem. Rep. Congo
87 D4 Akhalkalaki Georgia
79 C2 Akhḑar, Jabal mts Oman
111 C3 Akhisar Turkey
87 D4 Akhtubinsk Russia
130 B1 Akimiski Island Can.
66 D3 Akita Japan
114 A3 Akjoujt Maur.
77 D1 Akkol' Kazakh.
88 B2 Akmenrags pt Latvia
Akmola Kazakh. see Astana
117 B4 Akobo South Sudan
74 B2 Akola India
78 A3 Akordat Eritrea
127 G2 Akpatok Island Can.
92 □A3 Akranes Iceland
140 C2 Akron U.S.A.
75 B1 Aksai Chin terr. Asia
80 B2 Aksaray Turkey
76 B1 Aksay Kazakh.
91 D2 Aksay Russia
80 B2 Akşehir Turkey
76 C2 Akshiganak Kazakh.
77 E2 Aksu China
78 A3 Āksum Eth.
76 B2 Aktau Kazakh.
76 B1 Aktobe Kazakh.
77 D2 Aktogay Kazakh.
88 C3 Aktsyabrski Belarus
115 C4 Akure Nigeria
92 □B2 Akureyri Iceland
142 C2 Alabama r. U.S.A.
142 C2 Alabama state U.S.A.
111 C3 Alaçatı Turkey
81 C1 Alagir Russia
151 E3 Alagoinhas Brazil
107 C1 Alagón Spain
79 B2 Al Aḩmadī Kuwait
77 E2 Alakol', Ozero salt l. Kazakh.
92 J2 Alakurtti Russia
78 B3 Al 'Alayyah Saudi Arabia
80 A2 Al 'Āmirīyah Egypt
135 C3 Alamo U.S.A.
138 B2 Alamogordo U.S.A.
144 A2 Alamos Sonora Mex.
144 B2 Alamos Sonora Mex.
144 B2 Alamos r. Mex.
136 B3 Alamosa U.S.A.
93 G3 Åland Islands Fin.
80 B2 Alanya Turkey
73 B4 Alappuzha India
80 B3 Al 'Aqabah Jordan
78 B2 Al 'Aqīq Saudi Arabia
107 C2 Alarcón, Embalse de resr Spain
80 B2 Al 'Arīsh Egypt
78 B2 Al Arţāwīyah Saudi Arabia
61 C2 Alas Indon.
111 C3 Alaşehir Turkey
128 A2 Alaska state U.S.A.
124 F3 Alaska, Gulf of U.S.A.
81 C2 Älät Azer.
87 D3 Alatyr' Russia
150 A2 Alausí Ecuador
93 H3 Alavus Fin.
52 B2 Alawoona Austr.
108 A2 Alba Italy
107 C2 Albacete Spain
110 B1 Alba Iulia Romania
109 C2 Albania country Europe
50 A3 Albany Austr.
130 B1 Albany r. Can.
143 D2 Albany GA U.S.A.
141 E2 Albany NY U.S.A.
134 B2 Albany OR U.S.A.
Al Başrah Iraq see Basra
51 D1 Albatross Bay Austr.
116 A2 Al Bawītī Egypt
115 E1 Al Bayḑā' Libya
78 B3 Al Bayḑā' Yemen
143 D1 Albemarle U.S.A.
143 E1 Albemarle Sound sea chan. U.S.A.
108 A2 Albenga Italy
51 C2 Alberga watercourse Austr.
119 D2 Albert, Lake Dem. Rep. Congo/Uganda
128 C2 Alberta prov. Can.
100 B2 Albert Kanaal canal Belgium
137 E2 Albert Lea U.S.A.
104 C3 Albi France
78 A2 Al Bi'r Saudi Arabia
78 B3 Al Birk Saudi Arabia
78 B2 Al Biyāḑh reg. Saudi Arabia
106 C2 Alboran Sea Europe
Alborz, Reshteh-ye mts Iran see Elburz Mountains
106 B2 Albufeira Port.
138 B1 Albuquerque U.S.A.
79 C2 Al Buraymī Oman
53 C3 Albury Austr.
106 B2 Alcácer do Sal Port.
106 C1 Alcalá de Henares Spain
106 C2 Alcalá la Real Spain
108 B3 Alcamo Sicily Italy
107 C1 Alcañiz Spain
106 B2 Alcántara Spain
106 C2 Alcaraz Spain
106 C2 Alcaraz, Sierra de mts Spain
106 C2 Alcaudete Spain
106 C2 Alcázar de San Juan Spain
91 D2 Alchevs'k Ukr.
155 E1 Alcobaça Brazil
107 C2 Alcoy-Alcoi Spain
107 D2 Alcúdia Spain
145 C2 Aldama Mex.
83 J3 Aldan Russia
83 J2 Aldan r. Russia
95 C4 Alderney i. Channel Is
114 A3 Aleg Maur.
155 D2 Alegre Brazil
152 C3 Alegrete Brazil
83 K3 Aleksandrovsk-Sakhalinskiy Russia
91 D1 Alekseyevka Belgorodskaya Oblast' Russia
91 D1 Alekseyevka Belgorodskaya Oblast' Russia
89 E3 Aleksin Russia
109 D2 Aleksinac Serbia
118 B3 Alèmbé Gabon
155 D2 Além Paraíba Brazil
93 F3 Ålen Norway
104 C2 Alençon France
80 B2 Aleppo Syria
150 A3 Alerta Peru
128 B2 Alert Bay Can.
105 C3 Alès France
110 B1 Aleşd Romania
108 A2 Alessandria Italy
93 E3 Ålesund Norway
124 C3 Aleutian Islands U.S.A.
83 L3 Alevina, Mys c. Russia
128 A2 Alexander Archipelago is U.S.A.
122 A2 Alexander Bay S. Africa
142 C2 Alexander City U.S.A.
55 O2 Alexander Island Antarctica
53 C3 Alexandra Austr.
54 A3 Alexandra N.Z.
111 B2 Alexandreia Greece
Alexandretta Turkey see İskenderun
116 A1 Alexandria Egypt
110 C2 Alexandria Romania
123 C3 Alexandria S. Africa
142 B2 Alexandria LA U.S.A.
137 D1 Alexandria MN U.S.A.
141 D3 Alexandria VA U.S.A.
52 A3 Alexandrina, Lake Austr.
111 C2 Alexandroupoli Greece
131 E1 Alexis r. Can.
128 B2 Alexis Creek Can.
77 E1 Aleysk Russia
107 C1 Alfaro Spain
81 C3 Al Fāw Iraq
101 D2 Alfeld (Leine) Ger.
155 C2 Alfenas Brazil
Al Fujayrah U.A.E. see Fujairah
Al Furāt r. Iraq/Syria see Euphrates
106 B2 Algeciras Spain
107 C2 Algemesí Spain
78 A3 Algena Eritrea
Alger Alg. see Algiers
114 C2 Algeria country Africa
79 C3 Al Ghayḑah Yemen
108 A2 Alghero Sardinia Italy
116 B2 Al Ghurdaqah Egypt
79 B2 Al Ghwaybiyah Saudi Arabia
115 C1 Algiers Alg.
123 C3 Algoa Bay S. Africa
137 E2 Algona U.S.A.
106 C1 Algorta Spain
81 C2 Al Ḩadīthah Iraq
79 C2 Al Ḩajar al Gharbī mts Oman
107 C2 Alhama de Murcia Spain
80 A2 Al Ḩammām Egypt
78 B2 Al Ḩanākīyah Saudi Arabia
81 C2 Al Ḩasakah Syria
81 C2 Al Ḩayy Iraq
79 C3 Al Ḩibāk des. Saudi Arabia
78 B2 Al Ḩillah Saudi Arabia
79 B2 Al Ḩinnāh Saudi Arabia
Al Ḩudaydah Yemen see Hodeidah
79 B2 Al Hufūf Saudi Arabia
115 D2 Al Ḩulayq al Kabīr hills Libya
79 C2 'Alīābād Iran
111 C3 Aliağa Turkey
111 B2 Aliakmonas r. Greece
107 C2 Alicante Spain
139 D3 Alice U.S.A.
109 C3 Alice, Punta pt Italy
51 C2 Alice Springs Austr.
75 B2 Aligarh India
81 C2 Alīgūdarz Iran
69 E1 Alihe China

118 B3 **Alima** *r.* Congo
111 C3 **Aliova** *r.* Turkey
117 C3 **Ali Sabieh** Djibouti
Al Iskandarīyah Egypt *see* **Alexandria**
116 B1 **Al Ismā'īlīyah** Egypt
123 C3 **Aliwal North** S. Africa
115 E2 **Al Jaghbūb** Libya
78 B2 **Al Jahrah** Kuwait
115 D1 **Al Jawsh** Libya
106 B2 **Aljezur** Port.
Al Jīzah Egypt *see* **Giza**
79 B2 **Al Jubayl** Saudi Arabia
79 C2 **Al Jumaylīyah** Qatar
78 B2 **Al Junaynah** Saudi Arabia
106 B2 **Aljustrel** Port.
78 B2 **Al Kahfah** Saudi Arabia
79 C2 **Al Kāmil** Oman
80 B2 **Al Karak** Jordan
79 C2 **Al Khābūrah** Oman
78 B2 **Al Khamāsīn** Saudi Arabia
116 B2 **Al Khārijah** Egypt
79 C2 **Al Khaşab** Oman
78 B3 **Al Khawkhah** Yemen
79 C2 **Al Khawr** Qatar
115 D1 **Al Khums** Libya
79 B2 **Al Khunn** Saudi Arabia
79 C2 **Al Kir'ānah** Qatar
100 B1 **Alkmaar** Neth.
115 E2 **Al Kufrah** Libya
81 C2 **Al Kūt** Iraq
Al Kuwayt Kuwait *see* **Kuwait**
Al Lādhiqīyah Syria *see* **Latakia**
75 C2 **Allahabad** India
83 K2 **Allakh-Yun'** Russia
141 D2 **Allegheny** *r.* U.S.A.
140 C3 **Allegheny Mountains** U.S.A.
97 B1 **Allen, Lough** *l.* Ireland
145 B2 **Allende** *Coahuila* Mex.
145 B2 **Allende** *Nuevo León* Mex.
141 D2 **Allentown** U.S.A.
101 D1 **Aller** *r.* Ger.
136 C2 **Alliance** *NE* U.S.A.
140 C2 **Alliance** *OH* U.S.A.
78 B2 **Al Līth** Saudi Arabia
96 C2 **Alloa** U.K.
131 C2 **Alma** Can.
Alma-Ata Kazakh. *see* **Almaty**
106 B2 **Almada** Port.
106 C2 **Almadén** Spain
Al Madīnah Saudi Arabia *see* **Medina**
116 B1 **Al Mafraq** Jordan
78 B3 **Al Maḩwīt** Yemen
78 B2 **Al Majma'ah** Saudi Arabia
135 B2 **Almanor, Lake** U.S.A.
107 C2 **Almansa** Spain
80 B2 **Al Manşūrah** Egypt
79 C2 **Al Mariyyah** U.A.E.
115 E1 **Al Marj** Libya
77 D2 **Almaty** Kazakh.
106 C1 **Almazán** Spain
151 C2 **Almeirim** Brazil
100 C1 **Almelo** Neth.
155 D1 **Almenara** Brazil
106 B1 **Almendra, Embalse de** *resr* Spain
106 B2 **Almendralejo** Spain
106 C2 **Almería** Spain
106 C2 **Almería, Golfo de** *b.* Spain
87 E3 **Al'met'yevsk** Russia
78 B2 **Al Mindak** Saudi Arabia
116 B2 **Al Minyā** Egypt
79 B2 **Al Mish'āb** Saudi Arabia
106 B2 **Almodôvar** Port.
106 B2 **Almonte** Spain
75 B2 **Almora** India
79 B2 **Al Mubarrez** Saudi Arabia
79 C2 **Al Muḑaibī** Oman
80 B3 **Al Mudawwarah** Jordan
Al Mukallā Yemen *see* **Mukalla**
Al Mukhā Yemen *see* **Mocha**
106 C2 **Almuñécar** Spain
78 A2 **Al Muwayliḩ** Saudi Arabia
111 B3 **Almyros** Greece
96 B2 **Alness** U.K.
98 C1 **Alnwick** U.K.
49 G4 **Alofi** Niue
111 B3 **Alonnisos** *i.* Greece
59 C3 **Alor** *i.* Indon.
59 C3 **Alor, Kepulauan** *is* Indon.
60 B1 **Alor Star** Malaysia
Alost Belgium *see* **Aalst**
86 C2 **Alozero (abandoned)** Russia
140 C1 **Alpena** U.S.A.
139 C2 **Alpine** U.S.A.
105 D2 **Alps** *mts* Europe
79 B3 **Al Qa'āmīyāt** *reg.* Saudi Arabia
115 D1 **Al Qaddāḩīyah** Libya
Al Qāhirah Egypt *see* **Cairo**
78 B2 **Al Qā'īyah** Saudi Arabia
81 C2 **Al Qāmishlī** Syria
80 B2 **Al Qaryatayn** Syria
79 B3 **Al Qaţn** Yemen
106 B2 **Alqueva, Barragem de** *resr* Port.
80 B2 **Al Qunayţirah (abandoned)** Syria
78 B3 **Al Qunfidhah** Saudi Arabia
116 B2 **Al Quşayr** Egypt
78 B2 **Al Quwayīyah** Saudi Arabia
101 D2 **Alsfeld** Ger.
92 H2 **Alta** Norway
92 H2 **Altaelva** *r.* Norway
68 B1 **Altai Mountains** Asia
143 D2 **Altamaha** *r.* U.S.A.
151 C2 **Altamira** Brazil
109 C2 **Altamura** Italy
68 B1 **Altay** China
68 C1 **Altay** Mongolia
105 D2 **Altdorf** Switz.
107 C2 **Altea** Spain
101 F2 **Altenburg** Ger.
100 C2 **Altenkirchen (Westerwald)** Ger.
111 C3 **Altınoluk** Turkey
111 D3 **Altıntaş** Turkey
152 B2 **Altiplano** *plain* Bol.
154 B1 **Alto Araguaia** Brazil
154 B1 **Alto Garças** Brazil
121 C2 **Alto Molócuè** Moz.
129 E3 **Altona** Can.
141 D2 **Altoona** U.S.A.
154 B1 **Alto Sucuriú** Brazil
154 B1 **Alto Taquari** Brazil
102 C2 **Altötting** Ger.
68 B2 **Altun Shan** *mts* China
134 B2 **Alturas** U.S.A.
139 D2 **Altus** U.S.A.
88 C2 **Alūksne** Latvia
78 A2 **Al 'Ulā** Saudi Arabia
115 D1 **Al 'Uqaylah** Libya
Al Uqşur Egypt *see* **Luxor**
91 C3 **Alushta** Ukr.
139 D1 **Alva** U.S.A.
145 C3 **Alvarado** Mex.
93 F3 **Älvdalen** Sweden
93 F3 **Älvdalen** *val.* Sweden
92 H2 **Älvsbyn** Sweden
78 A2 **Al Wajh** Saudi Arabia
74 B2 **Alwar** India
81 C2 **Al Widyān** *plat.* Iraq/Saudi Arabia
Alxa Youqi China *see* **Ehen Hudag**
Alxa Zuoqi China *see* **Bayan Hot**
51 C1 **Alyangula** Austr.
88 B3 **Alytus** Lith.
136 C1 **Alzada** U.S.A.
100 D3 **Alzey** Ger.
50 C2 **Amadeus, Lake** *imp. l.* Austr.
81 C2 **'Amādīyah/Amêdî** Iraq
127 G2 **Amadjuak Lake** Can.
106 B2 **Amadora** Port.
78 B2 **Amā'ir** Saudi Arabia
93 F4 **Åmål** Sweden
111 B3 **Amaliada** Greece
59 D3 **Amamapare** Indon.
154 A2 **Amambaí** Brazil
154 B2 **Amambaí** *r.* Brazil
69 E3 **Amami-Ō-shima** *i.* Japan
69 E3 **Amami-shotō** *is* Japan
77 C1 **Amankel'dy** Kazakh.
109 C3 **Amantea** Italy
151 C1 **Amapá** Brazil
106 B2 **Amareleja** Port.
139 C1 **Amarillo** U.S.A.
108 B2 **Amaro, Monte** *mt.* Italy
80 B1 **Amasya** Turkey
150 C1 **Amazon** *r.* S. America
151 D1 **Amazon, Mouths of the** Brazil
Amazonas *r.* S. America *see* **Amazon**
74 B1 **Ambala** India
121 □D3 **Ambalavao** Madag.
121 □D2 **Ambanja** Madag.
150 A2 **Ambato** Ecuador
121 □D2 **Ambato Boeny** Madag.
121 □D3 **Ambato Finandrahana** Madag.
121 □D2 **Ambatolampy** Madag.
121 □D2 **Ambatondrazaka** Madag.
101 E3 **Amberg** Ger.
146 B3 **Ambergris Caye** *i.* Belize
75 C2 **Ambikapur** India
121 □D2 **Ambilobe** Madag.
98 B1 **Ambleside** U.K.
121 □D3 **Amboasary** Madag.
121 □D3 **Ambohimahasoa** Madag.
59 C3 **Ambon** Indon.
59 C3 **Ambon** *i.* Indon.
121 □D3 **Ambositra** Madag.
121 □D3 **Ambovombe** Madag.
135 C4 **Amboy** U.S.A.
120 A1 **Ambriz** Angola
145 B2 **Amealco** Mex.
144 B2 **Ameca** Mex.
100 B1 **Ameland** *i.* Neth.
134 D2 **American Falls** U.S.A.
134 D2 **American Falls Reservoir** U.S.A.
135 D2 **American Fork** U.S.A.
49 G3 **American Samoa** *terr.* S. Pacific Ocean
143 D2 **Americus** U.S.A.
100 B1 **Amersfoort** Neth.
55 F2 **Amery Ice Shelf** Antarctica
137 E2 **Ames** U.S.A.
111 B3 **Amfissa** Greece
83 J2 **Amga** Russia
66 C1 **Amgu** Russia
115 C2 **Amguid** Alg.
83 K3 **Amgun'** *r.* Russia
131 D2 **Amherst** Can.
104 C2 **Amiens** France
73 B3 **Amindivi Islands** India
122 A1 **Aminuis** Namibia
74 A2 **Amir Chah** Pak.
129 D2 **Amisk Lake** Can.
139 C3 **Amistad Reservoir** Mex./U.S.A.
98 A2 **Amlwch** U.K.

80 B2 **'Ammān** Jordan
81 D2 **Āmol** Iran
111 C3 **Amorgos** *i.* Greece
142 C2 **Amory** U.S.A.
130 C2 **Amos** Can.
Amoy China *see* **Xiamen**
155 C2 **Amparo** Brazil
107 D1 **Amposta** Spain
75 B2 **Amravati** India
74 B1 **Amritsar** India
100 B1 **Amstelveen** Neth.
100 B1 **Amsterdam** Neth.
103 C2 **Amstetten** Austria
115 E3 **Am Timan** Chad
76 B2 **Amudar'ya** *r.* Asia
126 E1 **Amund Ringnes Island** Can.
126 C2 **Amundsen Gulf** Can.
55 M2 **Amundsen Sea** Antarctica
61 C2 **Amuntai** Indon.
Amur *r.* China *see* **Heilong Jiang**
78 A3 **'Amur, Wadi** *watercourse* Sudan
83 I2 **Anabar** *r.* Russia
83 I2 **Anabarskiy Zaliv** *b.* Russia
134 D1 **Anaconda** U.S.A.
139 D1 **Anadarko** U.S.A.
80 B1 **Anadolu Dağları** *mts* Turkey
83 M2 **Anadyr'** *r.* Russia
81 C2 **'Ānah** Iraq
145 B2 **Anáhuac** Mex.
60 B1 **Anambas, Kepulauan** *is* Indon.
137 E2 **Anamosa** U.S.A.
80 B2 **Anamur** Turkey
67 B4 **Anan** Japan
73 B3 **Anantapur** India
74 B1 **Anantnag** India
90 B2 **Anan'yiv** Ukr.
91 D3 **Anapa** Russia
154 C1 **Anápolis** Brazil
152 B3 **Añatuya** Arg.
97 B1 **An Baile Thiar** Ireland
65 B2 **Anbyon** N. Korea
104 B2 **Ancenis** France
108 B2 **Ancona** Italy
153 A5 **Ancud** Chile
Anda China *see* **Daqing**
93 E3 **Åndalsnes** Norway
142 C2 **Andalusia** U.S.A.
73 D3 **Andaman Islands** India
63 A2 **Andaman Sea** Indian Ocean
121 □D2 **Andapa** Madag.
100 B2 **Andelst** Neth.
92 G2 **Andenes** Norway
100 B2 **Andenne** Belgium
100 B2 **Anderlecht** Belgium
126 C2 **Anderson** *r.* Can.
126 B2 **Anderson** *AK* U.S.A.
140 B2 **Anderson** *IN* U.S.A.
143 D2 **Anderson** *SC* U.S.A.
148 D3 **Andes** *mts* S. America
77 D2 **Andijon** Uzbek.
121 □D2 **Andilamena** Madag.
121 □D2 **Andilanatoby** Madag.
121 □D2 **Andoany** Madag.
Andong China *see* **Dandong**
65 B2 **Andong** S. Korea
107 D1 **Andorra** *country* Europe
107 D1 **Andorra la Vella** Andorra
99 C3 **Andover** U.K.
154 B2 **Andradina** Brazil
89 D2 **Andreapol'** Russia
155 D2 **Andrelândia** Brazil
139 C2 **Andrews** U.S.A.
109 C2 **Andria** Italy
121 □D3 **Androka** Madag.
146 C2 **Andros** *i.* Bahamas
111 B3 **Andros** *i.* Greece
143 E4 **Andros Town** Bahamas
73 B3 **Andrott** *i.* India
90 B1 **Andrushivka** Ukr.
92 G2 **Andselv** Norway
106 C2 **Andújar** Spain
120 A2 **Andulo** Angola
114 C3 **Anéfis** Mali
115 D3 **Aney** Niger
83 H3 **Angara** *r.* Russia
69 C1 **Angarsk** Russia
93 G3 **Ånge** Sweden
144 A2 **Ángel de la Guarda, Isla** *i.* Mex.
64 B1 **Angeles** Phil.
150 B1 **Angel Falls** Venez.
93 F4 **Ängelholm** Sweden
92 G3 **Ångermanälven** *r.* Sweden
104 B2 **Angers** France
129 E1 **Angikuni Lake** Can.
98 A2 **Anglesey** *i.* U.K.
121 C2 **Angoche** Moz.
120 A2 **Angola** *country* Africa
140 C2 **Angola** U.S.A.
128 A2 **Angoon** U.S.A.
104 C2 **Angoulême** France
77 D2 **Angren** Uzbek.
147 D3 **Anguilla** *terr.* West Indies
75 C2 **Angul** India
93 F4 **Anholt** *i.* Denmark
71 B3 **Anhua** China
70 B2 **Anhui** *prov.* China
154 B1 **Anhumas** Brazil
154 C1 **Anicuns** Brazil
66 D1 **Aniva, Mys** *c.* Russia
65 B2 **Anjŭ** N. Korea
70 A2 **Ankang** China
80 B2 **Ankara** Turkey
70 B2 **Anlu** China
91 E1 **Anna** Russia
115 C1 **Annaba** Alg.
101 F2 **Annaberg-Buchholz** Ger.
78 B3 **An Nābiyah** Yemen
78 B2 **An Nafūd** *des.* Saudi Arabia
81 C2 **An Najaf** Iraq
96 C3 **Annan** U.K.
141 D3 **Annapolis** U.S.A.
75 C2 **Annapurna I** *mt.* Nepal
140 C2 **Ann Arbor** U.S.A.
150 C1 **Anna Regina** Guyana
81 C2 **An Nāşirīyah** Iraq
105 D2 **Annecy** France
78 B3 **An Nimāş** Saudi Arabia
62 B1 **Anning** China
142 C2 **Anniston** U.S.A.
105 C2 **Annonay** France
79 B2 **An Nu'ayrīyah** Saudi Arabia
121 □D2 **Anorontany, Tanjona** *hd* Madag.
71 B3 **Anpu** China
70 B2 **Anqing** China
102 C2 **Ansbach** Ger.
70 C1 **Anshan** China
71 A3 **Anshun** China
114 C3 **Ansongo** Mali
150 A3 **Antabamba** Peru
80 B2 **Antakya** Turkey
121 □E2 **Antalaha** Madag.
80 B2 **Antalya** Turkey
80 B2 **Antalya Körfezi** *g.* Turkey
121 □D2 **Antananarivo** Madag.
55 Q3 **Antarctic Peninsula** Antarctica
96 B2 **An Teallach** *mt.* U.K.
106 C2 **Antequera** Spain
138 B2 **Anthony** U.S.A.
114 B2 **Anti-Atlas** *mts* Morocco
105 D3 **Antibes** France
131 D2 **Anticosti, Île d'** *i.* Can.
131 D2 **Antigonish** Can.
147 D3 **Antigua** *i.* Antigua
147 D3 **Antigua and Barbuda** *country* West Indies
145 C2 **Antiguo-Morelos** Mex.
111 B3 **Antikythira** *i.* Greece
Antioch Turkey *see* **Antakya**
49 F6 **Antipodes Islands** N.Z.
152 A3 **Antofagasta** Chile
154 C3 **Antonina** Brazil
97 C1 **Antrim** U.K.
97 C1 **Antrim Hills** U.K.
121 □D2 **Antsalova** Madag.
121 □D2 **Antsirabe** Madag.
121 □D2 **Antsirañana** Madag.
121 □D2 **Antsohihy** Madag.
Antwerp Belgium *see* **Antwerpen**
100 B2 **Antwerpen** Belgium
An Uaimh Ireland *see* **Navan**
74 B2 **Anupgarh** India
73 C4 **Anuradhapura** Sri Lanka
51 C3 **Anxious Bay** Austr.
70 B2 **Anyang** China
65 B2 **Anyang** S. Korea
108 B2 **Anzio** Italy
66 D2 **Aomori** Japan
54 B2 **Aoraki/Mount Cook** *mt.* N.Z.
108 A1 **Aosta** Italy
143 D3 **Apalachee Bay** U.S.A.
150 B2 **Apaporis** *r.* Col.
154 B2 **Aparecida do Tabuado** Brazil
64 B1 **Aparri** Phil.
86 C2 **Apatity** Russia
144 B3 **Apatzingán** Mex.
100 B1 **Apeldoorn** Neth.
100 C1 **Apen** Ger.
108 A2 **Apennines** *mts* Italy
49 G3 **Apia** Samoa
154 C2 **Apiaí** Brazil
64 B2 **Apo, Mount** *vol.* Phil.
101 E2 **Apolda** Ger.
52 B3 **Apollo Bay** Austr.
143 D3 **Apopka, Lake** U.S.A.
154 B1 **Aporé** Brazil
154 B1 **Aporé** *r.* Brazil
80 B2 **Apostolos Andreas, Cape** Cyprus
133 E3 **Appalachian Mountains** U.S.A.
53 D2 **Appin** Austr.
140 B2 **Appleton** U.S.A.
108 B2 **Aprilia** Italy
91 D3 **Apsheronsk** Russia
154 B2 **Apucarana** Brazil
154 B2 **Apucarana, Serra da** *hills* Brazil
78 A2 **Aqaba, Gulf of** Asia
154 A1 **Aquidauana** *r.* Brazil
117 A4 **Arab, Bahr el** *watercourse* Sudan
Arabian Gulf Asia *see* **The Gulf**
78 B2 **Arabian Peninsula** Asia
56 G5 **Arabian Sea** Indian Ocean
151 E3 **Aracaju** Brazil
151 E2 **Aracati** Brazil
154 B2 **Araçatuba** Brazil
155 D1 **Aracruz** Brazil
155 D1 **Araçuaí** Brazil
110 B1 **Arad** Romania
115 E3 **Arada** Chad
156 C6 **Arafura Sea** Austr./Indon.
154 B1 **Aragarças** Brazil
107 C1 **Aragón** *r.* Spain
151 D2 **Araguaia** *r.* Brazil
151 D2 **Araguaína** Brazil
154 C1 **Araguari** Brazil
115 C2 **Arak** Alg.
81 C2 **Ārāk** Iran

62 A1 **Arakan Yoma** *mts* Myanmar
81 C1 **Arak's** *r.* Armenia
76 C2 **Aral Sea** *salt l.* Kazakh./Uzbek.
76 C2 **Aral'sk** Kazakh.
Aral'skoye More *salt l.* Kazakh./Uzbek. *see* **Aral Sea**
106 C1 **Aranda de Duero** Spain
109 D2 **Aranđelovac** Serbia
97 B2 **Aran Islands** Ireland
106 C1 **Aranjuez** Spain
122 A1 **Aranos** Namibia
139 D3 **Aransas Pass** U.S.A.
67 B4 **Arao** Japan
114 B3 **Araouane** Mali
151 E2 **Arapiraca** Brazil
154 B2 **Arapongas** Brazil
154 C3 **Araquari** Brazil
78 B1 **'Ar'ar** Saudi Arabia
154 C2 **Araraquara** Brazil
151 C2 **Araras** Brazil
154 B3 **Araras, Serra das** *mts* Brazil
52 B3 **Ararat** Austr.
81 C2 **Ararat, Mount** Turkey
155 D2 **Araruama, Lago de** *lag.* Brazil
155 E1 **Arataca** Brazil
Aratürük China *see* **Yiwu**
150 A1 **Arauca** Col.
154 C1 **Araxá** Brazil
81 C2 **Arbīl/Hewlêr** Iraq
96 C2 **Arbroath** U.K.
74 A2 **Arbū-ye Shamālī, Dasht-e** *des.* Afgh.
104 B3 **Arcachon** France
143 D3 **Arcadia** U.S.A.
134 B2 **Arcata** U.S.A.
145 B3 **Arcelia** Mex.
86 D2 **Archangel** Russia
51 D1 **Archer** *r.* Austr.
134 D2 **Arco** U.S.A.
106 B2 **Arcos de la Frontera** Spain
127 F2 **Arctic Bay** Can.
160 **Arctic Ocean**
126 C2 **Arctic Red** *r.* Can.
81 C2 **Ardabīl** Iran
81 C1 **Ardahan** Turkey
93 E3 **Årdalstangen** Norway
100 B3 **Ardennes** *plat.* Belgium
81 D2 **Ardestān** Iran
53 C2 **Ardlethan** Austr.
139 D2 **Ardmore** U.S.A.
96 A2 **Ardnamurchan, Point of** U.K.
52 A2 **Ardrossan** Austr.
96 B3 **Ardrossan** U.K.
135 B3 **Arena, Point** U.S.A.
93 E4 **Arendal** Norway
101 E1 **Arendsee (Altmark)** Ger.
150 A3 **Arequipa** Peru
151 C2 **Arere** Brazil
106 C1 **Arévalo** Spain
108 B2 **Arezzo** Italy
104 B2 **Argentan** France
153 B4 **Argentina** *country* S. America
153 A6 **Argentino, Lago** *l.* Arg.
104 C2 **Argenton-sur-Creuse** France
110 C2 **Argeș** *r.* Romania
74 A1 **Arghandāb Rōd** *r.* Afgh.
111 B3 **Argolikos Kolpos** *b.* Greece
111 B3 **Argos** Greece
111 B3 **Argostoli** Greece
107 C1 **Arguis** Spain
69 E1 **Argun'** *r.* China/Russia
50 B1 **Argyle, Lake** Austr.
122 A2 **Ariamsvlei** Namibia
152 A2 **Arica** Chile
96 A2 **Arinagour** U.K.
155 C1 **Arinos** Brazil
150 C3 **Aripuanã** Brazil
150 B2 **Aripuanã** *r.* Brazil
150 B2 **Ariquemes** Brazil
154 B1 **Ariranhá** *r.* Brazil
138 A2 **Arizona** *state* U.S.A.
144 A1 **Arizpe** Mex.
78 B2 **'Arjah** Saudi Arabia
92 G2 **Arjeplog** Sweden
142 B2 **Arkadelphia** U.S.A.
77 C1 **Arkalyk** Kazakh.
142 B2 **Arkansas** *r.* U.S.A.
142 B1 **Arkansas** *state* U.S.A.
137 D3 **Arkansas City** U.S.A.
Arkhangel'sk Russia *see* **Archangel**
97 C2 **Arklow** Ireland
102 C1 **Arkona, Kap** *c.* Ger.
82 G1 **Arkticheskogo Instituta, Ostrova** *is* Russia
105 C3 **Arles** France
115 C3 **Arlit** Niger
100 B3 **Arlon** Belgium
97 C1 **Armagh** U.K.
116 B2 **Armant** Egypt
81 C1 **Armavir** Russia
81 C1 **Armenia** *country* Asia
150 A1 **Armenia** Col.
144 B3 **Armeria** Mex.
53 D2 **Armidale** Austr.
130 B1 **Armstrong** Can.
80 B1 **Armyans'k** Ukr.
80 B2 **Arnauti, Cape** Cyprus
100 B2 **Arnhem** Neth.
51 C1 **Arnhem, Cape** Austr.
51 C1 **Arnhem Bay** Austr.
51 C1 **Arnhem Land** *reg.* Austr.
108 B2 **Arno** *r.* Italy
52 A2 **Arno Bay** Austr.
130 C2 **Arnprior** Can.
100 D2 **Arnsberg** Ger.
101 E2 **Arnstadt** Ger.
122 A2 **Aroab** Namibia
101 D2 **Arolsen** Ger.
78 A3 **Aroma** Sudan
108 A1 **Arona** Italy
144 B2 **Aros** *r.* Mex.
75 C2 **Arrah** India
81 C2 **Ar Ramādī** Iraq
96 B3 **Arran** *i.* U.K.
97 B1 **Arranmore Island** Ireland
80 B2 **Ar Raqqah** Syria
104 C1 **Arras** France
78 B2 **Ar Rass** Saudi Arabia
145 C3 **Arriagá** Mex.
79 C2 **Ar Rimāl** *reg.* Saudi Arabia
Ar Riyāḍ Saudi Arabia *see* **Riyadh**
145 C2 **Arroyo Seco** Mex.
79 C2 **Ar Rustāq** Oman
80 C2 **Ar Ruṭbah** Iraq
81 D3 **Arsanajān** Iran
66 B2 **Arsen'yev** Russia
111 B3 **Arta** Greece
144 B3 **Arteaga** Mex.
66 B2 **Artem** Russia
91 D2 **Artemivs'k** Ukr.
104 C2 **Artenay** France
138 C2 **Artesia** U.S.A.
51 E2 **Arthur Point** Austr.
54 B2 **Arthur's Pass** N.Z.
152 C4 **Artigas** Uru.
129 D1 **Artillery Lake** Can.
90 B2 **Artsyz** Ukr.
77 D3 **Artux** China
81 C1 **Artvin** Turkey
59 C3 **Aru, Kepulauan** *is* Indon.
119 D2 **Arua** Uganda
147 D3 **Aruba** *terr.* West Indies
119 D3 **Arusha** Tanz.
69 C1 **Arvayheer** Mongolia
129 E1 **Arviat** Can.
92 G2 **Arvidsjaur** Sweden
93 F4 **Arvika** Sweden
87 D3 **Arzamas** Russia
107 C2 **Arzew** Alg.
100 C2 **Arzfeld** Ger.
101 F2 **Aš** Czech Rep.
115 C4 **Asaba** Nigeria
74 B1 **Asadābād** Afgh.
66 D2 **Asahi-dake** *vol.* Japan
66 D2 **Asahikawa** Japan
78 B3 **Āsalē** *l.* Eth.
75 C2 **Asansol** India
131 C2 **Asbestos** Can.
109 C2 **Ascea** Italy
152 B2 **Ascensión** Bol.
113 D7 **Ascension** *i.* S. Atlantic Ocean
145 D3 **Ascensión, Bahía de la** *b.* Mex.
101 D3 **Aschaffenburg** Ger.
100 C2 **Ascheberg** Ger.
101 E2 **Aschersleben** Ger.
108 B2 **Ascoli Piceno** Italy
92 G3 **Åsele** Sweden
110 B2 **Asenovgrad** Bulg.
76 B3 **Aşgabat** Turkm.
50 A2 **Ashburton** *watercourse* Austr.
54 B2 **Ashburton** N.Z.
142 B2 **Ashdown** U.S.A.
143 D1 **Asheville** U.S.A.
53 D1 **Ashford** Austr.
99 D3 **Ashford** U.K.
Ashgabat Turkm. *see* **Aşgabat**
98 C1 **Ashington** U.K.
67 B4 **Ashizuri-misaki** *pt* Japan
136 D3 **Ashland** *KS* U.S.A.
140 C3 **Ashland** *KY* U.S.A.
140 C2 **Ashland** *OH* U.S.A.
134 B2 **Ashland** *OR* U.S.A.
140 A1 **Ashland** *WI* U.S.A.
88 C3 **Ashmyany** Belarus
78 B3 **Ash Sharawrah** Saudi Arabia
Ash Shāriqah U.A.E. *see* **Sharjah**
81 C2 **Ash Sharqāṭ** Iraq
81 C2 **Ash Shaṭrah** Iraq
79 B3 **Ash Shiḥr** Yemen
79 C2 **Ash Şhināş** Oman
78 B2 **Ash Shu'bah** Saudi Arabia
78 B2 **Ash Shumlūl** Saudi Arabia
140 C2 **Ashtabula** U.S.A.
131 D1 **Ashuanipi Lake** Can.
106 B2 **Asilah** Morocco
108 A2 **Asinara, Golfo dell'** *b. Sardinia* Italy
82 G3 **Asino** Russia
88 C3 **Asipovichy** Belarus
78 B2 **'Asīr** *reg.* Saudi Arabia
93 F4 **Askim** Norway
68 C1 **Askiz** Russia
116 B3 **Asmara** Eritrea
93 F4 **Åsnen** *l.* Sweden
116 B2 **Asoteriba, Jebel** *mt.* Sudan
103 D2 **Aspang-Markt** Austria
136 B3 **Aspen** U.S.A.
54 A2 **Aspiring, Mount** N.Z.
117 C3 **Assab** Eritrea
Aş Şaḩrā' al Gharbīyah *des.* Egypt *see* **Western Desert**
Aş Şaḩrā' ash Sharqīyah *des.* Egypt *see* **Eastern Desert**
78 B2 **As Salamiyah** Saudi Arabia
81 C2 **As Samāwah** Iraq
79 C2 **Aş Şanām** *reg.* Saudi Arabia
115 E2 **As Sarīr** *reg.* Libya
100 C1 **Assen** Neth.
100 B2 **Assesse** Belgium
115 D1 **As Sidrah** Libya

129 D3 **Assiniboia** Can.
128 C2 **Assiniboine, Mount** Can.
154 B2 **Assis** Brazil
78 B2 **Aş Şubayḩīyah** Kuwait
81 C2 **As Sulaymānīyah/Slêmânî** Iraq
78 B2 **As Sulaymī** Saudi Arabia
78 B2 **As Sulayyil** Saudi Arabia
78 B2 **As Sūq** Saudi Arabia
80 B2 **As Suwaydā'** Syria
79 C2 **As Suwayq** Oman
As Suways Egypt *see* **Suez**
111 B3 **Astakos** Greece
77 D1 **Astana** Kazakh.
81 C2 **Āstārā** Iran
108 A2 **Asti** Italy
74 B1 **Astor** Pak.
106 B1 **Astorga** Spain
134 B1 **Astoria** U.S.A.
87 D4 **Astrakhan'** Russia
88 C3 **Astravyets** Belarus
111 C3 **Astypalaia** *i.* Greece
152 C3 **Asunción** Para.
116 B2 **Aswān** Egypt
116 B2 **Asyūţ** Egypt
Atacama, Desierto de *des.* Chile *see* **Atacama Desert**
152 B3 **Atacama, Salar de** *salt flat* Chile
152 B3 **Atacama Desert** *des.* Chile
114 C4 **Atakpamé** Togo
111 B3 **Atalanti** Greece
150 A3 **Atalaya** Peru
77 C3 **Atamyrat** Turkm.
78 B3 **'Ataq** Yemen
114 A2 **Atâr** Maur.
135 B3 **Atascadero** U.S.A.
77 D2 **Atasu** Kazakh.
111 C3 **Atavyros** *mt.* Greece
116 B3 **Atbara** Sudan
116 B3 **Atbara** *r.* Sudan
77 C1 **Atbasar** Kazakh.
137 D3 **Atchison** U.S.A.
108 B2 **Aterno** *r.* Italy
108 B2 **Atessa** Italy
100 A2 **Ath** Belgium
128 C2 **Athabasca** Can.
129 C2 **Athabasca** *r.* Can.
129 D2 **Athabasca, Lake** Can.
111 B3 **Athens** Greece
143 D2 **Athens** *GA* U.S.A.
140 C3 **Athens** *OH* U.S.A.
143 D1 **Athens** *TN* U.S.A.
139 D2 **Athens** *TX* U.S.A.
Athina Greece *see* **Athens**
97 C2 **Athlone** Ireland
111 B2 **Athos** *mt.* Greece
97 C2 **Athy** Ireland
115 D3 **Ati** Chad
130 A2 **Atikokan** Can.
87 D3 **Atkarsk** Russia
143 D2 **Atlanta** U.S.A.
137 D2 **Atlantic** U.S.A.
141 E3 **Atlantic City** U.S.A.
158 **Atlantic Ocean**
122 A3 **Atlantis** S. Africa
114 B1 **Atlas Mountains** Africa
114 C1 **Atlas Saharien** *mts* Alg.
128 A2 **Atlin** Can.
128 A2 **Atlin Lake** Can.
142 C2 **Atmore** U.S.A.
139 D2 **Atoka** U.S.A.
75 C2 **Atrai** *r.* India
78 B2 **Aţ Ţā'if** Saudi Arabia
63 B2 **Attapu** Laos
130 B1 **Attawapiskat** Can.
130 B1 **Attawapiskat** *r.* Can.
130 B1 **Attawapiskat Lake** Can.
100 C2 **Attendorn** Ger.
116 B2 **Aţ Ţūr** Egypt
78 B3 **At Turbah** Yemen
76 B2 **Atyrau** Kazakh.
105 C3 **Aubenas** France
126 C2 **Aubry Lake** Can.
142 C2 **Auburn** *AL* U.S.A.
135 B3 **Auburn** *CA* U.S.A.
137 D2 **Auburn** *NE* U.S.A.
141 D2 **Auburn** *NY* U.S.A.
104 C2 **Aubusson** France
104 C3 **Auch** France
54 B1 **Auckland** N.Z.
48 F6 **Auckland Islands** *is* N.Z.
101 F2 **Aue** Ger.
102 C2 **Augsburg** Ger.
109 C3 **Augusta** *Sicily* Italy
143 D2 **Augusta** *GA* U.S.A.
137 D3 **Augusta** *KS* U.S.A.
141 F2 **Augusta** *ME* U.S.A.
50 A2 **Augustus, Mount** Austr.
100 A2 **Aulnoye-Aymeries** France
62 A2 **Aunglan** Myanmar
122 B2 **Auob** *watercourse* Namibia/S. Africa
74 B3 **Aurangabad** India
100 C1 **Aurich** Ger.
154 B1 **Aurilândia** Brazil
104 C3 **Aurillac** France
136 C3 **Aurora** *CO* U.S.A.
140 B2 **Aurora** *IL* U.S.A.
137 D2 **Aurora** *NE* U.S.A.
122 A2 **Aus** Namibia
137 E2 **Austin** *MN* U.S.A.
135 C3 **Austin** *NV* U.S.A.
139 D2 **Austin** *TX* U.S.A.
50 B2 **Australia** *country* Oceania
159 D7 **Australian-Antarctic Basin** Southern Ocean
53 C3 **Australian Capital Territory** *admin. div.* Austr.
102 C2 **Austria** *country* Europe
144 B3 **Autlán** Mex.
105 C2 **Autun** France
105 C2 **Auxerre** France
105 D2 **Auxonne** France
105 C2 **Avallon** France
131 E2 **Avalon Peninsula** Can.
154 C2 **Avaré** Brazil
49 H4 **Avarua** Cook Is
91 D2 **Avdiyivka** Ukr.
106 B1 **Aveiro** Port.
109 B2 **Avellino** Italy
100 A2 **Avesnes-sur-Helpe** France
93 G3 **Avesta** Sweden
108 B2 **Avezzano** Italy
96 C2 **Aviemore** U.K.
109 C2 **Avigliano** Italy
105 C3 **Avignon** France
106 C1 **Ávila** Spain
106 B1 **Avilés** Spain
109 C3 **Avola** *Sicily* Italy
99 B2 **Avon** *r. England* U.K.
99 C3 **Avon** *r. England* U.K.
104 B2 **Avranches** France
54 B1 **Awanui** N.Z.
117 C4 **Āwash** Eth.
117 C3 **Āwash** *r.* Eth.
115 D2 **Awbārī** Libya
115 D2 **Awbārī, Idhān** *des.* Libya
117 C4 **Aw Dheegle** Somalia
96 B2 **Awe, Loch** *l.* U.K.
117 A4 **Aweil** South Sudan
126 E1 **Axel Heiberg Island** Can.
114 B4 **Axim** Ghana
150 A3 **Ayacucho** Peru
77 E2 **Ayagoz** Kazakh.
68 B2 **Ayakkum Hu** *salt l.* China
106 B2 **Ayamonte** Spain
83 K3 **Ayan** Russia
150 A3 **Ayaviri** Peru
76 A2 **Aybas** Kazakh.
91 D2 **Aydar** *r.* Ukr.
77 C2 **Aydarko'l ko'li** *l.* Uzbek.
111 C3 **Aydın** Turkey
99 C3 **Aylesbury** U.K.
106 C1 **Ayllón** Spain
129 D1 **Aylmer Lake** Can.
117 B4 **Ayod** South Sudan
83 M2 **Ayon, Ostrov** *i.* Russia
114 B3 **'Ayoûn el 'Atroûs** Maur.
51 D1 **Ayr** Austr.
96 B3 **Ayr** U.K.
98 A1 **Ayre, Point of** Isle of Man
76 C2 **Ayteke Bi** Kazakh.
110 C2 **Aytos** Bulg.
145 C3 **Ayutla** Mex.
63 B2 **Ayutthaya** Thai.
111 C3 **Ayvacık** Turkey
111 C3 **Ayvalık** Turkey
Azania *reg.* Somalia *see* **Jubaland**
114 C3 **Azaouagh, Vallée de** *watercourse* Mali/Niger
77 C2 **Azat, Gory** *h.* Kazakh.
114 B3 **Azawad** *reg.* Mali
Azbine *mts* Niger *see* **Aïr, Massif de l'**
81 C1 **Azerbaijan** *country* Asia
77 C1 **Azhibeksor, Ozero** *salt l.* Kazakh.
86 D2 **Azopol'ye** Russia
84 D5 **Azores** *aut. reg.* Port.
91 D2 **Azov** Russia
91 D2 **Azov, Sea of** Russia/Ukr.
Azraq, Bahr el *r.* Eth./Sudan *see* **Blue Nile**
106 B2 **Azuaga** Spain
146 B4 **Azuero, Península de** *pen.* Panama
153 C4 **Azul** Arg.
80 B2 **Az Zaqāzīq** Egypt
80 B2 **Az Zarqā'** Jordan
78 B3 **Az Zaydīyah** Yemen
114 C2 **Azzel Matti, Sebkha** *salt pan* Alg.
78 B2 **Az Zilfī** Saudi Arabia
78 B3 **Az Zuqur** *i.* Yemen

B

63 B2 **Ba, Sông** *r.* Vietnam
117 C4 **Baardheere** Somalia
77 C3 **Bābā, Kōh-e** *mts* Afgh.
110 C2 **Babadag** Romania
111 C2 **Babaeski** Turkey
117 C3 **Bāb al Mandab** *str.* Africa/Asia
61 C2 **Babana** Indon.
59 C3 **Babar** *i.* Indon.
119 D3 **Babati** Tanz.
89 E2 **Babayevo** Russia
128 B2 **Babine** *r.* Can.
128 B2 **Babine Lake** Can.
59 C3 **Babo** Indon.
81 D2 **Bābol** Iran
122 A3 **Baboon Point** S. Africa
88 C3 **Babruysk** Belarus
64 B1 **Babuyan** *i.* Phil.
64 B1 **Babuyan Islands** Phil.
151 D2 **Bacabal** Brazil
59 C3 **Bacan** *i.* Indon.
110 C1 **Bacău** Romania
52 B3 **Bacchus Marsh** Austr.

77 D3 **Bachu** China
129 E1 **Back** *r.* Can.
109 C1 **Bačka Palanka** Serbia
63 B3 **Bac Liêu** Vietnam
64 B1 **Bacolod** Phil.
130 C1 **Bacqueville, Lac** *l.* Can.
106 B2 **Badajoz** Spain
62 A1 **Badarpur** India
101 F1 **Bad Belzig** Ger.
101 E2 **Bad Berka** Ger.
101 D2 **Bad Berleburg** Ger.
101 E1 **Bad Bevensen** Ger.
100 C2 **Bad Ems** Ger.
103 D2 **Baden** Austria
102 B2 **Baden-Baden** Ger.
101 E2 **Bad Harzburg** Ger.
101 D2 **Bad Hersfeld** Ger.
102 C2 **Bad Hofgastein** Austria
101 D2 **Bad Homburg vor der Höhe** Ger.
74 A2 **Badin** Pak.
Bādiyat ash Shām *des.* Asia *see* **Syrian Desert**
101 E2 **Bad Kissingen** Ger.
100 C3 **Bad Kreuznach** Ger.
101 E2 **Bad Lauterberg im Harz** Ger.
101 D2 **Bad Lippspringe** Ger.
101 D3 **Bad Mergentheim** Ger.
101 D2 **Bad Nauheim** Ger.
100 C2 **Bad Neuenahr-Ahrweiler** Ger.
101 E2 **Bad Neustadt an der Saale** Ger.
101 E1 **Bad Oldesloe** Ger.
101 D2 **Bad Pyrmont** Ger.
78 A2 **Badr Ḩunayn** Saudi Arabia
101 D1 **Bad Salzuflen** Ger.
101 E2 **Bad Salzungen** Ger.
102 C1 **Bad Schwartau** Ger.
101 E1 **Bad Segeberg** Ger.
100 C3 **Bad Sobernheim** Ger.
101 E2 **Bad Staffelstein** Ger.
73 C4 **Badulla** Sri Lanka
100 D1 **Bad Zwischenahn** Ger.
65 A2 **Baengnyeong-do** *i.* S. Korea
106 C2 **Baeza** Spain
114 A3 **Bafatá** Guinea-Bissau
160 O2 **Baffin Bay** *sea* Can./Greenland
127 G2 **Baffin Island** Can.
118 B2 **Bafia** Cameroon
114 A3 **Bafing** *r.* Africa
114 A3 **Bafoulabé** Mali
118 B2 **Bafoussam** Cameroon
76 B3 **Bāfq** Iran
80 B1 **Bafra** Turkey
79 C2 **Bāft** Iran
119 C2 **Bafwasende** Dem. Rep. Congo
119 D3 **Bagamoyo** Tanz.
60 B1 **Bagan Datuk** Malaysia
120 B2 **Bagani** Namibia
60 B1 **Bagansiapiapi** Indon.
138 A2 **Bagdad** U.S.A.
152 C4 **Bagé** Brazil
97 C2 **Bagenalstown** Ireland
81 C2 **Baghdād** Iraq
77 C3 **Baghlān** Afgh.
104 C3 **Bagnères-de-Luchon** France
88 B3 **Bagrationovsk** Russia
Bagrax China *see* **Bohu**
64 B1 **Baguio** Phil.
115 C3 **Bagzane, Monts** *mts* Niger
Bahamas *country* West Indies *see* **The Bahamas**
146 C2 **Bahamas, The** *country* West Indies
75 C2 **Baharampur** India
Bahariya Oasis Egypt *see* **Bahrīyah, Wāḩāt al**
76 B3 **Baharly** Turkm.
60 B1 **Bahau** Malaysia
72 B2 **Bahawalnagar** Pak.
74 B2 **Bahawalpur** Pak.
153 B4 **Bahía Blanca** Arg.
144 A2 **Bahía Kino** Mex.
152 C3 **Bahía Negra** Para.
144 A2 **Bahía Tortugas** Mex.
117 B3 **Bahir Dar** Eth.
75 C2 **Bahraich** India
79 C2 **Bahrain** *country* Asia
116 A2 **Bahrīyah, Wāḩāt al** *oasis* Egypt
79 D2 **Bāhū Kālāt** Iran
110 B1 **Baia Mare** Romania
69 E1 **Baicheng** China
131 D2 **Baie-Comeau** Can.
Baie-du-Poste. Can. *see* **Mistissini**
131 C2 **Baie-St-Paul** Can.
65 B1 **Baihe** China
69 D1 **Baikal, Lake** Russia
110 B2 **Băilești** Romania
68 C2 **Baima** China
143 D2 **Bainbridge** U.S.A.
48 F2 **Bairiki** Kiribati
Bairin Youqi China *see* **Daban**
53 C3 **Bairnsdale** Austr.
71 A3 **Baise** China
65 B1 **Baishan** *Jilin* China
65 B1 **Baishan** *Jilin* China
65 B1 **Baitou Shan** *mt.* China/N. Korea
70 A2 **Baiyin** China
116 B3 **Baiyuda Desert** Sudan
103 D2 **Baja** Hungary
144 A1 **Baja California** *pen.* Mex.
78 B3 **Bājil** Yemen
114 A3 **Bakel** Senegal
135 C3 **Baker** *CA* U.S.A.
136 C1 **Baker** *MT* U.S.A.
134 C2 **Baker** *OR* U.S.A.
134 B1 **Baker, Mount** *vol.* U.S.A.
129 E1 **Baker Foreland** *hd* Can.
49 G2 **Baker Island** N. Pacific Ocean
129 E1 **Baker Lake** Can.
129 E1 **Baker Lake** Can.
135 C3 **Bakersfield** U.S.A.
91 C3 **Bakhchysaray** Ukr.
91 C1 **Bakhmach** Ukr.
Bākhtarān Iran *see* **Kermānshāh**
Bakı Azer. *see* **Baku**
111 C2 **Bakırköy** Turkey
92 □C2 **Bakkaflói** *b.* Iceland
118 C2 **Bakouma** C.A.R.
81 C1 **Baku** Azer.
64 A2 **Balabac** Phil.
64 A2 **Balabac** *i.* Phil.
64 A2 **Balabac Strait** Malaysia/Phil.
61 C2 **Balaiberkuak** Indon.
52 A2 **Balaklava** Austr.
91 C3 **Balaklava** Ukr.
91 D2 **Balakliya** Ukr.
87 D3 **Balakovo** Russia
76 C3 **Bālā Murghāb** Afgh.
145 C3 **Balancán** Mex.
111 C3 **Balan Dağı** *h.* Turkey
64 B1 **Balanga** Phil.
75 C2 **Balangir** India
79 C2 **Bālā Shahr** Iran
87 D3 **Balashov** Russia
103 D2 **Balaton, Lake** Hungary
103 D2 **Balatonboglár** Hungary
150 C2 **Balbina, Represa de** *resr* Brazil
97 C2 **Balbriggan** Ireland
52 A2 **Balcanoona** Austr.
110 C2 **Balchik** Bulg.
54 A3 **Balclutha** N.Z.
129 E2 **Baldock Lake** Can.
129 D2 **Baldy Mountain** *h.* Can.
138 B2 **Baldy Peak** U.S.A.
Baleares, Islas *is* Spain *see* **Balearic Islands**
107 D2 **Balearic Islands** *is* Spain
155 E1 **Baleia, Ponta da** *pt* Brazil
130 C1 **Baleine, Grande Rivière de la** *r.* Can.
131 D1 **Baleine, Rivière à la** *r.* Can.
75 C2 **Baleshwar** India
108 A2 **Balestrieri, Punta** *mt. Sardinia* Italy
61 C2 **Bali** *i.* Indon.
115 D4 **Bali** Nigeria
60 A1 **Balige** Indon.
75 C2 **Baligurha** India
111 C3 **Balıkesir** Turkey
61 C2 **Balikpapan** Indon.
59 D3 **Balimo** P.N.G.
102 B2 **Balingen** Ger.
Bali Sea Indon. *see* **Laut Bali**
76 B3 **Balkanabat** Turkm.
110 B2 **Balkan Mountains** Bulgaria/Serbia
77 D2 **Balkash** Kazakh.
77 D2 **Balkhash, Lake** Kazakh.
Balkhash, Ozero *l.* Kazakh. *see* **Balkhash, Lake**
50 B3 **Balladonia** Austr.
97 B2 **Ballaghaderreen** Ireland
92 G2 **Ballangen** Norway
52 B3 **Ballarat** Austr.
50 B2 **Ballard, Lake** *imp. l.* Austr.
96 C2 **Ballater** U.K.
114 B3 **Ballé** Mali
53 D1 **Ballina** Austr.
97 B1 **Ballina** Ireland
97 B2 **Ballinasloe** Ireland
139 D2 **Ballinger** U.S.A.
97 B2 **Ballinrobe** Ireland
97 B1 **Ballycastle** Ireland
97 C1 **Ballycastle** U.K.
97 D1 **Ballyclare** U.K.
97 C1 **Ballymena** U.K.
97 C1 **Ballymoney** U.K.
97 D1 **Ballynahinch** U.K.
97 B1 **Ballyshannon** Ireland
95 B2 **Ballyvoy** U.K.
51 D2 **Balonne** *r.* Austr.
74 B2 **Balotra** India
75 C2 **Balrampur** India
52 B2 **Balranald** Austr.
110 B2 **Balș** Romania
151 D2 **Balsas** Brazil
145 C3 **Balsas** Mex.
90 B2 **Balta** Ukr.
90 B2 **Bălți** Moldova
93 G4 **Baltic Sea** *g.* Europe
80 B2 **Balṭīm** Egypt
123 C1 **Baltimore** S. Africa
141 D3 **Baltimore** U.S.A.
88 A3 **Baltiysk** Russia
62 A1 **Balu** India
88 C2 **Balvi** Latvia
77 D2 **Balykchy** Kyrg.
87 E4 **Balykshi** Kazakh.
79 C2 **Bam** Iran
51 D1 **Bamaga** Austr.
130 A1 **Bamaji Lake** Can.
114 B3 **Bamako** Mali
118 C2 **Bambari** C.A.R.
101 E3 **Bamberg** Ger.
119 C2 **Bambili** Dem. Rep. Congo
119 C2 **Bambouti** C.A.R.
155 C2 **Bambuí** Brazil
118 B2 **Bamenda** Cameroon

74	A1	Bāmyān Afgh.
119	C2	Banalia Dem. Rep. Congo
151	C1	Bananal, Ilha do i. Brazil
74	B2	Banas r. India
111	C1	Banaz Turkey
62	B2	Ban Ban Laos
97	C1	Banbridge U.K.
99	C2	Banbury U.K.
130	C2	Bancroft Can.
119	C2	Banda Dem. Rep. Congo
75	C2	Banda India
59	C3	Banda, Kepulauan is Indon.
59	C3	Banda, Laut sea Indon.
60	A1	Banda Aceh Indon.
79	C2	Bandar-e 'Abbās Iran
81	C2	Bandar-e Anzalī Iran
79	C2	Bandar-e Būshehr Iran
81	C2	Bandar-e Chārak Iran
81	C2	Bandar-e Emām Khomeynī Iran
81	D3	Bandar-e Ganāveh Iran
79	C2	Bandar-e Jāsk Iran
79	C2	Bandar-e Kangān Iran
79	C2	Bandar-e Lengeh Iran
79	C2	Bandar-e Moqām Iran
60	B2	Bandar Lampung Indon.
61	C1	Bandar Seri Begawan Brunei
		Banda Sea Indon. see Banda, Laut
155	D2	Bandeiras, Pico de mt. Brazil
123	C1	Bandelierkop S. Africa
144	B1	Banderas, Bahía de b. Mex.
114	B3	Bandiagara Mali
111	C2	Bandırma Turkey
97	B3	Bandon Ireland
118	B3	Bandundu Dem. Rep. Congo
61	B2	Bandung Indon.
128	C2	Banff Can.
96	C2	Banff U.K.
114	B3	Banfora Burkina Faso
64	B2	Banga Phil.
73	B3	Bangalore India
118	C2	Bangassou C.A.R.
59	C3	Banggai Indon.
59	C3	Banggai, Kepulauan is Indon.
61	C1	Banggi i. Sabah Malaysia
60	B1	Bangka i. Indon.
61	C2	Bangkalan Indon.
60	B1	Bangkinang Indon.
60	B2	Bangko Indon.
63	B2	Bangkok Thai.
75	C2	Bangladesh country Asia
63	B2	Ba Ngoi Vietnam
97	D1	Bangor Northern Ireland U.K.
98	A2	Bangor Wales U.K.
141	F2	Bangor U.S.A.
63	A2	Bang Saphan Yai Thai.
64	A1	Bangued Phil.
118	B2	Bangui C.A.R.
121	B2	Bangweulu, Lake Zambia
62	B2	Ban Huai Khon Thai.
116	B2	Banī Suwayf Egypt
115	D1	Banī Walīd Libya
80	B2	Bāniyās Syria
109	C2	Banja Luka Bos. & Herz.
61	C2	Banjarmasin Indon.
114	A3	Banjul Gambia
128	A2	Banks Island B.C. Can.
126	C2	Banks Island N.W.T. Can.
48	F3	Banks Islands Vanuatu
129	E1	Banks Lake Can.
54	B2	Banks Peninsula N.Z.
62	A1	Bankura India
62	A1	Banmauk Myanmar
62	B2	Ban Mouang Laos
97	C1	Bann r. U.K.
62	B2	Ban Napè Laos
63	A3	Ban Na San Thai.

143	E4	Bannerman Town Bahamas
74	B1	Bannu Pak.
74	B2	Banswara India
63	A3	Ban Tha Kham Thai.
63	B2	Ban Tha Song Yang Thai.
63	B2	Ban Tôp Laos
97	B3	Bantry Ireland
97	B3	Bantry Bay Ireland
118	B2	Banyo Cameroon
107	D1	Banyoles Spain
61	C2	Banyuwangi Indon.
		Bao'an China see Shenzhen
69	C2	Baochang China
70	B2	Baoding China
70	A2	Baoji China
62	B1	Bao Lac Vietnam
63	B2	Bao Lôc Vietnam
66	B1	Baoqing China
62	A1	Baoshan China
70	B1	Baotou China
81	C2	Ba'qūbah Iraq
109	C2	Bar Montenegro
117	C4	Baraawe Somalia
147	C2	Baracoa Cuba
53	C2	Baradine Austr.
147	C3	Barahona Dom. Rep.
116	B3	Baraka watercourse Eritrea/Sudan
61	C1	Baram r. Sarawak Malaysia
74	B1	Baramulla India
88	C3	Baranavichy Belarus
78	A2	Baranis Egypt
90	B1	Baranivka Ukr.
128	A2	Baranof Island U.S.A.
59	C3	Barat Daya, Kepulauan is Indon.
155	D2	Barbacena Brazil
147	E3	Barbados country West Indies
107	D1	Barbastro Spain
104	B2	Barbezieux-St-Hilaire France
51	D2	Barcaldine Austr.
107	D1	Barcelona Spain
150	B1	Barcelona Venez.
105	D3	Barcelonnette France
150	B2	Barcelos Brazil
		Barcoo Creek watercourse Austr. see Cooper Creek
103	D2	Barcs Hungary
75	C2	Barddhaman India
103	E2	Bardejov Slovakia
79	C2	Bardsīr Iran
75	B2	Bareilly India
160	B2	Barents Sea Arctic Ocean
78	A3	Barentu Eritrea
75	C2	Barh India
141	F2	Bar Harbor U.S.A.
109	C2	Bari Italy
74	B1	Barī Kōt Afgh.
150	A1	Barinas Venez.
75	C2	Baripada India
75	D2	Barisal Bangl.
60	B2	Barisan, Pegunungan mts Indon.
61	C2	Barito r. Indon.
79	C2	Barkā Oman
88	C2	Barkava Latvia
51	C1	Barkly Tableland reg. Austr.
68	C2	Barkol China
110	C1	Bârlad Romania
105	D2	Bar-le-Duc France
50	A2	Barlee, Lake imp. l. Austr.
109	C2	Barletta Italy
53	C2	Barmedman Austr.
74	B2	Barmer India
99	A2	Barmouth U.K.
101	D1	Barmstedt Ger.
98	C1	Barnard Castle U.K.
53	B2	Barnato Austr.

82	G3	Barnaul Russia
127	C2	Barnes Icecap Can.
100	B1	Barneveld Neth.
98	C2	Barnsley U.K.
99	A3	Barnstaple U.K.
99	A3	Barnstaple Bay U.K.
143	D2	Barnwell U.S.A.
		Baroda India see Vadodara
150	B1	Barquisimeto Venez.
96	A2	Barra i. U.K.
53	D2	Barraba Austr.
151	D2	Barra do Corda Brazil
154	B1	Barra do Garças Brazil
150	C2	Barra do São Manuel Brazil
150	A3	Barranca Lima Peru
150	A2	Barranca Loreto Peru
152	C3	Barranqueras Arg.
150	A1	Barranquilla Col.
151	D3	Barreiras Brazil
154	C2	Barretos Brazil
130	C2	Barrie Can.
128	B2	Barrière Can.
52	B2	Barrier Range hills Austr.
53	D2	Barrington, Mount Austr.
129	D2	Barrington Lake Can.
53	C1	Barringun Austr.
97	C2	Barrow r. Ireland
51	C2	Barrow Creek Austr.
98	B1	Barrow-in-Furness U.K.
50	A2	Barrow Island Austr.
126	E2	Barrow Strait Can.
99	B3	Barry U.K.
130	C2	Barrys Bay Can.
74	B2	Barsalpur India
135	C4	Barstow U.S.A.
105	C2	Bar-sur-Aube France
80	B1	Bartın Turkey
51	D1	Bartle Frere, Mount Austr.
139	D1	Bartlesville U.S.A.
103	E1	Bartoszyce Pol.
61	C2	Barung i. Indon.
69	D1	Baruun-Urt Mongolia
91	D2	Barvinkove Ukr.
53	C2	Barwon r. Austr.
88	C3	Barysaw Belarus
110	C2	Basarabi Romania
105	D2	Basel Switz.
91	C2	Bashtanka Ukr.
64	B2	Basilan i. Phil.
99	D3	Basildon U.K.
99	C3	Basingstoke U.K.
81	C2	Başkale Turkey
130	C2	Baskatong, Réservoir resr Can.
		Basle Switz. see Basel
118	C2	Basoko Dem. Rep. Congo
81	C2	Basra Iraq
128	C2	Bassano Can.
114	C4	Bassar Togo
63	A2	Bassein Myanmar
147	D3	Basse-Terre Guadeloupe
147	D3	Basseterre St Kitts and Nevis
114	B3	Bassikounou Maur.
51	D3	Bass Strait Austr.
79	C2	Bastak Iran
101	E2	Bastheim Ger.
75	C2	Basti India
105	D3	Bastia Corsica France
100	B2	Bastogne Belgium
142	B2	Bastrop U.S.A.
		Basuo China see Dongfang
118	A2	Bata Equat. Guinea
83	J2	Batagay Russia
154	B2	Bataguassu Brazil
106	B2	Batalha Port.
60	B1	Batam Indon.
71	C3	Batan i. Phil.
118	C2	Batangafo C.A.R.

64	B1	**Batangas** Phil.
60	B2	**Batanghari** r. Indon.
71	C3	**Batan Islands** Phil.
141	D2	**Batavia** U.S.A.
91	D2	**Bataysk** Russia
130	B2	**Batchawana Mountain** h. Can.
50	C1	**Batchelor** Austr.
63	B2	**Bătdâmbâng** Cambodia
53	D3	**Batemans Bay** Austr.
142	B1	**Batesville** U.S.A.
89	D2	**Batetskiy** Russia
99	B3	**Bath** U.K.
74	B1	**Bathinda** India
53	C2	**Bathurst** Austr.
131	D2	**Bathurst** Can.
126	D2	**Bathurst Inlet** Can.
126	D2	**Bathurst Inlet (abandoned)** Can.
50	C1	**Bathurst Island** Austr.
126	E1	**Bathurst Island** Can.
78	B1	**Bāṭin, Wādī al** watercourse Asia
81	C2	**Batman** Turkey
115	C1	**Batna** Alg.
142	B2	**Baton Rouge** U.S.A.
144	B2	**Batopilas** Mex.
118	B2	**Batouri** Cameroon
154	E1	**Batovi** Brazil
92	I1	**Båtsfjord** Norway
73	C4	**Batticaloa** Sri Lanka
109	B2	**Battipaglia** Italy
129	D2	**Battle** r. Can.
140	B2	**Battle Creek** U.S.A.
135	C2	**Battle Mountain** U.S.A.
74	B1	**Battura Glacier** Pak.
117	B4	**Batu** mt. Eth.
60	A2	**Batu, Pulau-pulau** is Indon.
81	C1	**Bat'umi** Georgia
60	B1	**Batu Pahat** Malaysia
59	C3	**Baubau** Indon.
115	C3	**Bauchi** Nigeria
104	B2	**Baugé-en-Anjou** France
105	D2	**Baume-les-Dames** France
154	C2	**Bauru** Brazil
154	B1	**Baús** Brazil
88	B2	**Bauska** Latvia
102	C1	**Bautzen** Ger.
144	B2	**Bavispe** r. Mex.
87	E3	**Bavly** Russia
62	A1	**Bawdwin** Myanmar
61	C2	**Bawean** i. Indon.
114	B3	**Bawku** Ghana
146	C2	**Bayamo** Cuba
		Bayan Gol China see Dengkou
68	C1	**Bayanhongor** Mongolia
70	A2	**Bayan Hot** China
70	A1	**Bayannur** China
69	D2	**Bayan Shutu** China
69	D1	**Bayan-Uul** Mongolia
64	B2	**Bayawan** Phil.
80	C1	**Bayburt** Turkey
140	C2	**Bay City** MI U.S.A.
139	D3	**Bay City** TX U.S.A.
86	F2	**Baydaratskaya Guba** Russia
117	C4	**Baydhabo** Somalia
81	C2	**Bayji** Iraq
		Baykal, Ozero l. Russia see Baikal, Lake
83	I3	**Baykal'skiy Khrebet** mts Russia
76	C2	**Baykonyr** Kazakh.
87	E3	**Baymak** Russia
64	B1	**Bayombong** Phil.
104	B3	**Bayonne** France
111	C3	**Bayramiç** Turkey
101	E3	**Bayreuth** Ger.
78	B3	**Bayt al Faqih** Yemen
106	C2	**Baza** Spain
106	C2	**Baza, Sierra de** mts Spain
74	A1	**Bāzārak** Afgh.
76	A2	**Bazardyuzyu, Gora** mt. Azer./Russia
104	B3	**Bazas** France
74	A2	**Bazdar** Pak.
70	A2	**Bazhong** China
79	D2	**Bazmān** Iran
79	D2	**Bazmān, Kūh-e** mt. Iran
121	□D2	**Bé, Nosy** i. Madag.
99	D3	**Beachy Head** U.K.
123	C3	**Beacon Bay** S. Africa
50	B1	**Beagle Gulf** Austr.
121	□D2	**Bealanana** Madag.
97	B1	**Béal an Mhuirthead** Ireland
130	B2	**Beardmore** Can.
		Bear Island Arctic Ocean see Bjørnøya
134	E1	**Bear Paw Mountain** U.S.A.
147	C3	**Beata, Cabo** c. Dom. Rep.
147	C3	**Beata, Isla** i. Dom. Rep.
137	D2	**Beatrice** U.S.A.
135	C3	**Beatty** U.S.A.
53	D1	**Beaudesert** Austr.
52	B3	**Beaufort** Austr.
61	C1	**Beaufort** Sabah Malaysia
143	D2	**Beaufort** U.S.A.
160	L2	**Beaufort Sea** Can./U.S.A.
122	B3	**Beaufort West** S. Africa
96	B2	**Beauly** r. U.K.
100	B2	**Beaumont** Belgium
54	A3	**Beaumont** N.Z.
139	E2	**Beaumont** U.S.A.
105	C2	**Beaune** France
100	B2	**Beauraing** Belgium
129	E2	**Beauséjour** Can.
104	C2	**Beauvais** France
129	D2	**Beauval** Can.
129	D2	**Beaver** r. Can.
135	D3	**Beaver** U.S.A.
126	B2	**Beaver Creek** Can.
140	B2	**Beaver Dam** U.S.A.
129	E2	**Beaver Hill Lake** Can.
140	B1	**Beaver Island** U.S.A.
128	C2	**Beaverlodge** Can.
74	B2	**Beawar** India
154	C2	**Bebedouro** Brazil
101	D2	**Bebra** Ger.
106	B1	**Becerreá** Spain
114	B1	**Béchar** Alg.
140	C3	**Beckley** U.S.A.
117	B4	**Bedelê** Eth.
99	C2	**Bedford** U.K.
140	C3	**Bedford** U.S.A.
100	C1	**Bedum** Neth.
53	D2	**Beecroft Peninsula** Austr.
101	F1	**Beelitz** Ger.
53	D1	**Beenleigh** Austr.
80	B2	**Beersheba** Israel
139	D3	**Beeville** U.S.A.
53	C3	**Bega** Austr.
107	D1	**Begur, Cap de** c. Spain
128	C1	**Behchokò** Can.
81	D2	**Behshahr** Iran
69	E1	**Bei'an** China
71	A3	**Beihai** China
70	B2	**Beijing** China
100	C1	**Beilen** Neth.
96	A2	**Beinn Mhòr** h. U.K.
121	C2	**Beira** Moz.
80	B2	**Beirut** Lebanon
123	C1	**Beitbridge** Zimbabwe
106	B2	**Beja** Port.
115	C1	**Bejaïa** Alg.
106	B1	**Béjar** Spain
74	A2	**Beji** r. Pak.
103	E2	**Békés** Hungary
103	E2	**Békéscsaba** Hungary
121	□D3	**Bekily** Madag.
54	A2	**Bela** Pak.
123	C1	**Bela-Bela** S. Africa
118	B2	**Bélabo** Cameroon
109	D2	**Bela Crkva** Serbia
61	C1	**Belaga** Sarawak Malaysia
88	C3	**Belarus** country Europe
		Belau country N. Pacific Ocean see Palau
123	D2	**Bela Vista** Moz.
60	A1	**Belawan** Indon.
83	M2	**Belaya** r. Russia
103	D1	**Bełchatów** Pol.
130	C1	**Belcher Islands** Can.
117	C4	**Beledweyne** Somalia
151	D2	**Belém** Brazil
138	B2	**Belen** U.S.A.
89	E3	**Belev** Russia
97	D1	**Belfast** U.K.
141	F2	**Belfast** U.S.A.
105	D2	**Belfort** France
73	B3	**Belgaum** India
100	B2	**Belgium** country Europe
91	D1	**Belgorod** Russia
109	D2	**Belgrade** Serbia
134	D1	**Belgrade** U.S.A.
60	B2	**Belinyu** Indon.
61	B2	**Belitung** i. Indon.
146	B3	**Belize** Belize
146	B3	**Belize** country Central America
83	K1	**Bel'kovskiy, Ostrov** i. Russia
128	B2	**Bella Bella** Can.
104	C2	**Bellac** France
128	B2	**Bella Coola** Can.
53	C1	**Bellata** Austr.
136	C2	**Belle Fourche** U.S.A.
136	C2	**Belle Fourche** r. U.S.A.
143	D3	**Belle Glade** U.S.A.
104	B2	**Belle-Île** i. France
131	E1	**Belle Isle** i. Can.
131	E1	**Belle Isle, Strait of** Can.
130	C2	**Belleville** Can.
140	B3	**Belleville** IL U.S.A.
137	D3	**Belleville** KS U.S.A.
134	B1	**Bellevue** U.S.A.
134	B1	**Bellingham** U.S.A.
55	O2	**Bellingshausen Sea** Antarctica
105	D2	**Bellinzona** Switz.
108	B1	**Belluno** Italy
122	A3	**Bellville** S. Africa
155	E1	**Belmonte** Brazil
146	B3	**Belmopan** Belize
69	E1	**Belogorsk** Russia
121	□D3	**Beloha** Madag.
155	D1	**Belo Horizonte** Brazil
140	B2	**Beloit** U.S.A.
86	C2	**Belomorsk** Russia
91	D3	**Belorechensk** Russia
87	E3	**Beloretsk** Russia
		Belorussia country Europe see Belarus
86	F2	**Beloyarskiy** Russia
86	C2	**Beloye, Ozero** l. Russia
		Beloye More sea Russia see White Sea
86	C2	**Belozersk** Russia
77	C2	**Belukha, Gora** mt. Kazakh./Russia
86	D2	**Belush'ye** Russia
89	D2	**Belyy** Russia
82	F2	**Belyy, Ostrov** i. Russia
137	E1	**Bemidji** U.S.A.
118	C3	**Bena Dibele** Dem. Rep. Congo
53	C3	**Benalla** Austr.
106	B1	**Benavente** Spain
96	A2	**Benbecula** i. U.K.
134	B2	**Bend** U.S.A.

123 C3 **Bendearg** *mt.* S. Africa
90 B2 **Bender** Moldova
52 B3 **Bendigo** Austr.
121 C2 **Bene** Moz.
102 C2 **Benešov** Czech Rep.
109 B2 **Benevento** Italy
159 C2 **Bengal, Bay of** *sea* Indian Ocean
Bengaluru India *see* **Bangalore**
70 B2 **Bengbu** China
115 E1 **Benghazi** Libya
61 B1 **Bengkayang** Indon.
60 B2 **Bengkulu** Indon.
120 A2 **Benguela** Angola
96 B1 **Ben Hope** *h.* U.K.
152 B2 **Beni** *r.* Bol.
119 C2 **Beni** Dem. Rep. Congo
114 B1 **Beni Abbès** Alg.
107 C2 **Benidorm** Spain
114 B1 **Beni Mellal** Morocco
114 C3 **Benin** *country* Africa
114 C4 **Benin, Bight of** *g.* Africa
115 C4 **Benin City** Nigeria
153 C4 **Benito Juárez** Arg.
150 B2 **Benjamin Constant** Brazil
144 A1 **Benjamín Hill** Mex.
59 C3 **Benjina** Indon.
96 B2 **Ben Lawers** *mt.* U.K.
96 B2 **Ben Lomond** *h.* U.K.
96 C2 **Ben Macdui** *mt.* U.K.
96 A2 **Ben More** *h.* U.K.
54 B2 **Benmore, Lake** N.Z.
96 B1 **Ben More Assynt** *h.* U.K.
128 A2 **Bennett (abandoned)** Can.
83 K1 **Bennetta, Ostrov** *i.* Russia
96 B2 **Ben Nevis** *mt.* U.K.
141 E2 **Bennington** U.S.A.
123 C2 **Benoni** S. Africa
101 D3 **Bensheim** Ger.
138 A2 **Benson** U.S.A.
58 C3 **Benteng** Indon.
140 B2 **Benton Harbor** U.S.A.
142 B1 **Bentonville** U.S.A.
115 C4 **Benue** *r.* Nigeria
97 B1 **Benwee Head** Ireland
96 B2 **Ben Wyvis** *mt.* U.K.
70 C1 **Benxi** China
Beograd Serbia *see* **Belgrade**
75 C2 **Beohari** India
67 B4 **Beppu** Japan
109 C2 **Berane** Montenegro
109 C2 **Berat** Albania
59 C3 **Berau, Teluk** *b.* Indon.
116 B3 **Berber** Sudan
117 C3 **Berbera** Somalia
118 B2 **Berbérati** C.A.R.
104 C1 **Berck** France
91 D2 **Berdyans'k** Ukr.
90 B2 **Berdychiv** Ukr.
90 A2 **Berehove** Ukr.
59 D3 **Bereina** P.N.G.
76 B3 **Bereket** Turkm.
129 E2 **Berens River** Can.
90 A2 **Berezhany** Ukr.
90 C2 **Berezivka** Ukr.
90 B1 **Berezne** Ukr.
86 D2 **Bereznik** Russia
86 E3 **Berezniki** Russia
86 F2 **Berezovo** Russia
107 D1 **Berga** Spain
111 C3 **Bergama** Turkey
108 A1 **Bergamo** Italy
101 D1 **Bergen** Ger.
93 E3 **Bergen** Norway
102 C1 **Bergen auf Rügen** Ger.
100 B2 **Bergen op Zoom** Neth.
104 C3 **Bergerac** France
100 C2 **Bergheim** Ger.
100 C2 **Bergisch Gladbach** Ger.
122 A1 **Bergland** Namibia
92 H2 **Bergsviken** Sweden
83 M3 **Beringa, Ostrov** *i.* Russia
100 B2 **Beringen** Belgium
124 C3 **Bering Sea** N. Pacific Ocean
83 N2 **Bering Strait** Russia/U.S.A.
135 B3 **Berkeley** U.S.A.
100 B1 **Berkhout** Neth.
55 Q2 **Berkner Sub-glacial Island** Antarctica
110 B2 **Berkovitsa** Bulg.
92 I1 **Berlevåg** Norway
101 F1 **Berlin** Ger.
141 E2 **Berlin** U.S.A.
101 E2 **Berlingerode** Ger.
53 D3 **Bermagui** Austr.
144 B2 **Bermejíllo** Mex.
152 B3 **Bermejo** Bol.
131 D1 **Bermen, Lac** *l.* Can.
125 K4 **Bermuda** *terr.* N. Atlantic Ocean
105 D2 **Bern** Switz.
101 E2 **Bernburg (Saale)** Ger.
127 F2 **Bernier Bay** Can.
100 C3 **Bernkastel-Kues** Ger.
121 □D3 **Beroroha** Madag.
52 B2 **Berri** Austr.
107 D2 **Berrouaghia** Alg.
146 C2 **Berry Islands** Bahamas
100 C1 **Bersenbrück** Ger.
90 B2 **Bershad'** Ukr.
131 D1 **Berté, Lac** *l.* Can.
118 B2 **Bertoua** Cameroon
150 B2 **Beruri** Brazil
98 B1 **Berwick-upon-Tweed** U.K.
91 C2 **Beryslav** Ukr.
121 □D2 **Besalampy** Madag.
105 D2 **Besançon** France
129 D2 **Besnard Lake** Can.
142 C2 **Bessemer** U.S.A.
76 B2 **Besshoky, Gora** *h.* Kazakh.
106 B1 **Betanzos** Spain
118 B2 **Bétaré Oya** Cameroon
122 A2 **Bethanie** Namibia
123 C2 **Bethlehem** S. Africa
141 D2 **Bethlehem** U.S.A.
121 □D3 **Betioky** Madag.
77 D2 **Betpakdala** *plain* Kazakh.
121 □D3 **Betroka** Madag.
131 D2 **Betsiamites** Can.
121 □D2 **Betsiboka** *r.* Madag.
137 E2 **Bettendorf** U.S.A.
75 C2 **Bettiah** India
75 B2 **Betul** India
75 B2 **Betwa** *r.* India
98 B2 **Betws-y-coed** U.K.
98 C2 **Beverley** U.K.
101 D2 **Beverungen** Ger.
100 B1 **Beverwijk** Neth.
99 D3 **Bexhill** U.K.
111 C2 **Beykoz** Turkey
114 B4 **Beyla** Guinea
76 B2 **Beyneu** Kazakh.
80 B1 **Beypazarı** Turkey
Beyrouth Lebanon *see* **Beirut**
80 B2 **Beyşehir** Turkey
80 B2 **Beyşehir Gölü** *l.* Turkey
91 D2 **Beysug** *r.* Russia
88 C2 **Bezhanitsy** Russia
89 E2 **Bezhetsk** Russia
105 C3 **Béziers** France
75 C2 **Bhadrak** India
73 B3 **Bhadravati** India
75 C2 **Bhagalpur** India
74 A2 **Bhairi Hol** *mt.* Pak.
74 B1 **Bhakkar** Pak.
62 A1 **Bhamo** Myanmar
75 C3 **Bhanjanagar** India
74 B2 **Bharatpur** India
74 B2 **Bharuch** India
74 B2 **Bhavnagar** India
75 C3 **Bhawanipatna** India
123 D2 **Bhekuzulu** S. Africa
74 B2 **Bhilwara** India
73 B3 **Bhima** *r.* India
123 C3 **Bhisho** S. Africa
74 B2 **Bhiwani** India
123 C3 **Bhongweni** S. Africa
74 B2 **Bhopal** India
75 C2 **Bhubaneshwar** India
74 A2 **Bhuj** India
74 B2 **Bhusawal** India
75 D2 **Bhutan** *country* Asia
59 D3 **Biak** Indon.
59 D3 **Biak** *i.* Indon.
103 E1 **Biała Podlaska** Pol.
103 D1 **Białogard** Pol.
103 E1 **Białystok** Pol.
109 C3 **Bianco** Italy
104 B3 **Biarritz** France
105 D2 **Biasca** Switz.
66 D2 **Bibai** Japan
120 A2 **Bibala** Angola
102 B2 **Biberach an der Riß** Ger.
115 C4 **Bida** Nigeria
141 E2 **Biddeford** U.S.A.
99 A3 **Bideford** U.K.
101 D2 **Biedenkopf** Ger.
105 D2 **Biel/Bienne** Switz.
101 D1 **Bielefeld** Ger.
108 A1 **Biella** Italy
103 D2 **Bielsko-Biała** Pol.
63 B2 **Biên Hoa** Vietnam
130 C1 **Bienville, Lac** *l.* Can.
100 B3 **Bièvre** Belgium
118 B3 **Bifoun** Gabon
111 C2 **Biga** Turkey
123 D2 **Big Bend** Swaziland
129 D2 **Biggar** Can.
96 C3 **Biggar** U.K.
134 D1 **Big Hole** *r.* U.S.A.
136 B1 **Bighorn** *r.* U.S.A.
136 B2 **Bighorn Mountains** U.S.A.
139 C2 **Big Lake** U.S.A.
140 B2 **Big Rapids** U.S.A.
129 D2 **Big River** Can.
129 E2 **Big Sand Lake** Can.
137 D2 **Big Sioux** *r.* U.S.A.
139 C2 **Big Spring** U.S.A.
134 E1 **Big Timber** U.S.A.
130 B1 **Big Trout Lake** Can.
130 A1 **Big Trout Lake** Can.
109 C2 **Bihać** Bos. & Herz.
75 C2 **Bihar Sharif** India
110 B1 **Bihor, Vârful** *mt.* Romania
114 A3 **Bijagós, Arquipélago dos** *is* Guinea-Bissau
81 C2 **Bījār** Iran
109 C2 **Bijeljina** Bos. & Herz.
109 C2 **Bijelo Polje** Montenegro
71 A3 **Bijie** China
74 B2 **Bikaner** India
69 E1 **Bikin** Russia
118 B3 **Bikoro** Dem. Rep. Congo
79 C2 **Bilād Banī Bū 'Alī** Oman
75 C2 **Bilaspur** India
90 C2 **Bila Tserkva** Ukr.
63 A2 **Bilauktaung Range** *mts* Myanmar/Thai.
106 C1 **Bilbao** Spain
111 C2 **Bilecik** Turkey
103 E1 **Biłgoraj** Pol.
90 C2 **Bilhorod-Dnistrovs'kyy** Ukr.
119 C2 **Bili** Dem. Rep. Congo

Bilibino

83 M2 **Bilibino** Russia
134 E1 **Billings** U.S.A.
99 B3 **Bill of Portland** hd U.K.
115 D3 **Bilma** Niger
115 D3 **Bilma, Grand Erg de** des. Niger
51 E2 **Biloela** Austr.
91 C2 **Bilohirs'k** Ukr.
90 B1 **Bilohir"ya** Ukr.
91 C1 **Bilopillya** Ukr.
91 D1 **Bilovods'k** Ukr.
142 C2 **Biloxi** U.S.A.
51 C2 **Bilpa Morea Claypan** salt flat Austr.
101 E2 **Bilshausen** Ger.
115 E3 **Biltine** Chad
90 C2 **Bilyayivka** Ukr.
143 E3 **Bimini Islands** Bahamas
75 B2 **Bina-Etawa** India
59 C3 **Binaija, Gunung** mt. Indon.
118 B3 **Bindu** Dem. Rep. Congo
121 C2 **Bindura** Zimbabwe
107 D1 **Binéfar** Spain
53 D1 **Bingara** Austr.
100 C3 **Bingen am Rhein** Ger.
141 F1 **Bingham** U.S.A.
141 D2 **Binghamton** U.S.A.
81 C2 **Bingöl** Turkey
60 A1 **Binjai** Indon.
60 B2 **Bintuan** Indon.
61 C1 **Bintulu** Sarawak Malaysia
70 B2 **Binzhou** China
109 C2 **Biograd na Moru** Croatia
118 A2 **Bioko** i. Equat. Guinea
118 C1 **Birao** C.A.R.
75 C2 **Biratnagar** Nepal
128 C2 **Birch Mountains** Can.
51 C2 **Birdsville** Austr.
80 B2 **Birecik** Turkey
60 A1 **Bireun** Indon.
75 C2 **Birganj** Nepal
154 E2 **Birigui** Brazil
76 B3 **Birjand** Iran
98 B2 **Birkenhead** U.K.
114 B2 **Bir Lahlou** Western Sahara
99 C3 **Birmingham** U.K.
142 C2 **Birmingham** U.S.A.
114 A2 **Bîr Mogreïn** Maur.
115 C3 **Birnin-Kebbi** Nigeria
115 C3 **Birnin Konni** Niger
69 E1 **Birobidzhan** Russia
97 C2 **Birr** Ireland
96 C1 **Birsay** U.K.
78 A2 **Bi'r Shalatayn** Egypt
91 D1 **Biryuch** Russia
88 B2 **Biržai** Lith.
75 B2 **Bisalpur** India
138 B2 **Bisbee** U.S.A.
104 A2 **Biscay, Bay of** sea France/ Spain
102 C2 **Bischofshofen** Austria
130 B2 **Biscotasi Lake** Can.
77 D2 **Bishkek** Kyrg.
135 C3 **Bishop** U.S.A.
69 E1 **Bishui** China
150 B1 **Bisinaca** Col.
115 C1 **Biskra** Alg.
136 C1 **Bismarck** U.S.A.
48 D3 **Bismarck Sea** P.N.G.
107 D2 **Bissa, Djebel** mt. Alg.
114 A3 **Bissau** Guinea-Bissau
129 E2 **Bissett** Can.
128 C2 **Bistcho Lake** Can.
110 B1 **Bistriţa** Romania
110 C1 **Bistriţa** r. Romania
100 C3 **Bitburg** Ger.
105 D2 **Bitche** France
115 D3 **Bitkine** Chad

109 D2 **Bitola** Macedonia
109 C2 **Bitonto** Italy
122 A3 **Bitterfontein** S. Africa
134 D1 **Bitterroot** r. U.S.A.
134 C1 **Bitterroot Range** mts U.S.A.
91 D1 **Bityug** r. Russia
115 D3 **Biu** Nigeria
67 C3 **Biwa-ko** l. Japan
68 B1 **Biysk** Russia
115 C1 **Bizerte** Tunisia
92 □A2 **Bjargtangar** hd Iceland
92 G3 **Bjästa** Sweden
92 G2 **Bjerkvik** Norway
82 C2 **Bjørnøya** i. Arctic Ocean
114 B3 **Bla** Mali
137 E3 **Black** r. U.S.A.
51 D2 **Blackall** Austr.
98 B2 **Blackburn** U.K.
134 D2 **Blackfoot** U.S.A.
102 B2 **Black Forest** mts Ger.
136 C2 **Black Hills** U.S.A.
96 B2 **Black Isle** pen. U.K.
129 D2 **Black Lake** Can.
129 D2 **Black Lake** Can.
99 B3 **Black Mountains** hills U.K.
98 B2 **Blackpool** U.K.
62 B1 **Black River** r. Vietnam
140 A2 **Black River Falls** U.S.A.
140 C3 **Blacksburg** U.S.A.
80 B1 **Black Sea** Asia/Europe
97 A1 **Blacksod Bay** Ireland
97 C2 **Blackstairs Mountains** hills Ireland
114 B4 **Black Volta** r. Africa
97 C2 **Blackwater** r. Ireland
128 B1 **Blackwater Lake** Can.
50 A1 **Blackwood** r. Austr.
76 A2 **Blagodarnyy** Russia
110 B2 **Blagoevgrad** Bulg.
69 E1 **Blagoveshchensk** Russia
129 D2 **Blaine Lake** Can.
137 D2 **Blair** U.S.A.
96 C2 **Blair Atholl** U.K.
96 C2 **Blairgowrie** U.K.
143 D2 **Blakely** U.S.A.
105 D2 **Blanc, Mont** mt. France/Italy
153 B4 **Blanca, Bahía** b. Arg.
52 A1 **Blanche, Lake** imp. l. Austr.
152 B2 **Blanco** r. Bol.
131 E1 **Blanc-Sablon** Can.
92 □A2 **Blanda** r. Iceland
99 B3 **Blandford Forum** U.K.
135 E3 **Blanding** U.S.A.
107 D1 **Blanes** Spain
60 A1 **Blangkejeren** Indon.
100 C2 **Blankenheim** Ger.
100 C2 **Blankenrath** Ger.
103 D2 **Blansko** Czech Rep.
121 C2 **Blantyre** Malawi
98 C1 **Blaydon** U.K.
53 C2 **Blayney** Austr.
54 B2 **Blenheim** N.Z.
115 C1 **Blida** Alg.
130 B2 **Blind River** Can.
123 C2 **Bloemfontein** S. Africa
123 C2 **Bloemhof** S. Africa
123 C2 **Bloemhof Dam** S. Africa
92 □A2 **Blönduós** Iceland
97 B1 **Bloody Foreland** pt Ireland
138 B1 **Bloomfield** U.S.A.
140 B2 **Bloomington** IL U.S.A.
140 B3 **Bloomington** IN U.S.A.
140 C3 **Bluefield** U.S.A.
146 B3 **Bluefields** Nic.
53 C2 **Blue Mountains** Austr.
134 C1 **Blue Mountains** U.S.A.
116 B3 **Blue Nile** r. Eth./Sudan
126 D2 **Bluenose Lake** Can.

140 C3 **Blue Ridge** mts U.S.A.
97 B1 **Blue Stack Mountains** hills U.K.
54 A3 **Bluff** N.Z.
135 E3 **Bluff** U.S.A.
152 D3 **Blumenau** Brazil
52 A2 **Blyth** Austr.
98 C1 **Blyth** U.K.
135 D4 **Blythe** U.S.A.
142 C1 **Blytheville** U.S.A.
114 A4 **Bo** Sierra Leone
64 B1 **Boac** Phil.
151 D2 **Boa Esperança, Açude** resr Brazil
150 B1 **Boa Vista** Brazil
53 C2 **Bobadah** Austr.
71 B3 **Bobai** China
121 □D2 **Bobaomby, Tanjona** c. Madag.
114 B3 **Bobo-Dioulasso** Burkina Faso
89 F3 **Bobrov** Russia
91 C1 **Bobrovytsya** Ukr.
91 C2 **Bobrynets'** Ukr.
121 □D3 **Boby** mt. Madag.
150 B2 **Boca do Acre** Brazil
155 D1 **Bocaiúva** Brazil
118 B2 **Bocaranga** C.A.R.
103 E2 **Bochnia** Pol.
100 C2 **Bocholt** Ger.
100 C2 **Bochum** Ger.
101 E1 **Bockenem** Ger.
118 B2 **Boda** C.A.R.
83 I3 **Bodaybo** Russia
115 D3 **Bodélé** reg. Chad
92 H2 **Boden** Sweden
99 A3 **Bodmin** U.K.
99 A3 **Bodmin Moor** moorland U.K.
92 F2 **Bodø** Norway
111 C3 **Bodrum** Turkey
118 C3 **Boende** Dem. Rep. Congo
142 C2 **Bogalusa** U.S.A.
114 B3 **Bogandé** Burkina Faso
68 B2 **Bogda Shan** mts China
53 D1 **Boggabilla** Austr.
97 B2 **Boggeragh Mountains** hills Ireland
100 B3 **Bogny-sur-Meuse** France
97 C2 **Bog of Allen** reg. Ireland
53 C3 **Bogong, Mount** Austr.
60 B2 **Bogor** Indon.
89 E3 **Bogoroditsk** Russia
150 A1 **Bogotá** Col.
82 G3 **Bogotol** Russia
83 H3 **Boguchany** Russia
91 E2 **Boguchar** Russia
70 B2 **Bo Hai** g. China
100 A3 **Bohain-en-Vermandois** France
70 B2 **Bohai Wan** b. China
123 C2 **Bohlokong** S. Africa
102 C2 **Böhmer Wald** mts Ger.
91 D1 **Bohodukhiv** Ukr.
64 B2 **Bohol** i. Phil.
64 B2 **Bohol Sea** Phil.
68 B2 **Bohu** China
155 C2 **Boi, Ponta do** pt Brazil
154 B1 **Bois** r. Brazil
126 C2 **Bois, Lac des** l. Can.
134 C2 **Boise** U.S.A.
139 C1 **Boise City** U.S.A.
123 C2 **Boitumelong** S. Africa
101 E1 **Boizenburg/Elbe** Ger.
76 B3 **Bojnūrd** Iran
118 B3 **Bokatola** Dem. Rep. Congo
114 A3 **Boké** Guinea
118 C3 **Bokele** Dem. Rep. Congo
93 E4 **Boknafjorden** sea chan. Norway

115 D3 Bokoro Chad
63 A2 Bokpyin Myanmar
89 D2 Boksitogorsk Russia
122 B2 Bokspits Botswana
114 A3 Bolama Guinea-Bissau
63 B2 Bolaven, Phouphiang *plat.* Laos
104 C2 Bolbec France
77 E2 Bole China
118 B3 Boleko Dem. Rep. Congo
114 B3 Bolgatanga Ghana
90 B2 Bolhrad Ukr.
66 B1 Boli China
62 B2 Bolikhamxai Laos
110 C2 Bolintin-Vale Romania
137 E3 Bolivar U.S.A.
150 A1 Bolívar, Pico *mt.* Venez.
152 B2 Bolivia *country* S. America
89 E3 Bolkhov Russia
105 C3 Bollène France
93 G3 Bollnäs Sweden
53 C1 Bollon Austr.
101 E2 Bollstedt Ger.
93 F4 Bolmen *l.* Sweden
118 B3 Bolobo Dem. Rep. Congo
108 B2 Bologna Italy
89 D2 Bologovo Russia
89 D2 Bologoye Russia
118 B3 Bolomba Dem. Rep. Congo
83 H1 Bol'shevik, Ostrov *i.* Russia
86 E2 Bol'shezemel'skaya Tundra *lowland* Russia
66 B2 Bol'shoy Kamen' Russia
    Bol'shoy Kavkaz *mts* Asia/Europe *see* Caucasus
83 K2 Bol'shoy Lyakhovskiy, Ostrov *i.* Russia
100 B1 Bolsward Neth.
98 B2 Bolton U.K.
80 B1 Bolu Turkey
92 □A2 Bolungarvík Iceland
108 B1 Bolzano Italy
118 B3 Boma Dem. Rep. Congo
53 D2 Bomaderry Austr.
53 C3 Bombala Austr.
    Bombay India *see* Mumbai
155 C1 Bom Despacho Brazil
75 D2 Bomdila India
151 D3 Bom Jesus da Lapa Brazil
155 D2 Bom Jesus do Itabapoana Brazil
115 D1 Bon, Cap *c.* Tunisia
147 D3 Bonaire *i.* West Indies
147 D3 Bonaire *mun.* West Indies
50 B1 Bonaparte Archipelago *is* Austr.
131 E2 Bonavista Can.
131 E2 Bonavista Bay Can.
118 C2 Bondo Dem. Rep. Congo
114 B4 Bondoukou Côte d'Ivoire
58 C3 Bonerate, Kepulauan *is* Indon.
155 C1 Bonfinópolis de Minas Brazil
117 B4 Bonga Eth.
75 D2 Bongaigaon India
118 C2 Bongandanga Dem. Rep. Congo
118 C2 Bongo, Massif des *mts* C.A.R.
115 D3 Bongor Chad
114 B4 Bongouanou Côte d'Ivoire
63 B2 Bông Sơn Vietnam
139 D2 Bonham U.S.A.
105 D3 Bonifacio *Corsica* France
108 A2 Bonifacio, Strait of France/Italy
100 C2 Bonn Ger.
134 C1 Bonners Ferry U.S.A.
50 A3 Bonnie Rock Austr.
129 C2 Bonnyville Can.

108 A2 Bonorva *Sardinia* Italy
61 C1 Bontang Indon.
64 B1 Bontoc Phil.
58 B3 Bontosunggu Indon.
123 C3 Bontrug S. Africa
52 B2 Booligal Austr.
53 C1 Boomi Austr.
53 D1 Boonah Austr.
137 E2 Boone U.S.A.
142 C2 Booneville U.S.A.
137 E3 Boonville U.S.A.
53 C2 Boorowa Austr.
126 E2 Boothia, Gulf of Can.
126 E2 Boothia Peninsula Can.
100 C2 Boppard Ger.
144 B2 Boquilla, Presa de la *resr* Mex.
109 D2 Bor Serbia
117 B4 Bor South Sudan
80 B2 Bor Turkey
121 □E2 Boraha, Nosy *i.* Madag.
76 B2 Borankul Kazakh.
93 F4 Borås Sweden
79 C2 Borāzjān Iran
150 C2 Borba Brazil
104 B3 Bordeaux France
127 F2 Borden Peninsula Can.
52 B3 Bordertown Austr.
107 D2 Bordj Bou Arréridj Alg.
107 D2 Bordj Bounaama Alg.
115 C1 Bordj Messaouda Alg.
115 C2 Bordj Omer Driss Alg.
94 B1 Borðoy *i.* Faroe Is
92 □A3 Borgarnes Iceland
108 A1 Borgosesia Italy
87 D3 Borisoglebsk Russia
89 E2 Borisoglebskiy Russia
91 D1 Borisovka Russia
100 C2 Borken Ger.
92 G2 Borkenes Norway
100 C1 Borkum Ger.
100 C1 Borkum *i.* Ger.
93 G3 Borlänge Sweden
101 F2 Borna Ger.
61 C1 Borneo *i.* Asia
93 F4 Bornholm *i.* Denmark
111 C3 Bornova Turkey
90 B1 Borodyanka Ukr.
89 D2 Borovichi Russia
89 E2 Borovsk Russia
107 C2 Borriana Spain
51 C1 Borroloola Austr.
110 B1 Borşa Romania
90 B2 Borshchiv Ukr.
69 D1 Borshchovochnyy Khrebet *mts* Russia
101 E1 Börßum Ger.
    Bortala China *see* Bole
81 C2 Borüjerd Iran
65 B2 Boryeong S. Korea
90 A2 Boryslav Ukr.
90 C1 Boryspil' Ukr.
91 C1 Borzna Ukr.
69 D1 Borzya Russia
109 C1 Bosanska Dubica Bos. & Herz.
109 C1 Bosanska Gradiška Bos. & Herz.
109 C2 Bosanska Krupa Bos. & Herz.
109 C1 Bosanski Novi Bos. & Herz.
109 C2 Bosansko Grahovo Bos. & Herz.
123 C2 Boshof S. Africa
109 C2 Bosnia and Herzegovina *country* Europe
118 B2 Bosobolo Dem. Rep. Congo
111 B2 Bosporus *str.* Turkey
118 B2 Bossangoa C.A.R.
118 B2 Bossembélé C.A.R.
68 B2 Bosten Hu *l.* China

98 C2 Boston U.K.
141 E2 Boston U.S.A.
142 B1 Boston Mountains U.S.A.
53 D2 Botany Bay Austr.
110 B2 Botev *mt.* Bulg.
93 G3 Bothnia, Gulf of Fin./Sweden
110 C1 Botoşani Romania
123 C2 Botshabelo S. Africa
120 B3 Botswana *country* Africa
109 C3 Botte Donato, Monte *mt.* Italy
136 C1 Bottineau U.S.A.
100 C2 Bottrop Ger.
154 C2 Botucatu Brazil
114 B4 Bouaké Côte d'Ivoire
118 B2 Bouar C.A.R.
114 B1 Bou Arfa Morocco
131 D2 Bouctouche Can.
107 E2 Bougaa Alg.
114 B3 Bougouni Mali
100 B3 Bouillon Belgium
107 D2 Bouira Alg.
114 A2 Boujdour Western Sahara
136 B2 Boulder U.S.A.
135 D3 Boulder City U.S.A.
51 C2 Boulia Austr.
104 C2 Boulogne-Billancourt France
99 D3 Boulogne-sur-Mer France
118 B3 Boumango Gabon
118 B2 Boumba *r.* Cameroon
107 D2 Boumerdès Alg.
114 B4 Bouna Côte d'Ivoire
114 B4 Boundiali Côte d'Ivoire
134 D2 Bountiful U.S.A.
114 B3 Bourem Mali
104 C2 Bourganeuf France
105 D2 Bourg-en-Bresse France
104 C2 Bourges France
53 C2 Bourke Austr.
99 C3 Bournemouth U.K.
115 C1 Bou Saâda Alg.
115 D3 Bousso Chad
114 A3 Boutilimit Maur.
129 C3 Bow *r.* Can.
51 D2 Bowen Austr.
129 C3 Bow Island Can.
140 B3 Bowling Green KY U.S.A.
140 C2 Bowling Green OH U.S.A.
136 C1 Bowman U.S.A.
101 D3 Boxberg Ger.
100 B2 Boxtel Neth.
80 B1 Boyabat Turkey
    Boyang China *see* Poyang
97 B2 Boyle Ireland
97 C2 Boyne *r.* Ireland
136 B2 Boysen Reservoir U.S.A.
152 B3 Boyuibe Bol.
111 C3 Bozburun Turkey
111 C3 Bozcaada *i.* Turkey
111 C3 Bozdağ *mt.* Turkey
111 C3 Boz Dağları *mts* Turkey
111 C3 Bozdoğan Turkey
134 D1 Bozeman U.S.A.
118 B2 Bozoum C.A.R.
111 D3 Bozüyük Turkey
109 C2 Brač *i.* Croatia
130 C2 Bracebridge Can.
99 C3 Bracknell U.K.
109 C2 Bradano *r.* Italy
143 D3 Bradenton U.S.A.
98 C2 Bradford U.K.
141 D2 Bradford U.S.A.
139 D2 Brady U.S.A.
96 C2 Braemar U.K.
106 B1 Braga Port.
151 D2 Bragança Brazil
106 B1 Bragança Port.

155	C2	Bragança Paulista Brazil
89	D3	Brahin Belarus
73	C3	Brahmapur India
62	A1	Brahmaputra r. China/India
110	C1	Brăila Romania
137	E1	Brainerd U.S.A.
99	D3	Braintree U.K.
100	B2	Braives Belgium
101	C1	Brake (Unterweser) Ger.
100	D1	Bramsche Ger.
150	B2	Branco r. Brazil
101	F1	Brandenburg an der Havel Ger.
129	E3	Brandon Can.
97	A2	Brandon Mountain h. Ireland
122	B3	Brandvlei S. Africa
103	D1	Braniewo Pol.
130	B2	Brantford Can.
131	D2	Bras d'Or Lake Can.
155	C1	Brasil, Planalto do plat. Brazil
154	C1	Brasília Brazil
155	D1	Brasília de Minas Brazil
88	C2	Braslaw Belarus
110	C1	Braşov Romania
103	D2	Bratislava Slovakia
83	H3	Bratsk Russia
102	C2	Braunau am Inn Austria
101	E1	Braunschweig Ger.
92	☐A2	Brautarholt Iceland
		Bravo del Norte, Río r. Mex./U.S.A. see Rio Grande
135	C4	Brawley U.S.A.
97	C2	Bray Ireland
150	C2	Brazil country S. America
154	C1	Brazlândia Brazil
139	D2	Brazos r. U.S.A.
118	B3	Brazzaville Congo
109	C2	Brčko Bos. & Herz.
96	C2	Brechin U.K.
100	B2	Brecht Belgium
139	D2	Breckenridge U.S.A.
103	D2	Břeclav Czech Rep.
99	B3	Brecon U.K.
99	B3	Brecon Beacons reg. U.K.
100	B2	Breda Neth.
122	B3	Bredasdorp S. Africa
102	B2	Bregenz Austria
92	H1	Breivikbotn Norway
92	E3	Brekstad Norway
101	D1	Bremen Ger.
101	D1	Bremerhaven Ger.
134	B1	Bremerton U.S.A.
101	D1	Bremervörde Ger.
139	D2	Brenham U.S.A.
108	B1	Brennero Italy
102	C2	Brenner Pass Austria/Italy
99	D3	Brentwood U.K.
108	B1	Brescia Italy
108	B1	Bressanone Italy
96	☐	Bressay i. U.K.
104	B2	Bressuire France
88	B3	Brest Belarus
104	B2	Brest France
142	C3	Breton Sound b. U.S.A.
151	C2	Breves Brazil
53	C1	Brewarrina Austr.
134	C1	Brewster U.S.A.
89	E2	Breytovo Russia
109	C1	Brezovo Polje plain Croatia
118	C2	Bria C.A.R.
105	D3	Briançon France
90	B2	Briceni Moldova
99	B3	Bridgend U.K.
141	E2	Bridgeport CT U.S.A.
136	C2	Bridgeport NE U.S.A.
147	E3	Bridgetown Barbados
131	D2	Bridgewater Can.
99	B3	Bridgwater U.K.
98	C1	Bridlington U.K.
98	C1	Bridlington Bay U.K.
105	D2	Brig Switz.
134	D2	Brigham City U.S.A.
54	B3	Brighton N.Z.
99	C3	Brighton U.K.
105	D3	Brignoles France
101	D2	Brilon Ger.
109	C2	Brindisi Italy
91	D2	Brin'kovskaya Russia
53	D1	Brisbane Austr.
99	B3	Bristol U.K.
143	D1	Bristol U.S.A.
99	A3	Bristol Channel est. U.K.
128	B2	British Columbia prov. Can.
56	G7	British Indian Ocean Territory terr. Indian Ocean
95	B2	British Isles is Europe
123	C2	Brits S. Africa
122	B3	Britstown S. Africa
104	C2	Brive-la-Gaillarde France
106	C1	Briviesca Spain
103	D2	Brno Czech Rep.
143	D2	Broad r. U.S.A.
130	C1	Broadback r. Can.
96	C3	Broad Law h. U.K.
136	B1	Broadus U.S.A.
129	D2	Brochet Can.
129	D2	Brochet, Lac l. Can.
131	D2	Brochet, Lac au l. Can.
101	E1	Bröckel Ger.
126	D1	Brock Island Can.
130	C2	Brockville Can.
127	F2	Brodeur Peninsula Can.
96	B3	Brodick U.K.
103	D1	Brodnica Pol.
90	B1	Brody Ukr.
139	D1	Broken Arrow U.S.A.
137	D2	Broken Bow U.S.A.
52	B2	Broken Hill Austr.
99	B2	Bromsgrove U.K.
93	E4	Brønderslev Denmark
92	F2	Brønnøysund Norway
64	A2	Brooke's Point Phil.
142	B2	Brookhaven U.S.A.
134	B2	Brookings OR U.S.A.
137	D2	Brookings SD U.S.A.
129	C2	Brooks Can.
126	B2	Brooks Range mts U.S.A.
143	D3	Brooksville U.S.A.
96	B2	Broom, Loch inlet U.K.
50	B1	Broome Austr.
134	B2	Brothers U.S.A.
		Broughton Island Can. see Qikiqtarjuaq
90	C1	Brovary Ukr.
139	C2	Brownfield U.S.A.
128	C3	Browning U.S.A.
142	C1	Brownsville TN U.S.A.
139	D3	Brownsville TX U.S.A.
139	D2	Brownwood U.S.A.
92	☐A2	Brú Iceland
104	C1	Bruay-la-Buissière France
140	B1	Bruce Crossing U.S.A.
102	C2	Bruck an der Mur Austria
		Bruges Belgium see Brugge
100	A2	Brugge Belgium
128	C2	Brûlé Can.
151	D3	Brumado Brazil
93	F3	Brumunddal Norway
61	C1	Brunei country Asia
108	B1	Brunico Italy
101	D1	Brunsbüttel Ger.
143	D2	Brunswick GA U.S.A.
141	F2	Brunswick ME U.S.A.
53	D1	Brunswick Heads Austr.
136	C2	Brush U.S.A.
		Brussel Belgium see Brussels
100	B2	Brussels Belgium Bruxelles Belgium see Brussels
89	D3	Bryan U.S.A.
89	D3	Bryansk Russia
91	D2	Bryukhovetskaya Russia
103	D1	Brzeg Pol.
114	A3	Buba Guinea-Bissau
80	B2	Bucak Turkey
150	A1	Bucaramanga Col.
53	C3	Buchan Austr.
114	A4	Buchanan Liberia
110	C2	Bucharest Romania
65	B2	Bucheon S. Korea
101	D1	Buchholz in der Nordheide Ger.
110	C1	Bucin, Pasul pass Romania
101	D1	Bückeburg Ger.
138	A2	Buckeye U.S.A.
96	C2	Buckhaven U.K.
96	C2	Buckie U.K.
51	C1	Buckingham Bay Austr.
51	D2	Buckland Tableland reg. Austr.
52	A2	Buckleboo Austr.
141	F2	Bucksport U.S.A. Bucureşti Romania see Bucharest
89	D3	Buda-Kashalyova Belarus
103	D2	Budapest Hungary
75	B2	Budaun India
108	A3	Buddusò Sardinia Italy
99	A3	Bude U.K.
87	D4	Budennovsk Russia
89	D2	Budogoshch' Russia
108	A2	Budoni Sardinia Italy
118	A2	Buea Cameroon
144	B2	Buenaventura Mex.
106	C1	Buendía, Embalse de resr Spain
155	D1	Buenópolis Brazil
153	C4	Buenos Aires Arg.
153	A5	Buenos Aires, Lago l. Arg./Chile
141	D2	Buffalo NY U.S.A.
136	C1	Buffalo SD U.S.A.
136	B2	Buffalo WY U.S.A.
129	D2	Buffalo Narrows Can.
122	A2	Buffels watercourse S. Africa
110	C2	Buftea Romania
103	E1	Bug r. Pol.
61	C2	Bugel, Tanjung pt Indon.
109	C2	Bugojno Bos. & Herz.
64	A2	Bugsuk i. Phil.
87	E3	Buguruslan Russia
110	C1	Buhuşi Romania
99	B2	Builth Wells U.K.
120	A3	Buitepos Namibia
109	D2	Bujanovac Serbia
119	C3	Bujumbura Burundi
69	D1	Bukachacha Russia
119	C3	Bukavu Dem. Rep. Congo
60	B2	Bukittinggi Indon.
119	D3	Bukoba Tanz.
53	D2	Bulahdelah Austr.
121	B3	Bulawayo Zimbabwe
111	C3	Buldan Turkey
123	D2	Bulembu Swaziland
69	C1	Bulgan Mongolia
110	C2	Bulgaria country Europe
54	B2	Buller r. N.Z.
52	B1	Bulloo Downs Austr.
122	A1	Büllsport Namibia
58	C3	Bulukumba Indon.
118	B3	Bulungu Dem. Rep. Congo
118	C2	Bumba Dem. Rep. Congo
62	A1	Bumhkang Myanmar
118	B3	Buna Dem. Rep. Congo

50 A3 **Bunbury** Austr.
97 C1 **Buncrana** Ireland
119 D3 **Bunda** Tanz.
51 E2 **Bundaberg** Austr.
53 D2 **Bundarra** Austr.
74 B2 **Bundi** India
97 B1 **Bundoran** Ireland
53 C3 **Bungendore** Austr.
67 B4 **Bungo-suidō** *sea chan.* Japan
119 D2 **Bunia** Dem. Rep. Congo
118 C3 **Bunianga** Dem. Rep. Congo
63 B2 **Buôn Ma Thuôt** Vietnam
119 D3 **Bura** Kenya
78 B2 **Buraydah** Saudi Arabia
100 D2 **Burbach** Ger.
117 C4 **Burco** Somalia
100 B1 **Burdaard** Neth.
80 B2 **Burdur** Turkey
117 B3 **Burē** Eth.
99 D2 **Bure** *r.* U.K.
74 B1 **Burewala** Pak.
101 E1 **Burg** Ger.
110 C2 **Burgas** Bulg.
101 E1 **Burgdorf** *Niedersachsen* Ger.
101 E1 **Burgdorf** *Niedersachsen* Ger.
131 E2 **Burgeo** Can.
123 D1 **Burgersfort** S. Africa
100 A2 **Burgh-Haamstede** Neth.
145 C2 **Burgos** Mex.
106 C1 **Burgos** Spain
111 C3 **Burhaniye** Turkey
74 B2 **Burhanpur** India
101 D1 **Burhave (Butjadingen)** Ger.
131 E2 **Burin** Can.
151 D2 **Buriti Bravo** Brazil
155 C1 **Buritis** Brazil
51 C1 **Burketown** Austr.
114 B3 **Burkina Faso** *country* Africa
134 D2 **Burley** U.S.A.
136 C3 **Burlington** *CO* U.S.A.
137 E2 **Burlington** *IA* U.S.A.
143 E1 **Burlington** *NC* U.S.A.
141 E2 **Burlington** *VT* U.S.A.
Burma *country* Asia *see* **Myanmar**
134 B2 **Burney** U.S.A.
51 D4 **Burnie** Austr.
98 B2 **Burnley** U.K.
134 C2 **Burns** U.S.A.
128 B2 **Burns Lake** Can.
77 E2 **Burqin** China
52 A2 **Burra** Austr.
109 D2 **Burrel** Albania
97 B2 **Burren** *reg.* Ireland
53 C2 **Burrendong, Lake** *resr* Austr.
53 C2 **Burren Junction** Austr.
Burriana Spain *see* **Borriana**
53 C2 **Burrinjuck Reservoir** Austr.
144 B2 **Burro, Serranías del** *mts* Mex.
111 C2 **Bursa** Turkey
116 B2 **Būr Safājah** Egypt
Būr Sa'īd Egypt *see* **Port Said**
130 C1 **Burton, Lac** *l.* Can.
99 C2 **Burton upon Trent** U.K.
59 C3 **Buru** *i.* Indon.
119 C3 **Burundi** *country* Africa
119 C3 **Bururi** Burundi
91 C1 **Buryn'** Ukr.
99 D2 **Bury St Edmunds** U.K.
108 B3 **Busambra, Rocca** *mt. Sicily* Italy
65 B2 **Busan** S. Korea
118 C3 **Busanga** Dem. Rep. Congo
119 D3 **Bushenyi** Uganda
118 C2 **Businga** Dem. Rep. Congo
50 A3 **Busselton** Austr.
139 C3 **Bustamante** Mex.
118 C2 **Buta** Dem. Rep. Congo
119 C3 **Butare** Rwanda
123 C2 **Butha-Buthe** Lesotho
140 D2 **Butler** U.S.A.
59 C3 **Buton** *i.* Indon.
134 D1 **Butte** U.S.A.
60 B1 **Butterworth** Malaysia
96 A1 **Butt of Lewis** *hd* U.K.
129 E2 **Button Bay** Can.
64 B2 **Butuan** Phil.
91 E1 **Buturlinovka** Russia
75 C2 **Butwal** Nepal
101 D2 **Butzbach** Ger.
117 C4 **Buulobarde** Somalia
117 C5 **Buur Gaabo** Somalia
117 C4 **Buurhabaka** Somalia
76 C3 **Buxoro** Uzbek.
101 D1 **Buxtehude** Ger.
89 F2 **Buy** Russia
87 D4 **Buynaksk** Russia
69 D1 **Buyr Nuur** *l.* Mongolia
111 C3 **Büyükmenderes** *r.* Turkey
110 C1 **Buzău** Romania
121 C2 **Búzi** Moz.
87 E3 **Buzuluk** Russia
110 C2 **Byala** Bulg.
88 C3 **Byalynichy** Belarus
88 D3 **Byarezina** *r.* Belarus
88 B3 **Byaroza** Belarus
103 D1 **Bydgoszcz** Pol.
88 C3 **Byerazino** Belarus
88 C2 **Byeshankovichy** Belarus
89 D3 **Bykhaw** Belarus
127 F2 **Bylot Island** Can.
53 C2 **Byrock** Austr.
53 D1 **Byron Bay** Austr.
83 J2 **Bytantay** *r.* Russia
103 D1 **Bytom** Pol.
103 D1 **Bytów** Pol.

C

154 B2 **Caarapó** Brazil
64 B1 **Cabanatuan** Phil.
117 C3 **Cabdul Qaadir** Somalia
106 B2 **Cabeza del Buey** Spain
152 B2 **Cabezas** Bol.
150 A1 **Cabimas** Venez.
120 A1 **Cabinda** Angola
118 B3 **Cabinda** *prov.* Angola
155 D2 **Cabo Frio** Brazil
155 D2 **Cabo Frio, Ilha do** *i.* Brazil
130 C2 **Cabonga, Réservoir** *resr* Can.
51 E2 **Caboolture** Austr.
150 A2 **Cabo Pantoja** Peru
144 A1 **Caborca** Mex.
144 B2 **Cabo San Lucas** Mex.
131 D2 **Cabot Strait** Can.
155 D1 **Cabral, Serra do** *mts* Brazil
107 D2 **Cabrera, Illa de** *i.* Spain
106 B1 **Cabrera, Sierra de la** *mts* Spain
129 D2 **Cabri** Can.
107 C2 **Cabriel** *r.* Spain
152 C3 **Caçador** Brazil
109 D2 **Čačak** Serbia
108 A2 **Caccia, Capo** *c. Sardinia* Italy
151 C3 **Cáceres** Brazil
106 B2 **Cáceres** Spain
128 B2 **Cache Creek** Can.
114 A3 **Cacheu** Guinea-Bissau
151 C2 **Cachimbo, Serra do** *hills* Brazil
154 B1 **Cachoeira Alta** Brazil
155 D2 **Cachoeiro de Itapemirim** Brazil
114 A3 **Cacine** Guinea-Bissau
120 A2 **Cacolo** Angola
154 B1 **Caçu** Brazil
103 D2 **Čadca** Slovakia
101 D1 **Cadenberge** Ger.
145 B2 **Cadereyta** Mex.
140 B2 **Cadillac** U.S.A.
106 B2 **Cádiz** Spain
106 B2 **Cádiz, Golfo de** *g.* Spain
128 C2 **Cadotte Lake** Can.
104 B2 **Caen** France
98 A2 **Caernarfon** U.K.
98 A2 **Caernarfon Bay** U.K.
152 B3 **Cafayate** Arg.
64 B2 **Cagayan de Oro** Phil.
64 A2 **Cagayan de Tawi-Tawi** *i.* Phil.
108 B2 **Cagli** Italy
108 A3 **Cagliari** *Sardinia* Italy
108 A3 **Cagliari, Golfo di** *b. Sardinia* Italy
76 B2 **Çagyl** Turkm.
97 B3 **Caha Mountains** *hills* Ireland
97 A3 **Cahermore** Ireland
97 C2 **Cahir** Ireland
97 A3 **Cahirsiveen** Ireland
97 C2 **Cahore Point** Ireland
104 C3 **Cahors** France
90 B2 **Cahul** Moldova
121 C2 **Caia** Moz.
151 C3 **Caiabis, Serra dos** *hills* Brazil
120 B2 **Caianda** Angola
154 B1 **Caiapó, Serra do** *mts* Brazil
154 B1 **Caiapônia** Brazil
147 C2 **Caicos Islands** Turks and Caicos Is
96 C2 **Cairngorm Mountains** U.K.
98 A1 **Cairnryan** U.K.
51 D1 **Cairns** Austr.
116 B1 **Cairo** Egypt
98 C2 **Caistor** U.K.
120 A2 **Caiundo** Angola
150 A2 **Cajamarca** Peru
109 C1 **Čakovec** Croatia
123 C3 **Cala** S. Africa
150 B1 **Calabozo** Venez.
110 B2 **Calafat** Romania
153 A6 **Calafate** Arg.
107 C1 **Calahorra** Spain
104 C1 **Calais** France
141 F1 **Calais** U.S.A.
152 B3 **Calama** Chile
64 A1 **Calamian Group** *is* Phil.
107 C1 **Calamocha** Spain
120 A1 **Calandula** Angola
60 A1 **Calang** Indon.
64 B1 **Calapan** Phil.
110 C2 **Călărași** Romania
107 C1 **Calatayud** Spain
64 B1 **Calayan** *i.* Phil.
64 B1 **Calbayog** Phil.
151 E2 **Calcanhar, Ponta do** *pt* Brazil
151 C1 **Calçoene** Brazil
Calcutta India *see* **Kolkata**
106 B2 **Caldas da Rainha** Port.
154 C1 **Caldas Novas** Brazil
152 A3 **Caldera** Chile
134 C2 **Caldwell** U.S.A.
123 C3 **Caledon** *r.* Lesotho/S. Africa
122 A3 **Caledon** S. Africa
153 B5 **Caleta Olivia** Arg.
98 A1 **Calf of Man** *i.* Isle of Man
128 C2 **Calgary** Can.
150 A1 **Cali** Col.
Calicut India *see* **Kozhikode**
135 D3 **Caliente** U.S.A.
135 B2 **California** *state* U.S.A.
144 A1 **California, Gulf of** Mex.

135 B3 **California Aqueduct** *canal* U.S.A.
122 B3 **Calitzdorp** S. Africa
145 C2 **Calkiní** Mex.
52 B1 **Callabonna, Lake** *imp. l.* Austr.
96 B2 **Callander** U.K.
150 A3 **Callao** Peru
108 B3 **Caltagirone** *Sicily* Italy
108 B3 **Caltanissetta** *Sicily* Italy
120 A2 **Caluquembe** Angola
117 D3 **Caluula** Somalia
105 D3 **Calvi** *Corsica* France
107 D2 **Calvià** Spain
144 B2 **Calvillo** Mex.
122 A3 **Calvinia** S. Africa
109 C2 **Calvo, Monte** *mt.* Italy
144 B2 **Camacho** Mex.
120 A2 **Camacupa** Angola
146 C2 **Camagüey** Cuba
150 A3 **Camaná** Peru
154 B1 **Camapuã** Brazil
145 C2 **Camargo** Mex.
63 B3 **Ca Mau** Vietnam
63 B3 **Ca Mau, Mui** *c.* Vietnam
63 B2 **Cambodia** *country* Asia
99 A3 **Camborne** U.K.
105 C1 **Cambrai** France
99 B2 **Cambrian Mountains** *hills* U.K.
54 C1 **Cambridge** N.Z.
99 D2 **Cambridge** U.K.
141 E2 **Cambridge** *MA* U.S.A.
141 D3 **Cambridge** *MD* U.S.A.
137 E1 **Cambridge** *MN* U.S.A.
140 C2 **Cambridge** *OH* U.S.A.
131 D1 **Cambrien, Lac** *l.* Can.
53 D2 **Camden** Austr.
142 B2 **Camden** *AR* U.S.A.
141 F2 **Camden** *ME* U.S.A.
118 B2 **Cameroon** *country* Africa
118 B2 **Cameroon Highlands** *slope* Cameroon/Nigeria
151 D2 **Cametá** Brazil
64 B1 **Camiguin** *i.* Phil.
152 B3 **Camiri** Bol.
151 D2 **Camocim** Brazil
51 C1 **Camooweal** Austr.
63 A3 **Camorta** *i.* India
153 A5 **Campana, Isla** *i.* Chile
122 B2 **Campbell** S. Africa
54 B2 **Campbell, Cape** N.Z.
48 F6 **Campbell Island** N.Z.
128 B2 **Campbell River** Can.
140 B3 **Campbellsville** U.S.A.
131 D2 **Campbellton** Can.
96 B3 **Campbeltown** U.K.
145 C3 **Campeche** Mex.
145 C3 **Campeche, Bahía de** *g.* Mex.
52 B3 **Camperdown** Austr.
110 C1 **Câmpina** Romania
151 E2 **Campina Grande** Brazil
154 C2 **Campinas** Brazil
154 C1 **Campina Verde** Brazil
108 B2 **Campobasso** Italy
155 C2 **Campo Belo** Brazil
154 C1 **Campo Florido** Brazil
152 B3 **Campo Gallo** Arg.
154 B2 **Campo Grande** Brazil
151 D2 **Campo Maior** Brazil
106 B2 **Campo Maior** Port.
154 B2 **Campo Mourão** Brazil
155 C1 **Campos Altos** Brazil
155 C2 **Campos do Jordão** Brazil
155 D2 **Campos dos Goytacazes** Brazil
110 C1 **Câmpulung** Romania
138 A2 **Camp Verde** U.S.A.
128 C2 **Camrose** Can.
129 D2 **Camsell Portage** Can.
111 C2 **Çan** Turkey
126 F2 **Canada** *country* N. America
139 C1 **Canadian** U.S.A.
139 D1 **Canadian** *r.* U.S.A.
111 C2 **Çanakkale** Turkey
144 A1 **Cananea** Mex.
154 C2 **Cananéia** Brazil
Canarias, Islas *terr.* N. Atlantic Ocean *see* **Canary Islands**
114 A2 **Canary Islands** *terr.* N. Atlantic Ocean
155 C1 **Canastra, Serra da** *mts* Brazil
144 B2 **Canatlán** Mex.
143 D3 **Canaveral, Cape** U.S.A.
155 E1 **Canavieiras** Brazil
53 C3 **Canberra** Austr.
145 D2 **Cancún** Mex.
111 C3 **Çandarlı** Turkey
145 C3 **Candelaria** Mex.
129 D2 **Candle Lake** Can.
120 A2 **Cangamba** Angola
106 B1 **Cangas del Narcea** Spain
152 C4 **Canguçu** Brazil
70 B2 **Cangzhou** China
131 D1 **Caniapiscau** Can.
131 D1 **Caniapiscau** *r.* Can.
131 C1 **Caniapiscau, Réservoir de** *resr* Can.
108 B3 **Canicattì** *Sicily* Italy
151 E2 **Canindé** Brazil
144 B2 **Cañitas de Felipe Pescador** Mex.
80 B1 **Çankırı** Turkey
128 C2 **Canmore** Can.
96 A2 **Canna** *i.* U.K.
Cannanore India *see* **Kannur**
105 D3 **Cannes** France
99 B2 **Cannock** U.K.
53 C3 **Cann River** Austr.
152 C3 **Canoas** Brazil
129 D2 **Canoe Lake** Can.
154 B3 **Canoinhas** Brazil
136 B3 **Canon City** U.S.A.
129 D2 **Canora** Can.
53 C2 **Canowindra** Austr.
106 C1 **Cantábrica, Cordillera** *mts* Spain
106 B1 **Cantábrico, Mar** *sea* Spain
99 D3 **Canterbury** U.K.
54 B2 **Canterbury Bight** *b.* N.Z.
54 B2 **Canterbury Plains** N.Z.
63 B2 **Cân Thơ** Vietnam
151 D2 **Canto do Buriti** Brazil
Canton China *see* **Guangzhou**
142 C2 **Canton** *MS* U.S.A.
140 C2 **Canton** *OH* U.S.A.
139 C1 **Canyon** U.S.A.
134 D1 **Canyon Ferry Lake** U.S.A.
62 B1 **Cao Băng** Vietnam
154 C2 **Capão Bonito** Brazil
155 D2 **Caparaó, Serra do** *mts* Brazil
51 D4 **Cape Barren Island** Austr.
52 A3 **Cape Borda** Austr.
131 D2 **Cape Breton Island** Can.
114 B4 **Cape Coast** Ghana
141 E2 **Cape Cod Bay** U.S.A.
127 F2 **Cape Dorset** Can.
143 E2 **Cape Fear** *r.* U.S.A.
137 F3 **Cape Girardeau** U.S.A.
155 D1 **Capelinha** Brazil
100 B2 **Capelle aan den IJssel** Neth.
120 A1 **Capenda-Camulemba** Angola
122 A3 **Cape Town** S. Africa
112 C5 **Cape Verde** *country* Africa
51 D1 **Cape York Peninsula** Austr.
147 C3 **Cap-Haïtien** Haiti
151 D2 **Capim** *r.* Brazil
58 D1 **Capitol Hill** N. Mariana Is
109 C2 **Čapljina** Bos. & Herz.
109 B3 **Capo d'Orlando** *Sicily* Italy
108 A2 **Capraia, Isola di** *i.* Italy
108 A2 **Caprara, Punta** *pt Sardinia* Italy
108 B2 **Capri, Isola di** *i.* Italy
120 B2 **Caprivi Strip** *reg.* Namibia
150 B2 **Caquetá** *r.* Col.
110 B2 **Caracal** Romania
150 B1 **Caracas** Venez.
151 D2 **Caracol** Brazil
155 C2 **Caraguatatuba** Brazil
153 A4 **Carahue** Chile
155 D1 **Caraí** Brazil
155 D2 **Carangola** Brazil
110 B1 **Caransebeş** Romania
131 D2 **Caraquet** Can.
146 B3 **Caratasca, Laguna de** *lag.* Hond.
155 D1 **Caratinga** Brazil
150 B2 **Carauari** Brazil
107 C2 **Caravaca de la Cruz** Spain
155 E1 **Caravelas** Brazil
129 E3 **Carberry** Can.
144 A2 **Carbó** Mex.
107 C2 **Carbon, Cap** *c.* Alg.
153 B5 **Carbón, Laguna del** *l.* Arg.
108 A3 **Carbonara, Capo** *c. Sardinia* Italy
136 B3 **Carbondale** *CO* U.S.A.
140 B3 **Carbondale** *IL* U.S.A.
131 E2 **Carbonear** Can.
155 D1 **Carbonita** Brazil
107 C2 **Carcaixent** Spain
104 C3 **Carcassonne** France
128 A1 **Carcross** Can.
145 C3 **Cárdenas** Mex.
99 B3 **Cardiff** U.K.
99 A2 **Cardigan** U.K.
99 A2 **Cardigan Bay** U.K.
128 C3 **Cardston** Can.
110 B1 **Carei** Romania
104 B2 **Carentan** France
50 B2 **Carey, Lake** *imp. l.* Austr.
155 D2 **Cariacica** Brazil
146 B3 **Caribbean Sea** N. Atlantic Ocean
141 F1 **Caribou** U.S.A.
130 B1 **Caribou Lake** Can.
128 C2 **Caribou Mountains** Can.
144 B2 **Carichic** Mex.
100 B3 **Carignan** France
53 C2 **Carinda** Austr.
107 C1 **Cariñena** Spain
130 C2 **Carleton Place** Can.
123 C2 **Carletonville** S. Africa
97 C1 **Carlingford Lough** *inlet* Ireland/U.K.
98 B1 **Carlisle** U.K.
141 D2 **Carlisle** U.S.A.
155 D1 **Carlos Chagas** Brazil
97 C2 **Carlow** Ireland
135 C4 **Carlsbad** *CA* U.S.A.
138 C2 **Carlsbad** *NM* U.S.A.
129 D3 **Carlyle** Can.
128 A1 **Carmacks** Can.
129 E3 **Carman** Can.
99 A3 **Carmarthen** U.K.
99 A3 **Carmarthen Bay** U.K.
104 C3 **Carmaux** France
145 C3 **Carmelita** Guat.
144 A2 **Carmen, Isla** *i.* Mex.
104 B2 **Carnac** France
122 B3 **Carnarvon** S. Africa
97 C1 **Carndonagh** Ireland
50 B2 **Carnegie, Lake** *imp. l.* Austr.

96 B2 **Carn Eige** *mt.* U.K.
63 A3 **Car Nicobar** *i.* India
118 B2 **Carnot** C.A.R.
52 A2 **Carnot, Cape** Austr.
97 C2 **Carnsore Point** Ireland
151 D2 **Carolina** Brazil
48 D2 **Caroline Islands** *is* N. Pacific Ocean
59 D2 **Caroline Islands** N. Pacific Ocean
103 D2 **Carpathian Mountains** Europe
Carpații Meridionali *mts* Romania *see* **Transylvanian Alps**
51 C1 **Carpentaria, Gulf of** Austr.
105 D3 **Carpentras** France
97 B3 **Carrantuohill** *mt.* Ireland
105 E3 **Carrara** Italy
97 C2 **Carrickmacross** Ireland
97 B2 **Carrick-on-Shannon** Ireland
97 C2 **Carrick-on-Suir** Ireland
137 D1 **Carrington** U.S.A.
139 D3 **Carrizo Springs** U.S.A.
138 B2 **Carrizozo** U.S.A.
137 E2 **Carroll** U.S.A.
143 C2 **Carrollton** U.S.A.
129 D2 **Carrot River** Can.
135 C3 **Carson City** U.S.A.
150 A1 **Cartagena** Col.
107 C2 **Cartagena** Spain
146 B4 **Cartago** Costa Rica
137 E3 **Carthage** *MO* U.S.A.
139 E2 **Carthage** *TX* U.S.A.
131 E1 **Cartwright** Can.
151 E2 **Caruaru** Brazil
114 B1 **Casablanca** Morocco
154 C2 **Casa Branca** Brazil
144 B1 **Casa de Janos** Mex.
138 A2 **Casa Grande** U.S.A.
108 A1 **Casale Monferrato** Italy
109 C2 **Casarano** Italy
134 C2 **Cascade** U.S.A.
134 B2 **Cascade Range** *mts* Can./U.S.A.
106 B2 **Cascais** Port.
154 B2 **Cascavel** Brazil
108 B2 **Caserta** Italy
97 C2 **Cashel** Ireland
53 D1 **Casino** Austr.
107 C1 **Caspe** Spain
136 B2 **Casper** U.S.A.
76 A2 **Caspian Lowland** Kazakh./Russia
81 C1 **Caspian Sea** Asia/Europe
154 C2 **Cássia** Brazil
128 B2 **Cassiar (abandoned)** Can.
128 A2 **Cassiar Mountains** Can.
154 B1 **Cassilândia** Brazil
108 B2 **Cassino** Italy
96 B2 **Cassley** *r.* U.K.
151 D2 **Castanhal** Brazil
152 B4 **Castaño** *r.* Arg.
144 B2 **Castaños** Mex.
104 C3 **Casteljaloux** France
107 C2 **Castellón de la Plana** Spain
106 B2 **Castelo Branco** Port.
108 B3 **Castelvetrano** *Sicily* Italy
52 B3 **Casterton** Austr.
108 B2 **Castiglione della Pescaia** Italy
97 B2 **Castlebar** Ireland
96 A2 **Castlebay** U.K.
97 C1 **Castleblayney** Ireland
97 C1 **Castlederg** U.K.
96 C3 **Castle Douglas** U.K.
128 C3 **Castlegar** Can.
97 B2 **Castleisland** Ireland
52 B3 **Castlemaine** Austr.
97 B2 **Castlerea** Ireland
53 C2 **Castlereagh** *r.* Austr.
136 C3 **Castle Rock** U.S.A.
129 C2 **Castor** Can.
104 C3 **Castres** France
100 B1 **Castricum** Neth.
147 D3 **Castries** St Lucia
154 C2 **Castro** Brazil
153 A5 **Castro** Chile
106 B2 **Castro Verde** Port.
109 C3 **Castrovillari** Italy
150 A2 **Catacaos** Peru
155 D2 **Cataguases** Brazil
154 C1 **Catalão** Brazil
152 B3 **Catamarca** Arg.
64 B1 **Catanduanes** *i.* Phil.
154 C2 **Catanduva** Brazil
154 B3 **Catanduvas** Brazil
109 C3 **Catania** *Sicily* Italy
109 C3 **Catanzaro** Italy
64 B1 **Catarman** Phil.
64 B1 **Catbalogan** Phil.
145 C3 **Catemaco** Mex.
147 C2 **Cat Island** Bahamas
130 A1 **Cat Lake** Can.
145 D2 **Catoche, Cabo** *c.* Mex.
141 E2 **Catskill Mountains** U.S.A.
64 B2 **Cauayan** Phil.
150 A1 **Cauca** *r.* Col.
151 E2 **Caucaia** Brazil
81 C1 **Caucasus** *mts* Asia/Europe
100 A2 **Caudry** France
109 C3 **Caulonia** Italy
131 D2 **Causapscal** Can.
105 D3 **Cavaillon** France
151 D3 **Cavalcante** Brazil
97 C2 **Cavan** Ireland
154 B3 **Cavernoso, Serra do** *mts* Brazil
151 D2 **Caxias** Brazil
152 C3 **Caxias do Sul** Brazil
120 A1 **Caxito** Angola
151 C1 **Cayenne** Fr. Guiana
146 B3 **Cayman Islands** *terr.* West Indies
117 C4 **Caynaba** Somalia
120 B2 **Cazombo** Angola
144 B2 **Ceballos** Mex.
64 B1 **Cebu** Phil.
64 B1 **Cebu** *i.* Phil.
108 B2 **Cecina** Italy
137 F2 **Cedar** *r.* U.S.A.
135 D3 **Cedar City** U.S.A.
137 E2 **Cedar Falls** U.S.A.
129 D2 **Cedar Lake** Can.
137 E2 **Cedar Rapids** U.S.A.
144 A2 **Cedros, Isla** *i.* Mex.
51 C3 **Ceduna** Austr.
117 C4 **Ceeldheere** Somalia
117 C3 **Ceerigaabo** Somalia
108 B3 **Cefalù** *Sicily* Italy
145 B2 **Celaya** Mex.
58 C3 **Celebes** *i.* Indon.
156 B5 **Celebes Sea** Indon./Phil.
145 C2 **Celestún** Mex.
101 E1 **Celle** Ger.
95 B3 **Celtic Sea** Ireland/U.K.
59 D3 **Cenderawasih, Teluk** *b.* Indon.
150 A1 **Central, Cordillera** *mts* Col.
150 A3 **Central, Cordillera** *mts* Peru
64 B1 **Central, Cordillera** *mts* Phil.
118 C2 **Central African Republic** *country* Africa
74 A2 **Central Brahui Range** *mts* Pak.
137 D2 **Central City** U.S.A.
140 B3 **Centralia** *IL* U.S.A.
134 B1 **Centralia** *WA* U.S.A.
74 A2 **Central Makran Range** *mts* Pak.
59 D3 **Central Range** *mts* P.N.G.
89 E3 **Central Russian Upland** *hills* Russia
83 I2 **Central Siberian Plateau** Russia
111 B3 **Cephalonia** *i.* Greece
Ceram Sea Indon. *see* **Seram, Laut**
152 B3 **Ceres** Arg.
154 C1 **Ceres** Brazil
122 A3 **Ceres** S. Africa
104 C3 **Céret** France
106 C1 **Cerezo de Abajo** Spain
109 C2 **Cerignola** Italy
110 C2 **Cernavodă** Romania
145 C2 **Cerralvo** Mex.
144 B2 **Cerralvo, Isla** *i.* Mex.
145 B2 **Cerritos** Mex.
154 C2 **Cerro Azul** Brazil
145 C2 **Cerro Azul** Mex.
150 A3 **Cerro de Pasco** Peru
105 D3 **Cervione** *Corsica* France
106 B1 **Cervo** Spain
108 B2 **Cesena** Italy
88 C2 **Cēsis** Latvia
102 C2 **České Budějovice** Czech Rep.
101 F3 **Český les** *mts* Czech Rep.
111 C3 **Çeşme** Turkey
53 D2 **Cessnock** Austr.
109 C2 **Cetinje** Montenegro
109 C3 **Cetraro** Italy
106 B2 **Ceuta** N. Africa
105 C3 **Cévennes** *mts* France
Ceylon *country* Asia *see* **Sri Lanka**
79 D2 **Chābahār** Iran
150 A2 **Chachapoyas** Peru
89 D3 **Chachersk** Belarus
63 B2 **Chachoengsao** Thai.
115 D3 **Chad** *country* Africa
115 D3 **Chad, Lake** Africa
69 C1 **Chadaasan** Mongolia
68 C1 **Chadan** Russia
123 C1 **Chadibe** Botswana
136 C2 **Chadron** U.S.A.
65 B2 **Chaeryŏng** N. Korea
74 A2 **Chagai** Pak.
77 C3 **Chaghcharān** Afgh.
89 E2 **Chagoda** Russia
75 C2 **Chaibasa** India
63 B2 **Chainat** Thai.
63 B2 **Chaiyaphum** Thai.
152 C4 **Chajarí** Arg.
131 D1 **Chakonipau, Lac** *l.* Can.
150 A3 **Chala** Peru
131 D2 **Chaleur Bay** *inlet* Can.
74 B2 **Chalisgaon** India
111 C3 **Chalki** *i.* Greece
111 B3 **Chalkida** Greece
104 B2 **Challans** France
134 D2 **Challis** U.S.A.
105 C2 **Châlons-en-Champagne** France
105 C2 **Chalon-sur-Saône** France
138 B1 **Chama** U.S.A.
121 C2 **Chama** Zambia
74 A1 **Chaman** Pak.
74 B1 **Chamba** India
74 B2 **Chambal** *r.* India
137 D2 **Chamberlain** U.S.A.
141 D3 **Chambersburg** U.S.A.
105 D2 **Chambéry** France
121 C2 **Chambeshi** Zambia
140 B2 **Champaign** U.S.A.
141 E2 **Champlain, Lake** Can./U.S.A.
145 C3 **Champotón** Mex.

152 A3 **Chañaral** Chile
126 B2 **Chandalar** *r.* U.S.A.
142 C3 **Chandeleur Islands** U.S.A.
74 B1 **Chandigarh** India
138 A2 **Chandler** U.S.A.
75 B3 **Chandrapur** India
63 B2 **Chang, Ko** *i.* Thai.
Chang'an China *see* **Rong'an**
121 C3 **Changane** *r.* Moz.
121 C2 **Changara** Moz.
65 B1 **Changbai** China
65 B1 **Changbai Shan** *mts* China/N. Korea
69 E2 **Changchun** China
71 B3 **Changde** China
65 B2 **Ch'angdo** N. Korea
Chang Jiang *r.* China *see* **Yangtze**
65 B1 **Changjin** N. Korea
65 B1 **Changjin-gang** *r.* N. Korea
71 B3 **Changsha** China
71 B3 **Changting** China
65 B2 **Changwon** S. Korea
70 B2 **Changyuan** China
70 B2 **Changzhi** China
70 B2 **Changzhou** China
111 B3 **Chania** Greece
95 C4 **Channel Islands** English Chan.
135 C4 **Channel Islands** U.S.A.
131 E2 **Channel-Port-aux-Basques** Can.
63 B2 **Chanthaburi** Thai.
104 C2 **Chantilly** France
137 D3 **Chanute** U.S.A.
82 G3 **Chany, Ozero** *salt l.* Russia
71 B3 **Chaoyang** *Guangdong* China
Chaoyang China *see* **Huinan**
71 B3 **Chaozhou** China
144 B2 **Chapala, Laguna de** *l.* Mex.
76 B1 **Chapayevo** Kazakh.
152 C3 **Chapecó** Brazil
143 E1 **Chapel Hill** U.S.A.
130 B2 **Chapleau** Can.
89 E3 **Chaplygin** Russia
91 C2 **Chaplynka** Ukr.
75 C2 **Chapra** India
145 B2 **Charcas** Mex.
99 B3 **Chard** U.K.
104 B2 **Charente** *r.* France
77 C3 **Chārīkār** Afgh.
86 E2 **Charkayuvom** Russia
100 B2 **Charleroi** Belgium
141 D3 **Charles, Cape** U.S.A.
137 E2 **Charles City** U.S.A.
140 B3 **Charleston** *IL* U.S.A.
143 E2 **Charleston** *SC* U.S.A.
140 C3 **Charleston** *WV* U.S.A.
135 C3 **Charleston Peak** U.S.A.
51 D2 **Charleville** Austr.
105 C2 **Charleville-Mézières** France
143 D1 **Charlotte** U.S.A.
143 D3 **Charlotte Harbor** *b.* U.S.A.
141 D3 **Charlottesville** U.S.A.
131 D2 **Charlottetown** Can.
52 B3 **Charlton** Austr.
130 C1 **Charlton Island** Can.
51 D2 **Charters Towers** Austr.
104 C2 **Chartres** France
128 C2 **Chase** Can.
88 C3 **Chashniki** Belarus
54 A3 **Chaslands Mistake** *c.* N.Z.
65 B1 **Chasŏng** N. Korea
104 B2 **Chassiron, Pointe de** *pt* France
104 B2 **Châteaubriant** France
104 C2 **Château-du-Loir** France
104 C2 **Châteaudun** France
104 B2 **Châteaulin** France
105 D3 **Châteauneuf-les-Martigues** France
104 C2 **Châteauneuf-sur-Loire** France
105 C2 **Château-Thierry** France
128 C2 **Chateh** Can.
100 B2 **Châtelet** Belgium
104 C2 **Châtellerault** France
140 C2 **Chatham** Can.
49 G5 **Chatham Islands** *is* N.Z.
105 C2 **Châtillon-sur-Seine** France
143 D2 **Chattahoochee** *r.* U.S.A.
143 C1 **Chattanooga** U.S.A.
63 B2 **Châu Đôc** Vietnam
62 A1 **Chauk** Myanmar
105 D2 **Chaumont** France
105 C2 **Chauny** France
151 D2 **Chaves** Brazil
106 B1 **Chaves** Port.
130 C1 **Chavigny, Lac** *l.* Can.
89 D3 **Chavusy** Belarus
89 E2 **Chayevo** Russia
86 E3 **Chaykovskiy** Russia
102 C1 **Cheb** Czech Rep.
87 D3 **Cheboksary** Russia
140 C1 **Cheboygan** U.S.A.
114 B2 **Chegga** Maur.
134 B1 **Chehalis** U.S.A.
Cheju S. Korea *see* **Jeju**
65 B3 **Cheju-do** *i.* S. Korea
89 E2 **Chekhov** Russia
134 B1 **Chelan, Lake** U.S.A.
103 E1 **Chełm** Pol.
99 D3 **Chelmer** *r.* U.K.
103 D1 **Chełmno** Pol.
99 D3 **Chelmsford** U.K.
99 B3 **Cheltenham** U.K.
87 F3 **Chelyabinsk** Russia
101 F2 **Chemnitz** Ger.
114 B2 **Chenachane** Alg.
70 B1 **Chengde** China
70 A2 **Chengdu** China
71 A3 **Chengguan** China
71 B4 **Chengmai** China
Chengshou China *see* **Yingshan**
70 A2 **Chengxian** China
Chengyang China *see* **Juxian**
73 C3 **Chennai** India
71 B3 **Chenzhou** China
65 B2 **Cheonan** S. Korea
65 B2 **Cheorwon** S. Korea
99 B3 **Chepstow** U.K.
104 B2 **Cherbourg-Octeville** France
89 E3 **Cheremisinovo** Russia
69 C1 **Cheremkhovo** Russia
89 E2 **Cherepovets** Russia
91 C2 **Cherkasy** Ukr.
87 D4 **Cherkessk** Russia
91 C1 **Chernihiv** Ukr.
91 D2 **Cherninivka** Ukr.
90 B2 **Chernivtsi** Ukr.
90 B1 **Chernyakhiv** Ukr.
88 B3 **Chernyakhovsk** Russia
89 E3 **Chernyanka** Russia
83 I2 **Chernyshevskiy** Russia
137 D2 **Cherokee** U.S.A.
83 K2 **Cherskogo, Khrebet** *mts* Russia
91 E2 **Chertkovo** Russia
90 A1 **Chervonohrad** Ukr.
88 C3 **Chervyen'** Belarus
89 D3 **Cherykaw** Belarus
141 D3 **Chesapeake Bay** U.S.A.
86 D2 **Cheshskaya Guba** *b.* Russia
98 B2 **Chester** U.K.
140 B3 **Chester** *IL* U.S.A.
143 D2 **Chester** *SC* U.S.A.
98 C2 **Chesterfield** U.K.
129 E1 **Chesterfield Inlet** Can.
129 E1 **Chesterfield Inlet** Can.
141 F1 **Chesuncook Lake** U.S.A.
131 D2 **Chéticamp** Can.
145 D3 **Chetumal** Mex.
128 B2 **Chetwynd** Can.
98 B1 **Cheviot Hills** U.K.
136 C2 **Cheyenne** U.S.A.
136 C2 **Cheyenne** *r.* U.S.A.
136 C3 **Cheyenne Wells** U.S.A.
75 B2 **Chhatarpur** India
62 A2 **Chiang Dao** Thai.
62 A2 **Chiang Mai** Thai.
62 A2 **Chiang Rai** Thai.
108 A1 **Chiavenna** Italy
70 B3 **Chibi** China
121 C3 **Chiboma** Moz.
130 C2 **Chibougamau** Can.
123 D1 **Chibuto** Moz.
75 D1 **Chibuzhang Co** *l.* China
140 B2 **Chicago** U.S.A.
128 A2 **Chichagof Island** U.S.A.
99 C3 **Chichester** U.K.
50 A2 **Chichester Range** *mts* Austr.
139 D1 **Chickasha** U.S.A.
150 A2 **Chiclayo** Peru
153 B5 **Chico** *r.* Arg.
135 B3 **Chico** U.S.A.
131 C2 **Chicoutimi** Can.
108 B2 **Chieti** Italy
145 C3 **Chietla** Mex.
69 D2 **Chifeng** China
155 D1 **Chifre, Serra do** *mts* Brazil
145 C3 **Chignahuapán** Mex.
121 C3 **Chigubo** Moz.
74 A1 **Chihil Abdālān, Kōh-e** *mts* Afgh.
144 B2 **Chihuahua** Mex.
88 C2 **Chikhachevo** Russia
67 C3 **Chikuma-gawa** *r.* Japan
128 B2 **Chilanko** *r.* Can.
74 B1 **Chilas** Pak.
139 C2 **Childress** U.S.A.
153 A4 **Chile** *country* S. America
152 B3 **Chilecito** Arg.
75 C3 **Chilika Lake** India
121 B2 **Chililabombwe** Zambia
128 B2 **Chilko** *r.* Can.
128 B2 **Chilko Lake** Can.
153 A4 **Chillán** Chile
137 E3 **Chillicothe** *MO* U.S.A.
140 C3 **Chillicothe** *OH* U.S.A.
128 B3 **Chilliwack** Can.
153 A5 **Chiloé, Isla de** *i.* Chile
145 C3 **Chilpancingo** Mex.
53 C3 **Chiltern** Austr.
71 C3 **Chilung** Taiwan
119 D3 **Chimala** Tanz.
152 B4 **Chimbas** Arg.
150 A2 **Chimborazo** *mt.* Ecuador
150 A2 **Chimbote** Peru
87 E4 **Chimboy** Uzbek.
Chimkent Kazakh. *see* **Shymkent**
121 C2 **Chimoio** Moz.
77 C3 **Chimtargha, Qullai** *mt.* Tajik.
68 C2 **China** *country* Asia
145 C2 **China** Mex.
150 A3 **Chincha Alta** Peru
128 C2 **Chinchaga** *r.* Can.
145 D3 **Chinchorro, Banco** Mex.
121 C2 **Chinde** Moz.
65 B3 **Chindo** S. Korea
68 C2 **Chindu** China
62 A1 **Chindwin** *r.* Myanmar

65 B2 **Chinghwa** N. Korea
120 B2 **Chingola** Zambia
120 A2 **Chinguar** Angola
121 C2 **Chinhoyi** Zimbabwe
74 B1 **Chiniot** Pak.
144 B2 **Chinipas** Mex.
65 B2 **Chinju** S. Korea
118 C2 **Chinko** *r.* C.A.R.
138 B1 **Chinle** U.S.A.
67 C3 **Chino** Japan
104 C2 **Chinon** France
138 A2 **Chino Valley** U.S.A.
121 C2 **Chinsali** Zambia
108 B1 **Chioggia** Italy
111 C3 **Chios** Greece
111 C3 **Chios** *i.* Greece
121 C2 **Chipata** Zambia
120 A2 **Chipindo** Angola
121 C3 **Chipinge** Zimbabwe
73 B3 **Chiplun** India
99 B3 **Chippenham** U.K.
99 C3 **Chipping Norton** U.K.
77 C2 **Chirchiq** Uzbek.
121 C3 **Chiredzi** Zimbabwe
138 B2 **Chiricahua Peak** U.S.A.
146 B4 **Chiriquí, Golfo de** *b.* Panama
146 B4 **Chirripó** *mt.* Costa Rica
121 B2 **Chirundu** Zimbabwe
130 C1 **Chisasibi** Can.
137 E1 **Chisholm** U.S.A.
90 B2 **Chișinău** Moldova
87 E3 **Chistopol'** Russia
69 D1 **Chita** Russia
120 A2 **Chitado** Angola
121 C2 **Chitambo** Zambia
120 B1 **Chitato** Angola
121 C1 **Chitipa** Malawi
73 B3 **Chitradurga** India
74 B1 **Chitral** Pak.
146 B4 **Chitré** Panama
75 D2 **Chittagong** Bangl.
74 B2 **Chittaurgarh** India
121 C2 **Chitungwiza** Zimbabwe
120 B2 **Chiume** Angola
121 C2 **Chivhu** Zimbabwe
70 B2 **Chizhou** China
114 C1 **Chlef** Alg.
107 D2 **Chlef, Oued** *r.* Alg.
153 B4 **Choele Choel** Arg.
144 B2 **Choix** Mex.
103 D1 **Chojnice** Pol.
117 B3 **Ch'ok'ē Mountains** Eth.
117 B3 **Ch'ok'ē Terara** *mt.* Eth.
83 K2 **Chokurdakh** Russia
121 C3 **Chókwè** Moz.
104 B2 **Cholet** France
102 C1 **Chomutov** Czech Rep.
83 I2 **Chona** *r.* Russia
150 A2 **Chone** Ecuador
65 B1 **Ch'ŏngjin** N. Korea
65 B2 **Chŏngju** N. Korea
65 B2 **Chŏngp'yŏng** N. Korea
70 A3 **Chongqing** China
70 A2 **Chongqing** *mun.* China
71 A3 **Chongzuo** China
Chŏnju S. Korea *see* **Jeonju**
153 A5 **Chonos, Archipiélago de los** *is* Chile
154 B3 **Chopinzinho** Brazil
111 B3 **Chora Sfakion** Greece
98 B2 **Chorley** U.K.
91 C2 **Chornomors'ke** Ukr.
90 B2 **Chortkiv** Ukr.
65 B1 **Ch'osan** N. Korea
67 D3 **Chōshi** Japan
103 D1 **Choszczno** Pol.
114 A2 **Choûm** Maur.
69 D1 **Choybalsan** Mongolia
69 D1 **Choyr** Mongolia
54 B2 **Christchurch** N.Z.
99 C3 **Christchurch** U.K.
127 G2 **Christian, Cape** Can.
123 C2 **Christiana** S. Africa
54 A2 **Christina, Mount** N.Z.
153 B5 **Chubut** *r.* Arg.
90 B1 **Chudniv** Ukr.
89 D2 **Chudovo** Russia
Chudskoye Ozero *l.* Estonia/Russia *see* **Peipus, Lake**
126 B2 **Chugach Mountains** U.S.A.
67 B4 **Chūgoku-sanchi** *mts* Japan
66 B2 **Chuguyevka** Russia
91 D2 **Chuhuyiv** Ukr.
160 J3 **Chukchi Sea** Russia/U.S.A.
83 N2 **Chukotskiy Poluostrov** *pen.* Russia
135 C4 **Chula Vista** U.S.A.
82 G3 **Chulym** Russia
152 B3 **Chumbicha** Arg.
83 K3 **Chumikan** Russia
63 A2 **Chumphon** Thai.
65 B2 **Chuncheon** S. Korea
Chungking China *see* **Chongqing**
83 H2 **Chunya** *r.* Russia
150 A3 **Chuquibamba** Peru
152 B3 **Chuquicamata** Chile
105 D2 **Chur** Switz.
62 A1 **Churachandpur** India
129 E2 **Churchill** Can.
129 E2 **Churchill** *r. Man.* Can.
131 D1 **Churchill** *r. Nfld. and Lab.* Can.
129 E2 **Churchill, Cape** Can.
131 D1 **Churchill Falls** Can.
129 D2 **Churchill Lake** Can.
74 B2 **Churu** India
131 C2 **Chute-des-Passes** Can.
62 B1 **Chuxiong** China
90 B2 **Ciadîr-Lunga** Moldova
61 B2 **Ciamis** Indon.
60 B2 **Cianjur** Indon.
154 B2 **Cianorte** Brazil
103 E1 **Ciechanów** Pol.
146 C2 **Ciego de Ávila** Cuba
146 B2 **Cienfuegos** Cuba
107 C2 **Cieza** Spain
106 C2 **Cigüela** *r.* Spain
80 B2 **Cihanbeyli** Turkey
144 B3 **Cihuatlán** Mex.
106 C2 **Cíjara, Embalse de** *resr* Spain
61 B2 **Cilacap** Indon.
139 C1 **Cimarron** *r.* U.S.A.
90 B2 **Cimișlia** Moldova
108 B2 **Cimone, Monte** *mt.* Italy
140 C3 **Cincinnati** U.S.A.
111 C3 **Çine** Turkey
100 B2 **Ciney** Belgium
145 C3 **Cintalapa** Mex.
71 B3 **Ciping** China
126 B2 **Circle** *AK* U.S.A.
136 B1 **Circle** *MT* U.S.A.
58 B3 **Cirebon** Indon.
99 C3 **Cirencester** U.K.
108 A1 **Ciriè** Italy
109 C3 **Cirò Marina** Italy
109 C2 **Čitluk** Bos. & Herz.
122 A3 **Citrusdal** S. Africa
145 B2 **Ciudad Acuña** Mex.
145 B3 **Ciudad Altamirano** Mex.
150 B1 **Ciudad Bolívar** Venez.
144 B2 **Ciudad Camargo** Mex.
144 A2 **Ciudad Constitución** Mex.
145 C3 **Ciudad del Carmen** Mex.
144 B2 **Ciudad Delicias** Mex.
145 C2 **Ciudad de Valles** Mex.
150 B1 **Ciudad Guayana** Venez.
138 B3 **Ciudad Guerrero** Mex.
144 B3 **Ciudad Guzmán** Mex.
145 C3 **Ciudad Hidalgo** Mex.
145 C3 **Ciudad Ixtepec** Mex.
144 B1 **Ciudad Juárez** Mex.
145 C2 **Ciudad Mante** Mex.
145 C2 **Ciudad Mier** Mex.
144 B2 **Ciudad Obregón** Mex.
106 C2 **Ciudad Real** Spain
145 C2 **Ciudad Río Bravo** Mex.
106 B1 **Ciudad Rodrigo** Spain
145 C2 **Ciudad Victoria** Mex.
107 D1 **Ciutadella** Spain
111 C3 **Cıvan Dağ** *mt.* Turkey
108 B1 **Cividale del Friuli** Italy
108 B2 **Civitanova Marche** Italy
108 B2 **Civitavecchia** Italy
104 C2 **Civray** France
111 C3 **Çivril** Turkey
70 C2 **Cixi** China
99 D3 **Clacton-on-Sea** U.K.
128 C2 **Claire, Lake** Can.
105 C2 **Clamecy** France
122 A3 **Clanwilliam** S. Africa
52 A2 **Clare** Austr.
97 A2 **Clare Island** Ireland
141 E2 **Claremont** U.S.A.
97 B2 **Claremorris** Ireland
54 B2 **Clarence** N.Z.
131 E2 **Clarenville** Can.
128 C2 **Claresholm** Can.
137 D2 **Clarinda** U.S.A.
123 C3 **Clarkebury** S. Africa
143 D2 **Clark Hill Reservoir** U.S.A.
140 C3 **Clarksburg** U.S.A.
142 B2 **Clarksdale** U.S.A.
134 C1 **Clarks Fork** *r.* U.S.A.
142 B1 **Clarksville** *AR* U.S.A.
142 C1 **Clarksville** *TN* U.S.A.
154 B1 **Claro** *r.* Brazil
139 C1 **Clayton** U.S.A.
97 B3 **Clear, Cape** Ireland
137 E2 **Clear Lake** U.S.A.
135 B3 **Clear Lake** U.S.A.
128 C2 **Clearwater** Can.
129 C2 **Clearwater** *r.* Can.
143 D3 **Clearwater** U.S.A.
134 C1 **Clearwater** *r.* U.S.A.
139 D2 **Cleburne** U.S.A.
51 D2 **Clermont** Austr.
105 C2 **Clermont-Ferrand** France
52 A2 **Cleve** Austr.
142 B2 **Cleveland** *MS* U.S.A.
140 C2 **Cleveland** *OH* U.S.A.
143 D1 **Cleveland** *TN* U.S.A.
134 D1 **Cleveland, Mount** U.S.A.
143 D3 **Clewiston** U.S.A.
97 A2 **Clifden** Ireland
53 D1 **Clifton** Austr.
138 B2 **Clifton** U.S.A.
128 B2 **Clinton** Can.
137 E2 **Clinton** *IA* U.S.A.
137 E3 **Clinton** *MO* U.S.A.
139 D1 **Clinton** *OK* U.S.A.
96 A2 **Clisham** *h.* U.K.
98 B2 **Clitheroe** U.K.
97 B3 **Clonakilty** Ireland
51 D2 **Cloncurry** Austr.
97 C1 **Clones** Ireland
97 C2 **Clonmel** Ireland
100 D1 **Cloppenburg** Ger.
50 A2 **Cloud Break** Austr.
136 B2 **Cloud Peak** U.S.A.
139 C2 **Clovis** U.S.A.
129 D2 **Cluff Lake Mine** Can.
110 B1 **Cluj-Napoca** Romania
51 C2 **Cluny** Austr.

Cluses

105	D2	Cluses France
54	A3	Clutha r. N.Z.
96	B3	Clyde r. U.K.
96	B3	Clyde, Firth of est. U.K.
96	B3	Clydebank U.K.
127	G2	Clyde River Can.
144	B3	Coalcomán Mex.
135	C3	Coaldale (abandoned) U.S.A.
128	B2	Coal River Can.
150	B2	Coari Brazil
150	B2	Coari r. Brazil
142	B2	Coastal Plain U.S.A.
128	B2	Coast Mountains Can.
135	B2	Coast Ranges mts U.S.A.
96	B3	Coatbridge U.K.
127	F2	Coats Island Can.
55	R2	Coats Land reg. Antarctica
145	C3	Coatzacoalcos Mex.
146	A3	Cobán Guat.
53	C2	Cobar Austr.
97	B3	Cobh Ireland
152	B2	Cobija Bol.
141	D2	Cobourg Can.
50	C1	Cobourg Peninsula Austr.
53	C3	Cobram Austr.
101	E2	Coburg Ger.
152	B2	Cochabamba Bol.
100	C2	Cochem Ger.
		Cochin India see Kochi
128	C2	Cochrane Alta Can.
130	B2	Cochrane Ont. Can.
153	A5	Cochrane Chile
52	B2	Cockburn Austr.
		Cockburn Town Turks and
		Caicos Is see Grand Turk
98	B1	Cockermouth U.K.
122	B3	Cockscomb mt. S. Africa
146	B3	Coco r. Hond./Nic.
144	B2	Cocula Mex.
150	A1	Cocuy, Sierra Nevada del mt.
		Col.
141	E2	Cod, Cape U.S.A.
108	B2	Codigoro Italy
131	D1	Cod Island Can.
151	D2	Codó Brazil
136	B2	Cody U.S.A.
51	D1	Coen Austr.
100	C2	Coesfeld Ger.
134	C1	Coeur d'Alene U.S.A.
123	C3	Coffee Bay S. Africa
137	D3	Coffeyville U.S.A.
53	D2	Coffs Harbour Austr.
104	B2	Cognac France
118	A2	Cogo Equat. Guinea
52	B3	Cohuna Austr.
146	B4	Coiba, Isla de i. Panama
153	A5	Coihaique Chile
73	B3	Coimbatore India
106	B1	Coimbra Port.
52	B3	Colac Austr.
155	D1	Colatina Brazil
136	C3	Colby U.S.A.
99	D3	Colchester U.K.
129	C2	Cold Lake Can.
96	C3	Coldstream U.K.
139	D2	Coleman U.S.A.
52	B3	Coleraine Austr.
97	C1	Coleraine U.K.
123	C3	Colesberg S. Africa
144	B3	Colima Mex.
144	B3	Colima, Nevado de vol. Mex.
96	A2	Coll i. U.K.
53	C1	Collarenebri Austr.
50	B1	Collier Bay Austr.
54	B2	Collingwood N.Z.
97	B1	Collooney Ireland
105	D2	Colmar France
100	C2	Cologne Ger.
154	C2	Colômbia Brazil
150	A1	Colombia country S. America
73	B4	Colombo Sri Lanka
104	C3	Colomiers France
146	C4	Colón Panama
109	C3	Colonna, Capo c. Italy
96	A2	Colonsay i. U.K.
153	B4	Colorado r. Arg.
138	A2	Colorado r. Mex./U.S.A.
139	D3	Colorado r. U.S.A.
136	B3	Colorado state U.S.A.
135	C3	Colorado Plateau U.S.A.
136	C3	Colorado Springs U.S.A.
144	B2	Colotlán Mex.
136	B1	Colstrip U.S.A.
137	E3	Columbia MO U.S.A.
143	D2	Columbia SC U.S.A.
142	C1	Columbia TN U.S.A.
134	B1	Columbia r. U.S.A.
128	C2	Columbia, Mount Can.
134	D1	Columbia Falls U.S.A.
128	B2	Columbia Mountains Can.
134	C1	Columbia Plateau U.S.A.
143	D2	Columbus GA U.S.A.
140	B3	Columbus IN U.S.A.
142	C2	Columbus MS U.S.A.
137	D2	Columbus NE U.S.A.
138	B2	Columbus NM U.S.A.
140	C3	Columbus OH U.S.A.
134	C1	Colville U.S.A.
126	A2	Colville r. U.S.A.
126	C2	Colville Lake Can.
98	B2	Colwyn Bay U.K.
108	B2	Comacchio Italy
145	C3	Comalcalco Mex.
110	C1	Comăneşti Romania
130	C1	Comencho, Lac l. Can.
97	C2	Comeragh Mountains hills
		Ireland
75	D2	Comilla Bangl.
108	A2	Comino, Capo c. Sardinia
		Italy
145	C3	Comitán de Domínguez Mex.
104	C2	Commentry France
139	D2	Commerce U.S.A.
127	F2	Committee Bay Can.
108	A1	Como Italy
153	B5	Comodoro Rivadavia Arg.
121	D2	Comoros country Africa
104	C2	Compiègne France
144	B2	Compostela Mex.
90	B2	Comrat Moldova
114	A4	Conakry Guinea
155	E1	Conceição da Barra Brazil
151	D2	Conceição do Araguaia Brazil
155	D1	Conceição do Mato Dentro
		Brazil
152	B3	Concepción Arg.
153	A4	Concepción Chile
144	B2	Concepción Mex.
135	B4	Conception, Point U.S.A.
154	C2	Conchas Brazil
138	C1	Conchas U.S.A.
144	B2	Conchos r. Chihuahua Mex.
145	C2	Conchos r. Nuevo León/
		Tamaulipas Mex.
135	B3	Concord CA U.S.A.
141	E2	Concord NH U.S.A.
152	C4	Concordia Arg.
122	A2	Concordia S. Africa
137	D3	Concordia U.S.A.
53	C2	Condobolin Austr.
104	C3	Condom France
134	B1	Condon U.S.A.
108	B1	Conegliano Italy
104	C2	Confolens France
75	C2	Congdü China
118	B3	Congo country Africa
118	B3	Congo r. Congo/Dem. Rep.
		Congo
118	C3	Congo, Democratic Republic
		of the country Africa
129	C2	Conklin Can.
97	B1	Conn, Lough l. Ireland
97	B2	Connacht reg. Ireland
141	E2	Connecticut r. U.S.A.
141	E2	Connecticut state U.S.A.
97	B2	Connemara reg. Ireland
134	D1	Conrad U.S.A.
139	D2	Conroe U.S.A.
155	D2	Conselheiro Lafaiete Brazil
155	D1	Conselheiro Pena Brazil
98	C1	Consett U.K.
63	B3	Côn Sơn, Đao i. Vietnam
110	C2	Constanța Romania
106	B2	Constantina Spain
115	C1	Constantine Alg.
134	D2	Contact U.S.A.
150	A2	Contamana Peru
153	A6	Contreras, Isla i. Chile
126	D2	Contwoyto Lake Can.
142	B1	Conway AR U.S.A.
141	E2	Conway NH U.S.A.
51	C2	Coober Pedy Austr.
		Cook, Mount mt. N.Z. see
		Aoraki/Mount Cook
143	C1	Cookeville U.S.A.
49	H4	Cook Islands
		S. Pacific Ocean
131	E1	Cook's Harbour Can.
97	C1	Cookstown U.K.
54	B2	Cook Strait N.Z.
51	D1	Cooktown Austr.
53	C2	Coolabah Austr.
53	C2	Coolamon Austr.
53	D1	Coolangatta Austr.
50	B3	Coolgardie Austr.
53	C3	Cooma Austr.
52	B2	Coombah Austr.
53	C2	Coonabarabran Austr.
52	A3	Coonalpyn Austr.
53	C2	Coonamble Austr.
52	A1	Cooper Creek watercourse
		Austr.
134	B2	Coos Bay U.S.A.
53	C2	Cootamundra Austr.
145	C3	Copainalá Mex.
145	C3	Copala Mex.
93	F4	Copenhagen Denmark
109	C2	Copertino Italy
152	A3	Copiapó Chile
140	B1	Copper Harbor U.S.A.
		Coppermine Can. see
		Kugluktuk
126	D2	Coppermine r. Can.
122	B2	Copperton S. Africa
152	A3	Coquimbo Chile
110	B2	Corabia Romania
155	D1	Coração de Jesus Brazil
150	A3	Coracora Peru
53	D1	Coraki Austr.
50	A2	Coral Bay Austr.
127	F2	Coral Harbour Can.
156	D7	Coral Sea S. Pacific Ocean
48	D4	Coral Sea Islands Territory
		Austr.
52	B3	Corangamite, Lake Austr.
99	C2	Corby U.K.
153	A5	Corcovado, Golfo de sea chan.
		Chile
143	C2	Cordele U.S.A.
64	B1	Cordilleras Range mts Phil.
152	B4	Córdoba Arg.
145	C3	Córdoba Mex.
106	C2	Córdoba Spain

153	B4	Córdoba, Sierras de *mts* Arg.
111	A3	Corfu *i.* Greece
106	B2	Coria Spain
111	B3	Corinth Greece
142	C2	Corinth U.S.A.
155	D1	Corinto Brazil
97	B3	Cork Ireland
111	C2	Çorlu Turkey
154	B2	Cornélio Procópio Brazil
131	E2	Corner Brook Can.
53	C3	Corner Inlet *b.* Austr.
135	B3	Corning *CA* U.S.A.
141	D2	Corning *NY* U.S.A.
		Corn Islands *is* Nic. *see*
		Maíz, Islas del
108	B2	Corno Grande *mt.* Italy
130	C2	Cornwall Can.
126	E1	Cornwallis Island Can.
150	B1	Coro Venez.
154	C1	Coromandel Brazil
54	C1	Coromandel Peninsula N.Z.
129	C2	Coronation Can.
126	D2	Coronation Gulf Can.
152	C3	Coronel Oviedo Para.
153	B4	Coronel Suárez Arg.
150	A3	Coropuna, Nudo *mt.* Peru
109	D2	Çorovodë Albania
139	D3	Corpus Christi U.S.A.
152	B2	Corque Bol.
151	D3	Corrente Brazil
154	B1	Correntes Brazil
151	D3	Correntina Brazil
97	B2	Corrib, Lough *l.* Ireland
152	C3	Corrientes Arg.
144	B2	Corrientes, Cabo *c.* Mex.
53	C3	Corryong Austr.
		Corse *i.* France *see* Corsica
105	D3	Corse, Cap *c.* Corsica France
105	D3	Corsica *i.* France
139	D2	Corsicana U.S.A.
105	D3	Corte Corsica France
106	B2	Cortegana Spain
136	B3	Cortez U.S.A.
108	B1	Cortina d'Ampezzo Italy
141	D2	Cortland U.S.A.
108	B2	Cortona Italy
106	B2	Coruche Port.
		Çoruh Turkey *see* Artvin
80	B1	Çorum Turkey
152	C2	Corumbá Brazil
154	C1	Corumbá *r.* Brazil
134	B2	Corvallis U.S.A.
98	B2	Corwen U.K.
144	B2	Cosalá Mex.
145	C3	Cosamaloapan Mex.
109	C3	Cosenza Italy
105	C2	Cosne-Cours-sur-Loire France
107	C2	Costa Blanca *coastal area* Spain
107	D1	Costa Brava *coastal area* Spain
106	B2	Costa del Sol *coastal area* Spain
154	B1	Costa Rica Brazil
146	B3	Costa Rica *country* Central America
144	B2	Costa Rica Mex.
110	B2	Costeşti Romania
64	B2	Cotabato Phil.
114	B4	Côte d'Ivoire *country* Africa
150	A2	Cotopaxi, Volcán *vol.* Ecuador
99	B3	Cotswold Hills U.K.
134	B2	Cottage Grove U.S.A.
102	C1	Cottbus Ger.
104	B2	Coubre, Pointe de la *pt* France
52	A3	Couedic, Cape du Austr.

137	D2	Council Bluffs U.S.A.
88	B2	Courland Lagoon *b.* Lith./ Russia
128	B3	Courtenay Can.
104	B2	Coutances France
104	B2	Coutras France
100	B2	Couvin Belgium
99	C2	Coventry U.K.
140	C3	Covington U.S.A.
50	B3	Cowan, Lake *imp. l.* Austr.
96	C2	Cowdenbeath U.K.
53	C3	Cowes Austr.
134	B1	Cowlitz *r.* U.S.A.
53	C2	Cowra Austr.
154	B1	Coxim Brazil
75	D2	Cox's Bazar Bangl.
145	B3	Coyuca de Benítez Mex.
75	C1	Cozhê China
145	D2	Cozumel Mex.
145	D2	Cozumel, Isla de *i.* Mex.
123	C3	Cradock S. Africa
136	B2	Craig U.S.A.
102	C2	Crailsheim Ger.
110	B2	Craiova Romania
129	D2	Cranberry Portage Can.
53	C3	Cranbourne Austr.
128	C3	Cranbrook Can.
151	D2	Crateús Brazil
151	E2	Crato Brazil
136	C2	Crawford U.S.A.
140	B2	Crawfordsville U.S.A.
99	C3	Crawley U.K.
134	D1	Crazy Mountains U.S.A.
129	D2	Cree *r.* Can.
144	B2	Creel Mex.
129	D2	Cree Lake Can.
100	B1	Creil Neth.
105	D2	Crema Italy
108	B1	Cremona Italy
108	B1	Cres *i.* Croatia
134	B2	Crescent City U.S.A.
128	C3	Creston Can.
137	E2	Creston U.S.A.
142	C2	Crestview U.S.A.
111	B3	Crete *i.* Greece
107	D1	Creus, Cap de *c.* Spain
98	B2	Crewe U.K.
96	B2	Crianlarich U.K.
152	D3	Criciúma Brazil
96	C2	Crieff U.K.
108	B1	Crikvenica Croatia
91	C2	Crimea *disp. terr.* Ukr.
91	C2	Crimea *pen.* Ukr.
101	F2	Crimmitschau Ger.
154	C1	Cristalina Brazil
101	E1	Crivitz Ger.
		Crna Gora *country* Europe *see* Montenegro
109	D3	Crni Vrh *h.* Serbia
109	C1	Črnomelj Slovenia
97	B2	Croagh Patrick *h.* Ireland
109	C1	Croatia *country* Europe
61	C1	Crocker, Banjaran *mts* Malaysia
139	D2	Crockett U.S.A.
59	C3	Croker Island Austr.
99	D2	Cromer U.K.
54	A3	Cromwell N.Z.
137	D1	Crookston U.S.A.
53	C2	Crookwell Austr.
136	C1	Crosby U.S.A.
143	D3	Cross City U.S.A.
142	B2	Crossett U.S.A.
98	B1	Cross Fell *h.* U.K.
129	E2	Cross Lake Can.
143	C1	Crossville U.S.A.
109	C3	Crotone Italy
99	D3	Crowborough U.K.

142	B2	Crowley U.S.A.
128	C3	Crowsnest Pass Can.
146	C2	Cruz, Cabo *c.* Cuba
152	C3	Cruz Alta Brazil
152	B4	Cruz del Eje Arg.
155	D2	Cruzeiro Brazil
150	A2	Cruzeiro do Sul Brazil
52	A2	Crystal Brook Austr.
139	D3	Crystal City U.S.A.
140	B1	Crystal Falls U.S.A.
103	E2	Csongrád Hungary
120	B2	Cuando *r.* Angola/Zambia
120	A2	Cuangar Angola
118	B3	Cuango *r.* Angola/Dem. Rep. Congo
120	A1	Cuanza *r.* Angola
139	C3	Cuatro Ciénegas Mex.
144	B2	Cuauhtémoc Mex.
145	C2	Cuautla Mex.
146	B2	Cuba *country* West Indies
120	A2	Cubal Angola
120	B2	Cubango *r.* Angola/Namibia
150	A1	Cúcuta Col.
73	B3	Cuddalore India
		Cuddapah. India *see* Kadapa
106	C1	Cuéllar Spain
120	A2	Cuemba Angola
150	A2	Cuenca Ecuador
107	C1	Cuenca Spain
107	C1	Cuenca, Serranía de *mts* Spain
145	C3	Cuernavaca Mex.
139	C3	Cuero U.S.A.
151	C3	Cuiabá Brazil
151	C3	Cuiabá *r.* Brazil
96	A2	Cuillin Sound *sea chan.* U.K.
120	A1	Cuilo Angola
120	B2	Cuito *r.* Angola
120	A2	Cuito Cuanavale Angola
60	B1	Cukai Malaysia
53	C1	Culcairn Austr.
53	C1	Culgoa *r.* Austr.
144	B2	Culiacán Mex.
64	A1	Culion *i.* Phil.
107	C2	Cullera Spain
142	C2	Cullman U.S.A.
97	C1	Cullybackey U.K.
151	C3	Culuene *r.* Brazil
150	B1	Cumaná Venez.
141	D3	Cumberland U.S.A.
140	B3	Cumberland *r.* U.S.A.
129	D2	Cumberland Lake Can.
127	G2	Cumberland Peninsula Can.
142	C1	Cumberland Plateau U.S.A.
127	G2	Cumberland Sound *sea chan.* Can.
96	C3	Cumbernauld U.K.
135	B3	Cummings U.S.A.
96	B3	Cumnock U.K.
144	B1	Cumpas Mex.
145	C3	Cunduacán Mex.
120	A2	Cunene *r.* Angola
108	A2	Cuneo Italy
53	C1	Cunnamulla Austr.
108	A1	Cuorgnè Italy
96	C2	Cupar U.K.
147	D3	Curaçao *i.* West Indies
147	D3	Curaçao *terr.* West Indies
150	A2	Curaray *r.* Ecuador
153	A4	Curicó Chile
154	C2	Curitiba Brazil
52	A2	Curnamona Austr.
51	D3	Currie Austr.
51	E2	Curtis Island Austr.
151	C2	Curuá *r.* Brazil
60	B2	Curup Indon.
151	D2	Cururupu Brazil
155	D1	Curvelo Brazil

Cusco

150 A3 Cusco Peru
139 D1 Cushing U.S.A.
134 D1 Cut Bank U.S.A.
75 C2 Cuttack India
101 D1 Cuxhaven Ger.
64 B1 Cuyo Islands Phil.
Cuzco Peru *see* Cusco
119 C3 Cyangugu Rwanda
111 B3 Cyclades *is* Greece
129 C3 Cypress Hills Can.
80 B2 Cyprus *country* Asia
102 C2 Czech Republic *country*
Europe
103 D1 Czersk Pol.
103 D1 Częstochowa Pol.

D

Đa, Sông *r.* Vietnam *see*
Black River
69 D2 Daban China
114 A3 Dabola Guinea
Dacca Bangl. *see* Dhaka
102 C2 Dachau Ger.
117 C4 Dadaab Kenya
74 A2 Dadu Pak.
65 B2 Daegu S. Korea
65 B3 Daejeon S. Korea
65 B3 Daejeong S. Korea
64 B1 Daet Phil.
114 A3 Dagana Senegal
64 B1 Dagupan Phil.
74 B3 Dahanu India
69 D2 Da Hinggan Ling *mts* China
116 C3 Dahlak Archipelago *is* Eritrea
100 C2 Dahlem Ger.
78 B3 Dahm, Ramlat *des.* Saudi
Arabia /Yemen
60 B2 Daik Indon.
106 C2 Daimiel Spain
97 A2 Daingean Uí Chúis Ireland
123 Dajarra Austr.
114 A3 Dakar Senegal
Dākhilah, Wāḩāt ad *oasis*
Egypt
114 A2 Dakhla Western Sahara
Dakhla Oasis Egypt *see*
Dākhilah, Wāḩāt ad
63 A3 Dakoank India
88 C3 Dakol'ka *r.* Belarus
Đakovica Kosovo *see* Gjakovë
109 C1 Đakovo Croatia
120 B2 Dala Angola
68 C2 Dalain Hob China
93 G3 Dälälven *r.* Sweden
111 C3 Dalaman Turkey
111 C3 Dalaman *r.* Turkey
69 C2 Dalandzadgad Mongolia
63 B2 Đa Lạt Vietnam
74 A2 Dalbandin Pak.
96 C3 Dalbeattie U.K.
51 E2 Dalby Austr.
143 C1 Dale Hollow Lake U.S.A.
53 C3 Dalgety Austr.
139 C1 Dalhart U.S.A.
131 D2 Dalhousie Can.
62 B1 Dali China
70 C2 Dalian China
96 C3 Dalkeith U.K.
139 D2 Dallas U.S.A.
128 A2 Dall Island U.S.A.
109 C2 Dalmatia *reg.* Bos. & Herz./
Croatia
66 C2 Dal'negorsk Russia
66 B3 Dal'nerechensk Russia
114 B4 Daloa Côte d'Ivoire

51 D2 Dalrymple, Mount Austr.
92 □A3 Dalsmynni Iceland
143 D2 Dalton U.S.A.
75 C2 Daltonganj India
60 B1 Daludalu Indon.
92 □B2 Dalvík Iceland
50 C1 Daly *r.* Austr.
51 C1 Daly Waters Austr.
74 B2 Daman India
80 B2 Damanhūr Egypt
59 C3 Damar *i.* Indon.
80 B2 Damascus Syria
115 D3 Damaturu Nigeria
76 B3 Damāvand, Qolleh-ye *mt.* Iran
81 D2 Dāmghān Iran
79 C2 Dammam Saudi Arabia
101 D1 Damme Ger.
75 B2 Damoh India
114 B4 Damongo Ghana
59 C3 Dampir, Selat *sea chan.* Indon.
75 C2 Damqoq Zangbo *r.* China
117 C3 Danakil *reg.* Africa
114 B4 Danané Côte d'Ivoire
63 B2 Đa Nẵng Vietnam
141 E2 Danbury U.S.A.
65 A1 Dandong China
146 B3 Dangriga Belize
70 B2 Dangshan China
89 F2 Danilov Russia
89 E2 Danilovskaya Vozvyshennost'
hills Russia
70 B2 Danjiangkou China
89 E3 Dankov Russia
146 B3 Danlí Hond.
101 E1 Dannenberg (Elbe) Ger.
54 C2 Dannevirke N.Z.
62 B2 Dan Sai Thai.
Dantu China *see* Zhenjiang
110 A1 Danube *r.* Europe
110 C1 Danube Delta Romania/Ukr.
140 B2 Danville IL U.S.A.
140 C3 Danville KY U.S.A.
141 D3 Danville VA U.S.A.
71 A4 Danzhou China
71 B3 Daoxian China
114 C3 Dapaong Togo
64 B2 Dapitan Phil.
68 C2 Da Qaidam China
69 E1 Daqing China
80 B2 Dar'ā Syria
79 C2 Dārāb Iran
81 D2 Dārān Iran
75 C2 Darbhanga India
119 D3 Dar es Salaam Tanz.
117 A3 Darfur *reg.* Sudan
74 B1 Dargai Pak.
54 B1 Dargaville N.Z.
53 C3 Dargo Austr.
69 D1 Darhan Mongolia
150 A1 Darién, Golfo del *g.* Col.
75 C2 Darjiling India
52 B2 Darling *r.* Austr.
53 C1 Darling Downs *hills* Austr.
50 A3 Darling Range *hills* Austr.
98 C1 Darlington U.K.
53 C2 Darlington Point Austr.
103 D1 Darłowo Pol.
101 D3 Darmstadt Ger.
115 E1 Darnah Libya
52 B2 Darnick Austr.
107 C1 Daroca Spain
99 D3 Dartford U.K.
99 A3 Dartmoor U.K.
131 D2 Dartmouth Can.
99 B3 Dartmouth U.K.
59 D3 Daru P.N.G.
50 C1 Darwin Austr.
74 A2 Dasht *r.* Pak.

76 B2 Daşoguz Turkm.
61 C1 Datadian Indon.
111 C3 Datça Turkey
70 B1 Datong China
64 B2 Datu Piang Phil.
74 B1 Daud Khel Pak.
88 B2 Daugava *r.* Latvia
88 C2 Daugavpils Latvia
100 C2 Daun Ger.
129 D2 Dauphin Can.
129 E2 Dauphin Lake Can.
73 B3 Davangere India
64 B2 Davao Phil.
64 B2 Davao Gulf Phil.
99 C2 Davenport U.S.A.
123 C2 Daventry U.K.
146 B4 David Panama
129 D2 Davidson Can.
126 E3 Davidson Lake Can.
135 B3 Davis U.S.A.
131 D1 Davis Inlet (abandoned)
Can.
159 F3 Davis Sea Antarctica
160 P3 Davis Strait Can./Greenland
105 D2 Davos Switz.
63 A2 Dawei Myanmar
78 A2 Dawmat al Jandal
Saudi Arabia
79 C3 Dawqah Oman
126 B2 Dawson Can.
143 D2 Dawson U.S.A.
128 B2 Dawson Creek Can.
128 B2 Dawsons Landing Can.
68 C2 Dawu China
Dawukou China *see*
Shizuishan
104 B3 Dax France
68 C2 Da Xueshan *mts* China
80 C2 Dayr az Zawr Syria
143 D3 Dayton U.S.A.
143 D3 Daytona Beach U.S.A.
70 A2 Dazhou China
122 B3 De Aar S. Africa
80 B2 Dead Sea *salt l.* Asia
71 B3 De'an China
152 B4 Deán Funes Arg.
128 B2 Dease Lake Can.
126 D2 Dease Strait Can.
135 C3 Death Valley *depr.* U.S.A.
104 C2 Deauville France
61 C1 Debak Sarawak Malaysia
109 D2 Debar Macedonia
103 E2 Debrecen Hungary
117 B3 Debre Markos Eth.
117 B3 Debre Tabor Eth.
117 B4 Debre Zeyit Eth.
142 C2 Decatur AL U.S.A.
140 B3 Decatur IL U.S.A.
73 B3 Deccan *plat.* India
102 C1 Děčín Czech Rep.
137 E2 Decorah U.S.A.
88 C2 Dedovichi Russia
121 C2 Dedza Malawi
98 B2 Dee *r.* England/Wales U.K.
96 C2 Dee *r.* Scotland U.K.
53 D1 Deepwater Austr.
51 E2 Deer Lake Can.
134 D1 Deer Lodge U.S.A.
140 C2 Defiance U.S.A.
68 C2 Dêgê China
117 C4 Degeh Bur Eth.
102 C2 Deggendorf Ger.
91 E2 Degtevo Russia
75 B1 Dehra Dun India
75 C2 Dehri India
69 E2 Dehui China
100 A2 Deinze Belgium

110 B1 Dej Romania
140 B2 De Kalb U.S.A.
78 A3 Dekemhare Eritrea
118 C3 Dekese Dem. Rep. Congo
135 C3 Delano U.S.A.
135 D3 Delano Peak U.S.A.
123 C2 Delareyville S. Africa
129 D2 Delaronde Lake Can.
140 C2 Delaware U.S.A.
141 D3 Delaware r. U.S.A.
141 D3 Delaware state U.S.A.
141 D3 Delaware Bay U.S.A.
53 C3 Delegate Austr.
105 D2 Delémont Switz.
100 B1 Delft Neth.
100 C1 Delfzijl Neth.
121 D2 Delgado, Cabo c. Moz.
69 C1 Delgerhaan Mongolia
75 B2 Delhi India
60 B2 Deli i. Indon.
126 C2 Déline Can.
101 F2 Delitzsch Ger.
107 D2 Dellys Alg.
101 D1 Delmenhorst Ger.
109 B1 Delnice Croatia
83 L1 De-Longa, Ostrova is Russia
129 D3 Deloraine Can.
111 B3 Delphi tourist site Greece
139 C3 Del Rio U.S.A.
136 B3 Delta CO U.S.A.
135 D3 Delta UT U.S.A.
126 B2 Delta Junction U.S.A.
109 D3 Delvinë Albania
106 C1 Demanda, Sierra de la mts
Spain
118 C3 Demba Dem. Rep. Congo
117 B4 Dembī Dolo Eth.
89 D2 Demidov Russia
138 B2 Deming U.S.A.
111 C3 Demirci Turkey
110 C2 Demirköy Turkey
102 C1 Demmin Ger.
142 C2 Demopolis U.S.A.
60 B2 Dempo, Gunung vol. Indon.
89 D2 Demyansk Russia
122 B3 De Naawte S. Africa
100 B1 Den Burg Neth.
100 B2 Dendermonde Belgium
70 A1 Dengkou China
70 B2 Dengzhou China
Den Haag Neth. see
The Hague
50 A2 Deniliquin Austr.
100 B1 Den Helder Neth.
52 B3 Deniliquin Austr.
134 C2 Denio U.S.A.
137 D2 Denison IA U.S.A.
139 D2 Denison TX U.S.A.
111 C3 Denizli Turkey
53 D2 Denman Austr.
50 A3 Denmark Austr.
93 E4 Denmark country Europe
160 Q3 Denmark Strait Greenland/
Iceland
61 C2 Denpasar Indon.
139 D2 Denton U.S.A.
50 A3 D'Entrecasteaux, Point Austr.
136 B3 Denver U.S.A.
75 C2 Deogarh Odisha India
74 B2 Deogarh Rajasthan India
75 C2 Deoghar India
83 K2 Deputatskiy Russia
68 C3 Dêqên China
142 B2 De Queen U.S.A.
74 B1 Dera Bugti Pak.
74 B1 Dera Ghazi Khan Pak.
74 B1 Dera Ismail Khan Pak.
87 D4 Derbent Russia

50 B1 Derby Austr.
99 C2 Derby U.K.
99 D2 Dereham U.K.
97 B2 Derg, Lough l. Ireland
91 D1 Derhachi Ukr.
142 B2 DeRidder U.S.A.
91 D2 Derkul r. Russia/Ukr.
Derry U.K. see Londonderry
75 B1 Dêrub China
116 B3 Derudeb Sudan
122 B3 De Rust S. Africa
109 C2 Derventa Bos. & Herz.
98 C2 Derwent r. U.K.
98 B1 Derwent Water l. U.K.
77 C1 Derzhavinsk Kazakh.
152 B2 Desaguadero r. Bol.
129 D2 Deschambault Lake Can.
134 B1 Deschutes r. U.S.A.
117 B3 Desē Eth.
153 B5 Deseado Arg.
153 B5 Deseado r. Arg.
137 E2 Des Moines U.S.A.
137 E2 Des Moines r. U.S.A.
91 C1 Desna r. Russia/Ukr.
89 D3 Desnogorsk Russia
101 F2 Dessau-Roßlau Ger.
126 B2 Destruction Bay Can.
149 C3 Desventuradas, Islas is
S. Pacific Ocean
128 C1 Detah Can.
101 D2 Detmold Ger.
140 C2 Detroit U.S.A.
137 D1 Detroit Lakes U.S.A.
100 B2 Deurne Neth.
110 B1 Deva Romania
100 C1 Deventer Neth.
96 C2 Deveron r. U.K.
103 D2 Devět skal h. Czech Rep.
137 D1 Devils Lake U.S.A.
128 A2 Devils Paw mt. U.S.A.
99 C3 Devizes U.K.
74 B2 Devli India
110 C2 Devnya Bulg.
128 C2 Devon Can.
126 E1 Devon Island Can.
51 D4 Devonport Austr.
74 B2 Dewas India
137 F3 Dexter U.S.A.
70 A2 Deyang China
59 D3 Deyong, Tanjung pt Indon.
81 D2 Dezful Iran
70 B2 Dezhou China
79 C2 Dhahran Saudi Arabia
75 D2 Dhaka Bangl.
78 B3 Dhamār Yemen
75 C2 Dhamtari India
75 C2 Dhanbad India
75 C2 Dhankuta Nepal
62 A1 Dharmanagar India
75 C2 Dharmjaygarh India
73 B3 Dharwad India
74 B2 Dhasa India
78 B3 Dhubāb Yemen
74 B2 Dhule India
144 A1 Diablo, Picacho del mt. Mex.
51 C2 Diamantina watercourse Austr.
155 D1 Diamantina Brazil
151 D3 Diamantina, Chapada plat.
Brazil
151 C3 Diamantino Brazil
71 B3 Dianbai China
151 D3 Dianópolis Brazil
114 B4 Dianra Côte d'Ivoire
114 C3 Diapaga Burkina Faso
79 C2 Dibā al Ḥiṣn U.A.E.
118 C3 Dibaya Dem. Rep. Congo
62 A1 Dibrugarh India
136 C1 Dickinson U.S.A.

142 C1 Dickson U.S.A.
Dicle r. Turkey see Tigris
105 D3 Die France
129 D2 Diefenbaker, Lake Can.
114 B3 Diéma Mali
62 B2 Diên Châu Vietnam
101 D1 Diepholz Ger.
104 C2 Dieppe France
115 D3 Diffa Niger
131 D2 Digby Can.
105 D3 Digne-les-Bains France
105 C2 Digoin France
64 B2 Digos Phil.
59 D3 Digul r. Indon.
Dihang r. China/India see
Brahmaputra
Dihang r. China/India see
Yarlung Zangbo
105 D2 Dijon France
117 C3 Dikhil Djibouti
111 C3 Dikili Turkey
100 A2 Diksmuide Belgium
115 D3 Dikwa Nigeria
117 B4 Dīla Eth.
74 A1 Dilārām Afgh.
59 C3 Dili East Timor
101 D2 Dillenburg Ger.
134 D1 Dillon U.S.A.
118 C4 Dilolo Dem. Rep. Congo
72 D2 Dimapur India
Dimashq Syria see
Damascus
52 B3 Dimboola Austr.
110 C2 Dimitrovgrad Bulg.
87 D3 Dimitrovgrad Russia
64 B1 Dinagat i. Phil.
104 C2 Dinan France
100 B2 Dinant Belgium
111 D3 Dinar Turkey
81 D2 Dīnār, Kūh-e mt. Iran
73 B3 Dindigul India
123 D1 Dindiza Moz.
101 E2 Dingelstädt Ger.
75 C2 Dinggyê China
Dingle Ireland see
Daingean Uí Chúis
97 A2 Dingle Bay Ireland
96 B2 Dingwall U.K.
70 A2 Dingxi China
154 B3 Dionísio Cerqueira Brazil
114 A3 Diourbel Senegal
74 B1 Dir Pak.
51 D1 Direction, Cape Austr.
117 C4 Dirē Dawa Eth.
120 B2 Dirico Angola
115 D1 Dirj Libya
50 A2 Dirk Hartog Island Austr.
53 C1 Dirranbandi Austr.
78 B3 Dirs Saudi Arabia
50 B2 Disappointment, Lake imp. l.
Austr.
52 B3 Discovery Bay Austr.
143 E1 Dismal Swamp U.S.A.
99 D2 Diss U.K.
108 B3 Dittaino r. Sicily Italy
74 B2 Diu India
155 D2 Divinópolis Brazil
87 D4 Divnoye Russia
114 B4 Divo Côte d'Ivoire
80 B2 Divriği Turkey
140 B2 Dixon U.S.A.
128 A2 Dixon Entrance sea chan.
Can./U.S.A.
80 C2 Diyarbakır Turkey
74 A2 Diz Pak.
115 D2 Djado Niger
115 D2 Djado, Plateau du Niger
118 B3 Djambala Congo

115 C2 **Djanet** Alg.
115 C1 **Djelfa** Alg.
119 C2 **Djéma** C.A.R.
114 B3 **Djenné** Mali
118 B2 **Djibloho** Equat. Guinea
114 B3 **Djibo** Burkina Faso
117 C3 **Djibouti** *country* Africa
117 C3 **Djibouti** Djibouti
114 C4 **Djougou** Benin
92 □C3 **Djúpivogur** Iceland
91 E1 **Dmitriyevka** Russia
89 E3 **Dmitriyev-L'govskiy** Russia
89 E2 **Dmitrov** Russia
Dnepr *r.* Ukr. *see* **Dnieper**
91 C2 **Dnieper** *r.* Ukr.
90 B2 **Dniester** *r.* Ukr.
Dnipro *r.* Ukr. *see* **Dnieper**
91 C2 **Dniprodzerzhyns'k** Ukr.
91 D2 **Dnipropetrovs'k** Ukr.
91 C2 **Dniprorudne** Ukr.
Dnister *r.* Ukr. *see* **Dniester**
88 C2 **Dno** Russia
115 D4 **Doba** Chad
88 B2 **Dobele** Latvia
101 F2 **Döbeln** Ger.
59 C3 **Doberai, Jazirah** *pen.* Indon.
59 C3 **Dobo** Indon.
109 C2 **Doboj** Bos. & Herz.
110 C2 **Dobrich** Bulg.
89 F3 **Dobrinka** Russia
89 E3 **Dobroye** Russia
89 D3 **Dobrush** Belarus
155 E1 **Doce** *r.* Brazil
145 B2 **Doctor Arroyo** Mex.
144 B2 **Doctor Belisario Domínguez** Mex.
111 C3 **Dodecanese** *is* Greece
Dodekanisos *is* Greece *see* **Dodecanese**
136 C3 **Dodge City** U.S.A.
119 D3 **Dodoma** Tanz.
100 C2 **Doetinchem** Neth.
59 C3 **Dofa** Indon.
75 C1 **Dogai Coring** *salt l.* China
128 B2 **Dog Creek** Can.
67 B3 **Dōgo** *i.* Japan
115 C3 **Dogondoutchi** Niger
81 C2 **Doğubeyazıt** Turkey
79 C2 **Doha** Qatar
62 A2 **Doi Saket** Thai.
100 B1 **Dokkum** Neth.
88 C3 **Dokshytsy** Belarus
91 D2 **Dokuchayevs'k** Ukr.
131 C2 **Dolbeau-Mistassini** Can.
104 B2 **Dol-de-Bretagne** France
105 D2 **Dole** France
99 B2 **Dolgellau** U.K.
89 E3 **Dolgorukovo** Russia
89 E3 **Dolgoye** Russia
Dolisie Congo *see* **Loubomo**
59 D3 **Dolok, Pulau** *i.* Indon.
108 B1 **Dolomites** *mts* Italy
117 C4 **Dolo Odo** Eth.
126 D2 **Dolphin and Union Strait** Can.
90 A2 **Dolyna** Ukr.
102 C2 **Domažlice** Czech Rep.
93 E3 **Dombås** Norway
103 D2 **Dombóvár** Hungary
128 B2 **Dome Creek** Can.
147 D3 **Dominica** *country* West Indies
147 C3 **Dominican Republic** *country* West Indies
89 E2 **Domodedovo** Russia
111 B3 **Domokos** Greece
61 C2 **Dompu** Indon.
89 E3 **Don** *r.* Russia
96 C2 **Don** *r.* U.K.
97 D1 **Donaghadee** U.K.
52 B3 **Donald** Austr.
Donau *r.* Austria/Ger. *see* **Danube**
102 C2 **Donauwörth** Ger.
106 B2 **Don Benito** Spain
98 C2 **Doncaster** U.K.
120 A1 **Dondo** Angola
121 C2 **Dondo** Moz.
73 C4 **Dondra Head** Sri Lanka
97 B1 **Donegal** Ireland
97 B1 **Donegal Bay** Ireland
91 D2 **Donets'k** Ukr.
91 D2 **Donets'kyy Kryazh** *hills* Russia/Ukr.
50 A2 **Dongara** Austr.
62 B1 **Dongchuan** China
65 B2 **Dongducheon** S. Korea
71 A4 **Dongfang** China
66 B1 **Dongfanghong** China
58 B3 **Donggala** Indon.
65 A2 **Donggang** China
71 B3 **Dongguan** China
62 B2 **Đông Ha** Vietnam
65 B2 **Donghae** S. Korea
Dong Hai *sea* N. Pacific Ocean *see* **East China Sea**
62 B2 **Đông Hơi** Vietnam
118 B2 **Dongou** Congo
71 B3 **Dongshan** China
70 B2 **Dongsheng** China
70 C2 **Dongtai** China
71 B3 **Dongting Hu** *l.* China
Dong Ujimqin Qi China *see* **Uliastai**
70 B2 **Dongying** China
63 B2 **Don Kêv** Cambodia
54 B1 **Donnellys Crossing** N.Z.
99 B3 **Dorchester** U.K.
122 A1 **Dordabis** Namibia
104 B2 **Dordogne** *r.* France
100 B2 **Dordrecht** Neth.
123 C3 **Dordrecht** S. Africa
129 D2 **Doré Lake** Can.
101 D1 **Dorfmark** Ger.
68 C1 **Dörgön Nuur** *salt l.* Mongolia
114 B3 **Dori** Burkina Faso
122 A3 **Doring** *r.* S. Africa
96 B2 **Dornoch** U.K.
96 B2 **Dornoch Firth** *est.* U.K.
89 D3 **Dorogobuzh** Russia
90 B2 **Dorohoi** Romania
92 G3 **Dorotea** Sweden
50 A2 **Dorre Island** Austr.
53 D2 **Dorrigo** Austr.
100 C2 **Dortmund** Ger.
100 C2 **Dortmund-Ems-Kanal** *canal* Ger.
153 B5 **Dos Bahías, Cabo** *c.* Arg.
77 C3 **Dōshī** Afgh.
101 F1 **Dosse** *r.* Ger.
114 C3 **Dosso** Niger
143 C2 **Dothan** U.S.A.
101 D1 **Dötlingen** Ger.
105 C1 **Douai** France
118 A2 **Douala** Cameroon
104 B2 **Douarnenez** France
114 B3 **Douentza** Mali
98 A1 **Douglas** Isle of Man
122 B2 **Douglas** S. Africa
128 A2 **Douglas** *AK* U.S.A.
138 B2 **Douglas** *AZ* U.S.A.
143 D2 **Douglas** *GA* U.S.A.
136 B2 **Douglas** *WY* U.S.A.
71 C3 **Douliu** Taiwan
104 C1 **Doullens** France
154 B1 **Dourada, Serra** *hills* Brazil
154 B2 **Dourados** Brazil
154 B2 **Dourados, Serra dos** *hills* Brazil
106 B1 **Douro** *r.* Port.
99 D3 **Dover** U.K.
141 D3 **Dover** U.S.A.
95 D3 **Dover, Strait of** France/U.K.
141 F1 **Dover-Foxcroft** U.S.A.
79 C2 **Dowlatābād** *Būshehr* Iran
79 C2 **Dowlatābād** *Kermān* Iran
97 D1 **Downpatrick** U.K.
67 B3 **Dōzen** *is* Japan
130 C2 **Dozois, Réservoir** *resr* Can.
114 B2 **Drâa, Hamada du** *plat.* Alg.
154 B2 **Dracena** Brazil
100 C1 **Drachten** Neth.
110 B2 **Drăgănești-Olt** Romania
110 B2 **Drăgășani** Romania
88 C3 **Drahichyn** Belarus
123 C2 **Drakensberg** *mts* Lesotho/S. Africa
123 C2 **Drakensberg** *mts* S. Africa
158 B8 **Drake Passage** S. Atlantic Ocean
111 B2 **Drama** Greece
93 F4 **Drammen** Norway
109 C1 **Drava** *r.* Europe
128 C2 **Drayton Valley** Can.
101 D2 **Dreieich** Ger.
102 C1 **Dresden** Ger.
104 C2 **Dreux** France
100 B1 **Driemond** Neth.
109 C2 **Drina** *r.* Bos. & Herz./Serbia
109 C2 **Drniš** Croatia
110 B2 **Drobeta-Turnu Severin** Romania
101 D1 **Drochtersen** Ger.
97 C2 **Drogheda** Ireland
90 A2 **Drohobych** Ukr.
97 C1 **Dromore** U.K.
74 B1 **Drosh** Pak.
53 C3 **Drouin** Austr.
128 C2 **Drumheller** Can.
140 C1 **Drummond Island** U.S.A.
131 C2 **Drummondville** Can.
88 B3 **Druskininkai** Lith.
91 D2 **Druzhkivka** Ukr.
88 D2 **Druzhnaya Gorka** Russia
130 A2 **Dryden** Can.
50 B1 **Drysdale** *r.* Austr.
78 A2 **Ḍubā** Saudi Arabia
79 C2 **Dubai** U.A.E.
129 D1 **Dubawnt Lake** Can.
Dubayy U.A.E. *see* **Dubai**
78 A2 **Dubbagh, Jabal ad** *mt.* Saudi Arabia
53 C2 **Dubbo** Austr.
97 C2 **Dublin** Ireland
143 D2 **Dublin** U.S.A.
90 B1 **Dubno** Ukr.
141 D2 **Du Bois** U.S.A.
114 A4 **Dubréka** Guinea
109 C2 **Dubrovnik** Croatia
90 B1 **Dubrovytsya** Ukr.
89 D3 **Dubrowna** Belarus
137 E2 **Dubuque** U.S.A.
129 D2 **Duck Bay** Can.
101 E2 **Duderstadt** Ger.
82 G2 **Dudinka** Russia
99 B2 **Dudley** U.K.
106 B1 **Duero** *r.* Spain
131 C1 **Duffreboy, Lac** *l.* Can.
96 C2 **Dufftown** U.K.
109 C2 **Dugi Rat** Croatia
100 C2 **Duisburg** Ger.
123 C3 **Dukathole** S. Africa
79 C2 **Dukhān** Qatar
89 D2 **Dukhovshchina** Russia
Dukou China *see* **Panzhihua**

88 C2 Dūkštas Lith.
68 C2 Dulan China
152 B4 Dulce r. Arg.
100 C2 Dulovo Bulg.
110 C2 Dülmen Ger.
137 E1 Duluth U.S.A.
64 B2 Dumaguete Phil.
60 B1 Dumai Indon.
64 B1 Dumaran i. Phil.
142 B2 Dumas AR U.S.A.
139 C1 Dumas TX U.S.A.
96 B3 Dumbarton U.K.
103 D2 Ďumbier mt. Slovakia
96 C3 Dumfries U.K.
55 J3 Dumont d'Urville Sea
      Antarctica
116 B1 Dumyāṭ Egypt
      Duna r. Hungary see Danube
      Dunaj r. Slovakia see Danube
103 D2 Dunakeszi Hungary
      Dunărea r. Romania see
      Danube
103 D2 Dunaújváros Hungary
      Dunav r. Serbia see Danube
90 B2 Dunayivtsi Ukr.
96 C2 Dunbar U.K.
96 C1 Dunbeath U.K.
128 B3 Duncan Can.
139 D2 Duncan U.S.A.
96 C1 Duncansby Head U.K.
97 C1 Dundalk Ireland
97 C2 Dundalk Bay Ireland
123 D2 Dundee S. Africa
96 C2 Dundee U.K.
97 D1 Dundrum Bay U.K.
54 B3 Dunedin N.Z.
96 C2 Dunfermline U.K.
97 C1 Dungannon U.K.
74 B2 Dungarpur India
97 C2 Dungarvan Ireland
99 D3 Dungeness hd U.K.
53 D2 Dungiven U.K.
53 D2 Dungog Austr.
119 C2 Dungu Dem. Rep. Congo
60 B1 Dungun Malaysia
116 B2 Dungunab Sudan
69 E2 Dunhua China
68 C2 Dunhuang China
      Dunkerque France see
      Dunkirk
104 C1 Dunkirk France
141 D2 Dunkirk U.S.A.
97 C2 Dún Laoghaire Ireland
97 D1 Dunmurry U.K.
96 C1 Dunnet Head U.K.
96 C3 Duns U.K.
99 C3 Dunstable U.K.
110 B2 Dupnitsa Bulg.
136 C1 Dupree U.S.A.
51 B1 Durack r. Austr.
144 B2 Durango Mex.
106 C1 Durango Spain
136 B3 Durango U.S.A.
139 D2 Durant U.S.A.
153 C4 Durazno Uru.
123 D2 Durban S. Africa
104 C3 Durban-Corbières France
122 A3 Durbanville S. Africa
100 B2 Durbuy Belgium
100 C2 Düren Ger.
73 C2 Durg India
98 C1 Durham U.K.
143 E1 Durham U.S.A.
60 B1 Duri Indon.
109 C2 Durmitor mt. Montenegro
96 B1 Durness U.K.
109 C2 Durrës Albania
97 A3 Dursey Island Ireland

111 C3 Dursunbey Turkey
59 D3 D'Urville, Tanjung pt Indon.
54 B2 D'Urville Island N.Z.
71 A3 Dushan China
77 C3 Dushanbe Tajik.
100 C2 Düsseldorf Ger.
71 A3 Duyun China
91 D2 Dvorichna Ukr.
74 A2 Dwarka India
123 C1 Dwarsberg S. Africa
134 C1 Dworshak Reservoir U.S.A.
89 D3 Dyat'kovo Russia
96 C2 Dyce U.K.
127 G2 Dyer, Cape Can.
142 C1 Dyersburg U.S.A.
103 D2 Dyje r. Austria/Czech Rep.
103 D1 Dylewska Góra h. Pol.
91 D2 Dymytrov Ukr.
123 C3 Dyoki S. Africa
87 E3 Dyurtyuli Russia
69 D2 Dzamin Üüd Mongolia
120 D2 Dzaoudzi Mayotte
      Dzhambul Kazakh. see Taraz
91 C2 Dzhankoy Ukr.
91 D3 Dzhubga Russia
83 K3 Dzhugdzhur, Khrebet mts
      Russia
103 E1 Działdowo Pol.
69 D1 Dzuunmod Mongolia
88 C3 Dzyarzhynsk Belarus
88 C3 Dzyatlavichy Belarus

E

131 E1 Eagle r. Can.
134 C1 Eagle Cap mt. U.S.A.
130 A2 Eagle Lake Can.
134 B2 Eagle Lake U.S.A.
139 C3 Eagle Pass U.S.A.
126 B2 Eagle Plain Can.
130 A1 Ear Falls Can.
99 D3 Eastbourne U.K.
156 C3 East China Sea
      N. Pacific Ocean
129 C3 East Coast Bays N.Z.
131 C2 Eastend Can.
123 C3 Eastern Cape prov. S. Africa
116 B2 Eastern Desert Egypt
73 B3 Eastern Ghats mts India
129 E2 Easterville Can.
153 C6 East Falkland i. Falkland Is
100 C1 East Frisian Islands Ger.
96 B3 East Kilbride U.K.
99 C3 Eastleigh U.K.
140 C2 East Liverpool U.S.A.
123 C3 East London S. Africa
130 C1 Eastmain Can.
130 C1 Eastmain r. Can.
143 D2 Eastman U.S.A.
140 A3 East St Louis U.S.A.
      East Sea N. Pacific Ocean see
      Japan, Sea of
83 K2 East Siberian Sea Russia
59 C3 East Timor country Asia
140 A2 Eau Claire U.S.A.
130 C1 Eau Claire, Lac à l' l. Can.
59 D2 Eauripik atoll Micronesia
145 C2 Ebano Mex.
99 B3 Ebbw Vale U.K.
102 C1 Eberswalde Ger.
109 C2 Eboli Italy
118 B2 Ebolowa Cameroon
107 D1 Ebro r. Spain
144 A2 Echeverria, Pico mt. Mex.
67 C3 Echizen Japan
129 E2 Echoing r. Can.

100 C3 Echternach Lux.
52 B3 Echuca Austr.
106 B2 Écija Spain
102 B1 Eckernförde Ger.
127 F2 Eclipse Sound sea chan.
      Can.
150 A2 Ecuador country S. America
116 C3 Ed Eritrea
117 A3 Ed Da'ein Sudan
117 B3 Ed Damazin Sudan
116 B3 Ed Damer Sudan
116 B3 Ed Debba Sudan
116 B3 Ed Dueim Sudan
51 D4 Eddystone Point Austr.
100 B1 Ede Neth.
118 B2 Edéa Cameroon
154 C1 Edéia Brazil
53 C3 Eden Austr.
98 B1 Eden r. U.K.
123 C2 Edenburg S. Africa
97 C2 Edenderry Ireland
52 B3 Edenhope Austr.
111 B2 Edessa Greece
82 C1 Edgeøya i. Svalbard
139 D3 Edinburg U.S.A.
96 C3 Edinburgh U.K.
110 C2 Edirne Turkey
128 C2 Edmonton Can.
131 D2 Edmundston Can.
111 C3 Edremit Turkey
111 C3 Edremit Körfezi b. Turkey
128 C2 Edson Can.
119 C3 Edward, Lake Dem. Rep.
      Congo/Uganda
139 C2 Edwards Plateau U.S.A.
100 C1 Eenrum Neth.
48 F4 Éfaté i. Vanuatu
140 B3 Effingham U.S.A.
135 C3 Egan Range mts U.S.A.
103 E2 Eger Hungary
93 E4 Egersund Norway
92 □C2 Egilsstaðir Iceland
80 B2 Eğirdir Turkey
80 B2 Eğirdir Gölü l. Turkey
104 C2 Égletons France
      Egmont, Mount vol. N.Z. see
      Taranaki, Mount
83 M2 Egvekinot Russia
116 A2 Egypt country Africa
68 C2 Ehen Hudag China
100 C1 Eibergen Neth.
100 C1 Eifel hills Ger.
96 A2 Eigg i. U.K.
73 B4 Eight Degree Channel India/
      Maldives
50 B1 Eighty Mile Beach Austr.
80 B3 Eilat Israel
101 F2 Eilenburg Ger.
101 D2 Einbeck Ger.
100 B2 Eindhoven Neth.
150 B2 Eirunepé Brazil
120 B2 Eiseb watercourse Namibia
101 E2 Eisenach Ger.
102 C1 Eisenhüttenstadt Ger.
103 D2 Eisenstadt Austria
101 E2 Eisleben, Lutherstadt Ger.
      Eivissa Spain see Ibiza
      Eivissa i. Spain see Ibiza
107 C1 Ejea de los Caballeros Spain
121 □D3 Ejeda Madag.
      Ejin Qi China see
      Dalain Hob
93 H4 Ekenäs Fin.
92 J2 Ekostrovskaya Imandra,
      Ozero l. Russia
93 F4 Eksjö Sweden
122 A2 Eksteenfontein S. Africa
130 B1 Ekwan r. Can.

62	A2	Ela Myanmar
123	C2	Elandsdoorn S. Africa
111	B3	Elassona Greece
80	D2	Elazığ Turkey
108	B2	Elba, Isola d' i. Italy
150	A1	El Banco Col.
138	B2	El Barreal salt l. Mex.
109	D2	Elbasan Albania
150	B1	El Baúl Venez.
114	C1	El Bayadh Alg.
101	D1	Elbe r. Ger.
136	B3	Elbert, Mount U.S.A.
143	D2	Elberton U.S.A.
104	C2	Elbeuf France
80	B2	Elbistan Turkey
103	D1	Elblag Pol.
87	D4	El'brus mt. Russia
81	C2	Elburz Mountains Iran
150	B1	El Callao Venez.
139	D3	El Campo U.S.A.
135	C4	El Centro U.S.A.
152	B2	El Cerro Bol.
107	C2	Elche-Elx Spain
107	C2	Elda Spain
137	E3	Eldon U.S.A.
144	B2	El Dorado Mex.
142	B2	El Dorado AR U.S.A.
137	D3	El Dorado KS U.S.A.
114	B2	El Eglab plat. Alg.
106	C2	El Ejido Spain
89	E2	Elektrostal' Russia
		Elemi Triangle disp. terr.
		Africa see Ilemi Triangle
150	A2	El Encanto Col.
146	C2	Eleuthera i. Bahamas
117	A3	El Fasher Sudan
144	B2	El Fuerte Mex.
117	A3	El Geneina Sudan
116	B3	El Geteina Sudan
96	C2	Elgin U.K.
140	B2	Elgin U.S.A.
115	C1	El Goléa Alg.
44	A1	El Golfo de Santa Clara Mex.
119	D2	Elgon, Mount Kenya/Uganda
114	A2	El Hammâmi reg. Maur.
114	A2	El Hierro i. Canary Islands
145	C2	El Higo Mex.
114	C2	El Homr Alg.
110	C2	Elhovo Bulg.
87	D4	Elista Russia
141	E2	Elizabeth U.S.A.
143	E1	Elizabeth City U.S.A.
140	B3	Elizabethtown U.S.A.
114	B1	El Jadida Morocco
103	E1	Ełk Pol.
137	D1	Elk City U.S.A.
128	C2	Elkford Can.
140	B2	Elkhart U.S.A.
		El Khartum Sudan see
		Khartoum
140	D3	Elkins U.S.A.
128	C3	Elko Can.
134	C2	Elko U.S.A.
129	C2	Elk Point Can.
126	E1	Ellef Ringnes Island Can.
137	D1	Ellendale U.S.A.
134	B1	Ellensburg U.S.A.
54	B2	Ellesmere, Lake N.Z.
127	F1	Ellesmere Island Can.
98	B2	Ellesmere Port U.K.
126	E2	Ellice r. Can.
		Ellice Islands country
		S. Pacific Ocean see Tuvalu
123	C3	Elliotdale S. Africa
96	C2	Ellon U.K.
141	F2	Ellsworth U.S.A.
55	O2	Ellsworth Mountains Antarctica

111	C3	Elmalı Turkey
115	C1	El Meghaïer Alg.
141	D2	Elmira U.S.A.
107	C2	El Moral Spain
101	D1	Elmshorn Ger.
117	A3	El Muglad Sudan
64	A1	El Nido Phil.
117	B3	El Obeid Sudan
144	B2	El Oro Mex.
115	C1	El Oued Alg.
138	A2	Eloy U.S.A.
138	B2	El Paso U.S.A.
144	B1	El Porvenir Mex.
107	D1	El Prat de Llobregat Spain
139	D1	El Reno U.S.A.
145	B2	El Salado Mex.
144	B2	El Salto Mex.
146	B3	El Salvador country Central America
145	B2	El Salvador Mex.
138	B3	El Sauz Mex.
144	A1	El Socorro Mex.
145	C2	El Temascal Mex.
150	B1	El Tigre Venez.
147	D4	El Tocuyo Venez.
88	C2	Elva Estonia
106	B2	Elvas Port.
93	F3	Elverum Norway
119	E2	El Wak Kenya
99	D2	Ely U.K.
137	E1	Ely MN U.S.A.
135	D3	Ely NV U.S.A.
123	C2	eMalahleni S. Africa
93	G4	Emån r. Sweden
123	D3	eManzimtoti S. Africa
76	B2	Emba Kazakh.
123	C2	Embalenhle S. Africa
154	C1	Emborcação, Represa de resr Brazil
119	D3	Embu Kenya
100	C1	Emden Ger.
51	D2	Emerald Austr.
129	E3	Emerson Can.
111	C3	Emet Turkey
123	D2	eMgwenya S. Africa
115	D3	Emi Koussi mt. Chad
110	C2	Emine, Nos pt Bulg.
80	B2	Emirdağ Turkey
123	D2	eMjindini S. Africa
88	B2	Emmaste Estonia
100	B1	Emmeloord Neth.
100	C2	Emmelshausen Ger.
100	C1	Emmen Neth.
123	D2	eMondlo S. Africa
139	C3	Emory Peak U.S.A.
144	A2	Empalme Mex.
123	D2	Empangeni S. Africa
108	B2	Empoli Italy
137	D3	Emporia KS U.S.A.
141	D3	Emporia VA U.S.A.
		Empty Quarter des. Saudi Arabia see Rub' al Khālī
100	C1	Ems r. Ger.
100	C1	Emsdetten Ger.
123	C2	eMzinoni S. Africa
59	D3	Enarotali Indon.
144	B2	Encarnación Mex.
152	C3	Encarnación Para.
155	D1	Encruzilhada Brazil
58	C3	Ende Indon.
126	C2	Endicott Mountains U.S.A.
91	C2	Enerhodar Ukr.
87	D3	Engel's Russia
60	B2	Enggano i. Indon.
98	C2	England admin. div. U.K.
130	A1	English r. Can.
95	C4	English Channel France/U.K.
139	D1	Enid U.S.A.

100	B1	Enkhuizen Neth.
93	G4	Enköping Sweden
108	B3	Enna Sicily Italy
129	D1	Ennadai Lake Can.
117	A3	En Nahud Sudan
115	E3	Ennedi, Massif mts Chad
53	C1	Enngonia Austr.
97	B2	Ennis Ireland
139	D2	Ennis U.S.A.
97	C2	Enniscorthy Ireland
97	C1	Enniskillen U.K.
97	B2	Ennistymon Ireland
102	C2	Enns r. Austria
92	H2	Enontekiö Fin.
53	C3	Ensay Austr.
100	C1	Enschede Neth.
144	A1	Ensenada Mex.
70	A2	Enshi China
128	C1	Enterprise Can.
142	C2	Enterprise AL U.S.A.
134	C1	Enterprise OR U.S.A.
152	B3	Entre Ríos Bol.
106	B2	Entroncamento Port.
115	C4	Enugu Nigeria
150	A2	Envira Brazil
135	D3	Ephraim U.S.A.
134	C1	Ephrata U.S.A.
105	D2	Épinal France
99	C3	Epsom U.K.
118	A2	Equatorial Guinea country Africa
101	F3	Erbendorf Ger.
100	C3	Erbeskopf h. Ger.
81	C2	Erciş Turkey
65	B1	Erdao Jiang r. China
111	C2	Erdek Turkey
80	B2	Erdemli Turkey
152	C3	Erechim Brazil
69	D1	Ereentsav Mongolia
80	B2	Ereğli Konya Turkey
80	B1	Ereğli Zonguldak Turkey
80	B2	Erenhot China
		Erevan Armenia see Yerevan
101	E2	Erfurt Ger.
80	B2	Ergani Turkey
114	B2	'Erg Chech des. Alg./Mali
111	C2	Ergene r. Turkey
140	C2	Erie U.S.A.
140	C2	Erie, Lake Can./U.S.A.
66	D2	Erimo-misaki c. Japan
116	B3	Eritrea country Africa
101	E3	Erlangen Ger.
50	C2	Erldunda Austr.
123	C2	Ermelo S. Africa
80	B2	Ermenek Turkey
111	B3	Ermoupoli Greece
73	B4	Ernakulam India
73	B3	Erode India
100	B2	Erp Neth.
114	B1	Er Rachidia Morocco
117	B3	Er Rahad Sudan
97	B1	Errigal h. Ireland
97	A1	Erris Head Ireland
109	D2	Ersekë Albania
91	E1	Ertil' Russia
101	D2	Erwitte Ger.
102	F2	Erzgebirge mts Czech Rep./Ger.
80	B2	Erzincan Turkey
81	C2	Erzurum Turkey
93	E4	Esbjerg Denmark
135	D3	Escalante U.S.A.
144	B2	Escalón Mex.
140	B1	Escanaba U.S.A.
145	C3	Escárcega Mex.
107	C1	Escatrón Spain
100	A2	Escaut r. Belgium/France
101	E1	Eschede Ger.

100 B3 **Esch-sur-Alzette** Lux.
101 E2 **Eschwege** Ger.
100 C2 **Eschweiler** Ger.
135 C4 **Escondido** U.S.A.
144 B2 **Escuinapa** Mex.
111 C3 **Eşen** Turkey
81 D2 **Eşfahān** Iran
123 D2 **eSikhaleni** S. Africa
98 B1 **Esk** *r.* U.K.
131 D1 **Esker** Can.
92 □C2 **Eskifjörður** Iceland
93 G4 **Eskilstuna** Sweden
Eskimo Point Can. *see* **Arviat**
80 B2 **Eskişehir** Turkey
81 C2 **Eslāmābād-e Gharb** Iran
111 C3 **Esler Dağı** *mt.* Turkey
111 C3 **Eşme** Turkey
150 A1 **Esmeraldas** Ecuador
79 D2 **Espakeh** Iran
104 C3 **Espalion** France
130 B2 **Espanola** Can.
138 B1 **Espanola** U.S.A.
50 B3 **Esperance** Austr.
144 B2 **Esperanza** Mex.
106 B2 **Espichel, Cabo** *c.* Port.
155 D1 **Espinhaço, Serra do** *mts* Brazil
151 D3 **Espinosa** Brazil
48 F4 **Espiritu Santo** *i.* Vanuatu
144 A2 **Espíritu Santo, Isla** *i.* Mex.
93 H3 **Espoo** Fin.
153 A5 **Esquel** Arg.
114 B1 **Essaouira** Morocco
100 C2 **Essen** Ger.
150 C1 **Essequibo** *r.* Guyana
114 A2 **Es-Smara** Western Sahara
83 L3 **Esso** Russia
79 C2 **Estahbān** Iran
151 E3 **Estância** Brazil
123 C2 **Estcourt** S. Africa
107 C1 **Estella** Spain
106 B2 **Estepona** Spain
106 C1 **Esteras de Medinaceli** Spain
129 D2 **Esterhazy** Can.
152 B3 **Esteros** Para.
136 B2 **Estes Park** U.S.A.
129 D3 **Estevan** Can.
137 E2 **Estherville** U.S.A.
129 D2 **Eston** Can.
88 C2 **Estonia** *country* Europe
106 B1 **Estrela, Serra da** *mts* Port.
106 B2 **Estremoz** Port.
52 A1 **Etadunna** Austr.
104 C2 **Étampes** France
104 C1 **Étaples** France
75 B2 **Etawah** India
123 D2 **Ethandakukhanya** S. Africa
117 B4 **Ethiopia** *country* Africa
109 C3 **Etna, Mount** *vol. Sicily* Italy
128 A2 **Etolin Island** U.S.A.
120 A2 **Etosha Pan** *salt pan* Namibia
100 C3 **Ettelbruck** Lux.
100 B2 **Etten-Leur** Neth.
107 C1 **Etxarri-Aranatz** Spain
99 D3 **Eu** France
53 C2 **Euabalong** Austr.
Euboea *i.* Greece *see* **Evvoia**
50 B3 **Eucla** Austr.
143 C2 **Eufaula** U.S.A.
139 D1 **Eufaula Lake** *resr* U.S.A.
134 B2 **Eugene** U.S.A.
144 A2 **Eugenia, Punta** *pt* Mex.
53 C1 **Eulo** Austr.
53 C2 **Eumungerie** Austr.
139 C2 **Eunice** U.S.A.
80 C2 **Euphrates** *r.* Asia
134 B2 **Eureka** *CA* U.S.A.
134 C1 **Eureka** *MT* U.S.A.
135 C3 **Eureka** *NV* U.S.A.
52 B2 **Euriowie** Austr.
53 C3 **Euroa** Austr.
106 B2 **Europa Point** Gibraltar
128 B2 **Eutsuk Lake** Can.
130 C1 **Evans, Lac** *l.* Can.
53 D1 **Evans Head** Austr.
127 F2 **Evans Strait** Can.
136 A2 **Evanston** U.S.A.
140 B3 **Evansville** U.S.A.
123 C2 **Evaton** S. Africa
79 C2 **Evaz** Iran
83 L2 **Evensk** Russia
50 C2 **Everard Range** *hills* Austr.
75 C2 **Everest, Mount** China/Nepal
134 B1 **Everett** U.S.A.
100 A2 **Evergem** Belgium
143 D3 **Everglades** *swamp* U.S.A.
118 B2 **Evinayong** Equat. Guinea
93 E4 **Evje** Norway
106 B2 **Évora** Port.
104 C2 **Évreux** France
111 C2 **Evros** *r.* Greece/Turkey
111 B3 **Evrotas** *r.* Greece
80 B2 **Evrychou** Cyprus
111 B3 **Evvoia** *i.* Greece
119 E2 **Ewaso Ngiro** *r.* Kenya
152 B2 **Exaltación** Bol.
99 B3 **Exe** *r.* U.K.
99 B3 **Exeter** U.K.
99 B3 **Exmoor** *hills* U.K.
99 B3 **Exmouth** U.K.
50 A2 **Exmouth Gulf** Austr.
146 C2 **Exuma Cays** *is* Bahamas
117 C4 **Eyl** Somalia
51 C3 **Eyre Peninsula** Austr.
94 B1 **Eysturoy** *i.* Faroe Is
123 D2 **Ezakheni** S. Africa
123 C2 **Ezenzeleni** S. Africa
70 B2 **Ezhou** China
86 E2 **Ezhva** Russia
111 C3 **Ezine** Turkey

F

138 B2 **Fabens** U.S.A.
108 B2 **Fabriano** Italy
115 D3 **Fachi** Niger
114 C3 **Fada-N'Gourma** Burkina Faso
108 B2 **Faenza** Italy
59 C3 **Fafanlap** Indon.
110 B1 **Făgăraş** Romania
49 G3 **Fagatogo** American Samoa
93 E3 **Fagernes** Norway
93 G4 **Fagersta** Sweden
153 B6 **Fagnano, Lago** *l.* Arg./Chile
114 B3 **Faguibine, Lac** *l.* Mali
92 □B3 **Fagurhólsmýri** Iceland
126 B2 **Fairbanks** U.S.A.
137 D2 **Fairbury** U.S.A.
135 B3 **Fairfield** U.S.A.
96 □ **Fair Isle** *i.* U.K.
137 E2 **Fairmont** *MN* U.S.A.
140 C3 **Fairmont** *WV* U.S.A.
128 C2 **Fairview** Can.
59 D2 **Fais** *i.* Micronesia
74 B1 **Faisalabad** Pak.
136 C1 **Faith** U.S.A.
77 D3 **Faīzābād** Afgh.
75 C2 **Faizabad** India
59 C3 **Fakfak** Indon.
65 A1 **Faku** China
114 A4 **Falaba** Sierra Leone
139 D3 **Falcon Lake** Mex./U.S.A.
139 D3 **Falfurrias** U.S.A.
128 C2 **Falher** Can.
93 F4 **Falkenberg** Sweden
101 F2 **Falkenberg/Elster** Ger.
101 F1 **Falkensee** Ger.
96 C3 **Falkirk** U.K.
153 C6 **Falkland Islands** *terr.* S. Atlantic Ocean
93 F4 **Falköping** Sweden
135 C3 **Fallon** U.S.A.
141 E2 **Fall River** U.S.A.
137 D2 **Falls City** U.S.A.
99 A3 **Falmouth** U.K.
122 A3 **False Bay** S. Africa
93 F4 **Falster** *i.* Denmark
110 C1 **Fălticeni** Romania
93 G3 **Falun** Sweden
71 A3 **Fangcheng** China
71 C3 **Fangshan** Taiwan
69 E1 **Fangzheng** China
108 B2 **Fano** Italy
119 C2 **Faradje** Dem. Rep. Congo
121 □D3 **Farafangana** Madag.
116 A2 **Farāfirah, Wāḥāt al** *oasis* Egypt
76 C3 **Farāh** Afgh.
114 A3 **Faranah** Guinea
78 B3 **Farasān, Jazā'ir** *is* Saudi Arabia
127 J3 **Farewell, Cape** Greenland
54 B2 **Farewell, Cape** N.Z.
137 D1 **Fargo** U.S.A.
77 D2 **Farg'ona** Uzbek.
137 E2 **Faribault** U.S.A.
141 E2 **Farmington** *ME* U.S.A.
138 B1 **Farmington** *NM* U.S.A.
141 D3 **Farmville** U.S.A.
99 C3 **Farnborough** U.K.
128 C2 **Farnham, Mount** Can.
128 A1 **Faro** Can.
106 B2 **Faro** Port.
88 A2 **Fårö** *i.* Sweden
94 B1 **Faroe Islands** *terr.* N. Atlantic Ocean
79 C2 **Farrāshband** Iran
139 C2 **Farwell** U.S.A.
79 C2 **Fāryāb** Iran
79 C2 **Fasā** Iran
109 C2 **Fasano** Italy
90 B1 **Fastiv** Ukr.
75 B2 **Fatehgarh** India
75 C2 **Fatehpur** India
92 G2 **Fauske** Norway
92 □A3 **Faxaflói** *b.* Iceland
92 G3 **Faxälven** *r.* Sweden
115 D3 **Faya** Chad
142 B1 **Fayetteville** *AR* U.S.A.
143 E1 **Fayetteville** *NC* U.S.A.
142 C1 **Fayetteville** *TN* U.S.A.
74 B1 **Fazilka** India
114 A2 **Fdérik** Maur.
143 E2 **Fear, Cape** U.S.A.
54 C2 **Featherston** N.Z.
104 C2 **Fécamp** France
102 C1 **Fehmarn** *i.* Ger.
101 F1 **Fehrbellin** Ger.
155 D2 **Feia, Lagoa** *lag.* Brazil
150 A2 **Feijó** Brazil
54 C2 **Feilding** N.Z.
151 E3 **Feira de Santana** Brazil
107 D2 **Felanitx** Spain
145 D3 **Felipe C. Puerto** Mex.
155 D1 **Felixlândia** Brazil
99 D3 **Felixstowe** U.K.
101 D2 **Felsberg** Ger.
108 B1 **Feltre** Italy
93 F3 **Femunden** *l.* Norway
71 B3 **Fengcheng** *Jiangxi* China
65 A1 **Fengcheng** *Liaoning* China
62 A1 **Fengqing** China
70 B2 **Fengxian** China

Fengxiang China *see* **Lincang**
71 C3 **Fengyuan** Taiwan
70 B1 **Fengzhen** China
105 D3 **Feno, Capo di** *c.* *Corsica* France
121 □D2 **Fenoarivo Atsinanana** Madag.
91 D2 **Feodosiya** Ukr.
108 A3 **Fer, Cap de** *c.* Alg.
137 D1 **Fergus Falls** U.S.A.
109 D2 **Ferizaj** Kosovo
114 B4 **Ferkessédougou** Côte d'Ivoire
108 B2 **Fermo** Italy
131 D1 **Fermont** Can.
106 B1 **Fermoselle** Spain
97 B2 **Fermoy** Ireland
143 D2 **Fernandina Beach** U.S.A.
154 B2 **Fernandópolis** Brazil
128 C3 **Fernie** Can.
108 B2 **Ferrara** Italy
154 B2 **Ferreiros** Brazil
108 A2 **Ferro, Capo** *c.* *Sardinia* Italy
106 B1 **Ferrol** Spain
100 B1 **Ferwerd** Neth.
114 B1 **Fès** Morocco
118 B3 **Feshi** Dem. Rep. Congo
137 E3 **Festus** U.S.A.
111 C3 **Fethiye** Turkey
96 □ **Fetlar** *i.* U.K.
130 C1 **Feuilles, Rivière aux** *r.* Can.
Fez Morocco *see* **Fès**
121 □D3 **Fianarantsoa** Madag.
117 B4 **Fichē** Eth.
109 C2 **Fier** Albania
96 C2 **Fife Ness** *pt* U.K.
104 C3 **Figeac** France
106 B1 **Figueira da Foz** Port.
107 D1 **Figueres** Spain
114 B1 **Figuig** Morocco
48 F3 **Fiji** *country* S. Pacific Ocean
152 B3 **Filadelfia** Para.
55 Q2 **Filchner Ice Shelf** Antarctica
98 C1 **Filey** U.K.
111 B3 **Filippiada** Greece
93 F4 **Filipstad** Sweden
96 C2 **Findhorn** *r.* U.K.
140 C2 **Findlay** U.S.A.
51 D4 **Fingal** Austr.
141 D2 **Finger Lakes** U.S.A.
106 B1 **Finisterre, Cape** Spain
92 I3 **Finland** *country* Europe
93 H4 **Finland, Gulf of** Europe
128 B2 **Finlay** *r.* Can.
53 C3 **Finley** Austr.
101 E2 **Finne** *ridge* Ger.
92 H2 **Finnmarksvidda** *reg.* Norway
92 G2 **Finnsnes** Norway
93 G4 **Finspång** Sweden
96 A2 **Fionnphort** U.K.
Fırat *r.* Turkey *see* **Euphrates**
Firenze Italy *see* **Florence**
105 C2 **Firminy** France
75 B2 **Firozabad** India
74 B1 **Firozpur** India
79 C2 **Fīrūzābād** Iran
122 A2 **Fish** *watercourse* Namibia
122 B3 **Fish** *r.* S. Africa
99 A3 **Fishguard** U.K.
105 C2 **Fismes** France
Fisterra, Cabo *c.* Spain *see* **Finisterre, Cape**
141 E2 **Fitchburg** U.S.A.
129 C2 **Fitzgerald** Can.
50 B1 **Fitzroy Crossing** Austr.
108 B2 **Fivizzano** Italy
119 C3 **Fizi** Dem. Rep. Congo
92 G3 **Fjällsjöälven** *r.* Sweden
123 C3 **Flagstaff** S. Africa
138 A1 **Flagstaff** U.S.A.
130 C1 **Flaherty Island** Can.
98 C1 **Flamborough Head** U.K.
101 F1 **Fläming** *hills* Ger.
136 B2 **Flaming Gorge Reservoir** U.S.A.
134 D1 **Flathead** *r.* U.S.A.
134 D1 **Flathead Lake** U.S.A.
51 D1 **Flattery, Cape** Austr.
134 B1 **Flattery, Cape** U.S.A.
98 B2 **Fleetwood** U.K.
93 E4 **Flekkefjord** Norway
102 B1 **Flensburg** Ger.
104 B2 **Flers** France
51 D1 **Flinders** *r.* Austr.
50 A3 **Flinders Bay** Austr.
51 D3 **Flinders Island** Austr.
52 A2 **Flinders Ranges** *mts* Austr.
129 D2 **Flin Flon** Can.
140 C2 **Flint** U.S.A.
107 D1 **Florac** France
108 B2 **Florence** Italy
142 C2 **Florence** *AL* U.S.A.
138 A2 **Florence** *AZ* U.S.A.
134 B2 **Florence** *OR* U.S.A.
143 E2 **Florence** *SC* U.S.A.
150 A1 **Florencia** Col.
146 B3 **Flores** Guat.
58 C3 **Flores** *i.* Indon.
58 B3 **Flores, Laut** *sea* Indon.
Flores Sea Indon. *see* **Flores, Laut**
151 E2 **Floresta** Brazil
139 D3 **Floresville** U.S.A.
151 D2 **Floriano** Brazil
152 D3 **Florianópolis** Brazil
153 C4 **Florida** Uru.
143 D2 **Florida** *state* U.S.A.
143 D4 **Florida, Straits of** N. Atlantic Ocean
143 D4 **Florida Keys** *is* U.S.A.
111 B2 **Florina** Greece
93 E3 **Florø** Norway
129 D2 **Foam Lake** Can.
109 C2 **Foča** Bos. & Herz.
110 C1 **Focșani** Romania
71 B3 **Fogang** China
109 C2 **Foggia** Italy
131 E2 **Fogo Island** Can.
104 C3 **Foix** France
89 D3 **Fokino** Russia
130 B2 **Foleyet** Can.
108 B2 **Foligno** Italy
99 D3 **Folkestone** U.K.
143 D2 **Folkston** U.S.A.
108 B2 **Follonica** Italy
129 D2 **Fond-du-Lac** Can.
129 D2 **Fond du Lac** *r.* Can.
140 B2 **Fond du Lac** U.S.A.
106 B1 **Fondevila** Spain
108 B2 **Fondi** Italy
146 B3 **Fonseca, Golfo do** *b.* Central America
150 B2 **Fonte Boa** Brazil
104 B2 **Fontenay-le-Comte** France
92 □C2 **Fontur** *pt* Iceland
53 C2 **Forbes** Austr.
101 E3 **Forchheim** Ger.
93 E3 **Førde** Norway
53 C1 **Fords Bridge** Austr.
142 B2 **Fordyce** U.S.A.
142 C2 **Forest** U.S.A.
53 C3 **Forest Hill** Austr.
131 D2 **Forestville** Can.
96 C2 **Forfar** U.K.
134 B1 **Forks** U.S.A.
108 B2 **Forlì** Italy
107 D2 **Formentera** *i.* Spain
107 D2 **Formentor, Cap de** *c.* Spain
155 C2 **Formiga** Brazil
152 C3 **Formosa** Arg.
Formosa *country* Asia *see* **Taiwan**
154 C1 **Formosa** Brazil
96 C2 **Forres** U.K.
50 B3 **Forrest** Austr.
142 B1 **Forrest City** U.S.A.
51 D1 **Forsayth** Austr.
93 H3 **Forssa** Fin.
53 D2 **Forster** Austr.
136 B1 **Forsyth** U.S.A.
74 B2 **Fort Abbas** Pak.
130 B1 **Fort Albany** Can.
151 E2 **Fortaleza** Brazil
128 C2 **Fort Assiniboine** Can.
96 B2 **Fort Augustus** U.K.
134 D1 **Fort Benton** U.S.A.
135 B3 **Fort Bragg** U.S.A.
Fort Chimo Can. *see* **Kuujjuaq**
129 C2 **Fort Chipewyan** Can.
136 B2 **Fort Collins** U.S.A.
147 D3 **Fort-de-France** Martinique
137 E2 **Fort Dodge** U.S.A.
130 A2 **Fort Frances** Can.
Fort Franklin Can. *see* **Déline**
Fort George Can. *see* **Chisasibi**
126 C2 **Fort Good Hope** Can.
96 C2 **Forth** *r.* U.K.
96 C2 **Forth, Firth of** *est.* U.K.
152 C3 **Fortín Madrejón** Para.
143 D3 **Fort Lauderdale** U.S.A.
128 B1 **Fort Liard** Can.
129 C2 **Fort Mackay** Can.
129 C2 **Fort McMurray** Can.
126 C2 **Fort McPherson** Can.
136 C2 **Fort Morgan** U.S.A.
143 D3 **Fort Myers** U.S.A.
128 B2 **Fort Nelson** Can.
128 B2 **Fort Nelson** *r.* Can.
142 C2 **Fort Payne** U.S.A.
136 B1 **Fort Peck** U.S.A.
136 B1 **Fort Peck Reservoir** U.S.A.
143 D3 **Fort Pierce** U.S.A.
128 C1 **Fort Providence** Can.
129 D2 **Fort Qu'Appelle** Can.
128 C1 **Fort Resolution** Can.
Fort Rupert Can. *see* **Waskaganish**
128 B2 **Fort St James** Can.
128 B2 **Fort St John** Can.
128 C2 **Fort Saskatchewan** Can.
137 E3 **Fort Scott** U.S.A.
130 B1 **Fort Severn** Can.
76 B2 **Fort-Shevchenko** Kazakh.
128 B1 **Fort Simpson** Can.
129 C1 **Fort Smith** Can.
142 B1 **Fort Smith** U.S.A.
139 C2 **Fort Stockton** U.S.A.
138 C2 **Fort Sumner** U.S.A.
128 C2 **Fort Vermilion** Can.
142 C2 **Fort Walton Beach** U.S.A.
140 B2 **Fort Wayne** U.S.A.
96 B2 **Fort William** U.K.
139 D2 **Fort Worth** U.S.A.
126 B2 **Fort Yukon** U.S.A.
71 B3 **Foshan** China
92 F3 **Fosna** *pen.* Norway
93 E3 **Fosnavåg** Norway
92 □B3 **Foss** Iceland
92 □A2 **Fossá** Iceland
108 A2 **Fossano** Italy
53 C3 **Foster** Austr.
104 B2 **Fougères** France
96 □ **Foula** *i.* U.K.
111 C3 **Fournoi** *i.* Greece
114 A3 **Fouta Djallon** *reg.* Guinea
54 A3 **Foveaux Strait** N.Z.

136 C3 **Fowler** U.S.A.
50 C3 **Fowlers Bay** Austr.
128 C2 **Fox Creek** Can.
127 F2 **Foxe Basin** *g.* Can.
127 F2 **Foxe Channel** Can.
127 F2 **Foxe Peninsula** Can.
54 B2 **Fox Glacier** N.Z.
128 C2 **Fox Lake** Can.
128 A1 **Fox Mountain** Can.
54 C2 **Foxton** N.Z.
129 D2 **Fox Valley** Can.
97 C1 **Foyle, Lough** *b.* Ireland/U.K.
154 B3 **Foz de Areia, Represa de** *resr* Brazil
120 A2 **Foz do Cunene** Angola
154 B3 **Foz do Iguaçu** Brazil
107 D1 **Fraga** Spain
154 C2 **Franca** Brazil
109 C2 **Francavilla Fontana** Italy
104 C2 **France** *country* Europe
118 B3 **Franceville** Gabon
137 D2 **Francis Case, Lake** U.S.A.
155 D1 **Francisco Sá** Brazil
120 B3 **Francistown** Botswana
128 B2 **François Lake** Can.
101 D2 **Frankenberg (Eder)** Ger.
101 D3 **Frankenthal (Pfalz)** Ger.
101 E2 **Frankenwald** *mts* Ger.
140 C3 **Frankfort** U.S.A.
102 C1 **Frankfurt (Oder)** Ger.
101 D2 **Frankfurt am Main** Ger.
102 C2 **Fränkische Alb** *hills* Ger.
101 E3 **Fränkische Schweiz** *reg.* Ger.
141 D2 **Franklin** U.S.A.
126 C2 **Franklin Bay** Can.
134 C1 **Franklin D. Roosevelt Lake** U.S.A.
128 B1 **Franklin Mountains** Can.
126 E2 **Franklin Strait** Can.
82 E1 **Frantsa-Iosifa, Zemlya** *is* Russia
54 B2 **Franz Josef Glacier** N.Z.
Franz Josef Land *is* Russia *see* **Frantsa-Iosifa, Zemlya**
108 A3 **Frasca, Capo della** *c. Sardinia* Italy
128 B3 **Fraser** *r. B.C.* Can.
131 D1 **Fraser** *r. Nfld. and Lab.* Can.
122 B3 **Fraserburg** S. Africa
96 C2 **Fraserburgh** U.K.
130 B2 **Fraserdale** Can.
51 E2 **Fraser Island** Austr.
128 B2 **Fraser Lake** Can.
153 C4 **Fray Bentos** Uru.
93 E4 **Fredericia** Denmark
139 D2 **Frederick** U.S.A.
139 D2 **Fredericksburg** *TX* U.S.A.
141 D3 **Fredericksburg** *VA* U.S.A.
128 A2 **Frederick Sound** *sea chan.* U.S.A.
131 D2 **Fredericton** Can.
93 F4 **Frederikshavn** Denmark
Fredrikshamn Fin. *see* **Hamina**
93 F4 **Fredrikstad** Norway
140 B2 **Freeport** *IL* U.S.A.
139 D3 **Freeport** *TX* U.S.A.
146 C2 **Freeport City** Bahamas
139 D3 **Freer** U.S.A.
123 C2 **Free State** *prov.* S. Africa
114 A4 **Freetown** Sierra Leone
106 B2 **Fregenal de la Sierra** Spain
104 B2 **Fréhel, Cap** *c.* France
102 B2 **Freiburg im Breisgau** Ger.
102 C2 **Freising** Ger.
102 C2 **Freistadt** Austria
105 D3 **Fréjus** France
50 A3 **Fremantle** Austr.
137 D2 **Fremont** *NE* U.S.A.
140 C2 **Fremont** *OH* U.S.A.
151 C1 **French Guiana** *terr.* S. America
134 E1 **Frenchman** *r.* U.S.A.
49 I4 **French Polynesia** *terr.* S. Pacific Ocean
144 B2 **Fresnillo** Mex.
135 C3 **Fresno** U.S.A.
107 D2 **Freu, Cap des** *c.* Spain
105 D2 **Freyming-Merlebach** France
114 A3 **Fria** Guinea
152 B3 **Frias** Arg.
102 B2 **Friedrichshafen** Ger.
101 F1 **Friesack** Ger.
100 C1 **Friesoythe** Ger.
Frobisher Bay *Nunavut* Can. *see* **Iqaluit**
127 G2 **Frobisher Bay** Can.
101 F2 **Frohburg** Ger.
87 D4 **Frolovo** Russia
52 A2 **Frome, Lake** *imp. l.* Austr.
52 A2 **Frome Downs** Austr.
100 C2 **Fröndenberg/Ruhr** Ger.
145 C3 **Frontera** Mex.
144 B1 **Fronteras** Mex.
108 B2 **Frosinone** Italy
92 E3 **Frøya** *i.* Norway
Frunze Kyrg. *see* **Bishkek**
105 D2 **Frutigen** Switz.
103 D2 **Frýdek-Místek** Czech Rep.
71 B3 **Fu'an** China
106 C1 **Fuenlabrada** Spain
152 C3 **Fuerte Olimpo** Para.
114 A2 **Fuerteventura** *i.* Canary Islands
64 B1 **Fuga** *i.* Phil.
79 C2 **Fujairah** U.A.E.
67 C3 **Fuji** Japan
71 B3 **Fujian** *prov.* China
67 C3 **Fujinomiya** Japan
67 C3 **Fuji-san** *vol.* Japan
67 C3 **Fukui** Japan
67 B4 **Fukuoka** Japan
67 D3 **Fukushima** Japan
101 D2 **Fulda** Ger.
101 D2 **Fulda** *r.* Ger.
70 A3 **Fuling** China
137 E3 **Fulton** U.S.A.
105 C2 **Fumay** France
49 F3 **Funafuti** *atoll* Tuvalu
114 A1 **Funchal** Arquipélago da Madeira
106 B1 **Fundão** Port.
131 D2 **Fundy, Bay of** *g.* Can.
70 B2 **Funing** *Jiangsu* China
71 A3 **Funing** *Yunnan* China
115 C3 **Funtua** Nigeria
79 C2 **Fürgun, Kūh-e** *mt.* Iran
89 F2 **Furmanov** Russia
155 C2 **Furnas, Represa** *resr* Brazil
51 D4 **Furneaux Group** *is* Austr.
100 C1 **Fürstenau** Ger.
101 E3 **Fürth** Ger.
127 F2 **Fury and Hecla Strait** Can.
65 A1 **Fushun** China
65 B1 **Fusong** China
79 C2 **Fuwayriţ** Qatar
70 B2 **Fuyang** China
69 E1 **Fuyu** China
68 B1 **Fuyun** China
71 B3 **Fuzhou** *Fujian* China
71 B3 **Fuzhou** *Jiangxi* China
93 F4 **Fyn** *i.* Denmark
F.Y.R.O.M. *country* Europe *see* **Macedonia**

G

117 C4 **Gaalkacyo** Somalia
120 A2 **Gabela** Angola
115 D1 **Gabès** Tunisia
115 D1 **Gabès, Golfe de** *g.* Tunisia
118 B3 **Gabon** *country* Africa
123 C1 **Gaborone** Botswana
110 C2 **Gabrovo** Bulg.
114 A3 **Gabú** Guinea-Bissau
73 B3 **Gadag-Betigeri** India
75 C2 **Gadchiroli** India
101 E1 **Gadebusch** Ger.
142 C2 **Gadsden** U.S.A.
110 C2 **Găeşti** Romania
108 B2 **Gaeta** Italy
143 D1 **Gaffney** U.S.A.
115 C1 **Gafsa** Tunisia
89 E2 **Gagarin** Russia
114 B4 **Gagnoa** Côte d'Ivoire
131 D1 **Gagnon** Can.
81 C1 **Gagra** Georgia
122 A2 **Gaiab** *watercourse* Namibia
111 C3 **Gaïdouronisi** *i.* Greece
104 C3 **Gaillac** France
143 D3 **Gainesville** *FL* U.S.A.
143 D2 **Gainesville** *GA* U.S.A.
139 D2 **Gainesville** *TX* U.S.A.
98 C2 **Gainsborough** U.K.
52 A2 **Gairdner, Lake** *imp. l.* Austr.
96 B2 **Gairloch** U.K.
119 E3 **Galana** *r.* Kenya
103 D2 **Galanta** Slovakia
148 B3 **Galapagos Islands** Ecuador
96 C3 **Galashiels** U.K.
110 C1 **Galaţi** Romania
93 E3 **Galdhøpiggen** *mt.* Norway
145 B2 **Galeana** Mex.
128 C2 **Galena Bay** Can.
140 A2 **Galesburg** U.S.A.
122 B2 **Galeshewe** S. Africa
86 D3 **Galich** Russia
116 B1 **Galilee, Sea of** *l.* Israel
142 C1 **Gallatin** U.S.A.
73 C4 **Galle** Sri Lanka
150 A1 **Gallinas, Punta** *pt* Col.
109 C2 **Gallipoli** Italy
111 C2 **Gallipoli** Turkey
92 H2 **Gällivare** Sweden
138 B1 **Gallup** U.S.A.
117 C4 **Galmudug** *reg.* Somalia
114 A2 **Galtat-Zemmour** Western Sahara
97 B2 **Galtymore** *h.* Ireland
139 E3 **Galveston** U.S.A.
139 E3 **Galveston Bay** U.S.A.
97 B2 **Galway** Ireland
97 B2 **Galway Bay** Ireland
154 C1 **Gama** Brazil
123 D3 **Gamalakhe** S. Africa
114 A3 **Gambia, The** *country* Africa
52 A3 **Gambier Islands** Austr.
131 E2 **Gambo** Can.
118 B3 **Gamboma** Congo
128 C1 **Gamêtî** Can.
138 B1 **Ganado** U.S.A.
81 C1 **Gäncä** Azer.
Gand Belgium *see* **Ghent**
61 C2 **Gandadiwata, Bukit** *mt.* Indon.
118 C3 **Gandajika** Dem. Rep. Congo
131 E2 **Gander** Can.
131 E2 **Gander** *r.* Can.
101 D1 **Ganderkesee** Ger.
107 D1 **Gandesa** Spain
74 B2 **Gandhidham** India
74 B2 **Gandhinagar** India
74 B2 **Gandhi Sagar** *resr* India

107	C2	Gandia Spain
		Ganga r. Bangl./India see Ganges
153	B5	Gangán Arg.
74	B2	Ganganagar India
68	C3	Gangca China
75	C1	Gangdisê Shan mts China
75	C2	Ganges r. Bangl./India
105	C3	Ganges France
75	C2	Ganges, Mouths of the Bangl./India
65	B2	Gangneung S. Korea
75	C2	Gangtok India
105	C2	Gannat France
136	B2	Gannett Peak U.S.A.
122	A3	Gansbaai S. Africa
70	A1	Gansu prov. China
71	B3	Ganzhou China
114	B3	Gao Mali
97	B1	Gaoth Dobhair Ireland
114	A3	Gaoual Guinea
71	C3	Gaoxiong Taiwan
70	B2	Gaoyou China
70	B2	Gaoyou Hu l. China
105	D3	Gap France
75	C1	Gar China
76	B2	Garabogaz Turkm.
76	B2	Garabogazköl Turkm.
76	B2	Garabogazköl Aylagy b. Turkm.
53	C1	Garah Austr.
151	E2	Garanhuns Brazil
135	B2	Garberville U.S.A.
101	D1	Garbsen Ger.
154	C2	Garça Brazil
101	E1	Gardelegen Ger.
136	C3	Garden City U.S.A.
129	E2	Garden Hill Can.
77	C3	Gardêz Afgh.
88	B2	Gargždai Lith.
123	C3	Gariep Dam dam S. Africa
122	A3	Garies S. Africa
119	D3	Garissa Kenya
102	C2	Garmisch-Partenkirchen Ger.
52	B2	Garnpung Lake imp. l. Austr.
104	B3	Garonne r. France
117	C4	Garoowe Somalia
74	B2	Garoth India
118	B2	Garoua Cameroon
96	B2	Garry r. U.K.
126	E2	Garry Lake Can.
119	E3	Garsen Kenya
61	B2	Garut Indon.
140	B2	Gary U.S.A.
145	B2	Garza García Mex.
68	C2	Garzê China
104	B2	Gascony, Gulf of France
50	A2	Gascoyne r. Austr.
115	D3	Gashua Nigeria
131	D2	Gaspé Can.
131	D2	Gaspésie, Péninsule de la pen. Can.
143	E1	Gaston, Lake U.S.A.
143	D1	Gastonia U.S.A.
107	C2	Gata, Cabo de c. Spain
88	D2	Gatchina Russia
98	C1	Gateshead U.K.
139	D2	Gatesville U.S.A.
130	C2	Gatineau r. Can.
53	D1	Gatton Austr.
129	E2	Gauer Lake Can.
93	E4	Gausta mt. Norway
123	C2	Gauteng prov. S. Africa
111	B3	Gavdos i. Greece
93	G3	Gävle Sweden
89	E2	Gavrilov Posad Russia
89	E2	Gavrilov-Yam Russia
62	A1	Gawai Myanmar
52	A2	Gawler Austr.
52	A2	Gawler Ranges hills Austr.
75	C2	Gaya India
114	C3	Gaya Niger
140	C1	Gaylord U.S.A.
86	E2	Gayny Russia
80	B2	Gaza disp. terr. Asia
80	B2	Gaziantep Turkey
76	C2	Gazojak Turkm.
114	B4	Gbarnga Liberia
103	D1	Gdańsk Pol.
88	A3	Gdańsk, Gulf of Pol./Russia
88	C2	Gdov Russia
103	D1	Gdynia Pol.
117	B3	Gedaref Sudan
101	D2	Gedern Ger.
111	C3	Gediz r. Turkey
102	C1	Gedser Denmark
100	B2	Geel Belgium
52	B3	Geelong Austr.
101	E1	Geesthacht Ger.
75	C1	Gê'gyai China
129	D2	Geikie r. Can.
93	E3	Geilo Norway
62	B1	Gejiu China
108	B3	Gela Sicily Italy
91	D3	Gelendzhik Russia
		Gelibolu Turkey see Gallipoli
100	C2	Gelsenkirchen Ger.
118	B2	Gemena Dem. Rep. Congo
111	C2	Gemlik Turkey
117	C4	Genalē Wenz r. Eth.
153	B4	General Acha Arg.
153	B4	General Alvear Arg.
153	C4	General Belgrano Arg.
144	B2	General Cepeda Mex.
153	B4	General Pico Arg.
153	B4	General Roca Arg.
64	B2	General Santos Phil.
141	D2	Genesee r. U.S.A.
141	D2	Geneseo U.S.A.
105	D2	Geneva Switz.
141	D2	Geneva U.S.A.
105	D2	Geneva, Lake France/Switz.
		Genève Switz. see Geneva
106	B2	Genil r. Spain
100	B2	Genk Belgium
108	A2	Genoa Italy
		Genova Italy see Genoa
101	F1	Genthin Ger.
50	A3	Geographe Bay Austr.
65	B2	Geongju S. Korea
131	D1	George r. Can.
122	B3	George S. Africa
143	D3	George, Lake FL U.S.A.
141	E2	George, Lake NY U.S.A.
151	C1	Georgetown Guyana
60	B1	George Town Malaysia
143	E2	Georgetown SC U.S.A.
139	D2	Georgetown TX U.S.A.
55	I2	George V Land reg. Antarctica
81	C1	Georgia country Asia
143	D2	Georgia state U.S.A.
130	B2	Georgian Bay Can.
51	C2	Georgina watercourse Austr.
77	E2	Georgiyevka Kazakh.
87	D4	Georgiyevsk Russia
101	F2	Gera Ger.
151	D3	Geral de Goiás, Serra hills Brazil
54	B2	Geraldine N.Z.
50	A2	Geraldton Austr.
80	B1	Gerede Turkey
135	C2	Gerlach U.S.A.
103	E2	Gerlachovský štít mt. Slovakia
102	C1	Germany country Europe
100	C2	Gerolstein Ger.
101	E3	Gerolzhofen Ger.
101	D2	Gersfeld (Rhön) Ger.
75	C1	Gêrzê China
117	C4	Gestro Wenz, Wabê r. Eth.
141	D3	Gettysburg PA U.S.A.
136	D1	Gettysburg SD U.S.A.
109	D2	Gevgelija Macedonia
111	C3	Geyikli Turkey
122	B2	Ghaap Plateau S. Africa
115	C1	Ghadāmis Libya
75	C2	Ghaghara r. India
114	B4	Ghana country Africa
120	B3	Ghanzi Botswana
115	C1	Ghardaïa Alg.
115	D1	Gharyān Libya
115	D1	Ghāt Libya
75	B2	Ghaziabad India
75	C2	Ghazipur India
77	C3	Ghaznī Afgh.
100	A2	Ghent Belgium
110	B1	Gherla Romania
108	A2	Ghisonaccia Corsica France
74	B2	Ghotaru India
74	A2	Ghotki Pak.
91	E3	Giaginskaya Russia
97	C1	Giant's Causeway lava field U.K.
61	C2	Gianyar Indon.
109	C3	Giarre Sicily Italy
108	A1	Giaveno Italy
122	A2	Gibeon Namibia
106	B2	Gibraltar Gibraltar
106	B2	Gibraltar, Strait of Morocco/Spain
50	B2	Gibson Desert Austr.
68	C1	Gichgeniyn Nuruu mts Mongolia
117	B4	Gīdolē Eth.
104	C2	Gien France
101	D2	Gießen Ger.
101	E1	Gifhorn Ger.
128	C2	Gift Lake Can.
67	C3	Gifu Japan
96	B3	Gigha i. U.K.
106	B1	Gijón/Xixón Spain
138	A2	Gila r. U.S.A.
138	A2	Gila Bend U.S.A.
51	D1	Gilbert r. Austr.
49	F2	Gilbert Islands is Kiribati
134	D1	Gildford U.S.A.
53	C2	Gilgandra Austr.
74	B1	Gilgit Pak.
74	B1	Gilgit r. Pak.
53	C2	Gilgunnia Austr.
129	C2	Gillam Can.
136	B2	Gillette U.S.A.
99	D3	Gillingham U.K.
65	B2	Gimcheon S. Korea
129	E2	Gimli Can.
117	C4	Ginīr Eth.
109	C2	Ginosa Italy
53	C3	Gippsland reg. Austr.
74	A2	Girdar Dhor r. Pak.
80	B1	Giresun Turkey
74	A1	Girishk Afgh.
107	D1	Girona Spain
96	B3	Girvan U.K.
54	C1	Gisborne N.Z.
93	F4	Gislaved Sweden
119	C3	Gitarama Rwanda
108	B2	Giulianova Italy
110	C2	Giurgiu Romania
110	C1	Giuvala, Pasul pass Romania
105	C2	Givors France
123	D1	Giyani S. Africa
116	B2	Giza Egypt
109	D2	Gjakovë Kosovo
109	D2	Gjilan Kosovo

109 D2 **Gjirokastër** Albania
126 E2 **Gjoa Haven** Can.
93 F3 **Gjøvik** Norway
131 E2 **Glace Bay** Can.
134 B1 **Glacier Peak** *vol.* U.S.A.
51 E2 **Gladstone** Austr.
92 □A2 **Gláma** *mts* Iceland
109 C2 **Glamoč** Bos. & Herz.
100 C3 **Glan** *r.* Ger.
97 B2 **Glanaruddery Mountains** *hills* Ireland
96 B3 **Glasgow** U.K.
140 B3 **Glasgow** *KY* U.S.A.
136 B1 **Glasgow** *MT* U.S.A.
99 B3 **Glastonbury** U.K.
101 F2 **Glauchau** Ger.
86 E3 **Glazov** Russia
89 E3 **Glazunovka** Russia
96 B2 **Glen Coe** *val.* U.K.
138 A2 **Glendale** U.S.A.
53 D2 **Glen Davis** Austr.
136 C1 **Glendive** U.S.A.
52 B3 **Glenelg** *r.* Austr.
53 D1 **Glen Innes** Austr.
126 B2 **Glennallen** U.S.A.
96 C2 **Glenrothes** U.K.
141 E2 **Glens Falls** U.S.A.
96 C2 **Glen Shee** *val.* U.K.
97 B1 **Glenties** Ireland
138 B2 **Glenwood** U.S.A.
136 B3 **Glenwood Springs** U.S.A.
103 D1 **Gliwice** Pol.
138 A2 **Globe** U.S.A.
103 D1 **Głogów** Pol.
92 F2 **Glomfjord** Norway
93 F4 **Glomma** *r.* Norway
53 D2 **Gloucester** Austr.
99 B3 **Gloucester** U.K.
101 F1 **Glöwen** Ger.
77 E1 **Glubokoye** Kazakh.
101 D1 **Glückstadt** Ger.
103 C2 **Gmünd** Austria
102 C2 **Gmunden** Austria
101 D1 **Gnarrenburg** Ger.
103 D1 **Gniezno** Pol.
75 D2 **Goalpara** India
96 B3 **Goat Fell** *h.* U.K.
117 C4 **Goba** Eth.
120 A3 **Gobabis** Namibia
153 A5 **Gobernador Gregores** Arg.
69 D2 **Gobi** *des.* China/Mongolia
100 C2 **Goch** Ger.
122 A1 **Gochas** Namibia
74 B3 **Godavari** *r.* India
73 C3 **Godavari, Mouths of the** India
130 B2 **Goderich** Can.
74 B2 **Godhra** India
129 E2 **Gods** *r.* Can.
129 E2 **Gods Lake** Can.
Godthåb Greenland *see* **Nuuk**
Godwin-Austen, Mount China/Pak. *see* **K2**
130 C2 **Goéland, Lac au** *l.* Can.
131 D1 **Goélands, Lac aux** *l.* Can.
100 A2 **Goes** Neth.
154 C1 **Goiandira** Brazil
154 C1 **Goiânia** Brazil
154 B1 **Goiás** Brazil
154 B2 **Goioerê** Brazil
111 C2 **Gökçeada** *i.* Turkey
111 C3 **Gökçedağ** Turkey
121 B2 **Gokwe** Zimbabwe
93 E3 **Gol** Norway
62 A1 **Golaghat** India
111 C2 **Gölcük** Turkey
103 E1 **Gołdap** Pol.
101 F1 **Goldberg** Ger.
53 D1 **Gold Coast** Austr.
114 B4 **Gold Coast** Ghana
128 C2 **Golden** Can.
54 B2 **Golden Bay** N.Z.
128 B3 **Golden Hinde** *mt.* Can.
97 B2 **Golden Vale** *lowland* Ireland
135 C3 **Goldfield** U.S.A.
128 B3 **Gold River** Can.
143 E1 **Goldsboro** U.S.A.
135 C4 **Goleta** U.S.A.
68 C2 **Golmud** China
81 D2 **Golpāyegān** Iran
96 C2 **Golspie** U.K.
119 C3 **Goma** Dem. Rep. Congo
75 C2 **Gomati** *r.* India
115 D3 **Gombe** Nigeria
115 D3 **Gombi** Nigeria
Gomel' Belarus *see* **Homyel'**
144 B2 **Gómez Palacio** Mex.
147 C3 **Gonaïves** Haiti
147 C3 **Gonâve, Île de la** *i.* Haiti
81 D2 **Gonbad-e Kāvūs** Iran
117 B3 **Gonder** Eth.
75 C2 **Gondiya** India
111 C2 **Gönen** Turkey
65 B2 **Gongju** S. Korea
115 D4 **Gongola** *r.* Nigeria
53 C2 **Gongolgon** Austr.
75 D1 **Gongtang** China
145 C2 **Gonzáles** Mex.
139 D3 **Gonzales** U.S.A.
122 A3 **Good Hope, Cape of** S. Africa
134 D2 **Gooding** U.S.A.
136 C3 **Goodland** U.S.A.
53 C1 **Goodooga** Austr.
98 C2 **Goole** U.K.
53 C2 **Goolgowi** Austr.
52 A3 **Goolwa** Austr.
53 D1 **Goondiwindi** Austr.
134 B2 **Goose Lake** U.S.A.
102 B2 **Göppingen** Ger.
75 C2 **Gorakhpur** India
109 C2 **Goražde** Bos. & Herz.
111 C3 **Gördes** Turkey
89 D3 **Gordeyevka** Russia
51 D4 **Gordon, Lake** Austr.
115 D4 **Goré** Chad
117 B4 **Gorē** Eth.
54 A3 **Gore** N.Z.
97 C2 **Gorey** Ireland
81 D2 **Gorgān** Iran
81 C1 **Gori** Georgia
108 B1 **Gorizia** Italy
Gor'kiy Russia *see* **Nizhniy Novgorod**
103 E2 **Gorlice** Pol.
103 C1 **Görlitz** Ger.
109 D2 **Gornji Milanovac** Serbia
109 C2 **Gornji Vakuf** Bos. & Herz.
77 E1 **Gorno-Altaysk** Russia
110 C2 **Gornotrakiyska Nizina** *lowland* Bulg.
77 E1 **Gornyak** Russia
59 D3 **Goroka** P.N.G.
114 B3 **Gorom Gorom** Burkina Faso
59 C2 **Gorontalo** Indon.
89 E3 **Gorshechnoye** Russia
97 B2 **Gorumna Island** Ireland
91 D3 **Goryachiy Klyuch** Russia
65 B2 **Goryeong** S. Korea
103 D1 **Gorzów Wielkopolski** Pol.
53 D2 **Gosford** Austr.
66 D2 **Goshogawara** Japan
101 E2 **Goslar** Ger.
109 C2 **Gospić** Croatia
99 C3 **Gosport** U.K.
109 D2 **Gostivar** Macedonia
Göteborg Sweden *see* **Gothenburg**
101 E2 **Gotha** Ger.
93 F4 **Gothenburg** Sweden
136 C2 **Gothenburg** U.S.A.
93 G4 **Gotland** *i.* Sweden
111 B2 **Gotse Delchev** Bulg.
93 G4 **Gotska Sandön** *i.* Sweden
67 B4 **Gōtsu** Japan
101 D2 **Göttingen** Ger.
128 B2 **Gott Peak** Can.
100 B1 **Gouda** Neth.
114 A3 **Goudiri** Senegal
115 D3 **Goudoumaria** Niger
130 C2 **Gouin, Réservoir** *resr* Can.
53 C2 **Goulburn** Austr.
53 B3 **Goulburn** *r.* *N.S.W.* Austr.
53 B3 **Goulburn** *r.* *Vic.* Austr.
114 B3 **Goundam** Mali
107 D2 **Gouraya** Alg.
104 C3 **Gourdon** France
115 D3 **Gouré** Niger
122 B3 **Gourits** *r.* S. Africa
114 B3 **Gourma-Rharous** Mali
53 C3 **Gourock Range** *mts* Austr.
155 D1 **Governador Valadares** Brazil
143 E3 **Governor's Harbour** Bahamas
68 C2 **Govĭ Altayn Nuruu** *mts* Mongolia
75 C2 **Govind Ballash Pant Sagar** *resr* India
99 A3 **Gower** *pen.* U.K.
152 C3 **Goya** Arg.
81 C1 **Göyçay** Azer.
75 C1 **Gozha Co** *salt l.* China
122 B3 **Graaff-Reinet** S. Africa
101 E1 **Grabow** Ger.
109 C2 **Gračac** Croatia
87 E3 **Grachevka** Russia
101 F2 **Gräfenhainichen** Ger.
53 D1 **Grafton** Austr.
137 D1 **Grafton** U.S.A.
139 D2 **Graham** U.S.A.
128 A2 **Graham Island** Can.
55 P3 **Graham Land** *pen.* Antarctica
123 C3 **Grahamstown** S. Africa
151 D2 **Grajaú** Brazil
111 B2 **Grammos** *mt.* Greece
96 B2 **Grampian Mountains** U.K.
146 B3 **Granada** Nic.
106 C2 **Granada** Spain
141 E1 **Granby** Can.
114 A2 **Gran Canaria** *i.* Canary Islands
152 B3 **Gran Chaco** *reg.* Arg./Para.
136 C1 **Grand** *r.* U.S.A.
146 C2 **Grand Bahama** *i.* Bahamas
131 E2 **Grand Bank** Can.
158 C2 **Grand Banks of Newfoundland** N. Atlantic Ocean
Grand Canal *canal* China *see* **Jinghang Yunhe**
138 A1 **Grand Canyon** U.S.A.
138 A1 **Grand Canyon** *gorge* U.S.A.
146 B3 **Grand Cayman** *i.* Cayman Is
129 C2 **Grand Centre** Can.
134 C1 **Grand Coulee** U.S.A.
152 B2 **Grande** *r.* Bol.
154 B2 **Grande** *r.* Brazil
153 B6 **Grande, Bahía** *b.* Arg.
155 D2 **Grande, Ilha** *i.* Brazil
128 C2 **Grande Cache** Can.
128 C2 **Grande Prairie** Can.
114 B1 **Grand Erg Occidental** *des.* Alg.
115 C2 **Grand Erg Oriental** *des.* Alg.
131 D2 **Grande-Rivière** Can.
152 B4 **Grandes, Salinas** *salt flat* Arg.

156 D7 **Grande Terre** *i.* S. Pacific Ocean
131 D2 **Grand Falls** Can.
131 E2 **Grand Falls-Windsor** Can.
128 C3 **Grand Forks** Can.
137 D1 **Grand Forks** U.S.A.
128 C1 **Grandin, Lac** *l.* Can.
137 D2 **Grand Island** U.S.A.
142 B3 **Grand Isle** U.S.A.
136 B3 **Grand Junction** U.S.A.
114 B4 **Grand-Lahou** Côte d'Ivoire
131 D2 **Grand Lake** *N.B.* Can.
131 E2 **Grand Lake** *Nfld. and Lab.* Can.
137 E1 **Grand Marais** U.S.A.
106 B2 **Grândola** Port.
129 E2 **Grand Rapids** Can.
140 B2 **Grand Rapids** *MI* U.S.A.
137 E1 **Grand Rapids** *MN* U.S.A.
136 A2 **Grand Teton** *mt.* U.S.A.
147 C2 **Grand Turk** Turks and Caicos Is
134 C1 **Grangeville** U.S.A.
128 B2 **Granisle** Can.
134 E1 **Granite Peak** U.S.A.
108 B3 **Granitola, Capo** *c. Sicily* Italy
93 F4 **Gränna** Sweden
101 F1 **Gransee** Ger.
99 C2 **Grantham** U.K.
96 C2 **Grantown-on-Spey** U.K.
138 B1 **Grants** U.S.A.
134 B2 **Grants Pass** U.S.A.
104 B2 **Granville** France
129 D2 **Granville Lake** Can.
155 D1 **Grão Mogol** Brazil
123 D1 **Graskop** S. Africa
105 D3 **Grasse** France
107 D1 **Graus** Spain
92 F2 **Gravdal** Norway
104 B2 **Grave, Pointe de** *pt* France
129 D3 **Gravelbourg** Can.
130 C2 **Gravenhurst** Can.
53 D1 **Gravesend** Austr.
99 D3 **Gravesend** U.K.
105 D2 **Gray** France
103 D2 **Graz** Austria
146 C2 **Great Abaco** *i.* Bahamas
50 B3 **Great Australian Bight** *g.* Austr.
54 C1 **Great Barrier Island** N.Z.
51 D1 **Great Barrier Reef** Austr.
135 C3 **Great Basin** U.S.A.
126 D2 **Great Bear Lake** Can.
93 F4 **Great Belt** *sea chan.* Denmark
137 D3 **Great Bend** U.S.A.
63 A2 **Great Coco Island** Cocos Is
53 B3 **Great Dividing Range** *mts* Austr.
146 B2 **Greater Antilles** *is* Caribbean Sea
60 A3 **Greater Sunda Islands** *is* Indon.
134 D1 **Great Falls** U.S.A.
123 C3 **Great Fish** *r.* S. Africa
123 C3 **Great Fish Point** S. Africa
147 C2 **Great Inagua** *i.* Bahamas
122 B3 **Great Karoo** *plat.* S. Africa
123 C3 **Great Kei** *r.* S. Africa
99 B2 **Great Malvern** U.K.
122 A2 **Great Namaqualand** *reg.* Namibia
63 A3 **Great Nicobar** *i.* India
99 D2 **Great Ouse** *r.* U.K.
119 D3 **Great Rift Valley** Africa
119 D3 **Great Ruaha** *r.* Tanz.
134 D2 **Great Salt Lake** U.S.A.
135 D2 **Great Salt Lake Desert** U.S.A.
116 A2 **Great Sand Sea** *des.* Egypt/Libya
50 B2 **Great Sandy Desert** Austr.
128 C1 **Great Slave Lake** Can.
143 D1 **Great Smoky Mountains** U.S.A.
50 B2 **Great Victoria Desert** Austr.
70 B1 **Great Wall** *tourist site* China
99 D2 **Great Yarmouth** U.K.
106 B1 **Gredos, Sierra de** *mts* Spain
111 B3 **Greece** *country* Europe
136 C2 **Greeley** U.S.A.
82 F1 **Greem-Bell, Ostrov** *i.* Russia
140 B3 **Green** *r. KY* U.S.A.
136 B3 **Green** *r. WY* U.S.A.
140 B2 **Green Bay** U.S.A.
140 B1 **Green Bay** U.S.A.
140 C3 **Greenbrier** *r.* U.S.A.
140 B3 **Greencastle** U.S.A.
143 D1 **Greeneville** U.S.A.
141 E2 **Greenfield** U.S.A.
129 D2 **Green Lake** Can.
127 I2 **Greenland** *terr.* N. America
160 R2 **Greenland Sea** Greenland/Svalbard
96 B3 **Greenock** U.K.
135 D3 **Green River** *UT* U.S.A.
136 B2 **Green River** *WY* U.S.A.
140 B3 **Greensburg** *IN* U.S.A.
141 D2 **Greensburg** *PA* U.S.A.
143 E2 **Green Swamp** U.S.A.
138 A2 **Green Valley** U.S.A.
114 B4 **Greenville** Liberia
142 C2 **Greenville** *AL* U.S.A.
142 B2 **Greenville** *MS* U.S.A.
143 E1 **Greenville** *NC* U.S.A.
143 D2 **Greenville** *SC* U.S.A.
139 D2 **Greenville** *TX* U.S.A.
53 D2 **Greenwell Point** Austr.
143 D2 **Greenwood** U.S.A.
50 B2 **Gregory, Lake** *imp. l.* Austr.
51 D1 **Gregory Range** *hills* Austr.
102 C1 **Greifswald** Ger.
101 F2 **Greiz** Ger.
93 F4 **Grenaa** Denmark
142 C2 **Grenada** U.S.A.
147 D3 **Grenada** *country* West Indies
104 C3 **Grenade** France
53 C2 **Grenfell** Austr.
129 D2 **Grenfell** Can.
105 D2 **Grenoble** France
51 D1 **Grenville, Cape** Austr.
134 B1 **Gresham** U.S.A.
100 C1 **Greven** Ger.
111 B2 **Grevena** Greece
100 C2 **Grevenbroich** Ger.
101 E1 **Grevesmühlen** Ger.
136 B2 **Greybull** U.S.A.
128 A1 **Grey Hunter Peak** Can.
131 E1 **Grey Islands** Can.
54 B2 **Greymouth** N.Z.
52 B1 **Grey Range** *hills* Austr.
97 C2 **Greystones** Ireland
143 D2 **Griffin** U.S.A.
53 C2 **Griffith** Austr.
101 F2 **Grimma** Ger.
102 C1 **Grimmen** Ger.
98 C2 **Grimsby** U.K.
128 C2 **Grimshaw** Can.
92 □B2 **Grímsstaðir** Iceland
93 E4 **Grimstad** Norway
137 E2 **Grinnell** U.S.A.
123 C3 **Griqualand East** *reg.* S. Africa
122 B2 **Griqualand West** *reg.* S. Africa
127 F1 **Grise Fiord** Can.
96 C1 **Gritley** U.K.
123 C2 **Groblersdal** S. Africa
122 B2 **Groblershoop** S. Africa
Grodno Belarus *see* **Hrodna**
104 B2 **Groix, Île de** *i.* France
100 C1 **Gronau (Westfalen)** Ger.
92 F3 **Grong** Norway
100 C1 **Groningen** Neth.
122 B2 **Grootdrink** S. Africa
51 C1 **Groote Eylandt** *i.* Austr.
120 A2 **Grootfontein** Namibia
122 A2 **Groot Karas Berg** *plat.* Namibia
122 B3 **Groot Swartberge** *mts* S. Afric
123 C3 **Groot Winterberg** *mt.* S. Afric
101 D2 **Großenlüder** Ger.
102 C2 **Großer Rachel** *mt.* Ger.
103 C2 **Grosser Speikkogel** *mt.* Austria
108 B2 **Grosseto** Italy
101 D3 **Groß-Gerau** Ger.
102 C2 **Großglockner** *mt.* Austria
100 C1 **Groß Hesepe** Ger.
101 E2 **Großlohra** Ger.
122 A1 **Gross Ums** Namibia
131 E1 **Groswater Bay** Can.
130 B2 **Groundhog** *r.* Can.
49 I4 **Groupe Actéon** *is* Fr. Polynesia
135 B3 **Grover Beach** U.S.A.
141 E2 **Groveton** U.S.A.
87 D4 **Groznyy** Russia
109 C1 **Grubišno Polje** Croatia
103 D1 **Grudziądz** Pol.
122 A2 **Grünau** Namibia
92 □A3 **Grundarfjörður** Iceland
89 E3 **Gryazi** Russia
89 F2 **Gryazovets** Russia
103 D1 **Gryfice** Pol.
102 C1 **Gryfino** Pol.
146 C2 **Guacanayabo, Golfo de** *b.* Cuba
144 B2 **Guadalajara** Mex.
106 C1 **Guadalajara** *prov.* Spain
49 E3 **Guadalcanal** *i.* Solomon Is
107 C1 **Guadalope** *r.* Spain
106 B2 **Guadalquivir** *r.* Spain
132 B4 **Guadalupe** *i.* Mex.
106 B2 **Guadalupe, Sierra de** *mts* Spain
138 C2 **Guadalupe Peak** U.S.A.
144 B2 **Guadalupe Victoria** Mex.
144 B2 **Guadalupe y Calvo** Mex.
106 C1 **Guadarrama, Sierra de** *mts* Spain
147 D3 **Guadeloupe** *terr.* West Indies
106 B2 **Guadiana** *r.* Port./Spain
106 C2 **Guadix** Spain
154 B2 **Guaíra** Brazil
147 C3 **Guajira, Península de la** *pen.* Col.
150 A2 **Gualaceo** Ecuador
59 D2 **Guam** *terr.* N. Pacific Ocean
144 B2 **Guamúchil** Mex.
144 B2 **Guanacevi** Mex.
151 D3 **Guanambi** Brazil
150 B1 **Guanare** Venez.
146 B2 **Guane** Cuba
70 A2 **Guang'an** China
71 B3 **Guangchang** China
71 B3 **Guangdong** *prov.* China
71 A3 **Guangxi Zhuangzu Zizhiqu** *aut. reg.* China
70 A2 **Guangyuan** China
71 B3 **Guangzhou** China
155 D1 **Guanhães** Brazil
147 D4 **Guanipa** *r.* Venez.
71 A3 **Guanling** China
65 A1 **Guanshui** China
Guansuo China *see* **Guanling**
147 C2 **Guantánamo** Cuba

150 B3 Guaporé r. Bol./Brazil
154 B3 Guarapuava Brazil
154 C3 Guaraqueçaba Brazil
155 C2 Guaratinguetá Brazil
106 B1 Guarda Port.
154 C1 Guarda-Mor Brazil
106 C1 Guardo Spain
155 C2 Guarujá Brazil
144 B2 Guasave Mex.
146 A3 Guatemala country Central America
146 A3 Guatemala City Guat.
150 B1 Guaviare r. Col.
155 C2 Guaxupé Brazil
150 A2 Guayaquil Ecuador
150 B3 Guayaramerín Bol.
144 A2 Guaymas Mex.
68 C2 Guazhou China
117 B3 Guba Eth.
86 E1 Guba Dolgaya Russia
89 E3 Gubkin Russia
115 C1 Guelma Alg.
114 A2 Guelmim Morocco
130 B2 Guelph Can.
145 C2 Guémez Mex.
104 C2 Guéret France
95 C4 Guernsey terr. Channel Is
144 A2 Guerrero Negro Mex.
131 D1 Guers, Lac l. Can.
79 C2 Gūhrān Iran
118 B2 Guider Cameroon
108 B2 Guidonia Montecelio Italy
71 A3 Guigang China
100 A3 Guignicourt France
123 D1 Guija Moz.
99 C3 Guildford U.K.
71 B3 Guilin China
130 C1 Guillaume-Delisle, Lac l. Can.
106 B1 Guimarães Port.
114 A3 Guinea country Africa
113 F6 Guinea, Gulf of Africa
114 A3 Guinea-Bissau country Africa
104 B2 Guingamp France
104 B2 Guipavas France
154 B1 Guiratinga Brazil
150 B1 Güiria Venez.
100 A3 Guise France
64 B1 Guiuan Phil.
71 A3 Guiyang China
71 A3 Guizhou prov. China
74 B1 Gujranwala Pak.
74 B1 Gujrat Pak.
91 D2 Gukovo Russia
53 C2 Gulargambone Austr.
73 B3 Gulbarga India
88 C2 Gulbene Latvia
79 C2 Gulf, the Asia
111 B3 Gulf of Corinth sea chan. Greece
142 C2 Gulfport U.S.A.
69 E1 Gulian China
77 C2 Guliston Uzbek.
Gulja China see Yining
129 D2 Gull Lake Can.
111 C3 Güllük Turkey
119 D2 Gulu Uganda
120 B2 Gumare Botswana
76 B3 Gumdag Turkm.
65 B2 Gumi S. Korea
75 C2 Gumla India
100 C2 Gummersbach Ger.
74 B2 Guna India
53 C3 Gundagai Austr.
111 C3 Güney Turkey
118 B3 Gungu Dem. Rep. Congo
129 E2 Gunisao r. Can.
53 D2 Gunnedah Austr.
136 B3 Gunnison CO U.S.A.
135 D3 Gunnison UT U.S.A.
136 B3 Gunnison r. U.S.A.
65 B2 Gunsan S. Korea
73 B3 Guntakal India
60 A1 Gunungsitoli Indon.
60 A1 Gunungtua Indon.
102 C2 Günzburg Ger.
102 C2 Gunzenhausen Ger.
70 B2 Guojiaba China
74 B2 Gurgaon India
151 D2 Gurgueia r. Brazil
150 B1 Guri, Embalse de resr Venez.
154 C1 Gurinhatã Brazil
151 D2 Gurupi r. Brazil
74 B2 Guru Sikhar mt. India
Gur'yev Kazakh. see Atyrau
115 C3 Gusau Nigeria
65 A2 Gushan China
70 B2 Gushi China
83 I3 Gusinoozersk Russia
89 F2 Gus'-Khrustal'nyy Russia
108 A3 Guspini Sardinia Italy
128 A2 Gustavus U.S.A.
101 F1 Güstrow Ger.
101 D2 Gütersloh Ger.
121 C2 Gutu Mupandawana Zimbabwe
75 D2 Guwahati India
150 C1 Guyana country S. America
Guyi China see Sanjiang
139 C1 Guymon U.S.A.
53 D2 Guyra Austr.
70 A2 Guyuan China
144 B1 Guzmán Mex.
74 A2 Gwadar Pak.
128 A2 Gwaii Haanas Can.
75 B2 Gwalior India
121 B3 Gwanda Zimbabwe
65 B2 Gwangju S. Korea
117 D3 Gwardafuy, Gees c. Somalia
97 B1 Gweebarra Bay Ireland
121 B2 Gweru Zimbabwe
115 D3 Gwoza Nigeria
53 D2 Gwydir r. Austr.
75 C2 Gyangzê China
75 C1 Gyaring Co l. China
68 C2 Gyaring Hu l. China
86 G1 Gydan Peninsula Russia
Gydanskiy Poluostrov pen. Russia see Gydan Peninsula
Gyêgu China see Yushu
65 B2 Gyeonggi-man b. S. Korea
51 E2 Gympie Austr.
103 D2 Gyöngyös Hungary
103 D2 Gyr Hungary
129 E2 Gypsumville Can.
103 E2 Gyula Hungary
81 C1 Gyumri Armenia

H

88 B2 Haapsalu Estonia
100 B1 Haarlem Neth.
101 C2 Haarstrang ridge Ger.
54 A2 Haast N.Z.
78 B3 Ḥabbān Yemen
81 C2 Ḥabbānīyah, Hawr al l. Iraq
67 C4 Hachijō-jima i. Japan
66 D2 Hachinohe Japan
81 C1 Hacıqabul Azer.
121 C3 Hacufera Moz.
79 C2 Ḥadd, Ra's al pt Oman
96 C3 Haddington U.K.
115 D3 Hadejia Nigeria
93 E4 Haderslev Denmark
91 C1 Hadyach Ukr.
65 B2 Haeju N. Korea
65 B2 Haeju-man b. N. Korea
65 B3 Haenam S. Korea
78 B2 Ḥafar al Bāṭin Saudi Arabia
62 A1 Haflong India
92 □A3 Hafnarfjörður Iceland
78 A3 Hagar Nish Plateau Eritrea/Sudan
48 D2 Hagåtña Guam
100 C2 Hagen Ger.
101 E1 Hagenow Ger.
128 B2 Hagensborg Can.
141 D3 Hagerstown U.S.A.
93 F3 Hagfors Sweden
67 B4 Hagi Japan
62 B1 Ha Giang Vietnam
97 B2 Hag's Head Ireland
104 B2 Hague, Cap de la c. France
119 D3 Hai Tanz.
128 A2 Haida Gwaii Can.
62 B1 Hai Dương Vietnam
80 B2 Haifa Israel
71 B3 Haifeng China
71 B3 Haikou China
78 B2 Ḥā'il Saudi Arabia
92 H2 Hailuoto i. Fin.
71 A4 Hainan prov. China
69 D3 Hainan Dao i. China
128 A2 Haines U.S.A.
128 A1 Haines Junction Can.
101 E2 Hainich ridge Ger.
101 E2 Hainleite ridge Ger.
62 B1 Hai Phong Vietnam
147 C3 Haiti country West Indies
116 B3 Haiya Sudan
103 E2 Hajdúböszörmény Hungary
78 B3 Ḥajjah Yemen
79 C2 Ḥājjīābād Iran
62 A1 Haka Myanmar
81 C2 Hakkâri Turkey
66 D2 Hakodate Japan
Ḥalab Syria see Aleppo
78 B2 Halabān Saudi Arabia
81 C2 Ḥalabjah/Hełebce Iraq
116 B2 Ḥalā'ib Sudan
78 A2 Halaib Triangle terr. Egypt/Sudan
79 C3 Ḥalāniyāt, Juzur al is Oman
78 A2 Ḥālat 'Ammār Saudi Arabia
101 E2 Halberstadt Ger.
64 B1 Halcon, Mount Phil.
93 F4 Halden Norway
101 E1 Haldensleben Ger.
75 B2 Haldwani India
79 C2 Hāleh Iran
54 A3 Halfmoon Bay N.Z.
131 D2 Halifax Can.
98 C2 Halifax U.K.
141 D3 Halifax U.S.A.
65 B3 Halla-san mt. S. Korea
127 F2 Hall Beach Can.
100 B2 Halle Belgium
101 E2 Halle (Saale) Ger.
102 C2 Hallein Austria
137 D1 Hallock U.S.A.
127 G2 Hall Peninsula Can.
50 B1 Halls Creek Austr.
59 C2 Halmahera i. Indon.
93 F4 Halmstad Sweden
62 B1 Ha Long Vietnam
67 B4 Hamada Japan
81 C2 Hamadān Iran
80 B2 Ḥamāh Syria
67 C4 Hamamatsu Japan
93 F3 Hamar Norway
116 B2 Ḥamāṭah, Jabal mt. Egypt
73 C4 Hambantota Sri Lanka

101 D1 **Hamburg** Ger.
78 A2 **Ḩamḑ, Wādī al** *watercourse* Saudi Arabia
78 B3 **Ḩamḑah** Saudi Arabia
93 H3 **Hämeenlinna** Fin.
101 D1 **Hameln** Ger.
50 A2 **Hamersley Range** *mts* Austr.
65 B2 **Hamhŭng** N. Korea
68 C2 **Hami** China
116 B2 **Hamid** Sudan
52 B3 **Hamilton** Austr.
130 C2 **Hamilton** Can.
54 C1 **Hamilton** N.Z.
96 B3 **Hamilton** U.K.
142 C2 **Hamilton** *AL* U.S.A.
134 D1 **Hamilton** *MT* U.S.A.
140 C3 **Hamilton** *OH* U.S.A.
93 I3 **Hamina** Fin.
100 C2 **Hamm** Ger.
81 C2 **Ḩammār, Hawr al** *imp. l.* Iraq
101 D2 **Hammelburg** Ger.
92 G3 **Hammerdal** Sweden
92 H1 **Hammerfest** Norway
142 B2 **Hammond** U.S.A.
141 E3 **Hammonton** U.S.A.
115 D2 **Ḩamrā', Al Ḩamādah al** *plat.* Libya
78 A2 **Ḩanak** Saudi Arabia
66 D3 **Hanamaki** Japan
101 D2 **Hanau** Ger.
69 D2 **Hanbogd** Mongolia
70 B2 **Hancheng** China
140 B1 **Hancock** U.S.A.
70 B2 **Handan** China
135 C3 **Hanford** U.S.A.
68 C1 **Hangayn Nuruu** *mts* Mongolia
Hanggin Houqi China *see* **Xamba**
Hangö Fin. *see* **Hanko**
70 C2 **Hangzhou** China
70 C2 **Hangzhou Wan** *b.* China
Hanjia China *see* **Pengshui**
Hanjiang China *see* **Yangzhou**
93 H4 **Hanko** Fin.
135 D3 **Hanksville** U.S.A.
54 B2 **Hanmer Springs** N.Z.
129 C2 **Hanna** Can.
137 E3 **Hannibal** U.S.A.
101 D1 **Hannover** Ger.
101 D2 **Hannoversch Münden** Ger.
93 F4 **Hanöbukten** *b.* Sweden
62 B1 **Ha Nôi** Vietnam
Hanoi Vietnam *see* **Ha Nôi**
130 B2 **Hanover** Can.
122 B3 **Hanover** S. Africa
93 E4 **Hanstholm** Denmark
88 C3 **Hantsavichy** Belarus
75 C2 **Hanumana** India
74 B2 **Hanumangarh** India
70 A2 **Hanzhong** China
92 H2 **Haparanda** Sweden
100 B2 **Hapert** Neth.
131 D1 **Happy Valley-Goose Bay** Can.
78 A2 **Ḩaql** Saudi Arabia
79 B2 **Ḩaraḑh** Saudi Arabia
88 C2 **Haradok** Belarus
78 B3 **Ḩarajā** Saudi Arabia
121 C2 **Harare** Zimbabwe
79 C3 **Ḩarāsīs, Jiddat al** *des.* Oman
69 E1 **Harbin** China
131 E2 **Harbour Breton** Can.
74 B2 **Harda** India
Hardangerfjorden *sea chan.* Norway
100 C1 **Hardenberg** Neth.
100 B1 **Harderwijk** Neth.
122 A3 **Hardeveld** *mts* S. Africa
134 E1 **Hardin** U.S.A.
128 C1 **Hardisty Lake** Can.
100 C1 **Haren (Ems)** Ger.
117 C4 **Hārer** Eth.
117 C4 **Hargeysa** Somalia
110 C1 **Harghita-Mădăraş, Vârful** *mt.* Romania
68 C2 **Har Hu** *l.* China
74 B1 **Haripur** Pak.
74 A1 **Harī Rōd** *r.* Afgh./Iran
100 B1 **Harlingen** Neth.
139 D3 **Harlingen** U.S.A.
99 D3 **Harlow** U.K.
134 E1 **Harlowton** U.S.A.
110 C2 **Harmanli** Bulg.
134 C2 **Harney Basin** U.S.A.
134 C2 **Harney Lake** U.S.A.
93 G3 **Härnösand** Sweden
69 E1 **Har Nur** China
68 C1 **Har Nuur** *l.* Mongolia
114 B4 **Harper** Liberia
101 D1 **Harpstedt** Ger.
130 C1 **Harricana, Rivière d'** *r.* Can.
53 D2 **Harrington** Austr.
131 E1 **Harrington Harbour** Can.
96 A2 **Harris, Sound of** *sea chan.* U.K.
140 B3 **Harrisburg** *IL* U.S.A.
141 D2 **Harrisburg** *PA* U.S.A.
123 C2 **Harrismith** S. Africa
142 B1 **Harrison** U.S.A.
131 E1 **Harrison, Cape** Can.
126 A2 **Harrison Bay** U.S.A.
141 D3 **Harrisonburg** U.S.A.
137 E3 **Harrisonville** U.S.A.
98 C2 **Harrogate** U.K.
110 C2 **Hârşova** Romania
92 G2 **Harstad** Norway
122 B2 **Hartbees** *watercourse* S. Africa
103 D2 **Hartberg** Austria
141 E2 **Hartford** U.S.A.
99 A3 **Hartland Point** U.K.
98 C1 **Hartlepool** U.K.
128 B2 **Hartley Bay** Can.
123 B2 **Harts** *r.* S. Africa
143 D2 **Hartwell Reservoir** U.S.A.
68 C1 **Har Us Nuur** *l.* Mongolia
136 C1 **Harvey** U.S.A.
99 D3 **Harwich** U.K.
101 E2 **Harz** *hills* Ger.
110 C2 **Haskovo** Bulg.
73 B3 **Hassan** India
100 B2 **Hasselt** Belgium
115 C1 **Hassi Messaoud** Alg.
93 F4 **Hässleholm** Sweden
100 B2 **Hastière-Lavaux** Belgium
53 C3 **Hastings** Austr.
54 C1 **Hastings** N.Z.
99 D3 **Hastings** U.K.
137 E2 **Hastings** *MN* U.S.A.
137 D2 **Hastings** *NE* U.S.A.
Hatay Turkey *see* **Antakya**
129 D2 **Hatchet Lake** Can.
52 B2 **Hatfield** Austr.
68 C1 **Hatgal** Mongolia
62 B2 **Ha Tinh** Vietnam
143 E1 **Hatteras, Cape** U.S.A.
142 C2 **Hattiesburg** U.S.A.
100 C2 **Hattingen** Ger.
63 B3 **Hat Yai** Thai.
117 C4 **Haud** *reg.* Eth.
93 E4 **Haugesund** Norway
93 E4 **Haukeligrend** Norway
92 I2 **Haukipudas** Fin.
54 C1 **Hauraki Gulf** N.Z.
114 B1 **Haut Atlas** *mts* Morocco
131 D2 **Hauterive** Can.
114 B1 **Hauts Plateaux** Alg.
146 B2 **Havana** Cuba
99 C3 **Havant** U.K.
101 E1 **Havel** *r.* Ger.
101 F1 **Havelberg** Ger.
54 B2 **Havelock** N.Z.
54 C1 **Havelock North** N.Z.
99 A3 **Haverfordwest** U.K.
103 D2 **Havlíčkův Brod** Czech Rep.
92 H1 **Havøysund** Norway
111 C3 **Havran** Turkey
134 E1 **Havre** U.S.A.
131 D2 **Havre-Aubert** Can.
131 D1 **Havre-St-Pierre** Can.
124 E5 **Hawai'i** *i.* U.S.A.
124 E5 **Hawai'ian Islands** N. Pacific Ocean
98 B2 **Hawarden** U.K.
54 A2 **Hawea, Lake** N.Z.
54 B1 **Hawera** N.Z.
98 B1 **Hawes** U.K.
96 C3 **Hawick** U.K.
54 C1 **Hawke Bay** N.Z.
52 A2 **Hawker** Austr.
52 B1 **Hawkers Gate** Austr.
135 C3 **Hawthorne** U.S.A.
52 B2 **Hay** Austr.
128 C1 **Hay** *r.* Can.
134 C1 **Hayden** U.S.A.
129 E2 **Hayes** *r. Man.* Can.
126 E2 **Hayes** *r. Nunavut* Can.
79 C3 **Haymā'** Oman
77 C2 **Hayotboshi tog'i** *mt.* Uzbek.
111 C2 **Hayrabolu** Turkey
128 C1 **Hay River** Can.
137 D3 **Hays** U.S.A.
78 B3 **Ḩays** Yemen
90 B2 **Haysyn** Ukr.
99 C3 **Haywards Heath** U.K.
81 D2 **Hazar** Turkm.
74 A1 **Hazārah Jāt** *reg.* Afgh.
140 C3 **Hazard** U.S.A.
75 C2 **Hazaribagh** India
75 C2 **Hazaribagh Range** *mts* India
128 B2 **Hazelton** Can.
141 D2 **Hazleton** U.S.A.
78 B3 **Ḩazm al Jawf** Yemen
53 C3 **Healesville** Austr.
130 B2 **Hearst** Can.
70 B2 **Hebei** *prov.* China
53 C1 **Hebel** Austr.
142 B1 **Heber Springs** U.S.A.
131 D1 **Hebron** Can.
128 A2 **Hecate Strait** Can.
71 A3 **Hechi** China
93 F3 **Hede** Sweden
100 B1 **Heerenveen** Neth.
100 B1 **Heerhugowaard** Neth.
100 B2 **Heerlen** Neth.
Ḩefa Israel *see* **Haifa**
70 B2 **Hefei** China
70 B3 **Hefeng** China
69 E1 **Hegang** China
102 B1 **Heide** Ger.
122 A1 **Heide** Namibia
102 B2 **Heidelberg** Ger.
122 B3 **Heidelberg** S. Africa
102 B2 **Heilbronn** Ger.
69 E1 **Heilong Jiang** *r.* China
93 I3 **Heinola** Fin.
92 F3 **Helagsfjället** *mt.* Sweden
142 B2 **Helena** *AR* U.S.A.
134 D1 **Helena** *MT* U.S.A.
96 B2 **Helensburgh** U.K.
102 B1 **Helgoland** *i.* Ger.
102 B1 **Helgoländer Bucht** *g.* Ger.
Helixi China *see* **Ningguo**
92 □A3 **Hella** Iceland

100 B2 **Hellevoetsluis** Neth.
107 C2 **Hellín** Spain
76 C3 **Helmand** *r.* Afgh.
101 E2 **Helmbrechts** Ger.
122 A2 **Helmeringhausen** Namibia
100 B2 **Helmond** Neth.
96 C1 **Helmsdale** U.K.
96 C1 **Helmsdale** *r.* U.K.
101 E1 **Helmstedt** Ger.
65 B1 **Helong** China
93 F4 **Helsingborg** Sweden
Helsingfors Fin. *see* **Helsinki**
93 F4 **Helsingør** Denmark
93 H3 **Helsinki** Fin.
97 C2 **Helvick Head** Ireland
99 C3 **Hemel Hempstead** U.K.
101 D1 **Hemmoor** Ger.
92 F2 **Hemnesberget** Norway
70 B2 **Henan** *prov.* China
140 B3 **Henderson** *KY* U.S.A.
143 E1 **Henderson** *NC* U.S.A.
135 D3 **Henderson** *NV* U.S.A.
139 E2 **Henderson** *TX* U.S.A.
143 D1 **Hendersonville** U.S.A.
99 C3 **Hendon** U.K.
62 A1 **Hengduan Shan** *mts* China
100 C1 **Hengelo** Neth.
Hengnan China *see* **Hengyang**
70 B2 **Hengshui** China
71 A3 **Hengxian** China
71 B3 **Hengyang** China
Hengzhou China *see* **Hengxian**
91 C2 **Heniches'k** Ukr.
100 C2 **Hennef (Sieg)** Ger.
130 B1 **Henrietta Maria, Cape** Can.
139 D1 **Henryetta** U.S.A.
127 G2 **Henry Kater, Cape** Can.
101 D1 **Henstedt-Ulzburg** Ger.
120 A3 **Hentiesbaai** Namibia
71 A3 **Hepu** China
76 C3 **Herāt** Afgh.
129 D2 **Herbert** Can.
101 D2 **Herbstein** Ger.
99 B2 **Hereford** U.K.
139 C2 **Hereford** U.S.A.
101 D1 **Herford** Ger.
100 C2 **Herkenbosch** Neth.
96 □ **Herma Ness** *hd* U.K.
122 A3 **Hermanus** S. Africa
53 C2 **Hermidale** Austr.
134 C1 **Hermiston** U.S.A.
59 D3 **Hermit Islands** P.N.G.
144 A2 **Hermosillo** Mex.
154 B3 **Hernandarias** Para.
100 C2 **Herne** Ger.
93 E4 **Herning** Denmark
99 C3 **Hertford** U.K.
123 C2 **Hertzogville** S. Africa
51 E2 **Hervey Bay** Austr.
101 F2 **Herzberg (Elster)** Ger.
101 E3 **Herzogenaurach** Ger.
71 A3 **Heshan** China
128 A1 **Hess** *r.* Can.
101 D2 **Hessisch Lichtenau** Ger.
136 C1 **Hettinger** U.S.A.
101 E2 **Hettstedt** Ger.
98 B1 **Hexham** U.K.
71 B3 **Heyuan** China
52 B3 **Heywood** Austr.
70 B2 **Heze** China
71 B3 **Hezhou** China
137 D3 **Hiawatha** U.S.A.
137 E1 **Hibbing** U.S.A.
54 C1 **Hicks Bay** N.Z.
66 D2 **Hidaka-sanmyaku** *mts* Japan
145 C2 **Hidalgo** Mex.
144 B2 **Hidalgo del Parral** Mex.
154 C1 **Hidrolândia** Brazil
High Atlas *mts* Morocco *see* **Haut Atlas**
134 B2 **High Desert** U.S.A.
128 C2 **High Level** Can.
143 E1 **High Point** U.S.A.
128 C2 **High Prairie** Can.
128 C2 **High River** Can.
129 D2 **Highrock Lake** Can.
99 C3 **High Wycombe** U.K.
88 B2 **Hiiumaa** *i.* Estonia
78 A2 **Hijaz** *reg.* Saudi Arabia
54 C1 **Hikurangi** *mt.* N.Z.
101 E2 **Hildburghausen** Ger.
101 E2 **Hilders** Ger.
101 D1 **Hildesheim** Ger.
81 C2 **Hillah** Iraq
100 C2 **Hillesheim** Ger.
140 C3 **Hillsboro** *OH* U.S.A.
139 D2 **Hillsboro** *TX* U.S.A.
53 C2 **Hillston** Austr.
143 D2 **Hilton Head Island** U.S.A.
100 B1 **Hilversum** Neth.
68 B2 **Himalaya** *mts* Asia
67 B4 **Himeji** Japan
123 C2 **Himeville** S. Africa
51 D1 **Hinchinbrook Island** Austr.
74 A1 **Hindu Kush** *mts* Afgh./Pak.
143 D2 **Hinesville** U.S.A.
75 B2 **Hinganghat** India
81 C2 **Hınıs** Turkey
92 G2 **Hinnøya** *i.* Norway
106 B2 **Hinojosa del Duque** Spain
62 A2 **Hinthada** Myanmar
128 C2 **Hinton** Can.
75 C2 **Hirakud Reservoir** India
66 D2 **Hirosaki** Japan
67 B4 **Hiroshima** Japan
101 E3 **Hirschaid** Ger.
101 E2 **Hirschberg** Ger.
105 C2 **Hirson** France
93 E4 **Hirtshals** Denmark
74 B2 **Hisar** India
147 C2 **Hispaniola** *i.* Caribbean Sea
81 C2 **Hīt** Iraq
67 D3 **Hitachi** Japan
67 D3 **Hitachinaka** Japan
92 E3 **Hitra** *i.* Norway
49 I3 **Hiva Oa** *i.* Fr. Polynesia
93 G4 **Hjälmaren** *l.* Sweden
129 D1 **Hjalmar Lake** Can.
93 F4 **Hjørring** Denmark
123 D2 **Hlabisa** S. Africa
92 □B2 **Hlíð** Iceland
91 C2 **Hlobyne** Ukr.
123 C2 **Hlohlowane** S. Africa
123 C2 **Hlotse** Lesotho
91 C1 **Hlukhiv** Ukr.
88 C2 **Hlybokaye** Belarus
114 C4 **Ho** Ghana
62 B2 **Hoa Binh** Vietnam
122 A1 **Hoachanas** Namibia
51 D4 **Hobart** Austr.
139 D1 **Hobart** U.S.A.
139 C2 **Hobbs** U.S.A.
93 E4 **Hobro** Denmark
117 C4 **Hobyo** Somalia
63 B2 **Ho Chi Minh City** Vietnam
114 B3 **Ḥôḍ** *reg.* Maur.
78 B3 **Hodeidah** Yemen
103 E2 **Hódmezővásárhely** Hungary
Hoek van Holland Neth. *see* **Hook of Holland**
65 B2 **Hoeyang** N. Korea
101 E2 **Hof** Ger.
101 E2 **Hofheim in Unterfranken** Ger.
92 □B3 **Höfn** *Austurland* Iceland
92 □A2 **Höfn** *Vestfirðir* Iceland
92 □B3 **Hofsjökull** Iceland
67 B4 **Hōfu** Japan
93 G4 **Högsby** Sweden
101 D2 **Hohe Rhön** *mts* Ger.
100 C2 **Hohe Venn** *moorland* Belgium
70 B1 **Hohhot** China
75 C1 **Hoh Xil Shan** *mts* China
63 B2 **Hôi An** Vietnam
62 A1 **Hojai** India
54 B2 **Hokitika** N.Z.
66 D2 **Hokkaidō** *i.* Japan
128 B2 **Holberg** Can.
138 A2 **Holbrook** U.S.A.
137 D2 **Holdrege** U.S.A.
146 C2 **Holguín** Cuba
92 □B2 **Hóll** Iceland
Holland *country* Europe *see* **Netherlands**
140 B2 **Holland** U.S.A.
100 B1 **Hollum** Neth.
142 C2 **Holly Springs** U.S.A.
134 C4 **Hollywood** *CA* U.S.A.
143 D3 **Hollywood** *FL* U.S.A.
92 F2 **Holm** Norway
92 H3 **Holmsund** Sweden
122 A2 **Holoog** Namibia
93 E4 **Holstebro** Denmark
143 D1 **Holston** *r.* U.S.A.
98 A2 **Holyhead** U.K.
98 C1 **Holy Island** *England* U.K.
98 A2 **Holy Island** *Wales* U.K.
136 C2 **Holyoke** U.S.A.
101 D2 **Holzminden** Ger.
62 A1 **Homalin** Myanmar
101 D2 **Homberg (Efze)** Ger.
114 B3 **Hombori** Mali
127 G2 **Home Bay** Can.
143 D3 **Homestead** U.S.A.
92 F3 **Hommelvik** Norway
80 B2 **Homs** Syria
89 D3 **Homyel'** Belarus
122 A3 **Hondeklipbaai** S. Africa
145 D3 **Hondo** *r.* Belize/Mex.
139 D3 **Hondo** U.S.A.
146 B3 **Honduras** *country* Central America
93 F3 **Hønefoss** Norway
135 B2 **Honey Lake** U.S.A.
104 C2 **Honfleur** France
70 B3 **Honghu** China
71 A3 **Hongjiang** China
71 B3 **Hong Kong** China
71 B3 **Hong Kong** *aut. reg.* China
65 B1 **Hongwŏn** N. Korea
70 B2 **Hongze Hu** *l.* China
49 E3 **Honiara** Solomon Is
92 I1 **Honningsvåg** Norway
67 B3 **Honshū** *i.* Japan
134 B1 **Hood, Mount** *vol.* U.S.A.
50 A3 **Hood Point** Austr.
134 B1 **Hood River** U.S.A.
100 C1 **Hoogeveen** Neth.
100 C1 **Hoogezand-Sappemeer** Neth.
100 C2 **Hoog-Keppel** Neth.
100 B2 **Hook of Holland** Neth.
128 A2 **Hoonah** U.S.A.
100 B1 **Hoorn** Neth.
128 B3 **Hope** Can.
142 B2 **Hope** U.S.A.
83 N2 **Hope, Point** U.S.A.
131 D1 **Hopedale** Can.
131 D1 **Hope Mountains** Can.
52 B3 **Hopetoun** Austr.
122 B2 **Hopetown** S. Africa
141 D3 **Hopewell** U.S.A.
130 C1 **Hopewell Islands** Can.

50 B2 **Hopkins, Lake** *imp. l.* Austr.
140 B3 **Hopkinsville** U.S.A.
134 B1 **Hoquiam** U.S.A.
81 C1 **Horasan** Turkey
93 F4 **Hörby** Sweden
89 D3 **Horki** Belarus
91 D2 **Horlivka** Ukr.
79 D2 **Hormak** Iran
79 C2 **Hormuz, Strait of** Iran/Oman
103 D2 **Horn** Austria
92 □A2 **Horn** *c.* Iceland
153 B6 **Horn, Cape** Chile
141 D2 **Hornell** U.S.A.
130 B2 **Hornepayne** Can.
98 C2 **Hornsea** U.K.
90 B2 **Horodenka** Ukr.
91 C1 **Horodnya** Ukr.
90 B2 **Horodok** *Khmel'nyts'ka Oblast'* Ukr.
90 A2 **Horodok** *L'vivs'ka Oblast'* Ukr.
90 A1 **Horokhiv** Ukr.
Horqin Youyi Qianqi China *see* **Ulanhot**
131 E1 **Horse Islands** Can.
52 B3 **Horsham** Austr.
126 C2 **Horton** *r.* Can.
117 B4 **Hosa'ina** Eth.
74 A2 **Hoshab** Pak.
74 B1 **Hoshiarpur** India
77 E3 **Hotan** China
122 B2 **Hotazel** S. Africa
142 B2 **Hot Springs** *AR* U.S.A.
136 C2 **Hot Springs** *SD* U.S.A.
128 C1 **Hottah Lake** Can.
62 B1 **Houayxay** Laos
100 B2 **Houffalize** Belgium
70 B2 **Houma** China
142 B3 **Houma** U.S.A.
128 B2 **Houston** Can.
139 D3 **Houston** U.S.A.
122 B3 **Houwater** S. Africa
68 C1 **Hovd** Mongolia
99 C3 **Hove** U.K.
68 C1 **Hövsgöl Nuur** *l.* Mongolia
116 A3 **Howar, Wadi** *watercourse* Sudan
53 C3 **Howe, Cape** Austr.
49 G2 **Howland Island** N. Pacific Ocean
53 C3 **Howlong** Austr.
101 D2 **Höxter** Ger.
96 C1 **Hoy** *i.* U.K.
93 E3 **Høyanger** Norway
102 C1 **Hoyerswerda** Ger.
62 A2 **Hpapun** Myanmar
103 D1 **Hradec Králové** Czech Rep.
109 C2 **Hrasnica** Bos. & Herz.
91 C1 **Hrebinka** Ukr.
88 B3 **Hrodna** Belarus
62 A1 **Hsi-hseng** Myanmar
62 A1 **Hsipaw** Myanmar
70 A2 **Huachi** China
150 A3 **Huacho** Peru
69 D2 **Huade** China
65 B1 **Huadian** China
70 B2 **Huai'an** China
70 B2 **Huaibei** China
71 A3 **Huaihua** China
70 B2 **Huainan** China
70 B2 **Huaiyang** China
145 C3 **Huajuápan de León** Mex.
59 C3 **Huaki** Indon.
71 C3 **Hualian** Taiwan
150 A2 **Huallaga** *r.* Peru
120 A2 **Huambo** Angola
150 A3 **Huancayo** Peru
Huangcaoba China *see* **Xingyi**
70 B2 **Huangchuan** China
Huang Hai *sea* N. Pacific Ocean *see* **Yellow Sea**
Huang He *r.* China *see* **Yellow River**
71 A4 **Huangliu** China
70 B3 **Huangshan** China
70 B2 **Huangshi** China
70 A2 **Huangtu Gaoyuan** *plat.* China
71 C3 **Huangyan** China
65 B1 **Huanren** China
150 A2 **Huánuco** Peru
152 B2 **Huanuni** Bol.
150 A2 **Huaraz** Peru
150 A3 **Huarmey** Peru
152 A3 **Huasco** Chile
152 A3 **Huasco** *r.* Chile
144 B2 **Huatabampo** Mex.
145 C3 **Huatusco** Mex.
71 A3 **Huayuan** China
Hubballi India *see* **Hubli**
70 B2 **Hubei** *prov.* China
73 B3 **Hubli** India
100 C2 **Hückelhoven** Ger.
98 C2 **Hucknall** U.K.
98 C2 **Huddersfield** U.K.
93 G3 **Hudiksvall** Sweden
141 E2 **Hudson** *r.* U.S.A.
129 D2 **Hudson Bay** Can.
127 F3 **Hudson Bay** *sea* Can.
128 B2 **Hudson's Hope** Can.
127 G2 **Hudson Strait** Can.
63 B2 **Huê** Vietnam
146 A3 **Huehuetenango** Guat.
144 B2 **Huehueto, Cerro** *mt.* Mex.
145 C2 **Huejutla** Mex.
106 B2 **Huelva** Spain
107 C2 **Huércal-Overa** Spain
107 C1 **Huesca** Spain
106 C2 **Huéscar** Spain
50 B3 **Hughes (abandoned)** Austr.
139 D2 **Hugo** U.S.A.
122 B2 **Huhudi** S. Africa
122 A2 **Huib-Hoch Plateau** Namibia
71 B3 **Huichang** China
65 B1 **Huich'ŏn** N. Korea
120 A2 **Huíla, Planalto da** Angola
71 B3 **Huilai** China
62 B1 **Huili** China
65 B1 **Huinan** China
93 H3 **Huittinen** Fin.
145 C3 **Huixtla** Mex.
Huiyang China *see* **Huizhou**
62 B1 **Huize** China
71 B3 **Huizhou** China
78 B2 **Hujr** Saudi Arabia
122 B1 **Hukuntsi** Botswana
78 B2 **Ḩulayfah** Saudi Arabia
66 B1 **Hulin** China
130 C2 **Hull** Can.
Hulun China *see* **Hulun Buir**
69 D1 **Hulun Buir** China
69 D1 **Hulun Nur** *l.* China
91 D2 **Hulyaypole** Ukr.
69 E1 **Huma** China
150 B2 **Humaitá** Brazil
122 B3 **Humansdorp** S. Africa
98 C2 **Humber** *est.* U.K.
126 D3 **Humboldt** Can.
142 C1 **Humboldt** U.S.A.
135 C2 **Humboldt** *r.* U.S.A.
103 E2 **Humenné** Slovakia
53 C3 **Hume Reservoir** Austr.
138 A1 **Humphreys Peak** U.S.A.
92 □A2 **Húnaflói** *b.* Iceland
71 B3 **Hunan** *prov.* China
65 C1 **Hunchun** China
110 B1 **Hunedoara** Romania
101 D2 **Hünfeld** Ger.
103 D2 **Hungary** *country* Europe
52 B1 **Hungerford** Austr.
65 B2 **Hŭngnam** N. Korea
65 A1 **Hun He** *r.* China
99 D2 **Hunstanton** U.K.
101 D1 **Hunte** *r.* Ger.
51 D4 **Hunter Islands** Austr.
99 C2 **Huntingdon** U.K.
140 B2 **Huntington** *IN* U.S.A.
140 C3 **Huntington** *WV* U.S.A.
54 C1 **Huntly** N.Z.
96 C2 **Huntly** U.K.
130 C2 **Huntsville** Can.
142 C2 **Huntsville** *AL* U.S.A.
139 D2 **Huntsville** *TX* U.S.A.
59 D3 **Huon Peninsula** P.N.G.
70 B2 **Huozhou** China
137 D2 **Huron** U.S.A.
140 C2 **Huron, Lake** Can./U.S.A.
135 D3 **Hurricane** U.S.A.
92 □B2 **Húsavík** Iceland
110 C1 **Huşi** Romania
126 A2 **Huslia** U.S.A.
78 B3 **Ḩusn Āl 'Abr** Yemen
102 B1 **Husum** Ger.
69 C1 **Hutag-Öndör** Mongolia
60 A1 **Hutanopan** Indon.
137 D3 **Hutchinson** U.S.A.
70 C2 **Huzhou** China
92 □C3 **Hvalnes** Iceland
92 □B3 **Hvannadalshnúkur** *vol.* Iceland
109 C2 **Hvar** *i.* Croatia
120 B2 **Hwange** Zimbabwe
136 C2 **Hyannis** U.S.A.
68 C1 **Hyargas Nuur** *salt l.* Mongolia
50 A3 **Hyden** Austr.
73 B3 **Hyderabad** India
74 A2 **Hyderabad** Pak.
105 D3 **Hyères** France
105 D3 **Hyères, Îles d'** *is* France
65 B1 **Hyesan** N. Korea
128 B2 **Hyland Post** Can.
67 B3 **Hyōno-sen** *mt.* Japan
99 D3 **Hythe** U.K.
93 H3 **Hyvinkää** Fin.

I

150 B2 **Iaco** *r.* Brazil
110 C2 **Ialomiţa** *r.* Romania
110 C1 **Ianca** Romania
110 C1 **Iaşi** Romania
64 A1 **Iba** Phil.
115 C4 **Ibadan** Nigeria
150 A1 **Ibagué** Col.
150 A1 **Ibarra** Ecuador
78 B3 **Ibb** Yemen
100 C1 **Ibbenbüren** Ger.
115 C4 **Ibi** Nigeria
155 C1 **Ibiá** Brazil
155 D1 **Ibiraçu** Brazil
107 D2 **Ibiza** Spain
107 D2 **Ibiza** *i.* Spain
151 D3 **Ibotirama** Brazil
79 C2 **Ibrā'** Oman
79 C2 **Ibrī** Oman
150 A3 **Ica** Peru
92 □B2 **Iceland** *country* Europe
66 D3 **Ichinoseki** Japan
91 C1 **Ichnya** Ukr.
65 B2 **Ich'ŏn** N. Korea
139 E2 **Idabel** U.S.A.
134 D2 **Idaho** *state* U.S.A.

134 D2 **Idaho Falls** U.S.A.
100 C3 **Idar-Oberstein** Ger.
116 B2 **Idfū** Egypt
118 B3 **Idiofa** Dem. Rep. Congo
80 B2 **Idlib** Syria
154 B2 **Iepê** Brazil
100 A2 **Ieper** Belgium
119 D3 **Ifakara** Tanz.
121 □D3 **Ifanadiana** Madag.
115 C4 **Ife** Nigeria
114 C3 **Ifôghas, Adrar des** *hills* Mali
61 C1 **Igan** *Sarawak* Malaysia
154 C2 **Igarapava** Brazil
82 G2 **Igarka** Russia
74 B3 **Igatpuri** India
81 C2 **Iğdır** Turkey
108 A3 **Iglesias** *Sardinia* Italy
127 F2 **Igloolik** Can.
Igluligaarjuk Can. *see* **Chesterfield Inlet**
130 A2 **Ignace** Can.
88 C2 **Ignalina** Lith.
110 C2 **İğneada** Turkey
111 B3 **Igoumenitsa** Greece
86 E3 **Igra** Russia
86 F2 **Igrim** Russia
154 B3 **Iguaçu** *r.* Brazil
154 B3 **Iguaçu Falls** Arg./Brazil
145 C3 **Iguala** Mex.
107 D1 **Igualada** Spain
154 C2 **Iguape** Brazil
154 B2 **Iguatemi** Brazil
154 B2 **Iguatemi** *r.* Brazil
151 E2 **Iguatu** Brazil
118 A3 **Iguéla** Gabon
119 D3 **Igunga** Tanz.
121 □D3 **Ihosy** Madag.
110 B2 **Ihtiman** Bulg.
92 I3 **Iisalmi** Fin.
115 C4 **Ijebu-Ode** Nigeria
100 B1 **IJmuiden** Neth.
100 B1 **IJssel** *r.* Neth.
100 B1 **IJsselmeer** *l.* Neth.
123 C2 **Ikageng** S. Africa
111 C3 **Ikaria** *i.* Greece
118 C3 **Ikela** Dem. Rep. Congo
67 A4 **Iki-shima** *i.* Japan
121 □D3 **Ikongo** Madag.
65 B2 **Iksan** S. Korea
64 B1 **Ilagan** Phil.
81 C2 **Īlām** Iran
75 C2 **Ilam** Nepal
103 D1 **Iława** Pol.
79 C2 **Ilazārān, Kūh-e** *mt.* Iran
129 D2 **Île-à-la-Crosse** Can.
129 D2 **Île-à-la-Crosse, Lac** *l.* Can.
118 C3 **Ilebo** Dem. Rep. Congo
124 H6 **Île Clipperton** *terr.* N. Pacific Ocean
119 D2 **Ilemi Triangle** *disp. terr.* Africa
119 D2 **Ileret** Kenya
113 K11 **Îles Crozet** *is* Indian Ocean
49 I3 **Îles du Désappointement** *is* Fr. Polynesia
49 I4 **Îles Gambier** *is* Fr. Polynesia
99 D3 **Ilford** U.K.
99 A3 **Ilfracombe** U.K.
154 B2 **Ilha Grande** *resr* Brazil
155 D2 **Ilha Grande, Baía da** *b.* Brazil
154 B2 **Ilha Solteíra, Represa** *resr* Brazil
106 B1 **Ílhavo** Port.
151 E3 **Ilhéus** Brazil
64 B2 **Iligan** Phil.
152 A4 **Illapel** Chile
90 C2 **Illichivs'k** Ukr.
140 A3 **Illinois** *r.* U.S.A.
140 B3 **Illinois** *state* U.S.A.
90 B2 **Illintsi** Ukr.
115 C2 **Illizi** Alg.
89 D2 **Il'men', Ozero** *l.* Russia
101 E2 **Ilmenau** Ger.
150 A3 **Ilo** Peru
64 B1 **Iloilo** Phil.
92 J3 **Ilomantsi** Fin.
115 C4 **Ilorin** Nigeria
53 D1 **Iluka** Austr.
127 H2 **Ilulissat** Greenland
67 A4 **Imari** Japan
117 C4 **Īmī** Eth.
108 B2 **Imola** Italy
151 D2 **Imperatriz** Brazil
136 C2 **Imperial** U.S.A.
118 B2 **Impfondo** Congo
62 A1 **Imphal** India
111 C2 **İmroz** Turkey
150 B3 **Inambari** *r.* Peru
115 C2 **In Aménas** Alg.
59 C3 **Inanwatan** Indon.
92 I2 **Inari** Fin.
92 I2 **Inarijärvi** *l.* Fin.
67 D3 **Inawashiro-ko** *l.* Japan
80 B1 **İnce Burun** *pt* Turkey
65 B2 **Incheon** S. Korea
123 D2 **Incomati** *r.* Moz.
78 A3 **Inda Silasē** Eth.
144 B2 **Indé** Mex.
135 C3 **Independence** *CA* U.S.A.
137 E2 **Independence** *IA* U.S.A.
137 D3 **Independence** *KS* U.S.A.
137 E3 **Independence** *MO* U.S.A.
134 C2 **Independence Mountains** U.S.A.
76 B2 **Inderbor** Kazakh.
72 B2 **India** *country* Asia
141 D2 **Indiana** U.S.A.
140 B2 **Indiana** *state* U.S.A.
140 B3 **Indianapolis** U.S.A.
129 D2 **Indian Head** Can.
159 **Indian Ocean**
137 E2 **Indianola** *IA* U.S.A.
142 B2 **Indianola** *MS* U.S.A.
135 C3 **Indian Springs** U.S.A.
86 D2 **Indiga** Russia
83 K2 **Indigirka** *r.* Russia
109 D1 **Inđija** Serbia
135 C4 **Indio** U.S.A.
58 B3 **Indonesia** *country* Asia
74 B2 **Indore** India
61 B2 **Indramayu, Tanjung** *pt* Indon.
104 C2 **Indre** *r.* France
74 A2 **Indus** *r.* China/Pak.
74 A2 **Indus, Mouths of the** Pak.
80 B1 **İnebolu** Turkey
111 C2 **İnegöl** Turkey
144 B3 **Infiernillo, Presa** *resr* Mex.
53 D1 **Inglewood** Austr.
102 C2 **Ingolstadt** Ger.
75 C2 **Ingraj Bazar** India
123 D2 **Inhaca** Moz.
121 C3 **Inhambane** Moz.
97 A2 **Inishbofin** *i.* Ireland
97 B2 **Inishmore** *i.* Ireland
97 C1 **Inishowen** *pen.* Ireland
54 B2 **Inland Kaikoura Range** *mts* N.Z.
102 C2 **Inn** *r.* Europe
127 G1 **Innaanganeq** *c.* Greenland
96 B2 **Inner Sound** *sea chan.* U.K.
51 D1 **Innisfail** Austr.
102 C2 **Innsbruck** Austria
154 B1 **Inocência** Brazil
118 B3 **Inongo** Dem. Rep. Congo
103 D1 **Inowrocław** Pol.
114 C2 **In Salah** Alg.
62 A2 **Insein** Myanmar
86 F2 **Inta** Russia
137 E1 **International Falls** U.S.A.
130 C1 **Inukjuak** Can.
126 C2 **Inuvik** Can.
96 B2 **Inveraray** U.K.
54 A3 **Invercargill** N.Z.
53 D1 **Inverell** Austr.
96 B2 **Invergordon** U.K.
128 C2 **Invermere** Can.
131 D2 **Inverness** Can.
96 B2 **Inverness** U.K.
96 C2 **Inverurie** U.K.
52 A3 **Investigator Strait** Austr.
77 E1 **Inya** Russia
119 D3 **Inyonga** Tanz.
87 D3 **Inza** Russia
111 B3 **Ioannina** Greece
137 D3 **Iola** U.S.A.
96 A2 **Iona** *i.* U.K.
111 B3 **Ionian Islands** Greece
109 C3 **Ionian Sea** Greece/Italy
Ionioi Nisoi *is* Greece *see* **Ionian Islands**
111 C3 **Ios** *i.* Greece
137 E2 **Iowa** *state* U.S.A.
137 E2 **Iowa City** U.S.A.
154 C1 **Ipameri** Brazil
155 D1 **Ipatinga** Brazil
81 C1 **Ipatovo** Russia
123 C2 **Ipelegeng** S. Africa
150 A1 **Ipiales** Col.
154 B3 **Ipiranga** Brazil
60 B1 **Ipoh** Malaysia
154 B1 **Iporá** Brazil
118 C2 **Ippy** C.A.R.
111 C2 **İpsala** Turkey
53 D1 **Ipswich** Austr.
99 D2 **Ipswich** U.K.
127 G2 **Iqaluit** Can.
152 A3 **Iquique** Chile
150 A2 **Iquitos** Peru
Irakleio Greece *see* **Iraklion**
111 C3 **Iraklion** Greece
76 B3 **Iran** *country* Asia
61 C1 **Iran, Pegunungan** *mts* Indon.
79 D2 **Īrānshahr** Iran
144 B2 **Irapuato** Mex.
81 C2 **Iraq** *country* Asia
154 B3 **Irati** Brazil
80 B2 **Irbid** Jordan
86 F3 **Irbit** Russia
151 D3 **Irecê** Brazil
97 C2 **Ireland** *country* Europe
118 C3 **Irema** Dem. Rep. Congo
114 B3 **Irîgui** *reg.* Mali/Maur.
119 D3 **Iringa** Tanz.
151 C2 **Iriri** *r.* Brazil
95 B3 **Irish Sea** Ireland/U.K.
69 C1 **Irkutsk** Russia
52 A2 **Iron Knob** Austr.
140 B1 **Iron Mountain** U.S.A.
140 A1 **Ironwood** U.S.A.
64 B1 **Irosin** Phil.
67 C4 **Irō-zaki** *pt* Japan
90 C1 **Irpin'** Ukr.
62 A2 **Irrawaddy** *r.* Myanmar
63 A2 **Irrawaddy, Mouths of the** Myanmar
86 F2 **Irtysh** *r.* Kazakh./Russia
107 C1 **Irun** Spain
96 B3 **Irvine** U.K.
64 B2 **Isabela** Phil.
146 B3 **Isabelia, Cordillera** *mts* Nic.
92 □A2 **Ísafjörður** Iceland
67 B4 **Isahaya** Japan
105 E2 **Isar** *r.* Ger.
96 □ **Isbister** U.K.

Ischia, Isola d'

108 B2 Ischia, Isola d' *i.* Italy
67 C4 Ise Japan
118 C2 Isengi Dem. Rep. Congo
100 C2 Iserlohn Ger.
101 D1 Isernhagen Ger.
67 C4 Ise-wan *b.* Japan
114 C4 Iseyin Nigeria
Isfahan Iran *see* Eşfahān
66 C2 Ishikari-wan *b.* Japan
66 D3 Ishinomaki Japan
67 D3 Ishioka Japan
140 B1 Ishpeming U.S.A.
111 C2 Işıklar Dağı *mts* Turkey
111 C3 Işıklı Turkey
123 D2 Isipingo S. Africa
119 C2 Isiro Dem. Rep. Congo
110 B2 Iskar *r.* Bulg.
80 B2 İskenderun Turkey
82 G3 Iskitim Russia
128 A2 Iskut *r.* Can.
74 B1 Islamabad Pak.
52 A2 Island Lagoon *imp. l.* Austr.
129 E2 Island Lake Can.
54 B1 Islands, Bay of N.Z.
96 A3 Islas Malvinas *terr.* S. Atlantic Ocean *see* Falkland Islands
98 A1 Islay *i.* U.K.
98 A1 Isle of Man *i.* Irish Sea.
77 D3 Ismoili Somoní, Qullai *mt.* Tajik.
109 C3 Isola di Capo Rizzuto Italy
110 C2 Isperih Bulg.
80 B2 Israel *country* Asia
105 C2 Issoire France
111 C2 Istanbul Turkey
Istanbul Boğazı *str.* Turkey *see* Bosporus
111 B3 Istiaia Greece
105 C3 Istres France
108 B1 Istria *pen.* Croatia
151 D3 Itaberaba Brazil
155 D1 Itabira Brazil
155 D2 Itabirito Brazil
151 E3 Itabuna Brazil
150 C2 Itacoatiara Brazil
154 B2 Itaguajé Brazil
154 C2 Itaí Brazil
154 B1 Itaipu, Represa de *resr* Brazil
151 C2 Itaituba Brazil
152 D3 Itajaí Brazil
155 C2 Itajubá Brazil
108 B2 Italy *country* Europe
155 D1 Itamarandiba Brazil
155 D1 Itambacuri Brazil
155 D1 Itambé, Pico de *mt.* Brazil
62 A1 Itanagar India
154 C2 Itanhaém Brazil
155 D1 Itanhém Brazil
155 D1 Itaobim Brazil
154 C1 Itapajipe Brazil
155 E1 Itapebi Brazil
151 D2 Itapecuru Mirim Brazil
155 D2 Itapemirim Brazil
155 D2 Itaperuna Brazil
155 D1 Itapetinga Brazil
154 C2 Itapetininga Brazil
154 C2 Itapeva Brazil
151 E3 Itapicuru *r.* Brazil
154 C1 Itapuranga Brazil
154 C2 Itararé Brazil
75 B2 Itarsi India
154 B1 Itarumã Brazil
155 D2 Itaúna Brazil
71 C3 Itbayat *i.* Phil.
141 D2 Ithaca U.S.A.
101 D1 Ith Hils *ridge* Ger.
118 C2 Itimbiri *r.* Dem. Rep. Congo
155 D1 Itinga Brazil

154 B1 Itiquira Brazil
154 A1 Itiquira *r.* Brazil
67 C4 Itō Japan
154 C2 Itu Brazil
150 B2 Itui *r.* Brazil
154 C1 Ituiutaba Brazil
119 C3 Itula Dem. Rep. Congo
154 C1 Itumbiara Brazil
154 B1 Iturama Brazil
101 D1 Itzehoe Ger.
83 N2 Iul'tin Russia
154 B2 Ivaí *r.* Brazil
92 I2 Ivalo Fin.
88 C3 Ivanava Belarus
52 B2 Ivanhoe Austr.
90 B1 Ivankiv Ukr.
90 A2 Ivano-Frankivs'k Ukr.
89 F2 Ivanovo Russia
88 C3 Ivatsevichy Belarus
111 C2 Ivaylovgrad Bulg.
86 F2 Ivdel' Russia
154 B2 Ivinheima *r.* Brazil
154 B2 Ivinhema Brazil
127 H2 Ivittuut Greenland
Ivory Coast *country* Africa *see* Côte d'Ivoire
108 A1 Ivrea Italy
111 C3 Ivrindi Turkey
127 F2 Ivujivik Can.
67 D3 Iwaki Japan
67 B4 Iwakuni Japan
66 D2 Iwamizawa Japan
66 D2 Iwanai Japan
88 C3 Iwye Belarus
123 C3 Ixopo S. Africa
144 B2 Ixtlán Mex.
145 D2 Izamal Mex.
81 C1 Izberbash Russia
86 E3 Izhevsk Russia
86 E2 Izhma Russia
89 E3 Izmalkovo Russia
90 B2 Izmayil Ukr.
111 C3 İzmir Turkey
111 C2 İznik Gölü *l.* Turkey
152 B2 Izozog, Bañados del *swamp* Bol.
67 B3 Izumo Japan
90 B2 Izyaslav Ukr.
91 D2 Izyum Ukr.

J

Jabal, Bahr el *r.* South Sudan/Uganda *see* White Nile
106 C2 Jabalón *r.* Spain
75 B2 Jabalpur India
50 C1 Jabiru Austr.
109 C2 Jablanica Bos. & Herz.
151 E2 Jaboatão dos Guararapes Brazil
154 C2 Jaboticabal Brazil
107 C1 Jaca Spain
145 C2 Jacala Mex.
151 C2 Jacareacanga Brazil
155 C2 Jacareí Brazil
155 D1 Jacinto Brazil
141 E1 Jackman U.S.A.
142 C2 Jackson AL U.S.A.
140 C2 Jackson MI U.S.A.
142 B2 Jackson MS U.S.A.
142 C1 Jackson TN U.S.A.
136 A2 Jackson WY U.S.A.
54 A2 Jackson Head N.Z.
142 B2 Jacksonville AR U.S.A.
143 D2 Jacksonville FL U.S.A.
140 A3 Jacksonville IL U.S.A.

143 E2 Jacksonville NC U.S.A.
139 D2 Jacksonville TX U.S.A.
147 C3 Jacmel Haiti
74 A2 Jacobabad Pak.
151 D3 Jacobina Brazil
131 D2 Jacques-Cartier, Mont *mt.* Can.
151 D2 Jacundá Brazil
154 C2 Jacupiranga Brazil
109 C2 Jadovnik *mt.* Bos. & Herz.
150 A2 Jaén Peru
106 C2 Jaén Spain
52 A3 Jaffa, Cape Austr.
73 B4 Jaffna Sri Lanka
73 C3 Jagdalpur India
123 C2 Jagersfontein S. Africa
154 C2 Jaguariaíva Brazil
79 C2 Jahrom Iran
74 B2 Jaipur India
74 B2 Jaisalmer India
75 C2 Jajarkot Nepal
109 C2 Jajce Bos. & Herz.
60 B2 Jakarta Indon.
128 A1 Jakes Corner Can.
92 G2 Jäkkvik Sweden
92 H3 Jakobstad Fin.
77 D3 Jalālābād Afgh.
77 D2 Jalal-Abad Kyrg.
74 B1 Jalandhar India
Jalapa Mex. *see* Xalapa
154 B2 Jales Brazil
74 B2 Jalgaon India
115 C4 Jalingo Nigeria
74 B3 Jalna India
144 B2 Jalpa Mex.
75 C2 Jalpaiguri India
145 C2 Jalpan Mex.
114 B1 Jālū Libya
146 C3 Jamaica *country* West Indies
146 C3 Jamaica Channel Haiti/Jamaica
75 C2 Jamalpur Bangl.
60 B2 Jambi Indon.
137 D2 James *r. ND/SD* U.S.A.
141 D3 James *r.* VA U.S.A.
130 B1 James Bay Can.
52 A2 Jamestown Austr.
137 D1 Jamestown ND U.S.A.
141 D2 Jamestown NY U.S.A.
74 B1 Jammu India
74 B1 Jammu and Kashmir *state* India
74 B2 Jamnagar India
93 I3 Jämsä Fin.
75 C2 Jamshedpur India
75 C2 Jamuna *r.* Bangl.
75 C2 Janakpur Nepal
155 D1 Janaúba Brazil
81 D2 Jandaq Iran
140 B2 Janesville U.S.A.
65 B3 Jangheung S. Korea
65 B2 Jangseong S. Korea
80 B2 Janin West Bank
114 A3 Janjanbureh Gambia
84 F1 Jan Mayen *terr.* Arctic Ocean
81 D1 Jaňňa Turkm.
122 B3 Jansenville S. Africa
155 D1 Januária Brazil
74 B2 Jaora India
67 C3 Japan *country* Asia
156 C3 Japan, Sea of N. Pacific Ocean
150 B2 Japurá *r.* Brazil
154 C1 Jaraguá Brazil
154 B2 Jaraguari Brazil
70 A2 Jarantai China
152 C3 Jardim Brazil
103 D1 Jarocin Pol.
103 E1 Jarosław Pol.

92 F3 **Järpen** Sweden
150 B3 **Jaru** Brazil
Jarud China *see* **Lubei**
49 H3 **Jarvis Island** S. Pacific Ocean
103 E2 **Jasło** Pol.
128 C2 **Jasper** Can.
140 B3 **Jasper** *IN* U.S.A.
139 E2 **Jasper** *TX* U.S.A.
103 D2 **Jastrzębie-Zdrój** Pol.
103 D2 **Jászberény** Hungary
154 B1 **Jataí** Brazil
74 A2 **Jati** Pak.
154 C2 **Jaú** Brazil
150 B2 **Jaú** *r.* Brazil
145 C2 **Jaumave** Mex.
75 C2 **Jaunpur** India
154 B1 **Jauru** Brazil
61 B2 **Java** *i.* Indon.
Java Sea Indon. *see* **Jawa, Laut**
Jawa *i.* Indon. *see* **Java**
159 D4 **Jawa, Laut** *sea* Indon.
117 C4 **Jawhar** Somalia
103 D1 **Jawor** Pol.
103 D1 **Jaworzno** Pol.
59 D3 **Jaya, Puncak** *mt.* Indon.
59 D3 **Jayapura** Indon.
78 B3 **Jāzān** Saudi Arabia
79 C2 **Jaz Mūrīān, Hāmūn-e** *imp. l.* Iran
128 B1 **Jean Marie River** Can.
131 D1 **Jeannin, Lac** *l.* Can.
116 A3 **Jebel Abyad Plateau** Sudan
65 B2 **Jecheon** S. Korea
96 C3 **Jedburgh** U.K.
78 A2 **Jeddah** Saudi Arabia
101 E1 **Jeetze** *r.* Ger.
135 C3 **Jefferson, Mount** U.S.A.
137 E3 **Jefferson City** U.S.A.
65 B3 **Jeju** S. Korea
65 B3 **Jeju-haehyeop** *sea chan.* S. Korea
88 C2 **Jēkabpils** Latvia
103 D1 **Jelenia Góra** Pol.
88 B2 **Jelgava** Latvia
61 C2 **Jember** Indon.
101 E2 **Jena** Ger.
Jengish Chokusu *mt.* China/Kyrg. *see* **Pobeda Peak**
Jengish Chokusu *mt.* China/Kyrg. *see* **Pobeda Peak**
142 B2 **Jennings** U.S.A.
65 B2 **Jeonju** S. Korea
151 D3 **Jequié** Brazil
155 D1 **Jequitaí** Brazil
155 D1 **Jequitinhonha** Brazil
155 E1 **Jequitinhonha** *r.* Brazil
147 C3 **Jérémie** Haiti
144 B2 **Jerez** Mex.
106 B2 **Jerez de la Frontera** Spain
109 D3 **Jergucat** Albania
115 C1 **Jerid, Chott el** *salt l.* Tunisia
134 D2 **Jerome** U.S.A.
95 C4 **Jersey** *terr.* Channel Is
151 D2 **Jerumenha** Brazil
80 B2 **Jerusalem** Israel/West Bank
53 D3 **Jervis Bay Territory** *admin. div.* Austr.
108 B1 **Jesenice** Slovenia
108 B2 **Jesi** Italy
101 F2 **Jessen (Elster)** Ger.
75 C2 **Jessore** Bangl.
143 D2 **Jesup** U.S.A.
145 C3 **Jesús Carranza** Mex.
109 C2 **Jezercë, Maja** *mt.* Albania
74 B2 **Jhalawar** India
74 B1 **Jhang** Pak.
75 B2 **Jhansi** India
75 C2 **Jharsuguda** India
74 B1 **Jhelum** Pak.
70 C2 **Jiading** China
69 E1 **Jiamusi** China
71 B3 **Ji'an** *Jiangxi* China
65 B1 **Ji'an** *Jilin* China
62 A1 **Jianchuan** China
Jiandaoyu China *see* **Guojiaba**
70 B2 **Jiangsu** *prov.* China
71 B3 **Jiangxi** *prov.* China
70 A2 **Jiangyou** China
70 B3 **Jianli** China
70 B2 **Jianqiao** China
71 B3 **Jianyang** *Fujian* China
70 A2 **Jianyang** *Sichuan* China
70 C2 **Jiaozhou** China
70 B2 **Jiaozuo** China
70 C2 **Jiaxing** China
71 C3 **Jiayi** Taiwan
68 C2 **Jiayuguan** China
Jiddah Saudi Arabia *see* **Jeddah**
92 G2 **Jiehkkevárri** *mt.* Norway
70 B2 **Jiexiu** China
68 C2 **Jigzhi** China
103 D2 **Jihlava** Czech Rep.
117 C4 **Jijiga** Eth.
116 A2 **Jilf al Kabīr, Haḍabat al** *plat.* Egypt
117 C4 **Jilib** Somalia
69 E2 **Jilin** China
65 B1 **Jilin** *prov.* China
65 A1 **Jilin Hada Ling** *mts* China
117 B4 **Jīma** Eth.
144 B2 **Jiménez** *Chihuahua* Mex.
145 C2 **Jiménez** *Tamaulipas* Mex.
70 B2 **Jinan** China
70 B2 **Jincheng** China
53 C3 **Jindabyne** Austr.
65 B3 **Jin-do** *i.* S. Korea
103 D2 **Jindřichův Hradec** Czech Rep.
71 B3 **Jingdezhen** China
70 B2 **Jinghang Yunhe** *canal* China
62 B1 **Jinghong** China
70 B2 **Jingmen** China
70 A2 **Jingning** China
70 A2 **Jingtai** China
71 A3 **Jingxi** China
65 B1 **Jingyu** China
70 A2 **Jingyuan** China
70 B2 **Jingzhou** China
65 B2 **Jinhae** S. Korea
71 B3 **Jinhua** China
70 B2 **Jining** China
119 D2 **Jinja** Uganda
117 B4 **Jinka** Eth.
71 B3 **Jinmen** Taiwan
146 B3 **Jinotepe** Nic.
71 A3 **Jinping** China
Jinsha Jiang *r.* China *see* **Yangtze**
70 B3 **Jinshi** China
70 B2 **Jinzhong** China
70 C1 **Jinzhou** China
150 B2 **Ji-Paraná** *r.* Brazil
75 C1 **Jirang** China
65 B2 **Jiri-san** *mt.* S. Korea
79 C2 **Jīroft** Iran
71 A3 **Jishou** China
110 B2 **Jiu** *r.* Romania
70 A2 **Jiuding Shan** *mt.* China
70 B3 **Jiujiang** China
66 B1 **Jixi** China
77 C2 **Jizzax** Uzbek.
151 E2 **João Pessoa** Brazil
155 C1 **João Pinheiro** Brazil
74 B2 **Jodhpur** India
92 I3 **Joensuu** Fin.
67 C3 **Jōetsu** Japan
121 C3 **Jofane** Moz.
88 C2 **Jõgeva** Estonia
123 C2 **Johannesburg** S. Africa
134 C2 **John Day** U.S.A.
134 B1 **John Day** *r.* U.S.A.
128 C2 **John D'Or Prairie** Can.
143 E1 **John H. Kerr Reservoir** U.S.A.
96 C1 **John o' Groats** U.K.
143 D1 **Johnson City** U.S.A.
128 A1 **Johnson's Crossing** Can.
49 H1 **Johnston Atoll** N. Pacific Ocean
96 B3 **Johnstone** U.K.
141 D2 **Johnstown** U.S.A.
60 B1 **Johor Bahru** Malaysia
88 C2 **Jõhvi** Estonia
154 C3 **Joinville** Brazil
105 D2 **Joinville** France
92 G2 **Jokkmokk** Sweden
92 □B2 **Jökulsá á Fjöllum** *r.* Iceland
140 B2 **Joliet** U.S.A.
130 C2 **Joliette** Can.
64 B2 **Jolo** Phil.
64 B2 **Jolo** *i.* Phil.
61 C2 **Jombang** Indon.
75 C2 **Jomsom** Nepal
88 B2 **Jonava** Lith.
142 B1 **Jonesboro** *AR* U.S.A.
142 B2 **Jonesboro** *LA* U.S.A.
127 F1 **Jones Sound** *sea chan.* Can.
93 F4 **Jönköping** Sweden
131 C2 **Jonquière** Can.
145 C3 **Jonuta** Mex.
137 E3 **Joplin** U.S.A.
80 B2 **Jordan** *country* Asia
80 B2 **Jordan** *r.* Asia
136 B1 **Jordan** U.S.A.
134 C2 **Jordan Valley** U.S.A.
62 A1 **Jorhat** India
93 E4 **Jørpeland** Norway
115 C4 **Jos** Nigeria
145 C3 **José Cardel** Mex.
131 D1 **Joseph, Lac** *l.* Can.
50 B1 **Joseph Bonaparte Gulf** Austr.
115 C4 **Jos Plateau** Nigeria
93 E3 **Jotunheimen** *mts* Norway
122 B3 **Joubertina** S. Africa
123 C2 **Jouberton** S. Africa
93 I3 **Joutseno** Fin.
134 B1 **Juan de Fuca Strait** Can./U.S.A.
Juanshui China *see* **Tongcheng**
145 B2 **Juárez** Mex.
151 D2 **Juazeiro** Brazil
151 E2 **Juazeiro do Norte** Brazil
117 B4 **Juba** South Sudan
117 C4 **Jubaland** *reg.* Somalia
117 C5 **Jubba** *r.* Somalia
78 B2 **Jubbah** Saudi Arabia
145 C3 **Juchitán** Mex.
102 C2 **Judenburg** Austria
101 D2 **Jühnde** Ger.
146 B3 **Juigalpa** Nic.
100 C1 **Juist** *i.* Ger.
155 D2 **Juiz de Fora** Brazil
150 A3 **Juliaca** Peru
75 C2 **Jumla** Nepal
74 B2 **Junagadh** India
139 D2 **Junction** U.S.A.
137 D3 **Junction City** U.S.A.
154 C2 **Jundiaí** Brazil
128 A2 **Juneau** U.S.A.
53 C2 **Junee** Austr.
105 D2 **Jungfrau** *mt.* Switz.
141 D2 **Juniata** *r.* U.S.A.

92 G3 **Junsele** Sweden
134 C2 **Juntura** U.S.A.
154 C2 **Juquiá** Brazil
117 A4 **Jur** *r.* South Sudan
105 D2 **Jura** *mts* France/Switz.
96 B2 **Jura** *i.* U.K.
96 B3 **Jura, Sound of** *sea chan.* U.K.
88 B2 **Jurbarkas** Lith.
88 B2 **Jūrmala** Latvia
150 B2 **Juruá** *r.* Brazil
150 C2 **Juruena** *r.* Brazil
150 B2 **Jutaí** *r.* Brazil
101 F2 **Jüterbog** Ger.
146 B2 **Juventud, Isla de la** *i.* Cuba
70 B2 **Juxian** China
79 C2 **Jūyom** Iran
122 B1 **Jwaneng** Botswana
93 I3 **Jyväskylä** Fin.

K

74 B1 **K2** *mt.* China/Pak.
119 C3 **Kabalo** Dem. Rep. Congo
119 C3 **Kabare** Dem. Rep. Congo
130 B2 **Kabinakagami Lake** Can.
118 C3 **Kabinda** Dem. Rep. Congo
118 B2 **Kabo** C.A.R.
120 B2 **Kabompo** Zambia
119 C3 **Kabongo** Dem. Rep. Congo
77 C3 **Kābul** Afgh.
64 B2 **Kaburuang** *i.* Indon.
121 B2 **Kabwe** Zambia
74 A2 **Kachchh, Gulf of** India
74 B2 **Kachchh, Rann of** *marsh* India
83 I3 **Kachug** Russia
81 C1 **Kaçkar Dağı** *mt.* Turkey
73 B3 **Kadapa** India
111 C2 **Kadıköy** Turkey
114 B3 **Kadiolo** Mali
73 B3 **Kadmat** *atoll* India
121 B2 **Kadoma** Zimbabwe
63 A2 **Kadonkani** Myanmar
117 A3 **Kadugli** Sudan
115 C3 **Kaduna** Nigeria
89 E2 **Kaduy** Russia
86 E2 **Kadzherom** Russia
114 A3 **Kaédi** Maur.
118 B1 **Kaélé** Cameroon
65 B2 **Kaesŏng** N. Korea
114 A3 **Kaffrine** Senegal
121 B2 **Kafue** Zambia
120 B2 **Kafue** *r.* Zambia
118 B2 **Kaga Bandoro** C.A.R.
91 E2 **Kagal'nitskaya** Russia
67 B4 **Kagoshima** Japan
90 C2 **Kaharlyk** Ukr.
61 C2 **Kahayan** *r.* Indon.
118 B3 **Kahemba** Dem. Rep. Congo
101 E2 **Kahla** Ger.
79 C2 **Kahnūj** Iran
92 H2 **Kahperusvaarat** *mts* Fin.
80 B2 **Kahramanmaraş** Turkey
79 C2 **Kahūrak** Iran
59 C3 **Kai, Kepulauan** *is* Indon.
115 C4 **Kaiama** Nigeria
54 B2 **Kaiapoi** N.Z.
59 C3 **Kai Besar** *i.* Indon.
70 B2 **Kaifeng** China
Kaihua China *see* **Wenshan**
122 B2 **Kaiingveld** *reg.* S. Africa
59 C3 **Kai Kecil** *i.* Indon.
54 B2 **Kaikoura** N.Z.
114 A4 **Kailahun** Sierra Leone
71 A3 **Kaili** China
59 C3 **Kaimana** Indon.
54 C1 **Kaimanawa Mountains** N.Z.
67 C4 **Kainan** Japan
115 C3 **Kainji Reservoir** Nigeria
54 B1 **Kaipara Harbour** N.Z.
74 B2 **Kairana** India
115 D1 **Kairouan** Tunisia
54 B1 **Kaitaia** N.Z.
54 C1 **Kaitawa** N.Z.
Kaitong China *see* **Tongyu**
59 C3 **Kaiwatu** Indon.
65 A1 **Kaiyuan** *Liaoning* China
62 B1 **Kaiyuan** *Yunnan* China
92 I3 **Kajaani** Fin.
51 D2 **Kajabbi** Austr.
122 B2 **Kakamas** S. Africa
119 D2 **Kakamega** Kenya
91 C2 **Kakhovka** Ukr.
91 C2 **Kakhovs'ke Vodoskhovyshche** *resr* Ukr.
73 C3 **Kakinada** India
128 C1 **Kakisa** Can.
119 C3 **Kakoswa** Dem. Rep. Congo
126 B2 **Kaktovik** U.S.A.
Kalaallit Nunaat *terr.* N. America *see* **Greenland**
59 C3 **Kalabahi** Indon.
120 B2 **Kalabo** Zambia
91 E1 **Kalach** Russia
119 D2 **Kalacha Dida** Kenya
62 A1 **Kaladan** *r.* India/Myanmar
120 B3 **Kalahari Desert** Africa
92 H3 **Kalajoki** Fin.
111 B2 **Kalamaria** Greece
111 B3 **Kalamata** Greece
140 B2 **Kalamazoo** U.S.A.
111 B3 **Kalampaka** Greece
91 C2 **Kalanchak** Ukr.
115 E1 **Kalanshiyū ar Ramlī al Kabīr, Sarīr** *des.* Libya
63 B2 **Kalasin** Thai.
79 C2 **Kalāt** Iran
74 A2 **Kalat** Pak.
50 A2 **Kalbarri** Austr.
Kalburgi India *see* **Gulbarga**
111 C3 **Kale** Turkey
80 B1 **Kalecik** Turkey
118 C3 **Kalema** Dem. Rep. Congo
119 C3 **Kalemie** Dem. Rep. Congo
62 A1 **Kalemyo** Myanmar
Kalgan China *see* **Zhangjiakou**
50 B3 **Kalgoorlie** Austr.
109 C2 **Kali** Croatia
110 C2 **Kaliakra, Nos** *pt* Bulg.
119 C3 **Kalima** Dem. Rep. Congo
61 C2 **Kalimantan** *reg.* Indon.
88 B3 **Kaliningrad** Russia
91 D2 **Kalininskaya** Russia
88 C3 **Kalinkavichy** Belarus
134 D1 **Kalispell** U.S.A.
103 D1 **Kalisz** Pol.
91 E2 **Kalitva** *r.* Russia
92 H2 **Kalix** Sweden
92 H2 **Kalixälven** *r.* Sweden
111 C3 **Kalkan** Turkey
120 A3 **Kalkfeld** Namibia
92 I3 **Kallavesi** *l.* Fin.
92 F3 **Kallsjön** *l.* Sweden
93 G4 **Kalmar** Sweden
93 G4 **Kalmarsund** *sea chan.* Sweden
120 B2 **Kalomo** Zambia
128 B2 **Kalone Peak** Can.
75 B1 **Kalpa** India
73 B3 **Kalpeni** *atoll* India
75 B2 **Kalpi** India
101 D1 **Kaltenkirchen** Ger.
89 E3 **Kaluga** Russia
93 F4 **Kalundborg** Denmark
90 A2 **Kalush** Ukr.
89 E2 **Kalyazin** Russia
111 C3 **Kalymnos** *i.* Greece
119 C3 **Kama** Dem. Rep. Congo
62 A2 **Kama** Myanmar
86 E3 **Kama** *r.* Russia
66 D3 **Kamaishi** Japan
80 B2 **Kaman** Turkey
120 A2 **Kamanjab** Namibia
78 B3 **Kamarān** *i.* Yemen
74 A2 **Kamarod** Pak.
50 B3 **Kambalda** Austr.
119 C4 **Kambove** Dem. Rep. Congo
183 L3 **Kamchatka Peninsula** Russia
110 C2 **Kamchia** *r.* Bulg.
110 B2 **Kamenitsa** *mt.* Bulg.
108 B2 **Kamenjak, Rt** *pt* Croatia
91 D1 **Kamenka** Russia
91 E2 **Kamenolomni** Russia
83 M2 **Kamenskoye** Russia
91 E2 **Kamensk-Shakhtinskiy** Russia
86 F3 **Kamensk-Ural'skiy** Russia
122 A3 **Kamiesberge** *mts* S. Africa
122 A3 **Kamieskroon** S. Africa
129 D1 **Kamilukuak Lake** Can.
119 C3 **Kamina** Dem. Rep. Congo
129 E1 **Kaminak Lake** Can.
90 A1 **Kamin'-Kashyrs'kyy** Ukr.
128 B2 **Kamloops** Can.
118 C3 **Kamonia** Dem. Rep. Congo
119 D2 **Kampala** Uganda
60 B1 **Kampar** *r.* Indon.
60 B1 **Kampar** Malaysia
100 B1 **Kampen** Neth.
119 C3 **Kampene** Dem. Rep. Congo
63 A2 **Kamphaeng Phet** Thai.
63 B2 **Kâmpóng Cham** Cambodia
63 B2 **Kâmpóng Chhnăng** Cambodi
Kâmpóng Saôm Cambodia *se* **Sihanoukville**
63 B2 **Kâmpóng Spœ** Cambodia
63 B2 **Kâmpôt** Cambodia
129 D2 **Kamsack** Can.
86 E3 **Kamskoye Vodokhranilishche** *resr* Russia
117 C4 **Kamsuuma** Somalia
90 B2 **Kam"yanets'-Podil's'kyy** Ukr.
90 A1 **Kam"yanka-Buz'ka** Ukr.
88 B3 **Kamyanyets** Belarus
91 D2 **Kamyshevatskaya** Russia
87 D3 **Kamyshin** Russia
135 D3 **Kanab** U.S.A.
118 C3 **Kananga** Dem. Rep. Congo
87 D3 **Kanash** Russia
140 C3 **Kanawha** *r.* U.S.A.
67 C3 **Kanazawa** Japan
62 A1 **Kanbalu** Myanmar
63 A2 **Kanchanaburi** Thai.
73 B3 **Kanchipuram** India
77 C3 **Kandahār** Afgh.
86 C2 **Kandalaksha** Russia
61 C2 **Kandangan** Indon.
74 A2 **Kandh Kot** Pak.
114 C3 **Kandi** Benin
74 B2 **Kandla** India
53 C2 **Kandos** Austr.
121 □D2 **Kandreho** Madag.
73 C4 **Kandy** Sri Lanka
76 B2 **Kandyagash** Kazakh.
127 G1 **Kane Bassin** *b.* Greenland
91 D2 **Kanevskaya** Russia
122 B1 **Kang** Botswana
127 H2 **Kangaatsiaq** Greenland
114 B3 **Kangaba** Mali
80 B2 **Kangal** Turkey
60 B1 **Kangar** Malaysia
52 A3 **Kangaroo Island** Austr.
75 C2 **Kangchenjunga** *mt.* India/Nepal

65 B2 **Kangdong** N. Korea
61 C2 **Kangean, Kepulauan** *is* Indon.
127 I2 **Kangeq** *c.* Greenland
127 H2 **Kangerlussuaq** *inlet* Greenland
127 I2 **Kangerlussuaq** *inlet* Greenland
127 H2 **Kangersuatsiaq** Greenland
65 B1 **Kanggye** N. Korea
131 D1 **Kangiqsualujjuaq** Can.
127 G2 **Kangiqsujuaq** Can.
127 G2 **Kangirsuk** Can.
75 C2 **Kangmar** China
65 A1 **Kangping** China
72 D2 **Kangto** *mt.* China/India
62 A1 **Kani** Myanmar
86 D2 **Kanin, Poluostrov** *pen.* Russia
86 D2 **Kanin Nos** Russia
91 C2 **Kaniv** Ukr.
93 H3 **Kankaanpää** Fin.
140 B2 **Kankakee** U.S.A.
114 B3 **Kankan** Guinea
75 C2 **Kanker** India
73 B3 **Kannur** India
115 C3 **Kano** Nigeria
122 B3 **Kanonpunt** *pt* S. Africa
67 B4 **Kanoya** Japan
75 C2 **Kanpur** India
136 C3 **Kansas** *r.* U.S.A.
137 D3 **Kansas** *state* U.S.A.
137 E3 **Kansas City** U.S.A.
83 H3 **Kansk** Russia
114 C3 **Kantchari** Burkina Faso
91 D2 **Kantemirovka** Russia
97 B2 **Kanturk** Ireland
123 D2 **Kanyamazane** S. Africa
123 C1 **Kanye** Botswana
120 A2 **Kaokoveld** *plat.* Namibia
114 A3 **Kaolack** Senegal
120 B2 **Kaoma** Zambia
118 C3 **Kapanga** Dem. Rep. Congo
100 B2 **Kapellen** Belgium
121 B2 **Kapiri Mposhi** Zambia
127 H2 **Kapisillit** Greenland
130 B1 **Kapiskau** *r.* Can.
61 C1 **Kapit** *Sarawak* Malaysia
63 A3 **Kapoe** Thai.
117 B4 **Kapoeta** South Sudan
103 D2 **Kaposvár** Hungary
77 D2 **Kapshagay** Kazakh.
77 D2 **Kapshagay, Vodokhranilishche** *resr* Kazakh.
61 B2 **Kapuas** *r.* Indon.
52 A2 **Kapunda** Austr.
130 B2 **Kapuskasing** Can.
103 D2 **Kapuvár** Hungary
88 C3 **Kapyl'** Belarus
114 C4 **Kara** Togo
111 C3 **Kara Ada** *i.* Turkey
76 C1 **Karabalyk** Kazakh.
80 B1 **Karabük** Turkey
76 C2 **Karabutak** Kazakh.
110 C2 **Karacaköy** Turkey
89 D3 **Karachev** Russia
74 A2 **Karachi** Pak.
Kara Deniz *sea* Asia/Europe *see* **Black Sea**
77 D2 **Karagandy** Kazakh.
77 D2 **Karagayly** Kazakh.
83 L3 **Karaginskiy Zaliv** *b.* Russia
81 D2 **Karaj** Iran
64 B2 **Karakelong** *i.* Indon.
77 D2 **Kara-Köl** Kyrg.
77 D2 **Karakol** Kyrg.
74 B1 **Karakoram Range** *mts* Asia
Karakum, Peski *des.* Kazakh. *see* **Karakum Desert**
76 B2 **Karakum Desert** Kazakh.
76 C3 **Karakum Desert** Turkm.
Karakumy, Peski *des.* Turkm. *see* **Karakum Desert**
80 B2 **Karaman** Turkey
77 E2 **Karamay** China
54 B2 **Karamea** N.Z.
54 B2 **Karamea Bight** *b.* N.Z.
80 B2 **Karapınar** Turkey
122 A2 **Karasburg** Namibia
86 F1 **Kara Sea** Russia
92 I2 **Karasjok** Norway
82 G3 **Karasuk** Russia
77 D2 **Karatau** Kazakh.
77 C2 **Karatau, Khrebet** *mts* Kazakh.
86 F2 **Karatayka** Russia
67 A4 **Karatsu** Japan
60 B2 **Karawang** Indon.
81 C2 **Karbalā'** Iraq
103 E2 **Karcag** Hungary
111 B3 **Karditsa** Greece
88 B2 **Kärdla** Estonia
110 C2 **Kardzhali** Bulg.
122 B3 **Kareeberge** *mts* S. Africa
75 B2 **Kareli** India
74 B1 **Kargil** India
121 B2 **Kariba** Zimbabwe
121 B2 **Kariba, Lake** *resr* Zambia/Zimbabwe
61 B2 **Karimata, Pulau-pulau** *is* Indon.
61 B2 **Karimata, Selat** *str.* Indon.
73 B3 **Karimnagar** India
61 C2 **Karimunjawa, Pulau-pulau** *is* Indon.
91 C2 **Karkinits'ka Zatoka** *g.* Ukr.
91 D2 **Karlivka** Ukr.
109 C1 **Karlovac** Croatia
102 C1 **Karlovy Vary** Czech Rep.
93 F4 **Karlshamn** Sweden
93 G4 **Karlskrona** Sweden
102 B2 **Karlsruhe** Ger.
93 F4 **Karlstad** Sweden
101 D3 **Karlstadt** Ger.
89 D3 **Karma** Belarus
93 E4 **Karmøy** *i.* Norway
74 B2 **Karnal** India
75 D2 **Karnaphuli Reservoir** Bangl.
110 C2 **Karnobat** Bulg.
74 A2 **Karodi** Pak.
121 B2 **Karoi** Zimbabwe
121 C1 **Karonga** Malawi
116 B3 **Karora** Eritrea
111 C3 **Karpathos** *i.* Greece
111 B3 **Karpenisi** Greece
86 D2 **Karpogory** Russia
50 A2 **Karratha** Austr.
81 C1 **Kars** Turkey
88 C2 **Kārsava** Latvia
86 E2 **Karskiye Vorota, Proliv** *str.* Russia
Karskoye More *sea* Russia *see* **Kara Sea**
101 E1 **Karstädt** Ger.
111 C2 **Kartal** Turkey
87 F3 **Kartaly** Russia
73 B3 **Karwar** India
83 I3 **Karymskoye** Russia
111 B3 **Karystos** Greece
80 A2 **Kaş** Turkey
130 B1 **Kasabonika Lake** Can.
118 C4 **Kasaji** Dem. Rep. Congo
121 C2 **Kasama** Zambia
120 B2 **Kasane** Botswana
118 B3 **Kasangulu** Dem. Rep. Congo
73 B3 **Kasaragod** India
129 D1 **Kasba Lake** Can.
120 B2 **Kasempa** Zambia
119 C4 **Kasenga** Dem. Rep. Congo
119 C3 **Kasese** Dem. Rep. Congo
119 D2 **Kasese** Uganda
81 D2 **Kāshān** Iran
Kashgar China *see* **Kashi**
77 D3 **Kashi** China
67 D3 **Kashima-nada** *b.* Japan
89 E2 **Kashin** Russia
89 E3 **Kashira** Russia
89 E3 **Kashirskoye** Russia
67 C3 **Kashiwazaki** Japan
76 B3 **Kāshmar** Iran
74 B1 **Kashmir** *reg.* Asia
74 A2 **Kashmore** Pak.
119 C3 **Kashyukulu** Dem. Rep. Congo
87 D3 **Kasimov** Russia
93 H3 **Kaskinen** Fin.
119 C3 **Kasongo** Dem. Rep. Congo
118 B3 **Kasongo-Lunda** Dem. Rep. Congo
111 C3 **Kasos** *i.* Greece
Kaspiyskoye More *l.* Asia/Europe *see* **Caspian Sea**
116 B3 **Kassala** Sudan
101 D2 **Kassel** Ger.
80 B1 **Kastamonu** Turkey
111 B2 **Kastoria** Greece
89 D3 **Kastsyukovichy** Belarus
119 D3 **Kasulu** Tanz.
121 C2 **Kasungu** Malawi
141 F1 **Katahdin, Mount** U.S.A.
118 C3 **Katako-Kombe** Dem. Rep. Congo
50 A3 **Katanning** Austr.
63 A3 **Katchall** *i.* India
111 B2 **Katerini** Greece
128 A2 **Kate's Needle** *mt.* Can./U.S.A.
121 C2 **Katete** Zambia
62 A1 **Katha** Myanmar
50 C1 **Katherine** *r.* Austr.
74 B2 **Kathiawar** *pen.* India
75 C2 **Kathmandu** Nepal
122 B2 **Kathu** S. Africa
74 B1 **Kathua** India
114 B3 **Kati** Mali
75 C2 **Katihar** India
54 C1 **Katikati** N.Z.
123 C3 **Katikati** S. Africa
120 B2 **Katima Mulilo** Namibia
52 A1 **Kati Thanda-Lake Eyre (North)** *imp. l.* Austr.
52 A1 **Kati Thanda-Lake Eyre (South)** *imp. l.* Austr.
123 C2 **Katlehong** S. Africa
75 C2 **Katni** India
111 B3 **Kato Achaïa** Greece
53 D2 **Katoomba** Austr.
103 D1 **Katowice** Pol.
78 A2 **Kātrīnā, Jabal** *mt.* Egypt
93 G4 **Katrineholm** Sweden
115 C3 **Katsina** Nigeria
115 C4 **Katsina-Ala** Nigeria
77 C3 **Kattaqo'rg'on** Uzbek.
93 F4 **Kattegat** *str.* Denmark/Sweden
100 B1 **Katwijk aan Zee** Neth.
124 E5 **Kaua'i** *i.* U.S.A.
93 H3 **Kauhajoki** Fin.
88 B3 **Kaunas** Lith.
115 C3 **Kaura-Namoda** Nigeria
92 H2 **Kautokeino** Norway
111 B2 **Kavala** Greece
66 C2 **Kavalerovo** Russia
73 C3 **Kavali** India
73 B3 **Kavaratti** *atoll* India
110 C2 **Kavarna** Bulg.
81 D2 **Kavīr, Dasht-e** *des.* Iran
67 C3 **Kawagoe** Japan
54 B1 **Kawakawa** N.Z.
67 C3 **Kawanishi** Japan

130 C2 **Kawartha Lakes** Can.
67 C3 **Kawasaki** Japan
54 C1 **Kawerau** N.Z.
63 A2 **Kawkareik** Myanmar
62 A1 **Kawlin** Myanmar
63 A2 **Kawmapyin** Myanmar
63 A2 **Kawthaung** Myanmar
77 D3 **Kaxgar He** *r.* China
114 B3 **Kaya** Burkina Faso
61 C1 **Kayan** *r.* Indon.
136 B2 **Kaycee** U.S.A.
138 A1 **Kayenta** U.S.A.
114 A3 **Kayes** Mali
77 D2 **Kaynar** Kazakh.
80 B2 **Kayseri** Turkey
81 D1 **Kazakhskiy Zaliv** *b.* Kazakh.
76 C2 **Kazakhstan** *country* Asia
87 D3 **Kazan'** Russia
80 A1 **Kazanlak** Bulg.
76 A2 **Kazbek** *mt.* Georgia/Russia
81 D3 **Kāzerūn** Iran
103 E2 **Kazincbarcika** Hungary
86 F2 **Kazym-Mys** Russia
111 B3 **Kea** *i.* Greece
97 C1 **Keady** U.K.
137 D2 **Kearney** U.S.A.
138 A2 **Kearny** U.S.A.
116 A3 **Kebkabiya** Sudan
92 G2 **Kebnekaise** *mt.* Sweden
117 C4 **K'ebrī Dehar** Eth.
61 B2 **Kebumen** Indon.
128 B2 **Kechika** *r.* Can.
103 D2 **Kecskemét** Hungary
88 B2 **Kdainiai** Lith.
114 A3 **Kédougou** Senegal
103 D1 **Kędzierzyn-Koźle** Pol.
128 B1 **Keele** *r.* Can.
128 A1 **Keele Peak** Can.
Keelung Taiwan *see* **Chilung**
141 E2 **Keene** U.S.A.
122 A2 **Keetmanshoop** Namibia
129 E3 **Keewatin** Can.
Kefallonia *i.* Greece *see* **Cephalonia**
59 C3 **Kefamenanu** Indon.
92 □A3 **Keflavík** Iceland
77 D2 **Kegen** Kazakh.
128 C2 **Keg River** Can.
62 A1 **Kehsi Mansam** Myanmar
98 C2 **Keighley** U.K.
88 B2 **Keila** Estonia
122 B2 **Keimoes** S. Africa
92 I3 **Keitele** *l.* Fin.
52 B3 **Keith** Austr.
103 E2 **Kékes** *mt.* Hungary
92 J2 **Kelesuayv, Gora** *h.* Russia
102 C2 **Kelheim** Ger.
80 B1 **Kelkit** *r.* Turkey
128 B1 **Keller Lake** Can.
134 C1 **Kellogg** U.S.A.
92 I2 **Kelloselkä** Fin.
97 C2 **Kells** Ireland
88 B2 **Kelm** Lith.
115 D4 **Kélo** Chad
128 C3 **Kelowna** Can.
96 C3 **Kelso** U.K.
134 B1 **Kelso** U.S.A.
60 B1 **Keluang** Malaysia
129 D2 **Kelvington** Can.
86 C2 **Kem'** Russia
128 B2 **Kemano (abandoned)** Can.
111 C3 **Kemer** Turkey
82 G3 **Kemerovo** Russia
92 H2 **Kemi** Fin.
92 I2 **Kemijärvi** Fin.
92 I2 **Kemijoki** *r.* Fin.
136 A2 **Kemmerer** U.S.A.
92 I3 **Kempele** Fin.
53 D2 **Kempsey** Austr.
130 C2 **Kempt, Lac** *l.* Can.
102 C2 **Kempten (Allgäu)** Ger.
123 C2 **Kempton Park** S. Africa
61 C2 **Kemujan** *i.* Indon.
129 D2 **Kenaston** Can.
98 B1 **Kendal** U.K.
59 C3 **Kendari** Indon.
61 C2 **Kendawangan** Indon.
115 D3 **Kendégué** Chad
75 C2 **Kendujhargarh** India
114 A4 **Kenema** Sierra Leone
118 B3 **Kenge** Dem. Rep. Congo
62 A1 **Kengtung** Myanmar
122 B2 **Kenhardt** S. Africa
114 B1 **Kenitra** Morocco
97 B3 **Kenmare** Ireland
136 C1 **Kenmare** U.S.A.
97 A3 **Kenmare River** *inlet* Ireland
100 C3 **Kenn** Ger.
137 E3 **Kennett** U.S.A.
134 C1 **Kennewick** U.S.A.
129 E3 **Kenora** Can.
140 B2 **Kenosha** U.S.A.
138 C2 **Kent** U.S.A.
77 C2 **Kentau** Kazakh.
140 B3 **Kentucky** *r.* U.S.A.
140 C3 **Kentucky** *state* U.S.A.
140 B3 **Kentucky Lake** U.S.A.
119 D2 **Kenya** *country* Africa
119 D3 **Kenya, Mount** Kenya
137 E2 **Keokuk** U.S.A.
111 C3 **Kepsut** Turkey
52 B3 **Kerang** Austr.
91 D2 **Kerch** Ukr.
59 D3 **Kerema** P.N.G.
128 C3 **Keremeos** Can.
116 B3 **Keren** Eritrea
81 C2 **Kerend-e Gharb** Iran
Kerepakupai Merú Venez. *see* **Angel Falls**
159 C7 **Kerguelen Plateau** Indian Ocean
119 D3 **Kericho** Kenya
54 B1 **Kerikeri** N.Z.
60 B2 **Kerinci, Gunung** *vol.* Indon.
111 A3 **Kerkyra** Greece
Kerkyra *i.* Greece *see* **Corfu**
116 B3 **Kerma** Sudan
49 G4 **Kermadec Islands** S. Pacific Ocean
79 C1 **Kermān** Iran
81 C2 **Kermānshāh** Iran
139 C2 **Kermit** U.S.A.
135 C3 **Kern** *r.* U.S.A.
100 C2 **Kerpen** Ger.
129 D2 **Kerrobert** Can.
139 D2 **Kerrville** U.S.A.
Keryneia Cyprus *see* **Kyrenia**
130 B1 **Kesagami Lake** Can.
111 C2 **Keşan** Turkey
66 D3 **Kesennuma** Japan
74 B2 **Keshod** India
100 C2 **Kessel** Neth.
98 B1 **Keswick** U.K.
103 D2 **Keszthely** Hungary
82 G3 **Ket'** *r.* Russia
61 C2 **Ketapang** Indon.
128 A2 **Ketchikan** U.S.A.
134 D2 **Ketchum** U.S.A.
99 C2 **Kettering** U.K.
93 H3 **Keuruu** Fin.
100 C2 **Kevelaer** Ger.
140 B2 **Kewanee** U.S.A.
140 B1 **Keweenaw Bay** U.S.A.
140 B1 **Keweenaw Peninsula** U.S.A.
143 D3 **Key Largo** U.S.A.
141 D3 **Keyser** U.S.A.
143 D4 **Key West** U.S.A.
123 C2 **Kgotsong** S. Africa
69 E1 **Khabarovsk** Russia
80 B1 **Khadyzhensk** Russia
62 A1 **Khagrachari** Bangl.
74 A2 **Khairpur** Pak.
122 B1 **Khakhea** Botswana
68 C1 **Khamar-Daban, Khrebet** *mts* Russia
74 B2 **Khambhat** India
73 B3 **Khambhat, Gulf of** India
74 B2 **Khamgaon** India
78 B3 **Khamis Mushayṭ** Saudi Arabia
78 B3 **Khamr** Yemen
77 C3 **Khānābād** Afgh.
74 B2 **Khandwa** India
83 K2 **Khandyga** Russia
74 B1 **Khanewal** Pak.
66 B2 **Khanka, Lake** China/Russia
74 B2 **Khanpur** Pak.
77 D2 **Khantau** Kazakh.
83 H2 **Khantayskoye, Ozero** *l.* Russia
86 F2 **Khanty-Mansiysk** Russia
63 A3 **Khao Chum Thong** Thai.
63 A2 **Khao Laem, Ang Kep Nam** Thai.
87 D4 **Kharabali** Russia
75 C2 **Kharagpur** India
81 D3 **Kharāmeh** Iran
79 C2 **Khārān** *r.* Iran
116 B2 **Khārijah, Wāḥāt al** *oasis* Egypt
91 D2 **Kharkiv** Ukr.
Khar'kov Ukr. *see* **Kharkiv**
86 D3 **Kharovsk** Russia
116 B3 **Khartoum** Sudan
87 D4 **Khasavyurt** Russia
79 D2 **Khāsh** Iran
78 A3 **Khashm el Girba** Sudan
78 A3 **Khashm el Girba Dam** Sudan
74 D2 **Khasi Hills** India
123 C3 **Khayamnandi** S. Africa
78 A2 **Khaybar** Saudi Arabia
122 A3 **Khayelitsha** S. Africa
107 D2 **Khemis Miliana** Alg.
63 B2 **Khemmarat** Thai.
115 C1 **Khenchela** Alg.
91 C2 **Kherson** Ukr.
83 H2 **Kheta** *r.* Russia
69 D1 **Khilok** Russia
89 E2 **Khimki** Russia
74 A2 **Khipro** Pak.
89 E3 **Khlevnoye** Russia
90 B2 **Khmel'nyts'kyy** Ukr.
89 E3 **Khokhol'skiy** Russia
74 B2 **Khokhropar** Pak.
89 D2 **Kholm** Russia
89 D2 **Kholm-Zhirkovskiy** Russia
79 C2 **Khonj** Iran
63 B2 **Khon Kaen** Thai.
62 A1 **Khonsa** India
83 K2 **Khonuu** Russia
86 E2 **Khorey-Ver** Russia
69 D1 **Khorinsk** Russia
91 C2 **Khorol** Ukr.
81 C2 **Khorramābād** Iran
81 C2 **Khorramshahr** Iran
77 D3 **Khorugh** Tajik.
74 A1 **Khōst** Afgh.
62 A1 **Khreum** Myanmar
76 B1 **Khromtau** Kazakh.
90 B2 **Khrystynivka** Ukr.
77 C2 **Khŭjand** Tajik.
63 B2 **Khu Khan** Thai.
78 A2 **Khulays** Saudi Arabia
75 C2 **Khulna** Bangl.

79 B2 **Khurayş** Saudi Arabia
74 B1 **Khushab** Pak.
90 A2 **Khust** Ukr.
123 C2 **Khutsong** S. Africa
74 A2 **Khuzdar** Pak.
81 D2 **Khvānsār** Iran
79 C2 **Khvormūj** Iran
81 C2 **Khvoy** Iran
89 D2 **Khvoynaya** Russia
77 D3 **Khyber Pass** Afgh./Pak.
53 D2 **Kiama** Austr.
119 C3 **Kiambi** Dem. Rep. Congo
119 D3 **Kibiti** Tanz.
109 D2 **Kičevo** Macedonia
114 C3 **Kidal** Mali
99 B2 **Kidderminster** U.K.
114 A3 **Kidira** Senegal
54 C1 **Kidnappers, Cape** N.Z.
102 C1 **Kiel** Ger.
103 E1 **Kielce** Pol.
98 B1 **Kielder Water** U.K.
90 C1 **Kiev** Ukr.
114 A3 **Kiffa** Maur.
119 D3 **Kigali** Rwanda
119 C3 **Kigoma** Tanz.
88 B2 **Kihnu** *i.* Estonia
92 I2 **Kiiminki** Fin.
67 B4 **Kii-suidō** *sea chan.* Japan
109 D1 **Kikinda** Serbia
119 C3 **Kikondja** Dem. Rep. Congo
59 D3 **Kikori** P.N.G.
59 D3 **Kikori** *r.* P.N.G.
118 B3 **Kikwit** Dem. Rep. Congo
65 B1 **Kilchu** N. Korea
118 B3 **Kilembe** Dem. Rep. Congo
139 E2 **Kilgore** U.S.A.
119 D3 **Kilimanjaro** *vol.* Tanz.
80 B2 **Kilis** Turkey
90 B2 **Kiliya** Ukr.
97 B2 **Kilkee** Ireland
97 D1 **Kilkeel** U.K.
97 C2 **Kilkenny** Ireland
111 B2 **Kilkis** Greece
97 B1 **Killala Bay** Ireland
97 B2 **Killaloe** Ireland
129 C2 **Killam** Can.
97 B2 **Killarney** Ireland
139 D2 **Killeen** U.S.A.
96 B2 **Killin** U.K.
97 B1 **Killybegs** Ireland
96 B3 **Kilmarnock** U.K.
53 B3 **Kilmore** Austr.
119 D3 **Kilosa** Tanz.
97 B2 **Kilrush** Ireland
119 C3 **Kilwa** Dem. Rep. Congo
119 D3 **Kilwa Masoko** Tanz.
119 D3 **Kimambi** Tanz.
52 A2 **Kimba** Austr.
136 C2 **Kimball** U.S.A.
128 C3 **Kimberley** Can.
122 B2 **Kimberley** S. Africa
50 B1 **Kimberley Plateau** Austr.
65 B1 **Kimch'aek** N. Korea
127 G2 **Kimmirut** Can.
89 E3 **Kimovsk** Russia
118 B3 **Kimpese** Dem. Rep. Congo
89 E2 **Kimry** Russia
61 C1 **Kinabalu, Gunung** *mt. Sabah* Malaysia
128 C2 **Kinbasket Lake** Can.
130 B2 **Kincardine** Can.
62 A1 **Kinchang** Myanmar
119 C3 **Kinda** Dem. Rep. Congo
98 C2 **Kinder Scout** *h.* U.K.
129 D2 **Kindersley** Can.
114 A3 **Kindia** Guinea
119 C3 **Kindu** Dem. Rep. Congo
86 D3 **Kineshma** Russia
78 A2 **King Abdullah Economic City** Saudi Arabia
51 E2 **Kingaroy** Austr.
135 B3 **King City** U.S.A.
130 C1 **King George Islands** Can.
88 C2 **Kingisepp** Russia
51 D3 **King Island** Austr.
50 B1 **King Leopold Ranges** *hills* Austr.
138 A1 **Kingman** U.S.A.
135 B3 **Kings** *r.* U.S.A.
52 A3 **Kingscote** Austr.
99 D2 **King's Lynn** U.K.
48 F3 **Kingsmill Group** *is* Kiribati
50 B1 **King Sound** *b.* Austr.
134 D2 **Kings Peak** U.S.A.
143 D1 **Kingsport** U.S.A.
130 C2 **Kingston** Can.
146 C3 **Kingston** Jamaica
141 E2 **Kingston** U.S.A.
52 A3 **Kingston South East** Austr.
98 C2 **Kingston upon Hull** U.K.
147 D3 **Kingstown** St Vincent
139 D3 **Kingsville** U.S.A.
99 B3 **Kingswood** U.K.
96 B2 **Kingussie** U.K.
126 E2 **King William Island** Can.
123 C3 **King William's Town** S. Africa
67 D3 **Kinka-san** *i.* Japan
93 F4 **Kinna** Sweden
97 B3 **Kinsale** Ireland
118 B3 **Kinshasa** Dem. Rep. Congo
143 E1 **Kinston** U.S.A.
88 B2 **Kintai** Lith.
114 B4 **Kintampo** Ghana
96 B3 **Kintyre** *pen.* U.K.
62 A1 **Kin-U** Myanmar
130 C2 **Kipawa, Lac** *l.* Can.
83 I3 **Kirensk** Russia
89 E3 **Kireyevsk** Russia
Kirghizia *country* Asia *see* **Kyrgyzstan**
49 G3 **Kiribati** *country* Pacific Ocean
80 B2 **Kırıkkale** Turkey
89 E2 **Kirillov** Russia
Kirin China *see* **Jilin**
Kirinyaga *mt.* Kenya *see* **Kenya, Mount**
89 D2 **Kirishi** Russia
49 H2 **Kiritimati** *atoll* Kiribati
111 C3 **Kırkağaç** Turkey
96 C2 **Kirkcaldy** U.K.
96 B3 **Kirkcudbright** U.K.
92 J2 **Kirkenes** Norway
130 B2 **Kirkland Lake** Can.
137 E2 **Kirksville** U.S.A.
81 C2 **Kirkūk** Iraq
96 C1 **Kirkwall** U.K.
89 D3 **Kirov** *Kaluzhskaya Oblast'* Russia
86 D3 **Kirov** *Kirovskaya Oblast'* Russia
Kirovabad Azer. *see* **Gäncä**
86 E3 **Kirovo-Chepetsk** Russia
91 C2 **Kirovohrad** Ukr.
86 C2 **Kirovsk** Russia
91 D2 **Kirovs'ke** Ukr.
96 C2 **Kirriemuir** U.K.
86 E3 **Kirs** Russia
74 A2 **Kirthar Range** *mts* Pak.
92 H2 **Kiruna** Sweden
67 C3 **Kiryū** Japan
89 E2 **Kirzhach** Russia
119 C2 **Kisangani** Dem. Rep. Congo
118 B3 **Kisantu** Dem. Rep. Congo
60 A1 **Kisaran** Indon.
82 G3 **Kiselevsk** Russia
75 C2 **Kishanganj** India
115 C4 **Kishi** Nigeria
Kishinev Moldova *see* **Chişinău**
77 D1 **Kishkenekol'** Kazakh.
74 B1 **Kishtwar** India
119 D3 **Kisii** Kenya
103 D2 **Kiskunfélegyháza** Hungary
103 D2 **Kiskunhalas** Hungary
87 D4 **Kislovodsk** Russia
117 C5 **Kismaayo** Somalia
119 C3 **Kisoro** Uganda
111 B3 **Kissamos** Greece
114 A4 **Kissidougou** Guinea
143 D3 **Kissimmee** U.S.A.
143 D3 **Kissimmee, Lake** U.S.A.
129 D2 **Kississing Lake** Can.
119 D3 **Kisumu** Kenya
114 B3 **Kita** Mali
66 D3 **Kitakami** Japan
66 D3 **Kitakami-gawa** *r.* Japan
67 B4 **Kita-Kyūshū** Japan
119 D2 **Kitale** Kenya
66 D2 **Kitami** Japan
130 B2 **Kitchener** Can.
93 J3 **Kitee** Fin.
119 D2 **Kitgum** Uganda
128 B2 **Kitimat** Can.
118 B3 **Kitona** Dem. Rep. Congo
119 D3 **Kitunda** Tanz.
128 B2 **Kitwanga** Can.
121 B2 **Kitwe** Zambia
101 E3 **Kitzingen** Ger.
92 I3 **Kiuruvesi** Fin.
119 C3 **Kivu, Lac** Dem. Rep. Congo/Rwanda
110 C2 **Kıyıköy** Turkey
86 E3 **Kizel** Russia
111 C3 **Kızılca Dağ** *mt.* Turkey
87 D4 **Kizlyar** Russia
92 I1 **Kjøllefjord** Norway
92 G2 **Kjøpsvik** Norway
102 C1 **Kladno** Czech Rep.
102 C2 **Klagenfurt am Wörthersee** Austria
88 B2 **Klaipda** Lith.
94 B1 **Klaksvík** Faroe Is
134 B2 **Klamath** *r.* U.S.A.
134 B2 **Klamath Falls** U.S.A.
134 B2 **Klamath Mountains** U.S.A.
60 B1 **Klang** Malaysia
102 C2 **Klatovy** Czech Rep.
122 A3 **Klawer** S. Africa
128 A2 **Klawock** U.S.A.
128 B2 **Kleena Kleene** Can.
122 B2 **Kleinbegin** S. Africa
122 A2 **Kleinsee** S. Africa
123 C2 **Klerksdorp** S. Africa
89 D3 **Kletnya** Russia
100 C2 **Kleve** Ger.
89 D3 **Klimavichy** Belarus
89 D3 **Klimovo** Russia
89 E2 **Klimovsk** Russia
89 E2 **Klin** Russia
101 F2 **Klínovec** *mt.* Czech Rep.
93 G4 **Klintehamn** Sweden
89 D3 **Klintsy** Russia
109 C2 **Ključ** Bos. & Herz.
103 D1 **Kłodzko** Pol.
100 C1 **Kloosterhaar** Neth.
103 D2 **Klosterneuburg** Austria
101 E1 **Klötze (Altmark)** Ger.
103 D1 **Kluczbork** Pol.
128 A2 **Klukwan** U.S.A.
88 C3 **Klyetsk** Belarus
98 C1 **Knaresborough** U.K.
93 F3 **Knästen** *h.* Sweden
129 E2 **Knee Lake** Can.
101 E1 **Knesebeck** Ger.

101 E3 **Knetzgau** Ger.
109 C2 **Knin** Croatia
103 C2 **Knittelfeld** Austria
109 D2 **Knjaževac** Serbia
100 A2 **Knokke-Heist** Belgium
143 D1 **Knoxville** U.S.A.
122 B3 **Knysna** S. Africa
76 B1 **Kobda** Kazakh.
67 C4 **Kōbe** Japan
København Denmark *see* **Copenhagen**
100 C2 **Koblenz** Ger.
59 C3 **Kobroör** *i.* Indon.
88 B3 **Kobryn** Belarus
109 D2 **Kočani** Macedonia
111 C2 **Kocasu** *r.* Turkey
75 C2 **Koch Bihar** India
73 B4 **Kochi** India
67 B4 **Kōchi** Japan
87 D4 **Kochubey** Russia
75 C2 **Kodarma** India
117 B4 **Kodok** South Sudan
90 B2 **Kodyma** Ukr.
111 C2 **Kodzhaele** *mt.* Bulg./Greece
122 A2 **Koës** Namibia
122 C2 **Koffiefontein** S. Africa
114 B4 **Koforidua** Ghana
67 C3 **Kōfu** Japan
131 D1 **Kogaluk** *r.* Can.
117 B5 **Kogelo** Kenya
74 B1 **Kohat** Pak.
62 A1 **Kohima** India
88 C2 **Kohtla-Järve** Estonia
114 A4 **Koidu-Sefadu** Sierra Leone
92 H3 **Kokkola** Fin.
140 B2 **Kokomo** U.S.A.
77 E2 **Kokpekty** Kazakh.
77 C1 **Kokshetau** Kazakh.
131 D1 **Koksoak** *r.* Can.
123 C3 **Kokstad** S. Africa
Koktokay China *see* **Fuyun**
58 C3 **Kolaka** Indon.
86 C2 **Kola Peninsula** Russia
92 H2 **Kolari** Fin.
114 A3 **Kolda** Senegal
93 E4 **Kolding** Denmark
107 D2 **Koléa** Alg.
86 D2 **Kolguyev, Ostrov** *i.* Russia
73 B3 **Kolhapur** India
88 B2 **Kolkasrags** *pt* Latvia
75 C2 **Kolkata** India
73 B4 **Kollam** India
Köln Ger. *see* **Cologne**
103 D1 **Kołobrzeg** Pol.
114 B3 **Kolokani** Mali
89 E2 **Kolomna** Russia
90 B2 **Kolomyya** Ukr.
122 B2 **Kolonkwaneng** Botswana
82 G3 **Kolpashevo** Russia
89 E3 **Kolpny** Russia
Kol'skiy Poluostrov *pen.* Russia *see* **Kola Peninsula**
78 B3 **Koluli** Eritrea
119 C4 **Kolwezi** Dem. Rep. Congo
83 L2 **Kolyma** *r.* Russia
83 L2 **Kolymskaya Nizmennost'** *lowland* Russia
83 M2 **Kolymskiy, Khrebet** *mts* Russia
67 C3 **Komaki** Japan
83 M3 **Komandorskiye Ostrova** *is* Russia
103 D2 **Komárno** Slovakia
123 D2 **Komati** *r.* S. Africa/Swaziland
67 C3 **Komatsu** Japan
119 C3 **Kombe** Dem. Rep. Congo
90 C2 **Kominternivs'ke** Ukr.
109 C2 **Komiža** Croatia
103 D2 **Komló** Hungary
118 B3 **Komono** Congo
111 C2 **Komotini** Greece
122 B3 **Komsberg** *mts* S. Africa
83 H1 **Komsomolets, Ostrov** *i.* Russia
89 F2 **Komsomol'sk** Russia
91 C2 **Komsomol's'k** Ukr.
87 D4 **Komsomol'skiy** Russia
69 E1 **Komsomol'sk-na-Amure** Russia
89 E2 **Konakovo** Russia
75 C3 **Kondagaon** India
86 F2 **Kondinskoye** Russia
119 D3 **Kondoa** Tanz.
86 C2 **Kondopoga** Russia
89 E3 **Kondrovo** Russia
127 I2 **Kong Christian IX Land** *reg.* Greenland
127 I2 **Kong Frederik VI Kyst** *coastal area* Greenland
119 C3 **Kongolo** Dem. Rep. Congo
93 E4 **Kongsberg** Norway
93 F3 **Kongsvinger** Norway
77 D3 **Kongur Shan** *mt.* China
100 C2 **Königswinter** Ger.
103 D1 **Konin** Pol.
109 C2 **Konjic** Bos. & Herz.
122 A2 **Konkiep** *watercourse* Namibia
91 C1 **Konotop** Ukr.
102 B2 **Konstanz** Ger.
115 C3 **Kontagora** Nigeria
63 B2 **Kon Tum** Vietnam
63 B2 **Kon Tum, Cao Nguyên** *plat.* Vietnam
80 B2 **Konya** Turkey
100 C3 **Konz** Ger.
86 E3 **Konzhakovskiy Kamen', Gora** *mt.* Russia
134 C1 **Kooskia** U.S.A.
128 C3 **Kootenay Lake** Can.
122 B3 **Kootjieskolk** S. Africa
92 □B2 **Kópasker** Iceland
108 B1 **Koper** Slovenia
93 G4 **Kopparberg** Sweden
109 C1 **Koprivnica** Croatia
89 F3 **Korablino** Russia
73 C3 **Koraput** India
101 D2 **Korbach** Ger.
109 D2 **Korçë** Albania
109 C2 **Korčula** Croatia
109 C2 **Korčula** *i.* Croatia
70 C2 **Korea Bay** *g.* China/N. Korea
65 B2 **Korea, North** *country* Asia
65 B2 **Korea, South** *country* Asia
65 B3 **Korea Strait** Japan/S. Korea
91 D2 **Korenovsk** Russia
90 B1 **Korets'** Ukr.
111 C2 **Körfez** Turkey
114 B4 **Korhogo** Côte d'Ivoire
Korinthos Greece *see* **Corinth**
103 D2 **Kris-hegy** *h.* Hungary
109 D2 **Koritnik** *mt.* Albania/Kosovo
67 D3 **Kōriyama** Japan
80 B2 **Korkuteli** Turkey
68 B2 **Korla** China
103 D2 **Körmend** Hungary
114 B3 **Koro** Mali
131 D1 **Koroc** *r.* Can.
91 D1 **Korocha** Russia
119 D3 **Korogwe** Tanz.
59 C2 **Koror** Palau
90 B1 **Korosten'** Ukr.
90 B1 **Korostyshiv** Ukr.
115 D3 **Koro Toro** Chad
91 C2 **Korsun'-Shevchenkivs'kyy** Ukr.
103 E1 **Korsze** Pol.
100 A2 **Kortrijk** Belgium
83 L3 **Koryakskaya Sopka, Vulkan** *vol.* Russia
83 M2 **Koryakskoye Nagor'ye** *mts* Russia
86 D2 **Koryazhma** Russia
91 C1 **Koryukivka** Ukr.
111 C3 **Kos** Greece
111 C3 **Kos** *i.* Greece
65 B2 **Kosan** N. Korea
103 D1 **Kościan** Pol.
53 C3 **Kosciuszko, Mount** Austr.
68 B1 **Kosh-Agach** Russia
103 E2 **Košice** Slovakia
92 H2 **Koskullskulle** Sweden
65 B2 **Kosŏng** N. Korea
109 D2 **Kosovo** *country* Europe
Kosovska Mitrovica Kosovo *see* **Mitrovicë**
48 E2 **Kosrae** *atoll* Micronesia
114 B4 **Kossou, Lac de** *l.* Côte d'Ivoire
76 C1 **Kostanay** Kazakh.
110 B2 **Kostenets** Bulg.
123 C2 **Koster** S. Africa
117 B3 **Kosti** Sudan
86 C2 **Kostomuksha** Russia
90 B1 **Kostopil'** Ukr.
89 F2 **Kostroma** Russia
89 F2 **Kostroma** *r.* Russia
102 C1 **Kostrzyn nad Odrą** Pol.
103 D1 **Koszalin** Pol.
103 D2 **Kszeg** Hungary
74 B2 **Kota** India
60 B2 **Kotaagung** Indon.
61 C2 **Kotabaru** Indon.
61 C1 **Kota Belud** *Sabah* Malaysia
60 B1 **Kota Bharu** Malaysia
60 B2 **Kotabumi** Indon.
61 C1 **Kota Kinabalu** *Sabah* Malaysia
61 C1 **Kota Samarahan** *Sarawak* Malaysia
86 D3 **Kotel'nich** Russia
87 D4 **Kotel'nikovo** Russia
83 K1 **Kotel'nyy, Ostrov** *i.* Russia
101 E2 **Köthen (Anhalt)** Ger.
93 I3 **Kotka** Fin.
86 D2 **Kotlas** Russia
109 C2 **Kotor Varoš** Bos. & Herz.
87 D3 **Kotovo** Russia
91 E1 **Kotovsk** Russia
90 B2 **Kotovs'k** Ukr.
83 H2 **Kotuy** *r.* Russia
100 A2 **Koudekerke** Neth.
114 B3 **Koudougou** Burkina Faso
122 B3 **Kougaberge** *mts* S. Africa
118 B3 **Koulamoutou** Gabon
114 B3 **Koulikoro** Mali
114 A3 **Koundâra** Guinea
151 C1 **Kourou** Fr. Guiana
114 B3 **Kouroussa** Guinea
115 D3 **Kousséri** Cameroon
114 B3 **Koutiala** Mali
93 I3 **Kouvola** Fin.
92 J2 **Kovdor** Russia
90 A1 **Kovel'** Ukr.
89 F2 **Kovrov** Russia
54 B2 **Kowhitirangi** N.Z.
Koyamutthoor India *see* **Coimbatore**
111 C3 **Köyceğiz** Turkey
86 D2 **Koyda** Russia
126 A2 **Koyukuk** *r.* U.S.A.
111 B2 **Kozani** Greece
90 C1 **Kozelets'** Ukr.
89 E3 **Kozel'sk** Russia
73 B3 **Kozhikode** India
90 B2 **Kozyatyn** Ukr.
63 A3 **Krabi** Thai.

63 A2 **Kra Buri** Thai.
63 B2 **Krâchéh** Cambodia
93 E4 **Kragerø** Norway
100 B1 **Kraggenburg** Neth.
109 D2 **Kragujevac** Serbia
60 B2 **Krakatau** *i.* Indon.
103 D1 **Kraków** Pol.
91 D2 **Kramators'k** Ukr.
93 G3 **Kramfors** Sweden
111 B3 **Kranidi** Greece
86 E1 **Krasino** Russia
88 C2 **Krāslava** Latvia
101 F2 **Kraslice** Czech Rep.
89 D3 **Krasnapollye** Belarus
89 D3 **Krasnaya Gora** Russia
87 D3 **Krasnoarmeysk** Russia
91 D2 **Krasnoarmiys'k** Ukr.
86 D2 **Krasnoborsk** Russia
91 D2 **Krasnodar** Russia
91 D2 **Krasnodarskoye Vodokhranilishche** *resr* Russia
91 D2 **Krasnodon** Ukr.
88 C2 **Krasnogorodsk** Russia
91 D2 **Krasnohrad** Ukr.
91 C2 **Krasnohvardiys'ke** Ukr.
86 E3 **Krasnokamsk** Russia
89 D2 **Krasnomayskiy** Russia
91 C2 **Krasnoperekops'k** Ukr.
87 D3 **Krasnoslobodsk** Russia
86 E3 **Krasnoufimsk** Russia
83 H3 **Krasnoyarsk** Russia
89 F2 **Krasnoye-na-Volge** Russia
89 D3 **Krasnyy** Russia
89 E2 **Krasnyy Kholm** Russia
87 C4 **Krasnyy Luch** Ukr.
91 E2 **Krasnyy Sulin** Russia
90 B2 **Krasyliv** Ukr.
100 C2 **Krefeld** Ger.
91 C2 **Kremenchuk** Ukr.
91 C2 **Kremenchuts'ke Vodoskhovyshche** *resr* Ukr.
103 D2 **Křemešník** *h.* Czech Rep.
91 D2 **Kreminna** Ukr.
103 D2 **Krems an der Donau** Austria
89 D2 **Kresttsy** Russia
88 B2 **Kretinga** Lith.
100 C2 **Kreuzau** Ger.
100 C2 **Kreuztal** Ger.
118 A2 **Kribi** Cameroon
111 B3 **Krikellos** Greece
66 D1 **Kril'on, Mys** *c.* Russia
73 C3 **Krishna** *r.* India
73 C3 **Krishna, Mouths of the** India
75 C2 **Krishnanagar** India
93 E4 **Kristiansand** Norway
93 F4 **Kristianstad** Sweden
92 E3 **Kristiansund** Norway
93 F4 **Kristinehamn** Sweden
Kriti *i.* Greece *see* **Crete**
111 C3 **Kritiko Pelagos** *sea* Greece
Krivoy Rog Ukr. *see* **Kryvyy Rih**
109 C1 **Križevci** Croatia
108 B1 **Krk** *i.* Croatia
92 F3 **Krokom** Sweden
91 C1 **Krolevets'** Ukr.
101 E2 **Kronach** Ger.
63 B2 **Krŏng Kaôh Kŏng** Cambodia
127 I2 **Kronprins Frederik Bjerge** *nunataks* Greenland
123 C2 **Kroonstad** S. Africa
87 D4 **Kropotkin** Russia
103 E2 **Krosno** Pol.
103 D1 **Krotoszyn** Pol.
60 B2 **Krui** Indon.
109 C2 **Krujë** Albania
111 C2 **Krumovgrad** Bulg.
Krung Thep Thai. *see* **Bangkok**
88 C3 **Krupki** Belarus
109 D2 **Kruševac** Serbia
101 F2 **Krušné hory** *mts* Czech Rep.
128 A2 **Kruzof Island** U.S.A.
89 D3 **Krychaw** Belarus
91 D3 **Krymsk** Russia
91 C2 **Kryvyy Rih** Ukr.
114 B2 **Ksabi** Alg.
107 D2 **Ksar el Boukhari** Alg.
114 B1 **Ksar el Kebir** Morocco
89 E3 **Kshenskiy** Russia
78 B2 **Kū', Jabal al** *h.* Saudi Arabia
61 C1 **Kuala Belait** Brunei
60 B1 **Kuala Kerai** Malaysia
60 B1 **Kuala Lipis** Malaysia
60 B1 **Kuala Lumpur** Malaysia
61 C2 **Kualapembuang** Indon.
60 B1 **Kuala Terengganu** Malaysia
60 B2 **Kualatungal** Indon.
61 C1 **Kuamut** *Sabah* Malaysia
65 A1 **Kuandian** China
60 B1 **Kuantan** Malaysia
91 D2 **Kuban'** *r.* Russia
89 E2 **Kubenskoye, Ozero** *l.* Russia
110 C2 **Kubrat** Bulg.
61 C1 **Kubuang** Indon.
61 C1 **Kuching** *Sarawak* Malaysia
109 C2 **Kuçovë** Albania
61 C1 **Kudat** *Sabah* Malaysia
61 C2 **Kudus** Indon.
102 C2 **Kufstein** Austria
127 F2 **Kugaaruk** Can.
126 D2 **Kugluktuk** Can.
92 I3 **Kuhmo** Fin.
79 C2 **Kūhrān, Kūh-e** *mt.* Iran
Kuitin China *see* **Kuytun**
120 A2 **Kuito** Angola
92 I2 **Kuivaniemi** Fin.
65 B2 **Kujang** N. Korea
109 D2 **Kukës** Albania
111 C3 **Kula** Turkey
75 D2 **Kula Kangri** *mt.* Bhutan/China
76 B2 **Kulandy** Kazakh.
88 B2 **Kuldīga** Latvia
122 B1 **Kule** Botswana
101 E2 **Kulmbach** Ger.
77 C3 **Kŭlob** Tajik.
76 B2 **Kul'sary** Kazakh.
77 D1 **Kulunda** Russia
127 I2 **Kulusuk** Greenland
67 C3 **Kumagaya** Japan
67 B4 **Kumamoto** Japan
109 D2 **Kumanovo** Macedonia
114 B4 **Kumasi** Ghana
118 A2 **Kumba** Cameroon
78 B2 **Kumdah** Saudi Arabia
87 E3 **Kumertau** Russia
93 G4 **Kumla** Sweden
115 D3 **Kumo** Nigeria
62 A1 **Kumon Range** *mts* Myanmar
62 B2 **Kumphawapi** Thai.
Kumul China *see* **Hami**
66 D2 **Kunashir, Ostrov** *i.* Russia
120 A2 **Kunene** *r.* Angola/Namibia
77 D2 **Kungei Alatau** *mts* Kazakh./Kyrg.
93 F4 **Kungsbacka** Sweden
118 B2 **Kungu** Dem. Rep. Congo
86 E3 **Kungur** Russia
62 A1 **Kunhing** Myanmar
77 D3 **Kunlun Shan** *mts* China
62 B1 **Kunming** China
50 B1 **Kununurra** Austr.
92 I3 **Kuopio** Fin.
109 C1 **Kupa** *r.* Croatia/Slovenia
59 C3 **Kupang** Indon.
88 B2 **Kupiškis** Lith.
111 C2 **Küplü** Turkey
128 A2 **Kupreanof Island** U.S.A.
91 D2 **Kup"yans'k** Ukr.
77 E2 **Kuqa** China
67 B4 **Kurashiki** Japan
67 B3 **Kurayoshi** Japan
89 E3 **Kurchatov** Russia
81 C2 **Kurdistan** *reg.* Asia
67 B4 **Kure** Japan
88 B2 **Kuressaare** Estonia
86 F3 **Kurgan** Russia
93 H3 **Kurikka** Fin.
156 C3 **Kuril Trench** N. Pacific Ocean
89 E3 **Kurkino** Russia
117 B3 **Kurmuk** Sudan
73 B3 **Kurnool** India
53 D2 **Kurri Kurri** Austr.
89 E3 **Kursk** Russia
122 B2 **Kuruman** S. Africa
122 B2 **Kuruman** *watercourse* S. Africa
67 B4 **Kurume** Japan
83 I3 **Kurumkan** Russia
73 C4 **Kurunegala** Sri Lanka
111 C3 **Kuşadası** Turkey
111 C3 **Kuşadası, Gulf of** *b.* Turkey
111 C2 **Kuş Gölü** *l.* Turkey
91 D2 **Kushchevskaya** Russia
66 D2 **Kushiro** Japan
75 C2 **Kushtia** Bangl.
76 C1 **Kusmuryn** Kazakh.
66 D2 **Kussharo-ko** *l.* Japan
111 C3 **Kütahya** Turkey
81 C1 **Kutaisi** Georgia
109 C1 **Kutjevo** Croatia
103 D1 **Kutno** Pol.
118 B3 **Kutu** Dem. Rep. Congo
126 D2 **Kuujjua** *r.* Can.
131 D1 **Kuujjuaq** Can.
130 C1 **Kuujjuarapik** Can.
92 I2 **Kuusamo** Fin.
120 A2 **Kuvango** Angola
89 D2 **Kuvshinovo** Russia
78 B2 **Kuwait** *country* Asia
79 B2 **Kuwait** Kuwait
Kuybyshev Russia *see* **Samara**
91 D2 **Kuybysheve** Ukr.
87 D3 **Kuybyshevskoye Vodokhranilishche** *resr* Russia
77 E2 **Kuytun** China
111 C3 **Kuyucak** Turkey
87 D3 **Kuznetsk** Russia
90 B1 **Kuznetsovs'k** Ukr.
92 H1 **Kvalsund** Norway
123 D2 **KwaDukuza** S. Africa
123 D2 **KwaMashu** S. Africa
Kwangju S. Korea *see* **Gwangju**
65 B1 **Kwanmo-bong** *mt.* N. Korea
123 C3 **KwaNobuhle** S. Africa
122 B3 **KwaNonzame** S. Africa
123 C3 **Kwatinidubu** S. Africa
123 C2 **KwaZamokuhle** S. Africa
123 D2 **KwaZulu-Natal** *prov.* S. Africa
121 B2 **Kwekwe** Zimbabwe
118 B3 **Kwenge** *r.* Dem. Rep. Congo
103 D1 **Kwidzyn** Pol.
118 B3 **Kwilu** *r.* Angola/Dem. Rep. Congo
59 C3 **Kwoka** *mt.* Indon.
53 C3 **Kyabram** Austr.
62 A2 **Kyaikto** Myanmar
69 D1 **Kyakhta** Russia
52 A2 **Kyancutta** Austr.
62 A1 **Kyaukpadaung** Myanmar
62 A2 **Kyaukpyu** Myanmar
88 B3 **Kybartai** Lith.
62 A2 **Kyebogyi** Myanmar
62 A2 **Kyeintali** Myanmar
74 B1 **Kyelang** India
Kyiv Ukr. *see* **Kiev**

90	C1	Kyivs'ke Vodoskhovyshche *resr* Ukr.
		Kyklades *is Greece see*
		Cyclades
129	D2	Kyle Can.
96	B2	Kyle of Lochalsh U.K.
100	C3	Kyll *r.* Ger.
111	B3	Kyllini *mt.* Greece
111	B3	Kymi Greece
52	B3	Kyneton Austr.
119	D2	Kyoga, Lake Uganda
53	D1	Kyogle Austr.
67	C4	Kyōto Japan
111	B3	Kyparissia Greece
111	B3	Kyra Panagia *i.* Greece
80	B2	Kyrenia Cyprus
77	D2	Kyrgyzstan *country* Asia
101	F1	Kyritz Ger.
92	H3	Kyrönjoki *r.* Fin.
86	E2	Kyrta Russia
86	D2	Kyssa Russia
111	B3	Kythira *i.* Greece
111	B3	Kythnos *i.* Greece
128	B2	Kyuquot Can.
67	B4	Kyūshū *i.* Japan
110	B2	Kyustendil Bulg.
92	H3	Kyyjärvi Fin.
68	C1	Kyzyl Russia
76	C2	Kyzylkum Desert Kazakh./ Uzbek.
77	C2	Kyzylorda Kazakh.

L

145	C3	La Angostura, Presa de *resr* Mex.
117	C4	Laascaanood Somalia
150	B1	La Asunción Venez.
114	A2	Laâyoune Western Sahara
87	D4	Laba *r.* Russia
144	B2	La Babia Mex.
146	B3	La Bahía, Islas de *is* Hond.
152	B3	La Banda Arg.
104	B2	La Baule-Escoublac France
114	A3	Labé Guinea
128	A1	Laberge, Lake Can.
129	C2	La Biche, Lac *l.* Can.
87	D4	Labinsk Russia
64	B1	Labo Phil.
104	B3	Labouheyre France
131	D1	Labrador *reg.* Can.
131	D1	Labrador City Can.
158	C1	Labrador Sea Can./Greenland
150	B2	Lábrea Brazil
61	C1	Labuan Malaysia
60	B1	Labuhanbilik Indon.
59	C3	Labuna Indon.
63	A2	Labutta Myanmar
86	F2	Labytnangi Russia
109	C2	Laç Albania
105	C2	La Capelle France
		Laccadive Islands India *see* Lakshadweep
129	C2	Lac du Bonnet Can.
146	B3	La Ceiba Hond.
53	B2	Lachlan *r.* Austr.
141	E1	Lachute Can.
105	D3	La Ciotat France
129	C2	Lac la Biche Can.
		La la Martre Can. *see* Whati
141	E1	Lac-Mégantic Can.
128	C2	Lacombe Can.
146	B4	La Concepción Panama
145	C3	La Concordia Mex.
108	A3	Laconi *Sardinia* Italy
141	E2	Laconia U.S.A.
128	C2	La Crete Can.
140	A2	La Crosse U.S.A.
144	B2	La Cruz Mex.
144	B2	La Cuesta Mex.
75	B1	Ladakh Range *mts* India/Pak.
122	B3	Ladismith S. Africa
79	D2	Lādīz Iran
86	C2	Ladoga, Lake Russia
		Ladozhskoye Ozero *l.* Russia *see* Ladoga, Lake
128	B3	Ladysmith Can.
123	C2	Ladysmith S. Africa
59	D3	Lae P.N.G.
152	B3	La Esmeralda Bol.
93	F4	Læsø *i.* Denmark
143	C2	La Fayette U.S.A.
140	B2	Lafayette *IN* U.S.A.
142	B2	Lafayette *LA* U.S.A.
115	C4	Lafia Nigeria
104	B2	La Flèche France
143	D1	La Follette U.S.A.
131	C1	Laforge Can.
79	C2	Lāft Iran
108	A3	La Galite *i.* Tunisia
81	C1	Lagan' Russia
118	B2	Lagdo, Lac de *l.* Cameroon
152	C3	Lages Brazil
115	C1	Laghouat Alg.
155	D1	Lagoa Santa Brazil
114	A2	La Gomera *i.* Canary Islands
114	C4	Lagos Nigeria
106	B2	Lagos Port.
134	C1	La Grande U.S.A.
130	C1	La Grande 3, Réservoir *resr* Can.
131	C1	La Grande 4, Réservoir *resr* Can.
50	B1	La Grange Austr.
143	C2	La Grange U.S.A.
150	B1	La Gran Sabana *plat.* Venez.
152	D3	Laguna Brazil
144	A2	Laguna, Picacho de la *mt.* Mex.
150	A2	Lagunas Peru
		La Habana Cuba *see* Havana
61	C1	Lahad Datu *Sabah* Malaysia
60	B2	Lahat Indon.
78	B3	Laḥij Yemen
81	C2	Lāhījān Iran
100	C2	Lahnstein Ger.
74	B1	Lahore Pak.
74	A2	Lahri Pak.
93	I3	Lahti Fin.
115	D4	Laï Chad
53	D1	Laidley Austr.
104	B2	L'Aigle France
111	B3	Laimos, Akrotirio *pt* Greece
122	B3	Laingsburg S. Africa
92	H2	Lainioälven *r.* Sweden
96	B1	Lairg U.K.
108	B1	Laives Italy
70	B2	Laiwu China
70	C2	Laiyang China
70	B2	Laizhou China
70	B2	Laizhou Wan *b.* China
50	C1	Lajamanu Austr.
144	B2	La Junta Mex.
136	C3	La Junta U.S.A.
121	C2	Lake Cabora Bassa *resr* Moz.
53	C2	Lake Cargelligo Austr.
53	D2	Lake Cathie Austr.
142	B2	Lake Charles U.S.A.
143	D2	Lake City *FL* U.S.A.
143	E2	Lake City *SC* U.S.A.
108	A1	Lake Como Italy
128	B3	Lake Cowichan Can.
108	B1	Lake Garda Italy
138	A2	Lake Havasu City U.S.A.
143	D3	Lakeland U.S.A.
128	C2	Lake Louise Can.
134	B1	Lake Oswego U.S.A.
54	A2	Lake Paringa N.Z.
142	B2	Lake Providence U.S.A.
54	B2	Lake Pukaki N.Z.
53	C3	Lakes Entrance Austr.
134	B2	Lakeview U.S.A.
136	B3	Lakewood CO U.S.A.
141	E2	Lakewood NJ U.S.A.
143	D3	Lake Worth U.S.A.
74	A2	Lakhpat India
74	B1	Lakki Marwat Pak.
111	B3	Lakonikos Kolpos *b.* Greece
92	H1	Lakselv Norway
73	B3	Lakshadweep India
107	C1	L'Alcora Spain
145	C3	La Libertad Guat.
106	B1	Lalín Spain
75	B2	Lalitpur India
129	D2	La Loche Can.
100	B2	La Louvière Belgium
108	A2	La Maddalena *Sardinia* Italy
61	C1	Lamag *Sabah* Malaysia
		La Manche *str.* France/U.K. *see* English Channel
136	C3	Lamar U.S.A.
108	A3	La Marmora, Punta *mt. Sardinia* Italy
128	C1	La Martre, Lac *l.* Can.
118	B3	Lambaréné Gabon
122	A3	Lambert's Bay S. Africa
92	□A2	Lambeyri Iceland
106	B1	Lamego Port.
150	A3	La Merced Peru
79	C2	Lāmerd Iran
52	B3	Lameroo Austr.
139	C2	Lamesa U.S.A.
111	B3	Lamia Greece
137	E2	Lamoni U.S.A.
62	A2	Lampang Thai.
139	D2	Lampasas U.S.A.
145	B2	Lampazos Mex.
99	A2	Lampeter U.K.
62	A2	Lamphun Thai.
119	E3	Lamu Kenya
62	A2	Lan, Loi *mt.* Myanmar/Thai.
96	C3	Lanark U.K.
63	A2	Lanbi Kyun *i.* Myanmar
		Lancang Jiang *r.* China *see* Mekong
98	B1	Lancaster U.K.
135	C4	Lancaster CA U.S.A.
140	C3	Lancaster OH U.S.A.
141	D2	Lancaster PA U.S.A.
143	D2	Lancaster SC U.S.A.
127	F2	Lancaster Sound *str.* Can.
		Lanchow China *see* Lanzhou
102	C2	Landeck Austria
136	B2	Lander U.S.A.
99	A3	Land's End *pt* U.K.
102	C2	Landshut Ger.
93	F4	Landskrona Sweden
143	C2	Lanett U.S.A.
122	B2	Langberg *mts* S. Africa
137	D1	Langdon U.S.A.
93	F4	Langeland *i.* Denmark
101	D1	Langen Ger.
100	C1	Langeoog Ger.
100	C1	Langeoog *i.* Ger.
101	D2	Langgöns Ger.
92	□A3	Langjökull Iceland
105	C3	Langogne France
104	B3	Langon France
105	D2	Langres France
60	A1	Langsa Indon.
62	B1	Lang Sơn Vietnam

101 D1 Langwedel Ger.
129 D2 Lanigan Can.
153 A4 Lanín, Volcán *vol.* Arg./Chile
81 C2 Länkäran Azer.
104 B2 Lannion France
140 C2 Lansing U.S.A.
71 B3 Lanxi China
117 B4 Lanya South Sudan
114 A2 Lanzarote *i.* Canary Islands
70 A2 Lanzhou China
64 B1 Laoag City Phil.
62 B1 Lao Cai Vietnam
70 B2 Laohekou China
68 C2 Laojunmiao China
65 B1 Laoling China
65 B1 Lao Ling *mts* China
68 C2 Lao Mangnai China
105 C2 Laon France
62 B2 Laos *country* Asia
65 B1 Laotougou China
154 C3 Lapa Brazil
114 A2 La Palma *i.* Canary Islands
146 C4 La Palma Panama
150 B1 La Paragua Venez.
152 B2 La Paz Bol.
144 A2 La Paz Mex.
150 B2 La Pedrera Col.
66 D1 La Pérouse Strait Japan/Russia
145 C2 La Pesca Mex.
144 B2 La Piedad Mex.
153 C4 La Plata Arg.
153 C4 La Plata, Río de *sea chan.* Arg./Uru.
106 B1 La Pola Spain
93 I3 Lappeenranta Fin.
92 G2 Lappland *reg.* Europe
111 C2 Lâpseki Turkey
83 J1 Laptev Sea Russia
 Laptevykh, More *sea* Russia
 see Laptev Sea
92 H3 Lapua Fin.
152 B3 La Quiaca Arg.
79 C2 Lār Iran
114 B1 Larache Morocco
136 B2 Laramie U.S.A.
136 B2 Laramie Mountains U.S.A.
154 B3 Laranjeiras do Sul Brazil
59 C3 Larantuka Indon.
59 C3 Larat *i.* Indon.
107 D2 Larba Alg.
106 C1 Laredo Spain
139 D3 Laredo U.S.A.
96 B3 Largs U.K.
152 B3 La Rioja Arg.
111 B3 Larisa Greece
74 A2 Larkana Pak.
80 B2 Larnaca Cyprus
97 D1 Larne U.K.
100 B2 La Roche-en-Ardenne Belgium
104 B2 La Rochelle France
104 B2 La Roche-sur-Yon France
107 C2 La Roda Spain
147 D3 La Romana Dom. Rep.
129 D2 La Ronge Can.
129 D2 La Ronge, Lac *l.* Can.
50 C1 Larrimah Austr.
55 J2 Larsen Ice Shelf Antarctica
93 F4 Larvik Norway
130 C2 La Sarre Can.
138 B2 Las Cruces U.S.A.
153 C4 Las Flores Arg.
153 B4 Las Heras Arg.
62 A1 Lashio Myanmar
74 A1 Lashkar Gāh Afgh.
109 C3 La Sila *reg.* Italy
152 B3 Las Lomitas Arg.
144 B2 Las Nieves Mex.

114 A2 Las Palmas de Gran Canaria Canary Islands
108 A2 La Spezia Italy
133 B5 Las Plumas Arg.
129 D2 Last Mountain Lake Can.
152 B3 Las Tórtolas, Cerro *mt.* Arg./Chile
118 B3 Lastoursville Gabon
109 C2 Lastovo *i.* Croatia
144 A2 Las Tres Vírgenes, Volcán *vol.* Mex.
146 C2 Las Tunas Cuba
144 B2 Las Varas *Chihuahua* Mex.
144 B2 Las Varas *Nayarit* Mex.
138 B1 Las Vegas *NM* U.S.A.
135 C3 Las Vegas *NV* U.S.A.
131 E1 La Tabatière Can.
80 B2 Latakia Syria
104 B3 La Teste-de-Buch France
108 B2 Latina Italy
147 D3 La Tortuga, Isla *i.* Venez.
64 B1 La Trinidad Phil.
89 E2 Latskoye Russia
131 C2 La Tuque Can.
88 B2 Latvia *country* Europe
102 C1 Lauchhammer Ger.
106 C1 Laudio Spain
101 E3 Lauf an der Pegnitz Ger.
105 D2 Laufen Switz.
51 D4 Launceston Austr.
99 A3 Launceston U.K.
62 A1 Launggyaung Myanmar
51 D1 Laura Austr.
142 C2 Laurel *MS* U.S.A.
134 E1 Laurel *MT* U.S.A.
109 C2 Lauria Italy
143 E2 Laurinburg U.S.A.
105 D2 Lausanne Switz.
61 C2 Laut *i.* Indon.
61 C2 Laut Bali *sea* Indon.
101 D2 Lauterbach (Hessen) Ger.
61 C2 Laut Kecil, Kepulauan *is* Indon.
100 C1 Lauwersmeer *l.* Neth.
104 B2 Laval France
107 C2 La Vall d'Uixó Spain
50 B2 Laverton Austr.
155 D2 Lavras Brazil
123 D2 Lavumisa Swaziland
61 C1 Lawas *Sarawak* Malaysia
62 A1 Lawksawk Myanmar
114 B3 Lawra Ghana
137 D3 Lawrence U.S.A.
142 C1 Lawrenceburg U.S.A.
139 D2 Lawton U.S.A.
78 A2 Lawz, Jabal al *mt.* Saudi Arabia
93 F4 Laxå Sweden
74 B1 Layyah Pak.
109 D2 Lazarevac Serbia
144 A1 Lázaro Cárdenas *Baja California* Mex.
144 B3 Lázaro Cárdenas *Michoacán* Mex.
88 B3 Lazdijai Lith.
136 C2 Lead U.S.A.
129 D2 Leader Can.
136 B3 Leadville U.S.A.
 Leaf Bay Can. *see* Tasiujaq
129 D2 Leaf Rapids Can.
97 B2 Leane, Lough *l.* Ireland
137 E3 Leavenworth U.S.A.
80 B2 Lebanon *country* Asia
137 E3 Lebanon *MO* U.S.A.
141 E2 Lebanon *NH* U.S.A.
134 B2 Lebanon *OR* U.S.A.
141 D2 Lebanon *PA* U.S.A.
89 E3 Lebedyan' Russia

91 C1 Lebedyn Ukr.
104 B2 Le Blanc France
103 D1 Lębork Pol.
119 C2 Lebowakgomo S. Africa
106 B2 Lebrija Spain
153 A4 Lebu Chile
104 B2 Le Bugue France
109 C2 Lecce Italy
108 A1 Lecco Italy
102 C2 Lech *r.* Austria/Ger.
111 B3 Lechaina Greece
71 B3 Lechang China
102 B1 Leck Ger.
104 C2 Lectoure France
106 B1 Ledesma Spain
104 C2 Le Dorat France
128 C2 Leduc Can.
137 E1 Leech Lake U.S.A.
98 C2 Leeds U.K.
98 B2 Leek U.K.
100 C1 Leer (Ostfriesland) Ger.
143 D3 Leesburg U.S.A.
142 B2 Leesville U.S.A.
53 C2 Leeton Austr.
122 B3 Leeu-Gamka S. Africa
100 B1 Leeuwarden Neth.
50 A3 Leeuwin, Cape Austr.
147 D3 Leeward Islands Caribbean Sea
111 B3 Lefkada Greece
111 B3 Lefkada *i.* Greece
 Lefkosia Cyprus *see* Nicosia
64 B1 Legazpi Phil.
108 B1 Legnago Italy
103 D1 Legnica Pol.
75 B1 Leh India
104 C2 Le Havre France
72 B1 Lehututu Botswana
103 D2 Leibnitz Austria
99 C2 Leicester U.K.
51 C1 Leichhardt *r.* Austr.
100 B1 Leiden Neth.
100 A2 Leie *r.* Belgium
52 A2 Leigh Creek Austr.
93 E3 Leikanger Norway
101 D2 Leine *r.* Ger.
97 C2 Leinster *reg.* Ireland
101 F2 Leipzig Ger.
92 F2 Leiranger Norway
106 B2 Leiria Port.
93 E4 Leirvik Norway
97 C2 Leixlip Ireland
71 B3 Leiyang China
71 B3 Leizhou China
71 A3 Leizhou Bandao *pen.* China
118 B3 Lékana Congo
100 B1 Lelystad Neth.
153 B6 Le Maire, Estrecho de *sea chan.* Arg.
 Léman, Lac *l.* France/Switz. *see* Geneva, Lake
104 C2 Le Mans France
137 D2 Le Mars U.S.A.
154 C2 Leme Brazil
 Lemesos Cyprus *see* Limassol
101 D1 Lemförde Ger.
127 G2 Lemieux Islands Can.
136 C1 Lemmon U.S.A.
135 C3 Lemoore U.S.A.
131 C1 Le Moyne, Lac *l.* Can.
62 A1 Lemro *r.* Myanmar
109 C2 Le Murge *hills* Italy
83 J2 Lena *r.* Russia
100 C1 Lengerich Ger.
71 B3 Lengshuijiang China
91 D2 Lenine Ukr.
 Leningrad Russia *see* St Petersburg

91	D2	Leningradskaya Russia
77	D3	Lenin Peak Kyrg./Tajik.
		Leninsk Kazakh. see Baykonyr
89	E3	Leninskiy Russia
100	A2	Lens Belgium
104	C1	Lens France
83	I2	Lensk Russia
103	D2	Lenti Hungary
109	C3	Lentini Sicily Italy
114	B3	Léo Burkina Faso
103	D2	Leoben Austria
99	B2	Leominster U.K.
144	B2	León Mex.
146	B3	León Nic.
106	B1	León Spain
122	A1	Leonardville Namibia
50	B2	Leonora Austr.
155	D2	Leopoldina Brazil
123	C1	Lephalale S. Africa
123	C1	Lephepe Botswana
123	C3	Lephoi S. Africa
71	B3	Leping China
105	C2	Le Puy-en-Velay France
150	A2	Lérida Col.
106	C1	Lerma Spain
111	C3	Leros i. Greece
130	C1	Le Roy, Lac l. Can.
93	F4	Lerum Sweden
96	□	Lerwick U.K.
111	C3	Lesbos i. Greece
147	C3	Les Cayes Haiti
69	C3	Leshan China
86	D2	Leshukonskoye Russia
109	D2	Leskovac Serbia
104	B2	Lesneven France
89	E2	Lesnoye Russia
83	H3	Lesosibirsk Russia
123	C2	Lesotho country Africa
66	B1	Lesozavodsk Russia
104	B2	Les Sables-d'Olonne France
147	D3	Lesser Antilles is Caribbean Sea
81	C1	Lesser Caucasus mts Asia
128	C2	Lesser Slave Lake Can.
58	B3	Lesser Sunda Islands is Indon.
105	C3	Les Vans France
		Lesvos i. Greece see Lesbos
103	D1	Leszno Pol.
99	C3	Letchworth Garden City U.K.
128	C3	Lethbridge Can.
150	C1	Lethem Guyana
59	C3	Leti, Kepulauan is Indon.
150	B2	Leticia Col.
123	C1	Letlhakeng Botswana
104	C1	Le Touquet-Paris-Plage France
99	D3	Le Tréport France
63	A2	Letsok-aw Kyun i. Myanmar
123	C2	Letsopa S. Africa
97	C1	Letterkenny Ireland
105	C3	Leucate, Étang de l. France
60	A1	Leuser, Gunung mt. Indon.
100	B2	Leuven Belgium
92	F3	Levanger Norway
139	C2	Levelland U.S.A.
50	B1	Lévêque, Cape Austr.
100	C2	Leverkusen Ger.
103	D2	Levice Slovakia
54	C2	Levin N.Z.
131	C2	Lévis Can.
89	E3	Lev Tolstoy Russia
99	D3	Lewes U.K.
96	A1	Lewis, Isle of i. U.K.
140	C3	Lewisburg U.S.A.
134	D1	Lewis Range mts U.S.A.
134	C1	Lewiston ID U.S.A.
141	E2	Lewiston ME U.S.A.
134	E1	Lewistown U.S.A.
140	C3	Lexington KY U.S.A.
136	D2	Lexington NE U.S.A.
141	D3	Lexington VA U.S.A.
64	B1	Leyte i. Phil.
109	C2	Lezhë Albania
89	F2	Lezhnevo Russia
89	E3	L'gov Russia
68	C2	Lharigarbo China
75	D2	Lhasa China
75	C2	Lhazê China
60	A1	Lhokseumawe Indon.
111	B3	Liakoura mt. Greece
67	B3	Liancourt Rocks i. N. Pacific Ocean
71	B3	Lianhua China
71	B3	Lianjiang China
70	C1	Lianshan China
70	B2	Lianyungang China
71	B3	Lianzhou China
70	B2	Liaocheng China
70	C1	Liaodong Bandao pen. China
70	C1	Liaodong Wan b. China
65	A1	Liao He r. China
70	C1	Liaoning prov. China
65	A1	Liaoyang China
65	A1	Liaoyuan China
128	B1	Liard r. Can.
134	C1	Libby U.S.A.
118	B2	Libenge Dem. Rep. Congo
136	C3	Liberal U.S.A.
103	D1	Liberec Czech Rep.
114	B4	Liberia country Africa
146	B3	Liberia Costa Rica
150	B1	Libertad Venez.
100	B3	Libin Belgium
104	B3	Libourne France
118	A2	Libreville Gabon
115	D2	Libya country Africa
115	E2	Libyan Desert Egypt/Libya
116	A1	Libyan Plateau Egypt/Libya
108	B3	Licata Sicily Italy
		Licheng China see Lipu
121	C2	Lichinga Moz.
101	E2	Lichte Ger.
123	C2	Lichtenburg S. Africa
101	E2	Lichtenfels Ger.
88	C3	Lida Belarus
93	F4	Lidköping Sweden
50	C2	Liebig, Mount Austr.
105	D2	Liechtenstein country Europe
100	B2	Liège Belgium
92	J3	Lieksa Fin.
119	C2	Lienart Dem. Rep. Congo
63	B2	Liên Nghia Vietnam
102	C2	Lienz Austria
88	B2	Liepāja Latvia
102	C2	Liezen Austria
97	C2	Liffey r. Ireland
97	C1	Lifford Ireland
53	C1	Lightning Ridge Austr.
121	C2	Ligonha r. Moz.
105	D3	Ligurian Sea France/Italy
119	C4	Likasi Dem. Rep. Congo
128	B2	Likely Can.
121	C1	Likhoslavl' Russia
61	B1	Liku Indon.
105	D3	L'Île-Rousse Corsica France
71	B3	Liling China
93	F4	Lilla Edet Sweden
100	B2	Lille Belgium
105	C1	Lille France
		Lille Bælt sea chan. Denmark see Little Belt
93	F3	Lillehammer Norway
93	F4	Lillestrøm Norway
128	B2	Lillooet Can.
121	C2	Lilongwe Malawi
64	B2	Liloy Phil.
150	A3	Lima Peru
140	C2	Lima U.S.A.
80	B2	Limassol Cyprus
97	C1	Limavady U.K.
153	B4	Limay r. Arg.
101	F2	Limbach-Oberfrohna Ger.
88	B2	Limbaži Latvia
118	A2	Limbe Cameroon
100	D2	Limburg an der Lahn Ger.
122	B2	Lime Acres S. Africa
154	C2	Limeira Brazil
97	B2	Limerick Ireland
93	E4	Limfjorden sea chan. Denmark
111	C3	Limnos i. Greece
104	C2	Limoges France
136	C3	Limon U.S.A.
104	C3	Limoux France
123	C1	Limpopo prov. S. Africa
121	C3	Limpopo r. S. Africa/ Zimbabwe
64	A1	Linapacan i. Phil.
153	A4	Linares Chile
145	C2	Linares Mex.
106	C2	Linares Spain
62	B1	Lincang China
		Linchuan China see Fuzhou
98	C2	Lincoln U.K.
140	B2	Lincoln IL U.S.A.
141	F1	Lincoln ME U.S.A.
137	D2	Lincoln NE U.S.A.
151	C1	Linden Guyana
142	C1	Linden U.S.A.
119	C2	Lindi r. Dem. Rep. Congo
119	D3	Lindi Tanz.
		Lindisfarne i. U.K. see Holy Island
80	A2	Lindos Greece
141	D2	Lindsay Can.
49	H2	Line Islands Kiribati
64	B1	Linfen China
70	B2	Lingayen Phil.
70	B2	Lingbao China
123	C3	Lingelethu S. Africa
123	C3	Lingelihle S. Africa
100	C1	Lingen (Ems) Ger.
60	B2	Lingga, Kepulauan is Indon.
71	B3	Lingling China
71	A3	Lingshan China
71	A4	Lingshui China
114	A3	Linguère Senegal
63	B2	Linh, Ngok mt. Vietnam
155	D1	Linhares Brazil
93	G4	Linköping Sweden
66	B1	Linkou China
70	B2	Linqing China
154	C2	Lins Brazil
136	C1	Linton U.S.A.
69	D2	Linxi China
69	C2	Linxia China
70	B2	Linyi Shandong China
70	B2	Linyi Shandong China
70	B2	Linying China
102	C2	Linz Austria
105	C3	Lion, Golfe du g. France
108	B3	Lipari Italy
108	B3	Lipari, Isole is Italy
89	E3	Lipetsk Russia
110	B1	Lipova Romania
101	D2	Lippstadt Ger.
71	B3	Lipu China
76	C1	Lisakovsk Kazakh.
118	C3	Lisala Dem. Rep. Congo
		Lisboa Port. see Lisbon
106	B2	Lisbon Port.
97	C1	Lisburn U.K.
97	B2	Liscannor Bay Ireland

104 C2 **Lisieux** France
99 A3 **Liskeard** U.K.
89 E3 **Liski** Russia
53 D1 **Lismore** Austr.
97 C1 **Lisnaskea** U.K.
97 B2 **Listowel** Ireland
71 A3 **Litang** *Guangxi* China
68 C2 **Litang** *Sichuan* China
140 B3 **Litchfield** *IL* U.S.A.
137 E1 **Litchfield** *MN* U.S.A.
53 D2 **Lithgow** Austr.
111 B3 **Lithino, Akrotirio** *pt* Greece
88 B2 **Lithuania** *country* Europe
102 C1 **Litoměřice** Czech Rep.
146 C2 **Little Abaco** *i.* Bahamas
73 D3 **Little Andaman** *i.* India
93 E4 **Little Belt** *sea chan.* Denmark
137 E1 **Little Falls** U.S.A.
139 C2 **Littlefield** U.S.A.
99 C3 **Littlehampton** U.K.
122 A2 **Little Karas Berg** *plat.*
            Namibia
122 B3 **Little Karoo** *plat.* S. Africa
96 A2 **Little Minch** *sea chan.* U.K.
136 C1 **Little Missouri** *r.* U.S.A.
63 A3 **Little Nicobar** *i.* India
142 B3 **Little Rock** U.S.A.
141 E2 **Littleton** U.S.A.
70 B2 **Liujiachang** China
71 A3 **Liupanshui** China
71 A3 **Liuzhou** China
111 B3 **Livadeia** Greece
88 C2 **Līvāni** Latvia
50 B1 **Liveringa** Austr.
138 C2 **Livermore, Mount** U.S.A.
131 D2 **Liverpool** Can.
98 B2 **Liverpool** U.K.
127 F2 **Liverpool, Cape** Can.
53 C2 **Liverpool Range** *mts* Austr.
134 E1 **Livingston** *MT* U.S.A.
139 E2 **Livingston** *TX* U.S.A.
139 D2 **Livingston, Lake** U.S.A.
120 B2 **Livingstone** Zambia
109 C2 **Livno** Bos. & Herz.
89 E3 **Livny** Russia
140 C2 **Livonia** U.S.A.
108 B2 **Livorno** Italy
119 D3 **Liwale** Tanz.
70 B2 **Liyang** China
99 A4 **Lizard Point** U.K.
108 B1 **Ljubljana** Slovenia
93 G3 **Ljungan** *r.* Sweden
93 F4 **Ljungby** Sweden
93 G3 **Ljusdal** Sweden
93 G3 **Ljusnan** *r.* Sweden
99 B3 **Llandeilo** U.K.
99 B3 **Llandovery** U.K.
99 B2 **Llandrindod Wells** U.K.
98 B2 **Llandudno** U.K.
99 A3 **Llanelli** U.K.
98 A2 **Llangefni** U.K.
139 C2 **Llano Estacado** *plain* U.S.A.
150 B1 **Llanos** *plain* Col./Venez.
107 D1 **Lleida** Spain
99 A2 **Lleyn Peninsula** U.K.
107 C2 **Llíria** Spain
128 B2 **Lloyd George, Mount** Can.
129 D2 **Lloyd Lake** Can.
129 C2 **Lloydminster** Can.
152 B3 **Llullaillaco, Volcán** *vol.*
            Chile
123 C3 **Lobatse** Botswana
120 A2 **Lobito** Angola
101 F1 **Loburg** Ger.
96 B2 **Lochaber** *reg.* U.K.
104 C2 **Loches** France
96 B1 **Lochgilphead** U.K.
96 B1 **Lochinver** U.K.

96 A2 **Lochmaddy** U.K.
96 C2 **Lochnagar** *mt.* U.K.
52 A2 **Lock** Austr.
96 C3 **Lockerbie** U.K.
139 D3 **Lockhart** U.S.A.
141 D2 **Lock Haven** U.S.A.
141 D2 **Lockport** U.S.A.
63 B2 **Lôc Ninh** Vietnam
105 C3 **Lodève** France
86 C2 **Lodeynoye Pole** Russia
92 F2 **Løding** Norway
119 D2 **Lodwar** Kenya
103 D1 **Łódź** Pol.
62 B2 **Loei** Thai.
122 A3 **Loeriesfontein** S. Africa
92 F2 **Lofoten** *is* Norway
134 D2 **Logan** U.S.A.
126 B2 **Logan, Mount** Can.
140 B2 **Logansport** U.S.A.
108 B1 **Logatec** Slovenia
106 C1 **Logroño** Spain
101 D1 **Löhne** Ger.
101 D1 **Lohne (Oldenburg)** Ger.
62 A2 **Loikaw** Myanmar
104 B2 **Loire** *r.* France
150 A2 **Loja** Ecuador
106 C2 **Loja** Spain
92 I2 **Lokan tekojärvi** *resr* Fin.
74 B1 **Lôkâr** Afgh.
100 B2 **Lokeren** Belgium
122 B1 **Lokgwabe** Botswana
119 D2 **Lokichar** Kenya
119 D2 **Lokichokio** Kenya
89 D2 **Loknya** Russia
115 C4 **Lokoja** Nigeria
89 D3 **Lokot'** Russia
88 C2 **Loksa** Estonia
119 D3 **Loks Land** *i.* Can.
119 D3 **Loliondo** Tanz.
93 F4 **Lolland** *i.* Denmark
122 B2 **Lolwane** S. Africa
110 B2 **Lom** Bulg.
93 E3 **Lom** Norway
119 C2 **Lomami** *r.* Dem. Rep. Congo
153 C4 **Lomas de Zamora** Arg.
61 C2 **Lombok** *i.* Indon.
61 C2 **Lombok, Selat** *sea chan.*
            Indon.
114 C4 **Lomé** Togo
118 C3 **Lomela** *r.* Dem. Rep. Congo
100 B2 **Lommel** Belgium
96 B2 **Lomond, Loch** *l.* U.K.
88 C2 **Lomonosov** Russia
135 B4 **Lompoc** U.S.A.
63 B2 **Lom Sak** Thai.
103 E1 **Łomża** Pol.
130 B2 **London** Can.
99 C3 **London** U.K.
140 C3 **London** U.S.A.
97 C1 **Londonderry** U.K.
50 B1 **Londonderry, Cape** Austr.
154 B2 **Londrina** Brazil
83 M2 **Longa, Proliv** *sea chan.* Russia
61 C1 **Long Akah** *Sarawak* Malaysia
143 E2 **Long Bay** U.S.A.
142 B2 **Long Beach** U.S.A.
97 C2 **Longford** Ireland
61 C2 **Longiram** Indon.
147 C2 **Long Island** Bahamas
130 C1 **Long Island** Can.
59 D3 **Long Island** P.N.G.
141 E2 **Long Island** U.S.A.
130 B2 **Longlac** Can.
130 B2 **Long Lake** Can.
136 B2 **Longmont** U.S.A.
70 A2 **Longnan** China
140 C2 **Long Point** Can.
71 B3 **Longquan** China

131 E2 **Long Range Mountains** Can.
51 D2 **Longreach** Austr.
99 D2 **Long Stratton** U.K.
98 B1 **Longtown** U.K.
105 D2 **Longuyon** France
139 E2 **Longview** *TX* U.S.A.
134 B1 **Longview** *WA* U.S.A.
70 A2 **Longxi** China
71 B3 **Longxi Shan** *mt.* China
63 B2 **Long Xuyên** Vietnam
71 B3 **Longyan** China
82 C1 **Longyearbyen** Svalbard
102 B2 **Lons-le-Saunier** France
143 E2 **Lookout, Cape** U.S.A.
97 B2 **Loop Head** Ireland
63 B2 **Lop Buri** Thai.
64 B1 **Lopez** Phil.
68 C2 **Lop Nur** *salt flat* China
118 B3 **Lopori** *r.* Dem. Rep. Congo
74 A2 **Lora, Hāmūn-i-** *dry lake* Afgh./
            Pak.
106 B2 **Lora del Río** Spain
140 C2 **Lorain** U.S.A.
74 A1 **Loralai** Pak.
107 C2 **Lorca** Spain
48 E5 **Lord Howe Island** Austr.
138 B2 **Lordsburg** U.S.A.
155 C2 **Lorena** Brazil
152 B2 **Loreto** Brazil
144 A2 **Loreto** Mex.
104 B2 **Lorient** France
96 B2 **Lorn, Firth of** *est.* U.K.
52 B3 **Lorne** Austr.
138 B1 **Los Alamos** U.S.A.
139 D3 **Los Aldamas** Mex.
153 A4 **Los Ángeles** Chile
135 C4 **Los Angeles** U.S.A.
135 B3 **Los Banos** U.S.A.
152 B3 **Los Blancos** Arg.
91 E1 **Losevo** Russia
109 C2 **Lošinj** *i.* Croatia
144 B2 **Los Mochis** Mex.
118 B2 **Losombo** Dem. Rep. Congo
147 D3 **Los Roques, Islas** *is* Venez.
96 C2 **Lossiemouth** U.K.
150 B1 **Los Teques** Venez.
152 A4 **Los Vilos** Chile
104 C3 **Lot** *r.* France
96 C1 **Loth** U.K.
119 D2 **Lotikipi Plain** Kenya/Sudan
118 C3 **Loto** Dem. Rep. Congo
89 E2 **Lotoshino** Russia
62 B1 **Louangnamtha** Laos
62 B2 **Louangphabang** Laos
118 B3 **Loubomo** Congo
104 B2 **Loudéac** France
71 B3 **Loudi** China
118 B3 **Loudima** Congo
114 A3 **Louga** Senegal
99 C2 **Loughborough** U.K.
97 B2 **Loughrea** Ireland
105 D2 **Louhans** France
97 B2 **Louisburgh** Ireland
142 B2 **Louisiana** *state* U.S.A.
140 C3 **Louisville** *KY* U.S.A.
142 C2 **Louisville** *MS* U.S.A.
86 C2 **Loukhi** Russia
130 C1 **Loups Marins, Lacs des** *lakes*
            Can.
104 B2 **Lourdes** France
151 C1 **Lourenço** Brazil
106 B1 **Lousã** Port.
53 C2 **Louth** Austr.
98 C2 **Louth** U.K.
       Louvain Belgium *see* **Leuven**
89 D2 **Lovat'** *r.* Russia
110 B2 **Lovech** Bulg.
136 B2 **Loveland** U.S.A.

135	C2	**Lovelock** U.S.A.
139	C2	**Lovington** U.S.A.
119	C3	**Lowa** Dem. Rep. Congo
141	E2	**Lowell** U.S.A.
128	C3	**Lower Arrow Lake** Can.
54	B2	**Lower Hutt** N.Z.
97	C1	**Lower Lough Erne** l. U.K.
128	B2	**Lower Post** Can.
99	D2	**Lowestoft** U.K.
103	D1	**Łowicz** Pol.
141	D2	**Lowville** U.S.A.
52	B2	**Loxton** Austr.
		Loyang China *see* **Luoyang**
48	F4	**Loyauté, Îles** *is* New Caledonia
89	D3	**Loyew** Belarus
92	C3	**Leypskardtinden** *mt.* Norway
109	C2	**Loznica** Serbia
91	D2	**Lozova** Ukr.
120	B2	**Luacano** Angola
70	B2	**Lu'an** China
120	A1	**Luanda** Angola
121	C2	**Luangwa** r. Zambia
121	B2	**Luanshya** Zambia
106	B1	**Luarca** Spain
120	B2	**Luau** Angola
103	E1	**Lubaczów** Pol.
120	A2	**Lubango** Angola
119	C3	**Lubao** Dem. Rep. Congo
103	E1	**Lubartów** Pol.
101	E1	**Lübbecke** Ger.
139	C2	**Lubbock** U.S.A.
101	E1	**Lübeck** Ger.
69	E2	**Lubei** China
87	E3	**Lubenka** Kazakh.
103	D1	**Lubin** Pol.
103	E1	**Lublin** Pol.
91	C1	**Lubny** Ukr.
61	C1	**Lubok Antu** Sarawak Malaysia
101	E1	**Lübow** Ger.
101	E1	**Lübtheen** Ger.
119	C3	**Lubudi** Dem. Rep. Congo
60	B2	**Lubuklinggau** Indon.
119	C4	**Lubumbashi** Dem. Rep. Congo
120	B2	**Lubungu** Zambia
119	C3	**Lubutu** Dem. Rep. Congo
120	A1	**Lucala** Angola
97	C2	**Lucan** Ireland
120	B1	**Lucapa** Angola
96	B3	**Luce Bay** U.K.
154	B2	**Lucélia** Brazil
64	B1	**Lucena** Phil.
106	C2	**Lucena** Spain
103	D2	**Lučenec** Slovakia
109	C2	**Lucera** Italy
105	D2	**Lucerne** Switz.
101	E1	**Lüchow (Wendland)** Ger.
120	A2	**Lucira** Angola
101	F1	**Luckenwalde** Ger.
122	B2	**Luckhoff** S. Africa
75	C2	**Lucknow** India
120	B2	**Lucusse** Angola
		Lüda China *see* **Dalian**
100	C2	**Lüdenscheid** Ger.
101	E1	**Lüder** Ger.
120	A3	**Lüderitz** Namibia
74	B1	**Ludhiana** India
140	B2	**Ludington** U.S.A.
99	B2	**Ludlow** U.K.
135	C4	**Ludlow** U.S.A.
110	C2	**Ludogorie** reg. Bulg.
93	G3	**Ludvika** Sweden
102	B2	**Ludwigsburg** Ger.
101	F1	**Ludwigsfelde** Ger.
101	D3	**Ludwigshafen am Rhein** Ger.
101	E1	**Ludwigslust** Ger.
88	C2	**Ludza** Latvia
118	C3	**Luebo** Dem. Rep. Congo
120	A2	**Luena** Angola
70	A2	**Lüeyang** China
71	B3	**Lufeng** China
139	E2	**Lufkin** U.S.A.
88	C2	**Luga** Russia
88	C2	**Luga** r. Russia
105	D2	**Lugano** Switz.
121	C2	**Lugenda** r. Moz.
97	C2	**Lugnaquilla** h. Ireland
106	B1	**Lugo** Spain
110	B1	**Lugoj** Romania
91	D2	**Luhans'k** Ukr.
119	D3	**Luhombero** Tanz.
90	B1	**Luhyny** Ukr.
120	B2	**Luiana** Angola
118	C3	**Luilaka** r. Dem. Rep. Congo
105	D2	**Luino** Italy
92	I2	**Luiro** r. Fin.
118	C3	**Luiza** Dem. Rep. Congo
70	B2	**Lujiang** China
109	C2	**Lukavac** Bos. & Herz.
118	B3	**Lukenie** r. Dem. Rep. Congo
138	A2	**Lukeville** U.S.A.
89	E3	**Lukhovitsy** Russia
103	E1	**Łuków** Pol.
120	B2	**Lukulu** Zambia
92	H2	**Luleå** Sweden
92	H2	**Luleälven** r. Sweden
110	C2	**Lüleburgaz** Turkey
70	B2	**Lüliang Shan** mts China
61	C2	**Lumajang** Indon.
75	C1	**Lumajangdong Co** salt l. China
120	B2	**Lumbala Kaquengue** Angola
120	B2	**Lumbala N'guimbo** Angola
143	E2	**Lumberton** U.S.A.
61	C1	**Lumbis** Indon.
106	B1	**Lumbrales** Spain
63	B2	**Lumphăt** Cambodia
129	D2	**Lumsden** Can.
54	A3	**Lumsden** N.Z.
93	F4	**Lund** Sweden
121	C2	**Lundazi** Zambia
99	A3	**Lundy** i. U.K.
101	E1	**Lüneburg** Ger.
101	E1	**Lüneburger Heide** reg. Ger.
100	C2	**Lünen** Ger.
105	D2	**Lunéville** France
120	B2	**Lunga** r. Zambia
114	A4	**Lungi** Sierra Leone
62	A1	**Lunglei** India
120	B2	**Lungwebungu** r. Zambia
74	B2	**Luni** r. India
88	C3	**Luninyets** Belarus
114	A4	**Lunsar** Sierra Leone
77	D3	**Luntai** China
71	A3	**Luodian** China
71	B3	**Luoding** China
70	B2	**Luohe** China
70	B2	**Luoyang** China
121	B2	**Lupane** Zimbabwe
110	B1	**Lupeni** Romania
121	C2	**Lupilichi** Moz.
101	F2	**Luppa** Ger.
121	D2	**Lúrio** Moz.
121	D2	**Lurio** r. Moz.
121	B2	**Lusaka** Zambia
118	C3	**Lusambo** Dem. Rep. Congo
109	C2	**Lushnjë** Albania
136	C2	**Lusk** U.S.A.
76	B2	**Lüt, Kavīr-e** des. Iran
99	C3	**Luton** U.K.
61	C1	**Lutong** Sarawak Malaysia
129	C1	**Łutselk'e** Can.
90	B1	**Luts'k** Ukr.
122	B2	**Lutzputs** S. Africa
122	A3	**Lutzville** S. Africa
117	C4	**Luuq** Somalia
137	D2	**Luverne** U.S.A.
119	C3	**Luvua** r. Dem. Rep. Congo
123	D1	**Luvuvhu** r. S. Africa
119	D2	**Luwero** Uganda
59	C3	**Luwuk** Indon.
100	C3	**Luxembourg** country Europe
100	C3	**Luxembourg** Lux.
105	D2	**Luxeuil-les-Bains** France
123	C3	**Luxolweni** S. Africa
116	B2	**Luxor** Egypt
100	B2	**Luyksgestel** Neth.
86	D2	**Luza** Russia
		Luzern Switz. *see* **Lucerne**
71	A3	**Luzhou** China
154	C1	**Luziânia** Brazil
151	D2	**Luzilândia** Brazil
64	B1	**Luzon** i. Phil.
71	C3	**Luzon Strait** Phil./Taiwan
90	A2	**L'viv** Ukr.
		L'vov Ukr. *see* **L'viv**
88	C3	**Lyakhavichy** Belarus
92	G3	**Lycksele** Sweden
88	C3	**Lyel'chytsy** Belarus
88	C3	**Lyepyel'** Belarus
99	B3	**Lyme Bay** U.K.
141	D3	**Lynchburg** U.S.A.
129	D2	**Lynn Lake** Can.
129	D1	**Lynx Lake** Can.
105	C2	**Lyon** France
89	D2	**Lyozna** Belarus
86	E3	**Lys'va** Russia
91	D2	**Lysychans'k** Ukr.
98	B2	**Lytham St Anne's** U.K.
88	C3	**Lyuban'** Belarus
89	E2	**Lyubertsy** Russia
90	B1	**Lyubeshiv** Ukr.
89	F2	**Lyubim** Russia
91	D2	**Lyubotyn** Ukr.
89	D2	**Lyubytino** Russia
89	D3	**Lyudinovo** Russia

M

80	B2	**Ma'ān** Jordan
88	C2	**Maardu** Estonia
100	B2	**Maas** r. Neth.
64	B1	**Maasin** Phil.
100	B2	**Maaseik** Belgium
100	B2	**Maastricht** Neth.
121	C3	**Mabalane** Moz.
150	C1	**Mabaruma** Guyana
121	C3	**Mabote** Moz.
122	B2	**Mabule** Botswana
122	B1	**Mabutsane** Botswana
155	D2	**Macaé** Brazil
121	C2	**Macaloge** Moz.
126	E2	**MacAlpine Lake** Can.
71	B3	**Macao** aut. reg. China
151	C1	**Macapá** Brazil
150	A2	**Macará** Ecuador
155	D1	**Macarani** Brazil
123	D1	**Macarretane** Moz.
151	E2	**Macau** Brazil
98	B2	**Macclesfield** U.K.
50	B2	**Macdonald, Lake** imp. l. Austr.
50	C2	**Macdonnell Ranges** mts Austr.
130	A1	**MacDowell Lake** Can.
106	B1	**Macedo de Cavaleiros** Port.
52	B3	**Macedon** mt. Austr.
109	D2	**Macedonia** country Europe
151	E2	**Maceió** Brazil
108	B2	**Macerata** Italy
52	A2	**Macfarlane, Lake** imp. l. Austr.

97 B3 Macgillycuddy's Reeks *mts*
  Ireland
74 A2 Mach Pak.
155 C2 Machado Brazil
121 C3 Machaíla Moz.
119 D3 Machakos Kenya
150 A2 Machala Ecuador
68 C2 Machali China
121 C3 Machanga Moz.
70 B2 Macheng China
141 F2 Machias U.S.A.
150 A1 Machiques Venez.
150 A3 Machu Picchu *tourist site* Peru
123 D2 Macia Moz.
110 C1 Măcin Romania
114 B3 Macina Mali
53 D1 Macintyre *r.* Austr.
51 D2 Mackay Austr.
50 B2 Mackay, Lake *imp. l.* Austr.
129 C1 MacKay Lake Can.
128 B2 Mackenzie Can.
128 A1 Mackenzie *r.* Can.
126 B2 Mackenzie Bay Can.
126 D1 Mackenzie King Island Can.
128 A1 Mackenzie Mountains Can.
129 D2 Macklin Can.
53 D2 Macksville Austr.
53 D1 Maclean Austr.
50 A2 MacLeod, Lake *dry lake* Austr.
140 A2 Macomb U.S.A.
108 A2 Macomer *Sardinia* Italy
105 C2 Mâcon France
143 D2 Macon GA U.S.A.
137 E3 Macon MO U.S.A.
53 C2 Macquarie *r.* Austr.
48 E6 Macquarie Island
  S. Pacific Ocean
53 C2 Macquarie Marshes Austr.
97 B3 Macroom Ireland
52 A1 Macumba *watercourse* Austr.
145 C3 Macuspana Mex.
144 B2 Macuzari, Presa *resr* Mex.
123 D2 Madadeni S. Africa
117 □D3 Madagascar *country* Africa
115 D2 Madama Niger
111 B2 Madan Bulg.
59 D3 Madang P.N.G.
150 C2 Madeira *r.* Brazil
114 A1 Madeira *terr.*
  N. Atlantic Ocean
131 D2 Madeleine, Îles de la *is* Can.
144 B2 Madera Mex.
135 B3 Madera U.S.A.
118 B3 Madingou Congo
140 B3 Madison IN U.S.A.
137 D2 Madison SD U.S.A.
140 B2 Madison WI U.S.A.
140 C3 Madison WV U.S.A.
134 D1 Madison *r.* U.S.A.
140 B3 Madisonville U.S.A.
61 C2 Madiun Indon.
119 D2 Mado Gashi Kenya
88 C2 Madona Latvia
78 A2 Madrakah Saudi Arabia
134 B2 Madras India *see* Chennai
145 C2 Madras U.S.A.
145 C2 Madre, Laguna *lag.* Mex.
145 B3 Madre del Sur, Sierra *mts*
  Mex.
144 B2 Madre Occidental, Sierra *mts*
  Mex.
145 B2 Madre Oriental, Sierra *mts*
  Mex.
106 C1 Madrid Spain
106 C2 Madridejos Spain
61 C2 Madura *i.* Indon.
61 C2 Madura, Selat *sea chan.*
  Indon.

73 B4 Madurai India
67 C3 Maebashi Japan
62 A2 Mae Hong Son Thai.
62 A1 Mae Sai Thai.
62 A2 Mae Sariang Thai.
62 A2 Mae Suai Thai.
123 C2 Mafeteng Lesotho
119 D3 Mafia Island Tanz.
119 D3 Mafinga Tanz.
154 C3 Mafra Brazil
83 L3 Magadan Russia
147 C4 Magangué Col.
144 A1 Magdalena Mex.
138 B2 Magdalena U.S.A.
144 A2 Magdalena, Bahía *b.* Mex.
101 E1 Magdeburg Ger.
153 A6 Magellan, Strait of Chile
97 C1 Magherafelt U.K.
87 E3 Magnitogorsk Russia
142 B2 Magnolia U.S.A.
131 D1 Magpie, Lac *l.* Can.
114 A3 Magta' Lahjar Maur.
151 D2 Maguarinho, Cabo *c.* Brazil
123 D2 Magude Moz.
62 A1 Magwe Myanmar
81 C2 Mahābād Iran
74 B2 Mahajan India
121 □D2 Mahajanga Madag.
61 C2 Mahakam *r.* Indon.
123 C1 Mahalapye Botswana
121 □D2 Mahalevona Madag.
75 C2 Mahanadi *r.* India
121 □D2 Mahanoro Madag.
63 B2 Maha Sarakham Thai.
121 □D2 Mahavavy *r.* Madag.
78 B2 Mahd adh Dhahab
  Saudi Arabia
150 C1 Mahdia Guyana
113 K7 Mahé *i.* Seychelles
74 B2 Mahesana India
74 B2 Mahi *r.* India
54 C1 Mahia Peninsula N.Z.
89 D3 Mahilyow Belarus
74 B2 Mahuva India
110 C2 Mahya Dağı *mt.* Turkey
74 A1 Maidan Shahr Afgh.
129 D2 Maidstone Can.
99 D3 Maidstone U.K.
115 D3 Maiduguri Nigeria
75 C2 Mailani India
76 C3 Maimanah Afgh.
101 D2 Main *r.* Ger.
118 B3 Mai-Ndombe, Lac *l.*
  Dem. Rep. Congo
101 E3 Main-Donau-Kanal *canal*
  Ger.
141 F1 Maine *state* U.S.A.
62 A1 Maingkwan Myanmar
96 C1 Mainland *i.* Scotland U.K.
96 □ Mainland *i.* Scotland U.K.
121 □D2 Maintirano Madag.
101 D2 Mainz Ger.
150 B1 Maiquetía Venez.
53 C2 Maitland N.S.W. Austr.
52 A2 Maitland S.A. Austr.
146 B3 Maíz, Islas del *is* Nic.
67 C3 Maizuru Japan
61 C2 Majene Indon.
62 C3 Majorca *i.* Spain
48 E2 Majuro *atoll* Marshall Is
123 C2 Majwemasweu S. Africa
118 B3 Makabana Congo
58 B3 Makale Indon.
77 E2 Makanshy Kazakh.
109 C2 Makarska Croatia
58 B3 Makassar Indon.
61 C2 Makassar, Selat *str.* Indon.

76 B2 Makassar Strait Indon. *see*
  Makassar, Selat
123 D2 Makat Kazakh.
123 D2 Makatini Flats *lowland*
  S. Africa
114 A4 Makeni Sierra Leone
120 B3 Makgadikgadi *depr.* Botswana
87 D4 Makhachkala Russia
123 C1 Makhado S. Africa
76 B2 Makhambet Kazakh.
119 D3 Makindu Kenya
77 D1 Makinsk Kazakh.
91 D2 Makiyivka Ukr.
  Makkah Saudi Arabia *see*
  Mecca
131 E1 Makkovik Can.
103 E2 Makó Hungary
118 B2 Makokou Gabon
119 D3 Makongolosi Tanz.
122 B2 Makopong Botswana
79 D2 Makran *reg.* Iran/Pak.
74 A2 Makran Coast Range *mts* Pak.
89 E2 Maksatikha Russia
81 C2 Mākū Iran
62 A1 Makum India
67 B4 Makurazaki Japan
115 C4 Makurdi Nigeria
92 G2 Malå Sweden
146 B4 Mala, Punta *pt* Panama
118 A2 Malabo Equat. Guinea
60 A1 Malacca, Strait of Indon./
  Malaysia
134 D2 Malad City U.S.A.
88 C3 Maladzyechna Belarus
106 C2 Málaga Spain
97 B1 Málainn Mhóir Ireland
48 E3 Malaita *i.* Solomon Is
117 B4 Malakal South Sudan
48 F4 Malakula *i.* Vanuatu
61 C2 Malang Indon.
120 A1 Malanje Angola
93 G4 Mälaren *i.* Sweden
153 B4 Malargüe Arg.
80 B2 Malatya Turkey
121 C2 Malawi *country* Africa
  Malawi, Lake Africa *see*
  Nyasa, Lake
89 D2 Malaya Vishera Russia
64 B2 Malaybalay Phil.
81 C2 Maläyer Iran
60 B1 Malaysia *country* Asia
81 C2 Malazgirt Turkey
103 D1 Malbork Pol.
101 F1 Malchin Ger.
100 A2 Maldegem Belgium
49 H3 Malden Island Kiribati
56 G6 Maldives *country*
  Indian Ocean
153 C4 Maldonado Uru.
56 G6 Male Maldives
111 B3 Maleas, Akrotirio *pt* Greece
103 D2 Malé Karpaty *hills* Slovakia
134 C2 Malheur Lake U.S.A.
114 B3 Mali *country* Africa
114 A3 Mali Guinea
58 C3 Malili Indon.
119 E3 Malindi Kenya
97 C1 Malin Head Ireland
111 C2 Malkara Turkey
88 C3 Mal'kavichy Belarus
110 C2 Malko Tarnovo Bulg.
53 C3 Mallacoota Austr.
53 C3 Mallacoota Inlet *b.* Austr.
96 B2 Mallaig U.K.
129 E1 Mallery Lake Can.
  Mallorca *i.* Spain *see* Majorca
97 B2 Mallow Ireland
92 H2 Malmberget Sweden

Malmedy

100 C2	**Malmedy** Belgium	
122 A3	**Malmesbury** S. Africa	
93 F4	**Malmö** Sweden	
62 B1	**Malong** China	
118 C4	**Malonga** Dem. Rep. Congo	
93 E3	**Måløy** Norway	
89 E2	**Maloyaroslavets** Russia	
89 E2	**Maloye Borisovo** Russia	
85 H5	**Malta** *country* Europe	
88 C2	**Malta** Latvia	
134 E1	**Malta** U.S.A.	
122 A1	**Maltahöhe** Namibia	
98 C1	**Malton** U.K.	
	Maluku *is* Indon. *see* Moluccas	
59 C2	**Maluku, Laut** *sea* Indon.	
93 F3	**Malung** Sweden	
123 C2	**Maluti Mountains** Lesotho	
73 B3	**Malvan** India	
142 B2	**Malvern** U.S.A.	
90 B1	**Malyn** Ukr.	
83 L2	**Malyy Anyuy** *r.* Russia	
83 K2	**Malyy Lyakhovskiy, Ostrov** *i.* Russia	
123 C2	**Mamafubedu** S. Africa	
119 C2	**Mambasa** Dem. Rep. Congo	
118 B2	**Mambéré** *r.* C.A.R.	
123 C2	**Mamelodi** S. Africa	
150 B3	**Mamoré** *r.* Bol./Brazil	
114 A3	**Mamou** Guinea	
61 C2	**Mamuju** Indon.	
114 B4	**Man** Côte d'Ivoire	
98 A1	**Man, Isle of** *i.* Irish Sea	
150 B2	**Manacapuru** Brazil	
107 D2	**Manacor** Spain	
59 C2	**Manado** Indon.	
146 B3	**Managua** Nic.	
121 □D3	**Manakara** Madag.	
78 B3	**Manākhah** Yemen	
79 C2	**Manama** Bahrain	
59 D3	**Manam Island** P.N.G.	
121 □D3	**Mananara** *r.* Madag.	
121 □D2	**Mananara Avaratra** Madag.	
121 □D3	**Mananjary** Madag.	
114 A3	**Manantali, Lac de** *l.* Mali	
77 F2	**Manas Hu** *l.* China	
59 C3	**Manatuto** East Timor	
62 A2	**Man-aung Kyun** *i.* Myanmar	
150 B2	**Manaus** Brazil	
80 B2	**Manavgat** Turkey	
98 B2	**Manchester** U.K.	
141 E2	**Manchester** U.S.A.	
121 □D3	**Mandabe** Madag.	
93 E4	**Mandal** Norway	
59 D3	**Mandala, Puncak** *mt.* Indon.	
62 A1	**Mandalay** Myanmar	
69 D1	**Mandalgovi** Mongolia	
136 C1	**Mandan** U.S.A.	
118 B1	**Mandara Mountains** Cameroon/Nigeria	
108 A3	**Mandas** *Sardinia* Italy	
100 C2	**Manderscheid** Ger.	
74 B1	**Mandi** India	
114 B3	**Mandiana** Guinea	
75 C2	**Mandla** India	
121 □D2	**Mandritsara** Madag.	
74 B2	**Mandsaur** India	
50 A3	**Mandurah** Austr.	
73 B3	**Mandya** India	
108 B1	**Manerbio** Italy	
90 B1	**Manevychi** Ukr.	
109 C2	**Manfredonia** Italy	
114 B3	**Manga** Burkina Faso	
118 B3	**Mangai** Dem. Rep. Congo	
54 C1	**Mangakino** N.Z.	
110 C2	**Mangalia** Romania	
73 B3	**Mangalore** India	
	Mangaluru India *see* Mangalore	
123 C2	**Mangaung** S. Africa	
61 B2	**Manggar** Indon.	
76 B2	**Mangistau** Kazakh.	
121 C2	**Mangochi** Malawi	
59 C3	**Mangole** *i.* Indon.	
154 B3	**Mangueirinha** Brazil	
69 E1	**Mangui** China	
137 D3	**Manhattan** U.S.A.	
121 C3	**Manhiça** Moz.	
155 D2	**Manhuaçu** Brazil	
121 □D2	**Mania** *r.* Madag.	
108 B1	**Maniago** Italy	
150 B2	**Manicoré** Brazil	
131 D2	**Manicouagan** *r.* Can.	
131 D1	**Manicouagan, Petit Lac** *l.* Can.	
131 D1	**Manicouagan, Réservoir** *resr* Can.	
79 B2	**Manifah** Saudi Arabia	
64 B1	**Manila** Phil.	
53 D2	**Manilla** Austr.	
111 C3	**Manisa** Turkey	
140 B2	**Manistee** U.S.A.	
129 E2	**Manitoba** *prov.* Can.	
129 E2	**Manitoba, Lake** Can.	
140 B1	**Manitou Islands** U.S.A.	
130 B2	**Manitoulin Island** Can.	
140 B2	**Manitowoc** U.S.A.	
130 C2	**Maniwaki** Can.	
150 A1	**Manizales** Col.	
137 E2	**Mankato** U.S.A.	
114 B4	**Mankono** Côte d'Ivoire	
129 D3	**Mankota** Can.	
73 C4	**Mankulam** Sri Lanka	
74 B2	**Manmad** India	
73 B4	**Mannar, Gulf of** India/Sri Lanka	
101 D3	**Mannheim** Ger.	
128 C2	**Manning** Can.	
52 A2	**Mannum** Austr.	
129 C2	**Mannville** Can.	
59 C3	**Manokwari** Indon.	
119 C3	**Manono** Dem. Rep. Congo	
63 A2	**Manoron** Myanmar	
105 D3	**Manosque** France	
131 C1	**Manouane, Lac** *l.* Can.	
107 D1	**Manresa** Spain	
121 B2	**Mansa** Zambia	
127 F2	**Mansel Island** Can.	
92 I2	**Mansel'ya** *ridge* Fin./Russia	
53 C3	**Mansfield** Austr.	
98 C2	**Mansfield** U.K.	
142 B2	**Mansfield** *LA* U.S.A.	
140 C2	**Mansfield** *OH* U.S.A.	
141 D2	**Mansfield** *PA* U.S.A.	
150 A2	**Manta** Ecuador	
143 E1	**Manteo** U.S.A.	
104 C2	**Mantes-la-Jolie** France	
155 C2	**Mantiqueira, Serra da** *mts* Brazil	
108 B1	**Mantova** Italy *see* Mantua	
108 B1	**Mantua** Italy	
151 C2	**Manuelzinho** Brazil	
59 C3	**Manui** *i.* Indon.	
54 B1	**Manukau** N.Z.	
142 B2	**Many** U.S.A.	
119 D3	**Manyoni** Tanz.	
106 C2	**Manzanares** Spain	
144 B3	**Manzanillo** Mex.	
69 D1	**Manzhouli** China	
123 D2	**Manzini** Swaziland	
115 D3	**Mao** Chad	
107 D2	**Mao** Spain	
59 D3	**Maoke, Pegunungan** *mts* Indon.	
123 C2	**Maokeng** S. Africa	
65 A1	**Maokui Shan** *mt.* China	
71 B3	**Maoming** China	
121 C3	**Mapai** Moz.	
75 C1	**Mapam Yumco** *l.* China	
145 C3	**Mapastepec** Mex.	
144 B2	**Mapimí** Mex.	
144 B2	**Mapimí, Bolsón de** *des.* Mex.	
121 C3	**Mapinhane** Moz.	
129 D3	**Maple Creek** Can.	
121 C3	**Maputo** Moz.	
123 D2	**Maputo** *r.* Moz./S. Africa	
120 A1	**Maquela do Zombo** Angola	
153 B5	**Maquinchao** Arg.	
137 E2	**Maquoketa** U.S.A.	
150 B2	**Maraã** Brazil	
151 D2	**Marabá** Brazil	
151 C1	**Maracá, Ilha de** *i.* Brazil	
150 A1	**Maracaibo** Venez.	
150 A1	**Maracaibo, Lake** Venez.	
152 C3	**Maracaju, Serra de** *hills* Brazil	
150 B1	**Maracay** Venez.	
115 D2	**Marādah** Libya	
115 C3	**Maradi** Niger	
81 C2	**Marāgheh** Iran	
151 D2	**Marajó, Baía de** *est.* Brazil	
151 C2	**Marajó, Ilha de** *i.* Brazil	
79 C2	**Marāki** Iran	
119 D2	**Maralal** Kenya	
50 C3	**Maralinga** Austr.	
81 C2	**Marand** Iran	
150 A2	**Marañón** *r.* Peru	
143 D4	**Marathon** U.S.A.	
130 B2	**Marathon** Can.	
106 C2	**Marbella** Spain	
50 A2	**Marble Bar** Austr.	
123 C1	**Marble Hall** S. Africa	
101 D2	**Marburg** Ger.	
123 D3	**Marburg** S. Africa	
99 D2	**March** U.K.	
100 B2	**Marche-en-Famenne** Belgium	
106 B2	**Marchena** Spain	
152 B4	**Mar Chiquita, Laguna** *l.* Arg.	
141 E2	**Marcy, Mount** U.S.A.	
74 B1	**Mardan** Pak.	
153 C4	**Mar del Plata** Arg.	
81 C2	**Mardin** Turkey	
96 B2	**Maree, Loch** *l.* U.K.	
108 B3	**Marettimo, Isola** *i. Sicily* Italy	
89 D2	**Marevo** Russia	
138 C2	**Marfa** U.S.A.	
73 B3	**Margao** India	
50 A3	**Margaret River** Austr.	
147 D3	**Margarita, Isla de** *i.* Venez.	
123 D3	**Margate** S. Africa	
99 D3	**Margate** U.K.	
119 C2	**Margherita Peak** Dem. Rep. Congo/Uganda	
76 C3	**Märgö, Dasht-e** *des.* Afgh.	
91 C2	**Marhanets'** Ukr.	
62 A1	**Mari** Myanmar	
152 B3	**María Elena** Chile	
156 C5	**Mariana Trench** N. Pacific Ocean	
142 B2	**Marianna** *AR* U.S.A.	
143 C2	**Marianna** *FL* U.S.A.	
102 C2	**Mariánské Lázně** Czech Rep.	
144 B2	**Marías, Islas** *is* Mex.	
78 B3	**Ma'rib** Yemen	
109 C1	**Maribor** Slovenia	
117 A4	**Maridi** *watercourse* South Sudan	
55 M2	**Marie Byrd Land** *reg.* Antarctica	
147 D3	**Marie-Galante** *i.* Guadeloupe	
93 G3	**Mariehamn** Fin.	
122 A1	**Mariental** Namibia	
93 F4	**Mariestad** Sweden	
143 D2	**Marietta** *GA* U.S.A.	
140 C3	**Marietta** *OH* U.S.A.	

105 D3 Marignane France
83 K3 Marii, Mys pt Russia
88 B3 Marijampol Lith.
154 C2 Marília Brazil
106 B1 Marín Spain
109 C3 Marina di Gioiosa Ionica Italy
88 C3 Mar''ina Horka Belarus
140 B1 Marinette U.S.A.
154 B2 Maringá Brazil
106 B2 Marinha Grande Port.
140 B2 Marion IN U.S.A.
140 C2 Marion OH U.S.A.
143 E2 Marion SC U.S.A.
140 C3 Marion VA U.S.A.
143 D2 Marion, Lake U.S.A.
52 A3 Mariscal José Félix
152 B3 Estigarribia Para.
110 C2 Maritsa r. Bulg.
91 D2 Mariupol' Ukr.
117 C4 Marka Somalia
123 C1 Marken S. Africa
100 B1 Markermeer l. Neth.
83 I2 Markha r. Russia
91 D2 Markivka Ukr.
142 B2 Marksville U.S.A.
101 D3 Marktheidenfeld Ger.
101 F2 Marktredwitz Ger.
100 C2 Marl Ger.
100 A3 Marle France
139 D2 Marlin U.S.A.
104 C3 Marmande France
111 C2 Marmara, Sea of g. Turkey
      Marmara Denizi g. Turkey see
      Marmara, Sea of
111 C3 Marmaris Turkey
104 C2 Marne-la-Vallée France
121 □D2 Maroantsetra Madag.
121 □D2 Maroelaboer Ger.
121 □D2 Maromokotro mt. Madag.
121 □E2 Marondera Zimbabwe
151 C1 Maroni r. Fr. Guiana
118 B1 Maroua Cameroon
121 □D2 Marovoay Madag.
49 I3 Marquesas Islands is
      Fr. Polynesia
140 B1 Marquette U.S.A.
117 A3 Marra, Jebel mt. Sudan
117 A3 Marra, Jebel plat. Sudan
123 D2 Marracuene Moz.
114 B1 Marrakech Morocco
52 A1 Marree Austr.
121 C2 Marromeu Moz.
121 C2 Marrupa Moz.
116 B2 Marsá al 'Alam Egypt
115 D1 Marsá al Burayqah Libya
119 D2 Marsabit Kenya
108 B3 Marsala Sicily Italy
116 A1 Marsá Maţrūḩ Egypt
101 D2 Marsberg Ger.
108 B2 Marsciano Italy
53 C2 Marsden Austr.
105 D3 Marseille France
137 D2 Marshall MN U.S.A.
137 E3 Marshall MO U.S.A.
139 E2 Marshall TX U.S.A.
48 F2 Marshall Islands country
      N. Pacific Ocean
137 E2 Marshalltown U.S.A.
140 A2 Marshfield U.S.A.
143 E3 Marsh Harbour Bahamas
142 B3 Marsh Island U.S.A.
88 A2 Märsta Sweden
61 C2 Martapura Kalimantan Selatan
      Indon.
60 B2 Martapura Sumatera Selatan
      Indon.
141 E2 Martha's Vineyard i. U.S.A.

105 D2 Martigny Switz.
103 D2 Martin Slovakia
136 C2 Martin U.S.A.
145 C2 Martínez Mex.
147 D3 Martinique terr. West Indies
141 D3 Martinsburg U.S.A.
140 D3 Martinsville U.S.A.
76 B1 Martok Kazakh.
54 C2 Marton N.Z.
107 D1 Martorell Spain
106 C2 Martos Spain
105 C3 Marvejols France
76 C3 Mary Turkm.
51 E2 Maryborough Austr.
122 B2 Marydale S. Africa
141 D3 Maryland state U.S.A.
137 D3 Marysville U.S.A.
137 E2 Maryville MO U.S.A.
143 D1 Maryville TN U.S.A.
119 D3 Masai Steppe plain Tanz.
119 D3 Masaka Uganda
65 B2 Masan S. Korea
119 D4 Masasi Tanz.
64 B1 Masbate Phil.
64 B1 Masbate i. Phil.
123 C2 Maseru Lesotho
76 B3 Mashhad Iran
123 D2 Mashishing S. Africa
74 A2 Mashkel, Hamun-i- salt flat
      Pak.
123 C3 Masibambane S. Africa
79 C3 Masilah, Wādī al watercourse
      Yemen
123 C2 Masilo S. Africa
119 D2 Masindi Uganda
79 C2 Maşīrah, Jazīrat i. Oman
79 C3 Maşīrah, Khalīj b. Oman
81 C2 Masjed Soleymān Iran
97 B2 Mask, Lough l. Ireland
121 □E2 Masoala, Tanjona c. Madag.
137 E2 Mason City U.S.A.
      Masqaţ Oman see Muscat
108 B2 Massa Italy
141 E2 Massachusetts state U.S.A.
141 E2 Massachusetts Bay U.S.A.
121 C3 Massangena Moz.
120 A1 Massango Angola
116 B3 Massawa Eritrea
141 E2 Massena U.S.A.
128 A2 Masset Can.
105 C2 Massif Central mts France
140 C2 Massillon U.S.A.
121 C3 Massinga Moz.
123 D1 Massingir Moz.
78 A2 Mastābah Saudi Arabia
54 C2 Masterton N.Z.
74 A2 Mastung Pak.
78 A2 Mastūrah Saudi Arabia
88 B3 Masty Belarus
67 B4 Masuda Japan
      Masuku Gabon see Franceville
121 C3 Masvingo Zimbabwe
69 D1 Matad Mongolia
118 B3 Matadi Dem. Rep. Congo
146 B3 Matagalpa Nic.
130 C2 Matagami Can.
130 C2 Matagami, Lac l. Can.
139 D3 Matagorda Island U.S.A.
120 A2 Matala Angola
114 A3 Matam Senegal
144 B2 Matamoros Coahuila Mex.
145 C2 Matamoros Tamaulipas Mex.
119 D3 Matandu r. Tanz.
131 D2 Matane Can.
146 B2 Matanzas Cuba
73 C4 Matara Sri Lanka
61 C2 Mataram Indon.
50 C1 Mataranka Austr.

107 D1 Mataró Spain
123 C3 Matatiele S. Africa
54 A3 Mataura N.Z.
49 G3 Matā'utu Wallis and Futuna Is
54 C1 Matawai N.Z.
152 B2 Mategua Bol.
145 B2 Matehuala Mex.
109 C2 Matera Italy
139 D3 Mathis U.S.A.
75 B2 Mathura India
64 B2 Mati Phil.
98 C2 Matlock U.K.
123 D2 Matola Moz.
      Matou China see Pingguo
67 B3 Matsue Japan
66 D2 Matsumae Japan
67 C4 Matsusaka Japan
67 B4 Matsuyama Japan
130 B1 Mattagami r. Can.
105 D2 Matterhorn mt. Italy/Switz.
134 C2 Matterhorn mt. U.S.A.
140 B3 Mattoon U.S.A.
150 B1 Maturín Venez.
123 C2 Matwabeng S. Africa
100 A2 Maubeuge France
104 C3 Maubourguet France
124 E5 Maui i. U.S.A.
140 C2 Maumee r. U.S.A.
120 B2 Maun Botswana
62 A1 Maungdaw Myanmar
50 C2 Maurice, Lake imp. l. Austr.
114 A3 Mauritania country Africa
113 K9 Mauritius country
      Indian Ocean
78 B2 Māwān, Khashm mt.
      Saudi Arabia
118 B3 Mawanga Dem. Rep. Congo
71 B3 Mawei China
62 A1 Mawkmai Myanmar
62 A1 Mawlaik Myanmar
63 A2 Mawlamyaing Myanmar
78 B2 Mawqaq Saudi Arabia
78 B3 Mawza' Yemen
108 A3 Maxia, Punta mt. Sardinia
      Italy
83 J2 Maya r. Russia
147 C2 Mayaguana i. Bahamas
96 B3 Maybole U.K.
104 B2 Mayenne France
104 B2 Mayenne r. France
128 C2 Mayerthorpe Can.
140 B3 Mayfield U.S.A.
87 D4 Maykop Russia
126 B2 Mayo Can.
118 B3 Mayoko Congo
121 D2 Mayotte terr. Africa
83 J3 Mayskiy Russia
140 C3 Maysville U.S.A.
118 B3 Mayumba Gabon
137 D1 Mayville U.S.A.
151 C2 Mazagão Brazil
118 B2 Mazamet France
77 D3 Mazar China
108 B3 Mazara del Vallo Sicily Italy
77 C3 Mazār-e Sharif Afgh.
144 A2 Mazatán Mex.
146 A3 Mazatenango Guat.
144 B2 Mazatlán Mex.
88 B2 Mažeikiai Lith.
88 B2 Mazirbe Latvia
73 C1 Mazu Dao i. Taiwan
121 B3 Mazunga Zimbabwe
88 C3 Mazyr Belarus
123 D2 Mbabane Swaziland
118 B2 Mbaïki C.A.R.
121 C1 Mbala Zambia
119 D2 Mbale Uganda
118 B2 Mbalmayo Cameroon

Mbandaka

118 B3	Mbandaka Dem. Rep. Congo
118 A2	Mbanga Cameroon
120 A1	M'banza Congo Angola
119 D3	Mbeya Tanz.
119 D4	Mbinga Tanz.
123 C3	Mbombela S. Africa
118 B2	Mbomo Congo
118 A2	Mbouda Cameroon
114 A3	Mbour Senegal
114 A3	Mbout Maur.
118 C3	Mbuji-Mayi Dem. Rep. Congo
119 D3	Mbuyuni Tanz.
139 D2	McAlester U.S.A.
139 D3	McAllen U.S.A.
128 B2	McBride Can.
134 C2	McCall U.S.A.
126 E2	McClintock Channel Can.
126 D2	McClure Strait Can.
142 B2	McComb U.S.A.
136 C2	McConaughy, Lake U.S.A.
136 C2	McCook U.S.A.
134 C2	McDermitt U.S.A.
134 D1	McDonald Peak U.S.A.
134 D1	McGuire, Mount U.S.A.
128 C2	McLennan Can.
128 B2	McLeod Lake Can.
134 B1	McMinnville OR U.S.A.
142 C1	McMinnville TN U.S.A.
137 D3	McPherson U.S.A.
123 C3	Mdantsane S. Africa
135 D3	Mead, Lake resr U.S.A.
129 D2	Meadow Lake Can.
140 C2	Meadville U.S.A.
66 D2	Meaken-dake vol. Japan
106 B1	Mealhada Port.
131 E1	Mealy Mountains Can.
128 C2	Meander River Can.
78 A2	Mecca Saudi Arabia
100 B2	Mechelen Belgium
100 B2	Mechelen Neth.
100 C2	Mechernich Ger.
100 C2	Meckenheim Ger.
106 B1	Meda Port.
60 A1	Medan Indon.
153 B5	Medanosa, Punta pt Arg.
73 C4	Medawachchiya Sri Lanka
107 D2	Médéa Alg.
150 A1	Medellín Col.
115 D1	Medenine Tunisia
134 B2	Medford U.S.A.
110 C2	Medgidia Romania
110 B1	Mediaş Romania
136 B2	Medicine Bow Mountains U.S.A.
136 B2	Medicine Bow Peak U.S.A.
129 C2	Medicine Hat Can.
137 D3	Medicine Lodge U.S.A.
155 D1	Medina Brazil
78 A2	Medina Saudi Arabia
106 C1	Medinaceli Spain
106 C1	Medina del Campo Spain
106 B1	Medina de Rioseco Spain
84 G5	Mediterranean Sea
129 C2	Medley Can.
87 E3	Mednogorsk Russia
83 L2	Medvezh'i, Ostrova is Russia
86 C2	Medvezh'yegorsk Russia
50 A2	Meekatharra Austr.
136 B2	Meeker U.S.A.
75 B2	Meerut India
100 A2	Meetkerke Belgium
111 B3	Megalopoli Greece
75 C2	Meghasani mt. India
80 A2	Megisti i. Greece
92 I1	Mehamn Norway
50 A2	Meharry, Mount Austr.
79 C2	Mehrän watercourse Iran
76 C3	Mehrestän Iran
74 B1	Mehtar Läm Afgh.
154 C1	Meia Ponte r. Brazil
118 B2	Meiganga Cameroon
65 B1	Meihekou China
	Meijiang China see Ningdu
62 A1	Meiktila Myanmar
101 E2	Meiningen Ger.
102 C1	Meißen Ger.
71 B3	Meizhou China
152 B3	Mejicana mt. Arg.
152 A3	Mejillones Chile
117 B3	Mek'elë Eth.
114 C2	Mekerrhane, Sebkha salt pan Alg.
114 B1	Meknès Morocco
63 B2	Mekong r. Asia
63 B3	Mekong, Mouths of the Vietnam
60 B1	Melaka Malaysia
53 B3	Melbourne Austr.
143 D3	Melbourne U.S.A.
108 A2	Mele, Capo c. Italy
131 C1	Mélèzes, Rivière aux r. Can.
115 D3	Melfi Chad
109 C2	Melfi Italy
129 D2	Melfort Can.
92 F3	Melhus Norway
106 B1	Melide Spain
114 B1	Melilla N. Africa
91 D2	Melitopol' Ukr.
101 D1	Melle Ger.
93 F4	Mellerud Sweden
101 E2	Mellrichstadt Ger.
100 D1	Mellum i. Ger.
152 C4	Melo Uru.
115 C1	Melrhir, Chott salt l. Alg.
99 C2	Melton Mowbray U.K.
104 C2	Melun France
129 D2	Melville Can.
51 D1	Melville, Cape Austr.
131 E1	Melville, Lake Can.
50 C1	Melville Island Austr.
126 D1	Melville Island Can.
127 F2	Melville Peninsula Can.
102 C2	Memmingen Ger.
61 B1	Mempawah Indon.
80 B3	Memphis tourist site Egypt
142 B1	Memphis TN U.S.A.
139 C2	Memphis TX U.S.A.
91 C1	Mena Ukr.
142 B2	Mena U.S.A.
114 C3	Ménaka Mali
	Mènam Khong r. Laos/Thai. see Mekong
105 C2	Mende France
116 B3	Mendefera Eritrea
145 C2	Méndez Mex.
119 D2	Mendi Eth.
59 D3	Mendi P.N.G.
99 B3	Mendip Hills U.K.
153 B4	Mendoza Arg.
111 C3	Menemen Turkey
60 B2	Menggala Indon.
62 B1	Mengzi China
131 D1	Menihek Can.
52 B2	Menindee Austr.
52 B2	Menindee Lake Austr.
52 A3	Meningie Austr.
104 C2	Mennecy France
140 B1	Menominee U.S.A.
120 A2	Menongue Angola
	Menorca i. Spain see Minorca
60 A2	Mentawai, Kepulauan is Indon.
60 B2	Mentok Indon.
50 B2	Menzies Austr.
100 C1	Meppel Neth.
100 C1	Meppen Ger.
123 D1	Mepuze Moz.
123 C2	Meqheleng S. Africa
108 B1	Merano Italy
59 D3	Merauke Indon.
52 B2	Merbein Austr.
135 B3	Merced U.S.A.
152 C3	Mercedes Arg.
127 G2	Mercy, Cape Can.
139 C1	Meredith, Lake U.S.A.
91 D2	Merefa Ukr.
116 A3	Merga Oasis Sudan
63 A2	Mergui Archipelago is Myanmar
110 C2	Meriç r. Greece/Turkey
145 D2	Mérida Mex.
106 B2	Mérida Spain
150 A1	Mérida Venez.
142 C2	Meridian U.S.A.
104 B3	Mérignac France
53 C3	Merimbula Austr.
116 B3	Merowe Sudan
50 A3	Merredin Austr.
96 B3	Merrick h. U.K.
140 B1	Merrill U.S.A.
140 B2	Merrillville U.S.A.
128 B2	Merritt Can.
53 C2	Merrygoen Austr.
116 B3	Mersa Fatma Eritrea
100 C3	Mersch Lux.
101 E2	Merseburg Ger.
98 B2	Mersey r. U.K.
80 B2	Mersin Turkey
60 B1	Mersing Malaysia
99 D3	Mers-les-Bains France
74 B2	Merta India
99 B3	Merthyr Tydfil U.K.
106 B2	Mértola Port.
76 B2	Mertvyy Kultuk, Sor dry lake Kazakh.
119 D3	Meru vol. Tanz.
100 C3	Merzig Ger.
138 A2	Mesa U.S.A.
109 C2	Mesagne Italy
101 D2	Meschede Ger.
89 E3	Meshchovsk Russia
91 E2	Meshkovskaya Russia
111 B2	Mesimeri Greece
111 B3	Mesolongi Greece
121 D2	Messalo r. Moz.
109 C3	Messina Sicily Italy
109 C3	Messina, Strait of Italy
111 B3	Messiniakos Kolpos g. Greece
110 B2	Mesta r. Bulg.
150 B1	Meta r. Col./Venez.
127 G2	Meta Incognita Peninsula Can.
152 B3	Metán Arg.
111 B3	Methoni Greece
109 C2	Metković Croatia
60 B2	Metro Indon.
117 B4	Metu Eth.
105 D2	Metz France
100 B2	Meuse r. Belgium/France
139 D2	Mexia U.S.A.
144 A1	Mexicali Mex.
144 B2	Mexico country Central America
137 E3	Mexico U.S.A.
125 I5	Mexico, Gulf of Mex./U.S.A.
145 C3	Mexico City Mex.
101 F1	Meyenburg Ger.
86 D2	Mezen' Russia
86 D2	Mezen' r. Russia
86 E1	Mezhdusharskiy, Ostrov i. Russia
103 E2	Meztúr Hungary
144 B2	Mezquitic Mex.
88 C2	Mežvidi Latvia

121 C2 **Mfuwe** Zambia
123 D2 **Mhlume** Swaziland
74 B2 **Mhow** India
145 C3 **Miahuatlán** Mex.
106 B2 **Miajadas** Spain
143 D3 **Miami** *FL* U.S.A.
139 E1 **Miami** *OK* U.S.A.
143 D3 **Miami Beach** U.S.A.
81 C2 **Mīāndoāb** Iran
121 □D2 **Miandrivazo** Madag.
81 C2 **Mīāneh** Iran
74 B1 **Mianwali** Pak.
70 A2 **Mianyang** China
121 □D2 **Miarinarivo** Madag.
87 F3 **Miass** Russia
128 C2 **Mica Creek** Can.
103 E2 **Michalovce** Slovakia
140 B1 **Michigan** *state* U.S.A.
140 B2 **Michigan, Lake** U.S.A.
140 B2 **Michigan City** U.S.A.
130 B2 **Michipicoten Island** Can.
130 B2 **Michipicoten River** Can.
89 F3 **Michurinsk** Russia
48 D2 **Micronesia, Federated States of** *country* N. Pacific Ocean
100 A2 **Middelburg** Neth.
123 C3 **Middelburg** *E. Cape* S. Africa
123 C2 **Middelburg** *Mpumalanga* S. Africa
100 B2 **Middelharnis** Neth.
134 B2 **Middle Alkali Lake** U.S.A.
73 D3 **Middle Andaman** *i.* India
136 D2 **Middle Loup** *r.* U.S.A.
140 C3 **Middlesboro** U.S.A.
98 C1 **Middlesbrough** U.K.
141 E2 **Middletown** *NY* U.S.A.
140 C3 **Middletown** *OH* U.S.A.
78 B3 **Mīdī** Yemen
130 C2 **Midland** Can.
140 C2 **Midland** *MI* U.S.A.
139 C2 **Midland** *TX* U.S.A.
97 B3 **Midleton** Ireland
94 B1 **Miðvágur** Faroe Is
109 D2 **Midzhur** *mt.* Bulgaria/Serbia
103 E1 **Mielec** Pol.
110 C1 **Miercurea-Ciuc** Romania
106 B1 **Mieres del Camín** Spain
101 E1 **Mieste** Ger.
145 C3 **Miguel Alemán, Presa** *resr* Mex.
144 B2 **Miguel Auza** Mex.
144 B2 **Miguel Hidalgo, Presa** *resr* Mex.
63 A2 **Migyaunglaung** Myanmar
89 E3 **Mikhaylov** Russia
Mikhaylovgrad Bulg. *see* **Montana**
66 B2 **Mikhaylovka** Russia
77 D1 **Mikhaylovskoye** Russia
93 I3 **Mikkeli** Fin.
86 E2 **Mikun'** Russia
67 C3 **Mikuni-sanmyaku** *mts* Japan
108 A1 **Milan** Italy
121 C2 **Milange** Moz.
Milano Italy *see* **Milan**
111 C3 **Milas** Turkey
137 D1 **Milbank** U.S.A.
99 D2 **Mildenhall** U.K.
52 B2 **Mildura** Austr.
62 B1 **Mile** China
136 B1 **Miles City** U.S.A.
141 D3 **Milford** *DE* U.S.A.
135 D3 **Milford** *UT* U.S.A.
99 A3 **Milford Haven** U.K.
54 A2 **Milford Sound** N.Z.
107 D2 **Miliana** Alg.
116 B3 **Milk, Wadi el** *watercourse* Sudan
83 L3 **Mil'kovo** Russia
129 C3 **Milk River** Can.
105 C3 **Millau** France
143 D2 **Milledgeville** U.S.A.
137 E1 **Mille Lacs** *lakes* U.S.A.
130 A2 **Mille Lacs, Lac des** *l.* Can.
137 D2 **Miller** U.S.A.
91 E2 **Millerovo** Russia
52 A2 **Millers Creek** Austr.
52 B3 **Millicent** Austr.
141 F1 **Millinocket** U.S.A.
53 D1 **Millmerran** Austr.
98 B1 **Millom** U.K.
128 C1 **Mills Lake** Can.
111 B3 **Milos** *i.* Greece
89 E3 **Miloslavskoye** Russia
91 E2 **Milove** Ukr.
52 B1 **Milparinka** Austr.
54 A3 **Milton** N.Z.
99 C2 **Milton Keynes** U.K.
140 B2 **Milwaukee** U.S.A.
104 B3 **Mimizan** France
118 B3 **Mimongo** Gabon
79 C2 **Mīnāb** Iran
58 C2 **Minahasa, Semenanjung** *pen.* Indon.
79 C2 **Mīnā' Jabal 'Alī** U.A.E.
60 B1 **Minas** Indon.
153 C4 **Minas** Uru.
155 D1 **Minas Novas** Brazil
145 C3 **Minatitlán** Mex.
62 A1 **Minbu** Myanmar
64 B2 **Mindanao** *i.* Phil.
101 D1 **Minden** Ger.
142 B2 **Minden** *LA* U.S.A.
137 D2 **Minden** *NE* U.S.A.
64 B1 **Mindoro** *i.* Phil.
64 A1 **Mindoro Strait** Phil.
118 B3 **Mindouli** Congo
99 B3 **Minehead** U.K.
154 B1 **Mineiros** Brazil
139 D2 **Mineral Wells** U.S.A.
77 E3 **Minfeng** China
119 C4 **Minga** Dem. Rep. Congo
81 C1 **Mingäçevir** Azer.
131 D1 **Mingan** Can.
52 B2 **Mingary** Austr.
70 B2 **Mingguang** China
62 A1 **Mingin** Myanmar
107 C2 **Minglanilla** Spain
119 D4 **Mingoyo** Tanz.
69 E1 **Mingshui** China
71 B3 **Mingxi** China
73 B4 **Minicoy** *atoll* India
50 A2 **Minilya** Austr.
131 D1 **Minipi Lake** Can.
130 A1 **Miniss Lake** Can.
115 C4 **Minna** Nigeria
137 E2 **Minneapolis** U.S.A.
129 E2 **Minnedosa** Can.
137 E2 **Minnesota** *r.* U.S.A.
137 E1 **Minnesota** *state* U.S.A.
106 B1 **Miño** *r.* Port./Spain
107 D1 **Minorca** *i.* Spain
136 C1 **Minot** U.S.A.
88 C3 **Minsk** Belarus
103 E1 **Mińsk Mazowiecki** Pol.
131 D2 **Minto** Can.
130 C1 **Minto, Lac** *l.* Can.
70 A2 **Minxian** China
155 D1 **Mirabela** Brazil
155 D1 **Miralta** Brazil
131 D2 **Miramichi** Can.
111 C3 **Mirampellou, Kolpos** *b.* Greece
152 C3 **Miranda** Brazil
152 C2 **Miranda** *r.* Brazil
106 C1 **Miranda de Ebro** Spain
106 B1 **Mirandela** Port.
154 B2 **Mirandópolis** Brazil
79 C3 **Mirbāţ** Oman
61 C1 **Miri** *Sarawak* Malaysia
153 C4 **Mirim, Lagoa** *l.* Brazil/Uru.
79 D2 **Mīrjāveh** Iran
83 I2 **Mirnyy** Russia
101 F1 **Mirow** Ger.
74 A2 **Mirpur Khas** Pak.
111 B3 **Mirtoö Pelagos** *sea* Greece
65 B2 **Miryang** S. Korea
75 C2 **Mirzapur** India
66 B1 **Mishan** China
146 B3 **Miskitos, Cayos** *is* Nic.
103 E2 **Miskolc** Hungary
59 C3 **Misoöl** *i.* Indon.
115 D1 **Mişrātah** Libya
130 B1 **Missinaibi** *r.* Can.
130 B2 **Missinaibi Lake** Can.
128 B3 **Mission** Can.
130 B1 **Missisa Lake** Can.
142 C3 **Mississippi** *r.* U.S.A.
142 C2 **Mississippi** *state* U.S.A.
142 C3 **Mississippi Delta** U.S.A.
134 D1 **Missoula** U.S.A.
137 E3 **Missouri** *r.* U.S.A.
137 E3 **Missouri** *state* U.S.A.
131 C2 **Mistassibi** *r.* Can.
130 C1 **Mistassini, Lac** *l.* Can.
131 D1 **Mistastin Lake** Can.
103 D2 **Mistelbach** Austria
131 D1 **Mistinibi, Lac** *l.* Can.
130 C1 **Mistissini** Can.
51 D2 **Mitchell** Austr.
51 D1 **Mitchell** *r.* Austr.
137 D2 **Mitchell** U.S.A.
97 B2 **Mitchelstown** Ireland
74 A2 **Mithi** Pak.
67 D3 **Mito** Japan
119 D3 **Mitole** Tanz.
109 D2 **Mitrovicë** Kosovo
53 D2 **Mittagong** Austr.
101 E2 **Mittelhausen** Ger.
101 D1 **Mittellandkanal** *canal* Ger.
101 F3 **Mitterteich** Ger.
150 A1 **Mitú** Col.
119 C4 **Mitumba, Chaîne des** *mts* Dem. Rep. Congo
119 C3 **Mitumba, Monts** *mts* Dem. Rep. Congo
118 B2 **Mitzic** Gabon
78 B2 **Miyah, Wādī al** *watercourse* Saudi Arabia
67 C4 **Miyake-jima** *i.* Japan
66 D3 **Miyako** Japan
67 B4 **Miyakonojō** Japan
76 B2 **Miyaly** Kazakh.
Miyang China *see* **Mile**
67 B4 **Miyazaki** Japan
115 D1 **Mizdah** Libya
97 B3 **Mizen Head** Ireland
90 A2 **Mizhhirr"ya** Ukr.
93 G4 **Mjölby** Sweden
93 F3 **Mjøsa** *l.* Norway
119 D3 **Mkomazi** Tanz.
103 C1 **Mladá Boleslav** Czech Rep.
109 D2 **Mladenovac** Serbia
103 E1 **Mława** Pol.
123 C3 **Mlungisi** S. Africa
90 B1 **Mlyniv** Ukr.
123 C2 **Mmabatho** S. Africa
123 C2 **Mmathethe** Botswana
135 E3 **Moab** U.S.A.
123 D2 **Moamba** Moz.
119 C3 **Moba** Dem. Rep. Congo
118 C2 **Mobayi-Mbongo** Dem. Rep. Congo
137 E3 **Moberly** U.S.A.

Mobile

142	C2	**Mobile** U.S.A.
142	C2	**Mobile Bay** U.S.A.
136	C1	**Mobridge** U.S.A.
121	D2	**Moçambique** Moz.
62	B1	**Móc Châu** Vietnam
78	B3	**Mocha** Yemen
123	C1	**Mochudi** Botswana
121	D2	**Mocimboa da Praia** Moz.
150	A1	**Moco** Col.
154	C2	**Mococa** Brazil
144	B2	**Mocorito** Mex.
144	B1	**Moctezuma** *Chihuahua* Mex.
145	B2	**Moctezuma** *San Luis Potosí* Mex.
144	B2	**Moctezuma** *Sonora* Mex.
121	C2	**Mocuba** Moz.
105	D2	**Modane** France
122	B2	**Modder** r. S. Africa
108	B2	**Modena** Italy
135	B3	**Modesto** U.S.A.
123	C1	**Modimolle** S. Africa
123	D1	**Modjadjiskloof** S. Africa
53	C3	**Moe** Austr.
100	C2	**Moers** Ger.
96	C3	**Moffat** U.K.
117	C4	**Mogadishu** Somalia
123	C1	**Mogalakwena** r. S. Africa
62	A1	**Mogaung** Myanmar
155	C2	**Mogi das Cruzes** Brazil
		Mogilev Belarus *see*
		Mahilyow
154	C2	**Mogi Mirim** Brazil
83	I3	**Mogocha** Russia
62	A1	**Mogok** Myanmar
103	D2	**Mohács** Hungary
123	C3	**Mohale's Hoek** Lesotho
74	B1	**Mohali** India
79	C2	**Moḩammadābād** Iran
107	D2	**Mohammadia** Alg.
141	E2	**Mohawk** r. U.S.A.
119	D3	**Mohoro** Tanz.
90	B2	**Mohyliv-Podil's'kyy** Ukr.
110	C1	**Moineşti** Romania
92	F2	**Mo i Rana** Norway
104	C3	**Moissac** France
135	C3	**Mojave** U.S.A.
135	C3	**Mojave Desert** U.S.A.
62	B1	**Mojiang** China
154	C2	**Moji-Guaçu** r. Brazil
54	B1	**Mokau** N.Z.
123	C2	**Mokhotlong** Lesotho
123	C1	**Mokopane** S. Africa
65	B3	**Mokpo** S. Korea
145	C2	**Molango** Mex.
		Moldavia *country* Europe *see*
		Moldova
92	E3	**Molde** Norway
90	B2	**Moldova** *country* Europe
110	B1	**Moldoveanu, Vârful** *mt.* Romania
90	B2	**Moldovei Centrale, Podișul** *plat.* Moldova
123	C1	**Molepolole** Botswana
88	C2	**Moltai** Lith.
109	C2	**Molfetta** Italy
107	C1	**Molina de Aragón** Spain
150	A3	**Mollendo** Peru
53	C2	**Molong** Austr.
122	B2	**Molopo** *watercourse* Botswana/S. Africa
118	B2	**Moloundou** Cameroon
59	C3	**Moluccas** is Indon.
		Molucca Sea Indon. *see*
		Maluku, Laut
52	B2	**Momba** Austr.
119	D3	**Mombasa** Kenya
154	B1	**Mombuca, Serra de** *hills* Brazil

93	F4	**Møn** i. Denmark
105	D3	**Monaco** *country* Europe
96	B2	**Monadhliath Mountains** U.K.
97	C1	**Monaghan** Ireland
89	D3	**Monastyrshchina** Russia
90	B2	**Monastyryshche** Ukr.
66	D2	**Monbetsu** Japan
108	A1	**Moncalieri** Italy
107	C1	**Moncayo** *mt.* Spain
86	C2	**Monchegorsk** Russia
100	C2	**Mönchengladbach** Ger.
144	B2	**Monclova** Mex.
131	D2	**Moncton** Can.
106	B1	**Mondego** r. Port.
108	A2	**Mondovì** Italy
111	B3	**Monemvasia** Greece
66	D1	**Moneron, Ostrov** i. Russia
137	E3	**Monett** U.S.A.
108	B1	**Monfalcone** Italy
106	B1	**Monforte de Lemos** Spain
62	B1	**Mông Cai** Vietnam
62	B1	**Mong Lin** Myanmar
68	C1	**Mongolia** *country* Asia
62	A1	**Mong Pawk** Myanmar
62	A1	**Mong Ping** Myanmar
120	B2	**Mongu** Zambia
135	C3	**Monitor Range** *mts* U.S.A.
114	C4	**Mono** r. Benin/Togo
135	C3	**Mono Lake** U.S.A.
109	C2	**Monopoli** Italy
107	C1	**Monreal del Campo** Spain
142	B2	**Monroe** LA U.S.A.
140	B2	**Monroe** WI U.S.A.
142	C2	**Monroeville** U.S.A.
114	A4	**Monrovia** Liberia
100	A2	**Mons** Belgium
122	B3	**Montagu** S. Africa
109	C3	**Montalto** mt. Italy
110	B2	**Montana** Bulg.
134	E1	**Montana** *state* U.S.A.
104	C3	**Montargis** France
141	E2	**Montauban** France
123	C2	**Montauk Point** U.S.A.
		Mont-aux-Sources *mt.* Lesotho
105	C2	**Montbard** France
105	C2	**Montbrison** France
100	B3	**Montcornet** France
104	B3	**Mont-de-Marsan** France
104	C2	**Montdidier** France
151	C2	**Monte Alegre** Brazil
105	D3	**Monte-Carlo** Monaco
152	C4	**Monte Caseros** Arg.
146	C3	**Montego Bay** Jamaica
105	C3	**Montélimar** France
109	C2	**Montella** Italy
145	C2	**Montemorelos** Mex.
104	B2	**Montendre** France
		Montenegro *country* Europe
121	C2	**Montepuez** Moz.
108	B2	**Montepulciano** Italy
135	B3	**Monterey** U.S.A.
135	B3	**Monterey Bay** U.S.A.
150	A1	**Montería** Col.
152	B2	**Montero** Bol.
145	B2	**Monterrey** Mex.
109	C2	**Montesano sulla Marcellana** Italy
109	C2	**Monte Sant'Angelo** Italy
151	E3	**Monte Santo** Brazil
108	A2	**Monte Santu, Capo di** c. Sardinia Italy
155	D1	**Montes Claros** Brazil
153	C4	**Montevideo** Uru.
137	D2	**Montevideo** U.S.A.
136	B3	**Monte Vista** U.S.A.
142	C2	**Montgomery** U.S.A.
105	D2	**Monthey** Switz.

142	B2	**Monticello** AR U.S.A.
135	E3	**Monticello** UT U.S.A.
104	C2	**Montignac** France
105	D2	**Montigny-le-Roi** France
106	B1	**Montilla** Spain
131	D2	**Mont-Joli** Can.
130	C2	**Mont-Laurier** Can.
104	C2	**Montluçon** France
131	C2	**Montmagny** Can.
104	C2	**Montmorillon** France
51	E2	**Monto** Austr.
134	D2	**Montpelier** ID U.S.A.
141	E2	**Montpelier** VT U.S.A.
105	C3	**Montpellier** France
130	C2	**Montréal** Can.
129	D2	**Montreal Lake** Can.
129	D2	**Montreal Lake** Can.
99	D3	**Montreuil** France
105	D2	**Montreux** Switz.
96	C2	**Montrose** U.K.
136	B3	**Montrose** U.S.A.
147	D3	**Montserrat** *terr.* West Indies
62	A1	**Monywa** Myanmar
108	A1	**Monza** Italy
107	D1	**Monzón** Spain
123	C1	**Mookane** Botswana
123	C1	**Mookgophong** S. Africa
53	D1	**Moonie** Austr.
53	C1	**Moonie** r. Austr.
52	A2	**Moonta** Austr.
50	A2	**Moore, Lake** imp. l. Austr.
137	D1	**Moorhead** U.S.A.
53	C3	**Mooroopna** Austr.
122	A3	**Moorreesburg** S. Africa
130	B1	**Moose** r. Can.
130	B1	**Moose Factory** Can.
141	F1	**Moosehead Lake** U.S.A.
129	D2	**Moose Jaw** Can.
137	E1	**Moose Lake** U.S.A.
129	D2	**Moosomin** Can.
130	B1	**Moosonee** Can.
52	B2	**Mootwingee** Austr.
123	C1	**Mopane** S. Africa
114	B3	**Mopti** Mali
150	A3	**Moquegua** Peru
93	F3	**Mora** Sweden
137	E1	**Mora** U.S.A.
75	B2	**Moradabad** India
121	□D2	**Moramanga** Madag.
103	D2	**Morava** r. Europe
96	B2	**Moray Firth** b. U.K.
100	C3	**Morbach** Ger.
74	B2	**Morbi** India
104	B3	**Morcenx** France
69	E1	**Mordaga** China
129	E3	**Morden** Can.
91	E1	**Mordovo** Russia
98	B1	**Morecambe** U.K.
98	B1	**Morecambe Bay** U.K.
53	C1	**Moree** Austr.
59	D3	**Morehead** P.N.G.
140	C3	**Morehead** U.S.A.
143	E2	**Morehead City** U.S.A.
145	B3	**Morelia** Mex.
107	C1	**Morella** Spain
106	B2	**Morena, Sierra** *mts* Spain
110	C2	**Moreni** Romania
128	A2	**Moresby, Mount** U.S.A.
142	B3	**Morgan City** U.S.A.
143	D1	**Morganton** U.S.A.
140	D3	**Morgantown** U.S.A.
105	D2	**Morges** Switz.
77	C3	**Morghāb, Daryā-ye** r. Afgh.
66	D2	**Mori** Japan
128	B2	**Morice Lake** Can.
66	D3	**Morioka** Japan
53	D2	**Morisset** Austr.
104	B2	**Morlaix** France

51 C1 **Mornington Island** Austr.
59 D3 **Morobe** P.N.G.
114 B1 **Morocco** *country* Africa
119 D3 **Morogoro** Tanz.
64 B2 **Moro Gulf** Phil.
122 B2 **Morokweng** S. Africa
121 □D3 **Morombe** Madag.
68 C1 **Mörön** Mongolia
121 □D3 **Morondava** Madag.
121 D2 **Moroni** Comoros
59 C2 **Morotai** *i.* Indon.
119 D2 **Moroto** Uganda
98 C1 **Morpeth** U.K.
86 F2 **Morrasale** Russia
154 C1 **Morrinhos** Brazil
129 E3 **Morris** Can.
137 D1 **Morris** U.S.A.
143 D1 **Morristown** U.S.A.
87 D3 **Morshansk** Russia
154 B1 **Mortes, Rio das** *r.* Brazil
52 B3 **Mortlake** Austr.
53 D3 **Moruya** Austr.
96 B2 **Morvern** *reg.* U.K.
53 C3 **Morwell** Austr.
102 B2 **Mosbach** Ger.
89 E2 **Moscow** Russia
134 C1 **Moscow** U.S.A.
100 C2 **Mosel** *r.* Ger.
105 D2 **Moselle** *r.* France
134 C1 **Moses Lake** U.S.A.
92 □A3 **Mosfellsbær** Iceland
54 B3 **Mosgiel** N.Z.
89 D2 **Moshenskoye** Russia
119 D3 **Moshi** Tanz.
92 F2 **Mosjøen** Norway
Moskva Russia *see* **Moscow**
103 D2 **Mosonmagyaróvár** Hungary
146 B3 **Mosquitos, Costa de** *coastal area* Nic.
146 B4 **Mosquitos, Golfo de los** *b.* Panama
93 F4 **Moss** Norway
122 B3 **Mossel Bay** S. Africa
122 B3 **Mossel Bay** S. Africa
118 B3 **Mossendjo** Congo
52 B2 **Mossgiel** Austr.
51 D1 **Mossman** Austr.
151 E2 **Mossoró** Brazil
53 D2 **Moss Vale** Austr.
102 C1 **Most** Czech Rep.
114 C1 **Mostaganem** Alg.
109 C2 **Mostar** Bos. & Herz.
152 C4 **Mostardas** Brazil
81 C2 **Mosul** Iraq
93 G4 **Motala** Sweden
96 C3 **Motherwell** U.K.
107 C2 **Motilla del Palancar** Spain
122 B1 **Motokwe** Botswana
106 C2 **Motril** Spain
110 B2 **Motru** Romania
63 A2 **Mottama, Gulf of** Myanmar
145 D2 **Motul** Mex.
111 C3 **Moudros** Greece
118 B3 **Mouila** Gabon
52 B3 **Moulamein** Austr.
105 C2 **Moulins** France
143 D2 **Moultrie** U.S.A.
143 E2 **Moultrie, Lake** U.S.A.
140 B3 **Mound City** U.S.A.
115 D4 **Moundou** Chad
137 E3 **Mountain Grove** U.S.A.
142 B1 **Mountain Home** *AR* U.S.A.
134 C2 **Mountain Home** *ID* U.S.A.
143 D1 **Mount Airy** U.S.A.
52 A3 **Mount Barker** Austr.
53 C3 **Mount Beauty** Austr.
121 C2 **Mount Darwin** Zimbabwe
141 F2 **Mount Desert Island** U.S.A.
123 C3 **Mount Fletcher** S. Africa
123 C3 **Mount Frere** S. Africa
52 B3 **Mount Gambier** Austr.
59 D3 **Mount Hagen** P.N.G.
53 C2 **Mount Hope** Austr.
51 C2 **Mount Isa** Austr.
50 A2 **Mount Magnet** Austr.
52 B2 **Mount Manara** Austr.
54 C1 **Mount Maunganui** N.Z.
111 B2 **Mount Olympus** Greece
137 E2 **Mount Pleasant** *IA* U.S.A.
140 C2 **Mount Pleasant** *MI* U.S.A.
139 E2 **Mount Pleasant** *TX* U.S.A.
99 A3 **Mount's Bay** U.K.
134 B2 **Mount Shasta** U.S.A.
140 B3 **Mount Vernon** *IL* U.S.A.
140 C2 **Mount Vernon** *OH* U.S.A.
134 B1 **Mount Vernon** *WA* U.S.A.
51 D2 **Moura** Austr.
115 E3 **Mourdi, Dépression du** *depr.* Chad
97 C1 **Mourne Mountains** *hills* U.K.
100 A2 **Mouscron** Belgium
115 D3 **Moussoro** Chad
58 C2 **Moutong** Indon.
115 C2 **Mouydir, Monts du** *plat.* Alg.
100 B3 **Mouzon** France
97 B1 **Moy** *r.* Ireland
117 B4 **Moyale** Eth.
123 C3 **Moyeni** Lesotho
76 B2 **Mo'ynoq** Uzbek.
77 D2 **Moyynty** Kazakh.
121 C3 **Mozambique** *country* Africa
113 I9 **Mozambique Channel** Africa
89 E2 **Mozhaysk** Russia
119 D3 **Mpanda** Tanz.
121 C2 **Mpika** Zambia
121 C1 **Mporokoso** Zambia
123 C2 **Mpumalanga** *prov.* S. Africa
62 A1 **Mrauk-U** Myanmar
88 C2 **Mshinskaya** Russia
107 D2 **M'Sila** Alg.
89 D2 **Msta** *r.* Russia
89 D2 **Mstinskiy Most** Russia
89 D3 **Mstsislaw** Belarus
123 C3 **Mthatha** S. Africa
89 E3 **Mtsensk** Russia
119 E4 **Mtwara** Tanz.
118 B3 **Muanda** Dem. Rep. Congo
63 B2 **Muang Không** Laos
62 B1 **Muang Ngoy** Laos
62 B2 **Muang Pakbeng** Laos
62 B1 **Muang Sing** Laos
62 B2 **Muang Vangviang** Laos
60 B1 **Muar** Malaysia
60 B2 **Muarabungo** Indon.
60 B2 **Muaradua** Indon.
61 C2 **Muaralaung** Indon.
60 A2 **Muarasiberut** Indon.
60 B2 **Muaratembesi** Indon.
61 C2 **Muarateweh** Indon.
119 D2 **Mubende** Uganda
115 D3 **Mubi** Nigeria
120 B2 **Muconda** Angola
155 E1 **Mucuri** Brazil
155 E1 **Mucuri** *r.* Brazil
66 A2 **Mudanjiang** China
66 A1 **Mudan Jiang** *r.* China
111 C2 **Mudanya** Turkey
101 E1 **Müden (Örtze)** Ger.
53 C2 **Mudgee** Austr.
63 A2 **Mudon** Myanmar
80 B1 **Mudurnu** Turkey
121 C2 **Mueda** Moz.
121 B2 **Mufulira** Zambia
120 B2 **Mufumbwe** Zambia
111 C3 **Muğla** Turkey
116 B2 **Muhammad Qol** Sudan
101 F2 **Mühlberg/Elbe** Ger.
101 E2 **Mühlhausen/Thüringen** Ger.
121 C2 **Muite** Moz.
65 B2 **Muju** S. Korea
90 A2 **Mukacheve** Ukr.
61 C1 **Mukah** *Sarawak* Malaysia
79 B3 **Mukalla** Yemen
63 B2 **Mukdahan** Thai.
50 A3 **Mukinbudin** Austr.
60 B2 **Mukomuko** Indon.
121 C2 **Mulanje, Mount** Malawi
101 F2 **Mulde** *r.* Ger.
144 A2 **Mulegé** Mex.
139 C2 **Muleshoe** U.S.A.
106 C2 **Mulhacén** *mt.* Spain
100 C2 **Mülheim an der Ruhr** Ger.
105 D2 **Mulhouse** France
66 B2 **Muling** China
66 B1 **Muling He** *r.* China
96 B2 **Mull** *i.* U.K.
53 C2 **Mullaley** Austr.
136 C2 **Mullen** U.S.A.
61 C1 **Muller, Pegunungan** *mts* Indon.
50 A2 **Mullewa** Austr.
97 C2 **Mullingar** Ireland
96 B3 **Mull of Galloway** *c.* U.K.
96 B3 **Mull of Kintyre** *hd* U.K.
96 A3 **Mull of Oa** *hd* U.K.
120 B2 **Mulobezi** Zambia
74 B1 **Multan** Pak.
73 B3 **Mumbai** India
120 B2 **Mumbwa** Zambia
145 D2 **Muna** Mex.
101 E2 **Münchberg** Ger.
München Ger. *see* **Munich**
140 B2 **Muncie** U.S.A.
50 B3 **Mundrabilla** Austr.
119 C2 **Mungbere** Dem. Rep. Congo
75 C2 **Munger** India
52 A1 **Mungeranie** Austr.
53 C1 **Mungindi** Austr.
102 C2 **Munich** Ger.
155 D2 **Muniz Freire** Brazil
101 E1 **Munster** *Niedersachsen* Ger.
100 C2 **Münster** *Nordrhein-Westfalen* Ger.
97 B2 **Munster** *reg.* Ireland
100 C2 **Münsterland** *reg.* Ger.
62 B1 **Mường Nhe** Vietnam
92 H2 **Muonio** Fin.
92 H2 **Muonioälven** *r.* Fin./Sweden
Muqdisho Somalia *see* **Mogadishu**
103 D2 **Mur** *r.* Austria
119 C3 **Muramvya** Burundi
119 D3 **Murang'a** Kenya
81 B2 **Murat** *r.* Turkey
111 C2 **Muratlı** Turkey
50 A2 **Murchison** *watercourse* Austr.
107 C2 **Murcia** Spain
111 C2 **Mürefte** Turkey
110 B1 **Mureşul** *r.* Romania
104 C3 **Muret** France
142 C1 **Murfreesboro** U.S.A.
77 D3 **Murghob** Tajik.
155 D2 **Muriaé** Brazil
120 B1 **Muriege** Angola
101 F1 **Müritz** *l.* Ger.
86 C2 **Murmansk** Russia
87 D3 **Murom** Russia
66 D2 **Muroran** Japan
106 B1 **Muros** Spain
67 B4 **Muroto** Japan
67 B4 **Muroto-zaki** *pt* Japan
143 D1 **Murphy** U.S.A.
53 C1 **Murra Murra** Austr.
52 A3 **Murray** *r.* Austr.

128 B2 **Murray** *r.* Can.
140 B3 **Murray** U.S.A.
143 D2 **Murray, Lake** U.S.A.
52 A3 **Murray Bridge** Austr.
122 B3 **Murraysburg** S. Africa
52 B3 **Murrayville** Austr.
52 B2 **Murrumbidgee** *r.* Austr.
121 C2 **Murrupula** Moz.
53 D2 **Murrurundi** Austr.
109 C1 **Murska Sobota** Slovenia
54 C1 **Murupara** N.Z.
49 I4 **Mururoa** *atoll* Fr. Polynesia
Murwara India *see* **Katni**
53 D1 **Murwillumbah** Austr.
115 D2 **Murzūq** Libya
115 D2 **Murzuq, Idhān** *des.* Libya
81 C2 **Muş** Turkey
110 B2 **Musala** *mt.* Bulg.
65 B1 **Musan** N. Korea
78 B3 **Musaymir** Yemen
79 C2 **Muscat** Oman
137 E2 **Muscatine** U.S.A.
50 C2 **Musgrave Ranges** *mts* Austr.
118 B3 **Mushie** Dem. Rep. Congo
60 B2 **Musi** *r.* Indon.
123 D1 **Musina** S. Africa
140 B2 **Muskegon** U.S.A.
139 D1 **Muskogee** U.S.A.
128 B2 **Muskwa** *r.* Can.
74 A1 **Muslimbagh** Pak.
78 A3 **Musmar** Sudan
119 D3 **Musoma** Tanz.
96 C3 **Musselburgh** U.K.
88 B2 **Mustjala** Estonia
53 D2 **Muswellbrook** Austr.
116 A2 **Mūţ** Egypt
121 C2 **Mutare** Zimbabwe
66 D2 **Mutsu** Japan
121 C2 **Mutuali** Moz.
92 I2 **Muurola** Fin.
70 A2 **Mu Us Shadi** *des.* China
120 A1 **Muxaluando** Angola
86 C2 **Muyezerskiy** Russia
119 D3 **Muyinga** Burundi
74 B1 **Muzaffargarh** Pak.
75 C2 **Muzaffarpur** India
144 B2 **Múzquiz** Mex.
75 C1 **Muz Shan** *mt.* China
119 C3 **Mwanza** Dem. Rep. Congo
119 D3 **Mwanza** Tanz.
118 C3 **Mweka** Dem. Rep. Congo
121 B2 **Mwenda** Zambia
118 C3 **Mwene-Ditu** Dem. Rep. Congo
121 C3 **Mwenezi** Zimbabwe
119 C3 **Mweru, Lake** Dem. Rep. Congo/Zambia
118 C3 **Mwimba** Dem. Rep. Congo
120 B2 **Mwinilunga** Zambia
88 C3 **Myadzyel** Belarus
62 A2 **Myanaung** Myanmar
62 A1 **Myanmar** *country* Asia
63 A2 **Myaungmya** Myanmar
63 A2 **Myeik** Myanmar
Myeik Kyunzu *is* Myanmar *see* **Mergui Archipelago**
62 A1 **Myingyan** Myanmar
62 A1 **Myitkyina** Myanmar
91 C2 **Mykolayiv** Ukr.
111 C3 **Mykonos** Greece
111 C3 **Mykonos** *i.* Greece
86 E2 **Myla** Russia
75 D2 **Mymensingh** Bangl.
67 C3 **Myōkō** Japan
65 B1 **Myŏnggan** N. Korea
88 C2 **Myory** Belarus
92 □B3 **Mýrdalsjökull** Iceland
91 C2 **Myrhorod** Ukr.
90 C2 **Myronivka** Ukr.
143 E2 **Myrtle Beach** U.S.A.
53 C3 **Myrtleford** Austr.
134 B2 **Myrtle Point** U.S.A.
89 E2 **Myshkin** Russia
103 C1 **Myślibórz** Pol.
73 B3 **Mysore** India
83 N2 **Mys Shmidta** Russia
Mysuru India *see* **Mysore**
63 B2 **My Tho** Vietnam
111 C3 **Mytilini** Greece
89 E3 **Mytishchi** Russia
123 C3 **Mzamomhle** S. Africa
121 C2 **Mzimba** Malawi
121 C2 **Mzuzu** Malawi

N

97 C2 **Naas** Ireland
122 A2 **Nababeep** S. Africa
87 E3 **Naberezhnyye Chelny** Russia
59 D3 **Nabire** Indon.
80 B2 **Nāblus** West Bank
121 D2 **Nacala** Moz.
63 A2 **Nachuge** India
139 E2 **Nacogdoches** U.S.A.
144 B1 **Nacozari de García** Mex.
74 B2 **Nadiad** India
90 A2 **Nadvirna** Ukr.
86 C2 **Nadvoitsy** Russia
86 G2 **Nadym** Russia
93 F4 **Næstved** Denmark
111 B3 **Nafpaktos** Greece
111 B3 **Nafplio** Greece
115 D1 **Nafūsah, Jabal** *hills* Libya
78 B2 **Nafy** Saudi Arabia
64 B1 **Naga** Phil.
130 B1 **Nagagami** *r.* Can.
67 C3 **Nagano** Japan
67 C3 **Nagaoka** Japan
75 D2 **Nagaon** India
74 B1 **Nagar** India
74 B2 **Nagar Parkar** Pak.
67 A4 **Nagasaki** Japan
67 B4 **Nagato** Japan
74 B2 **Nagaur** India
73 B4 **Nagercoil** India
74 A2 **Nagha Kalat** Pak.
75 B2 **Nagina** India
81 C1 **Nagorno-Karabakh** *disp. terr.* Azer.
67 C3 **Nagoya** Japan
75 B2 **Nagpur** India
68 C2 **Nagqu** China
103 D2 **Nagyatád** Hungary
103 D2 **Nagykanizsa** Hungary
128 B1 **Nahanni Butte** Can.
76 A3 **Nahāvand** Iran
101 E1 **Nahrendorf** Ger.
153 A5 **Nahuel Huapí, Lago** *l.* Arg.
131 D1 **Nain** Can.
81 D2 **Nā'īn** Iran
96 C2 **Nairn** U.K.
119 D3 **Nairobi** Kenya
119 D3 **Naivasha** Kenya
81 D2 **Najafābād** Iran
78 B2 **Najd** *reg.* Saudi Arabia
106 C1 **Nájera** Spain
65 C1 **Najin** N. Korea
78 B3 **Najrān** Saudi Arabia
Nakambé *r.* Burkina Faso/Ghana *see* **White Volta**
67 C3 **Nakatsugawa** Japan
78 A3 **Nakfa** Eritrea
66 B2 **Nakhodka** Russia
63 B2 **Nakhon Pathom** Thai.
63 B2 **Nakhon Ratchasima** Thai.
63 B2 **Nakhon Sawan** Thai.
63 A3 **Nakhon Si Thammarat** Thai.
130 B1 **Nakina** Can.
121 C1 **Nakonde** Zambia
93 F4 **Nakskov** Denmark
119 D3 **Nakuru** Kenya
128 C2 **Nakusp** Can.
75 D2 **Nalbari** India
87 D4 **Nal'chik** Russia
115 D1 **Nālūt** Libya
123 C2 **Namahadi** S. Africa
77 D2 **Namangan** Uzbek.
122 A2 **Namaqualand** *reg.* S. Africa
51 E2 **Nambour** Austr.
53 D2 **Nambucca Heads** Austr.
75 D1 **Nam Co** *salt l.* China
62 B1 **Nam Định** Vietnam
120 A3 **Namib Desert** Namibia
120 A2 **Namibe** Angola
120 A3 **Namibia** *country* Africa
72 D2 **Namjagbarwa Feng** *mt.* China
59 C3 **Namlea** Indon.
53 C2 **Namoi** *r.* Austr.
134 C2 **Nampa** U.S.A.
114 B3 **Nampala** Mali
65 B2 **Namp'o** N. Korea
121 C2 **Nampula** Moz.
62 A1 **Namrup** India
62 A1 **Namsang** Myanmar
92 F3 **Namsos** Norway
63 A2 **Nam Tok** Thai.
83 J2 **Namtsy** Russia
62 A1 **Namtu** Myanmar
100 B2 **Namur** Belgium
120 B2 **Namwala** Zambia
65 B2 **Namwon** S. Korea
62 A1 **Namya Ra** Myanmar
62 B2 **Nan** Thai.
128 B3 **Nanaimo** Can.
71 B3 **Nan'an** China
122 A1 **Nananib Plateau** Namibia
67 C3 **Nanao** Japan
71 B3 **Nanchang** *Jiangxi* China
71 B3 **Nanchang** *Jiangxi* China
70 A2 **Nanchong** China
63 A3 **Nancowry** *i.* India
105 D2 **Nancy** France
75 C1 **Nanda Devi** *mt.* India
71 A3 **Nandan** China
73 B3 **Nanded** India
74 B2 **Nandurbar** India
73 B3 **Nandyal** India
71 B3 **Nanfeng** China
118 B2 **Nanga Eboko** Cameroon
61 C2 **Nangahpinoh** Indon.
74 B1 **Nanga Parbat** *mt.* Pak.
61 C2 **Nangatayap** Indon.
70 B2 **Nangong** China
119 D3 **Nangulangwa** Tanz.
70 C2 **Nanhui** China
70 B2 **Nanjing** China
Nanking China *see* **Nanjing**
120 A2 **Nankova** Angola
71 B3 **Nan Ling** *mts* China
71 A3 **Nanning** China
127 H2 **Nanortalik** Greenland
71 A3 **Nanpan Jiang** *r.* China
75 C2 **Nanpara** India
71 B3 **Nanping** China
Nansei-shotō *is* Japan *see* **Ryukyu Islands**
104 B2 **Nantes** France
70 C2 **Nantong** China
141 F2 **Nantucket Island** U.S.A.
155 D1 **Nanuque** Brazil
64 B2 **Nanusa, Kepulauan** *is* Indon.

71	B3	Nanxiong China
70	B2	Nanyang China
70	B2	Nanzhang China
107	D2	Nao, Cabo de la c. Spain
131	C1	Naococane, Lac l. Can.
135	B3	Napa U.S.A.
126	D2	Napaktulik Lake Can.
127	H2	Napasoq Greenland
54	C1	Napier N.Z.
108	B2	Naples Italy
143	D3	Naples U.S.A.
150	A2	Napo r. Ecuador/Peru
		Napoli Italy see Naples
114	B3	Nara Mali
93	I4	Narach Belarus
52	B3	Naracoorte Austr.
145	C2	Naranjos Mex.
63	B3	Narathiwat Thai.
105	C3	Narbonne France
63	A2	Narcondam Island India
127	G1	Nares Strait Can./Greenland
122	A1	Narib Namibia
87	D4	Narimanov Russia
67	D3	Narita Japan
74	B2	Narmada r. India
74	B2	Narnaul India
108	B2	Narni Italy
90	B1	Narodychi Ukr.
89	E2	Naro-Fominsk Russia
53	D3	Narooma Austr.
88	C3	Narowlya Belarus
53	C2	Narrabri Austr.
53	C2	Narrandera Austr.
53	C2	Narromine Austr.
88	C2	Narva Estonia
88	C2	Narva Bay Estonia/Russia
92	G2	Narvik Norway
86	F2	Narvskoye Vodokhranilishche resr Estonia/Russia
86	E2	Nar'yan-Mar Russia
77	D2	Naryn Kyrg.
74	B2	Nashik India
141	E2	Nashua U.S.A.
142	C1	Nashville U.S.A.
49	I5	Nasinu Fiji
117	B4	Nasir South Sudan
128	B2	Nass r. Can.
146	C2	Nassau Bahamas
116	B2	Nasser, Lake resr Egypt
93	F4	Nässjö Sweden
130	C1	Nastapoca r. Can.
130	C1	Nastapoka Islands Can.
67	D3	Nasushiobara Japan
120	B3	Nata Botswana
151	E2	Natal Brazil
131	D1	Natashquan Can.
131	D1	Natashquan r. Can.
142	B2	Natchez U.S.A.
142	B2	Natchitoches U.S.A.
53	C3	Nathalia Austr.
107	D1	Nati, Punta pt Spain
114	C3	Natitingou Benin
151	D3	Natividade Brazil
67	D3	Natori Japan
131	D1	Natuashish Can.
61	B1	Natuna, Kepulauan is Indon.
61	B1	Natuna Besar i. Indon.
120	A3	Nauchas Namibia
101	F1	Nauen Ger.
88	B2	Naujoji Akmen Lith.
74	A2	Naukot Pak.
101	E2	Naumburg (Saale) Ger.
48	F3	Nauru country S. Pacific Ocean
145	C2	Nautla Mex.
88	C3	Navahrudak Belarus
106	B2	Navalmoral de la Mata Spain
106	B2	Navalvillar de Pela Spain
97	C2	Navan Ireland
88	C2	Navapolatsk Belarus
83	M2	Navarin, Mys c. Russia
153	B6	Navarino, Isla i. Chile
96	B1	Naver r. U.K.
73	B3	Navi Mumbai India
89	D3	Navlya Russia
110	C2	Năvodari Romania
77	C2	Navoiy Uzbek.
144	B2	Navojoa Mex.
144	B2	Navolato Mex.
74	A2	Nawabshah Pak.
62	A1	Nawnghkio Myanmar
62	A1	Nawngleng Myanmar
81	C2	Naxçıvan Azer.
111	C3	Naxos i. Greece
144	B2	Nayar Mex.
66	D2	Nayoro Japan
144	B2	Nazas Mex.
144	B2	Nazas r. Mex.
150	A3	Nazca Peru
80	B2	Nazerat Israel
111	C3	Nazilli Turkey
117	B4	Nazrēt Eth.
79	C2	Nazwá Oman
121	B1	Nchelenge Zambia
122	B1	Ncojane Botswana
120	A1	N'dalatando Angola
118	C2	Ndélé C.A.R.
118	B3	Ndendé Gabon
115	D3	Ndjamena Chad
121	B2	Ndola Zambia
97	C1	Neagh, Lough l. U.K.
50	C2	Neale, Lake imp. l. Austr.
111	B2	Nea Roda Greece
99	B3	Neath U.K.
53	C1	Nebine Creek r. Austr.
150	B1	Neblina, Pico da mt. Brazil
89	D2	Nebolchi Russia
136	C2	Nebraska state U.S.A.
137	D2	Nebraska City U.S.A.
108	B3	Nebrodi, Monti mts Sicily Italy
153	C4	Necochea Arg.
131	C1	Nedlouc, Lac l. Can.
135	D4	Needles U.S.A.
74	B2	Neemuch India
129	E2	Neepawa Can.
87	E3	Neftekamsk Russia
82	F2	Neftyugansk Russia
120	A1	Negage Angola
117	B4	Negēlē Eth.
150	A2	Negra, Punta pt Peru
63	A2	Negrais, Cape Myanmar
153	B5	Negro r. Arg.
150	C2	Negro r. S. America
152	C4	Negro r. Uru.
106	B2	Negro, Cabo c. Morocco
64	B2	Negros i. Phil.
69	E1	Nehe China
70	A3	Neijiang China
129	D2	Neilburg Can.
150	A1	Neiva Col.
129	E2	Nejanilini Lake Can.
80	B2	Nek'emtē Eth.
89	F2	Nekrasovskoye Russia
89	D2	Nelidovo Russia
73	B3	Nellore India
128	C3	Nelson Can.
129	E2	Nelson r. Can.
54	B2	Nelson N.Z.
53	C3	Nelson, Cape Austr.
53	D2	Nelson Bay Austr.
129	E2	Nelson House Can.
134	E1	Nelson Reservoir U.S.A.
114	B3	Néma Maur.
88	B2	Neman Russia
104	C2	Nemours France
66	D2	Nemuro Japan
90	B2	Nemyriv Ukr.
97	C2	Nenagh Ireland
99	D2	Nene r. U.K.
69	E1	Nenjiang China
137	E3	Neosho U.S.A.
75	C2	Nepal country Asia
75	C2	Nepalganj Nepal
135	D3	Nephi U.S.A.
97	B1	Nephin h. Ireland
97	B1	Nephin Beg Range hills Ireland
131	D2	Nepisiguit r. Can.
119	C2	Nepoko r. Dem. Rep. Congo
104	C3	Nérac France
53	D1	Nerang Austr.
69	D1	Nerchinsk Russia
89	F2	Nerekhta Russia
109	C2	Neretva r. Bos. & Herz./Croatia
120	B2	Neriquinha Angola
88	B3	Neris r. Lith.
89	E2	Nerl' r. Russia
86	F2	Nerokhi Russia
154	C1	Nerópolis Brazil
83	J3	Neryungri Russia
92	□C2	Neskaupstaður Iceland
96	B2	Ness, Loch l. U.K.
136	D3	Ness City U.S.A.
111	B2	Nestos r. Greece
100	B1	Netherlands country Europe
127	G2	Nettilling Lake Can.
101	F1	Neubrandenburg Ger.
105	D2	Neuchâtel Switz.
100	C2	Neuerburg Ger.
100	B3	Neufchâteau Belgium
105	D2	Neufchâteau France
104	C2	Neufchâtel-en-Bray France
101	D2	Neuhof Ger.
102	B1	Neumünster Ger.
102	B2	Neunkirchen Ger.
153	B4	Neuquén Arg.
153	B4	Neuquén r. Arg.
101	F1	Neuruppin Ger.
100	C2	Neuss Ger.
101	D1	Neustadt am Rübenberge Ger.
101	E3	Neustadt an der Aisch Ger.
101	F1	Neustrelitz Ger.
100	C2	Neuwied Ger.
137	E3	Nevada U.S.A.
135	C3	Nevada state U.S.A.
106	C2	Nevada, Sierra mts Spain
135	B2	Nevada, Sierra mts U.S.A.
88	C2	Nevel' Russia
105	C2	Nevers France
53	C2	Nevertire Austr.
109	C2	Nevesinje Bos. & Herz.
87	D4	Nevinnomyssk Russia
128	B2	New Aiyansh Can.
140	B3	New Albany U.S.A.
151	C1	New Amsterdam Guyana
141	E2	Newark NJ U.S.A.
140	C2	Newark OH U.S.A.
98	C2	Newark-on-Trent U.K.
141	E2	New Bedford U.S.A.
143	E1	New Bern U.S.A.
143	D2	Newberry U.S.A.
139	E2	New Boston U.S.A.
139	D3	New Braunfels U.S.A.
97	C2	Newbridge Ireland
48	E3	New Britain i. P.N.G.
131	D2	New Brunswick prov. Can.
99	C3	Newbury U.K.
64	A1	New Busuanga Phil.
48	E4	New Caledonia terr. S. Pacific Ocean
53	D2	Newcastle Austr.
123	C2	Newcastle S. Africa

97 D1 **Newcastle** U.K.
140 C2 **New Castle** U.S.A.
136 C2 **Newcastle** U.S.A.
98 B2 **Newcastle-under-Lyme** U.K.
98 C1 **Newcastle upon Tyne** U.K.
97 B2 **Newcastle West** Ireland
74 B2 **New Delhi** India
128 C3 **New Denver** Can.
53 D2 **New England Range** *mts* Austr.
131 E2 **Newfoundland** *i.* Can.
131 E1 **Newfoundland and Labrador** *prov.* Can.
131 D2 **New Glasgow** Can.
59 D3 **New Guinea** *i.* Indon./P.N.G.
141 E2 **New Hampshire** *state* U.S.A.
141 E2 **New Haven** U.S.A.
128 B2 **New Hazelton** Can.
New Hebrides *country* S. Pacific Ocean *see* **Vanuatu**
142 B2 **New Iberia** U.S.A.
48 E3 **New Ireland** *i.* P.N.G.
141 E3 **New Jersey** *state* U.S.A.
130 C2 **New Liskeard** Can.
50 A2 **Newman** Austr.
138 B2 **New Mexico** *state* U.S.A.
142 B3 **New Orleans** U.S.A.
140 C2 **New Philadelphia** U.S.A.
54 B1 **New Plymouth** N.Z.
99 C3 **Newport** *England* U.K.
99 B3 **Newport** *Wales* U.K.
142 B1 **Newport** *AR* U.S.A.
134 B2 **Newport** *OR* U.S.A.
141 E2 **Newport** *RI* U.S.A.
141 E2 **Newport** *VT* U.S.A.
134 C1 **Newport** *WA* U.S.A.
141 D3 **Newport News** U.S.A.
143 E3 **New Providence** *i.* Bahamas
99 A3 **Newquay** U.K.
142 B2 **New Roads** U.S.A.
97 C2 **New Ross** Ireland
97 C1 **Newry** U.K.
83 K1 **New Siberia Islands** Russia
52 B2 **New South Wales** *state* Austr.
137 E2 **Newton** *IA* U.S.A.
137 D3 **Newton** *KS* U.S.A.
99 B3 **Newton Abbot** U.K.
96 B3 **Newton Stewart** U.K.
97 B2 **Newtown** Ireland
99 B2 **Newtown** U.K.
136 C1 **New Town** U.S.A.
97 D1 **Newtownabbey** U.K.
97 D1 **Newtownards** U.K.
96 C3 **Newtown St Boswells** U.K.
97 C1 **Newtownstewart** U.K.
137 E2 **New Ulm** U.S.A.
141 E2 **New York** U.S.A.
141 D2 **New York** *state* U.S.A.
54 B2 **New Zealand** *country* Oceania
79 C2 **Neyrīz** Iran
76 B3 **Neyshābūr** Iran
145 C3 **Nezahualcóyotl, Presa** *resr* Mex.
61 B1 **Ngabang** Indon.
75 C2 **Ngamring** China
75 C1 **Ngangla Ringco** *salt l.* China
77 E3 **Nganglong Kangri** *mt.* China
75 C1 **Nganglong Kangri** *mts* China
75 C1 **Ngangzê Co** *salt l.* China
62 A2 **Ngao** Thai.
118 B2 **Ngaoundéré** Cameroon
54 C1 **Ngaruawahia** N.Z.
62 A2 **Ngathainggyaung** Myanmar
121 D2 **Ngazidja** *i.* Comoros
118 B3 **Ngo** Congo
115 D4 **Ngol Bembo** Nigeria
68 C2 **Ngoring Hu** *l.* China
115 D3 **Ngourti** Niger
115 D3 **Nguigmi** Niger
59 D2 **Ngulu** *atoll* Micronesia
115 D3 **Nguru** Nigeria
123 D2 **Ngwelezana** S. Africa
121 C2 **Nhamalabué** Moz.
63 B2 **Nha Trang** Vietnam
52 B3 **Nhill** Austr.
123 D2 **Nhlangano** Swaziland
51 C1 **Nhulunbuy** Austr.
141 D2 **Niagara Falls** Can.
114 C3 **Niamey** Niger
119 C2 **Niangara** Dem. Rep. Congo
114 B3 **Niangay, Lac** *l.* Mali
60 A1 **Nias** *i.* Indon.
146 B3 **Nicaragua** *country* Central America
146 B3 **Nicaragua, Lake** Nic.
105 D3 **Nice** France
73 D4 **Nicobar Islands** India
80 B2 **Nicosia** Cyprus
146 B4 **Nicoya, Golfo de** *b.* Costa Rica
88 B2 **Nida** Lith.
103 E1 **Nidzica** Pol.
102 B1 **Niebüll** Ger.
101 D2 **Niederaula** Ger.
118 B2 **Niefang** Equat. Guinea
101 F1 **Niemegk** Ger.
101 D1 **Nienburg (Weser)** Ger.
100 B1 **Nieuwe Niedorp** Neth.
151 C1 **Nieuw Nickerie** Suriname
122 A3 **Nieuwoudtville** S. Africa
100 A2 **Nieuwpoort** Belgium
80 B2 **Niğde** Turkey
115 C3 **Niger** *country* Africa
115 C4 **Niger** *r.* Africa
115 C4 **Niger, Mouths of the** Nigeria
115 C4 **Nigeria** *country* Africa
130 B2 **Nighthawk Lake** Can.
111 B2 **Nigrita** Greece
67 C3 **Niigata** Japan
67 B4 **Niihama** Japan
67 C4 **Nii-jima** *i.* Japan
67 C3 **Niitsu** Japan
100 B2 **Nijmegen** Neth.
100 C1 **Nijverdal** Neth.
92 J2 **Nikel'** Russia
83 M3 **Nikol'skoye** Russia
91 C2 **Nikopol'** Ukr.
80 B1 **Niksar** Turkey
79 D2 **Nīkshahr** Iran
109 C2 **Nikšić** Montenegro
116 B1 **Nile** *r.* Africa
140 B2 **Niles** U.S.A.
74 A1 **Nīlī** Afgh.
105 C3 **Nîmes** France
53 C3 **Nimmitabel** Austr.
117 B4 **Nimule** Sudan
53 C1 **Nindigully** Austr.
73 B4 **Nine Degree Channel** India
53 C3 **Ninety Mile Beach** Austr.
54 B1 **Ninety Mile Beach** N.Z.
70 C3 **Ningbo** China
71 B3 **Ningde** China
71 B3 **Ningdu** China
70 B2 **Ningguo** China
71 C3 **Ninghai** China
Ningjiang China *see* **Songyuan**
68 C2 **Ningjing Shan** *mts* China
70 A2 **Ningxia Huizu Zizhiqu** *aut. reg.* China
70 B2 **Ningyang** China
62 B1 **Ninh Binh** Vietnam
63 B2 **Ninh Hoa** Vietnam
66 D2 **Ninohe** Japan
137 D2 **Niobrara** *r.* U.S.A.
114 B3 **Niono** Mali
114 B3 **Nioro** Mali
104 B2 **Niort** France
129 D2 **Nipawin** Can.
130 B2 **Nipigon** Can.
130 B2 **Nipigon, Lake** Can.
131 D1 **Nipishish Lake** Can.
130 C2 **Nipissing, Lake** Can.
135 C3 **Nipton** U.S.A.
151 D3 **Niquelândia** Brazil
73 B3 **Nirmal** India
109 D2 **Niš** Serbia
109 D2 **Nišava** *r.* Serbia
108 B3 **Niscemi** *Sicily* Italy
67 B4 **Nishino-omote** Japan
155 D2 **Niterói** Brazil
96 C3 **Nith** *r.* U.K.
103 D2 **Nitra** Slovakia
49 G4 **Niue** *terr.* S. Pacific Ocean
92 H3 **Nivala** Fin.
100 B2 **Nivelles** Belgium
73 B3 **Nizamabad** India
87 E3 **Nizhnekamsk** Russia
83 H3 **Nizhneudinsk** Russia
82 G2 **Nizhnevartovsk** Russia
89 F3 **Nizhniy Kislyay** Russia
87 D3 **Nizhniy Lomov** Russia
87 D3 **Nizhniy Novgorod** Russia
86 E2 **Nizhniy Odes** Russia
86 E3 **Nizhniy Tagil** Russia
83 G2 **Nizhnyaya Tunguska** *r.* Russia
91 C1 **Nizhyn** Ukr.
119 D3 **Njinjo** Tanz.
119 D3 **Njombe** Tanz.
121 C2 **Nkhotakota** Malawi
118 A2 **Nkongsamba** Cameroon
123 C3 **Nkululeko** S. Africa
123 C3 **Nkwenkwezi** S. Africa
67 B4 **Nobeoka** Japan
52 B1 **Noccundra** Austr.
144 A1 **Nogales** Mex.
138 A2 **Nogales** U.S.A.
104 C2 **Nogent-le-Rotrou** France
89 E2 **Noginsk** Russia
74 B2 **Nohar** India
100 C3 **Nohfelden** Ger.
104 B2 **Noirmoutier, Île de** *i.* France
104 B2 **Noirmoutier-en-l'Île** France
67 C4 **Nojima-zaki** *c.* Japan
74 B2 **Nokha** India
93 H3 **Nokia** Fin.
74 A2 **Nok Kundi** Pak.
118 B2 **Nola** C.A.R.
86 D3 **Nolinsk** Russia
123 C3 **Nomonde** S. Africa
123 D2 **Nondweni** S. Africa
62 B2 **Nong Khai** Thai.
52 A2 **Nonning** Austr.
144 B2 **Nonoava** Mex.
65 B2 **Nonsan** S. Korea
63 B2 **Nonthaburi** Thai.
122 B3 **Nonzwakazi** S. Africa
77 C3 **Norak** Tajik.
141 D1 **Noranda** Can.
82 C1 **Nordaustlandet** *i.* Svalbard
128 C2 **Nordegg** Can.
100 C1 **Norden** Ger.
83 H1 **Nordenshel'da, Arkhipelag** *is* Russia
100 C1 **Norderney** Ger.
100 C1 **Norderney** *i.* Ger.
101 E1 **Norderstedt** Ger.
93 E3 **Nordfjordeid** Norway
101 E2 **Nordhausen** Ger.
101 D1 **Nordholz** Ger.
100 C1 **Nordhorn** Ger.
Nordkapp *c.* Norway *see* **North Cape**
92 F3 **Nordli** Norway

102 C2 **Nördlingen** Ger.
92 G3 **Nordmaling** Sweden
94 B1 **Norðoyar** *is* Faroe Is
97 C2 **Nore** *r.* Ireland
137 D2 **Norfolk** *NE* U.S.A.
141 D3 **Norfolk** *VA* U.S.A.
48 F4 **Norfolk Island** *terr.*
S. Pacific Ocean
93 E3 **Norheimsund** Norway
82 G2 **Noril'sk** Russia
75 C2 **Norkyung** China
139 D1 **Norman** U.S.A.
Normandes, Îles *is* English
Chan. *see* **Channel Islands**
51 D1 **Normanton** Austr.
93 G4 **Norrköping** Sweden
93 G4 **Norrtälje** Sweden
50 B3 **Norseman** Austr.
92 G3 **Norsjö** Sweden
98 C1 **Northallerton** U.K.
50 A2 **Northampton** Austr.
99 C2 **Northampton** U.K.
73 D3 **North Andaman** *i.* India
129 D2 **North Battleford** Can.
130 C2 **North Bay** Can.
130 C1 **North Belcher Islands** Can.
98 C1 **North Berwick** U.K.
92 I1 **North Cape** Norway
54 B1 **North Cape** N.Z.
130 A1 **North Caribou Lake** Can.
143 E1 **North Carolina** *state* U.S.A.
130 B2 **North Channel** *lake channel*
Can.
96 A3 **North Channel** U.K.
128 B3 **North Cowichan** Can.
136 C1 **North Dakota** *state* U.S.A.
99 C3 **North Downs** *hills* U.K.
143 E3 **Northeast Providence**
Channel Bahamas
101 D2 **Northeim** Ger.
122 A2 **Northern Cape** *prov.* S. Africa
129 E2 **Northern Indian Lake** Can.
97 C1 **Northern Ireland** *prov.* U.K.
48 D1 **Northern Mariana Islands**
terr. N. Pacific Ocean
50 C1 **Northern Territory** *admin. div.*
Austr.
96 C2 **North Esk** *r.* U.K.
137 E2 **Northfield** U.S.A.
99 D3 **North Foreland** *c.* U.K.
54 B1 **North Island** N.Z.
129 E2 **North Knife Lake** Can.
65 B1 **North Korea** *country* Asia
62 A1 **North Lakhimpur** India
128 B1 **North Nahanni** *r.* Can.
136 C2 **North Platte** U.S.A.
136 C2 **North Platte** *r.* U.S.A.
96 C1 **North Ronaldsay** *i.* U.K.
94 D2 **North Sea** Europe
130 A1 **North Spirit Lake** Can.
51 D3 **North Stradbroke Island**
Austr.
54 B1 **North Taranaki Bight** *b.* N.Z.
130 C1 **North Twin Island** Can.
98 B1 **North Tyne** *r.* U.K.
96 A2 **North Uist** *i.* U.K.
131 D2 **Northumberland Strait** Can.
122 C2 **North West** *prov.* S. Africa
50 A2 **North West Cape** Austr.
143 E3 **Northwest Providence**
Channel Bahamas
131 E1 **North West River** Can.
128 B1 **Northwest Territories**
admin. div. Can.
98 C1 **North York Moors** *moorland*
U.K.
140 C3 **Norton** U.S.A.
121 C2 **Norton** Zimbabwe

140 C2 **Norwalk** U.S.A.
93 —— **Norway** *country* Europe
129 E2 **Norway House** Can.
160 A3 **Norwegian Sea** N. Atlantic
Ocean
99 D2 **Norwich** U.K.
141 E2 **Norwich** *CT* U.S.A.
141 D2 **Norwich** *NY* U.S.A.
66 D2 **Noshiro** Japan
91 C1 **Nosivka** Ukr.
122 B2 **Nosop** *watercourse* Africa
86 E2 **Nosovaya** Russia
79 C2 **Noşratābād** Iran
Nossob *watercourse* Africa *see*
Nosop
103 D1 **Noteć** *r.* Pol.
93 E4 **Notodden** Norway
67 C3 **Noto-hantō** *pen.* Japan
131 D2 **Notre-Dame, Monts** *mts*
Can.
131 E2 **Notre Dame Bay** Can.
130 C2 **Nottaway** *r.* Can.
99 C2 **Nottingham** U.K.
114 A2 **Nouâdhibou** Maur.
114 A3 **Nouakchott** Maur.
114 A3 **Nouâmghâr** Maur.
48 F4 **Nouméa** New Caledonia
114 B3 **Nouna** Burkina Faso
154 B2 **Nova Esperança** Brazil
155 C2 **Nova Friburgo** Brazil
109 C1 **Nova Gradiška** Croatia
154 C2 **Nova Granada** Brazil
155 C2 **Nova Iguaçu** Brazil
91 C2 **Nova Kakhovka** Ukr.
155 D1 **Nova Lima** Brazil
154 B2 **Nova Londrina** Brazil
91 C2 **Nova Odesa** Ukr.
131 D2 **Nova Scotia** *prov.* Can.
155 D1 **Nova Venécia** Brazil
83 K1 **Novaya Sibir', Ostrov** *i.*
Russia
86 E1 **Novaya Zemlya** *is* Russia
103 D2 **Nové Zámky** Slovakia
91 C1 **Novhorod-Sivers'kyy** Ukr.
110 B2 **Novi Iskar** Bulg.
108 A2 **Novi Ligure** Italy
109 C2 **Novi Pazar** Serbia
109 C1 **Novi Sad** Serbia
87 D3 **Novoanninskiy** Russia
150 B3 **Novo Aripuanã** Brazil
91 D2 **Novoazovs'k** Ukr.
91 E2 **Novocherkassk** Russia
86 D2 **Novodvinsk** Russia
152 C3 **Novo Hamburgo** Brazil
154 C2 **Novo Horizonte** Brazil
90 B1 **Novohrad-Volyns'kyy** Ukr.
103 D2 **Novo mesto** Slovenia
89 E3 **Novomikhaylovskiy** Russia
89 E3 **Novomoskovsk** Russia
91 D2 **Novomoskovs'k** Ukr.
91 C2 **Novomyrhorod** Ukr.
91 C2 **Novooleksiyivka** Ukr.
150 B1 **Novo Paraíso** Brazil
91 D2 **Novopskov** Ukr.
91 D3 **Novorossiysk** Russia
88 C2 **Novorzhev** Russia
87 E3 **Novosergiyevka** Russia
91 D2 **Novoshakhtinsk** Russia
82 G3 **Novosibirsk** Russia
Novosibirskiye Ostrova *is*
Russia *see* **New Siberia Islands**
89 E3 **Novosil'** Russia
91 C1 **Novosokol'niki** Russia
91 C2 **Novotroyits'ke** Ukr.
91 C2 **Novoukrayinka** Ukr.
90 A1 **Novovolyns'k** Ukr.
89 D3 **Novozybkov** Russia
103 D2 **Nový Jičín** Czech Rep.

86 E2 **Novyy Bor** Russia
91 D1 **Novyy Oskol** Russia
86 G2 **Novyy Port** Russia
82 G2 **Novyy Urengoy** Russia
69 E1 **Novyy Urgal** Russia
103 D1 **Nowogard** Pol.
53 C2 **Nowra** Austr.
81 D2 **Nowshahr** Iran
74 B1 **Nowshera** Pak.
103 E2 **Nowy Sącz** Pol.
103 E2 **Nowy Targ** Pol.
105 C2 **Noyabr'sk** Russia
105 C2 **Noyon** France
92 G2 **Noyon** Mongolia
121 C2 **Nsanje** Malawi
118 B3 **Ntandembele**
Dem. Rep. Congo
111 B3 **Ntoro, Kavo** *pt* Greece
119 D3 **Ntungamo** Uganda
79 C2 **Nu'aym** *reg.* Oman
116 B2 **Nubian Desert** Sudan
129 E1 **Nueltin Lake** Can.
153 A5 **Nueva Lubecka** Arg.
145 B2 **Nueva Rosita** Mex.
144 B1 **Nuevo Casas Grandes** Mex.
144 B2 **Nuevo Ideal** Mex.
145 C2 **Nuevo Laredo** Mex.
117 C4 **Nugaal** *watercourse* Somalia
117 C4 **Nugaaleed, Dooxo** *val.*
Somalia
105 C2 **Nuits-St-Georges** France
Nu Jiang *r.* China/Myanmar
see **Salween**
49 G4 **Nuku'alofa** Tonga
49 I3 **Nuku Hiva** *i.* Fr. Polynesia
76 B2 **Nukus** Uzbek.
50 B2 **Nullagine** Austr.
50 B3 **Nullarbor Plain** Austr.
115 D4 **Numan** Nigeria
67 C3 **Numazu** Japan
93 E3 **Numedal** *val.* Norway
59 C3 **Numfoor** *i.* Indon.
53 C3 **Numurkah** Austr.
Nunap Isua *c.* Greenland *see*
Farewell, Cape
127 G3 **Nunavik** *reg.* Can.
129 E1 **Nunavut** *admin. div.* Can.
99 C2 **Nuneaton** U.K.
106 B1 **Nuñomoral** Spain
108 A2 **Nuoro** *Sardinia* Italy
78 B2 **Nuqrah** Saudi Arabia
52 A2 **Nuriootpa** Austr.
92 I3 **Nurmes** Fin.
Nürnberg Ger. *see* **Nuremberg**
62 A1 **Nu Shan** *mts* China
74 A2 **Nushki** Pak.
127 H2 **Nuuk** Greenland
127 H2 **Nuussuaq** Greenland
127 H2 **Nuussuaq** *pen.* Greenland
78 A2 **Nuwaybi' al Muzayyinah**
Egypt
122 B3 **Nuweveldberge** *mts* S. Africa
86 F2 **Nyagan'** Russia
75 D1 **Nyainqêntanglha Feng** *mt.*
China
75 D2 **Nyainqêntanglha Shan** *mts*
China
117 A3 **Nyala** Sudan
86 D2 **Nyandoma** Russia
118 B3 **Nyanga** *r.* Gabon
121 C2 **Nyanga** Zimbabwe
Nyang'oma *see* **Kogelo**
121 C1 **Nyasa, Lake** Africa
93 F4 **Nyborg** Denmark
92 I1 **Nyborg** Norway
93 G4 **Nybro** Sweden
119 D3 **Nyeri** Kenya

68 C3 **Nyingchi** China
103 E2 **Nyíregyháza** Hungary
93 F4 **Nykøbing Falster** Denmark
93 G4 **Nyköping** Sweden
53 C2 **Nymagee** Austr.
93 G4 **Nynäshamn** Sweden
53 C2 **Nyngan** Austr.
88 B3 **Nyoman** *r.* Belarus/Lith.
105 D3 **Nyons** France
86 E2 **Nyrob** Russia
134 C2 **Nyssa** U.S.A.
119 C3 **Nyunzu** Dem. Rep. Congo
91 C2 **Nyzhn'ohirs'kyy** Ukr.
119 D3 **Nzega** Tanz.
114 B4 **Nzérékoré** Guinea
120 A1 **N'zeto** Angola

O

136 C2 **Oahe, Lake** U.S.A.
124 E5 **O'ahu** *i.* U.S.A.
52 B2 **Oakbank** Austr.
142 B2 **Oakdale** U.S.A.
53 D1 **Oakey** Austr.
134 B1 **Oak Harbor** U.S.A.
140 C3 **Oak Hill** U.S.A.
135 B3 **Oakland** U.S.A.
50 B2 **Oakover** *r.* Austr.
134 B2 **Oakridge** U.S.A.
143 D1 **Oak Ridge** U.S.A.
54 B3 **Oamaru** N.Z.
64 B1 **Oas** Phil.
145 C3 **Oaxaca** Mex.
86 F2 **Ob'** *r.* Russia
118 B2 **Obala** Cameroon
96 B2 **Oban** U.K.
106 B1 **O Barco** Spain
53 C2 **Oberon** Austr.
101 F3 **Oberpfälzer Wald** *mts* Ger.
101 F3 **Oberviechtach** Ger.
59 C3 **Obi** *i.* Indon.
151 C2 **Óbidos** Brazil
66 D2 **Obihiro** Japan
69 E1 **Obluch'ye** Russia
89 E2 **Obninsk** Russia
119 C2 **Obo** C.A.R.
117 C3 **Obock** Djibouti
118 B3 **Obouya** Congo
89 E3 **Oboyan'** Russia
144 B2 **Obregón, Presa** *resr* Mex.
109 D2 **Obrenovac** Serbia
87 E3 **Obshchiy Syrt** *hills* Kazakh./Russia
86 G2 **Obskaya Guba** *sea chan.* Russia
114 B4 **Obuasi** Ghana
90 C1 **Obukhiv** Ukr.
86 D2 **Ob''yachevo** Russia
143 D3 **Ocala** U.S.A.
144 B2 **Ocampo** Mex.
106 C2 **Ocaña** Spain
150 A1 **Occidental, Cordillera** *mts* Col.
150 A3 **Occidental, Cordillera** *mts* Peru
141 D3 **Ocean City** U.S.A.
128 B2 **Ocean Falls** Can.
135 C4 **Oceanside** U.S.A.
91 C2 **Ochakiv** Ukr.
86 E3 **Ocher** Russia
101 E3 **Ochsenfurt** Ger.
143 D2 **Oconee** *r.* U.S.A.
145 C3 **Ocosingo** Mex.
58 C3 **Ocussi** *enclave* East Timor
116 B2 **Oda, Jebel** *mt.* Sudan
66 D2 **Ōdate** Japan
67 C3 **Odawara** Japan
93 E3 **Odda** Norway
106 B2 **Odemira** Port.
111 C3 **Ödemiş** Turkey
93 F4 **Odense** Denmark
101 D3 **Odenwald** *reg.* Ger.
102 C1 **Oderbucht** *b.* Ger.
Odesa Ukr. *see* **Odessa**
90 C2 **Odessa** Ukr.
139 C2 **Odessa** U.S.A.
114 B4 **Odienné** Côte d'Ivoire
103 D2 **Odra** *r.* Ger./Pol.
151 D2 **Oeiras** Brazil
100 D2 **Oelde** Ger.
136 C2 **Oelrichs** U.S.A.
101 F2 **Oelsnitz/Vogtland** Ger.
100 B1 **Oenkerk** Neth.
109 C2 **Ofanto** *r.* Italy
101 D2 **Offenbach am Main** Ger.
102 B2 **Offenburg** Ger.
117 C4 **Ogadēn** *reg.* Eth.
66 C3 **Oga-hantō** *pen.* Japan
67 C3 **Ōgaki** Japan
136 C2 **Ogallala** U.S.A.
115 C4 **Ogbomoso** Nigeria
134 D2 **Ogden** U.S.A.
141 D2 **Ogdensburg** U.S.A.
126 B2 **Ogilvie** *r.* Can.
126 B2 **Ogilvie Mountains** Can.
143 D2 **Oglethorpe, Mount** U.S.A.
130 B1 **Ogoki** *r.* Can.
130 B1 **Ogoki Reservoir** Can.
88 B2 **Ogre** Latvia
109 C1 **Ogulin** Croatia
140 B3 **Ohio** *r.* U.S.A.
140 C2 **Ohio** *state* U.S.A.
101 E2 **Ohrdruf** Ger.
109 D2 **Ohrid** Macedonia
111 B2 **Ohrid, Lake** *l.* Albania/Macedonia
151 C1 **Oiapoque** Brazil
141 D2 **Oil City** U.S.A.
100 A3 **Oise** *r.* France
67 B4 **Ōita** Japan
144 B2 **Ojinaga** Mex.
152 B3 **Ojos del Salado, Nevado** *mt.* Arg./Chile
89 F2 **Oka** *r.* Russia
120 A3 **Okahandja** Namibia
120 A3 **Okakarara** Namibia
128 C3 **Okanagan Falls** Can.
128 C3 **Okanagan Lake** Can.
134 C1 **Okanogan** U.S.A.
134 C1 **Okanogan** *r.* U.S.A.
74 B1 **Okara** Pak.
120 B2 **Okavango** *r.* Africa
120 B2 **Okavango Delta** *swamp* Botswana
67 C3 **Okaya** Japan
67 B4 **Okayama** Japan
67 C4 **Okazaki** Japan
143 D3 **Okeechobee, Lake** U.S.A.
143 D2 **Okefenokee Swamp** U.S.A.
99 A3 **Okehampton** U.K.
74 A2 **Okha** India
83 K3 **Okha** Russia
75 C2 **Okhaldhunga** Nepal
83 K3 **Okhota** *r.* Russia
83 K3 **Okhotsk** Russia
156 C2 **Okhotsk, Sea of** Japan/Russia
91 C1 **Okhtyrka** Ukr.
69 E3 **Okinawa** *i.* Japan
67 B3 **Oki-shotō** *is* Japan
139 D1 **Oklahoma** *state* U.S.A.
139 D1 **Oklahoma City** U.S.A.
139 D1 **Okmulgee** U.S.A.
78 A2 **Oko, Wadi** *watercourse* Sudan
118 B3 **Okondja** Gabon
128 C2 **Okotoks** Can.
89 D3 **Okovskiy Les** *for.* Russia
118 B3 **Okoyo** Congo
92 H1 **Øksfjord** Norway
62 A2 **Oktwin** Myanmar
86 D2 **Oktyabr'skiy** *Arkhangel'skaya Oblast'* Russia
83 L3 **Oktyabr'skiy** *Kamchatskiy Kray* Russia
87 E3 **Oktyabr'skiy** *Respublika Bashkortostan* Russia
86 F2 **Oktyabr'skoye** Russia
83 H1 **Oktyabr'skoy Revolyutsii, Ostrov** *i.* Russia
89 D2 **Okulovka** Russia
66 C2 **Okushiri-tō** *i.* Japan
92 □A3 **Ólafsvík** Iceland
93 G4 **Öland** *i.* Sweden
52 B2 **Olary** Austr.
153 B4 **Olavarría** Arg.
103 D1 **Oława** Pol.
108 A2 **Olbia** *Sardinia* Italy
126 B2 **Old Crow** Can.
101 D1 **Oldenburg** Ger.
102 C1 **Oldenburg in Holstein** Ger.
100 C1 **Oldenzaal** Neth.
97 B3 **Old Head of Kinsale** Ireland
128 C2 **Olds** Can.
129 D2 **Old Wives Lake** Can.
141 D2 **Olean** U.S.A.
103 E1 **Olecko** Pol.
83 J2 **Olekminsk** Russia
91 C2 **Oleksandriya** Ukr.
86 C2 **Olenegorsk** Russia
83 I2 **Olenek** Russia
83 I2 **Olenek** *r.* Russia
89 D2 **Olenino** Russia
90 B1 **Olevs'k** Ukr.
106 B2 **Olhão** Port.
122 A2 **Olifants** *watercourse* Namibia
123 D1 **Olifants** S. Africa
123 D1 **Olifants** *r. Northern* S. Africa
122 A3 **Olifants** *r. W. Cape* S. Africa
122 B2 **Olifantshoek** S. Africa
154 C2 **Olímpia** Brazil
151 E2 **Olinda** Brazil
123 C1 **Oliphants Drift** Botswana
107 C2 **Oliva** Spain
155 D2 **Oliveira** Brazil
106 B2 **Olivenza** Spain
152 B3 **Ollagüe** Chile
150 A2 **Olmos** Peru
140 B3 **Olney** U.S.A.
103 D2 **Olomouc** Czech Rep.
64 B1 **Olongapo** Phil.
104 B3 **Oloron-Ste-Marie** France
107 D1 **Olot** Spain
69 D1 **Olovyannaya** Russia
83 L2 **Oloy** *r.* Russia
100 C2 **Olpe** Ger.
103 E1 **Olsztyn** Pol.
110 B2 **Olt** *r.* Romania
81 C1 **Oltu** Turkey
111 B3 **Olympia** *tourist site* Greece
134 B1 **Olympia** U.S.A.
134 B1 **Olympus, Mount** U.S.A.
83 M3 **Olyutorskiy, Mys** *c.* Russia
97 C1 **Omagh** U.K.
137 D2 **Omaha** U.S.A.
79 C2 **Oman** *country* Asia
79 C2 **Oman, Gulf of** Asia
120 A3 **Omaruru** Namibia
120 B2 **Omatako** *watercourse* Namibia
116 B3 **Omdurman** Sudan
53 C3 **Omeo** Austr.
145 C3 **Ometepec** Mex.
78 A3 **Om Hajër** Eritrea

128 B2 **Omineca Mountains** Can.
67 C3 **Ōmiya** Japan
100 C1 **Ommen** Neth.
83 L2 **Omolon** *r.* Russia
100 B3 **Omont** France
82 F3 **Omsk** Russia
83 L2 **Omsukchan** Russia
110 C1 **Omu, Vârful** *mt.* Romania
67 A4 **Ōmura** Japan
141 D3 **Onancock** U.S.A.
140 C1 **Onaping Lake** Can.
131 C2 **Onatchiway, Lac** *l.* Can.
120 A2 **Oncócua** Angola
122 B3 **Onderstedorings** S. Africa
120 A2 **Ondjiva** Angola
86 C2 **Onega** Russia
86 C2 **Onega** *r.* Russia
141 D2 **Oneida Lake** U.S.A.
137 D2 **O'Neill** U.S.A.
141 D2 **Oneonta** U.S.A.
110 C1 **Onești** Romania
Onezhskoye, Ozero *l.* Russia *see* **Onezhskoye Ozero**
86 C2 **Onezhskoye Ozero** *l.* Russia
122 B2 **Ongers** *watercourse* S. Africa
65 B2 **Ongjin** N. Korea
73 C3 **Ongole** India
121 □D3 **Onilahy** *r.* Madag.
115 C4 **Onitsha** Nigeria
122 A2 **Onseepkans** S. Africa
50 A2 **Onslow** Austr.
143 E2 **Onslow Bay** U.S.A.
130 A1 **Ontario** *prov.* Can.
134 C2 **Ontario** U.S.A.
141 D2 **Ontario, Lake** Can./U.S.A.
51 C2 **Oodnadatta** Austr.
Oostende Belgium *see* **Ostend**
100 B2 **Oosterhout** Neth.
100 A2 **Oosterschelde** *est.* Neth.
100 B1 **Oost-Vlieland** Neth.
128 B2 **Ootsa Lake** Can.
128 B2 **Ootsa Lake** Can.
118 C3 **Opala** Dem. Rep. Congo
130 C1 **Opataca, Lac** *l.* Can.
103 D2 **Opava** Czech Rep.
143 C2 **Opelika** U.S.A.
142 B2 **Opelousas** U.S.A.
130 C1 **Opinaca, Réservoir** *resr* Can.
131 D1 **Opiscotéo, Lac** *l.* Can.
88 C2 **Opochka** Russia
144 A2 **Opodepe** Mex.
103 D1 **Opole** Pol.
106 B1 **Oporto** Port.
54 C1 **Opotiki** N.Z.
93 E3 **Oppdal** Norway
54 B1 **Opunake** N.Z.
120 A2 **Opuwo** Namibia
110 B1 **Oradea** Romania
Orahovac Kosovo *see* **Rahovec**
114 B1 **Oran** Alg.
152 B3 **Orán** Arg.
65 B1 **Ŏrang** N. Korea
53 C2 **Orange** Austr.
105 C3 **Orange** France
122 A2 **Orange** *r.* Namibia/S. Africa
139 E2 **Orange** U.S.A.
143 D2 **Orangeburg** U.S.A.
140 C2 **Orangeville** Can.
101 F1 **Oranienburg** Ger.
122 A2 **Oranjemund** Namibia
120 B3 **Orapa** Botswana
110 B1 **Orăștie** Romania
108 B2 **Orbetello** Italy
53 C3 **Orbost** Austr.
50 B1 **Ord, Mount** *h.* Austr.
106 B1 **Ordes** Spain
Ordos China *see* **Dongsheng**
80 B1 **Ordu** Turkey
Ordzhonikidze Russia *see* **Vladikavkaz**
91 C2 **Ordzhonikidze** Ukr.
93 G4 **Örebro** Sweden
134 B2 **Oregon** *state* U.S.A.
134 B1 **Oregon City** U.S.A.
87 C3 **Orekhovo-Zuyevo** Russia
89 E3 **Orel** Russia
83 K3 **Orel', Ozero** *l.* Russia
135 D2 **Orem** U.S.A.
111 C3 **Ören** Turkey
87 E3 **Orenburg** Russia
54 A3 **Orepuki** N.Z.
93 F4 **Öresund** *str.* Denmark/Sweden
99 D2 **Orford Ness** *hd* U.K.
111 C3 **Orhaneli** Turkey
111 C2 **Orhangazi** Turkey
83 I3 **Orhon Gol** *r.* Mongolia
152 B2 **Oriental, Cordillera** *mts* Bol.
150 A1 **Oriental, Cordillera** *mts* Col.
150 A3 **Oriental, Cordillera** *mts* Peru
107 C2 **Orihuela** Spain
91 D2 **Orikhiv** Ukr.
130 C2 **Orillia** Can.
150 B1 **Orinoco** *r.* Col./Venez.
150 B1 **Orinoco, Delta del** Venez.
93 H4 **Orissaare** Estonia
108 A3 **Oristano** *Sardinia* Italy
93 I3 **Orivesi** *l.* Fin.
151 C2 **Oriximiná** Brazil
145 C3 **Orizaba** Mex.
145 C3 **Orizaba, Pico de** *vol.* Mex.
92 E3 **Orkanger** Norway
93 F4 **Örkelljunga** Sweden
92 E3 **Orkla** *r.* Norway
96 C1 **Orkney Islands** U.K.
154 C2 **Orlândia** Brazil
143 D3 **Orlando** U.S.A.
104 C2 **Orléans** France
74 A2 **Ormara** Pak.
64 B1 **Ormoc** Phil.
98 B2 **Ormskirk** U.K.
92 G3 **Örnsköldsvik** Sweden
114 B3 **Orodara** Burkina Faso
134 C1 **Orofino** U.S.A.
Oroqen Zizhiqi China *see* **Alihe**
64 B2 **Oroquieta** Phil.
108 A2 **Orosei** *Sardinia* Italy
108 A2 **Orosei, Golfo di** *b. Sardinia* Italy
103 E2 **Orosháza** Hungary
135 B3 **Oroville** U.S.A.
52 A2 **Orroroo** Austr.
89 D3 **Orsha** Belarus
87 E3 **Orsk** Russia
93 E3 **Ørsta** Norway
106 B1 **Ortegal, Cabo** *c.* Spain
104 B3 **Orthez** France
106 B1 **Ortigueira** Spain
137 D1 **Ortonville** U.S.A.
83 J2 **Orulgan, Khrebet** *mts* Russia
Orūmīyeh, Daryācheh-ye *salt l.* Iran *see* **Urmia, Lake**
152 B2 **Oruro** Bol.
108 B2 **Orvieto** Italy
146 B4 **Osa, Península de** *pen.* Costa Rica
137 E3 **Osage** *r.* U.S.A.
67 C4 **Ōsaka** Japan
66 D3 **Ōsaki** Japan
110 B2 **Osam** *r.* Bulg.
101 E1 **Oschersleben (Bode)** Ger.
108 A2 **Oschiri** *Sardinia* Italy
89 E3 **Osetr** *r.* Russia
77 D2 **Osh** Kyrg.
120 A2 **Oshakati** Namibia
130 C2 **Oshawa** Can.
66 C2 **Ō-shima** *i.* Japan
67 C4 **Ō-shima** *i.* Japan
140 B2 **Oshkosh** U.S.A.
81 C2 **Oshnavīyeh** Iran
118 B3 **Oshwe** Dem. Rep. Congo
109 C1 **Osijek** Croatia
128 B2 **Osilinka** *r.* Can.
108 B2 **Osimo** Italy
123 D2 **oSizweni** S. Africa
137 E2 **Oskaloosa** U.S.A.
93 G4 **Oskarshamn** Sweden
89 E3 **Oskol** *r.* Russia
93 F4 **Oslo** Norway
93 F4 **Oslofjorden** *sea chan.* Norway
80 B1 **Osmancık** Turkey
111 C2 **Osmaneli** Turkey
80 B2 **Osmaniye** Turkey
88 C2 **Os'mino** Russia
100 D1 **Osnabrück** Ger.
115 C4 **Osogbo** Nigeria
153 A5 **Osorno** Chile
106 C1 **Osorno** Spain
128 C3 **Osoyoos** Can.
100 B2 **Oss** Neth.
51 D4 **Ossa, Mount** Austr.
83 L3 **Ossora** Russia
89 D2 **Ostashkov** Russia
101 D1 **Oste** *r.* Ger.
100 A2 **Ostend** Belgium
101 E1 **Osterburg (Altmark)** Ger.
93 F3 **Österdalälven** *r.* Sweden
101 D1 **Osterholz-Scharmbeck** Ger.
101 E2 **Osterode am Harz** Ger.
92 F3 **Östersund** Sweden
Ostfriesische Inseln *is* Ger. *see* **East Frisian Islands**
100 C1 **Ostfriesland** *reg.* Ger.
93 G3 **Östhammar** Sweden
103 D2 **Ostrava** Czech Rep.
103 D1 **Ostróda** Pol.
89 E3 **Ostrogozhsk** Russia
103 E1 **Ostrołęka** Pol.
101 F2 **Ostrov** Czech Rep.
88 C2 **Ostrov** Russia
103 E1 **Ostrowiec Świętokrzyski** Pol.
103 E1 **Ostrów Mazowiecka** Pol.
103 D1 **Ostrów Wielkopolski** Pol.
67 B4 **Ōsumi-kaikyō** *sea chan.* Japan
67 B4 **Ōsumi-shotō** *is* Japan
106 B2 **Osuna** Spain
141 D2 **Oswego** U.S.A.
99 B2 **Oswestry** U.K.
67 C3 **Ōta** Japan
54 B3 **Otago Peninsula** N.Z.
54 C2 **Otaki** N.Z.
66 D2 **Otaru** Japan
120 A2 **Otavi** Namibia
134 C1 **Othello** U.S.A.
120 A3 **Otjiwarongo** Namibia
117 B3 **Otoro, Jebel** *mt.* Sudan
93 E4 **Otra** *r.* Norway
109 C2 **Otranto, Strait of** Albania/Italy
67 C3 **Ōtsu** Japan
93 E3 **Otta** Norway
130 C2 **Ottawa** Can.
130 C2 **Ottawa** *r.* Can.
140 B2 **Ottawa** *IL* U.S.A.
137 D3 **Ottawa** *KS* U.S.A.
130 B1 **Otter Rapids** Can.
100 B2 **Ottignies** Belgium
137 E2 **Ottumwa** U.S.A.
150 A2 **Otuzco** Peru
52 B3 **Otway, Cape** Austr.
142 B2 **Ouachita** *r.* U.S.A.

142 B2 Ouachita, Lake U.S.A.
142 B2 Ouachita Mountains
        U.S.A.
118 C2 Ouadda C.A.R.
115 D3 Ouaddaï reg. Chad
114 B3 Ouagadougou Burkina Faso
114 B3 Ouahigouya Burkina Faso
114 B3 Oualâta Maur.
118 C2 Ouanda Djallé C.A.R.
114 B2 Ouarâne reg. Maur.
115 C1 Ouargla Alg.
114 B1 Ouarzazate Morocco
100 A2 Oudenaarde Belgium
122 B3 Oudtshoorn S. Africa
107 C2 Oued Tlélat Alg.
104 A2 Ouessant, Île d' i. France
118 B2 Ouesso Congo
114 B1 Oujda Morocco
107 D2 Ouled Farès Alg.
92 I2 Oulu Fin.
92 I3 Oulujärvi l. Fin.
108 A1 Oulx Italy
115 E3 Oum-Chalouba Chad
115 D3 Oum-Hadjer Chad
115 E3 Ounianga Kébir Chad
100 B2 Oupeye Belgium
106 B1 Ourense Spain
154 C2 Ourinhos Brazil
155 D2 Ouro Preto Brazil
100 B2 Ourthe r. Belgium
98 C2 Ouse r. U.K.
131 D2 Outardes, Rivière aux r.
        Can.
131 D1 Outardes Quatre, Réservoir
        resr Can.
96 A2 Outer Hebrides is U.K.
120 A3 Outjo Namibia
129 D2 Outlook Can.
92 I3 Outokumpu Fin.
52 B3 Ouyen Austr.
106 B1 Ovar Port.
92 H2 Överkalix Sweden
135 D3 Overton U.S.A.
92 H2 Övertorneå Sweden
106 B1 Oviedo Spain
93 E3 Øvre Årdal Norway
93 F3 Øvre Rendal Norway
90 B2 Ovruch Ukr.
118 B3 Owando Congo
67 C4 Owase Japan
138 A2 Owatonna U.S.A.
140 B3 Owensboro U.S.A.
135 C3 Owens Lake U.S.A.
130 B2 Owen Sound Can.
115 C4 Owerri Nigeria
140 C2 Owosso U.S.A.
134 C2 Owyhee U.S.A.
134 C2 Owyhee r. U.S.A.
54 C2 Oxford N.Z.
99 C3 Oxford U.K.
142 C2 Oxford U.S.A.
129 E2 Oxford Lake Can.
52 B2 Oxley Austr.
97 B1 Ox Mountains hills Ireland
135 C4 Oxnard U.S.A.
67 C3 Oyama Japan
118 B2 Oyem Gabon
129 C2 Oyen Can.
105 D2 Oyonnax France
64 B3 Ozamis Phil.
142 C2 Ozark U.S.A.
137 E3 Ozark Plateau U.S.A.
137 E3 Ozarks, Lake of the
        U.S.A.
83 L3 Ozernovskiy Russia
88 B3 Ozersk Russia
89 E3 Ozery Russia
87 D3 Ozinki Russia

P

127 H2 Paamiut Greenland
122 A3 Paarl S. Africa
103 D1 Pabianice Pol.
75 C2 Pabna Bangl.
74 A2 Pab Range mts Pak.
109 C3 Pachino Sicily Italy
145 C2 Pachuca Mex.
156   Pacific Ocean
103 D1 Paczków Pol.
60 B2 Padang Indon.
60 B1 Padang Endau Malaysia
60 B2 Padangpanjang Indon.
60 A1 Padangsidimpuan Indon.
101 D2 Paderborn Ger.
       Padova Italy see Padua
139 D3 Padre Island U.S.A.
52 B3 Padthaway Austr.
108 B1 Padua Italy
140 B3 Paducah KY U.S.A.
139 C2 Paducah TX U.S.A.
65 B1 Paegam N. Korea
       Paengnyŏng-do i. S. Korea see
       Baengnyeong-do
54 C1 Paeroa N.Z.
       Pafos Cyprus see Paphos
109 C2 Pag Croatia
64 B2 Pagadian Phil.
60 B2 Pagai Selatan i. Indon.
60 B2 Pagai Utara i. Indon.
59 D1 Pagan i. N. Mariana Is
61 C2 Pagatan Indon.
138 A1 Page U.S.A.
88 B2 Paggiai Lith.
136 B3 Pagosa Springs U.S.A.
88 C2 Paide Estonia
93 I3 Päijänne l. Fin.
75 C2 Paikü Co l. China
138 A1 Painted Desert U.S.A.
96 B3 Paisley U.K.
92 H2 Pajala Sweden
150 B1 Pakaraima Mountains
       S. America
150 C1 Pakaraima Mountains
       S. America
74 A2 Pakistan country Asia
62 A1 Pakokku Myanmar
88 B2 Pakruojis Lith.
103 D2 Paks Hungary
130 A1 Pakwash Lake Can.
62 B2 Pakxan Laos
63 B2 Pakxé Laos
115 C4 Pala Chad
60 B2 Palabuhanratu, Teluk b.
       Indon.
111 C3 Palaikastro Greece
111 B3 Palaiochora Greece
122 B1 Palamakoloi Botswana
107 D1 Palamós Spain
83 L3 Palana Russia
64 B1 Palanan Phil.
61 C2 Palangkaraya Indon.
74 B2 Palanpur India
120 B3 Palapye Botswana
83 L2 Palatka Russia
143 D3 Palatka U.S.A.
59 C2 Palau country N. Pacific Ocean
63 A2 Palaw Myanmar
64 A2 Palawan i. Phil.
93 H4 Paldiski Estonia
60 B2 Palembang Indon.
106 C1 Palencia Spain
145 C3 Palenque Mex.
108 B3 Palermo Sicily Italy
       Palestine disp. terr. Asia see
       Gaza
                    Palestine disp. terr. Asia see
                    West Bank
139 D2 Palestine U.S.A.
62 A1 Paletwa Myanmar
74 B2 Pali India
48 E2 Palikir Micronesia
109 C2 Palinuro, Capo c. Italy
111 B3 Paliouri, Akrotirio pt Greece
100 B3 Paliseul Belgium
92 I3 Paljakka h. Fin.
88 C2 Palkino Russia
73 B4 Palk Strait India/Sri Lanka
54 C2 Palliser, Cape N.Z.
49 I3 Palliser, Îles is Fr. Polynesia
106 B2 Palma del Río Spain
107 D2 Palma de Mallorca Spain
154 B3 Palmas Paraná Brazil
151 D3 Palmas Tocantins Brazil
114 B4 Palmas, Cape Liberia
154 C3 Palmeira Brazil
151 D2 Palmeirais Brazil
55 P2 Palmer Land reg. Antarctica
54 C2 Palmerston North N.Z.
109 C3 Palmi Italy
145 C2 Palmillas Mex.
150 A1 Palmira Col.
135 C4 Palm Springs U.S.A.
49 H2 Palmyra Atoll
       N. Pacific Ocean
117 B3 Paloich South Sudan
145 C3 Palomares Mex.
107 C2 Palos, Cabo de c. Spain
92 I3 Paltamo Fin.
58 B3 Palu Indon.
83 M2 Palyavaam r. Russia
104 C3 Pamiers France
77 D3 Pamir mts Asia
143 E1 Pamlico Sound sea chan.
       U.S.A.
152 B2 Pampa Grande Bol.
153 B4 Pampas reg. Arg.
150 A1 Pamplona Col.
107 C1 Pamplona Spain
111 D2 Pamukova Turkey
60 B2 Panaitan i. Indon.
73 B3 Panaji India
146 B4 Panama country
       Central America
146 C4 Panamá, Canal de Panama
146 C4 Panama, Gulf of Panama
146 C4 Panama City Panama
142 C2 Panama City U.S.A.
135 C3 Panamint Range mts U.S.A.
61 B1 Panarik Indon.
64 B1 Panay i. Phil.
109 D2 Pančevo Serbia
64 B1 Pandan Phil.
75 C2 Pandaria India
73 B3 Pandharpur India
88 B2 Panevėžys Lith.
61 C2 Pangkalanbuun Indon.
60 A1 Pangkalansusu Indon.
61 B2 Pangkalpinang Indon.
127 G2 Pangnirtung Can.
86 G2 Pangody Russia
89 F3 Panino Russia
74 B2 Panipat India
74 A2 Panjgur Pak.
65 C1 Pan Ling mts China
75 C2 Panna India
50 A2 Pannawonica Austr.
154 B2 Panorama Brazil
65 B1 Panshi China
145 C2 Pánuco Mex.
62 B1 Panzhihua China
109 C3 Paola Italy
63 B2 Paôy Pêt Cambodia
103 D2 Pápa Hungary

54 B1	**Papakura** N.Z.	
145 C2	**Papantla** Mex.	
49 I4	**Papeete** Fr. Polynesia	
100 C1	**Papenburg** Ger.	
80 B2	**Paphos** Cyprus	
59 D3	**Papua, Gulf of** P.N.G.	
59 D3	**Papua New Guinea** country Oceania	
50 A2	**Paraburdoo** Austr.	
154 C1	**Paracatu** Brazil	
155 C1	**Paracatu** r. Brazil	
52 A2	**Parachilna** Austr.	
109 D2	**Paraćin** Serbia	
155 D1	**Pará de Minas** Brazil	
135 B3	**Paradise** U.S.A.	
142 B1	**Paragould** U.S.A.	
151 C3	**Paraguaí** r. Brazil	
152 C3	**Paraguay** r. Arg./Para.	
153 C2	**Paraguay** country S. America	
155 D2	**Paraíba do Sul** r. Brazil	
154 B1	**Paraíso** Brazil	
145 C3	**Paraíso** Mex.	
114 C4	**Parakou** Benin	
151 C1	**Paramaribo** Suriname	
83 L3	**Paramushir, Ostrov** i. Russia	
152 B4	**Paraná** Arg.	
154 A3	**Paraná** r. S. America	
154 C3	**Paranaguá** Brazil	
154 B1	**Paranaíba** Brazil	
154 B2	**Paranaíba** r. Brazil	
154 B2	**Paranapanema** r. Brazil	
154 B2	**Paranapiacaba, Serra** mts Brazil	
154 B2	**Paranavaí** Brazil	
54 B2	**Paraparaumu** N.Z.	
155 D2	**Parati** Brazil	
154 B1	**Paraúna** Brazil	
105 C2	**Paray-le-Monial** France	
83 H3	**Parbhani** India	
101 E1	**Parchim** Ger.	
155 E1	**Pardo** r. Bahia Brazil	
154 B2	**Pardo** r. Mato Grosso do Sul Brazil	
154 C2	**Pardo** r. São Paulo Brazil	
103 O3	**Pardubice** Czech Rep.	
150 B3	**Parecis, Serra dos** hills Brazil	
130 C2	**Parent, Lac** l. Can.	
58 B3	**Parepare** Indon.	
89 D2	**Parfino** Russia	
111 B3	**Parga** Greece	
109 C2	**Parghelia** Italy	
147 D3	**Paria, Gulf of** Trin. and Tob./Venez.	
150 B1	**Parima, Serra** mts Brazil	
151 C2	**Parintins** Brazil	
104 C2	**Paris** France	
142 C1	**Paris** TN U.S.A.	
139 D2	**Paris** TX U.S.A.	
93 H3	**Parkano** Fin.	
138 A2	**Parker** U.S.A.	
140 C3	**Parkersburg** U.S.A.	
53 C2	**Parkes** Austr.	
140 A1	**Park Falls** U.S.A.	
137 D1	**Park Rapids** U.S.A.	
108 B2	**Parma** Italy	
151 D2	**Parnaíba** Brazil	
151 D2	**Parnaíba** r. Brazil	
54 B2	**Parnassus** N.Z.	
111 B3	**Parnonas** mts Greece	
88 B2	**Pärnu** Estonia	
65 B2	**Paro-ho** l. S. Korea	
52 B2	**Paroo** watercourse Austr.	
	Paropamisus mts Afgh. see **Safīd Kōh, Silsilah-ye**	
111 C3	**Paros** i. Greece	
144 B2	**Parras** Mex.	
126 C2	**Parry, Cape** Can.	
126 D1	**Parry Islands** Can.	
130 B2	**Parry Sound** Can.	
79 C2	**Pārsīān** Iran	
137 D3	**Parsons** U.S.A.	
101 D2	**Partenstein** Ger.	
104 B2	**Parthenay** France	
97 B2	**Partry Mountains** hills Ireland	
151 C2	**Paru** r. Brazil	
135 C4	**Pasadena** U.S.A.	
62 A2	**Pasawng** Myanmar	
142 C2	**Pascagoula** U.S.A.	
110 C1	**Pașcani** Romania	
134 C1	**Pasco** U.S.A.	
102 C1	**Pasewalk** Ger.	
129 D2	**Pasfield Lake** Can.	
64 B1	**Pasig** Phil.	
60 B1	**Pasir Putih** Malaysia	
74 A2	**Pasni** Pak.	
153 A5	**Paso Río Mayo** Arg.	
135 B3	**Paso Robles** U.S.A.	
155 D2	**Passa Tempo** Brazil	
102 C2	**Passau** Ger.	
152 C3	**Passo Fundo** Brazil	
155 C2	**Passos** Brazil	
88 C2	**Pastavy** Belarus	
150 A2	**Pastaza** r. Peru	
150 A1	**Pasto** Col.	
61 C2	**Pasuruan** Indon.	
88 B2	**Pasvalys** Lith.	
153 A6	**Patagonia** reg. Arg.	
75 C2	**Patan** Nepal	
54 B1	**Patea** N.Z.	
141 E2	**Paterson** U.S.A.	
	Pathein Myanmar see **Bassein**	
136 B2	**Pathfinder Reservoir** U.S.A.	
61 C2	**Pati** Indon.	
62 A1	**Patkai Bum** mts India/Myanmar	
111 C3	**Patmos** i. Greece	
75 C2	**Patna** India	
81 C2	**Patnos** Turkey	
154 B3	**Pato Branco** Brazil	
152 C4	**Patos, Lagoa dos** l. Brazil	
155 C1	**Patos de Minas** Brazil	
152 B4	**Patquía** Arg.	
111 B3	**Patras** Greece	
75 C2	**Patratu** India	
154 C1	**Patrocínio** Brazil	
63 B3	**Pattani** Thai.	
63 B2	**Pattaya** Thai.	
128 A2	**Pattullo, Mount** Can.	
129 D2	**Patuanak** Can.	
144 B3	**Pátzcuaro** Mex.	
104 B3	**Pau** France	
104 B2	**Pauillac** France	
62 A1	**Pauk** Myanmar	
151 D2	**Paulistana** Brazil	
151 E2	**Paulo Afonso** Brazil	
123 D2	**Paulpietersburg** S. Africa	
139 D1	**Pauls Valley** U.S.A.	
62 A2	**Paungde** Myanmar	
154 B1	**Pavão** Brazil	
108 A1	**Pavia** Italy	
88 B2	**Pāvilosta** Latvia	
110 C2	**Pavlikeni** Bulg.	
77 D1	**Pavlodar** Kazakh.	
91 D1	**Pavlohrad** Ukr.	
91 E1	**Pavlovsk** Russia	
91 D2	**Pavlovskaya** Russia	
60 B2	**Payakumbuh** Indon.	
134 C2	**Payette** U.S.A.	
134 C2	**Payette** r. U.S.A.	
86 F2	**Pay-Khoy, Khrebet** hills Russia	
152 C4	**Paysandú** Uru.	
81 C1	**Pazar** Turkey	
110 B2	**Pazardzhik** Bulg.	
111 C3	**Pazarköy** Turkey	
108 B1	**Pazin** Croatia	
63 A2	**Pe** Myanmar	
128 C2	**Peace** r. Can.	
128 C2	**Peace River** Can.	
135 E3	**Peale, Mount** U.S.A.	
142 C2	**Pearl** r. U.S.A.	
139 D3	**Pearsall** U.S.A.	
121 C2	**Pebane** Moz.	
	Peć Kosovo see **Pejë**	
155 D1	**Peçanha** Brazil	
86 E2	**Pechora** Russia	
86 E2	**Pechora** r. Russia	
88 C2	**Pechory** Russia	
139 C2	**Pecos** U.S.A.	
139 C3	**Pecos** r. U.S.A.	
103 D2	**Pécs** Hungary	
155 D1	**Pedra Azul** Brazil	
154 C2	**Pedregulho** Brazil	
151 D2	**Pedreiras** Brazil	
73 C4	**Pedro, Point** Sri Lanka	
151 D2	**Pedro Afonso** Brazil	
154 B1	**Pedro Gomes** Brazil	
152 C3	**Pedro Juan Caballero** Para.	
96 C3	**Peebles** U.K.	
143 E2	**Pee Dee** r. U.S.A.	
126 C2	**Peel** r. Can.	
98 A1	**Peel** Isle of Man	
128 C2	**Peerless Lake** Can.	
54 B2	**Pegasus Bay** N.Z.	
101 E3	**Pegnitz** Ger.	
62 A2	**Pegu** Myanmar	
62 A2	**Pegu Yoma** mts Myanmar	
153 B4	**Pehuajó** Arg.	
101 E1	**Peine** Ger.	
88 C2	**Peipus, Lake** Estonia/Russia	
154 B2	**Peixe** r. Brazil	
109 D2	**Pejë** Kosovo	
61 B2	**Pekalongan** Indon.	
60 B1	**Pekan** Malaysia	
60 B1	**Pekanbaru** Indon.	
	Peking China see **Beijing**	
130 B2	**Pelee Island** Can.	
59 C3	**Peleng** i. Indon.	
92 I2	**Pelkosenniemi** Fin.	
122 A2	**Pella** S. Africa	
59 D3	**Pelleluhu Islands** P.N.G.	
92 H2	**Pello** Fin.	
128 A1	**Pelly** r. Can.	
128 A1	**Pelly Mountains** Can.	
152 C4	**Pelotas** Brazil	
152 C3	**Pelotas, Rio das** r. Brazil	
141 F1	**Pemadumcook Lake** U.S.A.	
61 B1	**Pemangkat** Indon.	
60 A1	**Pematangsiantar** Indon.	
121 D2	**Pemba** Moz.	
120 B2	**Pemba** Zambia	
119 D3	**Pemba Island** Tanz.	
128 B2	**Pemberton** Can.	
137 D1	**Pembina** r. Can./U.S.A.	
130 C2	**Pembroke** Can.	
99 A3	**Pembroke** U.K.	
145 C2	**Peña Nevada, Cerro** mt. Mex.	
154 C2	**Penápolis** Brazil	
106 B1	**Peñaranda de Bracamonte** Spain	
107 C2	**Peñarroya** mt. Spain	
106 B2	**Peñarroya-Pueblonuevo** Spain	
106 B1	**Peñas, Cabo de** c. Spain	
153 A5	**Penas, Golfo de** g. Chile	
134 C1	**Pendleton** U.S.A.	
128 B2	**Pendleton Bay** Can.	
128 C2	**Pend Oreille Lake** U.S.A.	
74 B3	**Penganga** r. India	
123 D1	**Penge** S. Africa	
70 A2	**Penglai** China	
71 A3	**Pengshui** China	
106 B2	**Peniche** Port.	
98 B1	**Penicuik** U.K.	
108 B2	**Penne** Italy	

98 B1 Pennines *hills* U.K.
141 D2 Pennsylvania *state* U.S.A.
127 G2 Penny Icecap Can.
141 F2 Penobscot *r.* U.S.A.
52 B3 Penola Austr.
50 C3 Penong Austr.
49 H3 Penrhyn *atoll* Cook Is
98 B1 Penrith U.K.
142 C2 Pensacola U.S.A.
55 Q1 Pensacola Mountains
      Antarctica
61 C1 Pensiangan *Sabah* Malaysia
128 C3 Penticton Can.
96 C1 Pentland Firth *sea chan.* U.K.
99 B2 Penygadair *h.* U.K.
87 D3 Penza Russia
99 A3 Penzance U.K.
140 B2 Peoria U.S.A.
107 C1 Perales del Alfambra Spain
51 E2 Percy Isles Austr.
86 F2 Peregrebnoye Russia
150 A1 Pereira Col.
154 B2 Pereira Barreto Brazil
90 A2 Peremyshlyany Ukr.
89 E2 Pereslavl'-Zalesskiy Russia
91 C1 Pereyaslav-Khmel'nyts'kyy
      Ukr.
153 B4 Pergamino Arg.
92 H3 Perhonjoki *r.* Fin.
131 C1 Péribonka, Lac *l.* Can.
152 B3 Perico Arg.
144 B2 Pericos Mex.
104 C2 Périgueux France
147 C4 Perijá, Sierra de *mts* Venez.
153 A5 Perito Moreno Arg.
101 E1 Perleberg Ger.
86 E3 Perm' Russia
52 A2 Pernatty Lagoon *imp. l.* Austr.
105 C2 Péronne France
145 C3 Perote Mex.
104 C3 Perpignan France
99 A3 Perranporth U.K.
143 D2 Perry *FL* U.S.A.
143 D2 Perry *GA* U.S.A.
137 E2 Perry *IA* U.S.A.
139 C1 Perryton U.S.A.
137 F3 Perryville U.S.A.
99 B2 Pershore U.K.
91 D2 Pershotravens'k Ukr.
      Persian Gulf Asia *see*
      The Gulf
50 A3 Perth Austr.
96 C2 Perth U.K.
105 D3 Pertuis France
108 A2 Pertusato, Capo *c.* Corsica
      France
150 A2 Peru *country* S. America
157 H4 Peru-Chile Trench
      S. Pacific Ocean
108 B2 Perugia Italy
154 B2 Peruíbe Brazil
100 A2 Péruwelz Belgium
90 A2 Pervomays'k Ukr.
91 C2 Pervomays'ke Ukr.
89 F3 Pervomayskiy Russia
91 D2 Pervomays'kyy Ukr.
108 B2 Pesaro Italy
108 B2 Pescara Italy
108 B2 Pescara *r.* Italy
74 B1 Peshawar Pak.
109 D2 Peshkopi Albania
109 C1 Pesnica Slovenia
89 E2 Pestovo Russia
144 B3 Petatlán Mex.
140 B2 Petenwell Lake U.S.A.
52 A2 Peterborough Austr.
130 C2 Peterborough Can.
99 C2 Peterborough U.K.

96 D2 Peterhead U.K.
50 B2 Petermann Ranges *mts* Austr.
129 D2 Peter Pond Lake Can.
128 A2 Petersburg *AK* U.S.A.
141 D3 Petersburg *VA* U.S.A.
101 D1 Petershagen Ger.
131 E1 Petit Mécatina *r.* Can.
145 D2 Peto Mex.
140 C1 Petoskey U.S.A.
80 B2 Petra *tourist site* Jordan
66 B2 Petra Velikogo, Zaliv *b.* Russia
111 B2 Petrich Bulg.
151 D2 Petrolina Brazil
83 L3 Petropavlovsk-Kamchatskiy
      Russia
77 C1 Petropavlovskoye Kazakh.
110 B1 Petroșani Romania
89 F3 Petrovskoye Russia
86 C2 Petrozavodsk Russia
123 C2 Petrusburg S. Africa
123 C2 Petrus Steyn S. Africa
122 B3 Petrusville S. Africa
89 E2 Petushki Russia
60 A1 Peureula Indon.
83 M2 Pevek Russia
102 B2 Pforzheim Ger.
102 C2 Pfunds Austria
101 D3 Pfungstadt Ger.
123 C2 Phahameng S. Africa
123 D1 Phalaborwa S. Africa
74 B2 Phalodi India
63 B2 Phang Hoei, San Khao *mts* Thai.
63 A3 Phangnga Thai.
62 B1 Phăng Xi Păng *mt.* Vietnam
63 B2 Phan Rang-Thap Cham
      Vietnam
63 B2 Phan Thiết Vietnam
63 B3 Phatthalung Thai.
62 A2 Phayao Thai.
129 D2 Phelps Lake Can.
143 C2 Phenix City U.S.A.
63 A2 Phet Buri Thai.
63 B2 Phichit Thai.
141 D3 Philadelphia U.S.A.
136 C2 Philip U.S.A.
100 B2 Philippeville Belgium
100 A2 Philippine Neth.
64 B1 Philippines *country* Asia
64 B1 Philippine Sea
      N. Pacific Ocean
126 B2 Philip Smith Mountains
      U.S.A.
122 B3 Philipstown S. Africa
53 C3 Phillip Island Austr.
137 D3 Phillipsburg U.S.A.
123 C2 Phiritona S. Africa
63 B2 Phitsanulok Thai.
63 B2 Phnom Penh Cambodia
      Phnom Pénh Cambodia *see*
      Phnom Penh
138 A2 Phoenix U.S.A.
49 G3 Phoenix Islands Kiribati
63 B2 Phon Thai.
62 B1 Phôngsali Laos
62 B2 Phônsavan Laos
62 B2 Phônsavan *mt.* Laos
62 B2 Phrae Thai.
63 A3 Phuket Thai.
62 A2 Phumĭphon, Khuan Thai.
123 C2 Phuthaditjhaba S. Africa
62 A1 Phyu Myanmar
108 A1 Piacenza Italy
110 C1 Piatra Neamț Romania
151 D2 Piauí *r.* Brazil
108 B1 Piave *r.* Italy
117 B4 Pibor *r.* South Sudan
117 B4 Pibor Post South Sudan

142 C2 Picayune U.S.A.
152 B3 Pichanal Arg.
144 A2 Pichilingue Mex.
98 C1 Pickering U.K.
130 A1 Pickle Lake Can.
151 D2 Picos Brazil
153 B5 Pico Truncado Arg.
53 D2 Picton Austr.
150 B3 Piedras, Río de las *r.* Peru
145 C3 Piedras Negras Guat.
145 B2 Piedras Negras Mex.
93 I3 Pieksämäki Fin.
92 I3 Pielinen *l.* Fin.
136 C2 Pierre U.S.A.
123 D2 Pierrelatte France
123 D2 Pietermaritzburg S. Africa
110 B1 Pietrosa *mt.* Romania
128 C2 Pigeon Lake Can.
153 B4 Pigüé Arg.
92 I3 Pihtipudas Fin.
145 C3 Pijijiapan Mex.
136 C3 Pikes Peak U.S.A.
122 A3 Piketberg S. Africa
140 C3 Pikeville U.S.A.
103 D1 Piła Pol.
153 C4 Pilar Arg.
152 C3 Pilar Para.
50 A2 Pilbara *reg.* Austr.
53 C2 Pilliga Austr.
154 C1 Pilões, Serra dos *mts* Brazil
150 B3 Pimenta Bueno Brazil
153 C4 Pinamar Arg.
80 B2 Pınarbaşı Turkey
146 B2 Pinar del Río Cuba
103 E1 Pińczów Pol.
151 D2 Pindaré *r.* Brazil
      Pindos *mts* Greece *see*
      Pindus Mountains
111 B2 Pindus Mountains Greece
142 B2 Pine Bluff U.S.A.
50 C1 Pine Creek Austr.
136 B2 Pinedale U.S.A.
86 D2 Pinega Russia
129 D2 Pinehouse Lake Can.
111 B3 Pineios *r.* Greece
128 C2 Pine Point (abandoned) Can.
136 C2 Pine Ridge U.S.A.
123 C2 Pinetown S. Africa
70 B2 Pingdingshan China
71 B3 Pingguo China
71 B3 Pingjiang China
70 A2 Pingliang China
71 C3 P'ingtung Taiwan
71 A3 Pingxiang *Guangxi* China
71 B3 Pingxiang *Jiangxi* China
70 B2 Pingyin China
151 D2 Pinheiro Brazil
101 D1 Pinneberg Ger.
145 C2 Pinotepa Nacional Mex.
88 C3 Pinsk Belarus
135 D3 Pioche U.S.A.
119 C3 Piodi Dem. Rep. Congo
103 E1 Pionki Pol.
103 D1 Piotrków Trybunalski Pol.
137 D2 Pipestone U.S.A.
131 C2 Pipmuacan, Réservoir *resr* Can.
154 B2 Piquiri *r.* Brazil
154 C1 Piracanjuba Brazil
154 C2 Piracicaba Brazil
155 D1 Piracicaba *r.* Brazil
111 B3 Piraeus Greece
154 C2 Piraí do Sul Brazil
154 C2 Pirajuí Brazil
154 B1 Piranhas Brazil
151 E2 Piranhas *r.* Brazil
155 D1 Piranhas Brazil
154 C1 Pirapora Brazil
154 C1 Pirassununga Brazil

154 C1 **Pires do Rio** Brazil
151 D2 **Piripiri** Brazil
59 C3 **Piru** Indon.
108 B2 **Pisa** Italy
152 A2 **Pisagua** Chile
150 A3 **Pisco** Peru
102 C2 **Písek** Czech Rep.
79 D2 **Pīshīn** Iran
145 D2 **Pisté** Mex.
109 C2 **Pisticci** Italy
108 B2 **Pistoia** Italy
106 C1 **Pisuerga** *r.* Spain
134 B2 **Pit** *r.* U.S.A.
154 B2 **Pitanga** Brazil
155 D1 **Pitangui** Brazil
49 J4 **Pitcairn Island** *i.* Pitcairn Is
92 H2 **Piteå** Sweden
92 H2 **Piteälven** *r.* Sweden
110 B2 **Pitești** Romania
75 C2 **Pithoragarh** India
96 C2 **Pitlochry** U.K.
128 B2 **Pitt Island** Can.
137 E3 **Pittsburg** U.S.A.
141 D2 **Pittsburgh** U.S.A.
141 E2 **Pittsfield** U.S.A.
53 D1 **Pittsworth** Austr.
155 C2 **Piumhi** Brazil
150 A2 **Piura** Peru
90 C2 **Pivdennyy Buh** *r.* Ukr.
131 E2 **Placentia** Can.
135 B3 **Placerville** U.S.A.
146 C2 **Placetas** Cuba
139 C2 **Plainview** U.S.A.
154 C1 **Planaltina** Brazil
142 B2 **Plaquemine** U.S.A.
106 B1 **Plasencia** Spain
147 C4 **Plato** Col.
137 D2 **Platte** *r.* U.S.A.
141 E2 **Plattsburgh** U.S.A.
101 F1 **Plau am See** Ger.
101 F2 **Plauen** Ger.
101 F1 **Plauer See** *l.* Ger.
89 E3 **Plavsk** Russia
129 E2 **Playgreen Lake** Can.
63 B2 **Plây Ku** Vietnam
153 B4 **Plaza Huincul** Arg.
139 D3 **Pleasanton** U.S.A.
54 B2 **Pleasant Point** N.Z.
104 C2 **Pleaux** France
130 B1 **Pledger Lake** Can.
54 C1 **Plenty, Bay of** *g.* N.Z.
136 C1 **Plentywood** U.S.A.
86 D2 **Plesetsk** Russia
131 C1 **Plétipi, Lac** *l.* Can.
100 C2 **Plettenberg** Ger.
122 B3 **Plettenberg Bay** S. Africa
110 B2 **Pleven** Bulg.
109 C2 **Pljevlja** Montenegro
109 C2 **Ploče** Croatia
103 D1 **Płock** Pol.
109 C2 **Pločno** *mt.* Bos. & Herz.
104 B2 **Ploemeur** France
110 C2 **Ploiești** Romania
89 F2 **Ploskoye** Russia
104 B2 **Plouzané** France
110 B2 **Plovdiv** Bulg.
88 B2 **Plung** Lith.
88 C3 **Plyeshchanitsy** Belarus
99 A3 **Plymouth** U.K.
140 B2 **Plymouth** U.S.A.
147 D3 **Plymouth (abandoned)** Montserrat
88 C2 **Plyussa** Russia
102 C2 **Plzeň** Czech Rep.
114 B3 **Pô** Burkina Faso
108 B1 **Po** *r.* Italy
77 E2 **Pobeda Peak** China/Kyrg.
142 B1 **Pocahontas** U.S.A.
134 D2 **Pocatello** U.S.A.
90 B1 **Pochayiv** Ukr.
89 D3 **Pochep** Russia
89 D3 **Pochinok** Russia
145 C3 **Pochutla** Mex.
141 D3 **Pocomoke City** U.S.A.
155 C2 **Poços de Caldas** Brazil
89 D2 **Poddor'ye** Russia
91 D1 **Podgorenskiy** Russia
109 C2 **Podgorica** Montenegro
82 G3 **Podgornoye** Russia
83 H2 **Podkamennaya Tunguska** *r.* Russia
89 E2 **Podol'sk** Russia
109 D2 **Podujevë** Kosovo
Podujevo Kosovo *see* **Podujevë**
122 A2 **Pofadder** S. Africa
89 D3 **Pogar** Russia
109 D2 **Pogradec** Albania
65 B2 **Pohang** S. Korea
48 E2 **Pohnpei** *atoll* Micronesia
110 B2 **Poiana Mare** Romania
118 C3 **Poie** Dem. Rep. Congo
118 B3 **Pointe-Noire** Congo
126 D2 **Point Lake** Can.
140 C3 **Point Pleasant** U.S.A.
104 C2 **Poitiers** France
74 B2 **Pokaran** India
75 C2 **Pokhara** Nepal
83 J2 **Pokrovsk** Russia
91 D2 **Pokrovskoye** Russia
138 A1 **Polacca** U.S.A.
103 D1 **Poland** *country* Europe
88 C2 **Polatsk** Belarus
61 C2 **Polewali** Indon.
118 B2 **Poli** Cameroon
102 C1 **Police** Pol.
109 C2 **Policoro** Italy
105 D2 **Poligny** France
64 B1 **Polillo Islands** Phil.
90 B1 **Polis'ke (abandoned)** Ukr.
103 D1 **Polkowice** Pol.
109 C3 **Pollino, Monte** *mt.* Italy
91 D2 **Polohy** Ukr.
123 C1 **Polokwane** S. Africa
123 D1 **Polokwane** *r.* S. Africa
90 B1 **Polonne** Ukr.
134 D1 **Polson** U.S.A.
91 C2 **Poltava** Ukr.
66 B2 **Poltavka** Russia
91 D2 **Poltavskaya** Russia
88 C2 **Põlva** Estonia
111 B2 **Polygyros** Greece
106 B2 **Pombal** Port.
102 C1 **Pomeranian Bay** Ger./Pol.
108 B2 **Pomezia** Italy
92 I2 **Pomokaira** *reg.* Fin.
110 C2 **Pomorie** Bulg.
Pomorska, Zatoka *b.* Ger./Pol. *see* **Pomeranian Bay**
155 D1 **Pompéu** Brazil
139 D1 **Ponca City** U.S.A.
147 D3 **Ponce** Puerto Rico
127 F2 **Pond Inlet** Can.
106 B1 **Ponferrada** Spain
117 A4 **Pongo** *watercourse* South Sudan
123 D2 **Pongola** *r.* S. Africa
128 C2 **Ponoka** Can.
84 D5 **Ponta Delgada** Arquipélago dos Açores
154 B3 **Ponta Grossa** Brazil
154 C1 **Pontalina** Brazil
105 D2 **Pont-à-Mousson** France
105 D2 **Pontarlier** France
102 B2 **Pontcharra** France
142 B2 **Pontchartrain, Lake** U.S.A.
106 B2 **Ponte de Sor** Port.
129 D3 **Ponteix** Can.
150 C3 **Pontes e Lacerda** Brazil
106 B1 **Pontevedra** Spain
140 B2 **Pontiac** *IL* U.S.A.
140 C2 **Pontiac** *MI* U.S.A.
61 B2 **Pontianak** Indon.
104 B2 **Pontivy** France
151 C1 **Pontoetoe** Suriname
129 E2 **Ponton** Can.
99 B3 **Pontypool** U.K.
108 B2 **Ponziane, Isole** *is* Italy
99 C3 **Poole** U.K.
Poona India *see* **Pune**
52 B2 **Pooncarie** Austr.
152 B2 **Poopó, Lago de** *l.* Bol.
150 A1 **Popayán** Col.
83 I2 **Popigay** *r.* Russia
52 B2 **Popiltah** Austr.
129 E2 **Poplar** *r.* Can.
137 E3 **Poplar Bluff** U.S.A.
118 B3 **Popokabaka** Dem. Rep. Congo
110 C2 **Popovo** Bulg.
103 E2 **Poprad** Slovakia
151 D3 **Porangatu** Brazil
74 A2 **Porbandar** India
126 B2 **Porcupine** *r.* Can./U.S.A.
108 B1 **Poreč** Croatia
54 B2 **Porirua** N.Z.
88 C2 **Porkhov** Russia
104 B2 **Pornic** France
83 K3 **Poronaysk** Russia
111 B3 **Poros** Greece
93 E4 **Porsgrunn** Norway
97 C1 **Portadown** U.K.
97 D1 **Portaferry** U.K.
140 B2 **Portage** U.S.A.
129 E3 **Portage la Prairie** Can.
128 B3 **Port Alberni** Can.
106 B2 **Portalegre** Port.
139 C2 **Portales** U.S.A.
128 A2 **Port Alexander** U.S.A.
128 B2 **Port Alice** Can.
134 B1 **Port Angeles** U.S.A.
51 D4 **Port Arthur** Austr.
139 E3 **Port Arthur** U.S.A.
96 A3 **Port Askaig** U.K.
52 A2 **Port Augusta** Austr.
147 C3 **Port-au-Prince** Haiti
131 E1 **Port aux Choix** Can.
73 D3 **Port Blair** India
52 B3 **Port Campbell** Austr.
54 B3 **Port Chalmers** N.Z.
143 D3 **Port Charlotte** U.S.A.
147 C3 **Port-de-Paix** Haiti
128 A2 **Port Edward** Can.
155 D1 **Porteirinha** Brazil
151 C2 **Portel** Brazil
130 B2 **Port Elgin** Can.
123 C3 **Port Elizabeth** S. Africa
96 A3 **Port Ellen** U.K.
98 A1 **Port Erin** Isle of Man
122 A3 **Porterville** S. Africa
135 C3 **Porterville** U.S.A.
52 B3 **Port Fairy** Austr.
54 C1 **Port Fitzroy** N.Z.
118 A3 **Port-Gentil** Gabon
115 C4 **Port Harcourt** Nigeria
128 B2 **Port Hardy** Can.
Port Harrison Can. *see* **Inukjuak**
131 D2 **Port Hawkesbury** Can.
50 A2 **Port Hedland** Austr.
99 A2 **Porthmadog** U.K.
131 E1 **Port Hope Simpson** Can.
140 C2 **Port Huron** U.S.A.
106 B2 **Portimão** Port.
53 C2 **Portland** *N.S.W.* Austr.

52 B3 **Portland** *Vic.* Austr.
141 E2 **Portland** *ME* U.S.A.
134 B1 **Portland** *OR* U.S.A.
128 A2 **Portland Canal** *inlet* Can.
97 C2 **Portlaoise** Ireland
139 D3 **Port Lavaca** U.S.A.
52 A2 **Port Lincoln** Austr.
114 A4 **Port Loko** Sierra Leone
113 K9 **Port Louis** Mauritius
53 D2 **Port Macquarie** Austr.
128 B2 **Port McNeill** Can.
131 D2 **Port-Menier** Can.
59 D3 **Port Moresby** P.N.G.
122 A2 **Port Nolloth** S. Africa
Port-Nouveau-Québec Can. *see* **Kangiqsualujjuaq**
Porto Port. *see* **Oporto**
150 B2 **Porto Acre** Brazil
152 C4 **Porto Alegre** Brazil
151 C3 **Porto Artur** Brazil
151 C3 **Porto dos Gaúchos Óbidos** Brazil
150 C3 **Porto Esperidião** Brazil
108 B2 **Portoferraio** Italy
96 A1 **Port of Ness** U.K.
151 D2 **Porto Franco** Brazil
147 D3 **Port of Spain** Trin. and Tob.
108 B1 **Portogruaro** Italy
108 B2 **Portomaggiore** Italy
154 B2 **Porto Mendes** Brazil
152 C3 **Porto Murtinho** Brazil
151 D3 **Porto Nacional** Brazil
114 C4 **Porto-Novo** Benin
154 B2 **Porto Primavera, Represa** *resr* Brazil
155 E1 **Porto Seguro** Brazil
108 B2 **Porto Tolle** Italy
108 A2 **Porto Torres** *Sardinia* Italy
105 D3 **Porto-Vecchio** *Corsica* France
150 B2 **Porto Velho** Brazil
150 A2 **Portoviejo** Ecuador
52 B3 **Port Phillip Bay** Austr.
52 A2 **Port Pirie** Austr.
96 A2 **Portree** U.K.
128 B3 **Port Renfrew** Can.
97 C1 **Portrush** U.K.
116 B1 **Port Said** Egypt
143 C3 **Port St Joe** U.S.A.
123 C3 **Port St Johns** S. Africa
123 D3 **Port Shepstone** S. Africa
99 C3 **Portsmouth** U.K.
141 E2 **Portsmouth** *NH* U.S.A.
140 C3 **Portsmouth** *OH* U.S.A.
141 D3 **Portsmouth** *VA* U.S.A.
97 C1 **Portstewart** U.K.
116 B3 **Port Sudan** Sudan
142 C3 **Port Sulphur** U.S.A.
99 B3 **Port Talbot** U.K.
106 B2 **Portugal** *country* Europe
97 B2 **Portumna** Ireland
105 C3 **Port-Vendres** France
48 F4 **Port Vila** Vanuatu
93 I3 **Porvoo** Fin.
152 C3 **Posadas** Arg.
89 E2 **Poshekhon'ye** Russia
92 I2 **Posio** Fin.
58 C3 **Poso** Indon.
151 D3 **Posse** Brazil
101 E2 **Pößneck** Ger.
139 C2 **Post** U.S.A.
Poste-de-la-Baleine Can. *see* **Kuujjuarapik**
122 B2 **Postmasburg** S. Africa
109 C2 **Posušje** Bos. & Herz.
139 E1 **Poteau** U.S.A.
109 C2 **Potenza** Italy
151 D2 **Poti** *r.* Brazil
81 C1 **Poti** Georgia
115 D3 **Potiskum** Nigeria
141 D3 **Potomac, South Branch** *r.* U.S.A.
152 B2 **Potosí** Bol.
64 B1 **Pototan** Phil.
138 C3 **Potrero del Llano** Mex.
101 F1 **Potsdam** Ger.
141 E2 **Potsdam** U.S.A.
141 D2 **Pottstown** U.S.A.
141 D2 **Pottsville** U.S.A.
131 E2 **Pouch Cove** Can.
141 E2 **Poughkeepsie** U.S.A.
98 B2 **Poulton-le-Fylde** U.K.
155 C2 **Pouso Alegre** Brazil
63 B2 **Poŭthĭsăt** Cambodia
103 D2 **Považská Bystrica** Slovakia
109 C2 **Povlen** *mt.* Serbia
106 B1 **Póvoa de Varzim** Port.
136 B2 **Powell** U.S.A.
135 D3 **Powell, Lake** *resr* U.S.A.
128 B3 **Powell River** Can.
154 B1 **Poxoréo** Brazil
71 B3 **Poyang** China
71 B3 **Poyang Hu** *l.* China
109 D2 **Požarevac** Serbia
145 C2 **Poza Rica** Mex.
109 C1 **Požega** Croatia
109 D2 **Požega** Serbia
79 D2 **Pozm Tīāb** Iran
103 D1 **Poznań** Pol.
106 C2 **Pozoblanco** Spain
108 B2 **Pozzuoli** Italy
60 B2 **Prabumulih** Indon.
102 C2 **Prachatice** Czech Rep.
63 A2 **Prachuap Khiri Khan** Thai.
155 E1 **Prado** Brazil
102 C1 **Prague** Czech Rep.
Praha Czech Rep. *see* **Prague**
112 C5 **Praia** Cape Verde
139 C2 **Prairie Dog Town Fork** *r.* U.S.A.
140 A2 **Prairie du Chien** U.S.A.
60 A1 **Prapat** Indon.
154 C1 **Prata** Brazil
105 E3 **Prato** Italy
137 D3 **Pratt** U.S.A.
61 C2 **Praya** Indon.
63 B2 **Preăh Vihéar** Cambodia
89 F2 **Prechistoye** Russia
129 D2 **Preeceville** Can.
88 C2 **Preiļi** Latvia
53 C2 **Premer** Austr.
105 C2 **Prémery** France
101 F1 **Premnitz** Ger.
102 C1 **Prenzlau** Ger.
63 A2 **Preparis Island** Cocos Is
63 A2 **Preparis North Channel** Cocos Is
63 A2 **Preparis South Channel** Cocos Is
103 D2 **Přerov** Czech Rep.
138 A2 **Prescott** U.S.A.
109 D2 **Preševo** Serbia
152 B3 **Presidencia Roque Sáenz Peña** Arg.
151 D2 **Presidente Dutra** Brazil
154 B2 **Presidente Epitácio** Brazil
64 B2 **Presidente Manuel A Roxas** Phil.
154 B2 **Presidente Prudente** Brazil
138 C3 **Presidio** U.S.A.
103 E2 **Prešov** Slovakia
141 F1 **Presque Isle** U.S.A.
101 F2 **Pressel** Ger.
98 B2 **Preston** U.K.
134 D2 **Preston** U.S.A.
96 B3 **Prestwick** U.K.
155 C1 **Preto** *r.* Brazil
123 C2 **Pretoria** S. Africa
111 B3 **Preveza** Greece
63 B2 **Prey Vêng** Cambodia
109 C2 **Priboj** Serbia
135 D3 **Price** U.S.A.
88 B3 **Prienai** Lith.
122 B2 **Prieska** S. Africa
103 D2 **Prievidza** Slovakia
109 C2 **Prijedor** Bos. & Herz.
Prikaspiyskaya Nizmennost' *lowland* Kazakh./Russia *see* **Caspian Lowland**
109 D2 **Prilep** Macedonia
91 D2 **Primorsko-Akhtarsk** Russia
129 D2 **Primrose Lake** Can.
129 D2 **Prince Albert** Can.
122 B3 **Prince Albert** S. Africa
126 D2 **Prince Albert Peninsula** Can.
122 B3 **Prince Albert Road** S. Africa
126 C2 **Prince Alfred, Cape** Can.
122 A3 **Prince Alfred Hamlet** S. Africa
127 F2 **Prince Charles Island** Can.
55 E2 **Prince Charles Mountains** Antarctica
131 D2 **Prince Edward Island** *prov.* Can.
113 I11 **Prince Edward Islands** Indian Ocean
128 B2 **Prince George** Can.
126 E2 **Prince of Wales Island** Can.
128 A2 **Prince of Wales Island** U.S.A.
126 D2 **Prince of Wales Strait** Can.
126 D1 **Prince Patrick Island** Can.
126 E2 **Prince Regent Inlet** *sea chan.* Can.
128 A2 **Prince Rupert** Can.
51 D1 **Princess Charlotte Bay** Austr.
128 B2 **Princess Royal Island** Can.
128 B3 **Princeton** Can.
134 B2 **Prineville** U.S.A.
90 B1 **Pripet** *r.* Belarus/Ukr.
90 A1 **Pripet Marshes** Belarus/Ukr.
109 D2 **Prishtinë** Kosovo
Priština Kosovo *see* **Prishtinë**
101 F1 **Pritzwalk** Ger.
109 C2 **Privlaka** Croatia
89 F2 **Privolzhsk** Russia
109 D2 **Prizren** Kosovo
151 C1 **Professor van Blommestein Meer** *resr* Suriname
145 D2 **Progreso** Mex.
81 C1 **Prokhladnyy** Russia
109 D2 **Prokuplje** Serbia
87 D4 **Proletarskoye Vodokhranilishche** *l.* Russia
126 C3 **Prophet** *r.* Can.
128 B2 **Prophet River** Can.
51 D2 **Proserpine** Austr.
89 E3 **Protvino** Russia
110 C2 **Provadia** Bulg.
141 E2 **Providence** U.S.A.
146 B3 **Providencia, Isla de** *i.* Caribbean Sea
83 N2 **Provideniya** Russia
135 D2 **Provo** U.S.A.
129 C2 **Provost** Can.
154 B3 **Prudentópolis** Brazil
126 B2 **Prudhoe Bay** U.S.A.
100 C2 **Prüm** Ger.
105 D3 **Prunelli-di-Fiumorbo** *Corsic* France
103 E1 **Pruszków** Pol.
110 C1 **Prut** *r.* Europe
91 C1 **Pryluky** Ukr.
91 D2 **Prymors'k** Ukr.
139 D1 **Pryor** U.S.A.
Prypyats' *r.* Belarus *see* **Pripe**

103 E2 Przemyśl Pol.
111 C3 Psara i. Greece
81 C1 Psebay Russia
91 D3 Pshekha r. Russia
88 C2 Pskov Russia
88 C2 Pskov Russia
88 C2 Pskov, Lake Estonia/Russia
111 B2 Ptolemaïda Greece
150 A2 Ptuj Slovenia
150 A2 Pucallpa Peru
71 B3 Pucheng China
103 D1 Puck Pol.
92 I2 Pudasjärvi Fin.
86 C2 Pudozh Russia
   Puducherri India see
   Puducherry
73 B3 Puducherry India
145 C3 Puebla Mex.
136 C3 Pueblo U.S.A.
153 B4 Puelén Arg.
106 C2 Puente Genil Spain
153 A5 Puerto Aisén Chile
152 B2 Puerto Alegre Bol.
145 C4 Puerto Ángel Mex.
146 B4 Puerto Armuelles Panama
150 B1 Puerto Ayacucho Venez.
146 B3 Puerto Cabezas Nic.
150 B1 Puerto Carreño Col.
153 A5 Puerto Cisnes Chile
144 A2 Puerto Cortés Mex.
145 C3 Puerto Escondido Mex.
152 B2 Puerto Frey Bol.
150 B1 Puerto Inírida Col.
152 B2 Puerto Isabel Bol.
150 A2 Puerto Leguizamo Col.
144 A2 Puerto Libertad Mex.
146 B3 Puerto Limón Costa Rica
106 C2 Puertollano Spain
153 B5 Puerto Madryn Arg.
150 B3 Puerto Maldonado Peru
153 A5 Puerto Montt Chile
153 A6 Puerto Natales Chile
150 B1 Puerto Nuevo Col.
144 A1 Puerto Peñasco Mex.
152 C3 Puerto Pinasco Para.
147 C3 Puerto Plata Dom. Rep.
150 A2 Puerto Portillo Peru
150 A2 Puerto Princesa Phil.
147 D3 Puerto Rico terr. West Indies
158 B3 Puerto Rico Trench
         Caribbean Sea
146 A3 Puerto San José Guat.
153 B6 Puerto Santa Cruz Arg.
144 B2 Puerto Vallarta Mex.
87 C3 Pugachev Russia
74 B2 Pugal India
146 A3 Pukaki, Lake N.Z.
129 D2 Pukatawagan Can.
65 B1 Pukchin N. Korea
65 B1 Pukch'ŏng N. Korea
54 B1 Pukekohe N.Z.
65 B1 Puksubaek-san mt. N. Korea
108 B2 Pula Croatia
108 A3 Pula Sardinia Italy
152 B3 Pulacayo Bol.
77 C3 Pul-e Khumri Afgh.
92 I3 Pulkkila Fin.
134 C1 Pullman U.S.A.
64 B1 Pulog, Mount Phil.
150 A2 Puná, Isla i. Ecuador
54 B2 Punakaiki N.Z.
123 C1 Punda Maria S. Africa
73 B3 Pune India
65 B1 P'ungsan N. Korea
121 C2 Púngué r. Moz.
153 B4 Punta Alta Arg.
153 A6 Punta Arenas Chile
146 B3 Puntarenas Costa Rica
117 C4 Puntland reg. Somalia

150 A1 Punto Fijo Venez.
92 I3 Puolanka Fin.
82 G2 Pur r. Russia
75 C3 Puri India
100 B1 Purmerend Neth.
75 C2 Purnia India
75 C2 Puruliya India
150 B2 Purus r. Brazil/Peru
61 B2 Purwakarta Indon.
65 B1 Puryŏng N. Korea
        Pusan S. Korea see Busan
88 C2 Pushkinskiye Gory Russia
88 C2 Pustoshka Russia
62 A1 Putao Myanmar
71 B3 Putian China
        Puting China see De'an
61 C2 Puting, Tanjung pt Indon.
101 F1 Putlitz Ger.
58 A2 Putrajaya Malaysia
102 C1 Puttgarden Ger.
150 A2 Putumayo r. Col.
61 C1 Putusibau Indon.
91 C1 Putyvl' Ukr.
127 F2 Puvirnituq Can.
70 B2 Puyang China
104 C3 Puylaurens France
99 A2 Pwllheli U.K.
63 A2 Pyapon Myanmar
82 G2 Pyasina r. Russia
87 D4 Pyatigorsk Russia
91 C2 P"yatykhatky Ukr.
62 A2 Pyè Myanmar
88 C3 Pyetrykaw Belarus
93 H3 Pyhäjärvi l. Fin.
92 H3 Pyhäjoki r. Fin.
92 I3 Pyhäsalmi Fin.
62 A2 Pyinmana Myanmar
65 B2 Pyŏksŏng N. Korea
65 B2 P'yŏnggang N. Korea
65 B2 P'yŏngsan N. Korea
65 B2 P'yŏngyang N. Korea
135 C2 Pyramid Lake U.S.A.
80 B3 Pyramids of Giza tourist site
        Egypt
107 D1 Pyrenees mts Europe
111 B3 Pyrgos Greece
91 C1 Pyryatyn Ukr.
103 C1 Pyrzyce Pol.
88 C2 Pytalovo Russia
111 B3 Pyxaria mt. Greece

Q

127 G1 Qaanaaq Greenland
123 C3 Qacha's Nek Lesotho
68 C2 Qaidam Pendi basin China
74 A1 Qalāt Afgh.
78 B2 Qal'at Bīshah Saudi Arabia
129 E1 Qamanirjuaq Lake Can.
        Qamanittuaq Can. see
        Baker Lake
79 C3 Qamar, Ghubbat al b. Yemen
78 B3 Qam Hadīl Saudi Arabia
77 C3 Qarshi Uzbek.
78 B2 Qaryat al Ulyā Saudi Arabia
127 H2 Qasigiannguit Greenland
79 D2 Qaşr-e Qand Iran
81 C2 Qaşr-e Shīrīn Iran
127 H2 Qassimiut Greenland
78 B3 Qa'tabah Yemen
79 C2 Qatar country Asia
116 A2 Qattara Depression Egypt
81 C1 Qazax Azer.
81 C2 Qazvīn Iran
127 H2 Qeqertarsuaq i. Greenland
127 H2 Qeqertarsuatsiaat Greenland

127 H2 Qeqertarsuup Tunua b.
        Greenland
79 C2 Qeshm Iran
70 A3 Qianjiang Chongqing China
70 B2 Qianjiang Hubei China
65 A1 Qian Shan mts China
70 C2 Qidong China
68 B2 Qiemo China
71 A3 Qijiang China
68 C2 Qijiaojing China
127 G2 Qikiqtarjuaq Can.
74 A2 Qila Ladgasht Pak.
68 C2 Qilian Shan mts China
127 I2 Qillak i. Greenland
70 B3 Qimen China
127 G1 Qimusseriarsuaq b.
        Greenland
116 B2 Qinā Egypt
70 C2 Qingdao China
68 C2 Qinghai Hu salt l. China
68 C2 Qinghai Nanshan mts China
70 A2 Qingyang China
71 B3 Qingyuan Guangdong China
65 A1 Qingyuan Liaoning China
        Qingzang Gaoyuan plat.
        China see Tibet, Plateau of
70 B2 Qingzhou China
70 B2 Qinhuangdao China
70 A2 Qin Ling mts China
        Qinting China see Lianhua
70 B2 Qinyang China
71 A3 Qinzhou China
71 B4 Qionghai China
68 C2 Qionglai Shan mts China
71 B4 Qiongshan China
69 E1 Qiqihar China
79 C2 Qīr Iran
66 B1 Qitaihe China
70 B2 Qixian China
        Qogir Feng mt. China/Pak.
        see K2
81 D2 Qom Iran
        Qomolangma Feng mt. China/
        Nepal see Everest, Mount
76 B2 Qo'ng'irot Uzbek.
        Qoqek China see Tacheng
77 C2 Qo'qon Uzbek.
76 B2 Qoraqalpog'iston Uzbek.
100 C1 Quakenbrück Ger.
63 B2 Quang Ngai Vietnam
63 B2 Quang Tri Vietnam
71 B3 Quanzhou Fujian China
71 B3 Quanzhou Guangxi China
108 A3 Quartu Sant'Elena Sardinia
        Italy
138 A2 Quartzsite U.S.A.
81 C1 Quba Azer.
53 C3 Queanbeyan Austr.
131 C2 Québec Can.
130 C1 Québec prov. Can.
101 E2 Quedlinburg Ger.
128 A2 Queen Charlotte Can.
128 A2 Queen Charlotte Sound
        sea chan. Can.
128 B2 Queen Charlotte Strait Can.
126 D1 Queen Elizabeth Islands Can.
55 A1 Queen Elizabeth Land reg.
        Antarctica
126 E2 Queen Maud Gulf Can.
55 B2 Queen Maud Land reg.
        Antarctica
55 N1 Queen Maud Mountains
        Antarctica
52 B1 Queensland state Austr.
51 D4 Queenstown Austr.
54 A3 Queenstown N.Z.
123 C3 Queenstown S. Africa
121 C3 Quelimane Moz.

138 B2 **Quemado** U.S.A.
154 B2 **Querência do Norte** Brazil
145 B2 **Querétaro** Mex.
101 E2 **Querfurt** Ger.
128 B2 **Quesnel** Can.
128 B2 **Quesnel Lake** Can.
74 A1 **Quetta** Pak.
64 A2 **Quezon** Phil.
64 B1 **Quezon City** Phil.
120 A2 **Quibala** Angola
150 A1 **Quibdó** Col.
104 B2 **Quiberon** France
104 C3 **Quillan** France
153 C4 **Quilmes** Arg.
Quilon India *see* **Kollam**
51 D2 **Quilpie** Austr.
153 A4 **Quilpué** Chile
120 A1 **Quimbele** Angola
152 B3 **Quimilí** Arg.
104 B2 **Quimper** France
104 B2 **Quimperlé** France
137 E3 **Quincy** *IL* U.S.A.
141 E2 **Quincy** *MA* U.S.A.
107 C1 **Quinto** Spain
121 D2 **Quionga** Moz.
53 D2 **Quirindi** Austr.
120 A2 **Quitapa** Angola
150 A2 **Quito** Ecuador
151 E2 **Quixadá** Brazil
71 A3 **Qujing** China
52 A2 **Quorn** Austr.
79 C2 **Qurayat** Oman
77 C3 **Qŭrghonteppa** Tajik.
63 B2 **Quy Nhơn** Vietnam
71 B3 **Quzhou** China

R

103 D2 **Raab** *r.* Austria
92 H3 **Raahe** Fin.
100 C1 **Raalte** Neth.
61 C2 **Raas** *i.* Indon.
61 C2 **Raba** Indon.
114 B1 **Rabat** Morocco
48 E3 **Rabaul** P.N.G.
78 A2 **Rābigh** Saudi Arabia
131 E2 **Race, Cape** Can.
142 B3 **Raceland** U.S.A.
63 B3 **Rach Gia** Vietnam
140 B2 **Racine** U.S.A.
78 B3 **Radā'** Yemen
110 C1 **Rădăuți** Romania
140 B3 **Radcliff** U.S.A.
74 B2 **Radhanpur** India
130 C1 **Radisson** Can.
103 E1 **Radom** Pol.
103 D1 **Radomsko** Pol.
90 B1 **Radomyshl'** Ukr.
109 D2 **Radoviš** Macedonia
88 B2 **Radviliškis** Lith.
78 A2 **Raḑwá, Jabal** *mt.* Saudi Arabia
90 B1 **Radyvyliv** Ukr.
75 C2 **Rae Bareli** India
100 C2 **Raeren** Belgium
54 C1 **Raetihi** N.Z.
152 B4 **Rafaela** Arg.
118 C2 **Rafaï** C.A.R.
78 B2 **Rafḩā'** Saudi Arabia
79 C1 **Rafsanjān** Iran
64 B2 **Ragang, Mount** *vol.* Phil.
109 B3 **Ragusa** *Sicily* Italy
59 C3 **Raha** Indon.
88 D3 **Rahachow** Belarus
74 B2 **Rahimyar Khan** Pak.
109 D2 **Rahovec** Kosovo
73 B3 **Raichur** India
75 C2 **Raigarh** India
128 C2 **Rainbow Lake** Can.
134 B1 **Rainier, Mount** *vol.* U.S.A.
130 A2 **Rainy Lake** Can./U.S.A.
129 E3 **Rainy River** Can.
75 C2 **Raipur** India
93 H3 **Raisio** Fin.
73 C3 **Rajahmundry** India
61 C1 **Rajang** *r. Sarawak* Malaysia
74 B2 **Rajanpur** Pak.
73 B4 **Rajapalayam** India
74 B2 **Rajasthan Canal** India
74 B2 **Rajgarh** India
74 B2 **Rajkot** India
74 B2 **Rajpur** India
75 C2 **Rajshahi** Bangl.
54 B2 **Rakaia** *r.* N.Z.
90 A2 **Rakhiv** Ukr.
91 D1 **Rakitnoye** Russia
88 C2 **Rakke** Estonia
88 C2 **Rakvere** Estonia
143 E1 **Raleigh** U.S.A.
48 F2 **Ralik Chain** *is* Marshall Is
117 B4 **Ramciel** S. Sudan
74 B2 **Ramgarh** India
81 C2 **Rāmhormoz** Iran
Ramlat Rabyānah *des.* Libya *see* **Rebiana Sand Sea**
110 C1 **Râmnicu Sărat** Romania
110 B1 **Râmnicu Vâlcea** Romania
89 E3 **Ramon'** Russia
123 C1 **Ramotswa** Botswana
75 B2 **Rampur** India
62 A2 **Ramree Island** Myanmar
98 A1 **Ramsey** Isle of Man
99 D3 **Ramsgate** U.K.
75 C2 **Ranaghat** India
61 C1 **Ranau** *Sabah* Malaysia
153 A4 **Rancagua** Chile
75 C2 **Ranchi** India
93 F4 **Randers** Denmark
54 B2 **Rangiora** N.Z.
54 C1 **Rangitaiki** *r.* N.Z.
62 A2 **Rangoon** Myanmar
75 C2 **Rangpur** Bangl.
129 E1 **Rankin Inlet** Can.
53 C2 **Rankin's Springs** Austr.
96 B2 **Rannoch Moor** *moorland* U.K.
63 A3 **Ranong** Thai.
59 C3 **Ransiki** Indon.
61 C2 **Rantaupanjang** Indon.
60 A1 **Rantauprapat** Indon.
92 I2 **Ranua** Fin.
78 B2 **Ranyah, Wādī** *watercourse* Saudi Arabia
49 I4 **Rapa** *i.* Fr. Polynesia
136 C2 **Rapid City** U.S.A.
88 B2 **Rapla** Estonia
74 A2 **Rapur** India
49 H4 **Rarotonga** *i.* Cook Is
153 B5 **Rasa, Punta** *pt* Arg.
79 C2 **Ra's al Khaymah** U.A.E.
117 B3 **Ras Dejen** *mt.* Eth.
88 B2 **Raseiniai** Lith.
81 C2 **Rasht** Iran
74 A2 **Ras Koh** *mt.* Pak.
88 C2 **Rasony** Belarus
87 D3 **Rasskazovo** Russia
79 C2 **Ras Tannūrah** Saudi Arabia
101 D1 **Rastede** Ger.
93 F3 **Rätan** Sweden
74 B2 **Ratangarh** India
63 A2 **Rat Buri** Thai.
62 A1 **Rathedaung** Myanmar
101 F1 **Rathenow** Ger.
97 C1 **Rathlin Island** U.K.
74 B2 **Ratlam** India
73 B3 **Ratnagiri** India
73 C4 **Ratnapura** Sri Lanka
90 A1 **Ratne** Ukr.
138 C1 **Raton** U.S.A.
96 D2 **Rattray Head** U.K.
101 E1 **Ratzeburg** Ger.
92 □B2 **Raufarhöfn** Iceland
54 C1 **Raukumara Range** *mts* N.Z.
93 H3 **Rauma** Fin.
61 C2 **Raung, Gunung** *vol.* Indon.
75 C2 **Raurkela** India
134 D1 **Ravalli** U.S.A.
81 C2 **Ravānsar** Iran
108 B2 **Ravenna** Italy
102 B2 **Ravensburg** Ger.
74 B1 **Ravi** *r.* Pak.
74 B1 **Rawalpindi** Pak.
103 D1 **Rawicz** Pol.
50 B3 **Rawlinna** Austr.
136 B2 **Rawlins** U.S.A.
153 B5 **Rawson** Arg.
73 C3 **Rayagada** India
69 E1 **Raychikhinsk** Russia
78 B3 **Raydah** Yemen
87 E3 **Rayevskiy** Russia
134 B1 **Raymond** U.S.A.
53 D2 **Raymond Terrace** Austr.
139 D3 **Raymondville** U.S.A.
145 C2 **Rayón** Mex.
63 B2 **Rayong** Thai.
78 A2 **Rayyis** Saudi Arabia
104 B2 **Raz, Pointe du** *pt* France
81 C2 **Razāzah, Buḩayrat ar** *l.* Iraq
110 C2 **Razgrad** Bulg.
110 C2 **Razim, Lacul** *lag.* Romania
110 B2 **Razlog** Bulg.
104 B2 **Ré, Île de** *i.* France
99 C3 **Reading** U.K.
141 D2 **Reading** U.S.A.
115 E2 **Rebiana Sand Sea** *des.* Libya
66 D1 **Rebun-tō** *i.* Japan
50 B3 **Recherche, Archipelago of the** *is* Austr.
89 D3 **Rechytsa** Belarus
151 E2 **Recife** Brazil
123 C3 **Recife, Cape** S. Africa
100 C2 **Recklinghausen** Ger.
152 C3 **Reconquista** Arg.
142 B2 **Red** *r.* U.S.A.
131 E1 **Red Bay** Can.
135 B2 **Red Bluff** U.S.A.
98 C1 **Redcar** U.K.
129 C2 **Redcliff** Can.
52 B2 **Red Cliffs** Austr.
128 C2 **Red Deer** Can.
126 D3 **Red Deer** *r.* Can.
129 D2 **Red Deer Lake** Can.
134 B2 **Redding** U.S.A.
99 C2 **Redditch** U.K.
137 D2 **Redfield** U.S.A.
130 A1 **Red Lake** Can.
137 E1 **Red Lakes** U.S.A.
134 E1 **Red Lodge** U.S.A.
134 B2 **Redmond** U.S.A.
137 D2 **Red Oak** U.S.A.
106 B2 **Redondo** Port.
159 B2 **Red Sea** Africa/Asia
128 B1 **Redstone** *r.* Can.
100 B1 **Reduzum** Neth.
137 E2 **Red Wing** U.S.A.
137 D2 **Redwood Falls** U.S.A.
97 C2 **Ree, Lough** *l.* Ireland
134 B2 **Reedsport** U.S.A.
54 B2 **Reefton** N.Z.
102 C2 **Regen** Ger.
155 E1 **Regência** Brazil
102 C2 **Regensburg** Ger.
114 C2 **Reggane** Alg.
109 C3 **Reggio di Calabria** Italy

108 B2 **Reggio nell'Emilia** Italy
110 B1 **Reghin** Romania
129 D2 **Regina** Can.
122 A1 **Rehoboth** Namibia
101 F2 **Reichenbach im Vogtland** Ger.
143 E1 **Reidsville** U.S.A.
99 C3 **Reigate** U.K.
105 C2 **Reims** France
101 E1 **Reinbek** Ger.
129 D2 **Reindeer** *r.* Can.
129 E2 **Reindeer Island** Can.
129 D2 **Reindeer Lake** Can.
92 F2 **Reine** Norway
100 C3 **Reinsfeld** Ger.
123 C2 **Reitz** S. Africa
122 B2 **Reivilo** S. Africa
129 D1 **Reliance** Can.
107 D2 **Relizane** Alg.
79 C2 **Remeshk** Iran
105 D2 **Remiremont** France
100 C2 **Remscheid** Ger.
102 B1 **Rendsburg** Ger.
141 D1 **Renfrew** Can.
60 B2 **Rengat** Indon.
90 B2 **Reni** Ukr.
52 B2 **Renmark** Austr.
100 D2 **Rennerod** Ger.
104 B2 **Rennes** France
129 D1 **Rennie Lake** Can.
108 B2 **Reno** *r.* Italy
135 C3 **Reno** U.S.A.
70 A3 **Renshou** China
140 B2 **Rensselaer** U.S.A.
75 C2 **Renukut** India
54 B2 **Renwick** N.Z.
58 C3 **Reo** Indon.
136 D3 **Republican** *r.* U.S.A.
127 F2 **Repulse Bay** Can.
150 A2 **Requena** Peru
107 C2 **Requena** Spain
154 B2 **Reserva** Brazil
152 C3 **Resistencia** Arg.
110 B1 **Reșița** Romania
126 E2 **Resolute** Can.
127 G2 **Resolution Island** Can.
105 C2 **Rethel** France
111 B3 **Rethymno** Greece
113 K9 **Réunion** *terr.* Indian Ocean
107 D1 **Reus** Spain
102 B2 **Reutlingen** Ger.
128 C2 **Revelstoke** Can.
144 A3 **Revillagigedo, Islas** *is* Mex.
128 A2 **Revillagigedo Island** U.S.A.
75 C2 **Rewa** India
134 D2 **Rexburg** U.S.A.
92 □A3 **Reykjanestá** *pt* Iceland
92 □A3 **Reykjavík** Iceland
145 C2 **Reynosa** Mex.
88 C2 **Rēzekne** Latvia
Rhein *r.* Ger. *see* **Rhine**
100 C1 **Rheine** Ger.
101 F1 **Rheinsberg** Ger.
Rhin *r.* France *see* **Rhine**
100 C2 **Rhine** *r.* Europe
140 B1 **Rhinelander** U.S.A.
101 F1 **Rhinluch** *marsh* Ger.
101 F1 **Rhinow** Ger.
141 E2 **Rhode Island** *state* U.S.A.
111 C3 **Rhodes** Greece
111 C3 **Rhodes** *i.* Greece
110 B2 **Rhodope Mountains** Bulg./Greece
105 C3 **Rhône** *r.* France/Switz.
Rhuthun U.K. *see* **Ruthin**
98 B2 **Rhyl** U.K.
154 C1 **Rianápolis** Brazil
60 B1 **Riau, Kepulauan** *is* Indon.
106 B1 **Ribadeo** Spain
106 B1 **Ribadesella/Ribeseya** Spain
154 B2 **Ribas do Rio Pardo** Brazil
121 C2 **Ribáuè** Moz.
98 B2 **Ribble** *r.* U.K.
154 C2 **Ribeira** *r.* Brazil
154 C2 **Ribeirão Preto** Brazil
104 C2 **Ribérac** France
152 B2 **Riberalta** Bol.
90 B2 **Rîbnița** Moldova
102 C1 **Ribnitz-Damgarten** Ger.
140 A1 **Rice Lake** U.S.A.
123 D2 **Richards Bay** S. Africa
126 B2 **Richardson Mountains** Can.
135 D3 **Richfield** U.S.A.
134 C1 **Richland** U.S.A.
140 A2 **Richland Center** U.S.A.
53 D2 **Richmond** *N.S.W.* Austr.
51 D2 **Richmond** *Qld* Austr.
54 B2 **Richmond** N.Z.
122 B3 **Richmond** S. Africa
98 C1 **Richmond** U.K.
140 C3 **Richmond** *IN* U.S.A.
140 C3 **Richmond** *KY* U.S.A.
141 D3 **Richmond** *VA* U.S.A.
130 C2 **Rideau Lakes** Can.
135 C3 **Ridgecrest** U.S.A.
102 C1 **Riesa** Ger.
100 D1 **Rieste** Ger.
123 B2 **Riet** *r.* S. Africa
101 D2 **Rietberg** Ger.
108 B2 **Rieti** Italy
136 B3 **Rifle** U.S.A.
88 B2 **Rīga** Latvia
88 B2 **Riga, Gulf of** Estonia/Latvia
134 D2 **Rigby** U.S.A.
131 E1 **Rigolet** Can.
93 H3 **Riihimäki** Fin.
108 B1 **Rijeka** Croatia
134 C2 **Riley** U.S.A.
78 B2 **Rimah, Wādī ar** *watercourse* Saudi Arabia
103 E2 **Rimavská Sobota** Slovakia
128 C2 **Rimbey** Can.
108 B2 **Rimini** Italy
131 D2 **Rimouski** Can.
93 F3 **Ringebu** Norway
93 E4 **Ringkøbing** Denmark
92 G2 **Ringvassøya** *i.* Norway
101 D1 **Rinteln** Ger.
150 A2 **Riobamba** Ecuador
150 B3 **Rio Branco** Brazil
154 C3 **Rio Branco do Sul** Brazil
154 B2 **Rio Brilhante** Brazil
154 C2 **Rio Claro** Brazil
153 B4 **Río Colorado** Arg.
153 B4 **Río Cuarto** Arg.
155 D2 **Rio de Janeiro** Brazil
153 B6 **Río Gallegos** Arg.
153 B6 **Río Grande** Arg.
152 C4 **Rio Grande** Brazil
144 B2 **Río Grande** Mex.
139 D3 **Rio Grande** *r.* Mex./U.S.A.
139 D3 **Rio Grande City** U.S.A.
150 A1 **Ríohacha** Col.
150 A2 **Rioja** Peru
145 D2 **Río Lagartos** Mex.
105 C2 **Riom** France
152 B2 **Río Mulatos** Bol.
154 C3 **Rio Negro** Brazil
155 D1 **Rio Pardo de Minas** Brazil
138 B1 **Rio Rancho** U.S.A.
150 A2 **Río Tigre** Ecuador
154 B1 **Rio Verde** Brazil
145 C2 **Río Verde** Mex.
154 B1 **Rio Verde de Mato Grosso** Brazil
90 C1 **Ripky** Ukr.
98 C2 **Ripley** U.K.
107 D1 **Ripoll** Spain
98 C1 **Ripon** U.K.
66 D1 **Rishiri-tō** *i.* Japan
93 E4 **Risør** Norway
122 B2 **Ritchie** S. Africa
63 A2 **Ritchie's Archipelago** *is* India
134 C1 **Ritzville** U.S.A.
152 B3 **Rivadavia** Arg.
108 B1 **Riva del Garda** Italy
146 B3 **Rivas** Nic.
152 C4 **Rivera** Uru.
129 D2 **Riverhurst** Can.
52 B2 **Riverina** *reg.* Austr.
122 B3 **Riversdale** S. Africa
135 C4 **Riverside** U.S.A.
136 B2 **Riverton** U.S.A.
131 D2 **Riverview** Can.
104 C3 **Rivesaltes** France
131 D2 **Rivière-du-Loup** Can.
90 B1 **Rivne** Ukr.
54 B2 **Riwaka** N.Z.
78 B2 **Riyadh** Saudi Arabia
81 C1 **Rize** Turkey
70 B2 **Rizhao** China
105 C2 **Roanne** France
141 D3 **Roanoke** U.S.A.
143 E1 **Roanoke** *r.* U.S.A.
143 E1 **Roanoke Rapids** U.S.A.
52 A3 **Robe** Austr.
101 F1 **Röbel/Müritz** Ger.
130 C1 **Robert-Bourassa, Réservoir** *resr* Can.
92 H3 **Robertsfors** Sweden
122 A3 **Robertson** S. Africa
114 A4 **Robertsport** Liberia
131 C2 **Roberval** Can.
50 A2 **Robinson Ranges** *hills* Austr.
52 B2 **Robinvale** Austr.
129 D2 **Roblin** Can.
128 C2 **Robson, Mount** Can.
153 C4 **Rocha** Uru.
98 B2 **Rochdale** U.K.
154 B1 **Rochedo** Brazil
100 B2 **Rochefort** Belgium
104 B2 **Rochefort** France
137 E2 **Rochester** *MN* U.S.A.
141 E2 **Rochester** *NH* U.S.A.
141 D2 **Rochester** *NY* U.S.A.
140 B2 **Rockford** U.S.A.
51 E2 **Rockhampton** Austr.
143 D2 **Rock Hill** U.S.A.
50 A3 **Rockingham** Austr.
140 A2 **Rock Island** U.S.A.
136 B1 **Rock Springs** *MT* U.S.A.
139 C3 **Rocksprings** U.S.A.
136 B2 **Rock Springs** *WY* U.S.A.
136 C3 **Rocky Ford** U.S.A.
143 E1 **Rocky Mount** U.S.A.
128 C2 **Rocky Mountain House** Can.
124 G3 **Rocky Mountains** Can./U.S.A.
100 B3 **Rocroi** France
102 C1 **Rødbyhavn** Denmark
131 E1 **Roddickton** Can.
104 C3 **Rodez** France
89 F2 **Rodniki** Russia
Rodos Greece *see* **Rhodes**
Rodos *i.* Greece *see* **Rhodes**
50 A2 **Roebourne** Austr.
50 B1 **Roebuck Bay** Austr.
123 C1 **Roedtan** S. Africa
100 B2 **Roermond** Neth.
100 A2 **Roeselare** Belgium
127 F2 **Roes Welcome Sound** *sea chan.* Can.
142 B1 **Rogers** U.S.A.

Roggeveldberge

122	B3	**Roggeveldberge** esc. S. Africa
92	G2	**Rognan** Norway
134	B2	**Rogue** r. U.S.A.
88	B2	**Roja** Latvia
60	B1	**Rokan** r. Indon.
88	C2	**Rokiškis** Lith.
90	B1	**Rokytne** Ukr.
154	B2	**Rolândia** Brazil
137	E3	**Rolla** U.S.A.
51	D2	**Roma** Austr.
		Roma Italy see Rome
123	C2	**Roma** Lesotho
139	D3	**Roma** U.S.A.
143	E2	**Romain, Cape** U.S.A.
110	C1	**Roman** Romania
59	C3	**Romang, Pulau** i. Indon.
110	B1	**Romania** country Europe
91	C3	**Roman-Kosh** mt. Ukr.
69	D1	**Romanovka** Russia
105	D2	**Rombas** France
64	B1	**Romblon** Phil.
108	B2	**Rome** Italy
143	C2	**Rome** GA U.S.A.
141	D2	**Rome** NY U.S.A.
99	D3	**Romford** U.K.
105	C2	**Romilly-sur-Seine** France
91	C1	**Romny** Ukr.
104	C2	**Romorantin-Lanthenay** France
99	C3	**Romsey** U.K.
96	□	**Ronas Hill** U.K.
151	C3	**Roncador, Serra do** hills Brazil
106	B2	**Ronda** Spain
154	B2	**Rondon** Brazil
154	B1	**Rondonópolis** Brazil
74	B1	**Rondu** Pak.
71	A3	**Rong'an** China
71	A3	**Rongjiang** China
62	A1	**Rongklang Range** mts Myanmar
		Rongmei China see Hefeng
93	F4	**Rønne** Denmark
55	P2	**Ronne Ice Shelf** Antarctica
101	D1	**Ronnenberg** Ger.
100	A2	**Ronse** Belgium
75	B2	**Roorkee** India
100	B2	**Roosendaal** Neth.
135	E2	**Roosevelt** U.S.A.
128	B2	**Roosevelt, Mount** Can.
55	K2	**Roosevelt Sub-glacial Island** Antarctica
104	B3	**Roquefort** France
150	B1	**Roraima, Mount** Guyana
93	F3	**Røros** Norway
153	B4	**Rosario** Arg.
144	A1	**Rosario** Baja California Mex.
144	B2	**Rosario** Sinaloa Mex.
144	B2	**Rosario** Sonora Mex.
151	C3	**Rosário Oeste** Brazil
144	A2	**Rosarito** Mex.
109	C3	**Rosarno** Italy
104	B2	**Roscoff** France
97	B2	**Roscommon** Ireland
97	C2	**Roscrea** Ireland
147	D3	**Roseau** Dominica
137	D1	**Roseau** U.S.A.
134	B2	**Roseburg** U.S.A.
139	D3	**Rosenberg** U.S.A.
101	D1	**Rosengarten** Ger.
102	C2	**Rosenheim** Ger.
129	D2	**Rosetown** Can.
122	A2	**Rosh Pinah** Namibia
110	C2	**Roşiori de Vede** Romania
93	F4	**Roskilde** Denmark
89	D3	**Roslavl'** Russia
109	C3	**Rossano** Italy
97	B1	**Rossan Point** Ireland
55	K1	**Ross Ice Shelf** Antarctica
131	D2	**Rossignol, Lake** Can.
128	C3	**Rossland** Can.
97	C2	**Rosslare** Ireland
114	A3	**Rosso** Maur.
105	D3	**Rosso, Capo** c. Corsica France
99	B3	**Ross-on-Wye** U.K.
91	D1	**Rossosh'** Russia
128	A1	**Ross River** Can.
55	K2	**Ross Sea** Antarctica
92	F2	**Røssvatnet** l. Norway
79	C2	**Rostãq** Iran
129	D2	**Rosthern** Can.
102	C1	**Rostock** Ger.
89	E2	**Rostov** Russia
91	D2	**Rostov-na-Donu** Russia
92	H2	**Rosvik** Sweden
138	C2	**Roswell** U.S.A.
59	D2	**Rota** i. N. Mariana Is
59	C3	**Rote** i. Indon.
101	D1	**Rotenburg (Wümme)** Ger.
102	C2	**Roth** Ger.
98	C1	**Rothbury** U.K.
98	C2	**Rotherham** U.K.
96	B3	**Rothesay** U.K.
53	C2	**Roto** Austr.
105	D3	**Rotondo, Monte** mt. Corsica France
54	C1	**Rotorua** N.Z.
54	C1	**Rotorua, Lake** N.Z.
101	E2	**Rottenbach** Ger.
102	C2	**Rottenmann** Austria
100	B2	**Rotterdam** Neth.
102	B2	**Rottweil** Ger.
49	F3	**Rotuma** i. Fiji
105	C1	**Roubaix** France
104	C2	**Rouen** France
		Roulers Belgium see Roeselare
53	D2	**Round Mountain** Austr.
131	E2	**Round Pond** l. Can.
139	D2	**Round Rock** U.S.A.
134	E1	**Roundup** U.S.A.
96	C1	**Rousay** i. U.K.
130	C2	**Rouyn-Noranda** Can.
92	I2	**Rovaniemi** Fin.
91	D2	**Roven'ki** Russia
91	D2	**Roven'ky** Ukr.
108	B1	**Rovereto** Italy
63	B2	**Rôviěng Tbong** Cambodia
108	B1	**Rovigo** Italy
108	B1	**Rovinj** Croatia
53	C1	**Rowena** Austr.
64	B1	**Roxas** Capiz Phil.
64	B1	**Roxas** Oriental Mindoro Phil.
64	A1	**Roxas** Palawan Phil.
52	A2	**Roxby Downs** Austr.
138	C1	**Roy** U.S.A.
140	B1	**Royale, Isle** i. U.S.A.
99	D3	**Royal Tunbridge Wells** U.K.
104	B2	**Royan** France
99	C2	**Royston** U.K.
90	C2	**Rozdil'na** Ukr.
91	C2	**Rozdol'ne** Ukr.
100	B3	**Rozoy-sur-Serre** France
87	D3	**Rtishchevo** Russia
54	C1	**Ruapehu, Mount** vol. N.Z.
54	A3	**Ruapuke Island** N.Z.
78	B3	**Rub' al Khālī** des. Saudi Arabia
91	D2	**Rubizhne** Ukr.
77	E1	**Rubtsovsk** Russia
135	C2	**Ruby Mountains** U.S.A.
66	C2	**Rudnaya Pristan'** Russia
89	D3	**Rudnya** Russia
76	C1	**Rudnyy** Kazakh.
82	E1	**Rudol'fa, Ostrov** i. Russia
101	E2	**Rudolstadt** Ger.
119	D3	**Rufiji** r. Tanz.
153	B4	**Rufino** Arg.
121	B2	**Rufunsa** Zambia
70	C2	**Rugao** China
99	C2	**Rugby** U.K.
136	C1	**Rugby** U.S.A.
102	C1	**Rügen** i. Ger.
101	E2	**Ruhla** Ger.
88	B2	**Ruhnu** i. Estonia
100	C2	**Ruhr** r. Ger.
71	C3	**Rui'an** China
138	B2	**Ruidoso** U.S.A.
144	B2	**Ruiz** Mex.
119	D3	**Rukwa, Lake** Tanz.
96	A2	**Rum** i. U.K.
109	C1	**Ruma** Serbia
78	B2	**Rumāh** Saudi Arabia
117	A4	**Rumbek** South Sudan
105	D2	**Rumilly** France
50	C1	**Rum Jungle (abandoned)** Austr.
54	B2	**Runanga** N.Z.
98	B2	**Runcorn** U.K.
120	A2	**Rundu** Namibia
68	B2	**Ruoqiang** China
130	C1	**Rupert** r. Can.
130	C1	**Rupert Bay** Can.
121	C2	**Rusape** Zimbabwe
110	C2	**Ruse** Bulg.
77	D3	**Rūshon** Tajik.
136	C2	**Rushville** U.S.A.
53	C3	**Rushworth** Austr.
129	D2	**Russell** Can.
54	B1	**Russell** N.Z.
142	C2	**Russellville** AL U.S.A.
142	B1	**Russellville** AR U.S.A.
140	B3	**Russellville** KY U.S.A.
101	D2	**Rüsselsheim** Ger.
82	F2	**Russia** country Asia/Europe
123	C2	**Rustenburg** S. Africa
142	B2	**Ruston** U.S.A.
98	B2	**Ruthin** U.K.
141	E2	**Rutland** U.S.A.
119	E4	**Ruvuma** r. Moz./Tanz.
79	C2	**Ruweis** U.A.E.
77	C1	**Ruzayevka** Kazakh.
87	D3	**Ruzayevka** Russia
119	C3	**Rwanda** country Africa
89	E3	**Ryazan'** Russia
89	F3	**Ryazhsk** Russia
86	C2	**Rybachiy, Poluostrov** pen. Russia
89	E2	**Rybinsk** Russia
89	E2	**Rybinskoye Vodokhranilishche** resr Russia
103	D1	**Rybnik** Pol.
89	E3	**Rybnoye** Russia
99	D3	**Rye** U.K.
89	D3	**Ryl'sk** Russia
67	C3	**Ryōtsu** Japan
69	E3	**Ryukyu Islands** Japan
103	E1	**Rzeszów** Pol.
89	D2	**Rzhev** Russia

S

79	C2	**Sa'ādatābād** Iran
101	E2	**Saale** r. Ger.
101	E2	**Saalfeld/Saale** Ger.
102	B2	**Saarbrücken** Ger.
88	B2	**Saaremaa** i. Estonia
92	I2	**Saarenkylä** Fin.
93	I3	**Saarijärvi** Fin.
102	B2	**Saarlouis** Ger.
80	B2	**Sab' Ābār** Syria
107	D1	**Sabadell** Spain
61	C1	**Sabah** state Malaysia
61	C2	**Sabalana** i. Indon.

155 D1 Sabará Brazil
108 B2 Sabaudia Italy
115 D2 Sabḥā Libya
123 D2 Sabie r. Moz./S. Africa
145 B2 Sabinas Mex.
145 B2 Sabinas Hidalgo Mex.
131 D2 Sable, Cape Can.
143 D3 Sable, Cape U.S.A.
131 E2 Sable Island Can.
106 B1 Sabugal Port.
78 B3 Ṣabyā Saudi Arabia
65 B3 Sabzevār Iran
120 A2 Sachanga Angola
65 B3 Sacheon S. Korea
130 A1 Sachigo Lake Can.
126 C2 Sachs Harbour Can.
135 B3 Sacramento U.S.A.
138 B2 Sacramento Mountains U.S.A.
135 B2 Sacramento Valley U.S.A.
123 C3 Sada S. Africa
107 C1 Sádaba Spain
78 B3 Ṣa'dah Yemen
62 A1 Sadiya India
67 C3 Sadoga-shima i. Japan
107 D2 Sa Dragonera i. Spain
76 C3 Safēd Kōh, Silsilah-ye mts Afgh.
93 F4 Säffle Sweden
138 B2 Safford U.S.A.
99 D2 Saffron Walden U.K.
114 B1 Safi Morocco
86 D2 Safonovo Arkhangel'skaya Oblast' Russia
89 D2 Safonovo Smolenskaya Oblast' Russia
75 C2 Saga China
67 B4 Saga Japan
62 A1 Sagaing Myanmar
67 C3 Sagamihara Japan
75 B2 Sagar India
140 C2 Saginaw U.S.A.
140 C2 Saginaw Bay U.S.A.
106 B2 Sagres Port.
146 B2 Sagua la Grande Cuba
141 F1 Saguenay r. Can.
107 C2 Sagunto Spain
76 B2 Sagyndyk, Mys pt Kazakh.
106 B1 Sahagún Spain
114 C3 Sahara des. Africa
Saharan Atlas mts Alg. see Atlas Sahariei
75 B2 Saharanpur India
75 C2 Saharsa India
114 B3 Sahel reg. Africa
144 B2 Sahuayo Mex.
78 B2 Ṣāḥūq reg. Saudi Arabia
Saïda Lebanon see Sidon
75 C2 Saidpur Bangl.
Saigon Vietnam see Ho Chi Minh City
62 A1 Saiha India
69 D2 Saihan Tal China
67 B4 Saiki Japan
93 I3 Saimaa l. Fin.
Sain Alto Mex.
96 C3 St Abb's Head U.K.
99 C3 St Albans U.K.
99 B3 St Aldhelm's Head U.K.
96 C2 St Andrews U.K.
131 E1 St Anthony Can.
134 D2 St Anthony U.S.A.
52 B3 St Arnaud Austr.
131 E1 St-Augustin Can.
131 E1 St Augustin r. Can.
143 D3 St Augustine U.S.A.
99 A3 St Austell U.K.
104 C2 St-Avertin France
98 B1 St Bees Head U.K.

105 D3 St-Bonnet-en-Champsaur France
99 A3 St Bride's Bay U.K.
104 B2 St-Brieuc France
130 C2 St Catharines Can.
99 C3 St Catherine's Point U.K.
137 E3 St Charles U.S.A.
140 C2 St Clair, Lake /U.S.A.
105 D2 St-Claude France
137 E1 St Cloud U.S.A.
140 A3 St Croix i. U.S.A.
147 D3 St Croix i. Virgin Is (U.S.A.)
105 C2 St-Dizier France
131 D2 Ste-Anne-des-Monts Can.
105 D2 St-Égrève France
126 B2 St Elias Mountains Can.
131 D1 Ste-Marguerite r. Can.
129 E2 Sainte Rose du Lac Can.
104 C2 Saintes France
105 C2 St-Étienne France
108 A2 St-Florent Corsica France
105 C2 St-Flour France
136 C3 St Francis U.S.A.
104 C3 St-Gaudens France
53 C1 St George Austr.
135 D3 St George U.S.A.
143 D3 St George Island U.S.A.
105 C2 St-Georges Can.
147 D3 St George's Grenada
97 C3 St George's Channel Ireland/U.K.
105 D2 St Gotthard Pass Switz.
113 E8 St Helena i. S. Atlantic Ocean
113 E8 St Helena, Ascension and Tristan da Cunha terr. S. Atlantic Ocean
122 A3 St Helena Bay S. Africa
122 A3 St Helena Bay S. Africa
98 B2 St Helens U.K.
134 B1 St Helens, Mount vol. U.S.A.
95 C4 St Helier Channel Is
100 B2 St-Hubert Belgium
141 E1 St-Hyacinthe Can.
140 C1 St Ignace U.S.A.
130 B2 St Ignace Island Can.
99 A3 St Ives U.K.
128 A2 St James, Cape Can.
131 C2 St-Jean, Lac l. Can.
104 B2 St-Jean-d'Angély France
104 B2 St-Jean-de-Monts France
130 C2 St-Jean-sur-Richelieu Can.
141 E1 St-Jérôme Can.
134 C1 St Joe r. U.S.A.
131 D2 Saint John Can.
141 F1 St John r. U.S.A.
147 D3 St John's Antigua
131 E2 St John's Can.
138 B2 St Johns U.S.A.
141 E2 St Johnsbury U.S.A.
137 E3 St Joseph U.S.A.
130 B1 St Joseph, Lake Can.
130 B2 St Joseph Island Can.
104 C2 St-Junien France
94 B2 St Kilda i. U.K.
147 D3 St Kitts and Nevis country West Indies
105 D2 St-Laurent, Golfe du g. Can. see St Lawrence, Gulf of
151 C1 St-Laurent-du-Maroni Fr. Guiana
131 D2 St Lawrence inlet Can.
131 D2 St Lawrence, Gulf of Can.
83 N2 St Lawrence Island U.S.A.
104 B2 St-Lô France
114 A3 St-Louis Senegal
137 E3 St Louis U.S.A.
137 E1 St Louis r. U.S.A.

147 D3 St Lucia country West Indies
123 D2 St Lucia Estuary S. Africa
104 B2 St-Malo France
104 B2 St-Malo, Golfe de g. France
122 A3 St Martin, Cape S. Africa
141 D2 St Marys U.S.A.
130 C2 St-Maurice r. Can.
104 B2 St-Nazaire France
104 C1 St-Omer France
129 C2 St Paul Can.
137 E2 St Paul U.S.A.
137 E2 St Peter U.S.A.
95 C4 St Peter Port Channel Is
89 D2 St Petersburg Russia
143 D3 St Petersburg U.S.A.
131 E2 St-Pierre St Pierre and Miquelon
131 E2 St Pierre and Miquelon terr. N. America
104 B2 St-Pierre-d'Oléron France
105 C2 St-Pourçain-sur-Sioule France
131 D2 St-Quentin Can.
105 C2 St-Quentin France
131 D2 St-Siméon Can.
129 E2 St Theresa Point Can.
130 B2 St Thomas Can.
105 D3 St-Tropez France
105 D3 St-Tropez, Cap de c. France
52 A3 St Vincent, Gulf Austr.
147 D3 St Vincent and the Grenadines country West Indies
100 C2 St-Vith Belgium
129 D2 St Walburg Can.
104 C2 St-Yrieix-la-Perche France
59 D1 Saipan i. N. Mariana Is
152 B2 Sajama, Nevado mt. Bol.
122 B2 Sak watercourse S. Africa
67 C4 Sakai Japan
67 B4 Sakaide Japan
78 B2 Sakākah Saudi Arabia
136 C1 Sakakawea, Lake U.S.A.
111 D2 Sakarya r. Turkey
66 C3 Sakata Japan
65 B1 Sakchu N. Korea
83 K3 Sakhalin i. Russia
123 C2 Sakhile S. Africa
81 C1 Şäki Azer.
89 E3 Šakiai Lith.
69 E3 Sakishima-shotō is Japan
62 B2 Sakon Nakhon Thai.
122 B3 Sakrivier S. Africa
67 D3 Sakura Japan
91 C2 Saky Ukr.
93 G4 Sala Sweden
130 C2 Salaberry-de-Valleyfield Can.
88 B2 Salacgrīva Latvia
109 C2 Sala Consilina Italy
135 C4 Salada, Laguna salt l. Mex.
152 B4 Salado r. Arg.
145 C2 Salado r. Mex.
114 B4 Salaga Ghana
122 B1 Salajwe Botswana
115 D3 Salal Chad
78 A2 Salâla Sudan
79 C3 Ṣalālah Oman
145 B2 Salamanca Mex.
106 B1 Salamanca Spain
106 B1 Salas Spain
63 B2 Salavan Laos
59 C3 Salawati i. Indon.
104 C2 Salbris France
88 C3 Šalčininkai Lith.
106 C1 Saldaña Spain
122 A3 Saldanha S. Africa
88 B2 Saldus Latvia

Sale

53 C3 **Sale** Austr.
86 F2 **Salekhard** Russia
73 B3 **Salem** India
137 E3 **Salem** MO U.S.A.
134 B2 **Salem** OR U.S.A.
96 B2 **Salen** U.K.
109 B2 **Salerno** Italy
98 B2 **Salford** U.K.
151 E2 **Salgado** r. Brazil
103 D2 **Salgótarján** Hungary
151 E2 **Salgueiro** Brazil
136 B3 **Salida** U.S.A.
111 C3 **Salihli** Turkey
88 C3 **Salihorsk** Belarus
121 C2 **Salima** Malawi
121 C2 **Salimo** Moz.
137 D3 **Salina** U.S.A.
108 B3 **Salina, Isola** i. Italy
145 C3 **Salina Cruz** Mex.
155 D1 **Salinas** Brazil
144 B2 **Salinas** Mex.
135 B3 **Salinas** U.S.A.
107 D2 **Salines, Cap de ses** c. Spain
151 D2 **Salinópolis** Brazil
99 C3 **Salisbury** U.K.
141 D3 **Salisbury** MD U.S.A.
143 D1 **Salisbury** NC U.S.A.
99 B3 **Salisbury Plain** U.K.
151 D2 **Salitre** r. Brazil
92 I2 **Salla** Fin.
127 F2 **Salluit** Can.
75 C2 **Sallyana** Nepal
81 C2 **Salmās** Iran
134 D1 **Salmon** U.S.A.
134 C1 **Salmon** r. U.S.A.
128 C2 **Salmon Arm** Can.
134 C2 **Salmon River Mountains** U.S.A.
100 C3 **Salmtal** Ger.
93 H3 **Salo** Fin.
87 D4 **Sal'sk** Russia
122 B3 **Salt** watercourse S. Africa
138 A2 **Salt** r. U.S.A.
152 B3 **Salta** Arg.
145 B2 **Saltillo** Mex.
134 D2 **Salt Lake City** U.S.A.
154 C2 **Salto** Brazil
152 C4 **Salto** Uru.
155 E1 **Salto da Divisa** Brazil
152 C4 **Salto del Guairá** Para.
135 C4 **Salton Sea** salt l. U.S.A.
143 D2 **Saluda** U.S.A.
108 A2 **Saluzzo** Italy
151 E3 **Salvador** Brazil
79 C2 **Salwah** Saudi Arabia
62 A1 **Salween** r. China/Myanmar
62 A2 **Salween** r. China/Myanmar
81 C2 **Salyan** Azer.
102 C2 **Salzburg** Austria
101 E1 **Salzgitter** Ger.
101 D2 **Salzkotten** Ger.
101 E1 **Salzwedel** Ger.
144 B1 **Samalayuca** Mex.
66 D2 **Samani** Japan
64 B1 **Samar** i. Phil.
87 E3 **Samara** Russia
61 C2 **Samarinda** Indon.
77 C3 **Samarqand** Uzbek.
81 C2 **Sāmarrā'** Iraq
81 C1 **Şamaxı** Azer.
119 C3 **Samba** Dem. Rep. Congo
61 C1 **Sambaliung** mts Indon.
75 C2 **Sambalpur** India
61 C2 **Sambar, Tanjung** pt Indon.
61 B1 **Sambas** Indon.
121 □E2 **Sambava** Madag.
90 A2 **Sambir** Ukr.
153 C4 **Samborombón, Bahía** b. Arg.

65 B2 **Samcheok** S. Korea
81 C2 **Samdi Dag** mt. Turkey
119 D3 **Same** Tanz.
78 B2 **Samirah** Saudi Arabia
65 B1 **Samjiyŏn** N. Korea
49 G3 **Samoa** country S. Pacific Ocean
109 C1 **Samobor** Croatia
111 C3 **Samos** i. Greece
111 C2 **Samothraki** Greece
111 C2 **Samothraki** i. Greece
61 C2 **Sampit** Indon.
119 C3 **Sampwe** Dem. Rep. Congo
63 B2 **Sâmraông** Cambodia
139 E2 **Sam Rayburn Reservoir** U.S.A.
80 B1 **Samsun** Turkey
81 C1 **Sam'redia** Georgia
63 B3 **Samui, Ko** i. Thai.
63 B2 **Samut Songkhram** Thai.
114 B3 **San** Mali
78 B3 **Şan'ā'** Yemen
118 A2 **Sanaga** r. Cameroon
81 C2 **Sanandaj** Iran
146 B3 **San Andrés, Isla de** i. Caribbean Sea
138 B2 **San Andres Mountains** U.S.A.
145 C3 **San Andrés Tuxtla** Mex.
139 D3 **San Angelo** U.S.A.
139 D3 **San Antonio** U.S.A.
135 C4 **San Antonio, Mount** U.S.A.
152 B3 **San Antonio de los Cobres** Arg.
153 B5 **San Antonio Oeste** Arg.
108 B2 **San Benedetto del Tronto** Italy
144 A3 **San Benedicto, Isla** i. Mex.
135 C4 **San Bernardino** U.S.A.
135 C4 **San Bernardino Mountains** U.S.A.
143 C3 **San Blas, Cape** U.S.A.
152 B2 **San Borja** Bol.
144 B2 **San Buenaventura** Mex.
64 B1 **San Carlos** Phil.
147 D4 **San Carlos** Venez.
153 A5 **San Carlos de Bariloche** Arg.
147 C4 **San Carlos del Zulia** Venez.
135 C4 **San Clemente Island** U.S.A.
104 C2 **Sancoins** France
150 A1 **San Cristóbal** Venez.
145 C3 **San Cristóbal de las Casas** Mex.
146 C2 **Sancti Spíritus** Cuba
61 C1 **Sandakan** Sabah Malaysia
93 E3 **Sandane** Norway
111 B2 **Sandanski** Bulg.
96 C1 **Sanday** i. U.K.
139 C2 **Sanderson** U.S.A.
150 B3 **Sandia** Peru
135 C4 **San Diego** U.S.A.
80 B2 **Sandıklı** Turkey
93 E4 **Sandnes** Norway
92 F2 **Sandnessjøen** Norway
118 C3 **Sandoa** Dem. Rep. Congo
103 E1 **Sandomierz** Pol.
89 E2 **Sandovo** Russia
94 B1 **Sandoy** i. Faroe Is
139 D2 **Sandoway** U.S.A.
150 B3 **Sandpoint** U.S.A.
71 B3 **Sandu** China
94 B1 **Sandur** Faroe Is
140 C2 **Sandusky** U.S.A.
122 A3 **Sandveld** mts S. Africa
93 F4 **Sandvika** Norway
93 G3 **Sandviken** Sweden
131 E1 **Sandwich Bay** Can.
129 D2 **Sandy Bay** Can.
51 E2 **Sandy Cape** Austr.
130 A1 **Sandy Lake** Can.
130 A1 **Sandy Lake** Can.

144 A1 **San Felipe** Baja California Mex.
145 B2 **San Felipe** Guanajuato Mex.
150 B1 **San Felipe** Venez.
144 A2 **San Fernando** Baja California Mex.
145 C2 **San Fernando** Tamaulipas Mex.
64 B1 **San Fernando** La Union Phil.
64 B1 **San Fernando** Pampanga Phil.
106 B2 **San Fernando** Spain
147 D3 **San Fernando** Trin. and Tob.
150 B1 **San Fernando de Apure** Venez.
143 D3 **Sanford** FL U.S.A.
141 E2 **Sanford** ME U.S.A.
152 B4 **San Francisco** Arg.
135 B3 **San Francisco** U.S.A.
74 B3 **Sangamner** India
83 J2 **Sangar** Russia
108 A3 **San Gavino Monreale** Sardinia Italy
101 E2 **Sangerhausen** Ger.
61 C1 **Sanggau** Indon.
118 B3 **Sangha** r. Congo
109 C3 **San Giovanni in Fiore** Italy
64 B2 **Sangir** i. Indon.
59 C2 **Sangir, Kepulauan** is Indon.
65 B2 **Sangju** S. Korea
61 C1 **Sangkulirang** Indon.
73 B3 **Sangli** India
118 B2 **Sangmélima** Cameroon
121 C3 **Sango** Zimbabwe
136 B3 **Sangre de Cristo Range** mts U.S.A.
75 C2 **Sangsang** China
144 A2 **San Hipólito, Punta** pt Mex.
144 A2 **San Ignacio** Mex.
130 C1 **Sanikiluaq** Can.
71 A3 **Sanjiang** China
135 B3 **San Joaquin** r. U.S.A.
153 B5 **San Jorge, Golfo de** g. Arg.
146 B4 **San José** Costa Rica
64 B1 **San Jose** Nueva Ecija Phil.
64 B1 **San Jose** Occidental Mindoro Phil.
135 B3 **San Jose** U.S.A.
144 A2 **San José, Isla** i. Mex.
144 B2 **San José de Bavicora** Mex.
64 B1 **San Jose de Buenavista** Phil.
144 A2 **San José de Comondú** Mex.
144 B2 **San José del Cabo** Mex.
150 A1 **San José del Guaviare** Col.
152 B4 **San Juan** Arg.
146 B3 **San Juan** r. Costa Rica/Nic.
147 D3 **San Juan** r. Puerto Rico
135 D3 **San Juan** r. U.S.A.
145 C3 **San Juan Bautista Tuxtepec** Mex.
134 B1 **San Juan Islands** U.S.A.
144 B2 **San Juanito** Mex.
136 B3 **San Juan Mountains** U.S.A.
153 B5 **San Julián** Arg.
75 C2 **Sankh** r. India
105 D2 **Sankt Gallen** Switz.
105 D2 **Sankt Moritz** Switz.
Sankt-Peterburg Russia see St Petersburg
102 C2 **Sankt Veit an der Glan** Austria
100 C3 **Sankt Wendel** Ger.
80 B2 **Şanlıurfa** Turkey
138 B3 **San Lorenzo** Mex.
106 B2 **Sanlúcar de Barrameda** Spain
145 B2 **San Luis** Mex.
145 B2 **San Luis de la Paz** Mex.
138 A2 **San Luisito** Mex.
135 B3 **San Luis Obispo** U.S.A.

145 B2 **San Luis Potosí** Mex.
144 A1 **San Luis Río Colorado** Mex.
139 D3 **San Marcos** U.S.A.
108 B2 **San Marino** *country* Europe
108 B2 **San Marino** San Marino
144 B2 **San Martín de Bolaños** Mex.
153 A5 **San Martín de los Andes** Arg.
153 B5 **San Matías, Golfo** *g.* Arg.
70 B2 **Sanmenxia** China
146 B3 **San Miguel** El Salvador
152 B3 **San Miguel de Tucumán** Arg.
145 C3 **San Miguel Sola de Vega** Mex.
71 B3 **Sanming** China
153 B4 **San Nicolás de los Arroyos** Arg.
135 C4 **San Nicolas Island** U.S.A.
123 C2 **Sannieshof** S. Africa
103 E2 **Sanok** Pol.
64 B1 **San Pablo** Phil.
144 B2 **San Pablo Balleza** Mex.
152 B3 **San Pedro** Arg.
152 B2 **San Pedro** Bol.
114 B4 **San-Pédro** Côte d'Ivoire
144 A2 **San Pedro** Mex.
138 A2 **San Pedro** *watercourse* U.S.A.
106 B2 **San Pedro, Sierra de** *mts* Spain
144 B2 **San Pedro de las Colonias** Mex.
146 B3 **San Pedro Sula** Hond.
108 A3 **San Pietro, Isola di** *i. Sardinia* Italy
144 A1 **San Quintín, Cabo** *c.* Mex.
153 B4 **San Rafael** Arg.
108 A2 **Sanremo** Italy
146 B3 **San Salvador** El Salvador
152 B3 **San Salvador de Jujuy** Arg.
107 C1 **San Sebastián** Spain
107 C1 **San Sebastián** Spain
109 C2 **San Severo** Italy
109 C2 **Sanski Most** Bos. & Herz.
152 B2 **Santa Ana** Bol.
146 B3 **Santa Ana** El Salvador
144 A1 **Santa Ana** Mex.
135 C4 **Santa Ana** U.S.A.
144 B2 **Santa Bárbara** Mex.
135 C4 **Santa Barbara** U.S.A.
154 B2 **Santa Bárbara, Serra de** *hills* Brazil
152 B3 **Santa Catalina** Chile
150 B2 **Santa Clara** Col.
146 C2 **Santa Clara** Cuba
135 C4 **Santa Clarita** U.S.A.
109 C3 **Santa Croce, Capo** *c. Sicily* Italy
153 B6 **Santa Cruz** *r.* Arg.
152 B2 **Santa Cruz** Bol.
64 B1 **Santa Cruz** Phil.
135 B3 **Santa Cruz** U.S.A.
145 C3 **Santa Cruz Barillas** Guat.
155 E1 **Santa Cruz Cabrália** Brazil
107 C2 **Santa Cruz de Moya** Spain
114 A2 **Santa Cruz de Tenerife** Canary Islands
135 C4 **Santa Cruz Island** U.S.A.
48 F3 **Santa Cruz Islands** Solomon Is
152 B4 **Santa Fe** Arg.
138 B1 **Santa Fe** U.S.A.
154 B1 **Santa Helena de Goiás** Brazil
153 B4 **Santa Isabel** Arg.
154 B1 **Santa Luisa, Serra de** *hills* Brazil
152 C3 **Santa Maria** Brazil
144 B1 **Santa María** *r.* Mex.
135 B4 **Santa Maria** U.S.A.
123 D2 **Santa Maria, Cabo de** *c.* Moz.
106 B2 **Santa Maria, Cabo de** *c.* Port.
151 D2 **Santa Maria das Barreiras** Brazil
109 C3 **Santa Maria di Leuca, Capo** *c.* Italy
150 A1 **Santa Marta** Col.
135 C4 **Santa Monica** U.S.A.
151 C2 **Santana** *Amapá* Brazil
151 D3 **Santana** *Bahia* Brazil
106 C1 **Santander** Spain
108 A3 **Sant'Antioco** *Sardinia* Italy
108 A3 **Sant'Antioco, Isola di** *i. Sardinia* Italy
107 D2 **Sant Antoni de Portmany** Spain
151 C2 **Santarém** Brazil
106 B2 **Santarém** Port.
154 B1 **Santa Rita do Araguaia** Brazil
153 B4 **Santa Rosa** Arg.
152 C3 **Santa Rosa** Brazil
135 B3 **Santa Rosa** *CA* U.S.A.
138 C2 **Santa Rosa** *NM* U.S.A.
146 B3 **Santa Rosa de Copán** Hond.
135 B4 **Santa Rosa Island** U.S.A.
144 A2 **Santa Rosalía** Mex.
107 D2 **Sant Francesc de Formentera** Spain
152 C3 **Santiago** Brazil
153 A4 **Santiago** Chile
147 C3 **Santiago** Dom. Rep.
144 B2 **Santiago** Mex.
146 B4 **Santiago** Panama
64 B1 **Santiago** Phil.
106 B1 **Santiago de Compostela** Spain
144 B2 **Santiago Ixcuintla** Mex.
144 B2 **Santiago Papasquiaro** Mex.
107 D2 **Sant Joan de Labritja** Spain
107 D1 **Sant Jordi, Golf de** *g.* Spain
155 D2 **Santo Amaro de Campos** Brazil
155 C2 **Santo André** Brazil
152 C3 **Santo Ângelo** Brazil
154 B2 **Santo Antônio da Platina** Brazil
151 E3 **Santo Antônio de Jesus** Brazil
150 B2 **Santo Antônio do Içá** Brazil
155 C2 **Santo Antônio do Monte** Brazil
147 D3 **Santo Domingo** Dom. Rep.
138 B1 **Santo Domingo Pueblo** U.S.A.
111 C3 **Santorini** *i.* Greece
155 C2 **Santos** Brazil
152 C3 **Santo Tomé** Arg.
153 A5 **San Valentín, Cerro** *mt.* Chile
146 B3 **San Vicente** El Salvador
144 A1 **San Vicente** Mex.
150 A3 **San Vicente de Cañete** Peru
108 B2 **San Vincenzo** Italy
108 B3 **San Vito, Capo** *c. Sicily* Italy
71 A4 **Sanya** China
155 C2 **São Bernardo do Campo** Brazil
152 C3 **São Borja** Brazil
154 C2 **São Carlos** Brazil
151 C3 **São Félix do Araguaia** Brazil
151 C2 **São Félix do Xingu** Brazil
155 D2 **São Fidélis** Brazil
155 D1 **São Francisco** Brazil
151 E3 **São Francisco** *r.* Brazil
154 C3 **São Francisco, Ilha de** *i.* Brazil
154 C3 **São Francisco do Sul** Brazil
152 C4 **São Gabriel** Brazil
150 B2 **São Gabriel da Cachoeira** Brazil
155 D2 **São Gonçalo** Brazil
155 C1 **São Gotardo** Brazil
155 D2 **São João da Barra** Brazil
155 C2 **São João da Boa Vista** Brazil
106 B1 **São João da Madeira** Port.
155 D1 **São João do Paraíso** Brazil
155 D2 **São João Nepomuceno** Brazil
154 C2 **São Joaquim da Barra** Brazil
154 C2 **São José do Rio Preto** Brazil
155 C2 **São José dos Campos** Brazil
154 C3 **São José dos Pinhais** Brazil
155 C2 **São Lourenço** Brazil
151 D2 **São Luís** Brazil
154 C2 **São Manuel** Brazil
154 C1 **São Marcos** *r.* Brazil
151 D2 **São Marcos, Baía de** *b.* Brazil
155 E1 **São Mateus** Brazil
155 C2 **São Paulo** Brazil
151 D2 **São Raimundo Nonato** Brazil
155 C1 **São Romão** Brazil
155 C2 **São Sebastião, Ilha do** *i.* Brazil
154 C2 **São Sebastião do Paraíso** Brazil
154 B1 **São Simão** Brazil
154 B1 **São Simão, Barragem de** *resr* Brazil
59 C2 **Sao-Siu** Indon.
113 F6 **São Tomé** São Tomé and Príncipe
155 D2 **São Tomé, Cabo de** *c.* Brazil
113 F6 **São Tomé and Príncipe** *country* Africa
155 C2 **São Vicente** Brazil
106 B2 **São Vicente, Cabo de** *c.* Port.
59 C3 **Saparua** Indon.
89 F3 **Sapozhok** Russia
66 D2 **Sapporo** Japan
109 C2 **Sapri** Italy
81 C2 **Saqqez** Iran
81 C2 **Sarāb** Iran
63 B2 **Sara Buri** Thai.
109 C2 **Sarajevo** Bos. & Herz.
76 B1 **Saraktash** Russia
141 E2 **Saranac Lake** U.S.A.
109 D3 **Sarandë** Albania
64 B2 **Sarangani Islands** Phil.
87 D3 **Saransk** Russia
87 E3 **Sarapul** Russia
143 D3 **Sarasota** U.S.A.
90 B2 **Sarata** Ukr.
136 B2 **Saratoga** U.S.A.
141 E2 **Saratoga Springs** U.S.A.
61 C1 **Saratok** *Sarawak* Malaysia
87 D3 **Saratov** Russia
79 D2 **Sarāvān** Iran
61 C1 **Sarawak** *state* Malaysia
110 C2 **Saray** Turkey
111 C3 **Sarayköy** Turkey
79 D2 **Sarbāz** Iran
74 B2 **Sardarshahr** India
Sardegna *i.* Italy *see* **Sardinia**
108 A2 **Sardinia** *i.* Italy
92 G2 **Sarektjåkkå** *mt.* Sweden
77 C3 **Sar-e Pul** Afgh.
158 B3 **Sargasso Sea** N. Atlantic Ocean
74 B1 **Sargodha** Pak.
115 D4 **Sarh** Chad
79 D2 **Sarhad** *reg.* Iran
81 D2 **Sārī** Iran
111 C3 **Sarıgöl** Turkey
81 C1 **Sarıkamış** Turkey
61 C1 **Sarikei** *Sarawak* Malaysia
51 D2 **Sarina** Austr.
65 B2 **Sariwŏn** N. Korea
111 C2 **Sarıyer** Turkey
78 B2 **Sark, Safrā' as** *esc.* Saudi Arabia
77 D2 **Sarkand** Kazakh.

111 C2 **Şarköy** Turkey
59 D3 **Sarmi** Indon.
140 C2 **Sarnia** Can.
90 B1 **Sarny** Ukr.
60 B2 **Sarolangun** Indon.
111 B3 **Saronikos Kolpos** *g.* Greece
111 C2 **Saros Körfezi** *b.* Turkey
87 D3 **Sarov** Russia
105 D2 **Sarrebourg** France
106 B1 **Sarria** Spain
107 C1 **Sarrión** Spain
105 D3 **Sartène** *Corsica* France
103 D2 **Sárvár** Hungary
77 D1 **Saryarka** *plain* Kazakh.
76 B2 **Sarykamyshskoye Ozero** *salt l.* Turkm./Uzbek.
77 D2 **Saryozek** Kazakh.
77 D2 **Saryshagan** Kazakh.
82 F3 **Sarysu** *watercourse* Kazakh.
77 D3 **Sary-Tash** Kyrg.
75 C2 **Sasaram** India
67 A4 **Sasebo** Japan
129 D2 **Saskatchewan** *prov.* Can.
129 D2 **Saskatchewan** *r.* Can.
129 D2 **Saskatoon** Can.
83 I2 **Saskylakh** Russia
123 C2 **Sasolburg** S. Africa
87 D3 **Sasovo** Russia
114 B4 **Sassandra** Côte d'Ivoire
108 A2 **Sassari** *Sardinia* Italy
102 C1 **Sassnitz** Ger.
114 A3 **Satadougou** Mali
123 D1 **Satara** S. Africa
75 C2 **Satna** India
74 B2 **Satpura Range** *mts* India
67 B4 **Satsuma-Sendai** Japan
63 B2 **Sattahip** Thai.
110 B1 **Satu Mare** Romania
63 B3 **Satun** Thai.
144 B2 **Saucillo** Mex.
93 E4 **Sauda** Norway
92 □B2 **Sauðárkrókur** Iceland
78 B2 **Saudi Arabia** *country* Asia
105 C3 **Saugues** France
105 C2 **Saulieu** France
130 B2 **Sault Sainte Marie** Can.
140 C1 **Sault Sainte Marie** U.S.A.
77 C1 **Saumalkol'** Kazakh.
59 C3 **Saumlakki** Indon.
104 B2 **Saumur** France
120 B1 **Saurimo** Angola
109 D2 **Sava** *r.* Europe
49 G3 **Savai'i** *i.* Samoa
91 E1 **Savala** *r.* Russia
143 D2 **Savannah** *GA* U.S.A.
142 C1 **Savannah** *TN* U.S.A.
143 D2 **Savannah** *r.* U.S.A.
63 B2 **Savannakhét** Laos
130 A1 **Savant Lake** Can.
111 C3 **Savaştepe** Turkey
89 F2 **Savino** Russia
86 D2 **Savinskiy** Russia
108 A2 **Savona** Italy
93 I3 **Savonlinna** Fin.
92 I2 **Savukoski** Fin.
Savu Sea Indon. *see* **Sawu, Laut**
74 B2 **Sawai Madhopur** India
62 A2 **Sawankhalok** Thai.
136 B3 **Sawatch Range** *mts* U.S.A.
53 D2 **Sawtell** Austr.
59 C3 **Sawu, Laut** *sea* Indon.
79 C3 **Sayḩūt** Yemen
69 D2 **Saynshand** Mongolia
141 D2 **Sayre** U.S.A.
144 B3 **Sayula** *Jalisco* Mex.
145 C3 **Sayula** *Veracruz* Mex.
128 B2 **Sayward** Can.
89 E2 **Sazonovo** Russia
114 B2 **Sbaa** Alg.
98 B1 **Scafell Pike** *h.* U.K.
109 C3 **Scalea** Italy
96 C1 **Scapa Flow** *inlet* U.K.
130 C2 **Scarborough** Can.
147 D3 **Scarborough** Trin. and Tob.
98 C1 **Scarborough** U.K.
64 A1 **Scarborough Reef** *sea feature* S. China Sea
96 A2 **Scarinish** U.K.
Scarpanto *i.* Greece *see* **Karpathos**
105 D2 **Schaffhausen** Switz.
100 B1 **Schagen** Neth.
102 C2 **Schärding** Austria
100 A2 **Scharendijke** Neth.
101 D1 **Scharhörn** *i.* Ger.
101 D1 **Scheeßel** Ger.
131 D1 **Schefferville** Can.
135 D3 **Schell Creek Range** *mts* U.S.A.
141 E2 **Schenectady** U.S.A.
101 E3 **Scheßlitz** Ger.
100 C1 **Schiermonnikoog** *i.* Neth.
108 B1 **Schio** Italy
101 F2 **Schkeuditz** Ger.
101 E1 **Schladen** Ger.
101 E2 **Schleiz** Ger.
102 B1 **Schleswig** Ger.
101 D2 **Schloß Holte-Stukenbrock** Ger.
101 D2 **Schlüchtern** Ger.
101 E3 **Schlüsselfeld** Ger.
101 D2 **Schmallenberg** Ger.
101 D1 **Schneverdingen** Ger.
101 E1 **Schönebeck (Elbe)** Ger.
101 E1 **Schöningen** Ger.
100 B2 **Schoonhoven** Neth.
59 D3 **Schouten Islands** P.N.G.
102 B2 **Schwäbische Alb** *mts* Ger.
102 C2 **Schwandorf** Ger.
61 C2 **Schwaner, Pegunungan** *mts* Indon.
101 E1 **Schwarzenbek** Ger.
101 F2 **Schwarzenberg/Erzgebirge** Ger.
122 A2 **Schwarzrand** *mts* Namibia
Schwarzwald *mts* Ger. *see* **Black Forest**
102 C2 **Schwaz** Austria
102 C1 **Schwedt/Oder** Ger.
101 E2 **Schweinfurt** Ger.
101 E1 **Schwerin** Ger.
101 E1 **Schweriner See** *l.* Ger.
105 D2 **Schwyz** Switz.
108 B3 **Sciacca** *Sicily* Italy
95 B4 **Scilly, Isles of** U.K.
140 C3 **Scioto** *r.* U.S.A.
136 B1 **Scobey** U.S.A.
53 D2 **Scone** Austr.
55 R3 **Scotia Ridge** S. Atlantic Ocean
158 C8 **Scotia Sea** S. Atlantic Ocean
96 C2 **Scotland** *admin. div.* U.K.
128 B2 **Scott, Cape** Can.
123 D3 **Scottburgh** S. Africa
136 C3 **Scott City** U.S.A.
136 C2 **Scottsbluff** U.S.A.
142 C2 **Scottsboro** U.S.A.
96 B1 **Scourie** U.K.
141 D2 **Scranton** U.S.A.
98 C2 **Scunthorpe** U.K.
105 E2 **Scuol** Switz.
129 E2 **Seal** *r.* Can.
122 B3 **Seal, Cape** S. Africa
52 B3 **Sea Lake** Austr.
139 D3 **Sealy** U.S.A.
142 B1 **Searcy** U.S.A.
98 B1 **Seascale** U.K.
134 B1 **Seattle** U.S.A.
141 E2 **Sebago Lake** U.S.A.
144 A2 **Sebastián Vizcaíno, Bahía** *b.* Mex.
110 B1 **Sebeş** Romania
60 B2 **Sebesi** *i.* Indon.
88 C2 **Sebezh** Russia
80 B1 **Şebinkarahisar** Turkey
143 D3 **Sebring** U.S.A.
128 B3 **Sechelt** Can.
150 A2 **Sechura** Peru
73 B3 **Secunderabad** India
137 E3 **Sedalia** U.S.A.
105 C2 **Sedan** France
54 B2 **Seddon** N.Z.
138 A2 **Sedona** U.S.A.
101 E2 **Seeburg** Ger.
101 E1 **Seehausen (Altmark)** Ger.
122 A2 **Seeheim** Namibia
104 C2 **Sées** France
101 E2 **Seesen** Ger.
101 E1 **Seevetal** Ger.
123 C1 **Sefare** Botswana
60 B1 **Segamat** Malaysia
86 C2 **Segezha** Russia
114 B3 **Ségou** Mali
106 C1 **Segovia** Spain
115 D2 **Séguédine** Niger
114 B4 **Séguéla** Côte d'Ivoire
139 D3 **Seguin** U.S.A.
107 C2 **Segura** *r.* Spain
106 C2 **Segura, Sierra de** *mts* Spain
120 B3 **Sehithwa** Botswana
93 H3 **Seinäjoki** Fin.
104 C2 **Seine** *r.* France
104 B2 **Seine, Baie de** *b.* France
103 E1 **Sejny** Pol.
60 B2 **Sekayu** Indon.
114 B4 **Sekondi** Ghana
59 C3 **Selaru** *i.* Indon.
61 C2 **Selatan, Tanjung** *pt* Indon.
126 A2 **Selawik** U.S.A.
58 C3 **Selayar, Pulau** *i.* Indon.
98 C2 **Selby** U.K.
120 B3 **Selebi-Phikwe** Botswana
105 D2 **Sélestat** France
92 □A3 **Selfoss** Iceland
114 A3 **Sélibabi** Maur.
138 A1 **Seligman** U.S.A.
116 A2 **Selîma Oasis** Sudan
111 C3 **Selimiye** Turkey
114 B3 **Sélingué, Lac de** *l.* Mali
89 D2 **Selizharovo** Russia
93 E4 **Seljord** Norway
129 E2 **Selkirk** Can.
96 C3 **Selkirk** U.K.
128 C2 **Selkirk Mountains** Can.
142 C2 **Selma** *AL* U.S.A.
135 C3 **Selma** *CA* U.S.A.
89 D3 **Sel'tso** Russia
150 A2 **Selvas** *reg.* Brazil
134 C1 **Selway** *r.* U.S.A.
129 D1 **Selwyn Lake** Can.
128 A1 **Selwyn Mountains** Can.
51 C2 **Selwyn Range** *hills* Austr.
60 B2 **Semangka, Teluk** *b.* Indon.
61 C2 **Semarang** Indon.
61 B1 **Sematan** *Sarawak* Malaysia
118 B2 **Sembé** Congo
81 C2 **Şemdinli** Turkey
91 C1 **Semenivka** Ukr.
86 D3 **Semenov** Russia
61 C2 **Semeru, Gunung** *vol.* Indon.
77 E1 **Semey** Kazakh.
89 E3 **Semiluki** Russia
136 B2 **Seminoe Reservoir** U.S.A.
139 C2 **Seminole** U.S.A.

143 D2 **Seminole, Lake** U.S.A.
61 C1 **Semitau** Indon.
81 D2 **Semnān** Iran
61 C1 **Semporna** *Sabah* Malaysia
105 C2 **Semur-en-Auxois** France
150 B2 **Sena Madureira** Brazil
120 B2 **Senanga** Zambia
67 D3 **Sendai** Japan
114 A3 **Senegal** *country* Africa
114 A3 **Sénégal** *r.* Maur./Senegal
102 C1 **Senftenberg** Ger.
119 D3 **Sengerema** Tanz.
151 D3 **Senhor do Bonfim** Brazil
108 B2 **Senigallia** Italy
109 B2 **Senj** Croatia
92 G2 **Senja** *i.* Norway
122 B2 **Senlac** S. Africa
104 C2 **Senlis** France
63 B2 **Sênmônoŭrôm** Cambodia
117 B3 **Sennar** Sudan
130 C2 **Senneterre** Can.
123 C3 **Senqu** *r.* Lesotho
105 C2 **Sens** France
109 D1 **Senta** Serbia
128 B2 **Sentinel Peak** Can.
123 C1 **Senwabarwana** S. Africa
65 B2 **Seocheon** S. Korea
65 B2 **Seongnam** S. Korea
75 B2 **Seoni** India
65 B2 **Seosan** S. Korea
65 B2 **Seoul** S. Korea
155 D2 **Sepetiba, Baía de** *b.* Brazil
59 D3 **Sepik** *r.* P.N.G.
61 C1 **Sepinang** Indon.
131 D1 **Sept-Îles** Can.
59 C3 **Seram** *i.* Indon.
59 C3 **Seram, Laut** *sea* Indon.
60 B2 **Serang** Indon.
109 D2 **Serbia** *country* Europe
76 B3 **Serdar** Turkm.
89 E3 **Serebryanyye Prudy** Russia
60 B1 **Seremban** Malaysia
119 D3 **Serengeti Plain** Tanz.
87 D3 **Sergach** Russia
89 E2 **Sergiyev Posad** Russia
74 A1 **Serhetabat** Turkm.
61 C1 **Seria** Brunei
61 C1 **Serian** *Sarawak* Malaysia
111 B3 **Serifos** *i.* Greece
80 B2 **Serik** Turkey
59 C3 **Sermata, Kepulauan** *is* Indon.
86 F3 **Serov** Russia
120 B3 **Serowe** Botswana
106 B2 **Serpa** Port.
89 E3 **Serpukhov** Russia
151 D3 **Serra da Mesa, Represa** *resr* Brazil
154 B1 **Serranópolis** Brazil
100 A3 **Serre** *r.* France
111 B2 **Serres** Greece
151 E3 **Serrinha** Brazil
155 D1 **Serro** Brazil
154 C2 **Sertãozinho** Brazil
61 C2 **Seruyan** *r.* Indon.
68 C2 **Sêrxü** China
120 A2 **Sesfontein** Namibia
108 B2 **Sessa Aurunca** Italy
108 A2 **Sestri Levante** Italy
105 C3 **Sète** France
155 D1 **Sete Lagoas** Brazil
92 G2 **Setermoen** Norway
93 E4 **Setesdal** *val.* Norway
115 C1 **Sétif** Alg.
67 B4 **Seto-naikai** *sea* Japan
114 B1 **Settat** Morocco
98 B1 **Settle** U.K.
106 B2 **Setúbal** Port.
106 B2 **Setúbal, Baía de** *b.* Port.
130 A1 **Seul, Lac** *l.* Can.
76 A2 **Sevan, Lake** Armenia
Sevana Lich *l.* Armenia *see* **Sevan, Lake**
91 C3 **Sevastopol'** Ukr.
105 C3 **Sévérac-le-Château** France
130 B1 **Severn** *r.* Can.
122 B2 **Severn** S. Africa
99 B3 **Severn** *r.* U.K.
86 D2 **Severnaya Dvina** *r.* Russia
83 H1 **Severnaya Zemlya** *is* Russia
86 D2 **Severnyy** *Nenetskiy Avtonomnyy Okrug* Russia
86 F2 **Severnyy** *Respublika Komi* Russia
82 E1 **Severnyy, Ostrov** *i.* Russia
86 C2 **Severodvinsk** Russia
86 C2 **Severomorsk** Russia
91 D3 **Severskaya** Russia
135 D3 **Sevier** *r.* U.S.A.
135 D3 **Sevier Lake** U.S.A.
Sevilla Spain *see* **Seville**
106 B2 **Seville** Spain
128 A2 **Sewell Inlet** Can.
128 C2 **Sexsmith** Can.
144 B2 **Sextín** *r.* Mex.
86 G1 **Seyakha** Russia
113 J7 **Seychelles** *country* Indian Ocean
92 □C2 **Seyðisfjörður** Iceland
91 C1 **Seym** *r.* Russia/Ukr.
83 L2 **Seymchan** Russia
53 C3 **Seymour** Austr.
140 B3 **Seymour** *IN* U.S.A.
139 D2 **Seymour** *TX* U.S.A.
105 C2 **Sézanne** France
110 C1 **Sfântu Gheorghe** Romania
115 D1 **Sfax** Tunisia
's-Gravenhage Neth. *see* **The Hague**
96 A2 **Sgurr Alasdair** *h.* U.K.
70 A2 **Shaanxi** *prov.* China
91 D2 **Shabel'skoye** Russia
77 D3 **Shache** China
55 R1 **Shackleton Range** *mts* Antarctica
99 B3 **Shaftesbury** U.K.
75 C2 **Shahdol** India
77 C3 **Shāh Fōlād** *mt.* Afgh.
75 B2 **Shahjahanpur** India
81 D2 **Shahr-e Kord** Iran
81 D2 **Shahreẕā** Iran
77 C3 **Shahrisabz** Uzbek.
81 D2 **Shāhrūd** Iran
89 E2 **Shakhovskaya** Russia
91 E2 **Shakhty** Russia
86 D3 **Shakhun'ya** Russia
66 D2 **Shakotan-misaki** *c.* Japan
76 B2 **Shalkar** Kazakh.
68 C2 **Shaluli Shan** *mts* China
129 E2 **Shamattawa** Can.
139 C1 **Shamrock** U.S.A.
70 B2 **Shancheng** China
68 C2 **Shandan** China
70 B2 **Shandong** *prov.* China
70 C2 **Shandong Bandao** *pen.* China
121 B2 **Shangani** *r.* Zimbabwe
70 C2 **Shanghai** China
70 C2 **Shanghai** *mun.* China
71 B3 **Shanghang** China
70 A2 **Shangluo** China
71 B3 **Shangrao** China
70 B2 **Shangshui** China
70 C2 **Shangyu** China
69 E1 **Shangzhi** China
97 B2 **Shannon** *r.* Ireland
97 B2 **Shannon, Mouth of the** Ireland
71 B3 **Shantou** China
70 B2 **Shanxi** *prov.* China
71 B3 **Shaoguan** China
71 B3 **Shaowu** China
70 C2 **Shaoxing** China
71 B3 **Shaoyang** China
116 C2 **Shaqrā'** Saudi Arabia
90 B2 **Sharhorod** Ukr.
79 C2 **Sharjah** U.A.E.
88 C2 **Sharkawshchyna** Belarus
50 A2 **Shark Bay** Austr.
78 A2 **Sharm ash Shaykh** Egypt
140 C2 **Sharon** U.S.A.
86 D3 **Shar'ya** Russia
121 B3 **Shashe** *r.* Botswana/Zimbabwe
117 B4 **Shashemenē** Eth.
134 B2 **Shasta, Mount** *vol.* U.S.A.
134 B2 **Shasta Lake** U.S.A.
156 D3 **Shatsky Rise** *sea feature* N. Pacific Ocean
89 E2 **Shatura** Russia
129 D3 **Shaunavon** Can.
140 B2 **Shawano** U.S.A.
131 C2 **Shawinigan** Can.
139 D1 **Shawnee** U.S.A.
50 B2 **Shay Gap (abandoned)** Austr.
89 E3 **Shchekino** Russia
89 E2 **Shchelkovo** Russia
89 E3 **Shchigry** Russia
91 C1 **Shchors** Ukr.
88 B3 **Shchuchyn** Belarus
91 D1 **Shebekino** Russia
117 C4 **Shebelē Wenz, Wabē** *r.* Eth./Somalia
140 B2 **Sheboygan** U.S.A.
91 D3 **Shebsh** *r.* Russia
97 C2 **Sheelin, Lough** *l.* Ireland
98 C2 **Sheffield** U.K.
89 E2 **Sheksna** Russia
89 E2 **Sheksninskoye Vodokhranilishche** *resr* Russia
83 M2 **Shelagskiy, Mys** *pt* Russia
131 D2 **Shelburne** Can.
134 D1 **Shelby** U.S.A.
140 B3 **Shelbyville** *IN* U.S.A.
142 C1 **Shelbyville** *TN* U.S.A.
83 L2 **Shelikhova, Zaliv** *g.* Russia
129 D2 **Shellbrook** Can.
134 B1 **Shelton** U.S.A.
137 D2 **Shenandoah** U.S.A.
141 D3 **Shenandoah** *r.* U.S.A.
141 D3 **Shenandoah Mountains** U.S.A.
118 A2 **Shendam** Nigeria
86 D2 **Shenkursk** Russia
65 A1 **Shenyang** China
71 B3 **Shenzhen** China
90 B1 **Shepetivka** Ukr.
53 C3 **Shepparton** Austr.
99 D3 **Sheppey, Isle of** *i.* U.K.
131 D2 **Sherbrooke** *N.S.* Can.
131 C2 **Sherbrooke** *Que.* Can.
116 B3 **Shereiq** Sudan
136 B2 **Sheridan** U.S.A.
139 D2 **Sherman** U.S.A.
100 B2 **'s-Hertogenbosch** Neth.
96 □ **Shetland Islands** U.K.
76 B2 **Shetpe** Kazakh.
Shevchenko Kazakh. *see* **Aktau**
137 D1 **Sheyenne** *r.* U.S.A.
79 B3 **Shibām** Yemen
66 D2 **Shibetsu** Japan
77 C3 **Shibirghān** Afgh.
71 B3 **Shicheng** China
96 B2 **Shiel, Loch** *l.* U.K.

Shihezi

77 E2 Shihezi China
Shijiazhuang China see Fogang
70 B2 Shijiazhuang China
74 A2 Shikarpur Pak.
67 B4 Shikoku i. Japan
66 D2 Shikotsu-ko l. Japan
86 D2 Shilega Russia
75 C2 Shiliguri India
75 D2 Shillong India
89 F3 Shilovo Russia
117 C3 Shimbiris mt. Somalia
67 C3 Shimizu Japan
73 B3 Shimoga India
84 B4 Shimonoseki Japan
96 B1 Shin, Loch l. U.K.
67 C4 Shingū Japan
123 C1 Shingwedzi S. Africa
123 C1 Shingwedzi r. S. Africa
119 D3 Shinyanga Tanz.
67 C4 Shiono-misaki c. Japan
138 B1 Shiprock U.S.A.
71 A2 Shiqian China
70 A2 Shiquan China
Shiquanhe China see Gar
Shiquan He r. China/Pak. see Indus
67 C3 Shirane-san mt. Japan
81 D3 Shīrāz Iran
66 D2 Shiretoko-misaki c. Japan
66 D2 Shiriya-zaki c. Japan
74 B2 Shiv India
Shivamogga India see Shimoga
69 D2 Shiveegovĭ Mongolia
75 B2 Shivpuri India
70 B2 Shiyan China
70 B2 Shizhong China
70 A2 Shizuishan China
67 C4 Shizuoka Japan
89 D3 Shklow Belarus
109 C2 Shkodër Albania
83 H1 Shmidta, Ostrov i. Russia
135 C3 Shoshone U.S.A.
135 C3 Shoshone Mountains U.S.A.
123 C1 Shoshong Botswana
91 C1 Shostka Ukr.
70 B2 Shouxian China
138 A2 Show Low U.S.A.
91 C2 Shpola Ukr.
142 B2 Shreveport U.S.A.
99 B2 Shrewsbury U.K.
62 A1 Shuangjiang China
87 E4 Shubarkudyk Kazakh.
116 B1 Shubrā al Khaymah Egypt
89 D2 Shugozero Russia
120 B2 Shumba Zimbabwe
110 C2 Shumen Bulg.
88 C2 Shumilina Belarus
89 D3 Shumyachi Russia
126 A2 Shungnak U.S.A.
78 B3 Shuqrah Yemen
89 F2 Shushkodom Russia
81 C2 Shūshtar Iran
128 C2 Shuswap Lake Can.
89 F2 Shuya Russia
89 F2 Shuyskoye Russia
62 A1 Shwebo Myanmar
62 A1 Shwedwin Myanmar
62 A2 Shwegyin Myanmar
77 D2 Shyganak Kazakh.
77 C2 Shymkent Kazakh.
91 C2 Shyroke Ukr.
59 C3 Sia Indon.
74 A2 Siahan Range mts Pak.
74 B1 Sialkot Pak.
64 B2 Siargao i. Phil.
88 B2 Šiauliai Lith.
109 C2 Šibenik Croatia

83 I2 Siberia reg. Russia
60 A2 Siberut i. Indon.
74 A2 Sibi Pak.
110 B1 Sibiu Romania
60 A1 Sibolga Indon.
61 C1 Sibu Sarawak Malaysia
118 B2 Sibut C.A.R.
64 B1 Sibuyan i. Phil.
64 B1 Sibuyan Sea Phil.
128 C2 Sicamous Can.
63 A3 Sichon Thai.
70 A2 Sichuan prov. China
70 A3 Sichuan Pendi basin China
105 D3 Sicié, Cap c. France
Sicilia i. Italy see Sicily
108 B3 Sicilian Channel Italy/Tunisia
108 B3 Sicily i. Italy
150 A3 Sicuani Peru
111 C3 Sideros, Akrotirio pt Greece
74 B2 Sidhpur India
107 D2 Sidi Aïssa Alg.
107 D2 Sidi Ali Alg.
114 B1 Sidi Bel Abbès Alg.
114 A2 Sidi Ifni Morocco
60 A1 Sidikalang Indon.
96 C2 Sidlaw Hills U.K.
99 B3 Sidmouth U.K.
136 C1 Sidney MT U.S.A.
136 C2 Sidney NE U.S.A.
140 C2 Sidney OH U.S.A.
143 D2 Sidney Lanier, Lake U.S.A.
80 B2 Sidon Lebanon
154 B2 Sidrolândia Brazil
103 E1 Siedlce Pol.
100 C2 Sieg r. Ger.
100 D2 Siegen Ger.
63 B2 Siĕm Réab Cambodia
108 B2 Siena Italy
103 D1 Sieradz Pol.
153 B5 Sierra Grande Arg.
114 A4 Sierra Leone country Africa
144 B2 Sierra Mojada Mex.
138 A2 Sierra Vista U.S.A.
105 D2 Sierre Switz.
111 B3 Sifnos i. Greece
107 C2 Sig Alg.
127 H2 Sigguup Nunaa pen. Greenland
103 E2 Sighetu Marmației Romania
110 B1 Sighișoara Romania
60 A1 Sigli Indon.
92 □B2 Siglufjörður Iceland
102 B2 Sigmaringen Ger.
100 B3 Signy-l'Abbaye France
106 C1 Sigüenza Spain
114 B3 Siguiri Guinea
88 B2 Sigulda Latvia
63 B2 Sihanoukville Cambodia
92 I3 Siilinjärvi Fin.
80 B2 Siirt Turkey
60 B2 Sijunjung Indon.
74 B2 Sikar India
114 B3 Sikasso Mali
137 F3 Sikeston U.S.A.
66 B2 Sikhote-Alin' mts Russia
111 C3 Sikinos i. Greece
75 C2 Sikkim state India
144 B2 Silao Mex.
75 D2 Silchar India
77 D1 Siletyteniz, Ozero salt l. Kazakh.
75 C2 Silgarhi Nepal
80 B2 Silifke Turkey
75 C1 Siling Co salt l. China
110 C2 Silistra Bulg.
80 A1 Silivri Turkey
93 F3 Siljan l. Sweden

93 E4 Silkeborg Denmark
88 C2 Sillamäe Estonia
142 B1 Siloam Springs U.S.A.
123 D2 Silobela S. Africa
88 B2 Šilut Lith.
81 C2 Silvan Turkey
138 B2 Silver City U.S.A.
136 B3 Silverton U.S.A.
62 B1 Simao China
130 C2 Simard, Lac l. Can.
111 C3 Simav Turkey
111 C3 Simav Dağları mts Turkey
118 C2 Simba Dem. Rep. Congo
141 D2 Simcoe, Lake Can.
60 A1 Simeulue i. Indon.
91 C3 Simferopol' Ukr.
110 B1 Şimleu Silvaniei Romania
100 C3 Şimmern/Hunsrück Ger.
129 D2 Simonhouse Can.
51 C2 Simpson Desert Austr.
93 F4 Simrishamn Sweden
60 A1 Sinabang Indon.
116 B2 Sinai pen. Egypt
71 A3 Sinan China
65 B2 Sinanju N. Korea
62 A1 Sinbo Myanmar
150 A1 Sincelejo Col.
111 C3 Sındırgı Turkey
86 E2 Sindor Russia
111 C2 Sinekçi Turkey
106 B2 Sines Port.
106 B2 Sines, Cabo de c. Port.
75 C2 Singahi India
60 B1 Singapore country Asia
61 C2 Singaraja Indon.
119 D3 Singida Tanz.
62 A1 Singkaling Hkamti Myanmar
61 B1 Singkawang Indon.
60 A1 Singkil Indon.
53 D2 Singleton Austr.
62 A1 Singu Myanmar
108 A2 Siniscola Sardinia Italy
109 C2 Sinj Croatia
116 B3 Sinkat Sudan
Sinkiang Uighur Autonomous Region aut. reg. China see Xinjiang Uygur Zizhiqu
80 B1 Sinop Turkey
65 B1 Sinp'o N. Korea
61 C1 Sintang Indon.
100 B2 Sint Anthonis Neth.
100 A2 Sint-Laureins Belgium
147 D3 Sint Maarten i. West Indies
147 D3 Sint Maarten terr. West Indies
100 B2 Sint-Niklaas Belgium
137 D3 Sinton U.S.A.
65 A1 Sinŭiju N. Korea
103 D2 Siófok Hungary
105 D2 Sion Switz.
137 D2 Sioux Center U.S.A.
137 D2 Sioux City U.S.A.
137 D2 Sioux Falls U.S.A.
130 A1 Sioux Lookout Can.
65 A1 Siping China
129 E2 Sipiwesk Lake Can.
60 A2 Sipura i. Indon.
93 E4 Sira r. Norway
Siracusa Italy see Syracuse
51 C1 Sir Edward Pellew Group is Austr.
116 B1 Sirhān, Wādī an watercourse Saudi Arabia
79 C2 Sīrīk Iran
62 B2 Siri Kit, Khuan Thai.
128 B1 Sir James MacBrien, Mount Can.
79 C2 Sīrjān Iran
81 C2 Şırnak Turkey

74 B2 **Sirohi** India
74 B2 **Sirsa** India
115 D1 **Sirte** Libya
115 D1 **Sirte, Gulf of** Libya
88 B2 **Širvintos** Lith.
145 C2 **Sisal** Mex.
122 B2 **Sishen** S. Africa
81 C2 **Sisian** Armenia
129 D2 **Sisipuk Lake** Can.
63 B2 **Sisŏphŏn** Cambodia
105 D3 **Sisteron** France
75 C2 **Sitapur** India
123 D2 **Siteki** Swaziland
128 A2 **Sitka** U.S.A.
100 B2 **Sittard** Neth.
62 A2 **Sittaung** *r.* Myanmar
62 A1 **Sittwe** Myanmar
61 C2 **Situbondo** Indon.
80 B2 **Sivas** Turkey
62 A1 **Sivasagar** India
111 C3 **Sivaslı** Turkey
80 B2 **Siverek** Turkey
80 B2 **Sivrihisar** Turkey
116 A2 **Sīwah** Egypt
74 B1 **Siwalik Range** *mts* India/Nepal
105 D3 **Six-Fours-les-Plages** France
70 B2 **Sixian** China
123 C2 **Siyabuswa** S. Africa
Sjælland *i.* Denmark *see* **Zealand**
109 D2 **Sjenica** Serbia
92 G2 **Sjøvegan** Norway
91 C2 **Skadovs'k** Ukr.
93 F4 **Skagen** Denmark
93 E4 **Skagerrak** *str.* Denmark/Norway
134 B1 **Skagit** *r.* U.S.A.
128 A2 **Skagway** U.S.A.
74 B1 **Skardu** Pak.
103 E1 **Skarżysko-Kamienna** Pol.
103 D2 **Skawina** Pol.
128 B2 **Skeena** *r.* Can.
128 B2 **Skeena Mountains** Can.
98 D2 **Skegness** U.K.
92 H3 **Skellefteå** Sweden
92 H3 **Skellefteälven** *r.* Sweden
97 C2 **Skerries** Ireland
111 B3 **Skiathos** *i.* Greece
97 B3 **Skibbereen** Ireland
92 □B2 **Skíðadalsjökull** *glacier* Iceland
98 B1 **Skiddaw** *h.* U.K.
93 E4 **Skien** Norway
103 E1 **Skierniewice** Pol.
115 C1 **Skikda** Alg.
52 B3 **Skipton** Austr.
98 B2 **Skipton** U.K.
93 E4 **Skive** Denmark
92 H1 **Skjervøy** Norway
111 B3 **Skopelos** *i.* Greece
89 E3 **Skopin** Russia
109 D2 **Skopje** Macedonia
93 F4 **Skövde** Sweden
141 F2 **Skowhegan** U.S.A.
88 B2 **Skrunda** Latvia
128 A1 **Skukum, Mount** Can.
123 D1 **Skukuza** S. Africa
88 B2 **Skuodas** Lith.
96 A2 **Skye** *i.* U.K.
111 B3 **Skyros** Greece
111 B3 **Skyros** *i.* Greece
93 F4 **Slagelse** Denmark
97 C2 **Slaney** *r.* Ireland
88 C2 **Slantsy** Russia
109 C1 **Slatina** Croatia
110 B2 **Slatina** Romania
129 C1 **Slave** *r.* Can.
114 C4 **Slave Coast** Africa
128 C2 **Slave Lake** Can.
82 G3 **Slavgorod** Russia
109 C1 **Slavonski Brod** Croatia
90 B1 **Slavuta** Ukr.
90 C1 **Slavutych** Ukr.
91 D2 **Slavyansk-na-Kubani** Russia
89 D3 **Slawharad** Belarus
103 D1 **Sławno** Pol.
97 A2 **Slea Head** Ireland
130 C1 **Sleeper Islands** Can.
97 D1 **Slieve Donard** *h.* U.K.
Slieve Gamph *hills* Ireland *see* **Ox Mountains**
97 B1 **Sligo** Ireland
97 B1 **Sligo Bay** Ireland
93 G4 **Slite** Sweden
110 C2 **Sliven** Bulg.
110 C2 **Slobozia** Romania
128 C3 **Slocan** Can.
88 C3 **Slonim** Belarus
100 B1 **Sloten** Neth.
99 C3 **Slough** U.K.
103 D2 **Slovakia** *country* Europe
108 B1 **Slovenia** *country* Europe
91 D2 **Slov"yans'k** Ukr.
90 B1 **Sluch** *r.* Ukr.
103 D1 **Słupsk** Pol.
88 C3 **Slutsk** Belarus
97 A2 **Slyne Head** Ireland
131 D1 **Smallwood Reservoir** Can.
88 C3 **Smalyavichy** Belarus
88 C3 **Smarhon'** Belarus
129 D2 **Smeaton** Can.
109 D2 **Smederevo** Serbia
109 D2 **Smederevska Palanka** Serbia
91 C2 **Smila** Ukr.
88 C2 **Smiltene** Latvia
128 B2 **Smithers** Can.
143 E1 **Smithfield** U.S.A.
141 D3 **Smith Mountain Lake** U.S.A.
130 C2 **Smiths Falls** Can.
137 D3 **Smoky Hills** U.S.A.
92 E3 **Smøla** *i.* Norway
89 D3 **Smolensk** Russia
110 B2 **Smolyan** Bulg.
130 B2 **Smooth Rock Falls** Can.
Smyrna Turkey *see* **İzmir**
92 □B3 **Snæfell** *mt.* Iceland
98 A1 **Snaefell** *h.* Isle of Man
132 B2 **Snake** *r.* U.S.A.
134 D2 **Snake River Plain** U.S.A.
100 B1 **Sneek** Neth.
97 B3 **Sneem** Ireland
122 B3 **Sneeuberge** *mts* S. Africa
108 B1 **Snežnik** *mt.* Slovenia
91 C2 **Snihurivka** Ukr.
93 E3 **Snøhetta** *mt.* Norway
129 D1 **Snowbird Lake** Can.
98 A2 **Snowdon** *mt.* U.K.
Snowdrift Can. *see* **Łutselk'e**
129 C1 **Snowdrift** *r.* Can.
138 A2 **Snowflake** U.S.A.
129 D2 **Snow Lake** Can.
52 A2 **Snowtown** Austr.
53 C3 **Snowy** *r.* Austr.
53 C3 **Snowy Mountains** Austr.
139 C2 **Snyder** U.S.A.
121 □D2 **Soalala** Madag.
117 B4 **Sobat** *r.* South Sudan
89 F2 **Sobinka** Russia
151 D3 **Sobradinho, Barragem de** *resr* Brazil
151 D2 **Sobral** Brazil
87 C4 **Sochi** Russia
49 H4 **Society Islands** Fr. Polynesia
150 A1 **Socorro** Col.
138 B2 **Socorro** U.S.A.
144 A3 **Socorro, Isla** *i.* Mex.
56 F6 **Socotra** *i.* Yemen
63 B3 **Soc Trăng** Vietnam
106 C2 **Socuéllamos** Spain
92 I2 **Sodankylä** Fin.
134 D2 **Soda Springs** U.S.A.
93 G3 **Söderhamn** Sweden
93 G4 **Södertälje** Sweden
116 A3 **Sodiri** Sudan
117 B4 **Sodo** Eth.
93 G3 **Södra Kvarken** *str.* Fin./Sweden
100 D2 **Soest** Ger.
110 B2 **Sofia** Bulg.
Sofiya Bulg. *see* **Sofia**
68 C2 **Sog** China
93 E3 **Sognefjorden** *inlet* Norway
111 D2 **Söğüt** Turkey
100 B2 **Soignies** Belgium
105 C2 **Soissons** France
90 A1 **Sokal'** Ukr.
111 C3 **Söke** Turkey
81 C1 **Sokhumi** Georgia
114 C4 **Sokodé** Togo
89 F2 **Sokol** Russia
101 F2 **Sokolov** Czech Rep.
115 C3 **Sokoto** Nigeria
115 C3 **Sokoto** *r.* Nigeria
90 B2 **Sokyryany** Ukr.
73 B3 **Solapur** India
135 B3 **Soledad** U.S.A.
89 F2 **Soligalich** Russia
99 C2 **Solihull** U.K.
86 E3 **Solikamsk** Russia
87 E3 **Sol'-Iletsk** Russia
100 C2 **Solingen** Ger.
92 G3 **Sollefteå** Sweden
93 G4 **Sollentuna** Sweden
101 D2 **Solling** *hills* Ger.
89 E2 **Solnechnogorsk** Russia
60 B2 **Solok** Indon.
48 E3 **Solomon Islands** *country* S. Pacific Ocean
48 E3 **Solomon Sea** S. Pacific Ocean
105 D2 **Solothurn** Switz.
101 D1 **Soltau** Ger.
89 D2 **Sol'tsy** Russia
96 C3 **Solway Firth** *est.* U.K.
120 B2 **Solwezi** Zambia
111 C3 **Soma** Turkey
117 C4 **Somalia** *country* Africa
117 A4 **Somaliland** *disp. terr.* Somalia
120 B1 **Sombo** Angola
109 C1 **Sombor** Serbia
144 B2 **Sombrerete** Mex.
140 C3 **Somerset** U.S.A.
123 C3 **Somerset East** S. Africa
126 E2 **Somerset Island** Can.
122 A3 **Somerset West** S. Africa
101 E2 **Sömmerda** Ger.
75 C2 **Son** *r.* India
65 C1 **Sŏnbong** N. Korea
93 E4 **Sønderborg** Denmark
101 E2 **Sondershausen** Ger.
Søndre Strømfjord *inlet* Greenland *see* **Kangerlussuaq**
62 B1 **Sông Đa, Hồ** *resr* Vietnam
119 D4 **Songea** Tanz.
65 B1 **Sŏnggan** N. Korea
65 B1 **Songhua Hu** *resr* China
Sŏngjin N. Korea *see* **Kimch'aek**
63 B3 **Songkhla** Thai.
65 B2 **Songnim** N. Korea
120 A1 **Songo** Angola
121 C2 **Songo** Moz.
69 E1 **Songyuan** China

Sonid Youqi China *see* Saihan Tal
89 E2 Sonkovo Russia
62 B1 Sơn La Vietnam
74 A2 Sonmiani Pak.
101 E2 Sonneberg Ger.
138 A2 Sonoita Mex.
144 A2 Sonora *r.* Mex.
135 B3 Sonora *CA* U.S.A.
139 C2 Sonora *TX* U.S.A.
117 A4 Sopo *watercourse* South Sudan
103 D2 Sopron Hungary
108 B2 Sora Italy
130 C2 Sorel Can.
51 D4 Sorell Austr.
106 C1 Soria Spain
90 B2 Soroca Moldova
154 C2 Sorocaba Brazil
87 E3 Sorochinsk Russia
59 D2 Sorol *atoll* Micronesia
59 C3 Sorong Indon.
119 D2 Soroti Uganda
92 H1 Sørøya *i.* Norway
92 G2 Sorsele Sweden
64 B1 Sorsogon Phil.
86 C2 Sortavala Russia
92 G2 Sortland Norway
123 C2 Soshanguve S. Africa
89 E3 Sosna *r.* Russia
153 B4 Sosneado *mt.* Arg.
86 E2 Sosnogorsk Russia
86 D2 Sosnovka Russia
88 C2 Sosnovyy Bor Russia
103 D1 Sosnowiec Pol.
91 D2 Sosyka *r.* Russia
145 C2 Soto la Marina Mex.
118 B2 Souanké Congo
104 C3 Souillac France
Sŏul S. Korea *see* Seoul
104 B2 Soulac-sur-Mer France
104 B3 Soulom France
Soûr Lebanon *see* Tyre
107 D2 Sour el Ghozlane Alg.
129 D3 Souris *Man.* Can.
131 D2 Souris *P.E.I.* Can.
129 E3 Souris *r.* Can.
151 E2 Sousa Brazil
115 D1 Sousse Tunisia
104 B3 Soustons France
122 B3 South Africa *country* Africa
99 C3 Southampton U.K.
127 F2 Southampton Island Can.
73 D3 South Andaman *i.* India
52 A1 South Australia *state* Austr.
130 B2 South Baymouth Can.
140 B2 South Bend U.S.A.
143 D2 South Carolina *state* U.S.A.
156 B4 South China Sea N. Pacific Ocean
136 C2 South Dakota *state* U.S.A.
99 C3 South Downs *hills* U.K.
129 D2 Southend Can.
99 D3 Southend-on-Sea U.K.
54 B2 Southern Alps *mts* N.Z.
50 A3 Southern Cross Austr.
129 E2 Southern Indian Lake Can.
159 Southern Ocean
143 E1 Southern Pines U.S.A.
96 B3 Southern Uplands *hills* U.K.
149 F6 South Georgia and the South Sandwich Islands *terr.* S. Atlantic Ocean
96 A2 South Harris *pen.* U.K.
129 E1 South Henik Lake Can.
54 B2 South Island N.Z.
65 B2 South Korea *country* Asia
135 B3 South Lake Tahoe U.S.A.
55 Q4 South Orkney Islands S. Atlantic Ocean
81 C1 South Ossetia *disp. terr.* Georgia
136 C2 South Platte *r.* U.S.A.
98 B2 Southport U.K.
143 E2 Southport U.S.A.
96 C1 South Ronaldsay *i.* U.K.
123 D3 South Sand Bluff *pt* S. Africa
129 D2 South Saskatchewan *r.* Can.
129 E2 South Seal *r.* Can.
55 P3 South Shetland Islands Antarctica
98 C1 South Shields U.K.
117 A4 South Sudan *country* Africa
54 B1 South Taranaki Bight *b.* N.Z.
130 C1 South Twin Island Can.
96 A2 South Uist *i.* U.K.
53 D2 South West Rocks Austr.
99 D2 Southwold U.K.
109 C3 Soverato Italy
88 B2 Sovetsk Russia
86 F2 Sovetskiy Russia
91 C2 Sovyets'kyy Ukr.
123 C2 Soweto S. Africa
66 D1 Sōya-misaki *c.* Japan
90 C1 Sozh *r.* Europe
110 C2 Sozopol Bulg.
106 C1 Spain *country* Europe
99 C2 Spalding U.K.
135 D2 Spanish Fork U.S.A.
97 B2 Spanish Point Ireland
108 B3 Sparagio, Monte *mt. Sicily* Italy
135 C3 Sparks U.S.A.
140 A2 Sparta U.S.A.
143 D2 Spartanburg U.S.A.
111 B3 Sparti Greece
109 C3 Spartivento, Capo *c.* Italy
89 D3 Spas-Demensk Russia
89 F2 Spas-Klepiki Russia
66 B2 Spassk-Dal'niy Russia
89 F3 Spassk-Ryazanskiy Russia
111 B3 Spatha, Akrotirio *pt* Greece
136 C2 Spearfish U.S.A.
139 C1 Spearman U.S.A.
137 D2 Spencer U.S.A.
52 A2 Spencer Gulf *est.* Austr.
98 C1 Spennymoor U.K.
54 B2 Spenser Mountains N.Z.
101 D3 Spessart *reg.* Ger.
96 C2 Spey *r.* U.K.
102 B2 Speyer Ger.
100 C1 Spiekeroog *i.* Ger.
100 B2 Spijkenisse Neth.
128 C2 Spirit River Can.
103 E2 Spišská Nová Ves Slovakia
82 C1 Spitsbergen *i.* Svalbard
102 C2 Spittal an der Drau Austria
109 C2 Split Croatia
129 E2 Split Lake Can.
129 E2 Split Lake Can.
134 C1 Spokane U.S.A.
140 A1 Spooner U.S.A.
102 C1 Spree *r.* Ger.
122 A2 Springbok S. Africa
131 E2 Springdale Can.
142 B1 Springdale U.S.A.
101 D1 Springe Ger.
138 C1 Springer U.S.A.
138 B2 Springerville U.S.A.
136 C3 Springfield *CO* U.S.A.
140 B3 Springfield *IL* U.S.A.
141 E2 Springfield *MA* U.S.A.
137 E3 Springfield *MO* U.S.A.
140 C3 Springfield *OH* U.S.A.
134 B2 Springfield *OR* U.S.A.
123 C3 Springfontein S. Africa
131 D2 Springhill Can.
143 D3 Spring Hill U.S.A.
54 B2 Springs Junction N.Z.
98 D2 Spurn Head U.K.
128 B3 Squamish Can.
109 C3 Squillace, Golfo di *g.* Italy
Srbija *country* Europe *see* Serbia
109 C2 Srebrenica Bos. & Herz.
110 C2 Sredets Bulg.
83 L3 Sredinnyy Khrebet *mts* Russia
83 L2 Srednekolymsk Russia
Sredne-Russkaya Vozvyshennost' *hills* Russia *see* Central Russian Upland
Sredne-Sibirskoye Ploskogor'ye *plat.* Russia *see* Central Siberian Plateau
69 D1 Sretensk Russia
61 C1 Sri Aman *Sarawak* Malaysia
73 B4 Sri Jayewardenepura Kotte Sri Lanka
73 C3 Srikakulam India
73 C4 Sri Lanka *country* Asia
74 B1 Srinagar India
73 B3 Srivardhan India
101 D1 Stade Ger.
101 E1 Stadensen Ger.
100 C1 Stadskanaal Neth.
101 D2 Stadtallendorf Ger.
101 D1 Stadthagen Ger.
99 B2 Stafford U.K.
99 C3 Staines-upon-Thames U.K.
91 D2 Stakhanov Ukr.
Stalingrad Russia *see* Volgograd
103 E1 Stalowa Wola Pol.
99 C2 Stamford U.K.
141 E2 Stamford *CT* U.S.A.
139 D2 Stamford *TX* U.S.A.
122 A1 Stampriet Namibia
92 F2 Stamsund Norway
123 C2 Standerton S. Africa
140 C2 Standish U.S.A.
153 C6 Stanley Falkland Is
136 C1 Stanley U.S.A.
83 I3 Stanovoye Nagor'ye *mts* Russia
83 J3 Stanovoy Khrebet *mts* Russia
53 D1 Stanthorpe Austr.
103 E1 Starachowice Pol.
Stara Planina *mts* Bulgaria/ Serbia *see* Balkan Mountains
89 D2 Staraya Russa Russia
89 D2 Staraya Toropa Russia
110 C2 Stara Zagora Bulg.
103 D1 Stargard Szczeciński Pol.
142 C2 Starkville U.S.A.
91 D2 Starobil's'k Ukr.
89 D3 Starodub Russia
103 D1 Starogard Gdański Pol.
90 B2 Starokostyantyniv Ukr.
91 D2 Starominskaya Russia
91 D2 Staroshcherbinovskaya Russia
91 D2 Starotitarovskaya Russia
89 F3 Staroyur'yevo Russia
99 B3 Start Point U.K.
88 C3 Staryya Darohi Belarus
89 E3 Staryy Oskol Russia
101 E2 Staßfurt Ger.
141 D2 State College U.S.A.
143 D2 Statesboro U.S.A.
143 D1 Statesville U.S.A.
93 E4 Stavanger Norway
87 D4 Stavropol' Russia
87 D4 Stavropol'skaya Vozvyshennost' *hills* Russia

52 B3 **Stawell** Austr.
123 C2 **Steadville** S. Africa
136 B2 **Steamboat Springs** U.S.A.
101 E2 **Stedten** Ger.
128 C2 **Steen River** Can.
134 C2 **Steens Mountain** U.S.A.
100 C1 **Steenwijk** Neth.
126 D2 **Stefansson Island** Can.
101 E3 **Steigerwald** *mts* Ger.
129 E3 **Steinbach** Can.
100 C1 **Steinfurt** Ger.
120 A3 **Steinhausen** Namibia
92 F3 **Steinkjer** Norway
122 A2 **Steinkopf** S. Africa
122 B2 **Stella** S. Africa
105 D2 **Stenay** France
101 E1 **Stendal** Ger.
Stepanakert Azer. *see* **Xankändi**
131 E2 **Stephenville** Can.
139 D2 **Stephenville** U.S.A.
122 B3 **Sterling** S. Africa
136 C2 **Sterling** *CO* U.S.A.
140 B2 **Sterling** *IL* U.S.A.
87 E3 **Sterlitamak** Russia
101 E1 **Sternberg** Ger.
128 C2 **Stettler** Can.
140 C2 **Steubenville** U.S.A.
99 C3 **Stevenage** U.K.
129 E2 **Stevenson Lake** Can.
126 B2 **Stevens Village** U.S.A.
128 B2 **Stewart** Can.
126 B2 **Stewart** *r.* Can.
54 A3 **Stewart Island** N.Z.
127 F2 **Stewart Lake** Can.
102 C2 **Steyr** Austria
122 B3 **Steytlerville** S. Africa
128 A2 **Stikine** *r.* Can.
128 A2 **Stikine Plateau** Can.
122 B3 **Stilbaai** S. Africa
139 D1 **Stillwater** U.S.A.
109 D2 **Štip** Macedonia
96 C2 **Stirling** U.K.
92 F3 **Stjørdalshalsen** Norway
103 D2 **Stockerau** Austria
93 G4 **Stockholm** Sweden
98 B2 **Stockport** U.K.
135 B3 **Stockton** U.S.A.
98 C1 **Stockton-on-Tees** U.K.
63 B2 **Stœng Trêng** Cambodia
96 B1 **Stoer, Point of** U.K.
98 B2 **Stoke-on-Trent** U.K.
109 D2 **Stol** *mt.* Serbia
109 C2 **Stolac** Bos. & Herz.
100 C2 **Stolberg (Rheinland)** Ger.
88 C3 **Stolin** Belarus
101 F2 **Stollberg** Ger.
101 D1 **Stolzenau** Ger.
96 C2 **Stonehaven** U.K.
129 E2 **Stonewall** Can.
129 D2 **Stony Rapids** Can.
92 G2 **Storavan** *l.* Sweden
Store Bælt *sea chan.* Denmark *see* **Great Belt**
92 F3 **Støren** Norway
92 F2 **Storforshei** Norway
126 D2 **Storkerson Peninsula** Can.
137 D2 **Storm Lake** U.S.A.
93 E3 **Stornosa** *mt.* Norway
96 A1 **Stornoway** U.K.
86 E2 **Storozhevsk** Russia
90 B2 **Storozhynets'** Ukr.
92 F3 **Storsjön** *l.* Sweden
92 H2 **Storslett** Norway
92 G2 **Storuman** Sweden
99 C2 **Stour** *r. England* U.K.
99 C3 **Stour** *r. England* U.K.
130 A1 **Stout Lake** Can.
88 C3 **Stowbtsy** Belarus
97 C1 **Strabane** U.K.
102 C2 **Strakonice** Czech Rep.
102 C1 **Stralsund** Ger.
122 A3 **Strand** S. Africa
93 E3 **Stranda** Norway
97 D1 **Strangford Lough** *inlet* U.K.
96 B3 **Stranraer** U.K.
105 D2 **Strasbourg** France
140 C2 **Stratford** Can.
54 B1 **Stratford** N.Z.
139 C1 **Stratford** U.S.A.
99 C2 **Stratford-upon-Avon** U.K.
128 C2 **Strathmore** Can.
96 C2 **Strathspey** *val.* U.K.
102 C2 **Straubing** Ger.
51 C3 **Streaky Bay** Austr.
140 B2 **Streator** U.S.A.
110 B2 **Strehaia** Romania
153 B5 **Stroeder** Arg.
101 D1 **Ströhen** Ger.
109 C3 **Stromboli, Isola** *i.* Italy
96 C1 **Stromness** U.K.
92 G3 **Strömsund** Sweden
96 C1 **Stronsay** *i.* U.K.
53 D2 **Stroud** Austr.
99 B3 **Stroud** U.K.
100 C1 **Strücklingen (Saterland)** Ger.
109 D2 **Struga** Macedonia
88 C2 **Strugi-Krasnyye** Russia
122 B3 **Struis Bay** S. Africa
109 D2 **Strumica** Macedonia
122 B2 **Strydenburg** S. Africa
111 B2 **Strymonas** *r.* Greece
90 A2 **Stryy** Ukr.
128 B2 **Stuart Lake** Can.
130 A1 **Stull Lake** Can.
89 E3 **Stupino** Russia
140 B2 **Sturgeon Bay** U.S.A.
130 C2 **Sturgeon Falls** Can.
130 A2 **Sturgeon Lake** Can.
140 B2 **Sturgis** *MI* U.S.A.
136 C2 **Sturgis** *SD* U.S.A.
50 B1 **Sturt Creek** *watercourse* Austr.
52 B1 **Sturt Stony Desert** Austr.
123 C3 **Stutterheim** S. Africa
102 B2 **Stuttgart** Ger.
142 B2 **Stuttgart** U.S.A.
92 □A2 **Stykkishólmur** Iceland
90 B1 **Styr** *r.* Belarus/Ukr.
155 D1 **Suaçuí Grande** *r.* Brazil
116 B3 **Suakin** Sudan
78 A3 **Suara** Eritrea
109 C1 **Subotica** Serbia
110 C1 **Suceava** Romania
97 B2 **Suck** *r.* Ireland
152 B2 **Sucre** Bol.
154 B2 **Sucuriú** *r.* Brazil
89 E2 **Suda** Russia
91 C3 **Sudak** Ukr.
117 A3 **Sudan** *country* Africa
130 B2 **Sudbury** Can.
117 A4 **Sudd** *swamp* South Sudan
89 F2 **Sudislavl'** Russia
89 F2 **Sudogda** Russia
94 B1 **Suðuroy** *i.* Faroe Is
107 C2 **Sueca** Spain
116 B2 **Suez** Egypt
116 B2 **Suez, Gulf of** Egypt
80 B2 **Suez Canal** Egypt
141 D3 **Suffolk** U.S.A.
116 B2 **Sūhāj** Egypt
79 C2 **Şuḩār** Oman
69 D1 **Sühbaatar** Mongolia
101 E2 **Suhl** Ger.
109 C1 **Suhopolje** Croatia
70 B2 **Suide** China
66 B2 **Suifenhe** China
69 E1 **Suihua** China
70 A2 **Suining** China
70 B2 **Suiping** China
70 B2 **Suiyang** China
70 B2 **Suizhou** China
74 B2 **Sujangarh** India
74 B1 **Sujanpur** India
74 A2 **Sujawal** Pak.
60 B2 **Sukabumi** Indon.
61 B2 **Sukadana** Indon.
61 C2 **Sukaraja** Indon.
89 E3 **Sukhinichi** Russia
89 F2 **Sukhona** *r.* Russia
62 A2 **Sukhothai** Thai.
74 A2 **Sukkur** Pak.
89 E2 **Sukromny** Russia
59 C3 **Sula, Kepulauan** *is* Indon.
74 A1 **Sulaiman Range** *mts* Pak.
Sulawesi *i.* Indon. *see* **Celebes**
150 A2 **Sullana** Peru
137 E3 **Sullivan** U.S.A.
139 D2 **Sulphur Springs** U.S.A.
64 B2 **Sulu Archipelago** *is* Phil.
64 A2 **Sulu Sea** N. Pacific Ocean
101 E3 **Sulzbach-Rosenberg** Ger.
79 C2 **Sumāil** Oman
Sumatera *i.* Indon. *see* **Sumatra**
60 A1 **Sumatra** *i.* Indon.
58 C3 **Sumba** *i.* Indon.
61 C2 **Sumbawa** *i.* Indon.
61 C2 **Sumbawabesar** Indon.
119 D3 **Sumbawanga** Tanz.
120 A2 **Sumbe** Angola
96 □ **Sumburgh** U.K.
96 □ **Sumburgh Head** U.K.
61 C2 **Sumenep** Indon.
67 D4 **Sumisu-jima** *i.* Japan
131 D2 **Summerside** Can.
140 C3 **Summersville** U.S.A.
128 B2 **Summit Lake** Can.
103 D2 **Šumperk** Czech Rep.
81 C1 **Sumqayıt** Azer.
143 D2 **Sumter** U.S.A.
91 C1 **Sumy** Ukr.
75 D2 **Sunamganj** Bangl.
65 B2 **Sunan** N. Korea
79 C2 **Şunaynah** Oman
52 B3 **Sunbury** Austr.
141 D2 **Sunbury** U.S.A.
65 B3 **Suncheon** S. Korea
65 B2 **Sunch'ŏn** N. Korea
123 C2 **Sun City** S. Africa
60 B2 **Sunda, Selat** *str.* Indon.
136 C2 **Sundance** U.S.A.
75 C2 **Sundarbans** *coastal area* Bangl./India
98 C1 **Sunderland** U.K.
128 C2 **Sundre** Can.
93 G3 **Sundsvall** Sweden
123 D2 **Sundumbili** S. Africa
60 B2 **Sungailiat** Indon.
60 B2 **Sungaipenuh** Indon.
60 B1 **Sungai Petani** Malaysia
80 B1 **Sungurlu** Turkey
93 E3 **Sunndalsøra** Norway
134 C1 **Sunnyside** U.S.A.
135 B3 **Sunnyvale** U.S.A.
83 I2 **Suntar** Russia
74 A2 **Suntsar** Pak.
114 B4 **Sunyani** Ghana
82 D2 **Suoyarvi** Russia
138 A2 **Superior** *AZ* U.S.A.
137 D2 **Superior** *NE* U.S.A.
140 A1 **Superior** *WI* U.S.A.
140 B1 **Superior, Lake** Can./U.S.A.
89 D3 **Suponevo** Russia

81 C2 **Sūq ash Shuyūkh** Iraq
70 B2 **Suqian** China
78 A2 **Sūq Suwayq** Saudi Arabia
79 C2 **Şūr** Oman
74 A2 **Surab** Pak.
61 C2 **Surabaya** Indon.
61 C2 **Surakarta** Indon.
74 B2 **Surat** India
74 B2 **Suratgarh** India
63 A3 **Surat Thani** Thai.
89 D3 **Surazh** Russia
109 D2 **Surdulica** Serbia
74 B2 **Surendranagar** India
82 F2 **Surgut** Russia
64 B2 **Surigao** Phil.
63 B2 **Surin** Thai.
151 C1 **Suriname** *country* S. America
Surt Libya *see* **Sirte**
Surt, Khalīj *g.* Libya *see* **Sirte, Gulf of**
60 B2 **Surulangun** Indon.
89 F2 **Susanino** Russia
135 B2 **Susanville** U.S.A.
80 B1 **Suşehri** Turkey
131 D2 **Sussex** Can.
101 D1 **Süstedt** Ger.
100 C1 **Sustrum** Ger.
83 K2 **Susuman** Russia
111 C3 **Susurluk** Turkey
75 B1 **Sutak** India
122 B3 **Sutherland** S. Africa
99 C2 **Sutton Coldfield** U.K.
66 D2 **Suttsu** Japan
49 F4 **Suva** Fiji
89 E3 **Suvorov** Russia
103 E1 **Suwałki** Pol.
63 B2 **Suwannaphum** Thai.
143 D3 **Suwannee** *r.* U.S.A.
Suweis, Qanâ el *canal* Egypt *see* **Suez Canal**
65 B2 **Suwon** S. Korea
79 C2 **Sūzā** Iran
89 F2 **Suzdal'** Russia
70 B2 **Suzhou** *Anhui* China
70 C2 **Suzhou** *Jiangsu* China
67 C3 **Suzu** Japan
67 C3 **Suzu-misaki** *pt* Japan
82 B1 **Svalbard** *terr.* Arctic Ocean
91 D2 **Svatove** Ukr.
63 B2 **Svay Riĕng** Cambodia
93 F3 **Sveg** Sweden
88 C2 **Švenčionys** Lith.
93 F4 **Svendborg** Denmark
Sverdlovsk Russia *see* **Yekaterinburg**
109 D2 **Sveti Nikole** Macedonia
88 B3 **Svetlogorsk** Russia
88 B3 **Svetlyy** Russia
93 I3 **Svetogorsk** Russia
110 C2 **Svilengrad** Bulg.
110 B2 **Svinecea Mare, Vârful** *mt.* Romania
110 C2 **Svishtov** Bulg.
103 D2 **Svitavy** Czech Rep.
91 C2 **Svitlovods'k** Ukr.
69 E1 **Svobodnyy** Russia
92 F2 **Svolvær** Norway
88 C3 **Svyetlahorsk** Belarus
143 D2 **Swainsboro** U.S.A.
120 A3 **Swakopmund** Namibia
52 B3 **Swan Hill** Austr.
128 C2 **Swan Hills** Can.
129 D2 **Swan Lake** Can.
129 D2 **Swan River** Can.
53 D2 **Swansea** Austr.
99 B3 **Swansea** U.K.
123 C2 **Swartruggens** S. Africa
Swatow China *see* **Shantou**
123 D2 **Swaziland** *country* Africa
93 G3 **Sweden** *country* Europe
139 C2 **Sweetwater** U.S.A.
136 B2 **Sweetwater** *r.* U.S.A.
122 B3 **Swellendam** S. Africa
103 D1 **Świdnica** Pol.
103 D1 **Świdwin** Pol.
103 D1 **Świebodzin** Pol.
103 D1 **Świecie** Pol.
129 D2 **Swift Current** Can.
97 C1 **Swilly, Lough** *inlet* Ireland
99 C3 **Swindon** U.K.
102 C1 **Świnoujście** Pol.
105 D2 **Switzerland** *country* Europe
97 C2 **Swords** Ireland
88 C3 **Syanno** Belarus
89 D2 **Sychevka** Russia
53 D2 **Sydney** Austr.
131 D2 **Sydney** Can.
131 D2 **Sydney Mines** Can.
91 D2 **Syeverodonets'k** Ukr.
86 E2 **Syktyvkar** Russia
142 C2 **Sylacauga** U.S.A.
75 D2 **Sylhet** Bangl.
102 B1 **Sylt** *i.* Ger.
111 C3 **Symi** *i.* Greece
91 D2 **Synel'nykove** Ukr.
109 C3 **Syracuse** *Sicily* Italy
136 C3 **Syracuse** *KS* U.S.A.
141 D2 **Syracuse** *NY* U.S.A.
77 C2 **Syrdar'ya** *r.* Asia
80 B2 **Syria** *country* Asia
80 B2 **Syrian Desert** Asia
111 B3 **Syros** *i.* Greece
87 D3 **Syzran'** Russia
102 C1 **Szczecin** Pol.
103 D1 **Szczecinek** Pol.
103 E1 **Szczytno** Pol.
103 E2 **Szeged** Hungary
103 D2 **Székesfehérvár** Hungary
103 D2 **Szekszárd** Hungary
103 E2 **Szentes** Hungary
103 D2 **Szentgotthárd** Hungary
103 D2 **Szigetvár** Hungary
103 E2 **Szolnok** Hungary
103 D2 **Szombathely** Hungary

T

78 B2 **Tābah** Saudi Arabia
76 B3 **Ţabas** Iran
81 D3 **Tābask, Kūh-e** *mt.* Iran
150 B2 **Tabatinga** Brazil
114 B2 **Tabelbala** Alg.
129 C3 **Taber** Can.
102 C2 **Tábor** Czech Rep.
119 D3 **Tabora** Tanz.
114 B4 **Tabou** Côte d'Ivoire
81 C2 **Tabrīz** Iran
78 A2 **Tabūk** Saudi Arabia
77 E2 **Tacheng** China
102 C2 **Tachov** Czech Rep.
64 B1 **Tacloban** Phil.
150 A3 **Tacna** Peru
134 B1 **Tacoma** U.S.A.
152 C4 **Tacuarembó** Uru.
138 B3 **Tacupeto** Mex.
117 C3 **Tadjourah** Djibouti
80 B2 **Tadmur** Syria
129 E2 **Tadoule Lake** Can.
65 B2 **Taebaek** S. Korea
Taegu S. Korea *see* **Daegu**
Taejŏn S. Korea *see* **Daejeon**
107 C1 **Tafalla** Spain
152 B3 **Tafi Viejo** Arg.
79 D2 **Taftān, Kūh-e** *mt.* Iran
91 D2 **Taganrog** Russia
91 D2 **Taganrog, Gulf of** Russia/Ukr.
62 A1 **Tagaung** Myanmar
64 B1 **Tagaytay City** Phil.
64 B2 **Tagbilaran** Phil.
64 B1 **Tagudin** Phil.
64 B2 **Tagum** Phil.
106 B2 **Tagus** *r.* Port./Spain
60 B1 **Tahan, Gunung** *mt.* Malaysia
115 C2 **Tahat, Mont** *mt.* Alg.
69 E1 **Tahe** China
49 I4 **Tahiti** *i.* Fr. Polynesia
139 E1 **Tahlequah** U.S.A.
135 B3 **Tahoe, Lake** U.S.A.
135 B3 **Tahoe City** U.S.A.
126 D2 **Tahoe Lake** Can.
115 C3 **Tahoua** Niger
79 C2 **Tahrūd** Iran
128 B3 **Tahsis** Can.
70 B2 **Tai'an** China
71 C3 **Taibei** Taiwan
Taibus Qi China *see* **Baochang**
54 C1 **Taihape** N.Z.
70 C2 **Tai Hu** *l.* China
52 A3 **Tailem Bend** Austr.
71 C3 **Tainan** Taiwan
155 D1 **Taiobeiras** Brazil
60 B1 **Taiping** Malaysia
71 B3 **Taishan** China
153 A5 **Taitao, Península de** *pen.* Chile
71 C3 **T'aitung** Taiwan
92 I2 **Taivalkoski** Fin.
92 H2 **Taivaskero** *h.* Fin.
71 C3 **Taiwan** *country* Asia
71 B3 **Taiwan Strait** China/Taiwan
70 B2 **Taiyuan** China
71 C3 **Taizhong** Taiwan
70 B2 **Taizhou** *Jiangsu* China
71 C3 **Taizhou** *Zhejiang* China
78 B3 **Ta'izz** Yemen
77 D3 **Tajikistan** *country* Asia
75 B2 **Taj Mahal** *tourist site* India
Tajo *r.* Port. *see* **Tagus**
58 A1 **Tak** Thai.
54 B2 **Takaka** N.Z.
67 B4 **Takamatsu** Japan
67 C3 **Takaoka** Japan
54 B1 **Takapuna** N.Z.
67 C3 **Takasaki** Japan
122 B1 **Takatokwane** Botswana
67 C3 **Takayama** Japan
Takefu Japan *see* **Echizen**
60 A1 **Takengon** Indon.
63 B2 **Ta Khmau** Cambodia
66 D2 **Takikawa** Japan
128 B2 **Takla Lake** Can.
128 B2 **Takla Landing** Can.
77 E3 **Taklimakan Desert** China
Taklimakan Shamo *des.* China *see* **Taklimakan Desert**
128 A2 **Taku** *r.* Can./U.S.A.
63 A3 **Takua Pa** Thai.
115 C4 **Takum** Nigeria
88 C3 **Talachyn** Belarus
74 B1 **Talagang** Pak.
150 A2 **Talara** Peru
59 C2 **Talaud, Kepulauan** *is* Indon.
106 C2 **Talavera de la Reina** Spain
153 A4 **Talca** Chile
153 A4 **Talcahuano** Chile
89 E2 **Taldom** Russia
77 D2 **Taldykorgan** Kazakh.
59 C3 **Taliabu** *i.* Indon.
64 B1 **Talisay** Phil.
61 C2 **Taliwang** Indon.
81 C2 **Tall 'Afar** Iraq

143 D2 **Tallahassee** U.S.A.
88 B2 **Tallinn** Estonia
142 B2 **Tallulah** U.S.A.
104 B2 **Talmont-St-Hilaire** France
90 C2 **Tal'ne** Ukr.
117 B3 **Talodi** Sudan
91 E1 **Talovaya** Russia
126 E2 **Taloyoak** Can.
88 B2 **Talsi** Latvia
152 A3 **Taltal** Chile
129 C1 **Taltson** *r.* Can.
60 A1 **Talu** Indon.
53 C1 **Talwood** Austr.
114 B4 **Tamale** Ghana
115 C2 **Tamanrasset** Alg.
99 A3 **Tamar** *r.* U.K.
145 C2 **Tamazunchale** Mex.
114 A3 **Tambacounda** Senegal
61 B1 **Tambelan, Kepulauan** *is* Indon.
91 E1 **Tambov** Russia
145 C2 **Tamiahua, Laguna de** *lag.* Mex.
143 D3 **Tampa** U.S.A.
143 D3 **Tampa Bay** U.S.A.
93 H3 **Tampere** Fin.
145 C2 **Tampico** Mex.
69 D1 **Tamsagbulag** Mongolia
102 C2 **Tamsweg** Austria
53 D2 **Tamworth** Austr.
99 C2 **Tamworth** U.K.
119 E3 **Tana** *r.* Kenya
117 B3 **Tana, Lake** Eth.
67 C4 **Tanabe** Japan
92 I1 **Tana Bru** Norway
61 C2 **Tanahgrogot** Indon.
58 C3 **Tanahjampea** *i.* Indon.
50 C1 **Tanami Desert** Austr.
126 A2 **Tanana** U.S.A.
108 A1 **Tanaro** *r.* Italy
65 B1 **Tanch'ŏn** N. Korea
64 B2 **Tandag** Phil.
110 C2 **Țăndărei** Romania
153 C4 **Tandil** Arg.
74 A2 **Tando Adam** Pak.
74 A2 **Tando Muhammad Khan** Pak.
114 B2 **Tanezrouft** *reg.* Alg./Mali
119 D3 **Tanga** Tanz.
119 C3 **Tanganyika, Lake** Africa
Tanger Morocco *see* **Tangier**
101 E1 **Tangermünde** Ger.
75 C1 **Tanggula Shan** *mts* China
114 B1 **Tangier** Morocco
75 C1 **Tangra Yumco** *salt l.* China
70 B2 **Tangshan** China
68 C2 **Taniantaweng Shan** *mts* China
59 C3 **Tanimbar, Kepulauan** *is* Indon.
64 B2 **Tanjay** Phil.
60 A1 **Tanjungbalai** Indon.
61 B2 **Tanjungpandan** Indon.
60 B1 **Tanjungpinang** Indon.
61 C1 **Tanjungredeb** Indon.
61 C1 **Tanjungselor** Indon.
74 B1 **Tank** Pak.
115 C3 **Tanout** Niger
75 C2 **Tansen** Nepal
116 B1 **Ṭanṭā** Egypt
119 D3 **Tanzania** *country* Africa
69 E1 **Taonan** China
138 B1 **Taos** U.S.A.
114 B2 **Taoudenni** Mali
88 C2 **Tapa** Estonia
145 C3 **Tapachula** Mex.
151 C2 **Tapajós** *r.* Brazil
60 A1 **Tapaktuan** Indon.
145 C3 **Tapanatepec** Mex.
150 B2 **Tapauá** Brazil
114 B4 **Tapeta** Liberia
141 D3 **Tappahannock** U.S.A.
74 B2 **Tapti** *r.* India
150 B2 **Tapurucuara** Brazil
154 A1 **Taquarí** *r.* Brazil
154 B1 **Taquari, Serra do** *hills* Brazil
154 C2 **Taquaritinga** Brazil
115 D4 **Taraba** *r.* Nigeria
Țarābulus Libya *see* **Tripoli**
61 C1 **Tarakan** Indon.
88 A3 **Taran, Mys** *pt* Russia
54 B1 **Taranaki, Mount** *vol.* N.Z.
106 C1 **Tarancón** Spain
109 C2 **Taranto** Italy
109 C2 **Taranto, Golfo di** *g.* Italy
150 A2 **Tarapoto** Peru
91 E2 **Tarasovskiy** Russia
150 A2 **Tarauacá** Brazil
150 B2 **Tarauacá** *r.* Brazil
48 F2 **Tarawa** *atoll* Kiribati
77 D2 **Taraz** Kazakh.
107 C1 **Tarazona** Spain
77 E2 **Tarbagatay, Khrebet** *mts* Kazakh.
96 A2 **Tarbert** *Scotland* U.K.
96 B3 **Tarbert** *Scotland* U.K.
104 C3 **Tarbes** France
96 B2 **Tarbet** U.K.
51 C3 **Tarcoola** Austr.
53 D2 **Taree** Austr.
110 C2 **Târgoviște** Romania
110 B1 **Târgu Jiu** Romania
110 B1 **Târgu Mureș** Romania
110 C1 **Târgu Neamț** Romania
79 C2 **Tarif** U.A.E.
152 B3 **Tarija** Bol.
79 B3 **Tarīm** Yemen
77 E3 **Tarim Basin** China
77 E2 **Tarim He** *r.* China
Tarim Pendi *basin* China *see* **Tarim Basin**
59 D3 **Taritatu** *r.* Indon.
82 G2 **Tarko-Sale** Russia
114 B4 **Tarkwa** Ghana
64 B1 **Tarlac** Phil.
68 C2 **Tarlag** China
92 G2 **Tärnaby** Sweden
77 C3 **Tarnak Rōd** *r.* Afgh.
110 B1 **Târnăveni** Romania
103 E1 **Tarnobrzeg** Pol.
103 E1 **Tarnów** Pol.
75 C1 **Taro Co** *salt l.* China
114 B1 **Taroudannt** Morocco
69 E1 **Tarqi** China
108 B2 **Tarquinia** Italy
107 D1 **Tarragona** Spain
107 D1 **Tàrrega** Spain
80 B2 **Tarsus** Turkey
152 B3 **Tartagal** Arg.
104 B3 **Tartas** France
88 C2 **Tartu** Estonia
80 B2 **Țarțūs** Syria
155 D1 **Tarumirim** Brazil
89 E3 **Tarusa** Russia
108 B1 **Tarvisio** Italy
81 D3 **Tashk, Daryācheh-ye** *l.* Iran
Tashkent Uzbek. *see* **Toshkent**
127 I2 **Tasiilaq** Greenland
131 D1 **Tasiujaq** Can.
76 B1 **Taskala** Kazakh.
77 E2 **Taskesken** Kazakh.
54 B2 **Tasman Bay** N.Z.
51 D4 **Tasmania** *state* Austr.
54 B2 **Tasman Mountains** N.Z.
156 D8 **Tasman Sea** S. Pacific Ocean
103 D2 **Tatabánya** Hungary
90 B2 **Tatarbunary** Ukr.
83 K3 **Tatarskiy Proliv** *str.* Russia
67 C4 **Tateyama** Japan
128 C1 **Tathlina Lake** Can.
78 B3 **Tathlīth** Saudi Arabia
78 B2 **Tathlīth, Wādī** *watercourse* Saudi Arabia
53 C3 **Tathra** Austr.
62 A1 **Tatkon** Myanmar
128 B2 **Tatla Lake** Can.
103 D2 **Tatra Mountains** *mts* Pol./Slovakia
Tatry *mts* Pol./Slovakia *see* **Tatra Mountains**
154 C2 **Tatuí** Brazil
139 C2 **Tatum** U.S.A.
81 C2 **Tatvan** Turkey
151 D2 **Tauá** Brazil
155 C2 **Taubaté** Brazil
101 D3 **Tauberbischofsheim** Ger.
54 C1 **Taumarunui** N.Z.
62 A1 **Taunggyi** Myanmar
62 A2 **Taung-ngu** Myanmar
62 A2 **Taungup** Myanmar
99 B3 **Taunton** U.K.
100 C2 **Taunus** *hills* Ger.
54 C1 **Taupo** N.Z.
54 C1 **Taupo, Lake** N.Z.
88 B2 **Taurag** Lith.
54 C1 **Tauranga** N.Z.
80 B2 **Taurus Mountains** Turkey
111 C3 **Tavas** Turkey
86 F3 **Tavda** Russia
106 B2 **Tavira** Port.
99 A3 **Tavistock** U.K.
Tavoy Myanmar *see* **Dawei**
111 C3 **Tavşanlı** Turkey
99 A3 **Taw** *r.* U.K.
140 C2 **Tawas City** U.S.A.
61 C1 **Tawau** *Sabah* Malaysia
64 A2 **Tawi-Tawi** *i.* Phil.
145 C3 **Taxco** Mex.
76 B2 **Taxiatosh** Uzbek.
77 D3 **Taxkorgan** China
96 C2 **Tay** *r.* U.K.
96 C2 **Tay, Firth of** *est.* U.K.
96 B2 **Tay, Loch** *l.* U.K.
128 B2 **Taylor** Can.
139 D2 **Taylor** U.S.A.
140 B3 **Taylorville** U.S.A.
78 A2 **Taymā'** Saudi Arabia
83 H2 **Taymura** *r.* Russia
83 H2 **Taymyr, Ozero** *l.* Russia
Taymyr, Poluostrov *pen.* Russia *see* **Taymyr Peninsula**
83 G2 **Taymyr Peninsula** Russia
63 B2 **Tây Ninh** Vietnam
64 A1 **Taytay** Phil.
82 G2 **Taz** *r.* Russia
114 B1 **Taza** Morocco
129 D2 **Tazin Lake** Can.
86 G2 **Tazovskaya Guba** *sea chan.* Russia
81 C1 **Tbilisi** Georgia
91 E2 **Tbilisskaya** Russia
118 B3 **Tchibanga** Gabon
118 B2 **Tcholliré** Cameroon
103 D1 **Tczew** Pol.
144 B2 **Teacapán** Mex.
54 A3 **Te Anau** N.Z.
54 A3 **Te Anau, Lake** N.Z.
145 C3 **Teapa** Mex.
54 C1 **Te Awamutu** N.Z.
115 C1 **Tébessa** Alg.
60 B2 **Tebingtinggi** *Sumatera Selatan* Indon.
60 A1 **Tebingtinggi** *Sumatera Utara* Indon.
114 B4 **Techiman** Ghana

144 B3 **Tecomán** Mex.
144 B2 **Tecoripa** Mex.
145 B3 **Técpan** Mex.
144 B2 **Tecuala** Mex.
110 C1 **Tecuci** Romania
68 C1 **Teeli** Russia
98 C1 **Tees** *r.* U.K.
111 C3 **Tefenni** Turkey
61 B2 **Tegal** Indon.
146 B3 **Tegucigalpa** Hond.
115 C3 **Teguidda-n-Tessoumt** Niger
114 B4 **Téhini** Côte d'Ivoire
81 D2 **Tehrān** Iran
145 C3 **Tehuacán** Mex.
145 C3 **Tehuantepec, Gulf of** Mex.
145 C3 **Tehuantepec, Istmo de** *isth.* Mex.
99 A2 **Teifi** *r.* U.K.
Te Ika-a-Māui *i.* N.Z. *see* **North Island**
76 C3 **Tejen** Turkm.
76 C3 **Tejen** *r.* Turkm.
Tejo *r.* Spain *see* **Tagus**
145 B3 **Tejupilco** Mex.
54 B2 **Tekapo, Lake** N.Z.
145 D2 **Tekax** Mex.
116 B3 **Tekezē Wenz** *r.* Eritrea/Eth.
111 C2 **Tekirdağ** Turkey
54 C1 **Te Kuiti** N.Z.
75 C2 **Tel** *r.* India
81 C1 **Telavi** Georgia
80 B2 **Tel Aviv-Yafo** Israel
145 D2 **Telchac Puerto** Mex.
128 A2 **Telegraph Creek** Can.
154 B2 **Telêmaco Borba** Brazil
99 B2 **Telford** U.K.
60 A2 **Telo** Indon.
86 E2 **Telpoziz, Gora** *mt.* Russia
88 B2 **Telšiai** Lith.
61 B2 **Telukbatang** Indon.
60 A1 **Telukdalam** Indon.
60 B1 **Teluk Intan** Malaysia
130 C2 **Temagami Lake** Can.
61 C2 **Temanggung** Indon.
123 C2 **Temba** S. Africa
60 B2 **Tembilahan** Indon.
120 A1 **Tembo Aluma** Angola
99 B2 **Teme** *r.* U.K.
60 B1 **Temerluh** Malaysia
77 D1 **Temirtau** Kazakh.
53 C2 **Temora** Austr.
139 D2 **Temple** U.S.A.
97 C2 **Templemore** Ireland
145 C2 **Tempoal** Mex.
91 D2 **Temryuk** Russia
153 A4 **Temuco** Chile
54 B2 **Temuka** N.Z.
145 C2 **Tenabo** Mex.
73 C3 **Tenali** India
63 A2 **Tenasserim** Myanmar
99 A3 **Tenby** U.K.
117 C3 **Tendaho** Eth.
105 D3 **Tende** France
108 A2 **Tende, Col de** *pass* France/Italy
73 D4 **Ten Degree Channel** India
67 D3 **Tendō** Japan
114 B3 **Ténenkou** Mali
115 D3 **Ténéré, Erg du** *des.* Niger
115 D2 **Ténéré du Tafassâsset** *des.* Niger
114 A2 **Tenerife** *i.* Canary Islands
107 D2 **Ténès** Alg.
61 C2 **Tengah, Kepulauan** *is* Indon.
62 A1 **Tengchong** China
61 C2 **Tenggarong** Indon.
70 A2 **Tengger Shamo** *des.* China
71 B3 **Tengxian** China
119 C4 **Tenke** Dem. Rep. Congo
114 B3 **Tenkodogo** Burkina Faso
51 C1 **Tennant Creek** Austr.
142 C1 **Tennessee** *r.* U.S.A.
142 C1 **Tennessee** *state* U.S.A.
145 C3 **Tenosique** Mex.
53 D1 **Tenterfield** Austr.
154 B2 **Teodoro Sampaio** Brazil
155 D1 **Teófilo Otoni** Brazil
145 C3 **Teopisca** Mex.
144 B2 **Tepache** Mex.
54 B1 **Te Paki** N.Z.
144 B3 **Tepalcatepec** Mex.
144 B2 **Tepatitlán** Mex.
144 B2 **Tepehuanes** Mex.
109 D2 **Tepelenë** Albania
144 B2 **Tepic** Mex.
102 C1 **Teplice** Czech Rep.
89 E3 **Teploye** Russia
144 B2 **Tequila** Mex.
108 B2 **Teramo** Italy
89 E3 **Terbuny** Russia
90 B2 **Terebovlya** Ukr.
87 D4 **Terek** *r.* Russia
151 D2 **Teresina** Brazil
155 D2 **Teresópolis** Brazil
63 A3 **Teressa Island** India
80 B1 **Terme** Turkey
108 B3 **Termini Imerese** *Sicily* Italy
145 C3 **Términos, Laguna de** *lag.* Mex.
77 C3 **Termiz** Uzbek.
109 B2 **Termoli** Italy
59 C2 **Ternate** Indon.
100 A2 **Terneuzen** Neth.
108 B2 **Terni** Italy
90 B2 **Ternopil'** Ukr.
128 B2 **Terrace** Can.
130 B2 **Terrace Bay** Can.
122 B2 **Terra Firma** S. Africa
140 B3 **Terre Haute** U.S.A.
131 E2 **Terrenceville** Can.
100 B1 **Terschelling** *i.* Neth.
108 A3 **Tertenia** *Sardinia* Italy
107 C1 **Teruel** Spain
92 H2 **Tervola** Fin.
109 C2 **Tešanj** Bos. & Herz.
116 B3 **Teseney** Eritrea
66 D2 **Teshio-gawa** *r.* Japan
128 A1 **Teslin** Can.
128 A1 **Teslin Lake** Can.
154 B1 **Tesouro** Brazil
115 C3 **Tessaoua** Niger
121 C2 **Tete** Moz.
90 C1 **Teteriv** *r.* Ukr.
101 F1 **Teterow** Ger.
90 B2 **Tetiyiv** Ukr.
114 B1 **Tétouan** Morocco
109 D2 **Tetovo** Macedonia
152 B3 **Teuco** *r.* Arg.
144 B2 **Teul de González Ortega** Mex.
101 D1 **Teutoburger Wald** *hills* Ger.
Tevere *r.* Italy *see* **Tiber**
54 A3 **Teviot** N.Z.
Te Waipounamu *i.* N.Z. *see* **South Island**
51 E2 **Tewantin** Austr.
54 C2 **Te Wharau** N.Z.
139 E2 **Texarkana** U.S.A.
53 D1 **Texas** Austr.
139 D2 **Texas** *state* U.S.A.
139 E3 **Texas City** U.S.A.
100 B1 **Texel** *i.* Neth.
139 D2 **Texoma, Lake** U.S.A.
123 C2 **Teyateyaneng** Lesotho
89 F2 **Teykovo** Russia
89 F2 **Teza** *r.* Russia
75 D2 **Tezpur** India
62 A1 **Tezu** India
129 E1 **Tha-anne** *r.* Can.
123 C2 **Thabana-Ntlenyana** *mt.* Lesotho
123 C2 **Thaba Putsoa** *mt.* Lesotho
123 C1 **Thabazimbi** S. Africa
123 C2 **Thabong** S. Africa
63 A2 **Thagyettaw** Myanmar
62 B1 **Thai Binh** Vietnam
63 B2 **Thailand** *country* Asia
63 B2 **Thailand, Gulf of** Asia
62 B1 **Thai Nguyên** Vietnam
62 B2 **Thakhèk** Laos
63 A3 **Thalang** Thai.
74 B1 **Thal Desert** Pak.
101 E2 **Thale** Ger.
62 B2 **Tha Li** Thai.
123 C1 **Thamaga** Botswana
116 C3 **Thamar, Jabal** *mt.* Yemen
79 C3 **Thamarīt** Oman
130 B2 **Thames** *r.* Can.
54 C1 **Thames** N.Z.
99 D3 **Thames** *est.* U.K.
99 D3 **Thames** *r.* U.K.
63 A2 **Thanbyuzayat** Myanmar
62 A2 **Thandwè** Myanmar
62 B2 **Thanh Hoa** Vietnam
73 B3 **Thanjavur** India
63 A2 **Thanlyin** Myanmar
74 A2 **Thano Bula Khan** Pak.
62 B1 **Than Uyên** Vietnam
74 A2 **Thar Desert** India/Pak.
52 B1 **Thargomindah** Austr.
81 C2 **Tharthār, Buḩayrat ath** *l.* Iraq
111 B2 **Thasos** *i.* Greece
62 B1 **Thât Khê** Vietnam
62 A2 **Thaton** Myanmar
74 A2 **Thatta** Pak.
62 A1 **Thaungdut** Myanmar
62 A2 **Thayawadi** Myanmar
62 A2 **Thayetmyo** Myanmar
62 A1 **Thazi** Myanmar
146 C2 **The Bahamas** *country* West Indies
98 B1 **The Cheviot** *h.* U.K.
134 B1 **The Dalles** U.S.A.
99 C2 **The Fens** *reg.* U.K.
114 A3 **The Gambia** *country* Africa
The Great Oasis Egypt *see* **Khārijah, Wāḩāt al**
79 C2 **The Gulf** Asia
100 B1 **The Hague** Neth.
129 E1 **Thelon** *r.* Can.
101 E2 **Themar** Ger.
96 A1 **The Minch** *sea chan.* U.K.
150 B2 **Theodore Roosevelt** *r.* Brazil
129 D2 **The Pas** Can.
111 B2 **Thermaïkos Kolpos** *g.* Greece
136 B2 **Thermopolis** U.S.A.
53 C3 **The Rock** Austr.
130 B2 **Thessalon** Can.
111 B2 **Thessaloniki** Greece
99 D2 **Thetford** U.K.
131 C2 **Thetford Mines** Can.
62 A1 **The Triangle** *mts* Myanmar
131 D1 **Thévenet, Lac** *l.* Can.
99 D2 **The Wash** *b.* U.K.
139 D2 **The Woodlands** U.S.A.
142 B3 **Thibodaux** U.S.A.
129 E2 **Thicket Portage** Can.
137 D1 **Thief River Falls** U.S.A.
105 C2 **Thiers** France
119 D3 **Thika** Kenya
73 B4 **Thiladhunmathi** Maldives
75 C2 **Thimphu** Bhutan
105 D2 **Thionville** France
Thira *i.* Greece *see* **Santorini**
98 C1 **Thirsk** U.K.

73 B4 Thiruvananthapuram India
93 E4 Thisted Denmark
129 E1 Thlewiaza r. Can.
62 A2 Thoen Thai.
123 D1 Thohoyandou S. Africa
101 E1 Thomasburg Ger.
97 C2 Thomastown Ireland
143 D2 Thomasville U.S.A.
106 C2 Thommen Belgium
129 E2 Thompson Can.
128 E3 Thompson r. U.S.A.
134 C1 Thompson Falls U.S.A.
128 B2 Thompson Sound Can.
Thoothukudi India see
Tuticorin
96 C3 Thornhill U.K.
55 C2 Thorshavnheiane reg.
Antarctica
104 B2 Thouars France
128 C2 Three Hills Can.
63 A2 Three Pagodas Pass
Myanmar/Thai.
114 B4 Three Points, Cape Ghana
73 B3 Thrissur India
63 B2 Thu Dâu Môt Vietnam
100 B2 Thuin Belgium
127 G1 Thule Air Base Greenland
121 B3 Thuli Zimbabwe
130 B2 Thunder Bay Can.
63 A3 Thung Song Thai.
101 E2 Thüringer Becken reg. Ger.
101 E2 Thüringer Wald mts Ger.
97 C2 Thurles Ireland
96 C1 Thurso U.K.
96 C1 Thurso r. U.K.
151 D2 Tianguá Brazil
70 B2 Tianjin China
70 B2 Tianjin mun. China
71 A3 Tianlin China
70 B2 Tianmen China
70 A2 Tianshui China
154 B2 Tibagi r. Brazil
118 B2 Tibati Cameroon
108 B2 Tiber r. Italy
Tiberias, Lake Israel see
Galilee, Sea of
115 D2 Tibesti mts Chad
Tibet aut. reg. China see
Xizang Zizhiqu
68 B2 Tibet, Plateau of China
Tibet Autonomous
Region aut. reg. China see
Xizang Zizhiqu
115 D2 Tibisti, Sarir des. Libya
73 B3 Tibooburra Austr.
144 A2 Tiburón, Isla i. Mex.
114 B3 Tichît Maur.
114 A2 Tichla Western Sahara
145 D2 Ticul Mex.
114 A3 Tidjikja Maur.
100 B1 Tiel Neth.
65 A1 Tieling China
100 A2 Tielt Belgium
100 B2 Tienen Belgium
68 B2 Tien Shan mts China/Kyrg.
Tientsin China see Tianjin
93 G3 Tierp Sweden
145 C3 Tierra Blanca Mex.
145 C3 Tierra Colorada Mex.
153 B6 Tierra del Fuego, Isla Grande
de i. Arg./Chile
154 C2 Tietê Brazil
Tiflis Georgia see Tbilisi
142 D1 Tifton U.S.A.
Tighina Moldova see Bender
131 D2 Tignish Can.
150 A2 Tigre r. Ecuador/Peru
81 C2 Tigris r. Asia

145 C2 Tihuatlán Mex.
144 A1 Tijuana Mex.
91 E2 Tikhoretsk Russia
89 D2 Tikhvin Russia
89 D2 Tikhvinskaya Gryada ridge Russia
54 C1 Tikokino N.Z.
81 C2 Tikrīt Iraq
83 J2 Tiksi Russia
100 B2 Tilburg Neth.
152 B3 Tilcara Arg.
52 B1 Tilcha (abandoned) Austr.
114 C3 Tillabéri Niger
134 B1 Tillamook U.S.A.
63 A3 Tillanchong Island India
111 C3 Tilos i. Greece
52 B2 Tilpa Austr.
86 F2 Til'tim Russia
89 E3 Tim Russia
86 D2 Timanskiy Kryazh ridge Russia
54 B2 Timaru N.Z.
91 D2 Timashevsk Russia
114 B3 Timbedgha Maur.
50 C1 Timber Creek Austr.
114 B3 Timbuktu Mali
114 C2 Timimoun Alg.
111 B2 Timiou Prodromou, Akrotirio pt Greece
110 B1 Timiş r. Romania
110 B1 Timişoara Romania
110 B1 Timmins Can.
89 E2 Timokhino Russia
151 D2 Timon Brazil
59 C3 Timor i. East Timor/Indonesia
Timor-Leste country Asia see East Timor
58 C3 Timor Sea Austr./Indon.
93 G3 Timrå Sweden
114 B2 Tindouf Alg.
75 C2 Tingri China
93 F4 Tingsryd Sweden
59 D2 Tinian i. N. Mariana Is
152 B3 Tinogasta Arg.
111 C3 Tinos Greece
111 C3 Tinos i. Greece
115 C2 Tinrhert, Hamada de Alg.
62 A1 Tinsukia India
107 D2 Tipasa Alg.
97 B2 Tipperary Ireland
109 C2 Tirana Albania
Tiranë Albania see Tirana
108 B1 Tirano Italy
90 B2 Tiraspol Moldova
111 C3 Tire Turkey
96 A2 Tiree i. U.K.
74 B1 Tirich Mir mt. Pak.
73 B3 Tiruchchirappalli India
73 B3 Tirunelveli India
73 B3 Tirupati India
73 B3 Tiruppattur India
73 B3 Tiruppur India
109 D1 Tisa r. Serbia
129 D2 Tisdale Can.
107 D2 Tissemsilt Alg.
152 B2 Titicaca, Lake Bol./Peru
75 C2 Titlagarh India
110 C2 Titu Romania
143 D3 Titusville U.S.A.
108 B2 Tivoli Italy
79 C2 Ṭiwi Oman
145 D2 Tizimín Mex.
114 B1 Tizi Ouzou Alg.
114 B2 Tiznit Morocco
145 C3 Tlacotalpán Mex.
144 B2 Tlahualilo Mex.
145 C3 Tlapa Mex.
145 C3 Tlaxcala Mex.

145 C3 Tlaxiaco Mex.
114 B1 Tlemcen Alg.
123 C1 Tlokweng Botswana
128 B2 Toad River Can.
121 □D2 Toamasina Madag.
60 A1 Toba, Danau l. Indon.
74 A1 Toba and Kakar Ranges mts Pak.
147 D3 Tobago i. Trin. and Tob.
59 C2 Tobelo Indon.
130 B2 Tobermory Can.
96 A2 Tobermory U.K.
129 D2 Tobin Lake Can.
60 B2 Toboali Indon.
86 F3 Tobol'sk Russia
76 C1 Tobyl r. Kazakh./Russia
151 E2 Tocantinópolis Brazil
151 D2 Tocantins r. Brazil
143 D2 Toccoa U.S.A.
108 A1 Toce r. Italy
152 A3 Tocopilla Chile
53 C3 Tocumwal Austr.
144 A2 Todos Santos Mex.
128 B3 Tofino Can.
96 □ Toft U.K.
49 G4 Tofua i. Tonga
59 C3 Togian, Kepulauan is Indon.
114 C4 Togo country Africa
74 B2 Tohana India
126 B2 Tok U.S.A.
116 B3 Tokar Sudan
69 E3 Tokara-rettō is Japan
91 E1 Tokarevka Russia
49 G3 Tokelau terr. S. Pacific Ocean
91 D2 Tokmak Ukr.
77 D2 Tokmok Kyrg.
54 C1 Tokoroa N.Z.
68 B2 Toksun China
67 B4 Tokushima Japan
67 C3 Tōkyō Japan
121 □D3 Tôlañaro Madag.
154 B2 Toledo Brazil
106 C2 Toledo Spain
140 C2 Toledo U.S.A.
106 C2 Toledo, Montes de mts Spain
142 B2 Toledo Bend Reservoir U.S.A.
121 □D3 Toliara Madag.
58 C2 Tolitoli Indon.
108 B1 Tolmezzo Italy
104 B3 Tolosa Spain
145 C3 Toluca Mex.
87 D3 Tol'yatti Russia
140 A2 Tomah U.S.A.
66 D2 Tomakomai Japan
106 B2 Tomar Port.
103 E1 Tomaszów Lubelski Pol.
103 E1 Tomaszów Mazowiecki Pol.
144 B3 Tomatlán Mex.
142 C2 Tombigbee r. U.S.A.
155 D2 Tombos Brazil
Tombouctou Mali see Timbuktu
120 A2 Tombua Angola
123 C1 Tom Burke S. Africa
53 C2 Tomingley Austr.
58 C3 Tomini, Teluk g. Indon.
109 C2 Tomislavgrad Bos. & Herz.
50 A2 Tom Price Austr.
82 G3 Tomsk Russia
93 F4 Tomtabacken h. Sweden
145 C3 Tonalá Mex.
150 B2 Tonantins Brazil
59 C2 Tondano Indon.
49 G4 Tonga country S. Pacific Ocean
49 G4 Tongatapu Group is Tonga
71 B3 Tongcheng China
70 A2 Tongchuan China
71 A3 Tongdao China

Tongeren

100 B2 **Tongeren** Belgium
62 B1 **Tonghai** China
65 B1 **Tonghua** China
65 B2 **Tongjosŏn-man** *b. N. Korea*
62 B1 **Tongking, Gulf of** China/
    Vietnam
69 E2 **Tongliao** China
70 B2 **Tongling** China
52 B2 **Tongo** Austr.
71 A3 **Tongren** China
    Tongshan China *see* **Xuzhou**
    Tongtian He *r.* China *see*
    Yangtze
96 B1 **Tongue** U.K.
65 B3 **Tongyeong** S. Korea
69 E2 **Tongyu** China
65 A1 **Tongyuanpu** China
74 B2 **Tonk** India
63 B2 **Tonle Sap** *l.* Cambodia
135 C3 **Tonopah** U.S.A.
93 F4 **Tønsberg** Norway
135 D2 **Tooele** U.S.A.
52 B3 **Tooleybuc** Austr.
53 D1 **Toowoomba** Austr.
137 D3 **Topeka** U.S.A.
144 B2 **Topia** Mex.
144 B2 **Topolobampo** Mex.
86 C2 **Topozero, Ozero** *l.* Russia
134 B1 **Toppenish** U.S.A.
111 C3 **Torbalı** Turkey
76 B3 **Torbat-e Ḥeydarīyeh** Iran
76 C3 **Torbat-e Jām** Iran
106 C1 **Tordesillas** Spain
107 C1 **Tordesilos** Spain
107 D1 **Torelló** Spain
101 F2 **Torgau** Ger.
76 C2 **Torgay** Kazakh.
100 A2 **Torhout** Belgium
    Torino Italy *see* **Turin**
154 B1 **Toritorëu** Brazil
106 B1 **Tormes** *r.* Spain
92 H2 **Torneälven** *r.* Sweden
127 C3 **Torngat Mountains** Can.
92 H2 **Tornio** Fin.
106 B1 **Toro** Spain
130 C2 **Toronto** Can.
119 D2 **Tororo** Uganda
    Toros Dağları *mts* Turkey *see*
    Taurus Mountains
99 B3 **Torquay** U.K.
106 B2 **Torrão** Port.
106 B1 **Torre** *mt.* Port.
107 D1 **Torreblanca** Spain
106 C1 **Torrecerredo** *mt.* Spain
106 B1 **Torre de Moncorvo** Port.
106 C1 **Torrelavega** Spain
106 C2 **Torremolinos** Spain
52 A2 **Torrens, Lake** *imp. l.* Austr.
107 C2 **Torrent** Spain
144 B2 **Torreón** Mex.
106 B2 **Torres Novas** Port.
106 B2 **Torres Vedras** Port.
107 C2 **Torrevieja** Spain
96 B2 **Torridon** U.K.
106 C2 **Torrijos** Spain
141 E2 **Torrington** CT U.S.A.
136 C2 **Torrington** WY U.S.A.
107 D1 **Torroella de Montgrí** Spain
94 B1 **Tórshavn** Faroe Is
108 A3 **Tortolì** *Sardinia* Italy
107 D1 **Tortosa** Spain
103 D1 **Toruń** Pol.
97 B1 **Tory Island** Ireland
89 D2 **Torzhok** Russia
122 B3 **Tosca** S. Africa
108 B2 **Toscano, Arcipelago** *is* Italy
77 C2 **Toshkent** Uzbek.
89 D2 **Tosno** Russia

152 B3 **Tostado** Arg.
101 D1 **Tostedt** Ger.
80 B1 **Tosya** Turkey
86 D3 **Tot'ma** Russia
67 B3 **Tottori** Japan
114 B4 **Touba** Côte d'Ivoire
114 B1 **Toubkal, Jebel** *mt.* Morocco
114 B3 **Tougan** Burkina Faso
115 C1 **Touggourt** Alg.
105 D2 **Toul** France
105 D3 **Toulon** France
104 C3 **Toulouse** France
100 A2 **Tournai** Belgium
105 C2 **Tournus** France
151 E2 **Touros** Brazil
104 C2 **Tours** France
115 D2 **Tousside, Pic** *mt.* Chad
122 B3 **Touwsrivier** S. Africa
66 D2 **Towada** Japan
134 D1 **Townsend** U.S.A.
51 D1 **Townsville** Austr.
77 E2 **Toxkan He** *r.* China
66 D2 **Tōya-ko** *l.* Japan
67 C3 **Toyama** Japan
67 C3 **Toyota** Japan
115 C1 **Tozeur** Tunisia
81 C1 **T'q'varcheli** Georgia
    Trâblous Lebanon *see* **Tripoli**
80 B1 **Trabzon** Turkey
106 B2 **Trafalgar, Cabo** *c.* Spain
128 C3 **Trail** Can.
88 B3 **Trakai** Lith.
97 B2 **Tralee** Ireland
97 C2 **Tramore** Ireland
63 A3 **Trang** Thai.
59 C3 **Trangan** *i.* Indon.
55 I2 **Transantarctic Mountains**
    Antarctica
90 B2 **Transnistria** *disp. terr.*
    Moldova
110 B1 **Transylvanian Alps** *mts*
    Romania
108 B3 **Trapani** *Sicily* Italy
53 C3 **Traralgon** Austr.
63 B2 **Trat** Thai.
102 C2 **Traunstein** Ger.
140 B2 **Traverse City** U.S.A.
103 D2 **Třebíč** Czech Rep.
109 C2 **Trebinje** Bos. & Herz.
103 E2 **Trebišov** Slovakia
109 C1 **Trebnje** Slovenia
153 C4 **Treinta y Tres** Uru.
153 B5 **Trelew** Arg.
93 F4 **Trelleborg** Sweden
130 C2 **Tremblant, Mont** *h.* Can.
109 C2 **Tremiti, Isole** *is* Italy
134 D2 **Tremonton** U.S.A.
107 D1 **Tremp** Spain
103 D2 **Trenčín** Slovakia
153 B4 **Trenque Lauquén** Arg.
98 C2 **Trent** *r.* U.K.
108 B1 **Trento** Italy
141 D2 **Trenton** Can.
137 E2 **Trenton** MO U.S.A.
141 E2 **Trenton** NJ U.S.A.
131 E2 **Trepassey** Can.
153 B4 **Tres Arroyos** Arg.
155 C2 **Três Corações** Brazil
154 B2 **Três Lagoas** Brazil
153 A5 **Tres Lagos** Arg.
155 C1 **Três Marias, Represa** *resr*
    Brazil
155 C2 **Três Pontas** Brazil
153 B5 **Tres Puntas, Cabo** *c.* Arg.
155 D2 **Três Rios** Brazil
101 F1 **Treuenbrietzen** Ger.
108 A1 **Treviglio** Italy
108 B1 **Treviso** Italy

99 A3 **Trevose Head** U.K.
109 C3 **Tricase** Italy
53 C2 **Trida** Austr.
100 C3 **Trier** Ger.
108 B1 **Trieste** Italy
108 B1 **Triglav** *mt.* Slovenia
59 D3 **Trikora, Puncak** *mt.* Indon.
97 C2 **Trim** Ireland
73 C4 **Trincomalee** Sri Lanka
154 C1 **Trindade** Brazil
152 B2 **Trinidad** Bol.
147 D3 **Trinidad** *i.* Trin. and Tob.
136 C3 **Trinidad** U.S.A.
147 D3 **Trinidad and Tobago** *country*
    West Indies
131 E2 **Trinity Bay** Can.
111 B3 **Tripoli** Greece
80 B2 **Tripoli** Lebanon
115 D1 **Tripoli** Libya
113 D10 **Tristan da Cunha** *i.*
    S. Atlantic Ocean
    Trivandrum India *see*
    Thiruvananthapuram
108 B2 **Trivento** Italy
103 D2 **Trnava** Slovakia
109 C2 **Trogir** Croatia
109 C2 **Troia** Italy
100 C2 **Troisdorf** Ger.
131 C2 **Trois-Rivières** Can.
86 E2 **Troitsko-Pechorsk** Russia
151 C2 **Trombetas** *r.* Brazil
123 C3 **Trompsburg** S. Africa
92 G2 **Tromsø** Norway
92 F3 **Trondheim** Norway
128 C2 **Trout Lake** Can.
128 B1 **Trout Lake** N.W.T. Can.
130 A1 **Trout Lake** Ont. Can.
99 B3 **Trowbridge** U.K.
142 C2 **Troy** AL U.S.A.
141 E2 **Troy** NY U.S.A.
105 C2 **Troyes** France
109 D2 **Trstenik** Serbia
89 D3 **Trubchevsk** Russia
106 B1 **Truchas** Spain
79 C2 **Trucial Coast** U.A.E.
146 B3 **Trujillo** Hond.
150 A2 **Trujillo** Peru
106 B2 **Trujillo** Spain
147 C4 **Trujillo** Venez.
142 B1 **Trumann** U.S.A.
131 D2 **Truro** Can.
99 A3 **Truro** U.K.
138 B2 **Truth or Consequences**
    U.S.A.
103 D1 **Trutnov** Czech Rep.
93 F3 **Trysil** Norway
103 D1 **Trzebiatów** Pol.
68 B1 **Tsagaannuur** Mongolia
121 ☐D2 **Tsaratanana, Massif du** *mts*
    Madag.
110 C2 **Tsarevo** Bulg.
122 A2 **Tses** Namibia
122 B1 **Tsetseng** Botswana
68 C1 **Tsetserleg** *Arhangay* Mongolia
68 C1 **Tsetserleg** *Hövsgöl* Mongolia
122 B2 **Tshabong** Botswana
122 B1 **Tshane** Botswana
118 B3 **Tshela** Dem. Rep. Congo
118 C3 **Tshikapa** Dem. Rep. Congo
118 C3 **Tshikapa** *r.* Dem. Rep. Congo
123 D1 **Tshipise** S. Africa
118 C3 **Tshitanzu** Dem. Rep. Congo
118 C3 **Tshuapa** *r.* Dem. Rep. Congo
    Tshwane S. Africa *see* **Pretoria**
87 D4 **Tsimlyanskoye**
    Vodokhranilishche *resr* Russia
    Tsingtao China *see* **Qingdao**
    Tsining China *see* **Ulan Qab**

121 □D2 Tsiroanomandidy Madag.
123 C3 Tsomo S. Africa
67 C4 Tsu Japan
67 C3 Tsuchiura Japan
66 D2 Tsugarū-kaikyō str. Japan
120 A2 Tsumeb Namibia
122 A1 Tsumis Park Namibia
120 B2 Tsumkwe Namibia
67 C3 Tsuruga Japan
66 C3 Tsuruoka Japan
67 A4 Tsushima is Japan
Tsushima-kaikyō str. Japan/
   S. Korea see Korea Strait
67 B3 Tsuyama Japan
123 C2 Tswelelang S. Africa
91 C2 Tsyurupyns'k Ukr.
Tthenaagoo Can. see
   Nahanni Butte
59 C3 Tual Indon.
97 B2 Tuam Ireland
91 D3 Tuapse Russia
54 A3 Tuatapere N.Z.
96 A1 Tuath, Loch a' b. U.K.
138 A1 Tuba City U.S.A.
61 C2 Tuban Indon.
152 D3 Tubarão Brazil
102 B2 Tübingen Ger.
115 E1 Tubruq Libya
49 H4 Tubuai Fr. Polynesia
49 I4 Tubuai i. Fr. Polynesia
144 B3 Tubutama Mex.
152 C2 Tucavaca Bol.
128 B1 Tuchitua Can.
138 A2 Tucson U.S.A.
139 C1 Tucumcari U.S.A.
150 B2 Tucupita Venez.
151 D2 Tucuruí Brazil
151 D2 Tucuruí, Represa de resr Brazil
107 C1 Tudela Spain
106 B1 Tuela r. Port.
62 A1 Tuensang India
64 B1 Tuguegarao Phil.
106 B1 Tui Spain
59 C3 Tukangbesi, Kepulauan is
   Indon.
126 C2 Tuktoyaktuk Can.
88 B2 Tukums Latvia
145 E3 Tula Mex.
89 E3 Tula Russia
145 C2 Tulancingo Mex.
135 C3 Tulare U.S.A.
138 B2 Tularosa U.S.A.
110 C1 Tulcea Romania
90 B2 Tul'chyn Ukr.
129 E1 Tulemalu Lake Can.
139 C2 Tulia U.S.A.
142 C1 Tullahoma U.S.A.
97 C2 Tullamore Ireland
104 C2 Tulle France
59 D1 Tully Austr.
131 D1 Tulsa U.S.A.
150 A1 Tumaco Col.
123 C2 Tumahole S. Africa
   Tumakuru India see Tumkur
93 G4 Tumba Sweden
118 B3 Tumba, Lac l.
   Dem. Rep. Congo
53 C3 Tumbarumba Austr.
150 A2 Tumbes Peru
128 B2 Tumbler Ridge Can.
52 A2 Tumby Bay Austr.
65 B1 Tumen China
150 B1 Tumereng Guyana
64 A2 Tumindao i. Phil.
73 B3 Tumkur India
74 A2 Tump Pak.
151 C1 Tumucumaque, Serra hills
   Brazil

53 C3 Tumut Austr.
80 B2 Tunceli Turkey
53 D2 Tuncurry Austr.
119 D4 Tunduru Tanz.
110 C2 Tundzha r. Bulg.
128 B1 Tungsten (abandoned) Can.
115 D1 Tunis Tunisia
115 C1 Tunisia country Africa
150 A1 Tunja Col.
92 F3 Tunnsjøen l. Norway
   Tunxi China see Huangshan
154 B2 Tupã Brazil
154 C1 Tupaciguara Brazil
142 C2 Tupelo U.S.A.
152 B3 Tupiza Bol.
76 B2 Tupkaragan, Mys pt Kazakh.
83 H2 Tura Russia
86 F3 Tura r. Russia
78 B2 Turabah Saudi Arabia
83 J3 Turana, Khrebet mts Russia
54 C1 Turangi N.Z.
76 B2 Turan Lowland Asia
78 A1 Turayf Saudi Arabia
88 B2 Turba Estonia
74 A2 Turbat Pak.
150 A1 Turbo Col.
110 B1 Turda Romania
   Turfan China see Turpan
111 C3 Turgutlu Turkey
80 B1 Turhal Turkey
107 C2 Turia r. Spain
108 A1 Turin Italy
86 F3 Turinsk Russia
90 A1 Turiys'k Ukr.
119 D2 Turkana, Lake salt l. Eth./
   Kenya
80 B2 Turkey country Asia/Europe
77 C2 Turkistan Kazakh.
76 C3 Türkmenabat Turkm.
76 B2 Türkmenbaşy Turkm.
76 B2 Turkmenistan country Asia
147 C2 Turks and Caicos Islands terr.
   West Indies
93 H3 Turku Fin.
135 B3 Turlock U.S.A.
54 C2 Turnagain, Cape N.Z.
100 B2 Turnhout Belgium
129 D2 Turnor Lake Can.
110 B2 Turnu Măgurele Romania
68 B2 Turpan China
77 D2 Turugart Pass China/Kyrg.
142 C2 Tuscaloosa U.S.A.
142 C2 Tuskegee U.S.A.
73 B4 Tuticorin India
120 B3 Tutume Botswana
49 F3 Tuvalu country
   S. Pacific Ocean
78 B2 Tuwayq, Jabal hills
   Saudi Arabia
78 B2 Tuwayq, Jabal mts
   Saudi Arabia
78 A2 Tuwwal Saudi Arabia
144 B2 Tuxpan Nayarit Mex.
145 C2 Tuxpan Veracruz Mex.
145 C3 Tuxtla Gutiérrez Mex.
62 B1 Tuyên Quang Vietnam
63 B2 Tuy Hoa Vietnam
80 B2 Tuz, Lake salt l. Turkey
   Tuz Gölü salt l. Turkey see
   Tuz, Lake
81 C2 Tuz Khurmātū Iraq
109 C2 Tuzla Bos. & Herz.
91 E2 Tuzlov r. Russia
89 E2 Tver' Russia
98 B1 Tweed r. U.K.
122 A2 Twee Rivier Namibia
135 C4 Twentynine Palms U.S.A.
131 C2 Twillingate Can.

134 D2 Twin Falls U.S.A.
137 E1 Two Harbors U.S.A.
129 C2 Two Hills Can.
139 D2 Tyler U.S.A.
83 J3 Tynda Russia
93 F3 Tynset Norway
80 B2 Tyre Lebanon
111 B3 Tyrnavos Greece
52 B3 Tyrrell, Lake dry lake Austr.
108 B2 Tyrrhenian Sea France/Italy
86 F3 Tyumen' Russia
83 J2 Tyung r. Russia
99 A3 Tywi r. U.K.
123 D1 Tzaneen S. Africa

U

120 B2 Uamanda Angola
155 D2 Ubá Brazil
155 D1 Ubaí Brazil
151 E3 Ubaitaba Brazil
118 B3 Ubangi r. C.A.R./
   Dem. Rep. Congo
67 B4 Ube Japan
106 C2 Úbeda Spain
154 C1 Uberaba Brazil
154 C1 Uberlândia Brazil
106 B1 Ubiña, Peña mt. Spain
123 D2 Ubombo S. Africa
63 B2 Ubon Ratchathani Thai.
118 C3 Ubundu Dem. Rep. Congo
150 A2 Ucayali r. Peru
74 B2 Uch Pak.
66 D2 Uchiura-wan b. Japan
83 J3 Uchur r. Russia
128 B3 Ucluelet Can.
74 B2 Udaipur India
91 C1 Uday r. Ukr.
93 F4 Uddevalla Sweden
92 G2 Uddjaure l. Sweden
100 B1 Uden Neth.
74 B1 Udhampur India
108 B1 Udine Italy
89 E2 Udomlya Russia
62 B2 Udon Thani Thai.
73 B3 Udupi India
83 K3 Udyl', Ozero l. Russia
67 C3 Ueda Japan
58 C3 Uekuli Indon.
118 C2 Uele r. Dem. Rep. Congo
101 E1 Uelzen Ger.
119 C2 Uere r. Dem. Rep. Congo
87 E3 Ufa Russia
119 D3 Ugalla r. Tanz.
119 D2 Uganda country Africa
89 E2 Uglich Russia
89 D2 Uglovka Russia
89 D3 Ugra Russia
103 D2 Uherské Hradiště Czech Rep.
101 E2 Üichteritz Ger.
96 A2 Uig U.K.
120 A1 Uíge Angola
65 B2 Uijeongbu S. Korea
135 D2 Uinta Mountains U.S.A.
65 B2 Uiseong S. Korea
120 A3 Uis Mine Namibia
123 C3 Uitenhage S. Africa
100 C1 Uithuizen Neth.
74 B2 Ujjain India
89 F3 Ukholovo Russia
62 A1 Ukhrul India
86 E2 Ukhta Russia
135 B3 Ukiah U.S.A.
127 H2 Ukkusissat Greenland
88 B2 Ukmerg Lith.

90 C2 **Ukraine** *country* Europe
Ulaanbaatar Mongolia *see* **Ulan Bator**
68 C1 **Ulaangom** Mongolia
69 D1 **Ulan Bator** Mongolia
Ulanhad China *see* **Chifeng**
69 E1 **Ulanhot** China
87 D4 **Ulan-Khol** Russia
70 B1 **Ulan Qab** China
69 D1 **Ulan-Ude** Russia
75 D1 **Ulan Ul Hu** *l.* China
Uleåborg Fin. *see* **Oulu**
88 C2 **Ülenurme** Estonia
69 D1 **Uliastai** China
68 C1 **Uliastay** Mongolia
59 D2 **Ulithi** *atoll* Micronesia
65 B2 **Uljin** S. Korea
53 D3 **Ulladulla** Austr.
96 B2 **Ullapool** U.K.
65 C2 **Ulleung-do** *i.* S. Korea
98 B1 **Ullswater** *l.* U.K.
102 B2 **Ulm** Ger.
65 B2 **Ulsan** S. Korea
96 □ **Ulsta** U.K.
97 C1 **Ulster** *reg.* Ireland/U.K.
52 B3 **Ultima** Austr.
111 C3 **Ulubey** Turkey
111 C2 **Uludağ** *mt.* Turkey
126 D2 **Ulukhaktok** Can.
123 D2 **Ulundi** S. Africa
77 E2 **Ulungur Hu** *l.* China
50 C2 **Uluṟu** *h.* Austr.
98 B1 **Ulverston** U.K.
87 D3 **Ul'yanovsk** Russia
136 C3 **Ulysses** U.S.A.
90 C2 **Uman'** Ukr.
86 C2 **Umba** Russia
59 D3 **Umboi** *i.* P.N.G.
92 H3 **Umeå** Sweden
92 H3 **Umeälven** *r.* Sweden
127 I2 **Umiiviip Kangertiva** *inlet* Greenland
126 D2 **Umingmaktok** Can.
123 D2 **Umlazi** S. Africa
117 A3 **Umm Keddada** Sudan
78 A2 **Umm Lajj** Saudi Arabia
117 B3 **Umm Ruwaba** Sudan
115 E1 **Umm Sa'ad** Libya
134 B2 **Umpqua** *r.* U.S.A.
120 A2 **Umpulo** Angola
154 B2 **Umuarama** Brazil
109 C1 **Una** *r.* Bos. & Herz./Croatia
155 E1 **Una** Brazil
154 C1 **Unaí** Brazil
78 B2 **'Unayzah** Saudi Arabia
136 C1 **Underwood** U.S.A.
89 D3 **Unecha** Russia
53 C2 **Ungarie** Austr.
52 A2 **Ungarra** Austr.
127 G2 **Ungava, Péninsule d'** *pen.* Can.
127 G3 **Ungava Bay** Can.
90 B2 **Ungheni** Moldova
Unguja *i.* Tanz. *see* **Zanzibar Island**
154 B3 **União da Vitória** Brazil
150 B2 **Unini** *r.* Brazil
142 C1 **Union City** U.S.A.
122 B3 **Uniondale** S. Africa
141 D3 **Uniontown** U.S.A.
79 C2 **United Arab Emirates** *country* Asia
95 C3 **United Kingdom** *country* Europe
132 D3 **United States of America** *country* N. America
129 D2 **Unity** Can.
96 □ **Unst** *i.* U.K.
101 E2 **Unstrut** *r.* Ger.
89 E3 **Upa** *r.* Russia
119 C3 **Upemba, Lac** *l.* Dem. Rep. Congo
122 B2 **Upington** S. Africa
134 B2 **Upper Alkali Lake** U.S.A.
128 C2 **Upper Arrow Lake** Can.
134 B2 **Upper Klamath Lake** U.S.A.
128 B1 **Upper Liard** Can.
97 C1 **Upper Lough Erne** *l.* U.K.
93 G4 **Uppsala** Sweden
78 B2 **'Uqlat aş Şuqūr** Saudi Arabia
Urad Qianqi China *see* **Xishanzui**
76 B2 **Ural** *r.* Kazakh./Russia
53 D2 **Uralla** Austr.
87 E3 **Ural Mountains** Russia
76 B1 **Ural'sk** Kazakh.
Ural'skiy Khrebet *mts* Russia *see* **Ural Mountains**
119 D3 **Urambo** Tanz.
53 C3 **Urana** Austr.
129 D2 **Uranium City** Can.
86 F2 **Uray** Russia
98 C1 **Ure** *r.* U.K.
86 D3 **Uren'** Russia
144 A2 **Ures** Mex.
76 C2 **Urganch** Uzbek.
100 B1 **Urk** Neth.
111 C3 **Urla** Turkey
81 C2 **Urmia, Lake** *salt l.* Iran
Uroševac Kosovo *see* **Ferizaj**
144 B2 **Uruáchic** Mex.
151 D3 **Uruaçu** Brazil
144 B3 **Uruapan** Mex.
150 A3 **Urubamba** *r.* Peru
151 C2 **Urucará** Brazil
151 D2 **Uruçuí** Brazil
151 C2 **Urucurituba** Brazil
152 C3 **Uruguaiana** Brazil
153 C4 **Uruguay** *country* S. America
Urumchi China *see* **Ürümqi**
68 B2 **Ürümqi** China
53 D2 **Urunga** Austr.
110 C2 **Urziceni** Romania
67 B4 **Usa** Japan
82 E2 **Usa** *r.* Russia
111 C3 **Uşak** Turkey
82 G1 **Ushakova, Ostrov** *i.* Russia
77 E2 **Usharal** Kazakh.
77 D2 **Ushtobe** Kazakh.
153 B6 **Ushuaia** Arg.
86 E2 **Usinsk** Russia
88 C3 **Uskhodni** Belarus
89 E3 **Usman'** Russia
86 D2 **Usogorsk** Russia
104 C2 **Ussel** France
66 B2 **Ussuriysk** Russia
108 B3 **Ustica, Isola di** *i. Sicily* Italy
83 H3 **Ust'-Ilimsk** Russia
86 E2 **Ust'-Ilych** Russia
103 D1 **Ustka** Pol.
83 L3 **Ust'-Kamchatsk** Russia
77 E2 **Ust'-Kamenogorsk** Kazakh.
86 F2 **Ust'-Kara** Russia
86 E2 **Ust'-Kulom** Russia
83 I3 **Ust'-Kut** Russia
91 D2 **Ust'-Labinsk** Russia
88 C2 **Ust'-Luga** Russia
86 E2 **Ust'-Nem** Russia
83 K2 **Ust'-Nera** Russia
83 K2 **Ust'-Omchug** Russia
83 H3 **Ust'-Ordynskiy** Russia
86 E2 **Ust'-Tsil'ma** Russia
86 D2 **Ust'-Ura** Russia
76 B2 **Ustyurt Plateau** Kazakh./Uzbek.
89 E2 **Ustyuzhna** Russia
89 D2 **Usvyaty** Russia
135 D3 **Utah** *state* U.S.A.
135 D2 **Utah Lake** U.S.A.
93 I4 **Utena** Lith.
123 D2 **uThukela** *r.* S. Africa
141 D2 **Utica** U.S.A.
107 C2 **Utiel** Spain
128 C2 **Utikuma Lake** Can.
100 B1 **Utrecht** Neth.
106 B2 **Utrera** Spain
92 I2 **Utsjoki** Fin.
67 C3 **Utsunomiya** Japan
87 D4 **Utta** Russia
62 B2 **Uttaradit** Thai.
127 H2 **Uummannaq Fjord** *inlet* Greenland
93 H3 **Uusikaupunki** Fin.
139 D3 **Uvalde** U.S.A.
119 D3 **Uvinza** Tanz.
68 C1 **Uvs Nuur** *salt l.* Mongolia
67 B4 **Uwajima** Japan
78 A2 **'Uwayriḍ, Ḥarrat al** *lava field* Saudi Arabia
116 A2 **Uweinat, Jebel** *mt.* Sudan
83 H3 **Uyar** Russia
115 C4 **Uyo** Nigeria
152 B3 **Uyuni, Salar de** *salt flat* Bol.
76 C2 **Uzbekistan** *country* Asia
104 C2 **Uzerche** France
105 C3 **Uzès** France
90 C1 **Uzh** *r.* Ukr.
90 A2 **Uzhhorod** Ukr.
109 C2 **Užice** Serbia
89 E3 **Uzlovaya** Russia
111 C3 **Üzümlü** Turkey
111 C2 **Uzunköprü** Turkey

V

123 B2 **Vaal** *r.* S. Africa
123 C2 **Vaal Dam** S. Africa
123 C1 **Vaalwater** S. Africa
92 H3 **Vaasa** Fin.
103 D2 **Vác** Hungary
152 C3 **Vacaria** Brazil
154 B2 **Vacaria, Serra** *hills* Brazil
135 B3 **Vacaville** U.S.A.
74 B2 **Vadodara** India
92 I1 **Vadsø** Norway
105 D2 **Vaduz** Liechtenstein
94 B1 **Vágar** *i.* Faroe Is
94 B1 **Vágur** Faroe Is
103 D2 **Váh** *r.* Slovakia
49 F3 **Vaiaku** Tuvalu
88 B2 **Vaida** Estonia
136 B3 **Vail** U.S.A.
79 C2 **Vakīlābād** Iran
108 B1 **Valdagno** Italy
89 D2 **Valday** Russia
89 D2 **Valdayskaya Vozvyshennost'** *hills* Russia
106 B2 **Valdecañas, Embalse de** *resr* Spain
93 G4 **Valdemarsvik** Sweden
106 C2 **Valdepeñas** Spain
153 B5 **Valdés, Península** *pen.* Arg.
153 A4 **Valdivia** Chile
130 C2 **Val-d'Or** Can.
143 D2 **Valdosta** U.S.A.
128 C2 **Valemount** Can.
105 C3 **Valence** France
107 C2 **Valencia** Spain
150 B1 **Valencia** Venez.
107 D2 **Valencia, Golfo de** *g.* Spain
100 A2 **Valenciennes** France
136 C2 **Valentine** U.S.A.

64 B1 **Valenzuela** Phil.
150 A1 **Valera** Venez.
109 C2 **Valjevo** Serbia
88 C2 **Valka** Latvia
93 H3 **Valkeakoski** Fin.
100 B2 **Valkenswaard** Neth.
91 D2 **Valky** Ukr.
55 D2 **Valkyrie Dome** Antarctica
145 D2 **Valladolid** Mex.
106 C1 **Valladolid** Spain
93 E4 **Valle** Norway
145 C2 **Vallecillos** Mex.
150 B1 **Valle de la Pascua** Venez.
150 A1 **Valledupar** Col.
145 C2 **Valle Hermoso** Mex.
135 B3 **Vallejo** U.S.A.
152 A3 **Vallenar** Chile
85 H5 **Valletta** Malta
137 D1 **Valley City** U.S.A.
134 B2 **Valley Falls** U.S.A.
128 C2 **Valleyview** Can.
107 D1 **Valls** Spain
129 D3 **Val Marie** Can.
88 C2 **Valmiera** Latvia
88 C3 **Valozhyn** Belarus
154 B2 **Valparaíso** Brazil
153 A4 **Valparaíso** Chile
105 C3 **Valréas** France
59 D3 **Vals, Tanjung** *c.* Indon.
74 B2 **Valsad** India
122 B2 **Valspan** S. Africa
91 D1 **Valuyki** Russia
106 B2 **Valverde del Camino** Spain
81 C2 **Van** Turkey
81 C2 **Van, Lake** *salt l.* Turkey
141 F1 **Van Buren** U.S.A.
128 B3 **Vancouver** Can.
134 B1 **Vancouver** U.S.A.
128 B3 **Vancouver Island** Can.
140 B3 **Vandalia** U.S.A.
123 C2 **Vanderbijlpark** S. Africa
128 B2 **Vanderhoof** Can.
88 C2 **Vändra** Estonia
93 F4 **Vänern** *l.* Sweden
93 F4 **Vänersborg** Sweden
121 □D3 **Vangaindrano** Madag.
Van Gölü *salt l.* Turkey *see* **Van, Lake**
138 C2 **Van Horn** U.S.A.
59 D3 **Vanimo** P.N.G.
83 K3 **Vanino** Russia
104 B2 **Vannes** France
59 D3 **Van Rees, Pegunungan** *mts* Indon.
122 A3 **Vanrhynsdorp** S. Africa
93 H3 **Vantaa** Fin.
49 F4 **Vanua Levu** *i.* Fiji
48 E3 **Vanuatu** *country* S. Pacific Ocean
140 C2 **Van Wert** U.S.A.
122 B3 **Van Wyksvlei** S. Africa
122 B2 **Van Zylsrus** S. Africa
75 C2 **Varanasi** India
92 I1 **Varangerfjorden** *sea chan.* Norway
92 I1 **Varangerhalvøya** *pen.* Norway
109 C1 **Varaždin** Croatia
93 F4 **Varberg** Sweden
109 D2 **Vardar** *r.* Macedonia
93 E4 **Varde** Denmark
92 J1 **Vardø** Norway
100 D1 **Varel** Ger.
88 B3 **Varna** Lith.
108 A1 **Varese** Italy
155 C2 **Varginha** Brazil
93 I3 **Varkaus** Fin.
110 C2 **Varna** Bulg.
93 F4 **Värnamo** Sweden
155 D1 **Várzea da Palma** Brazil
86 C2 **Varzino** Russia
Vasa Fin. *see* **Vaasa**
88 C2 **Vasknarva** Estonia
110 C1 **Vaslui** Romania
93 G4 **Västerås** Sweden
93 G3 **Västerdalälven** *r.* Sweden
88 A2 **Västerhaninge** Sweden
93 G4 **Västervik** Sweden
108 B2 **Vasto** Italy
90 C1 **Vasyl'kiv** Ukr.
104 C2 **Vatan** France
108 B2 **Vatican City** Europe
92 □B3 **Vatnajökull** Iceland
110 C1 **Vatra Dornei** Romania
93 F4 **Vättern** *l.* Sweden
138 B2 **Vaughn** U.S.A.
105 C3 **Vauvert** France
49 G4 **Vava'u Group** *is* Tonga
88 B3 **Vawkavysk** Belarus
93 F4 **Växjö** Sweden
86 E1 **Vaygach, Ostrov** *i.* Russia
101 D1 **Vechta** Ger.
110 C2 **Vedea** *r.* Romania
100 C1 **Veendam** Neth.
100 B1 **Veenendaal** Neth.
129 C2 **Vegreville** Can.
106 B2 **Vejer de la Frontera** Spain
93 E4 **Vejle** Denmark
109 D2 **Velbŭzhdki Prokhod** *pass* Bulg./Macedonia
100 B2 **Veldhoven** Neth.
109 B2 **Velebit** *mts* Croatia
100 C2 **Velen** Ger.
109 C1 **Velenje** Slovenia
109 D2 **Veles** Macedonia
106 C2 **Vélez-Málaga** Spain
155 D1 **Velhas** *r.* Brazil
109 D2 **Velika Plana** Serbia
88 C2 **Velikaya** *r.* Russia
89 D2 **Velikiye Luki** Russia
89 D2 **Velikiy Novgorod** Russia
86 D2 **Velikiy Ustyug** Russia
110 C2 **Veliko Tarnovo** Bulg.
108 B2 **Veli Lošinj** Croatia
89 D2 **Velizh** Russia
86 D2 **Vel'sk** Russia
101 F1 **Velten** Ger.
91 D1 **Velykyy Burluk** Ukr.
108 B2 **Venafro** Italy
104 C2 **Vendôme** France
89 E3 **Venev** Russia
Venezia Italy *see* **Venice**
150 B1 **Venezuela** *country* S. America
150 A1 **Venezuela, Golfo de** *g.* Venez.
108 B1 **Venice** Italy
143 D3 **Venice** U.S.A.
108 B1 **Venice, Gulf of** Europe
100 C2 **Venlo** Neth.
100 B2 **Venray** Neth.
88 B2 **Venta** *r.* Latvia/Lith.
88 B2 **Venta** Lith.
123 C3 **Venterstad** S. Africa
99 C3 **Ventnor** U.K.
88 B2 **Ventspils** Latvia
135 C4 **Ventura** U.S.A.
139 C3 **Venustiano Carranza, Presa** *resr* Mex.
107 C2 **Vera** Spain
145 C3 **Veracruz** Mex.
74 B2 **Veraval** India
108 A1 **Verbania** Italy
108 A1 **Vercelli** Italy
105 D3 **Vercors** *reg.* France
92 F3 **Verdalsøra** Norway
154 B1 **Verde** *r. Goiás* Brazil
154 B2 **Verde** *r. Mato Grosso do Sul* Brazil
144 B2 **Verde** *r.* Mex.
138 A2 **Verde** *r.* U.S.A.
155 D1 **Verde Grande** *r.* Brazil
101 D1 **Verden (Aller)** Ger.
154 B1 **Verdinho, Serra do** *mts* Brazil
108 A2 **Verdon** *r.* France
105 D2 **Verdun** France
123 C2 **Vereeniging** S. Africa
106 B1 **Verín** Spain
91 D3 **Verkhnebakanskiy** Russia
92 J2 **Verkhnetulomskiy** Russia
91 E1 **Verkhniy Mamon** Russia
89 E3 **Verkhov'ye** Russia
90 A2 **Verkhovyna** Ukr.
83 J2 **Verkhoyanskiy Khrebet** *mts* Russia
129 C2 **Vermilion** Can.
137 D2 **Vermillion** U.S.A.
130 A2 **Vermillion Bay** Can.
141 E2 **Vermont** *state* U.S.A.
135 E2 **Vernal** U.S.A.
128 C2 **Vernon** Can.
139 D2 **Vernon** U.S.A.
143 D3 **Vero Beach** U.S.A.
111 B2 **Veroia** Greece
108 B1 **Verona** Italy
104 C2 **Versailles** France
104 B2 **Vertou** France
123 D2 **Verulam** S. Africa
100 B2 **Verviers** Belgium
105 C2 **Vervins** France
105 D3 **Vescovato** *Corsica* France
87 E3 **Veselaya, Gora** *mt.* Russia
91 C2 **Vesele** Ukr.
105 D2 **Vesoul** France
92 F2 **Vesterålen** *is* Norway
92 F2 **Vestfjorden** *sea chan.* Norway
94 B1 **Vestmanna** Faroe Is
93 E3 **Vestnes** Norway
108 B2 **Vesuvius** *vol.* Italy
89 E2 **Ves'yegonsk** Russia
93 G4 **Vetlanda** Sweden
86 D3 **Vetluga** Russia
100 A2 **Veurne** Belgium
105 D2 **Vevey** Switz.
91 D1 **Veydelevka** Russia
80 B1 **Vezirköprü** Turkey
151 D2 **Viana** Brazil
106 B1 **Viana do Castelo** Port.
Viangchan Laos *see* **Vientiane**
62 B1 **Viangphoukha** Laos
111 C3 **Viannos** Greece
154 C1 **Vianópolis** Brazil
108 B2 **Viareggio** Italy
93 E4 **Viborg** Denmark
109 C3 **Vibo Valentia** Italy
107 D1 **Vic** Spain
144 A1 **Vicente Guerrero** Mex.
108 B1 **Vicenza** Italy
105 C2 **Vichy** France
142 B2 **Vicksburg** U.S.A.
155 D2 **Viçosa** Brazil
52 A3 **Victor Harbor** Austr.
50 C1 **Victoria** *r.* Austr.
52 B3 **Victoria** *state* Austr.
128 B3 **Victoria** Can.
153 A4 **Victoria** Chile
113 K7 **Victoria** Seychelles
139 D3 **Victoria** U.S.A.
119 D3 **Victoria, Lake** Africa
52 B2 **Victoria, Lake** Austr.
62 A1 **Victoria, Mount** Myanmar
59 D3 **Victoria, Mount** P.N.G.
120 B2 **Victoria Falls** Zambia/Zimbabwe
126 D2 **Victoria Island** Can.
50 C1 **Victoria River Downs** Austr.
122 B3 **Victoria West** S. Africa

135 C4 **Victorville** U.S.A.
110 C2 **Videle** Romania
92 □A2 **Víðidalsá** Iceland
153 B5 **Viedma** Arg.
153 A5 **Viedma, Lago** *l.* Arg.
100 B2 **Vielsalm** Belgium
101 E2 **Vienenburg** Ger.
103 D2 **Vienna** Austria
105 C2 **Vienne** France
104 C2 **Vienne** *r.* France
62 B2 **Vientiane** Laos
100 C2 **Viersen** Ger.
104 C2 **Vierzon** France
144 B2 **Viesca** Mex.
109 C2 **Vieste** Italy
62 B2 **Vietnam** *country* Asia
62 B1 **Viêt Tri** Vietnam
64 B1 **Vigan** Phil.
108 A1 **Vigevano** Italy
106 B1 **Vigo** Spain
73 C3 **Vijayawada** India
92 □B3 **Vík** Iceland
129 C2 **Viking** Can.
150 C3 **Vila Bela da Santíssima Trindade** Brazil
106 B2 **Vila Franca de Xira** Port.
106 B1 **Vilagarcía de Arousa** Spain
106 B1 **Vilalba** Spain
106 B1 **Vila Nova de Gaia** Port.
107 D1 **Vilanova i la Geltrú** Spain
106 B1 **Vila Real** Port.
106 B1 **Vilar Formoso** Port.
155 D2 **Vila Velha** Brazil
150 A3 **Vilcabamba, Cordillera** *mts* Peru
92 G3 **Vilhelmina** Sweden
150 B3 **Vilhena** Brazil
88 C2 **Viljandi** Estonia
88 B3 **Vilkaviškis** Lith.
83 H1 **Vil'kitskogo, Proliv** *str.* Russia
144 B1 **Villa Ahumada** Mex.
106 B1 **Villablino** Spain
102 C2 **Villach** Austria
144 B2 **Villa de Cos** Mex.
152 B4 **Villa Dolores** Arg.
145 C3 **Villa Flores** Mex.
145 C2 **Villagrán** Mex.
145 C3 **Villahermosa** Mex.
144 A2 **Villa Insurgentes** Mex.
152 B4 **Villa María** Arg.
152 B3 **Villa Montes** Bol.
144 B2 **Villanueva** Mex.
106 B2 **Villanueva de la Serena** Spain
106 C2 **Villanueva de los Infantes** Spain
152 C3 **Villa Ocampo** Arg.
108 A3 **Villaputzu** *Sardinia* Italy
152 C3 **Villarrica** Para.
106 C2 **Villarrobledo** Spain
152 B3 **Villa Unión** Arg.
144 B2 **Villa Unión** *Durango* Mex.
144 B2 **Villa Unión** *Sinaloa* Mex.
150 A1 **Villavicencio** Col.
152 B3 **Villazon** Bol.
107 C2 **Villena** Spain
104 C3 **Villeneuve-sur-Lot** France
142 B2 **Ville Platte** U.S.A.
105 C2 **Villeurbanne** France
102 B2 **Villingen** Ger.
88 C3 **Vilnius** Lith.
91 C2 **Vil'nohirs'k** Ukr.
91 D2 **Vil'nyans'k** Ukr.
100 B2 **Vilvoorde** Belgium
88 C3 **Vilyeyka** Belarus
83 J2 **Vilyuy** *r.* Russia
93 G4 **Vimmerby** Sweden
153 A4 **Viña del Mar** Chile
107 D1 **Vinaròs** Spain
140 B3 **Vincennes** U.S.A.
55 G3 **Vincennes Bay** Antarctica
141 D3 **Vineland** U.S.A.
62 B2 **Vinh** Vietnam
63 B2 **Vinh Long** Vietnam
139 D1 **Vinita** U.S.A.
90 B2 **Vinnytsya** Ukr.
55 O2 **Vinson, Mount** *mt.* Antarctica
93 E3 **Vinstra** Norway
108 B1 **Vipiteno** Italy
64 B1 **Virac** Phil.
129 D3 **Virden** Can.
104 B2 **Vire** France
120 A2 **Virei** Angola
155 D1 **Virgem da Lapa** Brazil
138 A1 **Virgin** *r.* U.S.A.
123 C2 **Virginia** S. Africa
137 E1 **Virginia** U.S.A.
141 D3 **Virginia** *state* U.S.A.
141 D3 **Virginia Beach** U.S.A.
135 C3 **Virginia City** U.S.A.
147 D3 **Virgin Islands (U.K.)** *terr.* West Indies
147 D3 **Virgin Islands (U.S.A.)** *terr.* West Indies
63 B2 **Virôchey** Cambodia
109 C1 **Virovitica** Croatia
100 B3 **Virton** Belgium
88 B2 **Virtsu** Estonia
109 C2 **Vis** *i.* Croatia
88 C2 **Visaginas** Lith.
135 C3 **Visalia** U.S.A.
74 B2 **Visavadar** India
64 B1 **Visayan Sea** Phil.
93 G4 **Visby** Sweden
126 D2 **Viscount Melville Sound** *sea chan.* Can.
151 D2 **Viseu** Brazil
106 B1 **Viseu** Port.
73 C3 **Vishakhapatnam** India
88 C2 **Višķi** Latvia
109 C2 **Visoko** Bos. & Herz.
103 D1 **Vistula** *r.* Pol.
108 B2 **Viterbo** Italy
49 F4 **Viti Levu** *i.* Fiji
83 I3 **Vitim** *r.* Russia
155 D2 **Vitória** Brazil
151 D3 **Vitória da Conquista** Brazil
106 C1 **Vitoria-Gasteiz** Spain
104 B2 **Vitré** France
105 C2 **Vitry-le-François** France
89 D2 **Vitsyebsk** Belarus
105 D2 **Vittel** France
108 B3 **Vittoria** *Sicily* Italy
108 B1 **Vittorio Veneto** Italy
106 B1 **Viveiro** Spain
144 A2 **Vizcaíno, Sierra** *mts* Mex.
110 C2 **Vize** Turkey
73 C3 **Vizianagaram** India
100 B2 **Vlaardingen** Neth.
87 D4 **Vladikavkaz** Russia
89 F2 **Vladimir** Russia
66 B2 **Vladivostok** Russia
109 D2 **Vlasotince** Serbia
100 B1 **Vlieland** *i.* Neth.
100 A2 **Vlissingen** Neth.
109 C2 **Vlorë** Albania
102 C2 **Vöcklabruck** Austria
101 D2 **Vogelsberg** *hills* Ger.
119 D3 **Voi** Kenya
105 D2 **Voiron** France
131 D1 **Voisey's Bay** Can.
109 C1 **Vojvodina** *prov.* Serbia
92 J3 **Voknavolok** Russia
Volcano Bay Japan *see* **Uchiura-wan**
89 E2 **Volga** Russia
89 F2 **Volga** *r.* Russia
87 D4 **Volgodonsk** Russia
87 D4 **Volgograd** Russia
89 D2 **Volkhov** Russia
89 D1 **Volkhov** *r.* Russia
101 E2 **Volkstedt** Ger.
91 D2 **Volnovakha** Ukr.
90 B2 **Volochys'k** Ukr.
91 D2 **Volodars'ke** Ukr.
90 B1 **Volodars'k-Volyns'kyy** Ukr.
90 B1 **Volodymyrets'** Ukr.
90 A1 **Volodymyr-Volyns'kyy** Ukr.
89 E2 **Vologda** Russia
89 E2 **Volokolamsk** Russia
91 D1 **Volokonovka** Russia
111 B3 **Volos** Greece
88 C2 **Volosovo** Russia
89 D2 **Volot** Russia
89 E3 **Volovo** Russia
87 D3 **Vol'sk** Russia
114 C4 **Volta, Lake** *resr* Ghana
155 D2 **Volta Redonda** Brazil
87 D4 **Volzhskiy** Russia
92 □C2 **Vopnafjörður** Iceland
88 C3 **Voranava** Belarus
86 F2 **Vorkuta** Russia
88 B2 **Vormsi** *i.* Estonia
89 E3 **Voronezh** Russia
89 E3 **Voronezh** *r.* Russia
91 E1 **Vorontsovka** Russia
91 C2 **Vorskla** *r.* Russia
88 C2 **Võrtsjärv** *l.* Estonia
88 C2 **Võru** Estonia
122 B3 **Vosburg** S. Africa
105 D2 **Vosges** *mts* France
89 E2 **Voskresensk** Russia
93 E3 **Voss** Norway
83 H3 **Vostochnyy Sayan** *mts* Russia
86 E3 **Votkinsk** Russia
154 C2 **Votuporanga** Brazil
100 B3 **Vouziers** France
92 J2 **Voynitsa** Russia
91 C2 **Voznesens'k** Ukr.
93 E4 **Vrådal** Norway
66 B2 **Vrangel'** Russia
Vrangelya, Ostrov *i.* Russia *see* **Wrangel Island**
109 D2 **Vranje** Serbia
110 C2 **Vratnik** *pass* Bulg.
110 B2 **Vratsa** Bulg.
109 C1 **Vrbas** *r.* Bos. & Herz.
109 C1 **Vrbas** Serbia
122 A3 **Vredenburg** S. Africa
122 A3 **Vredendal** S. Africa
100 B3 **Vresse-sur-Semois** Belgium
109 D1 **Vršac** Serbia
122 B2 **Vryburg** S. Africa
123 D2 **Vryheid** S. Africa
89 D1 **Vsevolozhsk** Russia
Vučitrn Kosovo *see* **Vushtrri**
109 C1 **Vukovar** Croatia
86 E2 **Vuktyl** Russia
123 C2 **Vukuzakhe** S. Africa
109 B3 **Vulcano, Isola** *i.* Italy
63 B2 **Vung Tau** Vietnam
109 D2 **Vushtrri** Kosovo
74 B2 **Vyara** India
Vyatka Russia *see* **Kirov**
89 D2 **Vyaz'ma** Russia
93 I3 **Vyborg** Russia
88 C2 **Vyerkhnyadzvinsk** Belarus
87 D3 **Vyksa** Russia
90 B2 **Vylkove** Ukr.
90 A2 **Vynohradiv** Ukr.
89 D2 **Vypolzovo** Russia
89 D2 **Vyritsa** Russia
91 D2 **Vyselki** Russia
90 C1 **Vyshhorod** Ukr.
89 D2 **Vyshniy-Volochek** Russia

103 D2 Vyškov Czech Rep.
86 C2 Vytegra Russia

W

114 B3 Wa Ghana
100 B2 Waal r. Neth.
100 B2 Waalwijk Neth.
128 C2 Wabasca r. Can.
128 C2 Wabasca-Desmarais Can.
140 B3 Wabash r. U.S.A.
129 E2 Wabowden Can.
143 D3 Waccasassa Bay U.S.A.
101 D2 Wächtersbach Ger.
139 D2 Waco U.S.A.
115 D2 Waddān Libya
Waddeneilanden is Neth. see
West Frisian Islands
100 B1 Waddenzee sea chan. Neth.
128 B2 Waddington, Mount Can.
100 B1 Waddinxveen Neth.
129 D2 Wadena Can.
137 D1 Wadena U.S.A.
74 A2 Wadh Pak.
116 B2 Wadi Halfa Sudan
116 B3 Wad Madani Sudan
70 C2 Wafangdian China
100 B2 Wageningen Neth.
127 F2 Wager Bay Can.
53 C3 Wagga Wagga Austr.
137 D2 Wahoo U.S.A.
137 D1 Wahpeton U.S.A.
54 B2 Waiau r. N.Z.
59 C3 Waigeo i. Indon.
58 B3 Waikabubak Indon.
52 A2 Waikerie Austr.
54 B2 Waimate N.Z.
75 B3 Wainganga r. India
58 C3 Waingapu Indon.
129 C2 Wainwright Can.
54 C1 Waiouru N.Z.
54 B2 Waipara N.Z.
54 C1 Waipawa N.Z.
54 B2 Wairau r. N.Z.
54 C1 Wairoa N.Z.
54 B2 Waitaki r. N.Z.
54 B1 Waitara N.Z.
54 B1 Waiuku N.Z.
119 E2 Wajir Kenya
67 C3 Wakasa-wan b. Japan
54 A3 Wakatipu, Lake N.Z.
129 D2 Wakaw Can.
67 C4 Wakayama Japan
136 D3 WaKeeney U.S.A.
54 B2 Wakefield N.Z.
98 C2 Wakefield U.K.
48 F1 Wake Island N. Pacific Ocean
66 D1 Wakkanai Japan
123 D2 Wakkerstroom S. Africa
103 D1 Wałbrzych Pol.
53 D2 Walcha Austr.
100 C1 Walchum Ger.
103 D1 Wałcz Pol.
99 B2 Wales admin. div. U.K.
53 C2 Walgett Austr.
119 C3 Walikale Dem. Rep. Congo
135 C3 Walker Lake U.S.A.
52 A2 Wallaroo Austr.
98 B2 Wallasey U.K.
134 C1 Walla Walla U.S.A.
101 D3 Walldürn Ger.
53 C2 Wallendbeen Austr.
49 G3 Wallis and Futuna Islands
terr. S. Pacific Ocean
96 □ Walls U.K.
98 B1 Walney, Isle of i. U.K.

99 C2 Walsall U.K.
136 C3 Walsenburg U.S.A.
101 D1 Walsrode Ger.
143 D2 Walterboro U.S.A.
120 A3 Walvis Bay Namibia
119 C2 Wamba Dem. Rep. Congo
52 B1 Wanaaring Austr.
54 A2 Wanaka N.Z.
54 A2 Wanaka, Lake N.Z.
130 B2 Wanapitei Lake Can.
154 B3 Wanda Arg.
66 B1 Wanda Shan mts China
62 A1 Wanding China
54 C1 Wanganui N.Z.
53 C3 Wangaratta Austr.
65 B1 Wangqing China
62 A1 Wan Hsa-la Myanmar
71 B4 Wanning China
100 B2 Wanroij Neth.
99 C3 Wantage U.K.
70 A2 Wanyuan China
70 A2 Wanzhou China
73 B3 Warangal India
101 D2 Warburg Ger.
50 B2 Warburton Austr.
52 A1 Warburton watercourse Austr.
75 B2 Wardha India
96 C1 Ward Hill U.K.
128 B2 Ware Can.
101 F1 Waren (Müritz) Ger.
100 C2 Warendorf Ger.
53 D1 Warialda Austr.
122 A2 Warmbad Namibia
135 C3 Warm Springs U.S.A.
134 C2 Warner Lakes U.S.A.
143 D2 Warner Robins U.S.A.
152 B2 Warnes Bol.
52 B3 Warracknabeal Austr.
53 C2 Warrego r. Austr.
53 C2 Warren Austr.
142 B2 Warren AR U.S.A.
140 C2 Warren OH U.S.A.
141 D2 Warren PA U.S.A.
97 C1 Warrenpoint U.K.
137 E3 Warrensburg U.S.A.
122 B2 Warrenton S. Africa
115 C4 Warri Nigeria
98 B2 Warrington U.K.
52 B3 Warrnambool Austr.
103 E1 Warsaw Pol.
Warszawa Pol. see Warsaw
103 D1 Warta r. Pol.
53 D1 Warwick Austr.
99 C2 Warwick U.K.
135 C3 Wasco U.S.A.
136 C1 Washburn U.S.A.
141 D3 Washington DC U.S.A.
137 E2 Washington IA U.S.A.
140 B3 Washington IN U.S.A.
137 E3 Washington MO U.S.A.
143 E1 Washington NC U.S.A.
140 C2 Washington PA U.S.A.
134 B1 Washington state U.S.A.
141 E2 Washington, Mount U.S.A.
140 C3 Washington Court House
U.S.A.
74 A2 Washuk Pak.
130 C2 Waskaganish Can.
129 E2 Waskaiowaka Lake Can.
122 A2 Wasser Namibia
130 C2 Waswanipi, Lac l. Can.
58 C3 Watampone Indon.
141 E2 Waterbury U.S.A.
129 D2 Waterbury Lake Can.
97 C2 Waterford Ireland
97 C2 Waterford Harbour Ireland
137 E2 Waterloo U.S.A.
123 C1 Waterpoort S. Africa

141 D2 Watertown NY U.S.A.
137 D2 Watertown SD U.S.A.
140 B2 Watertown WI U.S.A.
141 F2 Waterville U.S.A.
99 C3 Watford U.K.
136 C1 Watford City U.S.A.
129 D2 Wathaman r. Can.
139 D1 Watonga U.S.A.
129 D2 Watrous Can.
119 C2 Watsa Dem. Rep. Congo
140 B2 Watseka U.S.A.
118 C3 Watsi Kengo
Dem. Rep. Congo
128 B1 Watson Lake Can.
135 B3 Watsonville U.S.A.
59 C3 Watubela, Kepulauan is
Indon.
59 D3 Wau P.N.G.
117 A4 Wau South Sudan
53 D2 Wauchope Austr.
140 B2 Waukegan U.S.A.
139 D2 Waurika U.S.A.
140 B2 Wausau U.S.A.
99 D2 Waveney r. U.K.
137 E2 Waverly U.S.A.
143 D2 Waycross U.S.A.
137 D2 Wayne U.S.A.
143 D2 Waynesboro GA U.S.A.
141 D3 Waynesboro VA U.S.A.
143 D1 Waynesville U.S.A.
74 B1 Wazirabad Pak.
98 C1 Wear r. U.K.
139 D2 Weatherford U.S.A.
134 B2 Weaverville U.S.A.
130 B1 Webequie Can.
117 C4 Webi Shabeelle r. Somalia
137 D1 Webster U.S.A.
137 E2 Webster City U.S.A.
55 Q2 Weddell Sea Antarctica
100 B2 Weert Neth.
53 C2 Wee Waa Austr.
100 C2 Wegberg Ger.
103 E1 Węgorzewo Pol.
101 F3 Weiden in der Oberpfalz Ger.
70 B2 Weifang China
70 C2 Weihai China
53 C1 Weilmoringle Austr.
101 E2 Weimar Ger.
70 A2 Weinan China
51 D1 Weipa Austr.
53 C1 Weir r. Austr.
140 C2 Weirton U.S.A.
62 B1 Weishan China
101 E2 Weißenfels Ger.
102 C2 Weißkugel mt. Austria/Italy
103 D1 Wejherowo Pol.
128 C1 Wekweètì Can.
140 C3 Welch U.S.A.
117 B3 Weldiya Eth.
123 C2 Welkom S. Africa
99 C2 Welland r. U.K.
51 C1 Wellesley Islands Austr.
54 B2 Wellington Austr.
54 B2 Wellington N.Z.
122 A3 Wellington S. Africa
137 D3 Wellington U.S.A.
153 A5 Wellington, Isla i. Chile
53 C3 Wellington, Lake Austr.
128 B2 Wells Can.
99 B3 Wells U.K.
134 D2 Wells U.S.A.
50 B2 Wells, Lake imp. l. Austr.
54 B1 Wellsford N.Z.
98 D2 Wells-next-the-Sea U.K.
102 C2 Wels Austria
99 B2 Welshpool U.K.
123 C2 Wembesi S. Africa
130 C1 Wemindji Can.

134 B1	Wenatchee U.S.A.	
154 C2	Wenceslau Braz Brazil	
71 C4	Wencheng China	
114 B4	Wenchi Ghana	
70 C2	Wendeng China	
101 E1	Wendisch Evern Ger.	
117 B4	Wendo Eth.	
134 D2	Wendover U.S.A.	
71 B3	Wengyuan China	
71 C3	Wenling China	
71 A3	Wenshan China	
52 B2	Wentworth Austr.	
71 C3	Wenzhou China	
123 C2	Wepener S. Africa	
122 B2	Werda Botswana	
101 F2	Werdau Ger.	
101 F1	Werder (Havel) Ger.	
101 F3	Wernberg-Köblitz Ger.	
101 E2	Wernigerode Ger.	
101 D2	Werra r. Ger.	
53 D2	Werris Creek Austr.	
101 D3	Wertheim Ger.	
100 C2	Wesel Ger.	
101 E1	Wesendorf Ger.	
101 D1	Weser r. Ger.	
101 D1	Weser sea chan. Ger.	
51 C1	Wessel, Cape Austr.	
51 C1	Wessel Islands Austr.	
123 C2	Wesselton S. Africa	
80 B2	West Bank disp. terr. Asia	
140 B2	West Bend U.S.A.	
99 C2	West Bromwich U.K.	
100 C2	Westerburg Ger.	
100 C1	Westerholt Ger.	
50 B2	Western Australia state Austr.	
122 B3	Western Cape prov. S. Africa	
116 A2	Western Desert Egypt	
73 B3	Western Ghats mts India	
114 A2	Western Sahara disp. terr. Africa	
100 A2	Westerschelde est. Neth.	
100 C1	Westerstede Ger.	
100 C2	Westerwald hills Ger.	
153 B6	West Falkland i. Falkland Is	
140 B3	West Frankfort U.S.A.	
100 B1	West Frisian Islands is Neth.	
147 D2	West Indies is Caribbean Sea	
96 A1	West Loch Roag b. U.K.	
128 C2	Westlock Can.	
100 B1	Westmalle Belgium	
142 B1	West Memphis U.S.A.	
140 C3	Weston U.S.A.	
99 B3	Weston-super-Mare U.K.	
143 D3	West Palm Beach U.S.A.	
137 E3	West Plains U.S.A.	
137 D2	West Point U.S.A.	
97 B2	Westport Ireland	
54 B2	Westport N.Z.	
129 D2	Westray Can.	
96 C1	Westray i. U.K.	
100 B1	West-Terschelling Neth.	
140 C3	West Virginia state U.S.A.	
53 C2	West Wyalong Austr.	
134 D2	West Yellowstone U.S.A.	
59 C3	Wetar i. Indon.	
128 C2	Wetaskiwin Can.	
101 D2	Wetzlar Ger.	
59 D3	Wewak P.N.G.	
97 C2	Wexford Ireland	
129 D2	Weyakwin Can.	
129 D3	Weyburn Can.	
101 D1	Weyhe Ger.	
99 B3	Weymouth U.K.	
54 C1	Whakatane N.Z.	
129 E1	Whale Cove Can.	
96 □	Whalsay i. U.K.	
54 B1	Whangarei N.Z.	
98 C2	Wharfe r. U.K.	

139 D3	Wharton U.S.A.	
128 C1	Whatì Can.	
136 B2	Wheatland U.S.A.	
138 B1	Wheeler Peak NM U.S.A.	
135 D3	Wheeler Peak NV U.S.A.	
140 C2	Wheeling U.S.A.	
98 B1	Whernside h. U.K.	
128 B2	Whistler Can.	
98 C1	Whitby U.K.	
142 B2	White r. U.S.A.	
50 B2	White, Lake imp. l. Austr.	
131 E2	White Bay Can.	
136 C1	White Butte mt. U.S.A.	
52 B2	White Cliffs Austr.	
128 C2	Whitecourt Can.	
134 D1	Whitefish U.S.A.	
98 B1	Whitehaven U.K.	
97 D1	Whitehead U.K.	
128 A1	Whitehorse Can.	
142 B3	White Lake U.S.A.	
135 C3	White Mountain Peak U.S.A.	
116 B3	White Nile r. South Sudan/Uganda	
86 C2	White Sea Russia	
134 D1	White Sulphur Springs U.S.A.	
143 E2	Whiteville U.S.A.	
114 B3	White Volta r. Burkina Faso/Ghana	
138 B2	Whitewater Baldy mt. U.S.A.	
130 B1	Whitewater Lake Can.	
129 D2	Whitewood Can.	
96 B3	Whithorn U.K.	
54 C1	Whitianga N.Z.	
135 C3	Whitney, Mount U.S.A.	
51 D2	Whitsunday Island Austr.	
52 A2	Whyalla Austr.	
100 A2	Wichelen Belgium	
137 D3	Wichita U.S.A.	
139 D2	Wichita Falls U.S.A.	
96 C1	Wick U.K.	
138 A2	Wickenburg U.S.A.	
97 C2	Wicklow Ireland	
97 D2	Wicklow Head Ireland	
97 C2	Wicklow Mountains Ireland	
98 B2	Widnes U.K.	
101 D1	Wiehengebirge hills Ger.	
100 C2	Wiehl Ger.	
103 D1	Wieluń Pol.	
	Wien Austria see Vienna	
103 D2	Wiener Neustadt Austria	
100 B1	Wieringerwerf Neth.	
100 D2	Wiesbaden Ger.	
100 C1	Wiesmoor Ger.	
103 D1	Wieżyca h. Pol.	
99 C3	Wight, Isle of i. U.K.	
96 B3	Wigtown U.K.	
100 B2	Wijchen Neth.	
52 B2	Wilcannia Austr.	
123 C3	Wild Coast S. Africa	
123 C2	Wilge r. S. Africa	
100 D1	Wilhelmshaven Ger.	
141 D2	Wilkes-Barre U.S.A.	
55 H3	Wilkes Land reg. Antarctica	
129 D2	Wilkie Can.	
138 B2	Willcox U.S.A.	
100 B2	Willebroek Belgium	
147 D3	Willemstad Curaçao	
52 B3	William, Mount Austr.	
52 A1	William Creek Austr.	
138 A1	Williams U.S.A.	
141 D3	Williamsburg U.S.A.	
128 B2	Williams Lake Can.	
140 C3	Williamson U.S.A.	
141 D2	Williamsport U.S.A.	
143 E1	Williamston U.S.A.	
122 B3	Williston S. Africa	
136 C1	Williston U.S.A.	
128 B2	Williston Lake Can.	

135 B3	Willits U.S.A.	
137 D1	Willmar U.S.A.	
122 B3	Willowmore S. Africa	
123 C3	Willowvale S. Africa	
50 B2	Wills, Lake imp. l. Austr.	
52 A3	Willunga Austr.	
52 A2	Wilmington Austr.	
141 D3	Wilmington DE U.S.A.	
143 E2	Wilmington NC U.S.A.	
100 D2	Wilnsdorf Ger.	
143 E1	Wilson U.S.A.	
53 C3	Wilson's Promontory pen. Austr.	
100 B3	Wiltz Lux.	
50 B2	Wiluna Austr.	
99 C3	Winchester U.K.	
140 C3	Winchester KY U.S.A.	
141 D3	Winchester VA U.S.A.	
98 B1	Windermere l. U.K.	
120 A3	Windhoek Namibia	
137 D2	Windom U.S.A.	
51 D2	Windorah Austr.	
136 B2	Wind River Range mts U.S.A.	
53 D2	Windsor Austr.	
130 B2	Windsor Can.	
147 D3	Windward Islands Caribbean Sea	
147 C3	Windward Passage Cuba/Haiti	
137 D3	Winfield U.S.A.	
100 A2	Wingene Belgium	
53 D2	Wingham Austr.	
130 B1	Winisk r. Can.	
130 B1	Winisk (abandoned) Can.	
130 B1	Winisk Lake Can.	
63 A2	Winkana Myanmar	
129 E3	Winkler Can.	
114 B4	Winneba Ghana	
140 B2	Winnebago, Lake U.S.A.	
135 C2	Winnemucca U.S.A.	
136 C2	Winner U.S.A.	
142 B2	Winnfield U.S.A.	
137 E1	Winnibigoshish, Lake U.S.A.	
129 E3	Winnipeg Can.	
129 E2	Winnipeg r. Can.	
129 E2	Winnipeg, Lake Can.	
129 D2	Winnipegosis, Lake Can.	
141 E2	Winnipesaukee, Lake U.S.A.	
142 B2	Winnsboro U.S.A.	
137 E2	Winona MN U.S.A.	
142 C2	Winona MS U.S.A.	
100 C1	Winschoten Neth.	
101 D1	Winsen (Aller) Ger.	
101 E1	Winsen (Luhe) Ger.	
138 A1	Winslow U.S.A.	
143 D1	Winston-Salem U.S.A.	
101 D2	Winterberg Ger.	
143 D3	Winter Haven U.S.A.	
100 C2	Winterswijk Neth.	
105 D2	Winterthur Switz.	
51 D2	Winton Austr.	
54 A3	Winton N.Z.	
52 A2	Wirrabara Austr.	
99 D2	Wisbech U.K.	
140 A2	Wisconsin r. U.S.A.	
140 B2	Wisconsin state U.S.A.	
140 B2	Wisconsin Rapids U.S.A.	
	Wisła r. Pol. see Vistula	
101 E1	Wismar Ger.	
98 D2	Withernsea U.K.	
100 B1	Witmarsum Neth.	
99 C3	Witney U.K.	
123 D2	Witrivier S. Africa	
101 F2	Wittenberg, Lutherstadt Ger.	
101 E1	Wittenberge Ger.	
101 E1	Wittenburg Ger.	
101 E1	Wittingen Ger.	
100 C3	Wittlich Ger.	
100 C1	Wittmund Ger.	

101	F1	Wittstock/Dosse Ger.
120	A3	Witvlei Namibia
101	D2	Witzenhausen Ger.
103	D1	Władysławowo Pol.
103	D1	Włocławek Pol.
53	C3	Wodonga Austr.
59	C3	Wokam i. Indon.
99	F2	Woking U.K.
101	F2	Wolfen Ger.
101	E1	Wolfenbüttel Ger.
101	D2	Wolfhagen Ger.
136	B1	Wolf Point U.S.A.
101	E1	Wolfsburg Ger.
100	C3	Wolfstein Ger.
131	D2	Wolfville Can.
102	C1	Wolgast Ger.
102	C1	Wolin Pol.
129	D2	Wollaston Lake Can.
129	D2	Wollaston Lake Can.
126	D2	Wollaston Peninsula Can.
53	D2	Wollongong Austr.
101	E2	Wolmirsleben Ger.
101	E1	Wolmirstedt Ger.
100	C1	Wolvega Neth.
99	B2	Wolverhampton U.K.
65	B2	Wonju S. Korea
128	B2	Wonowon Can.
65	B2	Wŏnsan N. Korea
53	C3	Wonthaggi Austr.
52	A2	Woocalla Austr.
51	C1	Woodah, Isle i. Austr.
99	D2	Woodbridge U.K.
136	B3	Woodland Park U.S.A.
50	C2	Woodroffe, Mount Austr.
51	C1	Woods, Lake imp. l. Austr.
129	E3	Woods, Lake of the Can./
		U.S.A.
53	C3	Woods Point Austr.
131	D2	Woodstock N.B. Can.
140	C2	Woodstock Ont. Can.
54	C2	Woodville N.Z.
139	D1	Woodward U.S.A.
53	D2	Woolgoolga Austr.
52	A2	Woomera Austr.
140	C2	Wooster U.S.A.
122	A3	Worcester S. Africa
99	B3	Worcester U.K.
141	E2	Worcester U.S.A.
102	C2	Wörgl Austria
98	B1	Workington U.K.
98	C2	Worksop U.K.
136	B2	Worland U.S.A.
101	D3	Worms Ger.
99	C3	Worthing U.K.
137	D2	Worthington U.S.A.
58	C3	Wotu Indon.
59	C3	Wowoni i. Indon.
83	N2	Wrangel Island Russia
128	A2	Wrangell U.S.A.
96	B1	Wrath, Cape U.K.
136	C2	Wray U.S.A.
122	A2	Wreck Point S. Africa
98	B2	Wrexham U.K.
136	B2	Wright U.S.A.
63	A2	Wrightmyo India
128	B1	Wrigley Can.
103	D1	Wrocław Pol.
103	D1	Września Pol.
70	B2	Wu'an China
70	A2	Wuhai China
70	B2	Wuhan China
70	B2	Wuhu China
		Wujin China see Changzhou
115	C4	Wukari Nigeria
62	B1	Wuliang Shan mts China
59	C3	Wuliaru i. Indon.
71	A3	Wumeng Shan mts China
130	B1	Wunnummin Lake Can.

101	F2	Wunsiedel Ger.
101	D1	Wunstorf Ger.
62	A1	Wuntho Myanmar
100	C2	Wuppertal Ger.
122	A3	Wuppertal S. Africa
101	E2	Würzburg Ger.
101	D3	Würzburg Ger.
101	F2	Wurzen Ger.
68	C2	Wuwei China
70	A2	Wuxi Chongqing China
70	C2	Wuxi Jiangsu China
		Wuxing China see Huzhou
71	A3	Wuxuan China
		Wuyang China see Zhenyuan
69	E1	Wuyiling China
71	B3	Wuyishan China
71	B3	Wuyi Shan mts China
70	A1	Wuyuan China
71	A4	Wuzhishan China
70	A2	Wuzhong China
71	B3	Wuzhou China
53	C2	Wyangala Reservoir Austr.
52	B3	Wycheproof Austr.
99	B3	Wye r. U.K.
50	B1	Wyndham Austr.
142	B1	Wynne U.S.A.
129	D2	Wynyard Can.
136	B2	Wyoming state U.S.A.
103	E1	Wyszków Pol.
140	C3	Wytheville U.S.A.

X

117	D3	Xaafuun Somalia
62	B2	Xaignabouli Laos
121	C3	Xai-Xai Moz.
145	C3	Xalapa Mex.
70	A1	Xamba China
62	A1	Xamgyi'nyilha China
62	B1	Xam Nua Laos
120	A2	Xangongo Angola
81	C2	Xankändi Azer.
111	B2	Xanthi Greece
150	B3	Xapuri Brazil
107	C2	Xàtiva Spain
		Xiaguan China see Dali
71	B3	Xiamen China
70	A2	Xi'an China
70	A3	Xianfeng China
		Xiangfan China see
		Xiangyang
		Xiangjiang China see
		Huichang
71	B3	Xiangtan China
70	B2	Xiantao China
70	A2	Xianyang China
70	B2	Xiaogan China
69	E1	Xiao Hinggan Ling mts
		China
70	C2	Xiaoshan China
62	B1	Xichang China
145	C2	Xicohténcatl Mex.
71	A3	Xifeng China
75	C2	Xigazê China
83	I4	Xilinhot China
70	B2	Xincai China
68	C2	Xinghai China
70	B2	Xinghua China
71	B3	Xingning China
70	A2	Xingping China
70	B2	Xingtai China
151	C2	Xingu r. Brazil
71	A3	Xingyi China
70	B3	Xinhua China
68	C2	Xining China

		Xinjiang Uygur Autonomous
		Region aut. reg. China see
		Xinjiang Uygur Zizhiqu
75	C1	Xinjiang Uygur Zizhiqu
		aut. reg. China
		Xinjing China see Jingxi
69	D2	Xinkou China
65	A1	Xinmin China
71	B3	Xinning China
70	B2	Xintai China
71	B3	Xinxiang China
70	B2	Xinyang China
70	B2	Xinyi China
71	C3	Xinying Taiwan
71	B3	Xinyu China
70	B2	Xinzhou China
71	C3	Xinzhu Taiwan
106	B1	Xinzo de Limia Spain
		Xiongshan China see
		Zhenghe
68	C2	Xiqing Shan mts China
151	D3	Xique-Xique Brazil
70	A1	Xishanzui China
71	A3	Xiushan China
71	B3	Xiuying China
70	B2	Xixia China
		Xixón Spain see Gijón/Xixón
68	B2	Xizang Zizhiqu aut. reg. China
76	B2	Xo'jayli Uzbek.
70	B2	Xuancheng China
71	A3	Xuanwei China
70	B2	Xuchang China
		Xucheng China see Xuwen
117	C4	Xuddur Somalia
		Xujiang China see
		Guangchang
71	B3	Xun Jiang r. China
71	B3	Xunwu China
107	C2	Xúquer, Riu r. Spain
71	B3	Xuwen China
71	A3	Xuyong China
70	B2	Xuzhou China

Y

117	B4	Yabēlo Eth.
69	D1	Yablonovyy Khrebet mts
		Russia
143	D1	Yadkin r. U.S.A.
75	C2	Yadong China
89	E2	Yagnitsa Russia
118	B1	Yagoua Cameroon
128	C3	Yahk Can.
144	B2	Yahualica Mex.
80	B2	Yahyalı Turkey
67	C4	Yaizu Japan
134	B1	Yakima U.S.A.
114	B3	Yako Burkina Faso
66	D2	Yakumo Japan
126	B3	Yakutat U.S.A.
83	J2	Yakutsk Russia
91	D2	Yakymivka Ukr.
63	B3	Yala Thai.
53	C3	Yallourn Austr.
111	C2	Yalova Turkey
91	C3	Yalta Ukr.
65	A1	Yalu Jiang r. China/N. Korea
67	D3	Yamagata Japan
67	B4	Yamaguchi Japan
		Yamal, Poluostrov pen. Russia
		see Yamal Peninsula
86	F1	Yamal Peninsula Russia
53	D1	Yamba Austr.
117	A4	Yambio South Sudan
110	C2	Yambol Bulg.
86	G2	Yamburg Russia

62 A1 **Yamethin** Myanmar
114 B4 **Yamoussoukro** Côte d'Ivoire
90 B2 **Yampil'** Ukr.
75 C2 **Yamuna** r. India
75 D3 **Yamzho Yumco** l. China
83 K2 **Yana** r. Russia
70 A2 **Yan'an** China
150 A3 **Yanaoca** Peru
78 A2 **Yanbu' al Baḩr** Saudi Arabia
70 C2 **Yancheng** China
50 A3 **Yanchep** Austr.
70 B2 **Yangcheng** China
71 B3 **Yangchun** China
65 B2 **Yanggok** N. Korea
71 B3 **Yangjiang** China
Yangôn Myanmar see
Rangoon
70 B2 **Yangquan** China
71 B3 **Yangshuo** China
70 C3 **Yangtze** r. China
69 E2 **Yangtze, Mouth of the** China
70 B2 **Yangzhou** China
65 B1 **Yanji** China
137 D2 **Yankton** U.S.A.
83 K2 **Yano-Indigirskaya**
Nizmennost' lowland Russia
83 K2 **Yanskiy Zaliv** g. Russia
53 C1 **Yantabulla** Austr.
70 C2 **Yantai** China
118 B2 **Yaoundé** Cameroon
59 D2 **Yap** i. Micronesia
59 D3 **Yapen** i. Indon.
59 D3 **Yapen, Selat** sea chan. Indon.
144 A2 **Yaqui** r. Mex.
51 D2 **Yaraka** Austr.
86 D3 **Yaransk** Russia
48 F2 **Yaren** Nauru
78 B3 **Yarim** Yemen
77 D3 **Yarkant He** r. China
75 D2 **Yarlung Zangbo** r. China
131 D2 **Yarmouth** Can.
86 F2 **Yarono** Russia
89 E2 **Yaroslavl'** Russia
66 B2 **Yaroslavskiy** Russia
53 C3 **Yarram** Austr.
89 D2 **Yartsevo** Russia
89 E3 **Yasnogorsk** Russia
63 B2 **Yasothon** Thai.
53 C2 **Yass** Austr.
111 C3 **Yatağan** Turkey
129 E1 **Yathkyed Lake** Can.
67 B4 **Yatsushiro** Japan
150 B2 **Yavari** r. Brazil/Peru
75 B2 **Yavatmal** India
90 A2 **Yavoriv** Ukr.
67 B4 **Yawatahama** Japan
81 C2 **Yazd** Iran
142 B2 **Yazoo City** U.S.A.
111 B3 **Ydra** i. Greece
63 A2 **Ye** Myanmar
77 C3 **Yecheng** China
144 B2 **Yécora** Mex.
89 E3 **Yefremov** Russia
89 E2 **Yegor'yevsk** Russia
117 B4 **Yei** South Sudan
86 F3 **Yekaterinburg** Russia
77 D1 **Yekibastuz** Kazakh.
89 E3 **Yelets** Russia
114 A3 **Yélimané** Mali
96 □ **Yell** i. U.K.
128 C1 **Yellowknife** Can.
70 B2 **Yellow River** r. China
69 E2 **Yellow Sea** N. Pacific Ocean
136 C1 **Yellowstone** r. U.S.A.
136 A2 **Yellowstone Lake** U.S.A.
88 C3 **Yel'sk** Belarus
78 B3 **Yemen** country Asia
86 E2 **Yemva** Russia

91 D2 **Yenakiyeve** Ukr.
62 A1 **Yenangyaung** Myanmar
62 B1 **Yên Bai** Vietnam
114 B4 **Yendi** Ghana
111 C3 **Yenice** Turkey
111 C3 **Yenifoça** Turkey
68 C1 **Yenisey** r. Russia
65 B2 **Yeongdeok** S. Korea
53 C2 **Yeoval** Austr.
99 B3 **Yeovil** U.K.
51 E2 **Yeppoon** Austr.
83 I2 **Yerbogachen** Russia
81 C1 **Yerevan** Armenia
77 D1 **Yereymentau** Kazakh.
87 D3 **Yershov** Russia
Yertis r. Kazakh./Russia see
Irtysh
65 B2 **Yesan** S. Korea
77 C1 **Yesil'** Kazakh.
77 D1 **Yesil'** r. Kazakh./Russia
111 C3 **Yeşilova** Turkey
99 A3 **Yes Tor** h. U.K.
53 D1 **Yetman** Austr.
62 A1 **Ye-U** Myanmar
104 B2 **Yeu, Île d'** i. France
91 C2 **Yevpatoriya** Ukr.
91 D2 **Yeya** r. Russia
91 D2 **Yeysk** Russia
88 C3 **Yezyaryshcha** Belarus
71 A3 **Yibin** China
70 B2 **Yichang** China
69 E1 **Yichun** Heilong. China
71 B3 **Yichun** Jiangxi China
110 C2 **Yıldız Dağları** mts Turkey
80 B2 **Yıldızeli** Turkey
70 A2 **Yinchuan** China
65 B1 **Yingchengzi** China
71 B3 **Yingde** China
70 C1 **Yingkou** China
70 B2 **Yingshan** Hubei China
70 A2 **Yingshan** Sichuan China
71 B3 **Yingtan** China
77 E2 **Yining** China
117 B4 **Yirga Alem** Eth.
70 B2 **Yishui** China
68 C2 **Yiwu** China
71 B3 **Yiyang** China
71 A3 **Yizhou** China
92 I2 **Yli-Kitka** l. Fin.
92 H2 **Ylitornio** Fin.
92 H3 **Ylivieska** Fin.
61 C2 **Yogyakarta** Indon.
118 B2 **Yoko** Cameroon
67 C3 **Yokohama** Japan
115 D4 **Yola** Nigeria
67 D3 **Yonezawa** Japan
71 B3 **Yong'an** China
71 B3 **Yongchun** China
70 A2 **Yongdeng** China
71 C3 **Yongkang** China
62 B1 **Yongsheng** China
71 B3 **Yongzhou** China
150 A1 **Yopal** Col.
50 A3 **York** Austr.
98 C2 **York** U.K.
137 D2 **York** NE U.S.A.
141 D3 **York** PA U.S.A.
51 D1 **York, Cape** Austr.
52 A3 **Yorke Peninsula** Austr.
52 A3 **Yorketown** Austr.
98 C2 **Yorkshire Wolds** hills U.K.
129 D2 **Yorkton** Can.
87 D3 **Yoshkar-Ola** Russia
97 C3 **Youghal** Ireland
53 C2 **Young** Austr.
52 A3 **Younghusband Peninsula** Austr.
140 C2 **Youngstown** U.S.A.

114 B3 **Youvarou** Mali
77 E2 **Youyi Feng** mt. China/Russia
80 B2 **Yozgat** Turkey
134 B2 **Yreka** U.S.A.
76 C2 **Yrgyz** Kazakh.
Yr Wyddfa mt. U.K. see
Snowdon
105 C2 **Yssingeaux** France
93 F4 **Ystad** Sweden
Ysyk-Köl Kyrg. see Balykchy
77 D2 **Ysyk-Köl** salt l. Kyrg.
92 □A3 **Ytri-Rangá** r. Iceland
62 B1 **Yuanjiang** China
71 B3 **Yuan Jiang** r. China
62 B1 **Yuanmou** China
135 B3 **Yuba City** U.S.A.
66 D2 **Yūbari** Japan
145 C3 **Yucatán** pen. Mex.
146 B2 **Yucatan Channel** Cuba/Mex.
50 C2 **Yuendumu** Austr.
71 B3 **Yueyang** China
86 F2 **Yugorsk** Russia
83 L2 **Yukagirskoye Ploskogor'ye**
plat. Russia
128 A1 **Yukon** admin. div. Can.
126 C2 **Yukon** r. Can./U.S.A.
71 B3 **Yulin** Guangxi China
70 A2 **Yulin** Shaanxi China
62 B1 **Yulong Xueshan** mt. China
138 A2 **Yuma** AZ U.S.A.
136 C2 **Yuma** CO U.S.A.
Yumen China see
Laojunmiao
80 B2 **Yunak** Turkey
70 B2 **Yuncheng** China
71 B3 **Yunfu** China
62 B1 **Yunnan** prov. China
52 A2 **Yunta** Austr.
70 B2 **Yunyang** China
67 B3 **Yurihonjō** Japan
150 A2 **Yurimaguas** Peru
77 E3 **Yurungkax He** r. China
71 C3 **Yu Shan** mt. Taiwan
68 C2 **Yushu** China
Yushuwan China see
Huaihua
81 C1 **Yusufeli** Turkey
77 E3 **Yutian** China
62 B1 **Yuxi** China
66 D2 **Yuzhno-Kuril'sk** Russia
83 K3 **Yuzhno-Sakhalinsk** Russia
77 C2 **Yuzhnoukrayins'k** Ukr.
82 E2 **Yuzhnyy, Ostrov** i. Russia
69 D2 **Yuzhou** China
104 C2 **Yvetot** France
100 B1 **Zaandam** Neth.
69 D1 **Zabaykal'sk** Russia
78 B3 **Zabid** Yemen
Zābol Iran see Mehrestān
79 D2 **Zābolī** Iran
144 B3 **Zacapu** Mex.
144 B2 **Zacatecas** Mex.
145 C3 **Zacatepec** Mex.
144 B3 **Zacatlán** Mex.
111 B3 **Zacharo** Greece
144 A2 **Zacoalco** Mex.
145 C2 **Zacualtipán** Mex.
109 C2 **Zadar** Croatia
63 A3 **Zadetkyi Kyun** i. Myanmar
89 E3 **Zadonsk** Russia
106 B2 **Zafra** Spain
109 C1 **Zagreb** Croatia
Zagros, Kūhhā-ye mts Iran see
Zagros Mountains
81 C2 **Zagros Mountains** Iran
79 D2 **Zāhedān** Iran
80 B2 **Zahlé** Lebanon
78 B3 **Ẓahrān** Saudi Arabia

Zaire country Africa see Congo, Democratic Republic of the
109 D2 Zaječar Serbia
89 E3 Zakharovo Russia
81 C2 Zākhū/Zaxo Iraq
111 B3 Zakynthos Greece
111 B3 Zakynthos i. Greece
103 D2 Zalaegerszeg Hungary
110 B1 Zalău Romania
78 B2 Ẓalim Saudi Arabia
117 A3 Zalingei Sudan
78 A2 Ẓalmā, Jabal aẓ mt. Saudi Arabia
128 C2 Zama City Can.
120 C2 Zambeze r. Moz.
120 C2 Zambezi r. Africa
Zambezi r. Moz. see Zambeze
120 B2 Zambezi Zambia
120 B2 Zambia country Africa
64 B2 Zamboanga Phil.
64 B2 Zamboanga Peninsula Phil.
106 B1 Zamora Spain
144 B3 Zamora de Hidalgo Mex.
103 E1 Zamość Pol.
75 B1 Zanda China
100 B2 Zandvliet Belgium
140 C3 Zanesville U.S.A.
81 C2 Zanjān Iran
75 B1 Zanskar Mountains India
Zante i. Greece see Zakynthos
119 D3 Zanzibar Tanz.
119 D3 Zanzibar Island Tanz.
89 E3 Zaokskiy Russia
115 C2 Zaouatallaz Alg.
89 D2 Zapadnaya Dvina r. Europe
89 D2 Zapadnaya Dvina Russia
68 B1 Zapadnyy Sayan reg. Russia
139 D3 Zapata U.S.A.
92 J2 Zapolyarnyy Russia
91 D2 Zaporizhzhya Ukr.
101 E2 Zappendorf Ger.
80 B2 Zara Turkey
145 B2 Zaragoza Mex.
107 C1 Zaragoza Spain
74 A1 Zarah Sharan Afgh.
76 B3 Zarand Iran
76 C3 Zaranj Afgh.
88 C2 Zarasai Lith.
89 E3 Zaraysk Russia
150 B1 Zaraza Venez.
115 C3 Zaria Nigeria
90 B1 Zarichne Ukr.
81 D3 Zarqān Iran
66 B2 Zarubino Russia
103 D1 Żary Pol.
115 D1 Zarzis Tunisia
123 C3 Zastron S. Africa
121 C3 Zavala Moz.
69 E1 Zavitinsk Russia
103 D1 Zawiercie Pol.
77 E2 Zaysan, Lake Kazakh.
Zaysan, Ozero l. Kazakh. see Zaysan, Lake
90 B1 Zdolbuniv Ukr.
93 F4 Zealand i. Denmark
100 A2 Zeebrugge Belgium
123 C2 Zeerust S. Africa
50 C2 Zeil, Mount Austr.
101 F2 Zeitz Ger.
88 B3 Zelenogradsk Russia
82 E1 Zemlya Aleksandry i. Russia
82 F1 Zemlya Vil'cheka i. Russia
107 D2 Zemmora Alg.
145 C3 Zempoaltépetl, Nudo de mt. Mex.
65 B1 Zengfeng Shan mt. China
105 D2 Zermatt Switz.
91 E2 Zernograd Russia
101 E2 Zeulenroda Ger.
101 D1 Zeven Ger.
100 C2 Zevenaar Neth.
83 J3 Zeya Russia
79 C2 Zeydābād Iran
83 J3 Zeyskoye Vodokhranilishche resr Russia
103 D1 Zgierz Pol.
88 B3 Zhabinka Belarus
76 A2 Zhalpaktal Kazakh.
77 C1 Zhaltyr Kazakh.
76 B2 Zhanakala Kazakh.
76 B2 Zhanaozen Kazakh.
Zhangde China see Anyang
71 C3 Zhanghua Taiwan
71 B3 Zhangjiajie China
70 B1 Zhangjiakou China
71 B3 Zhangping China
71 B3 Zhangshu China
68 C2 Zhangye China
71 B3 Zhangzhou China
87 D4 Zhanibek Kazakh.
71 B3 Zhanjiang China
71 B3 Zhao'an China
71 B3 Zhaoqing China
71 A3 Zhaotong China
75 C1 Zhari Namco salt l. China
77 E2 Zharkent Kazakh.
89 D2 Zharkovskiy Russia
77 E2 Zharma Kazakh.
90 C2 Zhashkiv Ukr.
Zhayyk r. Kazakh./Russia see Ural
71 C3 Zhejiang prov. China
82 F1 Zhelaniya, Mys c. Russia
89 E3 Zheleznogorsk Russia
76 B2 Zhem r. Kazakh.
70 A2 Zhenba China
71 A3 Zheng'an China
71 B3 Zhenghe China
70 B2 Zhengzhou China
70 B2 Zhenjiang China
71 A3 Zhenyuan China
91 E1 Zherdevka Russia
86 D2 Zheshart Russia
77 D2 Zhetysuskiy Alatau mts China/Kazakh.
77 C2 Zhezkazgan Karagandinskaya Oblast' Kazakh.
77 C2 Zhezkazgan Karagandinskaya Oblast' Kazakh.
68 C3 Zhigang China
83 J2 Zhigansk Russia
Zhi Qu r. China see Yangtze
Zhishan China see Lingling
76 C1 Zhitikara Kazakh.
88 D3 Zhlobin Belarus
90 B2 Zhmerynka Ukr.
74 A1 Zhob Pak.
83 L1 Zhokhova, Ostrov i. Russia
75 C2 Zhongba China
Zhonghe China see Xiushan
70 A2 Zhongning China
71 B3 Zhongshan Guangdong China
Zhongshan China see Liupanshui
70 A2 Zhongwei China
Zhongxin China see Xamgyi'nyilha
76 C2 Zhosaly Kazakh.
70 B2 Zhoukou China
70 C2 Zhoushan China
91 C2 Zhovti Vody Ukr.
65 A2 Zhuanghe China
70 B2 Zhucheng China
89 D3 Zhukovka Russia
89 E2 Zhukovskiy Russia
70 B2 Zhumadian China
Zhuoyang China see Suiping
71 B3 Zhuzhou Hunan China
71 B3 Zhuzhou Hunan China
90 A2 Zhydachiv Ukr.
88 C3 Zhytkavichy Belarus
90 B1 Zhytomyr Ukr.
103 D2 Žiar nad Hronom Slovakia
70 B2 Zibo China
103 D1 Zielona Góra Pol.
62 A1 Zigaing Myanmar
71 A3 Zigong China
114 A3 Ziguinchor Senegal
144 B3 Zihuatanejo Mex.
103 D2 Žilina Slovakia
83 H3 Zima Russia
145 C2 Zimapán Mex.
121 B2 Zimbabwe country Africa
114 A4 Zimmi Sierra Leone
110 C2 Zimnicea Romania
115 C3 Zinder Niger
78 B3 Zinjibār Yemen
103 D2 Zirc Hungary
62 A1 Ziro India
79 C2 Zīr Rūd Iran
103 D2 Zistersdorf Austria
145 B3 Zitácuaro Mex.
103 C1 Zittau Ger.
110 B2 Zlatitsa Bulg.
87 E3 Zlatoust Russia
103 D2 Zlín Czech Rep.
89 D3 Zlynka Russia
89 E3 Zmiyevka Russia
91 D2 Zmiyiv Ukr.
89 E3 Znamenka Orlovskaya Oblast' Russia
91 E1 Znamenka Tambovskaya Oblast' Russia
91 C2 Znam"yanka Ukr.
103 D2 Znojmo Czech Rep.
91 D1 Zolochiv Kharkivs'ka Oblast' Ukr.
90 A2 Zolochiv L'vivs'ka Oblast' Ukr.
91 C2 Zolotonosha Ukr.
89 E3 Zolotukhino Russia
121 C2 Zomba Malawi
80 B1 Zonguldak Turkey
105 D3 Zonza Corsica France
114 B4 Zorzor Liberia
115 D2 Zouar Chad
114 A2 Zouérat Maur.
109 D1 Zrenjanin Serbia
89 D2 Zubtsov Russia
105 D2 Zug Switz.
81 C1 Zugdidi Georgia
106 B2 Zújar r. Spain
100 C2 Zülpich Ger.
121 C2 Zumbo Moz.
145 C3 Zumpango Mex.
138 B1 Zuni Mountains U.S.A.
71 A3 Zunyi China
109 C1 Županja Croatia
105 D2 Zürich Switz.
100 C1 Zutphen Neth.
115 D1 Zuwārah Libya
90 C2 Zvenyhorodka Ukr.
121 C3 Zvishavane Zimbabwe
103 D2 Zvolen Slovakia
109 C2 Zvornik Bos. & Herz.
114 B4 Zwedru Liberia
123 C3 Zwelitsha S. Africa
103 D2 Zwettl Austria
101 F2 Zwickau Ger.
100 C1 Zwolle Neth.
83 L2 Zyryanka Russia

Acknowledgements

pages 34-35
Climatic map data:
Kottek, M., Grieser, J., Beck, C., Rudolf, B., and Rubel, F., 2006: World Map
of the Köppen-Geiger climate classification updated.
Meteorol. Z., 15, 259–263.
http://koeppen-geiger.vu-wien.ac.at

pages 36-37
World land cover map data:
© ESA 2010 and UCLouvain
Arino, O., Ramos, J., Kalogirou, V., Defourny, P., Achard, F., 2010.
GlobCover 2009. ESA Living Planet Symposium 2010, 28th June - 2nd July, Bergen, Norway, SP-686, ESA,
www.esa.int/due/globcover
http://due.esrin.esa.int/prjs/Results/20110202183257.pdf

pages 38-39
Population map data:
Center for International Earth Science Information Network (CIESIN), Columbia University; and Centro Internacional de Agricultura
Tropical (CIAT). 2005. Gridded Population of the World Version 3 (GPWv3). Palisades, NY: Socioeconomic
Data and Applications Center (SEDAC), Columbia University.
Available at: http://sedac.ciesin.columbia.edu/gpw
http://www.ciesin.columbia.edu